DEUTERONOMY

Richard D. Nelson

DEUTERONOMY

A Commentary

Westminster John Knox Press
LOUISVILLE • LONDON

© 2002 Richard D. Nelson

All rights reserved. No part of this book may be reproduced or transmitted in any form or by any means, electronic or mechanical, including photocopying, recording, or by any information storage or retrieval system, without permission in writing from the publisher. For information, address Witherspoon John Knox Press, 100 Witherspoon Street, Louisville, Kentucky 40202-1396.

Book design by Jennifer K. Cox

First edition
Published by Westminster John Knox Press
Louisville, Kentucky

This book is printed on acid-free paper that meets the American National Standards Institute Z39.48 standard. ♾

PRINTED IN THE UNITED STATES OF AMERICA

02 03 04 05 06 07 08 09 10 11 — 10 9 8 7 6 5 4 3 2 1

Cataloging-in-Publication Data can be obtained from the Library of Congress.

ISBN 0-664-21952-7

CONTENTS

ABBREVIATIONS

AB	Anchor Bible
ABD	*Anchor Bible Dictionary*. Edited by D. N. Freedman. 6 vols. New York, 1992
AnBib	Analecta biblica
AJBI	*Annual of the Japanese Biblical Institute*
ANET	*Ancient Near Eastern Texts Relating to the Old Testament*. Edited by J. Pritchard. 3d ed. Princeton, 1969
AOAT	Alter Orient und Altes Testament
ATANT	Abhandlungen zur Theologie des Alten und Neuen Testaments
BASOR	Bulletin of the American Schools of Oriental Research
BBB	Bonner biblische Beiträge
BEATAJ	Beiträge zur Erforschung des Alten Testaments und des antiken Judentum
BETL	Bibliotheca ephermeridum theolgicarum lovaniensium
BHS	*Biblia Hebraica Stuttgartensia*, Stuttgart, 1977
Bib	*Biblica*
BKAT	Biblischer Kommentar, Altes Testament
BN	*Biblische Notizen*
BWANT	Beiträge zur Wissenschaft vom Alten und Neuen Testament
BZ	*Biblische Zeitschrift*
BZAW	Beihefte zur Zeitschrift für die alttestamentliche Wissenschaft
CBQ	*Catholic Biblical Quarterly*
ConBOT	Coniectanea biblica, Old Testament
CTU	*Cuneiform Alphabetic Texts from Ugarit, Ras Ibn Hani, and Other Places*. Edited by M. Dietrich et al. Münster, 1995
DBAT	*Dielheimer Blätter zum Alten Testament und seiner Rezeption in der alten Kirche*
DDD	*Dictionary of Deities and Demons in the Bible*. Edited by K. van der Toorn et al. 2d ed. Leiden, 1999

DH	Deuteronomistic History/Historian
E	Elohist source
ET	English (where verse numbers differ from the Hebrew)
ETL	*Ephemerides theologicae lovanienses*
FAT	Forschungen zum Alten Testament
FRLANT	Forschungen zur Religion und Literatur des Alten und Neuen Testaments
FZPhTh	*Freiburger Zeitschrift für Philosophie und Theologie*
GKC	*Gesenius' Hebrew Grammar.* Edited by E. Kautzsch. Translated by A. E. Cowley. 2d ed. Oxford, 1910
GTA	Göttinger theologische Arbeiten
HALOT	L. Koehler et al. *The Hebrew and Aramaic Lexicon of the Old Testament.* Translated and edited by M. Richardson. 5 vols. Leiden, 1994–2000.
HSM	Harvard Semitic Monographs
HTR	*Harvard Theological Review*
HUCA	*Hebrew Union College Annual*
IBHS	B. K. Waltke and M. O'Connor, *An Introduction to Biblical Hebrew Syntax.* Winona Lake, Ind. 1990
Int	*Interpretation*
J	Yahwist source
JBL	*Journal of Biblical Literature*
JJS	*Journal of Jewish Studies*
JNES	*Journal of Near Eastern Studies*
JPS	Jewish Publication Society
JSOT	*Journal for the Study of the Old Testament*
JSOTSup	Journal for the Study of the Old Testament Supplement Series
LH	Laws of Hammurabi (*ANET*, 163–80)
LXX	Septuagint (the Greek version tradition as a whole)
LXX^A	Codex Alexandrinus
LXX^B	Codex Vaticanus
M.	Mishnah
MAL	Middle Assyrian Laws (*ANET*, 180–88)
MSS	Manuscripts
MT	Masoretic Text
NAB	New American Bible
NJB	New Jerusalem Bible
NJPS	New Jewish Publication Society Version
NRSV	New Revised Standard Version
OBO	Orbis biblicus et orientalis
OG	Old Greek (earliest recoverable Greek version)

OL	Old Latin version
OLP	*Orientalia lovaniensia periodica*
OTL	Old Testament Library
OtSt	*Oudtestamentische Studiën*
P	Priestly source/Writer
RB	*Revue biblique*
REB	Revised English Bible
RSV	Revised Standard Version
Sam.	Samaritan Pentateuch
SBAB	Stuttgarter biblischer Aufsatzbände
SBLDS	Society of Biblical Literature Dissertation Series
SBLSCS	Society of Biblical Literature Septuagint and Cognate Studies
SBS	Stuttgarter Bibelstudien
SBT	Studies in Biblical Theology
SBTS	Sources for Biblical and Theological Study
ScrHier	Scripta hierosolymitana
Sem	*Semitica*
SJOT	*Scandanavian Journal of the Old Testament*
Syr.	Syriac version
TDOT	*Theological Dictionary of the Old Testament.* Edited by G. Botterweck, H. Ringgren, and H.-J. Fabry. Translated by J. T. Willis et al. Grand Rapids, 1974–
Tg.	Targum
Tg. Neof.	Targum Neofiti
Tg. Onq.	Targum Onqelos
Tg. Ps.-J.	Targum Pseudo-Jonathan
ThWAT	*Theologisches Wörterbuch zum Alten Testament.* Edited by G. Botterweck, H. Ringgren, and H.-J. Fabry. Stuttgart, 1970–
TZ	*Theologische Zeitschrift*
UF	*Ugarit-Forschungen*
VT	*Vetus Testamentum*
VTE	Vassal Treaties of Esarhaddon (*ANET*, 534–41)
VTSup	Vetus Testamentum Supplements
Vulg.	Vulgate
WMANT	Wissenschaftliche Monographien zum Alten und Neuen Testament
ZABR	*Zeitschrift für altorientalische und biblische Rechtgeschichte*
ZAW	*Zeitschrift für die alttestamentliche Wissenschaft*
ZTK	*Zeitschrift für Theologie und Kirche*

BIBLIOGRAPHY

Commentaries

Braulik, Georg. *Deuteronomium*. 2 vols. Neue Echter Bibel 15, 28. Würzburg: Echter, 1986, 1992.

Christensen, Duane L. *Deuteronomy 1:1–21:9*. 2 ed. Word Biblical Commentary 6A. Nashville: Nelson, 2001.

Clements, Roland E. "The Book of Deuteronomy." Pages 269–538 in *The New Interpreter's Bible II*. Nashville: Abingdon, 1998.

Craigie, P. C. *The Book of Deuteronomy*. New International Commentary on the Old Testament. Grand Rapids: Eerdmans, 1976.

Mayes, A. D. H. *Deuteronomy*. New Century Bible. Repr. Grand Rapids: Eerdmans, 1981.

Merrill, Eugene H. *Deuteronomy*. New American Commentary 4. Nashville: Broadman & Holman, 1994.

Miller, Patrick D. *Deuteronomy*. Interpretation Commentaries. Louisville: John Knox, 1990.

Nielsen, Eduard. *Deuteronomium*. Handbuch zum Alten Testament 1/6. Tübingen: Mohr, 1995.

Perlitt, Lothar. *Deuteronomium*. BKAT 5/1–. Neukirchen-Vluyn: Neukirchener Verlag, 1990–.

Rad, Gerhard von. *Deuteronomy*. Translated by Dorothea Barton. OTL. Philadelphia: Westminster, 1966.

Rose, Martin. *5. Mose*. 2 vols. Zürcher Bibelkommentare 5. Zurich: Theologischer Verlag, 1994.

Tigay, Jeffrey H. *Deuteronomy*. JPS Torah Commentary. Philadelphia: Jewish Publication Society, 1996.

Weinfeld, Moshe. *Deuteronomy 1–11*. AB 5. New York: Doubleday, 1991.

Monographs, Collected Essays, and Articles

Braulik, Georg. *Die deuteronomischen Gesetze und der Dekalog: Studien zum Aufbau von Deuteronomium 12–26*. SBS 145. Stuttgart: Katholisches Bibelwerk, 1991.

_____. *Die Mittel deuteronomischer Rhetorik: Erhoben aus Deuteronomium 4,1–40.* AnBib 68. Rome: Biblical Institute Press, 1978.

_____. *Studien zum Buch Deuteronomium.* SBAB 24. Stuttgart: Katholisches Bibelwerk, 1997.

_____. *Studien zum Deuteronomium und seiner Nachgeschichte.* SBAB 33. Stuttgart: Katholisches Bibelwerk, 2001.

_____. *Studien zur Theologie des Deuteronomiums.* SBAB 2. Stuttgart: Katholisches Bibelwerk, 1988.

_____. *The Theology of Deuteronomy: Collected Essays by Georg Braulik.* Translated by U. Lindblad. N. Richland Hills, Tex.: BIBAL Press, 1994.

_____, ed. *Bundesdokument und Gesetz: Studien zum Deuteronomium.* Herders biblische Studien 4. Freiburg: Herder, 1995.

Brekelmans, Chris, and Johan Lust, eds. *Pentateuchal and Deuteronomistic Studies.* BETL 94. Leuven: Leuven University Press, 1990.

Buchholz, Joachim. *Die Ältesten Israels im Deuteronomium.* GTA 36. Göttingen: Vandenhoeck & Ruprecht, 1988.

Christensen, Duane L., ed. *A Song of Power and the Power of Song: Essays on the Book of Deuteronomy.* SBTS 3. Winona Lake, Ind.: Eisenbrauns, 1993.

Dahmen, Ulrich. *Leviten und Priester im Deuteronomium: Literarkritische und redaktionsgeschichtliche Studien.* BBB 110. Frankfurt: Athenäum, 1996.

Engelmann, Angelika. "Deuteronomium: Recht und Gerechtigkeit für Frauen im Gesetz." Pages 67–79 in *Kompendium Feministische Bibelauslegung.* Edited by Luise Schottroff and Marie-Theres Wacker. Gütersloh: Kaiser, 1998.

Gammie, John G. "Theology of Retribution in the Book of Deuteronomy." *CBQ* 32 (1970): 1–12.

García Martínez, Florentino, et al., eds. *Studies in Deuteronomy: In Honour of C. J. Labuschagne on the Occasion of His 65th Birthday.* VTSup 53. Leiden: Brill, 1994.

Gertz, J. C. *Die Gerichtsorganisation Israels im deuteronomischen Gesetz.* FRLANT 165. Göttingen: Vandenhoeck & Ruprecht, 1994.

Halpern, Baruch. "The Centralization Formula in Deuteronomy." *VT* 31 (1981): 20–38.

Hamilton, Jeffries M. *Social Justice and Deuteronomy: The Case of Deuteronomy 15.* SBLDS 136. Atlanta: Scholars Press, 1992.

Janzen, J. G. "On the Most Important Word in the Shema." *VT* 37 (1987): 280–300.

Keller, Martin. *Untersuchungen zur deuteronomisch-deuteronomistischen Namenstheologie.* BBB 105. Weinheim: Beltz Athenäum, 1996.

Knapp, Dietrich. *Deuteronomium 4: Literarische Analyse und theologische Interpretation.* GTA 35. Göttingen: Vandenhoeck & Ruprecht, 1987.

Kratz, R., and H. Spieckermann, eds. *Liebe und Gebot: Studien zum Deuteronomium.* FRLANT 190. Göttingen: Vandenhoeck & Ruprecht, 2000.

Lenchak, Timothy A. *Choose Life! A Rhetorical-Critical Investigation of Deuteronomy 28,69–30,20*. AnBib 129. Rome: Pontifical Biblical Institute Press, 1993.

Levenson, Jon D. "Who Inserted the Book of the Torah?" *HTR* 68 (1975): 203–33.

Levinson, Bernard M. *Deuteronomy and the Hermeneutics of Legal Innovation*. New York: Oxford University Press, 1997.

Lohfink, Norbert. *Das Hauptgebot: Eine Untersuchung literarischer Einleitungsfragen zu Dtn 5–11*. AnBib 20. Rome: Pontifical Biblical Institute Press, 1963.

———. "Der Neue Bund im Buch Deuteronomium?" *ZABR* 4 (1998): 100–25.

———. *Studien zum Deuteronomium und zur deuteronomistichen Literatur I–IV*. SBAB 8, 12, 20, 31. Stuttgart: Katholisches Bibelwerk, 1990–2000.

———. *Theology of the Pentateuch: Themes of the Priestly Narrative and Deuteronomy*. Translated by Linda M. Maloney. Minneapolis: Fortress Press, 1994.

———. *Die Väter Israels im Deuteronomium, mit einer Stellungnahme von Thomas Römer*. OBO 111. Freiburg: Universitätsverlag, 1991.

———, ed. *Das Deuteronomium: Enststehung, Gestalt und Botschaft*. BETL 68. Leuven: Leuven University Press, 1985.

Lundbom, Jack R. "The Inclusio and Other Framing Devices in Deuteronomy I–XXVIII." *VT* 46 (1996): 296–315.

Lust, Johan, and Marc Vervenne, eds. *Deuteronomy and Deuteronomic Literature*. BETL 133. Leuven: Leuven University Press, 1997.

Mayes, A. D. H. "On Describing the Purpose of Deuteronomy." *JSOT* 58 (1993): 13–33.

McBride, S. Dean. "Polity of the Covenant People: The Book of Deuteronomy." *Int* 41 (1987): 229–44.

McConville, J. G., *Law and Theology in Deuteronomy*. JSOTSup 33. Sheffield: JSOT Press, 1984.

McConville, J. G., and J. G. Millar. *Time and Place in Deuteronomy*. JSOTSup 179. Sheffield: Sheffield Academic Press, 1994.

Miller, Patrick D. "Deuteronomy and Psalms: Evoking a Biblical Conversation." *JBL* 118 (1999): 3–18.

Merendino, R. P. *Das deuteronomische Gesetz: Eine literarkritische, gattungs- und überlieferungsgeschichtliche Untersuchung zu Dt 12–26*. BBB 31. Bonn: Peter Hanstein, 1969.

Mittmann, Siegfried. *Deuteronomium 1:1–6:3 literarkritisch und traditionsgeschichtlich untersucht*. BZAW 139. Berlin: de Gruyter, 1975.

Morrow, William S. *Scribing the Center: Organization and Redaction in Deuteronomy 14:1–17:13*. Society of Biblical Literature Monograph Series 49. Atlanta: Scholars Press, 1995.

Nicholson, E. W. *Deuteronomy and Tradition: Literary and Historical Problems in the Book of Deuteronomy*. Philadelphia: Fortress Press, 1967.

O'Brien, M. A. "The Book of Deuteronomy." *Currents in Research: Biblical Studies* 3 (1995): 95–128.

Olson, Dennis T. *Deuteronomy and the Death of Moses: A Theological Reading*. Overtures to Biblical Theology. Minneapolis: Fortress Press, 1994.

Otto, Eckart. *Das Deuteronomium*. BZAW 284. Berlin: de Gruyter, 1999.

————. "False Weights in the Scales of Biblical Justice? Different Views of Women from Patriarchal Hierarchy to Religious Equality in the Book of Deuteronomy." Pages 128–46 in *Gender and Law in the Hebrew Bible and the Ancient Near East*. Edited by Victor H. Matthews et al. JSOTSup 262. Sheffield: Sheffield Academic Press, 1998.

————. "The Pre-Exilic Deuteronomy as a Revision of the Covenant Code." Pages 112–22 in *Kontinuum und Proprium: Studien zur Sozial- und Rechtsgeschichte des Alten Orients und des Alten Testaments*. Edited by Eckart Otto and Siegbert Uhlig. Orientalia biblica et christiana 8. Wiesbaden: Harrassowitz, 1996.

————. "Treueid und Gesetz: Die Ursprünge des Deuteronomiums im Horizont neuassyrischen Vertragsrechts." *ZABR* 2 (1996): 1–52.

Perlitt, Lothar. *Deuteronomium-Studien*. FAT 8. Tübingen: Mohr, 1994.

Plöger, Josef G. *Literarkritische, formgeschichtliche und stilkritische Untersuchungen zum Deuteronomium*. BBB 26. Bonn: Hanstein, 1967.

Pressler, Carolyn. "Sexual Violence and Deuteronomic Law." Pages 102–12 in *A Feminist Companion to Exodus to Deuteronomy*. Edited by Athalya Brenner. Feminist Companion to the Bible 6. Sheffield: Sheffield Academic Press, 1994.

————. *The View of Women Found in the Deuteronomic Family Laws*. BZAW 216. Berlin: de Gruyter, 1993.

Preuss, Horst-Dietrich. *Deuteronomium*. Erträge der Forschung 164. Darmstadt: Wissenschaftliche Buchgesellschaft, 1982.

Rad, Gerhard von. *Studies in Deuteronomy*. Translated by David Stalker. SBT 1/9. Chicago: Henry Regnery, 1966.

Römer, Thomas. *Israels Väter: Untersuchungen zur Väterthematik im Deutoronomium und in der deuteronomistischen Tradition*. OBO 99. Freiburg: Universitätsverlag, 1990.

————. "The Book of Deuteronomy." Pages 178–212 in *The History of Israel's Traditions: The Heritage of Martin Noth*. Edited by Steven L. McKenzie and Patrick M. Graham. JSOTSup 182. Sheffield: Sheffield Academic Press, 1994.

Rüterswörden, Udo. "Der Verfassungsentwurf des Deuteronomiums in der neueren Diskussion: Ein Überblick." Pages 313–28 in *Altes Testament Forschung und Wirkung: Festschrift für Henning Graf Reventlow*. Edited by

Peter Mommer and Winfried Thiel. Frankfurt: Peter Lang, 1994.

_____. *Von der politischen Gemeinschaft zur Gemeinde: Studien zu Dt 16, 18–18, 22*. BBB 65. Frankfurt: Athenäum, 1987.

Seitz, Gottfried. *Redaktionsgeschichtliche Studien zum Deuteronomium*. BZAW 93. Stuttgart: Kohlhammer, 1971.

Skweres, D. E. *Die Ruckverweise im Buch Deuteronomium*. AnBib 79. Rome: Biblical Institute Press, 1979.

Sonnet, Jean-Pierre. *The Book Within the Book: Writing in Deuteronomy*. Biblical Interpretation Series 14. Leiden: Brill, 1997.

Steinberg, Naomi. "The Deuteronomic Law Code and the Politics of State Centralization." Pages 365–75 in *The Bible and Liberation: Political and Social Hermeneutics*. Edited by Norman K. Gottwald and Richard A. Horsley. Maryknoll, N.Y.: Orbis, 1993.

Steymans, Hans Ulrich. *Deuteronomium 28 und die Adê zur Thronfolgeregelung Asarhaddons: Segen und Fluch im Alten Orient und in Israel*. OBO 145. Freiburg: Universitätsverlag, 1995.

Stulman, Louis. "Encroachment in Deuteronomy: An Analysis of the Social World of the D Code." *JBL* 109 (1990): 613–32.

Veijola, Timo, ed. *Das Deuteronomium und seine Querbeziehungen*. Schriften der Finnischen Exegetischen Gesellschaft 62. Göttingen: Vandenhoeck & Ruprecht, 1996.

Weinfeld, Moshe. *Deuteronomy and the Deuteronomic School*. Winona Lake, Ind.: Eisenbrauns, 1992.

Wevers, John. *Notes on the Greek Text of Deuteronomy*. SBLSCS 39. Atlanta: Scholars Press, 1995.

Wilson, Ian. *Out of the Midst of the Fire: Divine Presence in Deuteronomy*. SBLDS 151. Atlanta: Scholars Press, 1995.

Introduction

Deuteronomy presents itself as a farewell address delivered by Moses just before his death. He speaks in the land of Moab immediately prior to Israel's invasion of its new land across the Jordan. His act of lawgiving is accomplished at Yahweh's direction and is interpreted as the establishment of a renewed covenant in Moab (28:69 [ET 29:1]) following Israel's violation of the previous covenant made at Mount Horeb (5:2). This law was mediated through Moses after the people's terror caused by Yahweh's direct communication of the Decalogue (5:22–31). Moses begins his address by reviewing previous events (chs. 1–3) and the experience at Mount Horeb (ch. 5). He prefaces the law itself with admonitions, warnings, and encouragements in order to inspire attentive obedience (chs. 4, 6–11). Then he promulgates, explains, and motivates a wide-ranging law code (chs. 12–26) by which Israel is to shape its life in the land as Yahweh's faithful people. This law urges exclusive loyalty to Yahweh by demanding that all sacrificial worship be centralized at a single location (ch. 12). It also seeks to make Israel a just and humane society by promoting a balanced and effective system of officeholders (16:18–18:22) and by advocating concrete measures to aid the poor and disadvantaged. The covenant agreement (26:16–19) is supported by a series of blessings and curses contingent on obedience or disobedience (ch. 28). After teaching the law, Moses refers to the future implications of the covenant (chs. 27, 29–30) and recites two poems that anticipate the future (chs. 32–33). Narratives about the transition of leadership and the death of Moses (chs. 31, 34) point forward to Israel's conquest (Joshua) and life in the land (Judges, 1–2 Samuel, 1–2 Kings). Ultimately, Deuteronomy portrays itself not only as an oral address, but also as a "book of the law" (29:20 [ET 21]; 30:10; 31:26) transmitted to a new generation of readers, who themselves face challenges analogous to those that confronted their ancestors on the plains of Moab.[1]

---

1. For recent scholarship, see H. D. Preuss, *Deuteronomium* (Erträge der Forschung 164; Darmstadt: Wissenschaftliche Buchgesellschaft, 1982); M. A. O'Brien, "The Book of Deuteronomy," *Currents in Research: Biblical Studies* 3 (1995): 95–128; T. Römer, "The Book of Deuteronomy," in *The History of Israel's Traditions: The Heritage of Martin Noth* (ed. S. McKenzie and M. Graham; JSOTSup 182; Sheffield: Sheffield Academic Press, 1994), 178–212.

Shapes and Structures

The linguistic character of Deuteronomy is distinctive. The style is prolix and marked by stereotyped words and phrases.[2] Sentences tend to be long and complex. The mood is homiletical and didactic, with exhortations addressed directly to the audience in second-person language. Incessant repetition aims for rhetorical effect and ease of retention. The language seeks to arouse emotions and stimulate memory of the tradition in order to motivate acceptance and action, appealing to a sense of propriety, to Yahweh's character, to Israel's election and redemption, and to the impending consequences of promise and threat.

In the parenetic material (chs. 4, 5–11), two rhetorical arguments stand out. One is the "internal monologue" in which a possible false conclusion on the part of the audience is opposed by contradictory evidence (7:17–24; 8:17–18; 9:4–6). Another is the "presentation of evidence from history," which sets forth Yahweh's historical acts, calls on the audience to "know" their theological import, and then draws out the implications of this knowing (4:37–40; 7:8–11; 8:2–6; 9:4–7a). In 9:8–10:11 Moses returns to the incident of the golden calf to demonstrate Israel's constant obstinacy. A call to internalize and outwardly display the precepts of Deuteronomy, in order to teach them to children and mesh them into the patterns of daily life, brackets the parenetic section (6:6–9; 11:18–20).

This stress on motivation is not only present in the parenetic introduction, but is also woven into the law code itself. The laws are sprinkled with stereotypical motivational formulas such as "you shall sweep out the evil from among you" (13:6 [ET 5]; 17:7, 12; 19:19; 21:21; 22:21, 22, 24; 24:7) or "something repugnant to Yahweh" (17:1; 18:12; 22:5; 23:19 [ET 18]; 25:16). Motivations attached to laws include appeals to Israel's special status (14:2, 21), the effectiveness of the prayers of the oppressed (15:9; 24:13, 15), Yahweh's intention to bless (14:29; 15:6; 23:21 [ET 20]; 24:19), and Israel's previous experience in Egypt (15:15; 16:12; 23:8 [ET 7]; 24:18, 22). A recurrent feature of the law code is a distinctive "if . . . you" casuistic style, in which some or all of a case law is presented in second-person rather than third-person language in order to personalize the behavior being encouraged (e.g., 15:7–11, 12–17; 17:2–5; 22:1–3, 23–24). Deuteronomy's fundamental purpose of motivating obedience is disclosed in a frequently repeated line of reasoning: listen and obey so that you may benefit in the land (cf. 11:22–23; 16:20; 23:21 [ET 20]; 25:15; 30:20).[3]

Structurally, Deuteronomy is complex. The final form of the book is segmented by four parallel introductory formulas (1:1; 4:44; 28:69 [ET 29:1]; 33:1) given in the voice of the narrator (rather than that of Moses). "These are the

---

2. For a list of characteristic expressions, see M. Weinfeld, *Deuteronomy and the Deuteronomic School* (Winona Lake, Ind.: Eisenbrauns, 1992), 320–59.

3. A rhetorical schema with three elements (obey what is being commanded so that you may benefit in the land) appears in 4:1, 40; 5:31–33; 6:1–3; 11:8–9.

words that Moses spoke to all Israel" (1:1) is followed by historical retrospective and exhortation. "This is the law that Moses set before the Israelites" (4:44) leads into the Decalogue, homiletical encouragement, and the "statutes and ordinances" of the law code itself. "These are the words of the covenant that Yahweh commanded Moses to make with the Israelites" (28:69 [ET 29:1]) introduces the covenant oath in Moab, succession by Joshua, and the future witness of written law and the Song of Moses. "This is the blessing that Moses the man of God pronounced on Israel" (33:1) launches the Blessing of Moses and his death report.

In addition, three introductory formulas (4:45; 6:1; 12:1) spoken by Moses refer to "statutes and ordinances" and organize the core material of chapters 5–26. "These are the precepts, statutes, and ordinances" (4:45) introduces the Decalogue while referring to the whole law. "This is the commandment—the statutes and ordinances" (6:1) serves as a heading for Moses' homiletic admonitions. "These are the statutes and ordinances" (12:1) then introduces the law code itself. Another set of introductory formulas features an oratorical appeal for attention (cf. 20:3). "Hear, O Israel" in 5:1 (bracketed by 6:3) introduces the Decalogue and coordinates it with the "statutes and ordinances" of the entire law. "Hear, O Israel" in 6:4 introduces the challenge of loyal obedience in the new land (6:4–8:20). "Hear, O Israel" reappears in 9:1 to begin a challenge to national complacency (9:1–10:11) and is then continued by "and now, O Israel" in 10:12 to introduce a concluding call for obedience and love. In the law code itself, two pairs of repeated expressions serve both as topical dividers and as reminders that the law will apply when Israel enters the land. These are: "When Yahweh your God has cut off the nations . . . and you have dispossessed them" (12:29; 19:1), and "When you have come into the land that Yahweh your God is going to give you" (17:14; 26:1).

Deuteronomy exhibits evidence of scribal activity, involving numerous patterns of scribal integration and organization. Sometimes these patterns overlap, providing evidence for successive redactional activity. Repetitions to bracket sections of text are common.[4] There are also a large number of concentric or chiastic structures created by the repetition and reversal of words, phrases, or topics.[5] For instance, the Decalogue is presented in a concentric format in order to put the Sabbath commandment at the center and highlight it.

In the final form of Deuteronomy, large-scale brackets surround the whole book. Thus chapters 1–3 and 31 frame the discourse of Moses in order to locate it within Israel's ongoing history. Deuteronomy 4:25–28 and 29:21–28 [ET 22–29] warn of destruction and exile, and 4:29–31 and 30:1–10 forecast an

---

4. Examples include 5:1 and 31; 6:1 and 25; 8:7a and 10b; 9:7b and 24; 9:26 and 29; 11:26 and 32; 14:2 and 21; 17:2 and 7; 20:5a and 9a; 22:12 and 23:1 [ET 22:30]; 23:10 and 15 [ET 9, 14]; 24:8–9 and 18; 27:2b–3a and 8; 28:15 and 45; 31:1 and 32:45; 31:30 and 32:44; 31:30 and 32:45.

5. Examples include 5:12–15; 5:27–6:3; 6:10–18; 8:1–19; 9:12–16; 11:31–12:1; 12:13–19; 29:9–14 [ET 10–15]; 30:1–10; 31:9–27.

optimistic outcome for exile. Deuteronomy 11:26–28 and 30:15–20 conceive of the law as presenting a choice set before Israel. Deuteronomy 11:29–30 and chapter 27 frame the law code with a ritual of blessings and curses to be performed at Shechem. The shared language of 11:32–12:1 and 26:16–19 (e.g., "today," "statutes and ordinances," " be careful to do") supplies yet another envelope around the law code.

Circumstances of Composition

Deuteronomy is a book unified theologically by a common set of verbal expressions. However, it also displays signs of disunity and repeated redaction. There is no consensus about the compositional history of Deuteronomy, although there is general agreement about certain matters. Most scholars would agree that elements of the law code are revisions of similar laws in the Covenant Code (Exod 20:22–23:33). Chapters 1–3; 31:1–8; and 34:1b-6 are generally thought to derive from the Deuteronomistic Historian (DH), who was responsible for narrating Israel's story from the book of Joshua through 2 Kings. The Song of Moses (ch. 32) and the Blessing of Moses (ch. 33) were undoubtedly added to the book at a late stage in its development. As portrayals of the future, these two poems strengthen the conception that Deuteronomy embodies the final testament of a dying Moses. In addition, material commonly assigned to the Priestly Writer occurs in 1:3; 32:48–52; and 34:1a, 7–9, reflecting the eventual incorporation of Deuteronomy into the Pentateuch. For example, 32:48–52 is a resumptive parallel of Num 27:12–14 that serves to "restart" the Pentateuch's story after its interruption by Deuteronomy. Non-Priestly links to wider contexts are provided by 4:41–43 and 34:10–12.

Deuteronomy 4:1–40 presupposes the existence of chapters 1–3 ("And now," 4:1), but also offers a theological commentary on the following Decalogue and Deuteronomic law, which are understood as coordinated revelations of a single divine will. Portions of this chapter also parallel other, clearly secondary material envisioning future apostasy and exile (4:25–28; 29:21–28 [ET 22–29]; 30:11–20) and assuring the possibility of restoration contingent on repentance (4:29–31; 30:1–10). The parallel introductory headings of 4:44 and 45, along with efforts made in 5:1, 28–31 to associate the Decalogue with the "statutes and ordinances" of Deuteronomic law, indicate that the Ten Commandments were not originally part of the book. Covenant making at Shechem (11:29–30; ch. 27) and in Moab (28:69–29:20 [ET 29:1–21]) also represent supplements to the core of Deuteronomy intended to connect it to the life of its readers and motivate obedience to its precepts.

Moreover, redactional complexity is visible even within the primary material, namely chapters 6–11 (parenesis), 12–26 (law code), and 28 (blessings and curses). Some of the laws themselves are plainly pre-Deuteronomic. Various perspectives on cult centralization occur within successive layers in chapter 12. A later supplement to chapter 20 makes the sacral war law more severe. The golden calf story (9:8–10:11) is clearly a later supplement, interrupting its context. The notion that obedience to the law would not only lead to a good life once the land was acquired, but was even a preliminary requirement to permit a successful conquest (4:1; 6:18–19; 8:1; 11:8; 16:20) stands at odds with the predominant theology of Deuteronomy. Claims of special prerogatives for the tribe of Levi as a whole (10:8–9; 18:1–2, 5) fit poorly with what the book says elsewhere about the priesthood. Beyond these instances, however, Deut 6–26, 28 exhibit no obvious succession of layers or redactions. The book's language and theology are so unified that attempts to distinguish such layers and organize them chronologically have proven unrewarding and unpersuasive.

Deuteronomy restates or revises a number of laws from the Covenant Code (Exod 20:22–23:19). Because not all the laws of that earlier code are reformulated, it seems probable that Deuteronomy was not intended to supercede the Covenant Code completely or abrogate it. Rather Deuteronomy restates only some aspects in order to account for centralization (16:1–17 and Exod 23:14–17; Deut 19:1–13 and Exod 21:12–14; 26:1–11 and Exod 23:19a) and changes in economic and social relationships (e.g., Deut 15:1–11 elaborates the fallow year of Exod 23:10–11; Deut 15:12–18 and Exod 21:2–11), while preserving much of the wording in the original law.[6] Narrative portions of Deuteronomy also rely on or allude to texts in Exodus and Numbers, freely retelling those older traditions while often retaining verbal elements from the earlier sources. Allusions to incidents without explanation rely on audience familiarity with those texts or the traditions behind them.[7] Deuteronomy often makes passing references to what Yahweh has said or promised in the past. Sometimes these citations seem to point to texts in the Tetrateuch (1:11; 6:3; 11:25; 13:18 [ET 17]; 18:2; 19:8; 26:18).

A particularly puzzling feature of Deuteronomy is its frequent alternation between second-person singular and plural address, which only sometimes corresponds to irregularities in the text or differences in outlook. The critical implication of these shifts in grammatical number must be evaluated on a case-by-case basis. Alternation between singular and plural seems to be significant in determining successive redactional layers in chapters 4 and 12. At

6. Other restatements of the Covenant Code are 14:21b and Exod 23:19b; Deut 19:16–21 and Exod 23:1b; Deut 22:1–4 and Exod 23:4–5; Deut 22:28–29 and Exod 22:15–16 [ET 16–17]; Deut 23:20 [ET 19] and Exod 22:24 [ET 25]; Deut 24:10–13 and Exod 22:25–26 [ET 26–27]; Deut 24:17–18 and Exod 22:20–23 [ET 21–24].

7. In the DH portions, 1:9–18 relies on Exod 18:13–27 and Num 11:11–17; Deut 1:19–46 depends on the spy story of Nums 13–14; and the encounters with the nations east of the Jordan utilize Num 20:14–21; 21:21–31. In the parenetic section, much of Deut 7 is related to Exod 23:20–33. The golden calf narrative of Deut 9:8–10:11 reflects elements of Exod 32 and 34.

other times the variation seems to be a rhetorical device to highlight elements in the text or to indicate structural units. Sometimes a shift in number was caused by the presence of a traditional formula or a quotation from another text (cf. 11:19b quoting 6:7b). Occasionally a genuine change of addressee seems to be indicated. Deuteronomy uses the collective singular to address the entire community, but shifts to the plural to focus on the individuals who make up the community in order to highlight personal responsibility.

Internal evidence indicates that Deuteronomy was originally produced as a reforming law in a time of religious, political, and social crisis. Loyalty to Yahweh was being undermined by the worship of other gods and the problematic policies of the monarchy. Deuteronomy sees a need to limit the king's authority and wealth and to test and limit prophetic speech. Some classes of society have fallen into poverty or slavery, but Deuteronomy itself is addressed to free, independent landowners with significant financial resources. The book presupposes a monarchic society, with a structured judicial system, and knows about forced labor imposed on conquered peoples as well as siege warfare. The world of Deuteronomy is an urbanized culture of walled communities whose citizens gather to do public business in the gates. Its social horizon encompasses a population of farmers and herders, priests and Levites, slaves and dependent resident aliens, but not merchants, artisans, or professional soldiers. There are laws about worship, justice, and family life, but none concerning commerce, real estate, contracts, commercial loans, royal taxation, or forced labor. Deuteronomy counts on some degree of literacy among its audience.

Two factors anchor the origins of Deuteronomy in the first three-quarters of the seventh century. First, Deuteronomy's rhetoric is enhanced by ideas and language from the Assyrian loyalty oath (notably the Vassal Treaties of Esarhaddon, 672 B.C.E.). These parallels are clearest in the sanctions against treason in chapter 13 and the blessings and curses of chapter 28. The second historical anchor is Deuteronomy's association with the reform of Josiah (622 B.C.E.). To be sure, questions have been raised about the historical value of what is reported in 2 Kgs 22–23. To judge everything in these chapters as a Deuteronomistic fiction would undermine the association of Josiah's policies with the requirements of Deuteronomy. Such a judgment would also preclude any relationship between the curses of Deut. 28 and either Josiah's fearful reaction or Huldah's threats (2 Kgs 22:11, 13, 16–17). Without doubt, the report of the discovery of "the book of the law of Moses" (2 Kgs 22:3–23:3) parallels other accounts of "miraculous discovery" intended to give authority to a literary work.[8] However, elements within the ensuing report of Josiah's cultic reforms

---

8. B. J. Diebner and C. Nauerth, "Die Inventio des *spr htwrh* in 2 Kön 22: Struktur, Intention und Funktion von Auffindungslegenden," *DBAT* 18 (1984): 95–118. The "discovery plot" reuses elements of Joash's temple repair procedures (2 Kgs 12:4–16).

(2 Kgs 23:4–14) reflect interests and particulars that cannot simply be derived from Deuteronomy. These include the fate of non-Yahwistic priests (v. 5), particular cultic installations in Jerusalem (vv. 6–7, 8b, 10–13), and the technical details of desecration (vv. 6b, 14). The presence of these non-Deuteronomic interests suggests that DH used a source at this point and that the cultic reform of Josiah actually did take place.

Even apart from the question of Josiah's reform, Deuteronomy reflects the issues and crises of the period of Assyrian dominance over Judah. This was a time of cultural and economic crisis and of prophetic censure of oppressive social conditions. Life in the land was threatened by the prospect of exile, which was a common feature of Assyrian foreign policy. The presence throughout Deuteronomy of concepts associated with the prophet Hosea (e.g., covenant, Yahweh's love and redemption, Israel's satiation and forgetting of Yahweh, "grain, new wine, and oil") seems to reflect the influx of refugees into Judah from the destroyed northern kingdom. The roots of centralization may go back to the crisis of Hezekiah's policies and the effects of his rebellion in 701. The existence of a reform movement like that mirrored in Deuteronomy would be understandable as resistance to the religious and international policies of Manasseh. Such resistance, both inside and outside the royal court, is apparent in the assassination of Manasseh's son Amon by "his servants" and the subsequent installation of Josiah by the "people of the land" (2 Kgs 21:23–24). Such a reform movement could have taken root in the powerful, aristocratic scribal and priestly families of Jerusalem, whose position would have been threatened by Manasseh's religious and political policies and strengthened by Josiah's accession as a minor with the need for some sort of regency. Such an origin would be consistent with the presence in Deuteronomy of scribal patterns, priestly interests, legal concerns, and elements from the wisdom tradition.[9] Deuteronomy shows its own nationalistic fervor in the borders described in 11:24 and the ethnic pride attested in 15:6; 26:19; 28:1, 12–13.[10]

Origin within an originally clandestine movement made up of groups with different but overlapping interests (scribes, priests, sages, aristocrats) is the best explanation for Deuteronomy's particular literary character. Its cohesive ideological program is expressed in uniform language, but nevertheless reveals an abundance of theological inconsistencies and ambiguities. Deuteronomy has proven to be resistant to analysis into clearly defined and

9. The ideology of wisdom is apparent in the handling of laws such as 19:14 (Prov 22:28; 23:10) or 25:13–16 (Prov 11:1; 20:23) and the attitude behind 23:23–24 [ET 22–23] (cf. Qoh 5:1–5). See G. Braulik, "'Weisheit' im Buch Deuteronomium," in *Studien zum Buch Deuteronomium* (SBAB 24; Stuttgart: Katholisches Bibelwerk, 1997), 225–71.

10. For Deuteronomy as the product of a coalition reform movement, see R. Albertz, *A History of Israelite Religion in the Old Testament Period* (trans. J. Bowden; 2 vols.; OTL; Louisville, Ky.: Westminster John Knox, 1994), 1:195–231.

mutually exclusive stages of literary development. Differing viewpoints are present, but they cannot be coordinated into layers or assigned to different time periods.

It is better to postulate a process of scribal recopying and restructuring by a limited circle of contributors for a limited circle of readers over a relatively brief period of time. Perhaps the expression "microredaction" would be appropriate to describe such a process of accretion by small steps and changes by minor increments. These are the sorts of changes one would expect in a document intended for limited, internal distribution within a small group. One would expect an efflorescence of expansions, motivational clauses, supplements, internal quotations, and allusions—as well as importations from other documents—that cannot be associated with discrete layers or stages. This aptly describes the literary character of Deut 5–26, 28. The tools of traditional historical criticism are too blunt to tease apart such a richly ramified and intertwined growth. However, once Deuteronomy became publicly accessible and respected, presumably as the foundation for Josiah's reform, its text would have remained more or less stable. For this reason, subsequent monarchic and exilic additions may be discerned without difficulty.

Deuteronomy most likely began as a covert undertaking by dissident Jerusalem scribal circles during the reign of Manasseh and the minority of Josiah, with collaboration from aristocratic families, elements of the priesthood, and those schooled in wisdom. Traditional legal materials formed the basis for a document fashioned through a series of scribal microredactions. Older laws were formed into a program of religious, social, and political reform, fashioned in part on the model of Assyrian loyalty treaties. This process led to a legal code intended to serve as the basis for reform, one that centered on the centralization of sacrifice and its implications, a "constitutional proposal" to regulate various officeholders (16:18–18:22), and measures to improve the economic and social position of marginalized groups. In order to achieve acceptance, a number of authors and editors incorporated a persistent, repeated, motivational rhetoric into this law code, prefaced it with an introductory admonition (chs. 5–11), and concluded it with a catalog of blessings and curses derived in part from Assyrian culture (ch. 28).

In the friendlier domestic and international climate of Josiah's reign, this underground reform theology emerged as a freely accessible "published" document and temporarily became public policy. Later, blocks of material were added in order to adapt Deuteronomy to new situations and different literary contexts. These expansions highlighted covenant making at Shechem (ch. 27) and Moab (28:69–29:20 [ET 29:1–21]) and encouraged obedience (ch. 4, 29:21 [ET 22]–30:20). Chapters 1–3, 31, and elements of 34 connected Deuteronomy to the wider historical horizon of the Deuteronomistic History. The addition of the Song of Moses (ch. 32) offered a prophetic theology of history, and the

Blessing of Moses (ch. 33) emphasized Deuteronomy's nature as the final testament of the lawgiver.

Theological Themes

Deuteronomy epitomizes a movement that had an enormous effect on the history of Judah, on subsequent theological developments, and on the evolution of the biblical canon. The book offers a reforming, comprehensive reinterpretation of Israel's inherited traditions in the context of an unsettled present and a threatening future. It seeks to reevaluate traditional law at a moment of critical transition, explain that law, and motivate acceptance and obedience. The law in question is not new. It is purportedly law commanded by Yahweh and Moses in Israel's foundational period. Deuteronomy reinterprets inherited laws (the Covenant Code, the Decalogue, and pre-Deuteronomic laws in chs. 12–26), applying them to the new situation faced by the audience. In order to evoke a response of renewed commitment, this law code is presented in terms of a covenant put forward by Yahweh and accepted by Israel long ago.

As an idealistic proposal for reform, Deuteronomy possesses a utopian flavor, ignoring some of the obdurate realities of power politics, class struggle, and economics. Many of its commands would have been unenforceable by legal measures. Deuteronomy has an idealized, timeless quality, collapsing the contemporaries of Moses into the current audience of the book, as both generations are confronted by the demand to decide to obey "today." Deuteronomy is not "legalistic" in the sense of focusing only on the performance of required actions, but speaks to the heart, arguing from concrete laws and Yahweh's gracious deeds to generalized ethical principles and faithful attitudes.

Deuteronomy demands the centralization of sacrifice as the result of Yahweh's choice of a single place of worship and in order to protect Israel's relationship to Yahweh, its cultic purity, and its national unity. Centralization reflects the unity of a single Yahweh worshiped at one altar by a unified people. Although in late monarchic Judah the only realistic candidate for this central sanctuary would be Jerusalem, Deuteronomy does not make this identification. No doubt the authors felt that mention of a city absorbed into Israel only in the reign of David would be inappropriate for Moses. Deuteronomy confesses the reality of Yahweh's presence in association with this central altar without describing divine presence as habitation in a temple building. Yahweh has chosen to be present and available at the central shrine, electing it as a special "place" by placing the divine name there (12:5, 11, 14, 18, 21; 14:23–25, etc.). At that place, one worships "before Yahweh" (16:11, 16; 26:10, 13). What matters is not so much how Yahweh has chosen to be present, but that Israel assembles regularly at that place and that joyful sacrificial celebrations involving all social classes take place there. Deuteronomy says nothing about fixed, nationally sponsored sacrifices, but emphasizes private offerings made during pilgrimage festivals, performed to fulfill vows, and offered to express gratitude and obligation to Yahweh (12:5–27; 14:22–26; 16:1–17; 23:22–24 [ET 21–23]; 26:1–11). The consolidation of sacrifice also affects the use of the tithe, the disposition of firstling animals, the practice of jurisprudence, and the role of priests (e.g., 14:28–29; 15:19–23; 17:8–13; 18:1–8; 26:12–15).

Deuteronomy demands the eradication of anything that would compromise Yahweh's position as sole God of Israel. The worship of other gods is a capital offense (ch. 13; 17:2–7); idols and rival religious paraphernalia and practices must be eliminated (7:1–5, 25–26; 12:2–4, 29–31; 16:21–17:1; 18:9–14). Yahweh must be Israel's "one and only" God (6:4–5). Yahweh's exclusive claim on Israel's worship is based on a history of saving deeds involving promise to the patriarchs, redemption through the exodus, wilderness experience, and the gift of the land. Yahweh's claim on Israel rests on the special nature and character of Yahweh as jealous (4:24; 5:9; 6:15), merciful (4:31), living (5:26), consistent (7:9–10), just (10:17–18), as well as wrathful and terrible (7:4, 21; 29:19, 27 [ET 20, 28]). Yahweh dwells in heaven (26:15) and is the only true God (10:17).

Deuteronomy stresses Yahweh's election of an undeserving Israel (4:37–39; 7:6–11; 9:5; 10:14–15) and the loyalty owed by Israel in return. The exodus is central to Israel's identity as Yahweh's people, and important lessons from it and other foundational traditions must be remembered and passed on to future generations. Yahweh loves Israel (4:37; 7:7–8; 10:15; 23:6 [ET 5]) and is to be loved and feared in return (4:10; 5:26; 6:2, 5, 13, 24, etc.). As a chosen people, Israel is a holy people (14:2, 21; 28:9) and Yahweh's treasured possession (7:6; 26:19). Other metaphors that describe this special relationship include that of parent and child (8:5; 32:6, 18) and inheritance (4:20; 32:9). Election entails responsibility, and Deuteronomy emphasizes the rewards of obedience and the punishments that would result from a refusal to obey (e.g., 11:13–17). The opposing consequences of obedience and disobedience are especially clear in the blessings and curses in chapter 28. Although this law is not difficult to obey (10:12–13; 30:11–14), Israel has shown itself to be stubborn and rebellious (9:6–7, 13, 22–24; 10:16; 29:17–18 [ET 18–19]). Yet Israel's future is also bound up with divine promise (15:6; 26:18–19; 29:12 [ET 13]) and clemency (4:29–31; 30:1–10). Ultimately, this law is intended to offer life, not death (4:40; 6:3; 30:19–20).

Deuteronomy emphasizes humanitarian concerns and promotes a sense of responsibility to fellow Israelites. This outlook is evidenced in laws with a conspicuous humanitarian quality (15:1–18; 20:5–8; 22:1–8; 23:16–26 [ET 15–25] 24:6, 10–22; 25:1–4). This social ethic is based on a shared history of slavery and liberation. All Israelites are "brothers" (19:18–20; 22:1–4; 23:20–21 [ET 19–20]; 25:3). Slaves, both male and female, and debtors are treated as brothers (ch. 15). The king finds his proper role as a brother (17:15). Levitical priests enjoy their portion with their brothers (18:7). This overarching, idealized kinship takes the place of the earlier family structures on which social support and protection from economic catastrophe had depended, but which had broken down. Deuteronomy provides special protections for debtors, wage laborers, slaves, those without husband or father, economically dependent resident aliens, and even animals.[11] However, the ethos of Deuteronomy remains an "ingroup" social ethic of a group sharply defined against outsiders by sacral war (ch. 20), the elimination of foreign groups (7:1–5), and ethnic barriers (23:4–7 [ET 3–6]; 25:17–19). Social welfare depends on fair and effective government. Deuteronomy's "constitutional proposal" distributes authority among various officeholders and limits the possibility of abuse by a system of checks and balances (16:18–18:22). Much attention is given to a fair and effective system of justice (16:18–20; 17:2–13; 19:1–13, 15–21). Even the king is subject to the law (17:18–20).

Deuteronomy presents a law for life in the land given by Yahweh. This land comes as a gift promised to the ancestors (6:10, 18, 23; 8:1; 11:9, 21). It is a splendid land (6:10–11; 8:7–9; 11:9–12). The land is the place where Israel is to obey the law (6:1, 10; 12:1; 16:18; 17:14; 18:9; 19:1) in order to create the fair and just society described in it. The land is the place of secure "rest" (12:9–10; 25:19; cf. 5:14). However, continued occupation of the land and life there depends on obedience (4:26; 7:12–15; 11:8–9, 13–17; 25:15; 30:16–18). In the final form of Deuteronomy, the gift of the land is framed by the threat of expulsion from it and, subsequently, the possibility of return (4:25–31; 29:21 [ET 22] –30:10).

Deuteronomy presents itself as a covenant between Yahweh and Israel. As such it is protected by a catalog of blessings and curses (ch. 28). Deuteronomy 26:16–19 summarizes this covenant as a mutual agreement in which Yahweh assumes the role of being Israel's God and Israel takes on an obligation to obey the "statutes and ordinances" of Deuteronomy as Yahweh's people. This covenant is a counterpart to the one made at Horeb with the previous generation (4:13, 23; 5:2–3; 17:2; 28:69 [ET 29:1]) and was concluded in Moab on the very day Moses spoke the law there (28:69–29:20 [ET 29:1–21]). By "covenant" Deuteronomy of course means a compact with mutual responsibilities, but also something sustained by the sure promises of Yahweh (4:31; 7:9, 12; 8:18).

Deuteronomy confronts every serious reader with a moment of existential decision, the choice of whether to accept or reject its claim over one's life. This moment of decision is always "today," always on the threshold of new

---

11. Deut 12:12, 18–19; 14:28–29; 15:1–18; 16:11, 14; 22:4, 6–7, 10; 23:16–17, 20, 25–26 [ET 15–16, 19, 24–25]; 24:6, 10–15, 17–22; 25:1–4.

possibilities for richer life. The threat of impending curse means that one dare not postpone this decision. Incessantly, Deuteronomy urges the reader to respond, to choose obedience, and thus to receive the benefits and blessings that will result. Through skillful and impassioned motivational rhetoric, it seeks to make this decision self-evident and easy. To say yes is to act out one's choice in religious loyalty, in the practice of social justice, and in one's public and personal life. To say yes is to affirm one's allegiance to one, incomparable, loving God and to catch the vision that religious fidelity, personal morality, social responsibility, and trustworthy government hold together as a single aspiration for the human race.

March Forth
1:1–18

Setting the Scene

1:1 These are the words that Moses spoke to all Israel on the other side of the Jordan in the wilderness, in the Arabah opposite Suph, between Paran and Tophel, Laban, Hazeroth, and Di-zahab.[a] 2 It is eleven days from Horeb by the Mount Seir road to Kadesh-barnea. 3 It was in the fortieth year in the eleventh month on the first day of the month that Moses spoke to the Israelites according to everything that Yahweh had commanded him in regard to them,[b] 4 after he had struck down Sihon king of the Amorites who ruled[c] in Heshbon, and Og king of Bashan who ruled in Ashtaroth, in Edrei.[d] 5 On the other side of the Jordan in the land of Moab, Moses began[e] to state clearly[f] this law, saying:

6 Yahweh our God spoke to us at Horeb, saying, "You have stayed long enough at this mountain. 7 Set out, march forth,[g] and go into the hill country of the Amorites and to all their neighbors[h] in the Arabah, the hill country, the Shephelah, the Negeb, and the seacoast—the land of the Canaanites[i]—and the Lebanon, as far as the great river, the Euphrates River. 8 See, I hereby give[j] the land over to you. Go in and take over the land that Yahweh swore[k] to your ancestors, to Abraham, to Isaac, and to Jacob, to give to them[l] and to their descendants after them."

Moses Appoints Judges

9 At that time I said to you, "I cannot carry you by myself. 10 Yahweh your God has multiplied you, so that today you are as many as the stars in the sky. 11 May Yahweh, the God of your ancestors, make you a thousand times larger than you are and bless you, just as he promised you! 12 How can I carry[m] the weight and burden of you and your bickering by myself? 13 Choose for each of your tribes men who are wise, understanding, and experienced[n] and I will appoint them as your leaders."[o]

14 You answered me, "What you have proposed to do is good."

15 So I took the leaders of your tribes,[p] men who were wise and experienced, and appointed them as leaders over you, commanders of thousands, commanders of hundreds, commanders of fifties, commanders of tens, and officers for your tribes.[q] 16 I commanded your judges at that

time, "Hear out[r] your kindred and judge fairly between any person and a kindred or a resident alien. 17 Do not show partiality in judgment. Hear both small and great alike. Do not be afraid of anyone, for judgment belongs to God. Any matter that is too hard for you, you shall bring to me and I will hear it." 18 So I commanded you at that time about all the things that you should do.

a. Alternate translation joining v. 1b to v. 2 as an itinerary: "Through the wilderness . . . , it is eleven days . . . by the Mount Seir road."

b. Alternate translation: "to speak to them."

c. This understands *yāšab* as "sat on the throne" rather than as "lived" (3:2; 4:46; cf. Amos 1:8 with Amos 2:3).

d. Another option is to connect the end of v. 4 with the first phrase of v. 5: "in Edrei on the other side of the Jordan." MT "in Edrei" (with no "and") may be construed as the location of Og's defeat (cf. 3:1).

e. The verb *y'l* hip'il implies a deliberate and decisive initiative in a new situation. See A. Kapelrud, "*y'l*," *TDOT* 5:357–58.

f. This translation is required by the context. The pi'el of *b'r* is also used for writing something down clearly (27:8; Hab 2:2). Other possible translations are "explain" or "expound."

g. The verbal hendiadys with *pānâ* (turn) implies volition and decision (cf. vv. 24, 40). *Lākem* is a centripetal or reflexive dative, indicating that an action has a decisive effect on the grammatical subject: "make your way," *IBHS* 11.2.10d.

h. Alternate translation connecting the pronominal suffix to "hill country" rather than to "Amorites": "all its neighboring territories."

i. Taking this expression as a summary of v. 7a conforms with the masoretic punctuation. An alternate translation would understand "the land of Canaan" as a reference only to "the seacoast."

j. This translation reflects the performative speech indicated by the perfect tense, in which a legal transfer takes place in the speaking of the formula, *IBHS* 30.5.1d. The preposition *lipnê* implies "at your disposal" (cf. 2:31; 7:2, 23).

k. Follows MT, Syr., and Vulg. This is smoothed out to "I swore" by OG and Sam.

l. Follows MT and OG. Because the land was not actually given to the patriarchs, Sam. eliminates "to them and."

m. Modal use of the imperfect to denote capability, *IBHS* 31.4c.

n. Here, and in v. 15, the translation construes the participle actively in the sense of "those who know," corresponding to the parallel notions of "wise" and "understanding." It is possible to understand the participle in a passive way as "known" in the sense of "reputable."

o. The *bêt* of identity (*beth essestiae*) indicates "in the capacity of being your leaders," *IBHS* 11.2.53.

p. Follows MT, Sam., Syr., and Vulg. This phrase is awkward—these men have not yet actually become tribal leaders—and is probably a secondary expansion. OG simplifies to "I took from you."

q. Follows MT and Sam. in reading *lšbtykm*. OG has the phonetically similar *lšptykm*, "as your judges," a confusion of labials, probably reinforced by contamination from the next verse.

r. That is, hear both sides of the argument; literally "listen between" (cf. Judg 11:10). I use the translation "kindred" for the singular and plural of "brother."

Verse 1a is the first heading in an all-encompassing system of rubrics that organizes the final form of Deuteronomy. The other headings are 4:44–45 "This is the law"; 28:69 [ET 29:1], "These are the words of the covenant"; and 33:1, "This is the blessing." Verses 1–5 present an expanded introduction to an address by Moses that begins with v. 6 and is eventually interrupted by the action of 4:41–43. This introduction lays out the dramatic setting of Deuteronomy, just before the invasion, and establishes its genre as a valedictory testament. The dramatic moment is fixed in time by references to the exodus ("fortieth year"), Horeb, wilderness experience (Kadesh-barnea), and conquest east of the Jordan. The section stresses that the words that follow are indeed the words of Moses, authorized by Yahweh and shaped for easy comprehension (note f). Deuteronomy is not the promulgation of some new law, but an exposition and reaffirmation of the law that had already been given (vv. 3, 5).

Verse 6 reports that the subsequent narrative is a "retelling" of a story already known. For the fictional audience these events are something they have witnessed personally. For their part, the readers of Deuteronomy are also expected to be familiar with these traditions. Moses begins his long discourse with a claim to the land based on a geographical catalog and a divine conveyance rooted in ancestral promise (vv. 6–8). These verses also initiate the overall pattern of chapters 1–3 as one of imperative ("set out, march forth, and go") followed by journey and action. However, immediate obedience to the command of vv. 7–8 is delayed by preliminary preparations (vv. 9–18). This opening narrative establishes a juridical framework for the application of Deuteronomy's law in the land and partially answers the need for successors to Moses' various leadership roles. Israel enters the land as a numerous and organized people committed to the principles of wisdom and justice.[1]

1. Studies of chs. 1–3 include H. Cazelles, "Passages in the Singular within Discourse in the Plural of Dt 1–4," *CBQ* 29 (1967): 207–19; N. Lohfink, "Darstellungskunst und Theologie in Dtn 1:6–3:29," in *Studien zum Deuteronomium und zur deuteronomistischen Literatur I* (SBAB 8; Stuttgart: Katholisches Bibelwerk, 1990), 15–44; idem, "Geschichtstypologie in Deuteronomium 1–3," in *Lasset uns Brücken bauen* (ed. K.–D, Schunk and M. Augustin; BEATAJ 42; Frankfurt: Lang, 1998), 87–92; idem, "The Problem of Individual and Community in Deuteronomy 1;6–3:29," in *Theology of the Pentateuch: Themes of the Priestly Narrative and Deuteronomy* (trans. L. Maloney; Minneapolis: Fortress Press, 1994), 227–33; trans. of "Wie stellt sich das Problem Individuum—Gemeinschaft in Deuteronomium 1,6–3,29?" in *Studien zum Deuteronomium I*, 45–51; P. D. Miller, "The Wilderness Journey in Deuteronomy: Style, Structure, and Theology in

[1–5] The perspective of this introduction views Moses as a literary character, depicted in the third person (cf. 5:1; 27:1, 9, 11; 31:1, 7, 10, 25, 30; 32:44). Verse 5 brackets the paragraph by reversing the grammatical sequence of v. 1: verb followed by location. It also repeats "on the other side of the Jordan" and more narrowly identifies "these words" as "this law." The final form of vv. 1–5 exhibits a concentric pattern: "Moses spoke" (v. 1a), place (v. 1b), time (v. 3a), "Moses spoke" (v. 3b), time (v. 4), place (v. 5a), "Moses began to state clearly" (v. 5b).

Even so, the section reflects a complex history of composition. Successive additions have expanded the core nominal sentence of the title (v. 1a), piling up information in a composite way. These supplements serve to localize the address of Moses into various redactional horizons. It is difficult to reconstruct a detailed history of these overlapping and competing additions. Nonetheless, it seems clear that vv. 1a, 4, 5 reveal the interests of Deuteronomy and the Deuteronomistic History (DH), while vv. 1b, 2, 3 reflect the horizon of the Pentateuch as a whole. Geographically and temporally, vv. 1a, 4–5 look forward to lawgiving and conquest ("across the Jordan," Sihon and Og, Moab), while vv. 1b, 2–3 look back to the wilderness and Kadesh-barnea.[2]

The "all Israel" theme of v. 1a emphasizes the essential unity of the nation as the audience of Moses' address (5:1; 27:9, 14; 29:1 [E 2]; 31:1, 7, 11, 30; 32:45). This theme also brackets the entire book (cf. 1:1 with 34:12). The overloaded list of places with prepositions (v. 1b) sounds as if what was formerly an itinerary has been converted into a generalized geographic location. The place names are difficult to identify, and scholars disagree as to whether they reflect wilderness trek stations or sites around the Mount Nebo area. As localities in the wilderness, they would be at odds with the Beth-peor locale of 3:29; 4:46a; 34:6 and with the Moab situation of v. 5. Mapped as an itinerary, they

---

Deuteronomy 1–3," *Covenant Quarterly* 55 (1997): 50–68; L. Perlitt, "Deuteronomium 1–3 im Streit der exegetischen Methoden," in *Das Deuteronomium: Enstehung, Gestalt und Botschaft* (ed. N. Lohfink; BETL 68; Leuven: Leuven University Press, 1985), 149–63; T. Veijola, "Principal Observations on the Basic Story in Deuteronomy 1–3," in *A Song of Power and the Power of Song: Essays on the Book of Deuteronomy* (ed. D. Christensen; SBTS 3; Winona Lake, Ind.: Eisenbrauns, 1993), 137–46.

2. Z. Kallai, "Where Did Moses Speak (Deuteronomy I 1–5)?" *VT* 45 (1995): 188–97, suggests that vv. 1–5 are an integrated, purposeful literary construction, presenting a succinct preannouncement of the subject of Moses' discourse in vv. 1–4, followed by the full discourse itself beginning with a new start in v. 5 and continuing to the end of ch. 3. The place names and other references of vv. 1–4 allude briefly to the events from Horeb to Moab that are then recounted fully in the speech that follows. Thus vv. 1b–2 represent the wilderness period from Horeb to Kadesh-barnea (i.e., 1:6–46) by listing stages of the wilderness itinerary in reverse order (cf. "Arabah" in 2:8 and "Sea of Suph" [Red Sea] in 2:1). Verse 3 refers to the timetable of Moses speaking at divine command. Verse 4 uses the victories over the two Amorite kings to summarize the remainder of Moses' historical review.

seem to look backward in time from the Arabah via Paran to places nearer Horeb.[3] In any case, the literary effect is one of setting the scene in history, pulling present and past together. The text emphasizes that the speech of Moses takes place "in the wilderness" and not yet in the land, illustrating this fact by a list of wilderness names.

The timetable and itinerary of v. 2 are a geographical parenthesis, since Israel is not at Kadesh-barnea when Moses speaks. Roads were often designated by their destination, so the "Mount Seir road" would be a route from Horeb that continued beyond Kadesh-barnea onward to Seir. This notice does point forward to the upcoming narratives that begin with 1:19 ("to Kadesh-barnea") and repeatedly highlight that location (1:46; 2:14; 9:23). Seir, too, reappears in 1:44; 2:1, 5. The rhetorical point is that a wilderness journey that could have taken a mere matter of days turned out to consume an entire generation (v. 3; 1:46; 2:1, 14).

Verse 3 is part of a chain of dates involving Josh 4:19 and 5:10. It is usually related to the Priestly Writer and linked to 32:48–52, chapter 34, and the itinerary fragments of 10:6–7. The beginning of "the eleventh month" of "the fortieth year" means that Israel will soon be crossing the Jordan. This date connects Deuteronomy to the rest of the Pentateuch and emphasizes that it is a testament spoken on the very day of Moses' death.[4] Moreover, the "words of Moses" (v. 1) are unequivocally designated as Yahweh's words. In contrast to the calendrical "when" of v. 3, v. 4 offers a narrative "when" that foreshadows 2:26–3:7 and also signals that the crossing is at hand.

Verse 5 specifies that "the words" of v. 1 consist precisely in an act of law-giving. It aptly points to what follows as explicated law, characterized by the motivations and comments typical of Deuteronomy. The designation of the locale as Moab prepares for 28:69 [ET 29:1]; 34:1, 5, 6, 8. "Began" forms a unifying bracket with "finished" in 31:1; 32:45. The phrase "this law" will be picked up by the new major heading of 4:44. At this point the law is oral, a speech delivered before death (4:44–45). This notion of oral delivery stands in tension with statements that describe Deuteronomy as a written book (17:18–19; 27:3, 8; 28:58, 61; 29:20 [ET 21]; 30:10; 31:24, 26). If the verb *b'r* "state clearly," can also imply "write down" (note f), it would mediate this tension to a degree.

[6–8] "Long enough" (*rab lākem*) in v. 6 goads Israel from stagnation into action, setting in motion and unifying the upcoming plot (2:3; cf. 3:26). Here the phrase introduces a plot of disobedience and failure; in 2:3 it will begin a

---

3. Here "Arabah" means the valley north of the Dead Sea. Paran correlates with Kadesh-barnea (Num 13:3, 26) and is a general designation for the wilderness west of Edom (Num 10:12). Laban seems to be the Libnah of Num 33:20–21. Hazeroth ("enclosures") is a journey stage in Num 11:35; 33:16–18.

4. J. van Goudoever, "The Liturgical Significance of the Date in Dt 1,3," in *Das Deuteronomium*, ed. Lohfink, 145–48.

plot of obedience and success. Repetition of the verb *yāšab* "stay" in 1:6, 46; 3:29 performs a similar unifying function, segmenting the journey—by means of periods of stasis—into a negative expedition from Horeb to Kadesh (1:6 to 1:46) followed by a successful expedition ending at Beth peor (3:29). "Our God" stresses the relationship of Yahweh to the audience of Deuteronomy, while "to us" links them to the Horeb generation.

The imperatives of v. 7 initiate the journeys and actions of 1:19–3:7. "Set out" (*pānâ*) and "march forth" (*nāsaʿ*) continue to appear as imperative verbs in 1:40 and 2:3, 24, and as indicatives describing obedience in 1:19, 24; 2:1, 8; 3:1. (The translation of these verbs in this commentary varies with context.) This imperatival structure immediately sets Deuteronomy into a framework of command and obedience. However, the context is not yet instruction in the law but the course of history and possession of the land. This historical interest is plainly the redactional horizon of DH, although Deuteronomy itself also focuses on life "when you come into the land" (17:14; 18:9; 26:1). The geographical description piles up various sorts of data into an ever-widening perspective. "The hill country of the Amorites" points to the short-term goal of vv. 19–20 and "their neighbors" to the various enemies of Joshua.[5] This region is further defined by a geographical list that corresponds to the territory of Judah (cf. Josh 10:40; 11:16; 12:8) and then is summarized more expansively as "the land of the Canaanites." "And Lebanon" points to the horizon of DH in 3:25 and 1 Kgs 9:19 and begins a "line of extent" formula that affirms the imperialistic aspirations also expressed in Deut 11:24 and Josh 1:4 ("as far as the great river"; cf. Ps 72:8; 2 Sam 8:3–8; 10:15–18; 1 Kgs 5:1, 4 [ET 4:21, 24]; cf. 2 Kgs 14:25).[6]

Verse 8 introduces the campaign of chapters 1–3 as a paradigm of the entire conquest, as one guaranteed by long-standing divine promise. Through an act of "performative speech" (note j), Yahweh uses what sounds like a legal formula to give Israel its "occupancy permit." The rhetoric is repeatedly doubled and thus strongly emphatic: "hereby give" and "to give to them," "give the land" and "take over the land," "to you ancestors" and "to Abraham," etc., "to them" and "to their descendants." "Descendants" links promised possession to both the fictional listeners and the reader of Deuteronomy (cf. 11:9; 34:4).[7]

---

5. "Amorites" is more an ideological label (Ezek 16:3; Amos 2:9–10) than an ethnographic one and thus designates enemies on both sides of the Jordan (cf. Deut 3:2, 8).

6. For other "lines of extent," see the commentary on 3:8–11, 12–17.

7. On the "fathers" in Deuteronomy, see T. Römer, *Israels Väter: Untersuchungen zur Väterthematik im Deutoronomium und in der deuteronomistischen Tradition* (OBO 99; Freiburg: Universitätsverlag, 1990); idem, "Deuteronomy in Search of Origins" (trans. P. Daniels), in *Reconsidering Israel and Judah: Recent Studies on the Deuteronomistic History* (ed. G. N. Knoppers and J. G. McConville; SBTS 8; Winona Lake, Ind.: Eisenbrauns, 2000), 112–38. He proposes that older Deuteronomic references to the "fathers" refer to the exodus generation, and only later became the patriarchal ancestors.

[9–18] Moses shifts his reference from Yahweh's earlier speech to one of his own, stressing that this system of delegated justice was designed to be fair, was accepted at the grassroots level, and utilized highly talented people. This episode intervenes between the command of vv. 6–8 and its fulfillment in v. 19 and is often thought to represent a later stage of composition.[8] Nevertheless, its pattern of proposal/agreement/appointment used in a positive sense (vv. 13–15) is mirrored by the same pattern in vv. 22–23, but in a contrasting episode that ends in disobedience and failure.[9] Although this narrative clearly breaks into the connection between v. 7 and v. 19, it is hard to see where else an author or editor could have placed it without disturbing the ideological plot of what follows. Because the tradition of Exod 18 locates this event at Sinai, Deuteronomy certainly has to report it *before* Israel sets out for the hill country of the Amorites (vv. 7, 19). The repeated emphasis on "at that time" (vv. 9, 16, 18) reflects this chronological accent.

"At that time" repeatedly appears in chapters 1–3, sometimes introducing retrospection (2:34) and sometimes signaling digressions apparently added later (1:16, 18; 3:4, 8, 12, 18, 21, 23).[10] The literary effect of this repeated formula is to urge the reader to pay attention to the temporal circumstances. This particular event took place at Horeb; later examples of the formula will point to the time between Horeb and the "today" of Deuteronomy. Structurally, the argument made by Moses is bracketed by a repetition of "carry myself" in vv. 9 and 12.[11]

The problem of overwork, introduced abruptly by v. 9, is explained by Israel's population growth, which fulfills Yahweh's ancestral promise (10:22; cf. Gen 15.5). The wish of v. 11 may be an intrusive addition, but it is also rhetorically and psychologically understandable. "Bickering" (v. 12) translates *rîb* (legal disputation) and points specifically to the need for judges. The formulaic threefold talents of v. 13 (cf. Qoh 9:11) correspond to the threefold responsibilities of v. 12. There is some tension between Israel's authority to choose individuals from the tribes (v. 13) and Moses' appointment of those who

8. Appointment of these leaders is not explicitly part of Yahweh's command (vv. 6–8), nor do they appear in the following episodes.

9. G. Braulik traces a unifying pattern in the similarity between the three speeches given "at that time" in 1:9–13, 14, 16–17 (which follow the divine imperative of 1:6–8) and the three speeches "at that time" in 3:18–20, 21–22, 24–25 (which precede the divine command of 3:26–28). See "Weisheit im Buch Deuteronomium," in *Studien zum Buch Deuteronomium* (SBAB 24; Stuttgart: Katholisches Bibelwerk, 1997), 234–45.

10. S. E. Loewenstamm, "The Formula *Bā'et Hahi'* in the Introductory Speeches in Deuteronomy," in *From Babylon to Canaan: Studies in the Bible and Its Oriental Background* (Jerusalem: Magnes, 1992), 42–50.

11. For the poetics of this section, see D. L. Christensen, "Prose and Poetry in the Bible: The Narrative Poetics of Deuteronomy 1,9–18," *ZAW* 97 (1985): 179–89; and C. Schedl, "Prosa und Dichtung in der Bibel: Logotechnische Analyse von Dtn 1,9–18," *ZAW* 98 (1986): 271–75.

are already "leaders of your tribes" as "leaders" (v. 15). The point seems to be that the system was not arbitrarily imposed, but rather Israel agreed to it (v. 14). The officials were appointed from current tribal leaders selected by the people. Their titles (v. 15) sound as much military as juridical. "Commanders" (śārîm) of designated numerical divisions would seem appropriate for military units (20:9) or work gangs. "Officers" (šōṭĕrîm) deal with scribal affairs in both jurisprudence (16:18) and warfare (20:5, 8–9). In a stylistically pleasing move, the two offices are described by only two of the three attributes from v. 13. The justice system is comprehensive, reaching down to the level of tens.

By implication, the "leaders" who are "commanders" and "officers" are also the "judges" addressed in vv. 16–18. These verses exhibit a concentric structure: "I commanded . . . at that time" in vv. 16a and 18, "hear" in vv. 16b and 17b, and two occurrences of "judgment" surrounding another instance of "hear" in v. 17a. Verses 16b–17a stand out as a formulaic admonition, with positive apodictic commands surrounding an antithetical negative one. Fair decisions are insured by impartiality, even when a disdained resident alien is involved, and by the possibility of an appeal to Moses' special expertise. Judges similar to those addressed here will reappear in the legal portion of Deuteronomy (16:18–20), along with comparable concerns about favoritism (16:19) and making difficult decisions (17:8–13). Justice in the human sphere imitates that of Yahweh (10:17–18). Verse 18 is a generalizing summary that closes this section and redirects attention back to the wider horizon of Moses' narrative.

Deuteronomy's presentation takes into account previous traditions reflected in Num 11:11–17, 24b–30 (J), and Exod 18:13–27 (E). Verses 15–16, 17b parallel (and apparently derive from) Exod 18:18, 20–22, 25–26. Deuteronomy begins the story abruptly, but the Exodus version grows naturally out of its context. The Deuteronomic version eliminates Jethro and throws the process of judging and appealing to Moses into the future (cf. v. 17 with Exod 18:22, 26). The wisdom interest of v. 13 appears only in Deuteronomy. Deuteronomy also allows Israel a chance to agree to the plan (v. 14) and adds tribal interests and "officers" (cf. v. 15 with Exod 18:25). In Deut 1:16, the generic litigants of Exodus 18:16a (someone and a "neighbor") become the typical "kindred" ("brother") and "resident alien" so characteristic of Deuteronomy. Deuteronomy 1:9b, 12 ("carry," "burden") parallel Num 11:10–25 (cf. vv. 11, 14, 17b), but the direction of literary dependence is less clear than in the case of Exodus. In Num 11 Moses addresses his complaint to Yahweh rather than to the people.[12]

12. On the comparative age of these three texts, see H. Reviv, "The Traditions Concerning the Inception of the Legal System in Israel: Significance and Dating," *ZAW* 94 (1982): 566–75. For Deuteronomy's reinterpretation, see M. Z. Brettler, *The Creation of History in Ancient Israel* (New York: Routledge, 1995), 65–70.

A Failed Invasion
1:19–46

Scouting the Land

1:19 Then we marched forth from Horeb and went through all that great and terrible wilderness that you saw, on the road to the hill country of the Amorites, just as Yahweh our God had commanded us. We came to Kadesh-barnea. 20 I said to you, "You have come to the hill country of the Amorites, which Yahweh our God is going to give us. 21 See, Yahweh your God has given the land over to you. Go up, take possession, just as Yahweh the God of your ancestors promised you. Do not fear or be terrified." 22 Then you all came to me and said, "Let us send men ahead of us so they may scout out the land for us and bring us back word about the road by which we should go up and the cities that we will come to." 23 The proposal seemed good in my opinion, so I took twelve of you, one from each tribe. 24 They set out and went up toward the hill country and came to the Valley of Eshcol. They scouted it[a] out. 25 They took some of the fruit of the land with them and brought it down to us. They brought us back word[b] and said, "It is a good land that Yahweh our God is going to give us."

Mutiny

26 But you were not willing to go up. You rebelled against the command of Yahweh your God. 27 You grumbled[c] in your tents and said, "It is because[d] Yahweh hates us that he has brought us out of the land of Egypt, to put us into the power of the Amorites to destroy us. 28 What kind of place are we going up to? Our kindred have made our hearts melt, saying, 'A people greater and taller[e] than we are! Great cities fortified up to the sky! We even saw the Anakim there!'" 29 I said to you, "Do not be alarmed and do not fear them. 30 Yahweh your God, who goes before you, will be the one who fights for you, just as he did for you in Egypt right before your eyes,[f] 31 and in the wilderness, where you saw how Yahweh your God carried you, just as one carries a child, all the way that you went until you came to this place.[g] 32 But in spite of[h] this fact, you are without trust in Yahweh your God, 33 who goes before you on the way to reconnoiter a place for you to camp[i]—in the fire by night to show you the way you should go, and in the cloud by day."

34 When Yahweh heard the sound of your words, he became angry and swore, 35 "Not one of these people[j] shall see the good land that I swore

to give[k] to your ancestors, 36 except for Caleb son of Jephunneh. He shall see it, and I will give the land on which he stepped to him and to his children, because he remained fully loyal to Yahweh." 37 Yahweh was angry with me as well on your account, saying, "You shall not enter there either. 38 It is Joshua son of Nun, who stands ready to serve you, who shall enter there. Encourage him,[l] for he will cause Israel to inherit it. 39 And your small children, who you said would become booty and your children[m] who today do not yet know good from bad, they will enter there. To them I will give it, and they will take it over. 40 But as for you, turn back and march toward the wilderness in the direction of the Red Sea."

Israel Attacks on Its Own

41 Then you answered me, "We have sinned against Yahweh! We ourselves[n] will go up and fight, just as Yahweh our God commanded us." So you all girded on your battle gear and were ready[o] to go up to the hill country. 42 But Yahweh said to me, "Say to them, 'Do not go up and do not fight, for I am not in your midst so that[p] you should not be defeated before your enemies.'" 43 I spoke to you, but you did not listen. You rebelled against the command of Yahweh and acted arrogantly[q] and went up to the hill country. 44 The Amorites who lived in that hill country came out to engage you and pursued you just as bees do. They crushed[r] you through[s] Seir as far as Hormah. 45 Then you returned and wept before Yahweh, but Yahweh would not heed your voice or listen to you. 46 You remained at Kadesh many days.[t]

a. Follows MT. 1QDeut[a], Syr., Vulg. specify "the land."

b. Follows MT and Sam., but with reservations. This assumes that OG and Vulg. lost "they brought us back word" by haplography: *wy[šbw 'tnw dbr wy]'mrw*. However, it is possible that MT expanded a more original shorter text on the basis of v. 22b or Num 13:26 (P).

c. Perhaps the nip'al suggests "appear sullen," *HALOT* 3:1188.

d. Causal use of the preposition *b*, *IBHS* 36.2.2b.

e. Follows MT and Vulg. *wrm* as more appropriate to the huge Anakim (9:2). Sam. has *wrb*, "and more numerous," by confusion of *b* for *m*. OG conflates the two readings and follows the full formula as found in 2:21.

f. Follows MT. OG pedantically omits *l'ynykm*, "before your eyes," because this audience had not been in Egypt. "Did for you" translates the preposition *'et* as expressing advantage (cf. 10:21; R. J. Williams, *Hebrew Syntax: An Outline* [2d ed.; Toronto: University of Toronto Press, 1976], 341).

g. Verse 31a is second person singular and v. 31b is plural.

h. For *b* as "in spite of" see Num 14:11. *IBHS* explains this usage as a metaphorical *bêt* of price (p. 197 n. 28).

i. Follows MT. OG has transposed *lḥntkm* ("for you to camp") into *lnḥtkm* (hip'il of *nāḥâ*, "to lead you"), a reading that harmonizes with Exod 13:21. The awkward word order suggests that the fire provided light to show Israel its nighttime path. For the relation of this verse to Num 14:14 and Exod 13:21, see L. Perlitt, *Deuteronomium* (BKAT 5/2; Neukirchen-Vluyn: Neukirchener Verlag, 1991–), 111–14.

j. Follows OG. MT expands with an explanatory gloss: "this evil generation."

k. Follows MT. OG, Sam., and Vulg. omit "give" to correct the implication that the land had already been given to the patriarchs. Compare note 1 at v. 8.

l. The object pronoun is emphatic. The pi'el is delocative (i.e., based on a speech act): "say to him 'be strong,'" *IBHS* 24.2f.

m. Follows MT. OG (apparently supported by 4QDeut[h]) suffered haplography: *wṭp[km' 'šr 'mrtm lbz yhyh wbny]km 'šr*, dropping "who you said would become booty and your children." The *paidion neon* of OG most likely translates *ṭappĕkem* rather than *bĕnêkem*. An alternative is that the longer MT text represents a harmonizing expansion from Num 14:31 (P). Although Sam. omits "who today do not yet know good from bad," this phrase is retained here because there is no obvious source for it as an expansion.

n. "We" is in emphatic position implying "we and not our descendants."

o. This translation assumes that *hwn* hip'il originated as a sort of ad hoc formulation based on the parallel text of Num 14:40: *hnnw w'lynw* ("we are here and we will go up") giving rise to *wthynw l'lt* ("you were ready to go up"). The verb occurs only here in the Hebrew Bible and ancient translators did not understand it. The usual modern translation is "you considered it easy," based on a dubious Arabic cognate. Another proposal, grounded largely on context, is "equipped yourselves" (P. Grelot, "La racine *hwn* en Dt i 41," *VT* 12 [1962]: 198–201). Yet another suggestion is "were presumptuous" (R. Tournay, "A propos du verbe *hûn/hîn*," *RB* 103 [1994]: 321–25.) For a discussion, see E. Kutsch, "*hôn*," *TDOT* 3:365–66.

p. A negative purpose clause, GKC 109g.

q. To engage in "a presumptuous, premeditated offense against God and his religious and moral order" (J. Scharbert, "*zûdh*," *TDOT* 4:48). Such arrogance does not obey or fear God (cf. the object lesson of 17:12–13 and the prophet of 18:20).

r. Hip'il of *ktt*, "break into small pieces," thus "to make an enemy break formation and scatter in flight," exactly as in Num 14:45. See G. Warmuth, "*ktt*," *TDOT* 7:392–94.

s. Follows MT. OG, Vulg., and Syr. read "from Seir" by confusion of *b* and *m*, resulting in an "improved" text. Proposals to translate *b* as "from" based on Ugaritic usage are misguided. It is best to understand this *b* as "in the region of" or "through" (*IBHS* 11.2.5b). Since "Seir" refers to Edomite territory and is not present in Num 14:45, it is sometimes taken as a gloss from Deut 2:1, 4, 8.

t. Literally "You sat at Kadesh many days, as the days you sat," an idiom indicating an unspecified period: "so and so many days." For a similar construction, cf. 29:15 [ET 16].

Literary Structure

The plot moves from setting and command (vv. 19–21) through a deflecting, delaying sidetrack of spying (vv. 22–25) to the climax of rebellion (vv. 26–28). Then the fallout of this transgression is reported, first through the reactions of

Moses (vv. 29–33) and Yahweh (vv. 34–40), and then by an account of Israel's impudence and defeat (vv. 41–46). At every turn, Israel's disobedience and defeat are cast in the worst possible light so that they may stand in contrast to the victories of the next generation reported in chapters 2 and 3.

The episode begins and ends at Kadesh-barnea (vv. 19b, 46; the location derives from Num 13:26), and the action takes place in the hill country of the Amorites (vv. 19a, 20). The concluding return to Kadesh in v. 46 and the point-less circling of 2:1 convey the futility that Israel's rebellion has created. Israel fruitlessly heads back in the "direction of the Red Sea" to the "wilderness" that was the starting point in v. 19 (vv. 40, 2:1). The "Red Sea" is an ominous route, even though it refers to the Gulf of Aqaba, which is south of Kadesh. "Red Sea" hints at a reversal of exodus redemption. Nonetheless, Kadesh will also be the point of departure for a successful conquest a generation later (2:14).

Chapter 1 offers less narrative than does chapter 2. Speech is more impor-tant than action, and dialogue is used to advance the plot. Several overlapping literary features unify vv. 19–46. For example, discourse alternates in a chias-tic pattern between Moses (vv. 20–21), the people (v. 22), the spies (the center point, v. 25b), the people again (vv. 27–28), and Moses (vv. 29–33).[1] Yahweh then enters the dialogue (vv. 35–40), followed by the people (v. 41), and then Yahweh again (v. 42). In addition, a structure of reversal surrounds the people's fear and rebellion, which is described in vv. 26–27:

> The hopeful perspective of vv. 19–21a is cancelled by the
>   negative outcome of vv. 41–46.
> The "do not fear" of v. 21b is negated by the melted hearts of
>   v. 28a.
> The spies' good report of v. 25 is reversed by the quoted bad
>   report in v. 28b.[2]

Moreover, repetition of the phrase "rebel against the command" (vv. 26, 43) brackets the part of the story that narrates the peoples' defiance and defeat.

At the same time, this episode is well integrated with its context. The "I said to you," which introduces v. 20, is related to vv. 9 and 29 and refers to the com-mand of v. 7 (as does v. 26). The call to "see" (v. 21) links to v. 8. That Moses approves of the people's plan in v. 23 reverses the direction of approval of v. 14, while "I took" in the same verse alludes to v. 15.

The motif of journey provides both internal unity and a connection to the

---

1. J. G. Plöger, *Literarkritische, formgeschichtliche und stilkritische Untersuchungen zum Deuteronomium* (BBB 26; Bonn: Hanstein, 1967), 50–51. For Lohfink, the chiasm extends to a cor-respondence between vv. 6–8 and Yahweh's speeches in vv. 35–42 ("Darstellungskunst," 122).

2. Adapted from E. E. Carpenter, "Literary Structure and Unbelief: A Study of Deuteronomy 1:6–46," *Asbury Theological Journal* 42 (1987): 79.

larger context.[3] There is a sharp contrast between the "ways" (*derek*; also translated here as "road" and "direction") of obedience and disobedience. The "way" that brings Israel to the border of the land (v. 19) has been one on which Yahweh has guided and nurtured them (vv. 31, 33). However, they send out spies to report on the "way" (v. 22); and, in the end, this means they must return on the "way" toward the Red Sea (v. 40; 2:1). The motif of "way" continues in 2:8, 27; 3:1. Unity is also provided by the verb *'ālâ*, "go up." Israel is commanded to "go up" (v. 21), but instead the spies "went up" (v. 24) to report on how to "go up" (v. 22). Fearful and unwilling, Israel fails to "go up" (vv. 26, 28), only to attempt to do so later in defiant overconfidence (vv. 41, 42, 43).

Redactional and Compositional History

The text condenses an earlier narrative tradition found within Num 13–14 (J).[4] The parallels between Numbers and Deuteronomy are closer in the speeches than in the narrative sections. The Deuteronomy version stresses that the guilt of the people was obvious and inexcusable. They were at fault, not Moses or the spies. The disbelief of the people prevented a proper sacral war, and their arrogance led to an invalid one. Deuteronomy also emphasizes that the future lies with Joshua and the next generation.

The spies are unambiguously sent out at the *people's* instigation (contrast Num 13:1–2). Given Deuteronomy's theology of the land, there is no need to discover whether the land is good (Num 13:19–20). Interest in the number twelve (Deut 1:23; cf. Josh. 3:12) is absent from the J portion of Num 13. Deuteronomy dissolves the connection between Eshcol ("Grape Cluster Valley") and grapes (Num 13:23) and eliminates the giant cluster of grapes in order to focus on the people's shocking response to the spies' report. Deuteronomy's "fruit of the land" (v. 25) refers generally to agricultural products rather than specifically to grapes.

The menacing elements of the spies' report in Num 13:26–28 are delayed by the people's instant negative response in Deut 1:26–27, so that they do not appear until v. 28 (cf. Num 13:28). In Num 13:31 the *spies* come to the negative conclusion; in Deuteronomy the *people* do so. In Num 14:4 the people

---

3. T. Veerkamp, "Israels Wende: Eine Auslegung von Dt. 1,20–2,1," *Texte & Kontexte* 19 (1983): 5–24.

4. The issue is complicated by later influences from Deuteronomy on the text of Numbers. See S. Mittmann, *Deuteronomium 1:1–6:3 literarkritisch und traditionsgeschichtlich untersucht* (BZAW 139; Berlin: de Gruyter, 1975), 42–55; M. Rose, *Deuteronomist und Jahwist: Untersuchungen zu den Berührungspunkten beider Literaturwerke* (ATANT 67; Zurich: Theologischer Verlag, 1981), 281–93; E. Aurelius, *Der Fürbitte Israels: Eine Studie zum Mosebild im Alten Testament* (ConBOT 27; Stockholm: Almqvist & Wiksell, 1988), 130–41. The last two agree that Num 14:11–25 depends on Deut 1:34–40.

direct their complaint against the leadership of Moses ("let us chose a captain");
Deuteronomy stresses that their rebellion is "against the command of Yahweh"
(vv. 26, 43).

Caleb appears, but not explicitly as a spy as in Numbers. The reader seems
to be expected to know of Caleb's admonition in Num 13:30 without being told.
Between the reference to Caleb (Num 14:24; Deut 1:36) and the command to
turn back to the Red Sea (Num 14:25; Deut 1:40) comes material that reflects
the interests of DH: Yahweh's anger at Moses because of the people's sin, the
impending replacement of Moses by Joshua, and the introduction of the next
generation as those who will successfully conquer (Deut 1:37–39).

Deuteronomy 1:41–44 and Num 14:40–45 are close parallels. However, the
"Amalekites and Canaanites" of Numbers are "Amorites" in Deuteronomy, its
usual term for the enemy west of the Jordan (7:1; 20:17). The ark of Num 14:44
is absent from Deuteronomy. Apparently a (mis)reading of Num 14:40 has generated the unique verb form of Deut 1:41 (note o). Weeping after defeat and
Yahweh's refusal to respond to it (Deut 1:45) sharpen Deuteronomy's didactic
point that it was the people who were decisively at fault.

Secondary additions seem to be present. The singular address of v. 21 contrasts sharply with the plural of vv. 20 and 22 and repeats v. 8. It seems too early
in the plot for the standard formula "do not fear"; this appears in a more appropriate place in v. 29. The second person singular of v. 31a is also abrupt. Verse
24b may be a supplement since the antecedent of the feminine suffix ("it") is
remote ("land" in v. 22). The logical connection between vv. 26–28 and vv.
34–35 (Yahweh hears the grumbling words of the people) is interrupted by
Moses' admonition in vv. 29–33. This may be a later theological amplification
interpreting their fear as a lack of trust.

A Case Study in Disobedience

The text seeks to motivate faithful obedience by portraying the results of disobedience. In the context of chapters 1–3, this is one of a series of case studies
of life lived in either obedience or disobedience. Here disobedience leads to the
experience of an anti-exodus and a perverted sacral war that comprises a rebellion against Yahweh, not really against Moses (vv. 32, 43). In chapters 2 and 3,
case studies of successful obedience provide positive counterexamples.[5]

This narrative is a call to trust and faith: do not fear; Yahweh carries, leads,
accompanies, and protects you. The text evokes courage by portraying the negative consequences of faithless cowardice followed by arrogant bravado. It proclaims what readers are to believe and to do by combining traditional history

5. W. L. Moran, "The End of the Unholy War and the Anti-Exodus," *Bib* 44 (1963): 333–42;
repr. in *Song of Power*, ed. Christensen, 147–55.

with admonition, retelling the past in order to appeal for religious loyalty in the readers' present. In this way, Deuteronomy reuses inherited traditions of national unbelief and a promised future as illustrations of contemporary challenges. The allusion to what "you saw" (v. 19) calls on the imagination of readers and persuades them to make this story their own (cf. similar rhetoric in vv. 30–31; 3:21; 4:3, 9, 34; 6:22; 7:19; 9:17; 11:2–7; 29:1–2 [ET 2–3]).

By retelling this traditional story, Deuteronomy (in this case, DH) makes clear that national disasters are the result of Israel's disbelief and guilt. Such catastrophes cannot be interpreted as being Yahweh's fault. This text introduces themes that are important to DH, the author of Joshua through Kings: disobedience, presumption, transition to new leadership, conquest, defeat. However, this story also functions as an apt introduction to the book of Deuteronomy itself (cf. the reference to it in 9:23–24). The law proclaimed by Deuteronomy is set into the context of a relationship with Yahweh that had been annulled by past disobedience, yet was nevertheless revitalized for the next generation. Readers are invited to identify themselves with that new generation, a generation that once again has a new chance to choose obedience. From now on, however, things must be done Yahweh's "way" (vv. 19, 31, 33) and decisions must be based on trust in Yahweh's ability to act on behalf of the people.

[19–21] *Setting and command.* The itinerary of v. 19 restarts the journey begun by v. 7, the movement from Horeb (via Kadesh, v. 2) to Amorite territory. The contrast between the desert they have experienced (v. 19) and the good land that awaits them (vv. 20–21, 25) should have made their decision to attack obvious. The language of "we" and "us" expresses the solidarity of Moses with the people, but this first person plural will turn sour in the rebellious statements of vv. 28 and 41. His solidarity with the people will turn out to be a personal tragedy for Moses (v. 37).

[22–25] *Sidetrack.* Sending spies is the unanimous (cf. "you all," v. 22) suggestion of the people. This course of action may be common in sacral war stories (Josh 2; 7:2–3; Judg 1:23–25), but as an immediate follow-up to Moses' unambiguous command and promise, it hints at resistance to Yahweh's plan. The spies fulfill just part of the task assigned to them (v. 22), reporting only on the first issue, the character of the land. They echo what Moses has already said in vv. 20–21, adding that the land is a "good" one. Agricultural products are presented as evidence and as a visual aid to support their "word" (v. 25). The "word" they bring is really a confession of faith rather than useful military data (cf. the spies' report in Josh 2:24).

Because of this bounty and the spies' confession, it comes as a shock when Israel proves unwilling to attack. The sequence of the text sets up the reader to expect a positive response, for the content of the report as quoted so far refers only to "fruit" and "good." However, the people have really heard only the negative elements in the spies' report, something the narrator does not reveal to the reader until v. 28. Rebellion follows immediately, almost inexplicably, after the spies' positive report.

[26–28] *Rebellion.* Verse 26 gives the reader a rhetorical jolt, dramatically emphasizing the exact opposite of the trust and obedience that the situation calls for. According to the pattern of spy stories in Josh 2 and 7 or Judg 18, the reader naturally expects an attack as the next order of business.[6] That Israel's response is not a legitimate tactical decision but an abandonment of faith is made clear in vv. 27–28 (cf. Ps 106:24–26). The people furtively grumble in their tents, impugning Yahweh's motives and commitment. They engage in a "counter-confession" of unfaith, a perversion of Israel's creed (cf. Deut 9:28). They turn the exodus upside down (contrast 5:6; note the "back to Egypt" of Num 14:4). Yahweh "hates," rather than loves (contrast 4:37; 7:8). The question, "What kind of place?" denies the spies' witness that the land is "good." The people annul the faith required in sacral war with their accusation "to destroy us" (contrast, e.g., 7:23) and express a self-fulfilling reversal of proper sacral war formulas ("put us into the power of the Amorites"; cf. the lament of Josh 7:7). It is enemy hearts that are supposed to melt (Josh 2:11; 5:1), not those of Israel (cf. 20:8). In sacral war, Israel's weakness in contrast to the strength of the foe emphasizes Yahweh's power. Here the people have it backward, so that this item of confessional faith is used to support disbelief instead of wonder. The kinship shared with the spies (literally "our brothers") is used to underscore the reliability of their frightening report, and the giant-sized Anakim (1:28; 2:10, 21; 9:2) become symbols of the danger of entry and conquest.[7] Complaining "in tents" may refer ironically to the dispersion to tents that is supposed to take place after a sacral war (Josh 22:4, 8; 2 Sam 20:1; 1 Kgs 12:16). The people's unfaith converts the command to attack and the promise of land into an occasion for Yahweh's catastrophic wrath.

[29–33] *Reaction by Moses.* The text seeks to motivate a proper response by having Moses deliver an encouraging sacral war sermon, similar to that in 20:3–4. Fears are countered by the use of verbs typical of sacral war (vv. 29–30; cf. 20:3–4). The exodus event is all the evidence Israel will ever need about Yahweh's willingness to fight. Moses gives three reasons why Israel should have no dread or fear: the Lord has already fought for them (v. 30), carried them like a child (v. 31), and guided them on their journey (v. 33). These three reasons are bracketed by "goes before you" (vv. 30, 33). Moses' speech responds directly to Israel's grievances. Thus v. 31 counters v. 27 as a response to the objection about Yahweh's motives and attitude. Verse 33 answers the question

---

6. S. Wagner, "Die Kundschaftergeschichten im Alten Testament," *ZAW* 76 (1964): 255–69.

7. See L. Perlitt, "Riesen im Alten Testament: Ein literarisches Motiv im Wirkungsfeld des Deuteronomismus," in *Deuteronomium-Studien* (FAT 8; Tübingen: Mohr, 1994), 205–46.

of the first part of v. 28 about where the people are going. Verse 33 also makes clear that it is Yahweh who is truly the effective sacral war spy, the one who has carried out the assignment of v. 22 ("reconnoiter," "show the way"). From a literary standpoint, this speech introduces tension-building delay before the expected negative reaction of Yahweh (v. 34). From a theological perspective, this is a sort of short historical credo that counters the anticredo professed by the people (vv. 27–28). Israel's reaction springs from an incomprehensible lack of trust (v. 32).

Yahweh's promise to act "just as he did" in Egypt (v. 30) introduces a type-antitype organizational pattern of failure and success, highlighted by the phrase *ka'ăšer* ("just as") with the verb *'āśâ* ("act, do"). These same words appear in v. 44: because of their disloyalty, the Amorites will pursue Israel "just as bees do." The combination of *ka'ăšer* and *'āśâ* also characterizes the positive half of the story pattern in 2:12, 22, 29; 3:2, 6 and continues on into the book of Joshua. This historical typology is used to underscore the consistency of Yahweh's actions, the harmony of Israel's obedient actions with Yahweh's purpose, and the truth that the land is a divine gift.[8]

[34–40] *Reaction by Yahweh.* Verse 34 shifts the scene from Moses to Yahweh. It is directly related to v. 28, as though Moses has never spoken. Yahweh swears a counteroath to the one once sworn to the ancestors (1:8). Successful progress must be put on hold until this oath has run its course (cf. 2:14). Yahweh's counteroath operates according to a generational schema that contrasts the oath to the ancestors, the one made to the disobedient generation, and its implications for their children for whom the land is reserved. All those who are guilty are to be excluded from the land, while the fulfillment of Yahweh's promise must await a generation that has not been faithless.

Two parenthetical issues surface: Caleb in v. 36 and Moses and Joshua in vv. 37–38. The main topic does not resume until v. 39, where "and [but] your small children" fits perfectly as a continuation of v. 35. Caleb appears abruptly (v. 36) as a paradigm of the proper loyalty to Yahweh that the people lack. "Except for" (*zûlātî*) indicates his special position. The text relies on the reader to know the story of his favorable report (Num 13:30 J) and Yahweh's promise to him (Num 14:24 J).[9] Second, Moses and Joshua are introduced (vv. 37–38) to embody the contrast of generations. The destiny of Moses is linked emphatically to that of the doomed rebellious generation by the repeated *gam* ("as well," "either"). This shocking announcement underscores the enormity of the

---

8. Lohfink, "Geschichtstypologie in Deuteronomium 1–3," in *Lasset uns Brücken bauen, ed.* Schunk and Augustin, 87–92. The Joshua passages are 4:23; 8:2; 10:1, 28, 30, 39; 23:8; 24:5.

9. Caleb implies "the faithful one"; see O. Margalith. "*Keleb:* Homonym or Metaphor?" *VT* 33 (1983): 491–95; C. Brunet, "L'he'breu Kèlèb," *VT* 35 (1985): 485–88. "Remained fully loyal" translates a phrase meaning "follow Yahweh fully" or "fulfill [something] in obedience to Yahweh." This formula is the classic description of Caleb (Josh 14:8, 9, 14) and comes from Num 14:24.

people's fault.[10] Joshua stands in contrast with Moses. Joshua represents the generation of the audience and the time of the book's dramatic "today." The contrast with Moses is clear: Moses "shall not enter there" (v. 37); Joshua "shall enter there" (v. 38). Joshua's future is also linked to that of the loyal Caleb, since the feminine pronoun "it" (referring to "land") in v. 38 has its antecedent in vv. 35–36. The transfer of leadership to Joshua will bridge the gap between the doomed wilderness generation and their fortunate progeny.[11]

These "little ones" (v. 39) are the new generation to whom Moses is now speaking the words of Deuteronomy, and (by extension) the readers of Deuteronomy, who face a similar challenge. Emphatic pronouns create a syntax of contrast ("they," not "you"), and standard Deuteronomic formulas provide hope. It is divine favor to this next generation that protects Yahweh's original oath from the counteroath of v. 35. As "little ones" (*ṭap*), that is, "dependent children," this next generation had no responsibility for their elders' iniquitous decisions.

With v. 40, Yahweh again assumes the role of directing Israel's route (cf. v. 7). However, the optimistic *pĕnû ûsĕ 'û*, "turn and march," of v. 7 now becomes a negative deflection *away* from the land of promise into a sort of "suspended animation" at Kadesh (v. 46). Israel will obey this imperative to "turn and march in the direction of the Red Sea" only in 2:1, after they have engaged in an act of further rebellion.

[41–44] *Defeat.* The dialogic structure continues as Israel moves from the disobedience of inaction to the disobedience of self-chosen action. "We have sinned" is a favorite formula in DH (Judg 10:10, 15; 1 Sam 7:6; 12:10; 1 Kgs 8:47). The emphatic "we ourselves" (v. 41, note n) signals a disobedient contrast to the next generation of v. 39, for whom the privilege to enter and take over has now been reserved. The proposal to "go up" stands in sharp contrast to Israel's unwillingness to "go up" in v. 26a.

The issue at stake is more than just simple obedience; it concerns trust and fidelity. The people are indeed following Yahweh's earlier command, just as they claim, but the situation has changed in that Yahweh has issued a countercommand (v. 40). Yahweh's warning in v. 42 is unambiguous. In the future, the phrase "Yahweh said to me" (v. 42) will highlight other divine commands that

10. The tradition of Yahweh's anger against Moses was open to multiple interpretations. Seen here as a result of the people's misdeeds (as in 3:26 and 4:21), it is attributed to Moses' own fault in 32:51. Moses' plight of solidarity with corporate guilt may be compared with that of Josiah in 2 Kgs 23:25–27.

11. Lohfink proposes a special "encouragement formula" for installation into office; see "The Deuteronomistic Picture of the Transfer of Authority from Moses to Joshua," in *Theology of the Pentateuch,* 234–47; trans. of "Die deuteronomistische Darstellung des Übergangs der Führung Israels von Mose auf Josue," *Studien zum Deuteronomium I,* 83–97. Contrast D. McCarthy, "An Installation Genre?" *JBL* 90 (1971): 31–41.

dictate the direction of the campaign (2:9, 17, 31; 3:2). The key words of Yahweh's warning are: "I am not in your midst," the opposite of Deut 7:21 or Josh 3:10. Without Yahweh's presence there can be no successful sacral war.

Verse 43 fulfills the plan of v. 41—to "go up"—and directly violates Yahweh's "do not go up" in v. 42. Israel's "go it alone" antisacral war results in a reversal of the typical sacral war: the enemy pursues Israel rather than the other way around (v. 44). Afterward, the people weep in remorse (v. 45; cf. Judg 2:1–5; 2 Kgs 22:19), but Yahweh's refusal to "listen" is a punishment that suitably fits their crime of not listening (v. 43a). That they "returned" (v. 45) probably means that they physically came back from battle, but the phrase could also refer to an attempt at repentance. If so, it is too late. Now the story of conquest is frozen at Kadesh (v. 46), and progress toward the land is brought to a standstill by a return southward (2:1).

Through Edom and Moab
2:1–25

Turn North

2:1 Then we turned back and marched toward the wilderness in the direction of the Red Sea, just as Yahweh had spoken to me, and circled around[a] Mount Seir for many days.

2 Then Yahweh said to me, 3 "You have been circling around this hill country long enough. Turn north. 4 Command the people[b] saying, 'You are going to pass through the territory of your kindred, the descendants of Esau, who live in Seir. They will be afraid of you, so you[c] must be very careful. 5 Do not stir up yourselves against them, for I will not give you even as much of their land as a foot can step on, because I have given Mount Seir as property to Esau. 6 You shall purchase food from them for money so you may eat, and you shall also buy water from them for money so you may drink. 7 Indeed, Yahweh your God has blessed you in all your endeavors. He has watched over[d] your travel through[e] this great wilderness. Yahweh your God has been with you these forty years. You have not lacked a thing.' " 8 So we passed on away from[f] our kindred, the descendants of Esau, who live in Seir, away from[g] the road of the Arabah, from Elath and from Ezion-geber. We turned and passed along the road of the wilderness of Moab. 9 Then Yahweh said to me: "Do not beleaguer Moab or stir up yourself against it,[h] for I will not give you any of its land as property, because I have given Ar to the descendants of Lot as property."

10 The Emim had once lived there—a great and numerous people, and tall like the Anakim. 11 They also are regarded as Rephaim like the Anakim,[i] but the Moabites call them Emim. 12 The Horites had once lived in Seir, but the descendants of Esau dispossessed them, destroyed them before them, and settled in their place, just as Israel did in the land of its possession that Yahweh gave them.

Cross the Zered

13 "Now get up, cross the Wadi Zered." So we crossed the Wadi Zered. 14 The time we took to go from Kadesh-barnea until we crossed the Wadi Zered was thirty-eight years, until the whole generation of warriors had perished from the camp, just as Yahweh had sworn about them. 15 Moreover, Yahweh's hand was against them to roust them from the camp until they perished.

16 As soon as all the warriors had completely died off from among the people, 17 Yahweh spoke to me, saying, 18 "You are going to cross the boundary of Moab at Ar.[j] 19 You will approach opposite the Ammonites. Do not beleaguer them or stir up yourself against them, for I will not give you any of the land of the Ammonites as property, because I have given it to the descendants of Lot as property."

20 It also is regarded as Rephaim country. Rephaim once lived in it, but the Ammonites call them Zamzummim, 21 a great and numerous people, and tall like the Anakim. But Yahweh destroyed them before them so that they dispossessed them and settled in their place, 22 just as he did for the descendants of Esau, who live in Seir, when he destroyed the Horites before them so that they dispossessed them and settled in their place, as is the case to this day. 23 As for the Avvim, who lived in settlements near Gaza,[k] Caphtorites who came from Caphtor destroyed them and settled in their place.

Cross the Arnon

24 "Get up, march out, and cross the Wadi Arnon. See, I have given into your power Sihon the Amorite, king of Heshbon, and his land. Begin to take possession and stir up yourself against him in battle. 25 This day I am beginning[l] to put the dread and fear of you upon the peoples under the sky,[m] so that when[n] they hear a report about you, they will tremble and writhe because of you."

a. The verb *sābab* could mean "circle repeatedly," suggesting aimlessness, or "skirt around," implying avoidance.

b. The object-first word order emphasizes the command, perhaps expressing the unexpected, unusual nature of what is planned.

c. Follows MT. OG "they will be very careful of you" smooths the verse by keeping the same subject for this last verb and expanding with an object.

d. Literally "he has known" in the sense of providential watching over (Ps 1:6). OG translates this verb as an imperative: "know how you have traveled through."

e. *'et* with adverbial accusative of place, *IBHS* 10.3.1c.

f. In other words, "withdrew from." Follows MT (*m't*, "away from") as the contextually more difficult reading. This reflects the geographic concept of Num 20:14–21, but is inconsistent with Deut 2:4–6, which commands passage *through* Edom. OG (supported by Vulg.) harmonized this incongruity by reading the simple direct object marker: "we passed through our kindred."

g. Follows MT *mdrk*. OG (supported by Vulg.) harmonizes by reading "by the road," without the preposition "from" (see note f). MT states that Israel avoided the direct route north on the road through the Arabah and veered through Edom toward the east. This route took them toward "the road of the wilderness of Moab" running on the east.

h. Follows Sam. *bw*, "against it," as the shorter reading. MT and OG level to the plural pronoun of v. 5a and add a clarifying expansion, perhaps from v. 24: *bm mlḥmh*, "against them in battle." OG also supplements with "in battle" in vv. 5 and 19.

i. Follows MT. Sam. lost v. 11a by haplography from *rp'ym* to *k'nqym*.

j. Accusative of place, indicating the north border of Moab. Alternate translation taking *gĕbûl* as "territory" and Ar as an apposition: "pass through the territory of Moab, that is, Ar."

k. *'ad* is a static locative, "near," *IBHS* 11.2.12b. *Ḥăṣērîm*, "settlements, enclosures," implies something less than a full-fledged urban center enclosed by a defensive wall (cf. Josh 13:23).

l. Follows MT. OG and Sam. level to the imperative of v. 24: *hḥl*, "begin."

m. Follows OG and Syr. in omitting *kl*, "all," before "sky" (MT = "everywhere under the sky"). OG and some Hebrew witnesses do insert *kl* before "peoples" to achieve the more expected expression (*kol hā'ammîm*; cf. 4:19 and OG of 4:27).

n. *'ašer* introducing a purpose or result clause, *IBHS* 38.3b. This could also be translated simply "when" or "who/whoever."

Connections to Context

Deuteronomy 2:1–3:17 follows a pattern of divine command and human obedience, organized by encounters with five peoples on a journey from south to north.[1] The first three encounters are peaceful; the last two are sacral war victories. Two important changes in Israel's situation take place. The generation of those who had engaged in false sacral war has died off (at the Zered, vv.

---

1. For this five-part structure, see W. A. Sumner, "Israel's Encounter with Edom, Moab, Amman, Sihon, and Og According to the Deuteronomist," *VT* 18 (1968): 216–28. The shared elements are: movement, divine instructions through the repeated phrase "and Yahweh said/spoke to me," and the prehistory of the territories in question.

14–16), and Yahweh has begun to function as Divine Warrior (at the Arnon, v. 25). Fidelity to Yahweh, and not human military might, stands behind Israel's legitimate claim to the land. Moreover, Israel shares the territory east of the Jordan with other nations to whom Yahweh the Divine Warrior has given land and who have a right to their own territory.

Deuteronomy 2:1–25 is a bridge, binding the story of the failure of false sacral war (1:19–46) to its opposite, the successful prosecution of true sacral war (2:26–3:7). There are connections both backward and forward:

> Verse 1 fulfills the command of 1:40.
> "Yahweh said to me" (v. 2) stresses the existence of a divine
>   plan as a unifying structural element (1:42; 2:9, 17 (with
>   *dbr*), 31; 3:2, 26).
> The verb *'ābar*, "cross over, pass through," is used repeatedly
>   in chapters 2–3. The root *yrš*, "take over," occurs fourteen
>   times in chapters 1–3.[2]
> Kadesh (v. 14a) relates back to 1:19–20, 46.
> The motif of purchasing food and water from Edom (v. 6)
>   prepares for the preliminary negotiations with Sihon (vv.
>   26–28).

Israel carefully avoids battle with the "kinfolk" peoples of Edom, Moab, and Ammon, whose land Yahweh has not given to Israel. By contrast, this sharpens Yahweh's call for war against the Amorites, whose land Israel is to inherit.

Journey Plot, Avoidance Plot, Ethnographic Notes

Three intertwined literary features shape this text: a journey plot, an avoidance plot, and two ethnographic notes about other nations. The *journey plot* resumes after the interruption caused by the rebellion of the wilderness generation and provides the backbone for the action. The rhythm of this journey is one of divine command followed by obedient action. Yahweh's commands instigate obedient travel by Israel, described with the pronoun "we." Israel's journey leads toward war with the Amorite kings. These commands drive the journey plot: turn north (command, vv. 2–3; obedience, v. 8b), cross the Zered (command, v. 13a; obedience, v. 13b), cross the Arnon (command, v. 24). However, an *avoidance plot*, also shaped by divine command, complicates the journey plot. This avoidance plot evades conflict, first with Edom (command, vv. 4–7; obedience, v. 8a) and then with Moab and Ammon (commands only, v. 9 and

---

2. G. Braulik, "Die Funktion von Siebenergruppierungen im Endtext des Deuteronomiums," in *Studien zum Buch Deuteronomium*, p. 67 n. 14, traces a palindromic structure based on the verb "give" and seven uses of the noun *yĕruššâ*, "property," unifying 2:5, 9, 12 (as the center), 19; and 3:20.

vv. 17–19). The same basic message is repeated three times with slight variations: "do not (beleaguer or) stir up yourself against X, for I will not give you the land of X, because I have given it as property to X." Each command states the prohibition, offers a negative reason for it, and then provides a positive reason for that reason. The incident with Edom seems to have been the model for what is reported about Moab and Ammon. It is richer in detail and anchored in Num 20:14–21, which Deuteronomy used as a source. In addition, two *ethnographic notes* link Israel's story of land possession to broader international patterns of conquest and settlement: vv. 10–12, 20–23.

Each of these three narrative features supports and highlights the upcoming victories over Sihon and Og. The *journey plot* puts Israel at the place (the wilderness of Kedemoth, v. 26) where it encounters Sihon. Israel's obedient journey continues through 3:1 ("we turned") to confront Og in Bashan, then ends with "we remained" at Beth-peor (3:29). The *avoidance plot* creates a sharp contrast to the aggression against Sihon and Og and provides background for Moses' devious offer of peaceful coexistence with Sihon (vv. 27–29). Yahweh says, "I will not give you" the land of Edom, Moab, or Ammon, so "do not stir up yourselves against them." Instead, "stir up yourself against" Sihon, for "I have given into your power . . . his land" (vv. 24, 31). The two *ethnographic notes* make clear that Israel's conquest is legitimate, since it is only one part of a larger, wide-reaching realignment of ethnic geography ordained by Yahweh.

These three interwoven features probably reflect a complex history of composition, but this cannot be unraveled in a convincing manner. The journey plot and the avoidance plot are so well integrated that two of the avoidance plot prohibitions (vv. 9 and 19) also serve as triggers for journey plot commands (vv. 13 and 24). Not harassing Moab prefaces crossing the Zered into Moab; not harassing Ammon launches crossing the Arnon into Sihon's territory.

Theology

The *journey plot* of a divinely directed, goal-oriented expedition carries a straightforward theological message. Past disobedience led to failure, but Yahweh will give the land to this new and obedient generation.

The theology of the *avoidance plot* concerning the descendants of Esau and Lot is more subtle. The complete exclusion of the three kingdoms east of the Jordan from Israel's land claim asserts, by contrast, that the more northern "Amorite" area east of the Jordan is an integral part of the land of promise. Thus the Arnon (and not the Jordan) serves as the threshold between peace and sacral war, nonviolent avoidance and land acquisition. Kinship language implies that ethnic ties preclude warlike behavior. Esau's descendants are "brothers" (vv. 4, 8; the name "Edom" never occurs). The phrase "descendants of Lot" indicates knowledge of the traditions reflected in Gen 19:36–38.

At one level, the avoidance plot is a political statement, a reprimand against any imperialistic incursions into these territories by succeeding generations. At another level, it provides an etiological answer to the question of why these lands were never permanently subdued. However, vv. 5, 9, and 19 are also a confession about the nature and character of Yahweh as the supreme, universal God. Yahweh's sovereign rule involves protecting the sovereignty of those other nations. Yahweh gave them the territory they occupy in the same way that Israel has received its special land. This idea parallels the attitude of the Song of Moses (32:8) and the thought of Amos 9:7. Yahweh's land grants render those territories off limits for Israel's sacral war, but conversely that same reality confirms Israel's legitimate possession of its own land (vv. 12, 24, 29, 31, 36).

The theology of the *ethnographic notices* (vv. 10–12 and 20–23) builds on the concept of Yahweh's sovereign rule and makes it more explicit. These footnotes are not just erudite marginalia, but potent claims offering a theology of divine historical causation. Israel's particular salvation history—of destroying, dispossessing, and settling in place of the previous inhabitants of a land given by Yahweh—follows an earlier pattern set by Yahweh's actions on behalf of the Edomites and Ammonites. Looking backward to the fiasco of 1:19–46, the reader finds a certain irony, since those other nations have already succeeded, whereas Israel has so far failed.

Relationship to Numbers 20:14–21

The geography of Israel's route is somewhat ambiguous. On the one hand, Israel passes *through* Esau's territory and is commanded to purchase supplies and avoid any hostilities (vv. 4–6). But on the other hand, their route takes them *away from* their Edomite kindred and they slip off the main Arabah road eastward toward the "wilderness of Moab" (v. 8, notes f and g), that is, the territory east of settled Moab. The crossing of the Zered (v. 13) is not identified as the point of entry into Moab; instead it marks the time when the previous generation has completely died off (vv. 14–15). Israel's route thus intersects the Arnon upstream on the east, in the neighborhood of Ammonite territory (v. 19). This confusion seems to be the result of the author (DH) utilizing some of the material in Num 20:14–20, but overlaying it with other geographic and ideological concepts.[3]

In Numbers the Israelites ask to pass through Edom and pay for water, but

3. There can be little doubt about the direction of literary dependence. The motif of purchase fits the context of Num 20:19 much better than that of Deut 2:6. Because Numbers speaks only of Edom at this point, Deuteronomy's story about the descendants of Esau is richer in detail than its reports about Moab and Ammon. J. Van Seters, *The Life of Moses: The Yahwist as Historian in Exodus–Numbers* (Louisville, Ky.: Westminster John Knox, 1994), 383–404, reverses the direction of dependence.

this request is refused. The Edomites oppose them militarily, so Israel turns away to circle around the east of Edom. Deuteronomy uses the concepts of purchasing supplies and passing straight through in order to set up Yahweh's commands to avoid conflict with the descendants of Esau and Lot and to support the notion that their land is Yahweh's gift, off limits to Israel. However, the idea that Israel was driven off to circle around eastward by a show of Edomite military force would have been inconsistent with the author's interest in portraying a completely successful march toward sacral war, in every way the opposite of the debacle reported in 1:19–46. So the Edomite military threat described in Num 20:21 is transformed into the warning of Deut 2:4b and the strategic withdrawal of v. 8. Edom will fear Israel, and such fear could lead them to attempt military conflict. Israel must "be very careful" to avoid this, which means taking a route tending northeast in order to avoid the direct contact that would take place on the main "road of the Arabah," which headed straight north. This itinerary is similar to the route eastward around both Edom and Moab described in Judg 11:18.

Deuteronomy's version of events is both more nationalistic and more theological than that of Numbers. There is enough contact with Edom to make the point expressed in vv. 4–5 ("you are going to pass through . . . do not stir yourselves up against them"), but not enough contact to bring about an attack that would undercut the point of the upcoming victory against Sihon. The messengers of Num 20:14 and the negotiations of Num 20:17–19 are avoided for now, but these will be picked up to fashion the encounter with Sihon in Deut 2:27–29. Instead the concessions Israel offers in its negotiations with Edom (Num 20:17, 19) are converted into divine commands that reduce the possibility of conflict. Israel turns away, but this is because of Yahweh's command to be careful, not because of Edomite military opposition. In fact, the Edomites never speak or even appear in the Deuteronomic version. Blockage from Edom is simply unthinkable because Israel is moving at the command of Yahweh and the text is reporting only positive events. Israel is not afraid but is feared![4]

The text offers further evidence of a complex history of composition. The second-person singular language in v. 7 most likely marks that verse as a supplementary, theologically inspired addition to its plural context. Its connection to v. 6 is loose: you can pay for supplies and cross Edom without hesitation because of Yahweh's past blessings. Verses 3–6, 13, 24aα (the journey plot commands and the avoidance plot in regard to Edom) use second-person plural language, while vv. 9, 18–19 (the avoidance plot commands about Moab and

---

4. For further observations, see D. A. Glatt-Gilad, "The Re-interpretation of the Edomite-Israelite Encounter in Deuteronomy ii," *VT* 47 (1997): 441–55; and J. Maier, "Israel und 'Edom' in den Ausdeutungen zu Dtn 2:1–8," in *Judentum—Ausblicke und Einsichten* (ed. C. Thoma et al.; Judentum und Umwelt 43; Frankfurt: Peter Lang, 1993), 135–84.

Ammon) and v. 25 use second-person singular. At the same time, vv. 4–8a seem to break an original connection between vv. 3 and 8b ("turn," "we turned"), suggesting that the original text may have been vv. 2–3, 8b, 9aα, 13, 17, 24aα, essentially equivalent to the journey plot line. The ethnographic notes of vv. 10–12 and 20–23 almost certainly represent later supplements.

[1–9] Verse 1 provides a bridge between the previous catastrophe and the renewed journey to the place where the conquest can begin. Verse 1 fulfills the command of 1:40 verbatim and thus signals a return to obedience on Israel's part. However, the verse also introduces some confusion. Most of thirty-eight years is expended between the stay in Kadesh (1:19, 46) and arrival at the Zered (2:14), all spent circling "many days." This "circling" may represent nothing more than an aimless roving about, but it could be understood as "skirting around" Mount Seir (a synonym for Edom's territory) on the way to the goal of the land of promise (note a). Yet another possibility is that this "circling" may describe a static encirclement, a "besieging" of Mount Seir. If so this would be an ironic depiction of Israel spending years besieging a land it had not been promised, then paying money to pass through and leave it untouched.[5]

In any case, the command to "turn north" (v. 3) marks a decisive new beginning. The operation of a divine timetable is suggested by "long enough" (cf. 1:6). The command to "turn" continues the pattern of 1:7, 24, and 40, and reintroduces the format of command/response that shapes the larger story of chapters 1–3.

Yahweh's language to Moses (v. 4) emphasizes that the true audience is "the people" (note b). Because the plot has moved from false sacral war to true sacral war, the peoples that Israel confronts are now appropriately fearful (in contrast to 1:28). However, the fear of the Edomites must not prematurely force Israel into war. The text emphasizes the issue of kinship with "kindred" ("brothers") and "descendants of Esau" (vv. 4, 8; in contrast to Num 20:14–21, where the "king of Edom" appears). Edom would have been of intense interest for Judahite readers since the two nations interacted regularly. However, one suspects that such a positive attitude toward a people despised as the archetypal foe after 586 B.C.E. requires a preexilic origin for this text (cf. 23:8 [ET 7]). To place one's foot on land would establish a legal claim on it (v. 5; 11:24; Josh 14:9; cf. Deut 25:9–10).

Verse 7 reintroduces the theology of nurture (1:31), perhaps to counteract any impression that purchasing supplies would contradict Yahweh's wilderness providence, but also to motivate the trust Israel would need to enter this potentially risky situation. "Blessing in all your endeavors" is a common phrase in Deuteronomy (14:29; 16:15; 24:19; 28:12; 30:9), but elsewhere it refers to agricultural prosperity.

5. N. Lohfink, "Zu *sbb't* in Dtn 2,1.3," in *Studien zum Deuteronomium und zur deuteronomistischen Literatur III* (SBAB 20; Stuttgart: Katholisches Bibelwerk, 1995), 263–68.

Verse 8 marks the transition away from Edom and toward Moab. Israel's movement takes a positive direction, "away from Elath and Ezion-geber" (the starting points of the Arabah road) and thus away from the ominous Red Sea of 1:40 and 2:1. "Wilderness of Moab" leads to the cautions in the next verse. Verse 9 uses Ar (equivalent to the Hebrew noun for "city") to refer to the territory of Moab in general (as does v. 29, apparently). In v. 18, however, Ar identifies a specific city or region. The text thus uses Ar both to designate territory (vv. 9, 29; cf. Edom's Seir in vv. 5, 29) and to identify Israel's crossing point on the Arnon (v. 18).[6] "Descendants of Lot" indicates a shared kinship with Moab that is less direct than that with Esau (contrast v. 4, literally "your brothers"; cf. the hostility of 23:4–7 [ET 3–6]).

[10–12] The notices of vv. 10–12 and 20–23 are later than the textual matrix in which they are embedded. They are neither speeches of Yahweh like their context nor part of the itinerary report spoken by Moses. Each supplement has been inserted as further explanation following "I have given it to the descendants of Lot as property" (vv. 9b and 19b). The material is similar to Gen 14:5–6, which also speaks of the Horites in Mount Seir and Rephaim, Zuzim, and Emim in contexts east of the Jordan. The content is stylized, marked by "once lived" (vv. 10, 12, 20) and the verbal chain "dispossessed . . . destroyed . . . settled" (vv. 12, 21, 22). From a literary standpoint, these notices provide dramatic delay between the prohibitions that retard the movement of the plot (vv. 9, 19) and the positive commands that advance it (vv. 13, 24). Moreover, details about fabled and extinct peoples would have stimulated the reader's interest. By associating these aboriginal inhabitants with the Anakim, the text comments retroactively on Israel's fear of this group as attested in 1:28.

The text renders these alien peoples as terrifying as possible. As Anakim they are the mythic giants whose huge bones and megalithic architecture inspired fearsome folktales. "Emim" means "terrifying ones." Along with the Zamzummim, they are also counted among the numinous "Rephaim," divine princes and spirits of ancient heroes dwelling in the underworld.[7] Terrible as they were, however, Israel's neighbors were able to defeat them with Yahweh's help. Og will also turn out to be Rephaim (3:11), but will be easily defeated. The Horites, in contrast, are described as an ordinary, nonmythic people (cf. the genealogy in Gen 36:20–30). Scholars often connect them to the Hurrians, but the author was most likely thinking of them as "cave dwellers" (Hebrew $mĕʿārâ hōr$, "cave").

The analogical thinking behind the phrase "just as Israel did" (v. 12) is one of seven such historical comparisons made in chapters 1–3 (cf. 1:30; 2:21–22,

---

6. This matches an old poetic usage of Ar as a parallel for the Arnon region of Moab in Num 21:14–15. For a discussion of Ar, the Zered, and Jahaz (2:32), see J. M. Miller, "The Israelite Journey through (around) Moab and Moabite Toponymy," *JBL* 108 (1989): 577–95.

7. Ps 88:11 [ET 10]; Isa 14:9. See H. Rouillard, "Rephaim," *DDD* 692–700.

28–29; 3:2, 6, 21). Verse 12 equates Esau's dispossession of earlier peoples to what Israel did in its conquest of the land. Verses 21–22 go on to extend this pattern of analogy to include Yahweh's actions. Yahweh destroyed indigenous inhabitants on behalf of the Ammonites, "just as" Yahweh had done for the Edomites.[8]

[13–15] Moses does not report the trek from the Zered to the Arnon. The narrative space between vv. 13 and 17 is simply left blank, as geography is subordinated to theology. The imperative "cross the Wadi Zered" (v. 13) divides the failed wilderness generation of the past from the successful new generation. Once this replacement of generations has been completed (vv. 14–16), the narrative scene shifts immediately to the boundary of Moab (vv. 17–18) and the command to cross the Arnon (v. 24), the geographic dividing line between peace and war. Thus the Zered marks the expiration of punishment and the Arnon signifies the beginning of success.

The narrative gap left between the Zered and the Arnon is filled with a theological retrospective (vv. 14–15) that draws a sharp contrast between old failures and new opportunities. Verse 14 brings the theme of Yahweh's oath against the previous generation to completion (cf. 1:34–35, 39). Thirty-eight "lost years" were consumed by the pointless circular movement or encircling blockade of 2:1. In light of the former generation's poor military record, one suspects that the appellation "warriors" is ironic.[9] Verse 15 emphasizes that their extinction was not due to natural causes alone, but involved the direct action of Yahweh as Divine Warrior. Yahweh's warlike assault is described by the verb *hwm*, "roust out, throw into confusion," referring to the divinely induced panic of sacral war (cf. 7:23; Josh. 10:10).[10] Also characteristic of the vocabulary of sacral war is Yahweh's devastating "hand" (1 Sam 5:6, 7, 9, 11; 6:3, 5, 9) and "until they perished" (Josh 8:24; 10:20). Repetition underscores the totality of this annihilation. The root *tmm* (translated here as "perished" and "completely") appears three times in vv. 14–16. Verse 16 echoes v. 14b: "warriors . . . from the camp / from among the people" (*'anšê hammilḥāmâ . . . miqqereb hammaḥăneh / miqqereb hā'ām*). The text makes a shocking claim: Yahweh the

---

8. Deuteronomy 1:30 links Yahweh's Divine Warrior activity in the exodus with Israel's upcoming victories. On these analogies, usually expressed by *ka'ăšer* + *'āśâ* + *l*, see N. Lohfink, "Geschichtstypologisch orientierte Textstrukturen in den Büchern Deuteronomium und Josua," in *Deuteronomy and Deuteronomic Literature* (ed. M. Vervenne and J. Lust; BETL 133; Leuven: Leuven University Press, 1997), 133–60; repr. in *Studien zum Deuteronomium und zur deuteronomistischen Literatur IV* (SBAB 31; Stuttgart: Katholisches Bibelwerk, 2000), 75–103.

9. "Warriors" may also point to a narrower group than the entire generation targeted by Yahweh's oath (1:35). Debate over exactly who died off in the wilderness generated the confusion exhibited in Josh 5:2–7. See R. D. Nelson, *Joshua: A Commentary* (OTL; Louisville: Westminster John Knox, 1997), 75–77.

10. H.-P. Müller, "*hmm*," *TDOT* 3:419–22.

Divine Warrior prosecuted sacral war against the generation who had waged a rebellious and false sacral war.[11]

[16–19] The transition into Moab's "sphere of interest" (to the east of its settled territory) was described by vv. 9, 13. Verse 18, with its reference to "the boundary of Moab at Ar," situates Israel within range of the Ammonites. Ammonite territory is described as lying to the east of Israel's line of advance, which is thus not through Ammon but "opposite" it. We cannot identify the location where Israel is supposed to cross the Arnon (v. 24), which is treated as the north boundary of Moab. However, the general routing suggests a descent upstream (on the east) into one of its tributaries running south to north, followed by a journey northward along that system of valleys. Crossing the Arnon positions Israel for an inevitable conflict with Sihon (v. 24).

[20–23] There is a break in the narrative between Yahweh's admonition in vv. 18–19 and the command of v. 24 (similar to the gap between vv. 13 and 17). This gap is filled by a second group of ethnographic observations. From a literary perspective, the time consumed by making these comments may be thought of as giving Israel a sufficient amount of time in the narrative world to move from the locale of Yahweh's speech to the crossing point itself.[12]

The name Zamzummim sounds onomatopoeic: the "buzz-buzz people," perhaps a reference to their unintelligible speech or eerie and supernatural sounds. Verse 22 moves beyond the secular history of v. 12a into theological history, describing the obliteration of the Horites as an act of Yahweh performed on behalf of the descendants of Esau. In v. 23, however, the territorial gains of the Caphtorites are not explicitly credited to Yahweh. This may indicate that the territory of the Avvim remains fair game for Israelite expansion (cf. Josh 13:3; 18:23).

[24–25] With this decisive command and promise, Israel's journey (vv. 3, 8, 13) has reached a major goal. The Arnon marks the change from peace to war. Yet this command and promise is also part of a much larger narrative movement that began with Yahweh's command and promise in 1:7–8 and that will be carried forward by the command and promise of Josh 1:2–9 (cf. Deut 11:25). Language commonly used of the Divine Warrior assures victory and underscores Yahweh's initiative and sovereignty: "given into your power," "dread

---

11. For this "unholy war" schema, see Moran, "The End of the Unholy War." He points out that v. 15 repeats the key words of v. 14 in a chiastic pattern: *'ad-tōm . . . miqqereb hammaḥăneh / miqqereb hamaḥăneh 'ad tummām*, "until perished . . . from the camp / from the camp until perished."

12. N. Lohfink, "Die Stimmen in Deuteronomium 2," in *Studien zum Deuteronomium IV*, 47–74. He makes the distinction between "representational time" (time taken up by the process of narration) and "represented time" (the chronology of the narrated events themselves). Lohfink also understands these comments by the narrator as a literary strategy to relativize the authoritative voice of Moses.

and fear," "tremble and writhe."[13] The text utilizes the tradition of the nations' terror found in Exod 15:14–16 (v. 25 shares the language of Exod 15:14). That Sihon is an "Amorite" signals that he is fair game for conquest. The victory over Sihon was important for Israel to remember and retell, because both Ammon and Moab also claimed his former territory (Num 21:13–15; Judg 11:4–33; 1 Sam 11:1–11).

Defeating the Two Kings of the Amorites
2:26–3:7

King Sihon

2:26 So I sent messengers from the wilderness of Kedemoth to Sihon king of Heshbon with words of peace,[a] saying, 27 "Let me pass through your land. I will go only on the road.[b] I will not deviate right or left. 28 You shall sell me food for money so I may eat, and give me water for money so I may drink. Only let me pass through on foot 29 (just as the descendants of Esau who live in Seir did for me, as well as the Moabites who live in Ar) until I cross the Jordan into the land that Yahweh our God is giving us." 30 But Sihon king of Heshbon was not willing to let us pass through his territory,[c] because Yahweh your God had stiffened his spirit and hardened his heart in order to give him into your power, as is now the case.

31 Yahweh said to me, "See, I have begun to give Sihon and his land over to you. Begin to take over[d] his land." 32 Then Sihon came out to engage us, he and all his people[e] for battle at Jahaz. 33 Yahweh our God gave him over to us, and we struck down him and his sons[f] and all his people. 34 We captured all his cities at that time and devoted to destruction every city with its adult male population,[g] and also women and small children. We left no survivors. 35 Only we plundered the cattle for ourselves and the booty of the cities that we captured. 36 From Aroer, which is on the rim of the Wadi Arnon, and the city that is in the wadi, as far as Gilead, no town was too high for us. Yahweh our God gave everything over to us.[h] 37 Only you did not approach the land of the Ammonites, the whole region beside the Wadi Jabbok, and the cities of the hill country, and every place[i] that Yahweh our God had commanded about.

---

13. H.-P. Müller, "*pāḥad*," *TDOT* 11:522–23; G. Vanoni, "*rgz*," *ThWAT* 7:326–30; A. Baumann, "*ḥyl*," *TDOT* 4:344–47.

King Og

3:1 Then we turned and went up the road to Bashan. Og king of Bashan came out to engage us, he and all his people, for battle at Edrei. 2 Yahweh said to me, "Do not be afraid of him, for I have given[j] him into your power, and all his people and all his land. Deal with him just as you dealt with Sihon king of the Amorites, who ruled in Heshbon." 3 So Yahweh our God also gave Og king of Bashan and all his people into our power. We struck him down until no survivor was left[k] to him. 4 At that time we captured all his cities. There was no town that we did not take from them—sixty cities, the whole region[l] of Argob, the kingdom of Og in Bashan. 5 All these were fortified cities with high walls, gates, and bars, apart from very many towns of the country population.[m] 6 We devoted them to destruction, just as we had done to Sihon king of Heshbon, devoting to destruction every city with its adult male population, also women, and small children. 7 But all the cattle and the booty of the cities we plundered for ourselves.

a. Either an accusative of manner (*IBHS* 10.2.2e), or a double direct object (*IBHS* 10.2.3b, d).

b. Follows MT *bdrk bdrk*, the repetition indicating exclusivity, as translated here (*IBHS* 7.2.3c), or perhaps as a distributive plural, "on all of the roads." OG omits the repetition, either as a translational strategy or because of haplography. Vulg. interpreted the phrase as a public highway. *BHS* advocates reading "the King's Highway" and points to the parallel in Num 21:22.

c. This translates *bw*, literally "in or through him" (cf. Num 20:18a). The possessor serves as a metonymy for what he possesses.

d. Follows OG and Vulg. *hḥl lrš* on the assumption that MT *hḥl rš lršt* is a conflate text, merging the alternative readings *hḥl rš*, "begin, take over," and *hḥl lršt*, "begin to take over." OG reads *hḥl lrš* in v. 24a where MT has *hḥl rš*.

e. That is, his army; E. Lipiński, "'*am*," *TDOT* 11:176.

f. Follows Qere, Sam., OG, Syr., Vulg.; Kethib: "his son."

g. Follows MT and respects the masoretic punctuation: "every city-of-males—and women and small children." This expression means the city itself together with its male population fit for military service (cf. Judg 20:48); K.-M. Beyse, "*mt*," *TDOT* 9:99. Sam. offers '*ryw mtm hnšym whṭp*, "his cities, men, women, and small children," which reduces the difficulty of MT and harmonizes it with 3:6. OG construed *mtm* from the root *tmm* ("be complete"), translating "one after the other."

h. Follows MT as the less familiar formula. OG and Sam. adjust this to the more usual "into your hand (power)" (cf. vv. 24, 30). In the next verse, OG, Syr., Vulg. smooth "you did not approach" into "we did not approach."

i. Follows the more difficult MT (Syr., Vulg.) *wkl*, understanding the verb *ṣwh* negatively as "forbid" (cf. 4:23). OG and Tg. Ps.-J. lessen the difficulty by offering *kkl*, "according to all," and interpreting the verb in its usual positive sense of "command to do."

j. The perfect may indicate resolve ("I intend to give"), performative speech ("I hereby give"), or refer to an assured future, *IBHS* 30.5.1d and 1e.

k. Presumably *hiš'îr* is an infinitive construct, in spite of the masoretic vocalization as a perfect.

l. Alternate translation: "confederation."

m. Alternate translation: "open country." Two construct phrases are contrasted to indicate that all cities were destroyed: "cites fortified by walls" over against "cities of the *pĕrāzî*" (i.e., "the open-country-folk"; Ezek 38:11). "Gates" (dual) and "bars" signify a pair of doors secured by a crossbar.

Deuteronomy 2:26–36 and Num 21:21–31 are related. That the parallel text in Numbers reproduces no characteristically Deuteronomistic elements argues strongly that Numbers is primary.[1] The version in Deuteronomy is more expressly theological (e.g., the hardening of Sihon's heart and the sacral war oracle, 2:30–31). The Divine Warrior is more clearly at work in Deut 2:33 and 36 than in Num 21:24. Nor is the *ḥērem* of Deut 2:34–35 (introduced by a parenthetical "at that time") present in the Numbers parallel. The idea that the strength of the Ammonite border caused Israel problems (Num 21:24) is absent from Deuteronomy (cf. 2:4), as are the songs quoted in Num 21:27–30. Deuteronomy 2:27–28 also utilizes some details of Num 20:17, 19, texts that also helped form Deut 2:6.

Deuteronomy 2:26–3:7 evidences irregularities that reflect a complex history of composition. Deuteronomy 2:29a connects directly to 2:28a rather than to 2:28b and describes the Moabites selling supplies to Israel, something not reported earlier. Deuteronomy 2:37 sounds redundant, supplementing 2:19. Verse 3:4b gives the impression of being an inaccurate gloss triggered by the catchword "city" and separating v. 4a from v. 5.

This section is a doxological description of how Yahweh gave Israel two wonderful victories. Israel exhibited obedience, faith, and courage (2:33b, 34, 37; 3:3b), but Yahweh did everything that was really significant (2:30, 33a, 36b; 3:3a). Slaughter is total and the seizure of territory is complete. Yahweh pledges

1. Mittmann, *Deuteronomium 1:1–6:3*, 145–46; L. Perlitt, *Deuteronomium* (BKAT 5/3; Neukirchen-Vluyn: Neukirchener Verlag, 1994–), 200–201; Brettler, *Creation of History*, 71–76. In contrast, J. Van Seters, "The Conquest of Sihon's Kingdom: A Literary Examination," *JBL* 91 (1972): 182–197, contends that Num 21:21–35 used Deut 2:26–37 and Judg 11:19–26. For a response, see J. R. Bartlett, "Conquest of Sihon's Kingdom: A Literary Re-examination," *JBL* 97 (1978): 347–51. M. Rose, *Deuteronomist und Jahwist*, 308–13, also judges Deut 2:26–37 to be earlier than Num 21:21–31. On the other hand, there can be no question that Num 21:33–35a depends on Deut 3:1–3; M. Noth, *Numbers: A Commentary* (trans. J. Martin; OTL; Philadelphia: Westminster, 1968), 161–62; Rose, *Deuteronomist und Jahwist*, 306–7. On the whole, the material in Numbers parallel to Deut 1–3 is disordered, scattered, and mixed in with laws. In Deuteronomy it is presented in a compact way, well organized geographically, unified theologically, and adapted to the form of a retrospective speech.

absolute victory (2:24–25, 31; 3:2), the scope of which is underscored by *ḥērem* (2:34–35; 3:6–7), the vast amount of land acquired (2:36; 3:4), and the defensive strength of the captured cities (2:36; 3:5). The narratives follow the scribal convention of a "battle report," familiar from ancient royal inscriptions. As such it describes the confrontation of forces, the battle, and its outcome.[2] The battle report about Sihon is the more detailed of the two and exhibits more in the way of theological comment. The narrative of the victory over Og is largely a parallel replay of what happened to Sihon and was evidently constructed on the basis of it. The Og story merely seconds and underscores the primary story about Sihon ("just as you dealt," 3:2; "also," 3:3).

Glorious triumphs, given to a new generation, reverse in every way the previous generation's failure of nerve and obedience. The spies that triggered Israel's fear (1:23) are replaced by messengers that bring about Sihon's overconfident resistance (2:26). Once again "the land that Yahweh is giving us" (1:25; 2:29) may be approached, but this time Israel's rebellion (1:26) is replaced by Sihon's defiance (2:30). Given a second chance, Israel this time believes Yahweh's promise of victory and obeys the reassuring admonition "do not fear" (1:21; 3:2). The attacks of Sihon and Og parallel the earlier assault of the Amorites ("came out to engage us," 1:44; 2:32; 3:1), but this time overwhelming victory exemplifies true sacral war. The conquest of high and fortified cities (2:36; 3:5) cancels Israel's earlier discouragement about such obstacles (1:28). The new generation sees the beginning of what the old generation was forbidden to see and receive (1:35; 2:31).

The divine promise instituted at Horeb (1:6–8) now moves forward again toward fulfillment (2:31; 3:2). As a structural signal of this, the chain of imperatives that call on Israel to "see" the acts of Yahweh the Divine Warrior resumes (1:8, 21; 2:24, 31; cf. Josh 6:2; 8:1). Indeed, the "begin" of v. 31 (cf. vv. 24–25; Josh 3:7) indicates that these east Jordan campaigns are only the first episode of a larger story. The text's horizon points forward to the book of Joshua, where the plot begun in Deut 1:6–8 continues in Josh 1:2–4.[3]

The geography of this text is theologically meaningful. For example, using the title "king of the Amorite" for both monarchs (3:2, 8)[4] is significant, because all land that is "Amorite" is fair game for conquest (1:7, 20; cf. Josh 5:1;

---

2. Plöger, *Untersuchungen zum Deuteronomium*, 16–18.

3. DH understood the territory east of the Jordan to be part of the land given by Yahweh. Thus the Arnon is the threshold of sacral war (v. 24) and the enemy falls into the category of *ḥērem* under the terms of 20:17. Gilead is included in the land shown to Moses in 34:1. Yet 2:29 suggests that the eastern territories are not unequivocally part of the land of promise. They are not included in 1:6–8, and their capture is part of Moses' term of leadership, which does not include entering the "good land" (1:37; 3:25–28).

4. Also 1:4; 4:46–47; 31:4. Elsewhere Sihon is termed king of Heshbon, 2:24, 26, 30; 3:6; cf. 29:6 [ET 7].

10:5–6; 24:15). Chapters 2–3 systematize (and to some degree artificially synthesize) the area from the Arnon up to Bashan in the service of theology. This schematic geography assures readers that the territory taken from Sihon and Og included all the land east of the Jordan claimed by Israel. The "plateau" region is associated with Sihon, Bashan is connected to Og, and Gilead is split between them. The "plateau" (*mîšōr*, 3:10; cf. 4:43) is the tableland north of the Arnon and south of Wadi Heshbon. Gilead is the area north and south of the Jabbok. Bashan (3:4) refers to territory north of the downstream course of the Yarmuk (the Golan), along with the area encompassed by its upper tributaries, including Edrei.

This schematic geography unfolds further in 3:8–17, but one feature must be treated here. In DH Gilead usually refers to both sides of the Jabbok and is divided into northern and southern halves (Josh 12:2–5; 13:29–31; contrast 13:9–12). However, Deut 2:36 uses Gilead in a more restricted sense, as "Gilead territory not belonging to Og." In other words, the phrase "as far as Gilead" in 2:36 does not encompass all of Gilead. This becomes clear only when the reader discovers in 3:10 that "all of Gilead" also includes territory north of the Jabbok.

For preexilic readers, this theology of conquest meant that Israel had a legitimate claim on disputed territory east of the Jordan and north of the Arnon. For later audiences, however, that theology would have supported the yearning for a return home and hope for regained political independence. Remembering Yahweh's past deeds would build faith in an anticipated future. Certainly sin has brought catastrophe, but the generation responsible for that sin has been punished. Exilic readers may now hope for a better future and a return to secure possession of the land.

[2:26–37] Moses follows Yahweh's command to fight (2:24) with an unexpected offer of peace (2:26–29). Although this offer stands in some tension with the predominant plot line of predestined sacral war (2:24–25, 31–36), negotiation and aggression are joined together by the motif of Sihon's hardened heart (2:30). The offer of 2:26–29 turns out to be a tactical move by which Yahweh "sets up" Sihon for the kill by drawing him out from Heshbon. This incident also provides the author an opportunity to confess that Yahweh is in control of even the psychological aspects of human history. By rejecting such a modest request, Sihon becomes responsible for his own fate, justifying the defeat and conquest that results. The needs reflected in Moses' request for food and water are soon met by the triumphs of the Divine Warrior, who according to v. 36 "gave everything."

The first part of the Sihon episode offers a structural parallel to Israel's earlier interaction with Edom. The two episodes share the following elements: divine command about travel (2:2–3, 24), fear on the part of the foreigners (vv. 4b and 25), passing through (vv. 4a and 27), and buying supplies (vv. 6 and 28).

These parallels highlight the totally different outcomes. In contrast to 2:5, battle is joined and land is appropriated.

The geographical setting of the wilderness of Kedemoth (2:26) signals that Israel is still outside settled territory when Moses opens negotiations. Israel has not yet impinged on Sihon's realm, even though they have moved north of the Arnon frontier. (Kedemoth itself was located in the territory of Reuben, Josh 13:18.) In 2:29 Moses offers Sihon two inducements to consent to his request. First, Sihon would only be repeating what Edom and Moab have already safely done.[5] Second, Sihon has no reason to worry because the goal of Israel's march is to reach territory on the other side of the Jordan. Of course, what Moses says is true with regard to Israel's ultimate intention, but he keeps Israel's penultimate goal concealed. Moses seems to speak of crossing the Jordan personally ("I"), although both he and the reader already know that this is not going to happen (1:37–38).

Verse 30 reports Sihon's reaction. In the context of the exodus tradition, the hardening of his heart associates Sihon with Pharaoh, whose heart Yahweh also hardened. "Spirit" refers to Sihon's attitude and emotions; "heart" to his will and mind. The motif of Yahweh hardening hearts in order to lure enemies into destruction also occurs in Josh 11:20. Repetition of the verb "give" with Yahweh as subject (2:30, 31, 33, 36) shows that Yahweh is in control of the events that follow. The formula "as is now the case" (literally "as at this day") refers to the dramatic "today" of Deuteronomy as a speech of Moses.

The language of 2:31 is a resumptive repetition (*Wiederaufnahme*) of 2:24, one that picks up the main line of thought after the tactical sidetrack of 2:26–30. Paired rhetorical formulas coordinate the theological relationship between what Yahweh does as Divine Warrior ("give") and what Israel achieves in sacral war ("take over"). This victory oracle is in its expected narrative place in 2:31 and is fulfilled in 2:33, but its "premature" appearance in 2:24 makes clear that whatever option Sihon might have chosen, Yahweh's plan was already in place. Verse 33 emphasizes the total defeat of Sihon, both of his army ("people") and his dynastic hopes ("sons").[6]

In 2:34–35 the parenthetical formula "at that time" introduces *ḥērem* in order to underscore this defeat as a victory won by Yahweh as Divine Warrior, to whom all human captives belong by right of conquest. This practice of *ḥērem* accords with the usual pattern in DH in allowing Israel to take nonhuman booty

---

5. Moab's actions were not reported earlier. From a literary perspective, either this is a matter of "delayed exposition" or Moses is inflating his diplomatic speech!

6. Jahaz (v. 32) was a point of conflict between Israel and Moab (Mesha Inscription, *ANET*, 320–21). Sihon's connection with Heshbon (v. 26; 2:30) was an established tradition. It is the "city of Sihon" in an early song (Num 21:27–30) and its conquest is attested in Num 21:34.

(Josh 8:2, 27; 11:14). The *ḥērem* inventory of 2:35 (cf. 3:7) emphasizes the totality of the slaughter.[7]

Verse 36 expands on Num 21:24 ("from the Arnon to the Jabbok") by providing greater geographic detail in order to celebrate and accentuate the confession: "Yahweh our God gave everything." By specifying Aroer in the form of a standardized border formula,[8] the text emphasizes that Israel's claimed territory reaches the southernmost possible point (in contrast to competing Moabite claims). A sweeping "line of extent" reaches from there northward as far as Gilead in order to encompass all of Sihon's territory.[9] In this way, the text makes clear that Sihon's territory was not just the neighborhood of Heshbon, but extended south down to the Arnon, in agreement with the land claim set forth by Jephthah in Judg 11:22.

Verse 37 clarifies "as far as the Ammonites" from Num 21:24. Israel did not "approach" their land (in the hostile sense of Deut 20:2–3, 10), but this was not because the Ammonite border was strong (as in Num 21:24 NRSV), but instead was a consequence of Yahweh's prohibition. Excluded from Israel's territory is "the whole region beside the Wadi Jabbok" (*kol-yad naḥal yabbōq*). This phrase refers to territory upstream, where the region surrounding the Jabbok region marked Ammon's west and north border (3:16; Josh 12:2). The "hill country" in question refers to territory east of the "plateau" (*mîšōr*) that Israel had taken from Sihon (3:10).

[3:1–7] The more succinct Og story echoes the report about Sihon (cf. 2:32 and 3:1; 2:24–25 and 3:2 [note Sihon's full title]; 2:33 and 3:3; 2:34–36 and 3:4–7). Og is a suspiciously thin character, anchored in early tradition primarily by his "bed" and known as one of the Rephaim (3:11). He is only a reflection of Sihon, little more than his formulaic twin. Most likely this narrative was composed entirely by DH. Nevertheless, the names Sihon and Og developed into a fixed pair in the confession of Yahweh's saving deeds (29:6–7 [ET 7–8]; Ps 136:17–22, etc.).[10]

Deuteronomy 3:1a ("turned and went up") follows the pattern of 2:1, 8b. On the one hand, "turn" strengthens the next verb (as a verbal hendiadys, cf. NRSV "we headed up the road"), but it also portrays Israel's obedience. In contrast to

---

7. The "*ḥērem* inventory" is a formulaic list of what has been treated as *ḥērem* (Josh 8:2, 27; 11:14, Mesha Inscription lines 16–17 [*ANET*, 320–21]). See R. D. Nelson, "*Ḥerem* and the Deuteronomic Social Conscience," in *Deuteronomy and Deuteronomic Literature*, ed. Vervenne and Lust, 47.

8. The phrase is a fixed border formula: 2:36; 3:12; 4:48; Josh 12:2; 13:9; 16; 2 Kgs 10:33; cf. 2 Sam 24:5.

9. "Lines of extent" drawn "from" one point "as far as" another are common in geographical descriptions (11:24; Josh 13:3–6; Exod 23:31).

10. On the tradition history of these two figures and the hypothetical extent of their kingdoms, see J. R. Bartlett, "Sihon and Og, Kings of the Amorites," *VT* 20 (1970): 257–77.

the situation with Sihon, Israel is the invading aggressor. Verse 3b introduces a formula of *ḥērem* obedience that reappears in Josh 8:22; 10:28, 30, 33, 40; 11:8.

According to 1 Kgs 4:13, Solomon's sixth district included sixty cities of the "region" (or "confederation") of Argob. If that parenthetical notice can be trusted, Argob was properly a region *within* Bashan. However, 3:4 enlarges the "region of Argob," equating it with Bashan as a whole (cf. 3:13–14). The text piles up geographical expressions without precision in order to stress the totality of the conquest. The language of v. 5 echoes the curse in 28:52. In v. 6 the contrast of fortified and open settlements without walls (note m; cf. 1 Sam 6:18) also stresses total conquest: We captured even the strongest fortresses, and occupied other settlements as well, right down to the smallest hamlet.

Reaching Beth-peor: Allotment and Appeal 3:8–29

Land and Tribes East of the Jordan

3:8 So at that time we took from the control of the two kings of the Amorites the land on the other side of the Jordan, from the Wadi Arnon as far as Mount Hermon 9 (the Sidonians call Hermon Sirion, but the Amorites call it Senir), 10 all the cities of the plateau, all Gilead, and all Bashan as far as Salecah and Edrei, cities of the kingdom of Og in Bashan. 11 (Only Og king of Bashan was left of the remnant of the Rephaim. Look, his bed, an iron bed, is it not to be seen in Rabbah of the Ammonites? Its length is nine cubits and its breadth is four cubits, according to the ordinary cubit.)

12 I gave to the Reubenites and Gadites the land that we took over at that time, from Aroer, which is on[a] the Wadi Arnon, and half of the hill country of Gilead and its cities. 13 I gave to the half-tribe of Manasseh the rest of Gilead and all Bashan, the kingdom of Og, the whole region of Argob. (That whole Bashan used to be called Rephaim country.[b] 14 Jair son of Manasseh took the whole region of Argob as far as the border of the Geshurites and the Maacathites and he named them—that is, Bashan—Havvoth-jair after himself, as is the case to this day.) 15 To Machir I gave Gilead. 16 And to the Reubenites and the Gadites I gave from Gilead and as far as[c] the Wadi Arnon, the middle of the wadi and adjacent territory,[d] and as far as the Wadi Jabbok, the border of the

Ammonites, 17 and the Arabah and the Jordan and its adjacent territory, from Chinnereth as far as the sea of the Arabah (the Salt Sea), below the slopes of Pisgah on the east.

18 At that time I commanded you saying, "Yahweh your God has given you this land to take it over. As armed soldiers[e] you shall cross over before your kindred the Israelites, all valiant warriors. 19 Only your wives, your small children, and your cattle—I know that you have much cattle—shall remain in your cities that I have given to you. 20 When Yahweh gives rest like yours to your kindred and they too have taken over the land that Yahweh your God is giving them on the other side of the Jordan, then you may return, each to his own property that I have given to you."

21 And I commanded Joshua at that time saying, "Your eyes are the ones that have seen[f] everything that Yahweh your God[g] has done to these two kings. Yahweh will do the same thing to all the kingdoms into which you are going to cross. 22 Do not be afraid of them, for Yahweh your God is the one who fights for you."[h]

Moses Appeals, Yahweh Refuses

23 At that time I appealed to Yahweh, saying, 24 "O Lord Yahweh, you have begun to show your servant your greatness and your mighty hand, because[i] what god in heaven or on earth can do anything like your deeds and your powerful acts? 25 Let me cross over to see the good land that is on the other side of the Jordan, this good hill country and the Lebanon." 26 But Yahweh was angry[j] with me on your account and would not listen to me. Yahweh said to me, "Enough! Do not continue speaking to me about this matter! 27 Go up to[k] the promontory of Pisgah and lift up your eyes to the west, to the north, to the south, and to the east. Look well, for you will not cross over this Jordan. 28 But command[l] Joshua and make him brave and strong, because he is the one who shall cross over at the head of this people and he shall cause them to inherit the land that you see." 29 Then we remained in the valley opposite Beth-peor.

a. Follows MT. Sam., OG, Syr., Vulg. supplement with *śpt*, "the rim of," to harmonize with 2:36; 4:48.

b. This translation ignores the masoretic punctuation.

c. The conjunctions in both occurrences of *w'd* in this verse are uncertain (see *BHS*; for the first see 4QDeut[d]).

d. For the formula "and its adjacent territory," cf. Josh 13:23, 27; 15:12, 47.

e. An accusative of state describing the result of being "girded," *IBHS* 10.2.2d. *Ḥălûṣîm* refers to warriors who have belted on weapons and tucked up their skirts for action. Other suggestions include "as a vanguard" (based on context) or "drafted, selected," taking the meaning of the verbal root as "pull off" (cf. Deut 25:9–10).

f. The participle is the predicate of a verbless clause (*IBHS* 37.5a), and the definite article functions as a relative pronoun (*IBHS* 13.5.2d). "Your eyes" is emphasized by word order; cf. 4:3; 11:7.

g. Follows MT and OG (LXX^A). The disturbing plural of the second-person suffix may have triggered the loss of "your God" in Sam.

h. Verse 22 shifts to second person plural in order to address the people. For the logic behind the alternation of singular and plural address here, see N. Lohfink, "Zum Numeruswechsel in Dtn 3:21f.," *BN* 49 (1989): 39–52.

i. Taking the first *'ăšer* as causal. It also could function as a relative: "about whom [one says], what god. . . ?"

j. Unbridled fury that drives one to adverse words or deeds; see K.-D. Schunck, "*'ebrâ*," *TDOT* 10:425–30.

k. MT has no preposition. 4QDeut^d and OG read *'l*, "unto," probably as a dittography of *'lh*, "go up." This became *'l* in Sam. (Syr., Tg.). *Rō'š*, "head," can refer to a promontory or projection of a mountain rather than to its summit (cf. Judg 9:7).

l. "To commission for a task, give charge to," *HALOT* 3:1011; cf. Deut 31:14, 23. The usage seems to derive from Num 27:19, 23.

Moses brings his historical review to a close and turns to subjects important for Israel's future: land seizure and distribution, plans for war, and the future of his leadership. He begins with a summary of land acquisitions east of the Jordan (vv. 8–11), introduced by the formula "at that time." Conquest ("we captured," 2:34; 3:4) now leads to appropriation ("we took," 3:8; "we took over," 3:12). Moses next covers four other topics in four distinct sections, each also featuring the transitional phrase "at that time" and adding to this a first-person statement:

> Moses recalls allocation of land east of the Jordan (vv. 12–17; "I gave"). This solidifies disputed eastern frontiers.
>
> He commands the eastern tribes to aid in the remaining conquest (vv. 18–20; "I commanded you"). Yahweh has given them rich grazing land; now brotherly solidarity demands they help secure Yahweh's gift for the other tribes.
>
> He previews 31:3–8 and charges Joshua to have confidence in a future guaranteed by Yahweh's precedent-setting victories (vv. 21–22; "I commanded Joshua").
>
> Finally, he raises the issue of his own fate (vv. 23–28; "I appealed"). But Yahweh responds in anger. Moses cannot participate in Israel's future, but he will be permitted to view it from afar.

The five occurrences of "at that time" and the four "I" statements unify the composition, but some verses are only loosely connected to their context.

Verse 9 breaks into the description of the land in vv. 8 and 10. Verse 11 returns parenthetically to the topic addressed in 2:11, 20. Verses 13b–15 (Jair and Machir) and vv. 16–17 (a second look at Reuben and Gad) appear to be discursive embellishments resulting from a desire to pile up topographic information.

[8–11] This catalog summarizes the land taken from Sihon and Og. The original text consists of vv. 8 and 10. It reinforces the point that the goal identified in 2:24–3:7 has been achieved: "two kings," "from the Wadi Arnon as far as Mount Hermon." The acquired land is on the "other side" from the perspective of author and reader, but not according to the dramatic situation of Deuteronomy (contrast vv. 20 and 25).

A descriptive "line of extent" ("from . . . as far as") is drawn south to north from the Arnon. The terminal point Hermon marks the northernmost extent of the whole territory. This is an idealistic claim in the direction of Aram that ignores the existence of Maacah and Geshur (v. 14). The names Sirion and Senir (v. 9) are known from extrabiblical sources, but they do not refer specifically to Mount Hermon.[1] A second line of extent in v. 10 terminates at Salecah and Edrei, describing the east and south extent of Bashan. Salecah is the easternmost point; Edrei is to the south of Salecah and marks the border's east point on the Yarmuk.[2] These two lines of extent are filled out and connected by a threefold list: plateau, Gilead, Bashan. The plateau (*mîšōr*, 3:10; cf. 4:43) is the tableland north of the Arnon and south of Wadi Heshbon (for the cites of the plateau, see Josh 13:9, 16–20). This represents a land claim against Moab to the south. "All Gilead" is understood to extend both north and south of the Jabbok (in contrast to 2:36 and 3:15–16). "Bashan" refers to territory north of the downstream course of the Yarmuk (the Golan) along with the area encompassed by its upper tributaries, including Edrei and Salecah.

Supplementary information about Og (v. 11) became attached to the catchword of his name (v. 10). That he was the last of the mighty and numinous Rephaim (2:11, 20; 3:11, 13) increases the glory of Israel's victory. Rephaim were not just giant supermen, but mythic royal beings and numinous figures connected with the underworld.[3] Reference to Og's bed is intended to boost the text's trustworthiness and believability. If one doubts that he was one of the Rephaim, one should see how large his bed is: about 4 meters by 2 meters. The word *'ereś* is only used for a bed or couch; it never means a

1. For details see Perlitt, *Deuteronomium*, 237–38.

2. The identification of Salecah with Salkhad (map reference 311212) is geographically plausible, but philologically weak. Edrei is Der'a (253224).

3. A Ugaritic text mentions a deified king who is one of the Rephaim and "sits enthroned in Ashtaroth, judges in Hedrei" (*CTU* 1:108; cf. Josh 12:4; 13:12). Ashtaroth is linked to Og by Deut 1:4 and to the Rephaim by Gen 14:5. For a discussion and bibliography, see G. del Olmo Lete, "Og," *DDD* 638–40.

sarcophagus.[4] Although the word "iron" is not used for stone in Hebrew (ironstone, basalt), it often serves as a metaphor for strength. A mighty ("iron strong") dolmen (a horizontal stone slab set on two verticals) is probably intended. Or perhaps Og's "bed" was a ceremonial furnishing with iron fittings, part of the cult of a deified king practiced in the Ammonite capital.[5] The down-to-earth note that this is the "ordinary cubit," as opposed to the longer royal one, has the literary effect of emphasizing the concrete reality of this relic.

[12–17] Verses 12–14 describe land distribution from south to north; the original text is vv. 12–13a. Here the standard understanding about Gilead operates. Half is north of the Jabbok and the rest lies to the south. Verses 15–17 function as a mirror text, repeating the distribution in reverse order from north to south. Machir substitutes for Manasseh, and Gilead is restricted to territory exclusively north of the Jabbok. This mirror pattern unites disparate materials: "I gave to the Reubenites and Gadites" (v. 12) / "I gave to . . . Manasseh" (v. 13) // "to Machir I gave" (v. 15) / "to the Reubenites and Gadites I gave" (v. 16).

Verses 12–13 raise no difficulties. Reuben and Gad receive Sihon's kingdom, that is, the southern half of Gilead (v. 12); Manasseh obtains the northern half of Gilead along with Bashan (v. 13). However, vv. 14–16 introduce substantial confusion, in part resulting from a different definition of Gilead, understanding it as being completely north of the Jabbok.

With its assertion that Jair took Bashan, v. 14 conflates two originally separate items of traditional geography, namely Argob and Havvoth-jair. According to the Solomonic district list (1 Kgs 4:13) Havvoth-jair was in Gilead (cf. Num 32:41; Judg 10:4), while the sixty Argob cities made up a completely different region within Bashan. However, v. 14 simply identifies Argob with Havvoth-jair. Moreover, it follows v. 4 in incorrectly equating Argob, which was really only a region of Bashan, with the whole of Bashan. The unwieldy "named them" (with "region" as antecedent) suggests that mention of Havvoth-jair derives from Num 32:41 ("Jair the son of Manasseh went and took their villages, and named them Havvoth-jair"). The parenthetical "that is, Bashan" follows as an awkward attempt to explain "them" as being coterminous with all of Bashan. The resulting text has collapsed the "tent encampments" of Jair in

---

4. The notion of a sarcophagus is supported by Josephus, *Ant.* 5:125, who mentions the bones of giants on display, and Herodotus, *Hist.* 1:68, who speaks of Orestes' giant sarcophagus. For linguistic data, see A. Angerstorfer, "*'eres*," *TDOT* 11:379–83. For the suggestion that this was an actual bed, see A. R. Millard, "King Og's Bed and Other Ancient Ironmongery," in *Ascribe to the Lord: Biblical and Other Studies in Memory of Peter C. Craigie* (ed. L. Eslinger and G. Taylor; JSOTSup 67; Sheffield: JSOT Press, 1988), 481–92.

5. U. Hübner, "Og von Baschan und sein Bett in Rabbat-Ammon (Deuteronomium 3,11)," *ZAW* 105 (1993): 86–92, proposes a Neo-Babylonian cultic item.

Gilead into the fortified cities of Argob in Bashan.[6] Geshur in the Golan and Maachah south of Hermon mark the western edge of Manasseh's territory. These two nations remained independent in the early monarchy (2 Sam 10:6; 13:37; cf. 2 Kgs 25:23).

More confusion is introduced as v. 15 treats Gilead as coextensive with the territory of Machir, contradicting v. 13 and restricting Gilead to territory north of the Jabbok (the opposite of 2:36; cf. Josh 13:25). "From Gilead" in v. 16 shares this same conception, if one understands it as an expression intended to leave Gilead outside the territory of Reuben and Gad.

In v. 16 two lines of extent are drawn from the same starting point of Gilead, one "as far as" the Arnon and the second "as far as" the Jabbok (for this pattern, cf. Josh 1:4; 10:41). Each line of extent has supplementary information appended to it. The first line runs southward to the Arnon, which represents the south border of Reuben. "Middle of the wadi" seems to be a fragment of the longer formula found in 2:36; Josh 13:9, 16; 2 Sam 24:5. The second line of extent runs eastward to where the upper reaches of the Jabbok divided Gad from the Ammonites.

The west border is defined by the Arabah, that is, the valley of the Jordan (v. 17). Gad claimed an arm of territory along the Jordan up to Lake Chinnereth (Josh 12:3; 13:27). The geographical description closes with a subsidiary line of extent running southward down the Jordan Valley from Chinnereth to the east shore of the Dead Sea. The "slopes" (Deut 4:49; Josh 12:3; 13:20) refer to the watershed down the west side of the Pisgah escarpment ("the fissured place," which always occurs with a definite article). Pisgah seems to indicate a range of scarps rather than a single location.

[18–20] These eastern conquests and allotments are only foretastes of the upcoming main event on the "other side of the Jordan." These verses may be based on elements of Num 32:1, 16–27. This dependency is suggested by the unexpected change of address at the start of v. 18 and the parenthesis about cattle in v. 19.[7] This section is unified by a palindromic structure:

> Yahweh your God has *given you* this land *to take it over* (*lĕrištāh*)
>> You shall cross over before *your kindred* (v. 18)
>>> But your wives, your small children, and your cattle . . . shall remain (v. 19)
>> When Yahweh gives rest like yours to *your kindred* (v. 20)
> Then you may return, each to his own *property* (*lîruššātô*) that I have *given to you*

---

6. The confusion is compounded by Josh 13:30, which derives from this passage.

7. In Num 32:1 these cattle indicate the suitability of the land claimed by the eastern tribes, but in Deuteronomy they play no significant role. On the reciprocal literary relationship between these texts, see Noth, *Numbers*, 233–41; and Mittmann, *Deuteronomium 1:1–6:3*, 95–104.

Without warning Moses shifts to address the tribes east of the Jordan. They have a further mission based on Yahweh's gift to them and their solidarity with their "brothers." Their children (who had served as a faithless excuse in 1:39) may remain behind, along with other vulnerable elements of their household, as a sign of their secure possession of Yahweh's gift (contrast Num 32:17). "Cities" (v. 19) is a reminder that Israel has taken over both the land and its infrastructure (cf. 6:10–11; but according to Num 32:16 they must build their own). "Rest" is a classic theme of Deuteronomy's theology (12:8–12; 25:17–19). This story will continue and conclude in Josh 1:12–18; 21:43–45; 22:1–6.

[21–22] These verses raise the issue of the transfer of power to Joshua, pointing forward to 31:3–8. In 31:7 Moses repeats what he reports doing here, but "in the sight of all Israel." Courage to face the future is based on remembering the past. "Kings" and "kingdoms" prepare for the sort of foes Joshua will face (cf. Josh 8, 10–12). Joshua will quote the Divine Warrior credo of v. 22 when his own career is over (Josh 23:10). The verb "command" implies "commission" (note 1). However, Moses does not transfer leadership at this point, but instead addresses Yahweh about his own future (vv. 23–25).

A sequence of seven comparative, typological expressions concludes with v. 21 (cf. 1:30; 2:12, 21–22, 28–29; 3:2, 6). This last comparison is picked up in reversed form by 31:4 ("two kings" . . . "all the kingdoms" transposed into "them" . . . "Sihon and Og, the kings"). The reader is thus presented with an extended historical analogy: Yahweh will fight in the conquest in the same way as in the liberation from Egypt (1:30); he dispossessed earlier populations to give land to other nations just as he will for Israel (2:12, 21–22); he did to Og what he did to Sihon (3:2, 6); he will do to all enemy kings what he did to Sihon and Og (3:21; 31:4).[8]

[23–28] The topic of Israel's future beyond the Jordan leads into a plea on the part of Moses. His fate has already been announced in 1:37–38; now he resists. "Appeal" (v. 23; *ḥnn* hitpaʻel) suggests desperation and intense emotion. In v. 24 Moses uses the language of courtly submission ("my lord," "your servant"), but in so doing also echoes his own role as "servant of Yahweh" (34:5). "Begun" (referring to 2:25, 31) sounds like a hopeful suggestion that his experience with Yahweh's deeds may not really be over. He uses the hymnic language of Yahweh's incomparability (Ps 89:7–9 [ET 6–8] 113:5–6) to motivate a receptive hearing. The "hill country" and "Lebanon" of v. 25 hark back to the promise of 1:7.

Yahweh's angry response, however, immediately returns the topic to that of the succession of Joshua. Perhaps Yahweh's brusque *rab lāk*, "enough" (v. 26),

---

8. Lohfink, "Geschichtstypologisch orientierte Textstrukturen," in *Deuteronomy and Deuteronomic Literature*, ed. Vervenne and Lust, 140–44.

ironically reflects on the *rab lākem*, "long enough," of 1:6 and 2:3. Moses' "let me cross" (v. 25) is opposed by Yahweh's "you will not cross" (v. 27). However, Moses' parallel request to "see" is to be granted in an unanticipated way. Perhaps what Moses is to do ("lift up your eyes") alludes to Abraham's panoramic view of the land (Gen 13:14–15). Moses is to look not only across the Jordan, but also eastward, for that too is part of the conquered and distributed land.

As before (1:37–38), Yahweh's anger is "on your account" (v. 26), but nothing more specific is revealed about the reason for Moses' punishment (contrast 32:48–52; Num 20:12; 27:14). Here he simply suffers in solidarity with the people he leads. That even Moses must endure punishment emphasizes the seriousness of the people's past disobedience. From the perspective of DH, the fate of Moses may echo the undeserved death of the righteous Josiah.[9] For exilic readers, the punishment of an innocent individual along with the whole people would serve as a theological reflection on the nation's communal fate in defeat and exile.[10] The future lies with Joshua, who has a double task. He will lead Israel across the Jordan and "cause them to inherit the land" (v. 28; cf. 1:38).[11]

[29] At this point the narrative horizon of DH is brought to a halt; it will resume in 31:1. Reference to Beth-peor forms a ring composition, bracketing Moses' retrospective speech by circling back to the locale of law giving (1:5). Beth-peor also sets the scene for Moses' second address that will soon follow (4:46) and his eventual burial (34:6). However, Peor is also a place of ominous tradition, the scéne of an archetypal choice between fidelity and apostasy (4:3–4; Num 25:1–13; Hos 9:10). Now both the audience of Moses and the readers of Deuteronomy, primed for the challenges of the future, wait at the point of critical decision for Moses to speak the law.

---

9. T. W. Mann, "Theological Reflections on the Denial of Moses," *JBL* 98 (1979): 481–94.

10. Lohfink, "The Problem of Individual and Community," 227–33.

11. The two tasks of entering and causing to inherit are also differentiated in Josh 1:2–9. In "The Deuteronomistic Picture" (in *Theology of the Pentateuch*, 234–47), Lohfink understands "cause to inherit" (*nḥl* hip'il) as "distribute" and advances a complex thesis of how authority is transferred in Deuteronomy. Supposedly, Moses has to be commanded twice to install Joshua into office (1:38 and 3:28) because he is trying to hold onto his office. Instead of fully installing Joshua at 3:21–22 as he was expected to, Moses only encouraged him at that point in the story. Joshua is not fully installed until 31:7–8 and 23.

Exhortation to Obedience
4:1–40

Listen to the Statutes and Ordinances

4:1 And now, O Israel, listen to the statutes and ordinances that I am teaching you to do, so that you may live and enter and take over the land that Yahweh the God of your ancestors is going to give you. **2** Do not add to the word that I command you and do not subtract from it, keeping the commandments of Yahweh your God that I am commanding you.

3 Your eyes have seen what Yahweh did at Baal-peor, how Yahweh your God destroyed from among you everyone who followed the Baal of Peor. **4** But you who clung to Yahweh your God are all alive today.

5 See, I hereby teach[a] you statutes and ordinances just as Yahweh my God[b] has commanded me, for you to do in the land that you are going to enter to take it over. **6** Keep them and do them, for this will be your wisdom and discernment before the eyes of the peoples. When they hear about all these statutes, they will say, "Surely[c] this great nation is a wise and discerning people!" **7** For what great nation is there that has gods as near[d] to it as Yahweh our God is whenever we call to him? **8** And what great nation has statutes and ordinances as equitable as this whole law that I am setting before you today?

Be Careful Lest You Forget

9 Only[e] take care and be very careful about yourselves, lest you forget the things your eyes have seen and lest they slip away from your mind as long as you live. Inform your children and your children's children about them. **10** There was a day when you stood before Yahweh your God at Horeb, when Yahweh said to me, "Assemble the people for me,[f] so that I may make them hear my words, that they may learn to fear me all the days that they live on the earth and may teach their children." **11** You approached and stood at the foot of the mountain. The mountain was burning with fire up to the sky itself.[g] There was darkness, cloud, and gloom. **12** Then Yahweh spoke to you from the middle of the fire. You were hearing the sound of words, but seeing no shape. There was only a sound. **13** He declared to you his covenant, which he commanded you to do, the ten words, and wrote them on two stone tablets. **14** Yahweh commanded me at that time to teach you statutes and ordinances for you to do in the land that you are going to cross into to take it over.

Be Careful Lest You Make an Idol

15 Be very careful about yourselves, because you did not see any shape on the day[h] Yahweh spoke to you at Horeb from the middle of the fire, 16 lest you act corruptly and make an idol for yourselves, in the shape of any image, a replica of a male or female,[i] 17 a replica of any animal that is on the earth, a replica of any winged bird that flies in the sky, 18 a replica of any creeping thing that creeps[j] on the ground, a replica of any fish that is in the waters below the earth. 19 And [be careful] lest you raise your eyes skyward and see the sun, the moon, and the stars, all the host of heaven, and let yourself be led astray[k] and bow down to them and serve them, things that Yahweh your God allotted to all the peoples under the sky.[l] 20 But you are the ones[m] Yahweh has taken and brought out of the iron forge, out of Egypt, to become a people of his hereditary possession, as is the case today.

21 Yahweh was angry with me because of you, and swore that I would not cross the Jordan and that I would not enter the land[n] that Yahweh your God is giving you as a hereditary possession. 22 For I am to die in this land without crossing the Jordan, but you are going to cross over and take over this good land.

23 Be careful lest you forget the covenant of Yahweh your God, which he made with you, and you make yourselves an idol in the shape of anything against which Yahweh your God has commanded you. 24 For Yahweh your God is a consuming fire. He is a jealous God.

A Look to the Future

25 When you have children and grandchildren and have grown old in the land, and you act corruptly and make an idol in the shape of anything and do evil in the opinion of Yahweh your God so as to[o] offend him, 26 I call heaven and earth to witness against you today that you will certainly perish soon[p] from the land to which you are crossing the Jordan to take it over. You will not live long on it, but you will certainly be destroyed.[q] 27 Yahweh will scatter you among the peoples, and only a small number of you will be left among the nations to which Yahweh will drive you. 28 There you will serve gods[r] made by human hands, objects of wood and stone that cannot see or hear or eat or smell.

29 You[s] will seek Yahweh your God from there and you will find him, if only you search for him with all your heart and all your being. 30 In your distress when[t] all these things have happened to you,[u] in the days to come you will return to Yahweh your God and obey him. 31 For a merciful God is Yahweh your God. He will not desert you or destroy you.

He will not forget the covenant with your ancestors that he swore to them.

Israel's Unique Experience of Yahweh

32 Ask about former days that were before you, ever since[v] the day that God created humanity on the earth, and from one end of the sky to the other. Has anything[w] as great as this happened before? Has anything like it been heard of? 33 Has any people heard the voice of a god[x] speaking from the middle of fire, as you yourself have heard, and remained alive? 34 Or has any god ventured to go and take a nation for himself from the midst of another nation, by ordeals, by signs and wonders, by war, by a mighty hand and an outstretched arm, and by great deeds of terror, according to all Yahweh your God did[y] in Egypt before your eyes? 35 You yourself were shown it so you might know that it is Yahweh who is God; beside him there is no other. 36 From heaven he made you hear his voice to discipline you and on earth he showed you his great fire, and you heard his words from the middle of the fire. 37 And because he loved your ancestors, he chose their descendants after them;[z] and with his presence, with his great power, he brought you out of Egypt, 38 to dispossess before you nations greater and more powerful than you, to bring you in so as to give you their land as a hereditary possession, as is the case today. 39 So know today and recall in your heart that it is Yahweh who is God in heaven above and on earth below. There is no other. 40 Keep his statutes and his commandments, which I am commanding you today, that it may go well for you and your children after you, and so that you may live long in the land that Yahweh your God is giving you for all time.

a. A performative perfect as an act of promulgation, *IBHS* 30.5.1d; cf. 1:8.

b. Follows MT, supported by Syr. (although without the jarring pronominal suffix). OG dropped *'lhy*, "my God," to ease the difficulty.

c. The restrictive adverb *raq* with the situation to be qualified left unexpressed, thus giving it emphatic, affirmative force: "[we would not have thought so,] but this nation is nothing other than a wise people" (*IBHS* 39.3.5c).

d. Follows MT, which has a plural participle modifying "god." OG, Syr., Tg. interpret the expression as singular, each nation having its own god near to it.

e. Follows MT. The absence of *raq*, "only," in OG is probably a translation strategy. The restrictive adverb affirms a significant conclusion: "the bottom line is: do nothing other than take care" (*IBHS* 39.3.5c).

f. This translation takes the following *'ăšer* clause as a final clause, *IBHS* 38.3b. Alternate translation: "to me."

g. Literally "unto the heart of the sky" (MT and Sam.). Omission of *lb*, "heart," by OG (followed by Vulg.) is probably a translation strategy (J. W. Wevers, *Notes on the*

Greek Text of Deuteronomy [SBLSCS 39; Atlanta: Scholars Press, 1995], 73). "The mountain was burning" is a circumstantial sentence. "Darkness, cloud, and gloom" are loosely connected to the sentence as accusatives of manner.

h. *Běyôm* stands in construct with the following clause, *IBHS* 9.6c–e.

i. Alternative translation, seeking better parallelism by dividing the verse at *kol*: "an idol in the shape of anything, an image as a replica of male or female." The first construct chain uses the language of 5:8 rather than Exod 20:4.

j. Follows OG, Vulg.: *rmś 'šr rmś* as providing better parallelism. MT lost this by haplography: *kl [rmś 'šr] rmś*.

k. Nip'al of *ndh* in a tolerative sense, *IBHS* 23.4f; cf. 30:17.

l. Follows OG, Vulg., Syr. MT supplements: *tḥt kl-hšmym*, "everywhere under the sky."

m. "You" is in emphatic, contrastive position (cf. v. 14).

n. Follows OG and Tg. Ps.-J, as the shorter text. MT, Sam., Vulg., Syr. supplement with *ḥṭwbh*, "good."

o. Preposition *l* plus infinitive construct to express consequence or result, Williams, *Hebrew Syntax*, 198.

p. Follows MT. OG omits *mhr*, "soon," either as a correction because the perishing took some time (cf. OG at 9:3, 16) or due to homoioarchton: *m[hr m]'l*.

q. Alternate translation: "be completely destroyed."

r. Follows MT and Sam. as a shorter, less expected text. OG and Syr. expand to the standard formula *'lhym 'ḥrym*, "other gods."

s. Read as singular with Sam. and Vulg. The plural (MT, OG, Syr.) arose by dittography: *wbqšt[m] mšm*.

t. Relative *waw* with temporal force, *IBHS* 32.2.6b.

u. This translation follows the masoretic punctuation. NRSV connects "in the days to come" with Israel's distress (as 31:29) rather than its repentance. Sam. and OG divide vv. 29–30 differently: "all your being when you are in distress. All these things will happen to you. . . ."

v. The compound preposition *lmn* indicates a terminus a quo in space or time (cf. 9:7).

w. The preposition *k* is used in a quasi-nominal way to introduce a nominal phrase, *IBHS* 11.2.9a, d.

x. Follows MT. Sam., OG, Targ. supplement with *ḥyym*, "living," taken from 5:26. Alternate translation: "the voice of God."

y. Follows OG and Syr. as the shorter text. MT supplements with *lkm*, "for you." OG does translate this word in 11:5.

z. Literally "his seed after him." This could represent a distributive singular ("each one's seed") or refer only to Isaac (Gen 17:19) or Jacob. Sam., OG, Syr., Tg., Vulg. "correct" to the expected plural (cf. 10:15).

This chapter presents "reading instructions" for the rest of the book of Deuteronomy. "Statutes and ordinances" (vv. 1, 5, 14; cf. 40) point to the book's dramatic premise that it is a promulgation of law by Moses that begins in 5:1. Moses recalls history (vv. 3–4, 10–14, 15, 20, 21, 32–34), appeals to experience (vv. 7, 9–12, 15), and anticipates the future (vv. 25–31). He does so in order to encourage obedience to the law he is about to proclaim, to explain the relationship of the Decalogue "covenant" to the "statutes and ordinances" of the rest of Deuteronomy (vv. 13–14), and to warn of idolatry (vv. 15–19). His exhortation begins with a call to attention (v. 1). It employs effective rhetoric in the shape of positive motivations such as Yahweh's saving acts (vv. 20, 34, 37), negative ones like the threat of exile (vv. 25–28), rhetorical questions (vv. 7–8, 33–34), and similar devices (v. 32). The speech seeks to inculcate obedience to the chief commandment of exclusive worship (5:7), understood primarily in terms of the prohibition of images (5:8–10), but also motivated by a virtually monotheistic confession that there really are no other gods (vv. 35, 39).[1]

Chapter 4 forms a bridge between the historical review of chapters 1–3 and the start of Moses' promulgation of law in 5:1. It makes a sharp transition from history to parenesis and from a retrospective horizon to the "now" of Moses' act of speaking. The horizon of reference extends both backward and forward. The introductory "And now" (cf. 10:12) indicates a new beginning that looks back to the previous material. However, chapters 1–3 as such report nothing about the events at Baal-peor (4:3–4), nor do they point in any way to lawgiving, obedience to the law, or the theophany at Horeb. In other words, chapters 1–3 do not prepare for chapter 4, although chapter 4 looks back to them (vv. 3–4 to 3:29 and vv. 21–22 to 3:23–28). Chapter 4 also looks forward, not just to the Decalogue, but also to the dual structure of Deuteronomy as Decalogue plus Deuteronomic law (vv. 13–14). It is likely that chapter 4 was composed at a late stage, having both the DH introduction to Deuteronomy and Deuteronomy itself already in view.

Opinions about the literary history of this chapter range from complex theories of layered supplementation to assertions of overall literary unity.[2] The most obvious internal anomaly is the shift between second person plural and singular. Verses 1–28 are predominantly plural; vv. 29–40 change to singular

---

1. For the theology of this chapter, see B. B. Schmidt, "The Aniconic Tradition: On Reading Images and Viewing Texts," in *The Triumph of Elohim: From Yahwism to Judaisms* (ed. D. V. Edelman; Grand Rapids: Eerdmans, 1996), 75–105; A. Schenker, "Unwiderrufliche Umkehr und neuer Bund: Vergleich zwischen Dt 4:25–31, 30:1–14; Jer 31:31–34," *FZPhTh* 27 (1980): 93–106; P. Beauchamp, "Pour une théologie de la lettre (Dt 4)," *Recherches de science religieuse* 67 (1979): 481–94.

2. *Basic unity*: N. Lohfink, "Verkündigung des Hauptgebots in der jüngsten Schicht des Deuteronomiums (Dt 4,1–40)," in *Studien zum Deuteronomium I*, 167–91; G. Braulik, *Die Mittel deuteronomischer Rhetorik: Erhoben aus Deuteronomium 4,1–40* (AnBib 68; Rome: Biblical Institute Press, 1978), 7–81, 91–100. A. D. H. Mayes, "Deuteronomy 4 and the Literary Criticism of Deuteronomy," *JBL* 100 (1981): 23–51; repr. in *Song of Power*, ed. Christensen, 195–224, sees ch. 4 as secondary to DH in chs. 1–3 and discerns contributions from this same exilic editor

address.[3] Unquestionably, the course of argumentation is uneven. The thematic focus switches from theophany and Decalogue (vv. 9–14) to a denunciation of images (vv. 15–24), then to a consideration of Israel's future fate (vv. 25–31), and finally to the uniqueness of Yahweh (vv. 32–39). Another indication of development over time is the changing definition of "covenant." "Covenant" means the whole Decalogue in v. 13, the prohibition of images in v. 23, and the promise to the ancestors in v. 31.

On the one hand, chapter 4 must be understood as the result of a complex process of growth. The interest in lawgiving in vv. 1–14 points directly at the upcoming address of Moses. In contrast, the interest in images in vv. 15–20, 23–24 emerges as a reflective digression based on a single, unemphatic phrase in v. 12, "seeing no shape." The grim portrayal of exile in vv. 25–28 (mostly second person plural) converts abruptly into the positive viewpoint of vv. 29–31 (singular). This circumstance, along with the repeated initial *kî* of vv. 31 and 32, demonstrates that vv. 29–31 are a later supplement to vv. 25–28, advancing the theme of restoration found also in 30:1–10. Finally, in vv. 32–40 the exilic situation abruptly disappears from view and images are no longer at issue. In addition, parenthetical digressions seem evident in vv. 19 and 21–22.[4]

On the other hand, the final form is held together across these divisions by many unifying factors, which appear to be the result of exceptionally skillful redactional work. The whole address is enclosed by an envelope formed by the parallel language of vv. 1–2 and 40 and by the repetition of this same language

---

elsewhere in Deuteronomy. *Successive expansions*: D. Knapp, *Deuteronomium 4: Literarische Analyse und theologische Interpretation* (GTA 35; Göttingen: Vandenhoeck & Ruprecht, 1987), proposes three successive blocks, each with expansions: 1–4, 9–14 (expansion 5–8) + 15–16a, 19–28 (expansion 16b-18) + 29–35 (expansion 36–40). R. D. Nelson, *The Double Redaction of the Deuteronomistic History* (JSOTSup 18; Sheffield: JSOT Press, 1981), 90–94: DH in vv. 1–14, 21–22; a later addition on images in vv. 15–18, 23–28; an exilic DH2 in vv. 19–20; and an optimistic supplement from the author of 30:1–10 in vv. 29–31 (40).

3. C. H. Begg, "The Literary Criticism of Deut 4,1–40: Contributions to a Continuing Discussion," *ETL* 56 (1980): 10–55, uses number shifts to help distinguish three successive blocks: vv. 1–28 (basically plural), vv. 29–31 and vv. 32–40 (both basically singular). He explains other variations in number as quotations from older texts in Deuteronomy (e.g., vv. 19 and 24) and the result of of standardized phrasing. N. Lohfink, *Das Hauptgebot; Eine Untersuchung literarischer Einleitungsfragen zu Dtn 5–11* (AnBib 20; Rome, Biblical Institute Press, 1963), 30–31, 239–58, suggests that number change is an emphatic stylistic device used to contrast elements of the argument. Overall, he understands the singular of vv. 29–40 as speaking to the whole cultic community and the plural of vv. 1–28 as addressed to a collection of responsible individuals or to those who had participated in the events narrated.

4. On literary-critical issues, see K. Holter, "Literary Critical Studies of Deut 4: Some Criteriological Remarks," *BN* 81 (1996): 91–103; G. Braulik, "Literarkritik und archäologische Stratigraphie: zu R. Mittmanns Analyse von Deuteronomium 4:1–40," *Bib* 59 (1978): 351–83.

in vv. 5 and 14. Structurally, vv. 1–8 and 32–40 may be treated as brackets surrounding three paragraphs beginning with "be careful lest": vv. 9–14, 15–22, and 23–31. Phrases and themes recur persistently.[5] In addition, there are rhetorical harmonies in the use of foregrounded imperatives (vv. 1, 5, 9, 23, 32), the cautionary "lest" (*pen*; vv. 9, 16, 19, 23), arguments from history and audience experience (vv. 3–4, 9–14, 15, 20, 34–38), and rhetorical questions (vv. 7, 8, 33, 34). The verbal root '*śh* is employed repeatedly: the audience is to "do" the law (vv. 1, 5, 6, 13, 14), but not "make" images (vv. 16, 23, 25). The vocabulary of "great" and "nation" is also reiterated, first three times in vv. 6–8 and then again in a variety of ways in vv. 32, 34, 36–38. Similar arguments from universal and international realities are developed in vv. 6–8 and 32–34.[6]

Chapter 4 is connected thematically to elements of chapters 29–30 (cf. e.g., 4:19 and 29:25 [ET 26]; 30:17; 4:26 and 30:19). The most striking parallel is the extension of the chronological horizon to national disaster (4:25–28; 29:22–28 [ET 23–29]) followed by the possibility of restoration (4:29–31 and 30:1–10).[7]

[1–4] Verse 1 is a sort of mission statement for all that follows. The initial "And now" draws a parenetic conclusion from the previous narrative, and the imperative "listen" signals an introduction to the impending act of lawgiving (5:1; 6:4; 9:1; 20:3; 27:9). "Statutes and ordinances" (vv. 1, 5, 8, 14) refers to Moses' promulgation of law in Moab.[8] As a generalizing term for the whole of

5. Hearing and seeing (respectively: vv. 1, 6, 10, 12, 28, 30, 32, 33, 36 and 3, 9, 12, 15, 34–36); teaching and learning (vv. 1, 5, 10, 14); the emphatic "I" for Moses (vv. 1, 2 [twice], 8, 22, 40); "today" (vv. 4, 8, 20, 38–40); "keep/be careful" (vv. 2, 6, 9, 15, 23, 40); "forget" (vv. 9, 23, 31); "inform/know" (vv. 9, 35, 39); "fire" (vv. 11, 12, 15, 24, 33, 36); "shape" (vv. 12, 15, 16, 23, 25); "act corruptly" (vv. 16, 25).

6. Lohfink, "Verkündigung des Hauptgebots," 172–74, suggests a pattern of alternating extensions of chronological horizon: Baal-peor and conquest (vv. 3–4 and 5), Solomonic wisdom and temple nearness (vv. 6–8), Horeb (vv. 10–14), the monarchic world of image and astral cults (vv. 16–19), the exodus (v. 20), the exile (vv. 25–28), ending with the most distant past of the patriarchs and then the most remote future of restoration (vv. 29–31).

7. E. Otto, "Deuteronomium 4: Die Pentateuchredaktion im Deuteronomium," in *Das Deuteronomium und seine Querbeziehungen* (ed. T. Veijola; Schriften der Finnischen Exegetischen Gesellschaft 62; Göttingen: Vandenhoeck & Ruprecht, 1996), 196–222, asserts that ch. 4 corrects 29:1–14 [ET 2–15] (which according to Otto views the Horeb event negatively and replaces it with the Moab covenant) and reinterprets ch. 5 so that Yahweh only speaks the Decalogue and does not directly reveal Deuteronomic law.

8. "Statutes and ordinances" are not two sorts of laws, but a collective reference to the whole law (cf. 1 Sam 30:25). See G. Braulik, "Die Ausdrücke für 'Gesetz' im Buch Deuteronomium," in *Studien zur Theologie des Deuteronomiums* (SBAB 2; Stuttgart: Katholisches Bibelwerk, 1988), 11–38. According to N. Lohfink, "Die *ḥuqqîm ûmišpāṭîm* im Buch Deuteronomium und ihre Neubegrenzung durch Dtn 12:1," in *Studien zum Deuteronomium und zur deuteronomistischen Literatur II* (SBAB 12; Stuttgart: Katholisches Bibelwerk, 1991), 229–56, this phrase helps incorporate ch. 5 into Deuteronomy, integrates the pre-Deuteronomic laws of chs. 12–26 into the whole book, and binds the parenesis of chs. 6–11 to both Decalogue and Mosaic law.

Mosaic preaching, this phrase performs a framing role for chapters 5–11 (cf. 4:45, 5:1, 31; 6:1 and 11:32) and for chapters 12–26 (cf. 12:1 and 26:16–17).

Warnings similar to the so-called canonical formula of v. 2 (cf. 13:1 [ET 12:32]) are found in treaties and other scribal texts. The occurrence of this formula is evidence of scribal professionalism behind the text. The phrase displays an authorial consciousness that chapter 4 is introducing a larger, comprehensive whole, complete in itself. Since it is itself part of a redactional addition to Deuteronomy, however, v. 2 clearly intends to guard the spirit and sense of the law rather than the exact letter of the text. The "promulgation formula" ("I am commanding you," vv. 2, 40) recurs throughout Deuteronomy as an insistent call for obedience and decision.[9]

The incident referred to in vv. 3–4 (Num 25:1–13) was not mentioned in chapters 1–3. As a place of religious disloyalty, the name is pointedly given as *Baal*-peor, rather than the more neutral Beth-peor of 3:29 and 4:46. The episode illustrates Deuteronomy's basic point that disobedience leads to destruction (vv. 24, 26) but obedience leads to life (vv. 1, 40). "Your eyes have seen" introduces the subsequent rhetoric of eyewitness experience (vv. 9, 15, 34). "Cling" (*dābaq*) is an image of loyalty and allegiance (10:20; 11:22; 13:5 [ET 4]; 30:20).

[5–8] Verse 5 promulgates the law, v. 6a commands obedience to it, and vv. 6b-8 motivate observance. Verse 5 restarts the mode of introduction and the theme of v. 1 with parallel language (v. 1: "statutes and ordinances . . . teaching you to do . . . enter and take over the land"; v. 5: "teach you statutes and ordinances . . . for you to do in the land . . . to enter to take it over"). Verses 5–8 are held together as a unit by an inversion of "I hereby teach you statutes and ordinances" (v. 5) by "law that I am setting before you" (v. 8).[10] Verse 5 asserts that the act of lawgiving Moses is about to perform was a task divinely authorized and commanded at Horeb (cf. v. 14), a point underscored by his startling reference to Yahweh as "my God." Exilic readers might have heard the statement of the law's applicability "in the land" (again cf. v. 14) as a comforting limit on any unreasonable obligation to obey all its details in exile.[11] The

9. S. J. DeVries, "Development of the Deuteronomic Promulgation Formula," *Bib* 55 (1974): 301–16.

10. G. Braulik finds a "pattern of law establishment" (*Reschtsfeststellungsschema*) here: "see" (v. 5), statement of promulgation (v. 5), imperatives (v. 6aα), motivation introduced by *kî* (vv. 6aβ-8). He finds a similar pattern in vv. 32–40. The intention is to gain acceptance of the law that follows. See "Wisdom, Divine Presence and Law: Reflections on the Kerygma of Deut. 4:5–8," in *The Theology of Deuteronomy* (N. Richland Hills, Tex.: BIBAL Press, 1994), 1–25; trans. of "Weisheit, Gottesnähe und Gesetz: Zum Kerygma von Deuteronomium 4, 5–8," in *Studien zur Theologie des Deuteronomiums*, 53–93.

11. Even though exiled readers could not obey all of Deuteronomy, they could safeguard its demand for exclusive, aniconic worship in their polytheistic environment.

ambiguous "this" in v. 6a most likely refers to the action of doing the law, construing "wisdom" as a behavioral term. However, "this" could also point forward to the nations' positive evaluation in vv. 6b-8.

In vv. 6b-8 an appeal to ethnic pride and a reminder of Yahweh's saving acts motivate obedience. Three arguments for obedience are advanced based on the notion "great nation": recognition of Israel's wisdom (v. 6b), the nearness of Yahweh (v. 7), and the righteousness of the law (v. 8). What is at issue here is religious and ethical greatness, something pertinent even for dispossessed exiles. Verse 6b quotes international reaction, using the rhetorical strategy also employed in 28:37; 29:21-27 [ET 22-28]. The attractive notion of Deuteronomic law as much-admired wisdom would provide readers respectability over against the power and claimed cultural superiority of other peoples, something that would be especially meaningful for exiles. To Israel as a whole belongs the "wisdom and discernment" of the classic wise ruler (1:13; Isa 11:2; 29:14; cf. Joseph and Solomon). Thus Deuteronomic law represents a democratization of the special quality that enables just government.

Taken together, vv. 7-8 form an incomparability saying (cf. Mic 4:5; 2 Sam 7:23) similar in thought to vv. 32-34. The "great nation" argument of v. 6b is continued through two rhetorical questions about the incomparability of national deities and laws. In each case the expected answer is: "There is none." The comparison of competing deities involves "near and far" rather than true or false gods (v. 7). "Nearness" is a characteristic of effective prayer and worship ("call upon"). Even for exiles, divine nearness is assured, in spite of the loss of the temple and their distance from Yahweh's land. Yahweh's innate nearness also challenges the classic ideology of images, one purpose of which was to guarantee the nearness and availability of the god represented. The effectiveness of the "call" to Yahweh on the part of the poor is illustrated in 15:9 and 24:15 and leads implicitly into the second question about the social fairness of the law (v. 8). The word translated "equitable" is *ṣaddîq*, "righteous" (used elsewhere of persons rather than things). The law Moses will promulgate is one that helps debtors, slaves, and widows. The prologue and epilogue of the Hammurabi Code boast in a similar way of its wise and fair social ordering (*ANET*, 164, 177-78).

[9-14] For the introductory warning formula of v. 9, compare 12:13, 19, 30; 15:9. For the danger of forgetting, see 6:12; 8:11, 14, 19; 9:7. Teaching the next generation is a central concern of Deuteronomy (6:7-9, 20-25; 11:19; 31:13; 32:46).[12]

Verse 10 opens with an accusative designating a time more exactly (*yôm 'ăšer*, GKC 118i), explaining the circumstances of what Israel saw (v. 9). "Fear"

---

12. As well as of Assyrian vassal treaties. See VTE 25, *ANET*, 537, where there are also parallels to vv. 23 and 26.

designates active belief, reverent obedience. For rhetorical purposes, the argument presupposes that those addressed had been present at Horeb, conflating the generations of "that day" (vv. 10, 15) with the "today" generation of v. 8. This rhetorical sleight-of-hand makes possible an eyewitness argument that goes on to include the readers of Deuteronomy, who themselves experience the "today" of decision. The "you" who experienced the exodus and Horeb (vv. 11–13, 20) merges into the "you" addressed by Moses and by the written text. The fire of theophany (v. 11) sets the stage for repeated references to the amazing circumstances of Yahweh's address at Horeb (vv. 12, 15, 33, 36; cf. 5:4, 22).

The participles of v. 12 convey dramatic vividness. The contrast between "shape" (*těmûnâ*) and "voice" (*qôl*) at this point stresses the auditory character of this event. The notion of shape, unemphasized here, will be turned into an attack on idolatry in vv. 15–18 and again in vv. 25–28. For now, however, the topic is dropped. Instead v. 13 unwraps the content of the "voice" as the Decalogue understood in terms of a "covenant" (cf. v. 23; 9:9, 11, 15; 10:8) intended for obedience. Writing on stone indicates permanence and importance, while employing two tablets may imply making two copies, a practice sometimes followed in the recording of ancient treaties.

Verse 14 adds as a second outcome of the Horeb event the deferred promulgation by Moses of the "statutes and ordinances" that constitute Deuteronomy. Yahweh's command "at that time" links Decalogue and Deuteronomic law. The double content of the Horeb revelation is also described in 5:23–31. Here in 4:13–14, however, the "statutes and ordinances" give the impression of being a mediated exposition of the Decalogue worked out by Moses as lawgiver, rather than independent laws directly revealed to Moses by Yahweh, as is clearly the case in 5:31. The foregrounded, emphatic "me" that begins v. 14 contrasts with the surrounding occurrences of "you" and points forward to the diametrically opposed futures in store for Moses and Israel (vv. 21–22). The warning of vv. 9–14 is concluded by language parallel to that of vv. 1 and 5.

[15–20] Verse 15 restates the warning language of v. 9 ("be very careful") and picks up the notion of *těmûnâ*, "shape;" from v. 12. This verse begins an exposition or restatement of 5:8–10, characterizing exclusive worship narrowly in terms of images. Verse 15 states the foundational evidence, then vv. 16–19 draw the predictable deductions from it, so that the theological principle is derived from experience. Horeb demonstrated that images are inappropriate in the worship of Yahweh.

The argument begins with the claim that any image of Yahweh is based on a faulty presupposition, for no divine image can be Yahweh (v. 15). Verse 16 piles up the vocabulary of idolatry into construct chains (note i). "Act corruptly" in v. 16 (cf. v. 25) appropriately parallels the use of this verb in the golden calf episode (9:12). The argument then moves in vv. 17–18 through various possible candidates for idols. These various iconic possibilities build a bridge between Yahweh images and the wider topic of pagan gods, for birds and fish could hardly represent Yahweh. A comprehensive list seeks to express rigorous prohibition, as does the repeated and emphatic *kol*, "all" (vv. 15, 17 [twice], 18 [twice]; cf. 23, 25, and 5:8). The list of shapes in vv. 16–18 is set forth in language similar to that of the Priestly Writer, though not in the order found in Genesis, but rather according to the tripartite division set forth in 5:8. The sequence of possibilities (human, animal, bird, creeping thing, fish) moves farther and farther from what would be conceivable as an image of Yahweh. This list is summarized in v. 23. Yahweh is degendered to a degree in that the form of neither man nor woman is appropriate.

Verses 19–20 move beyond the fabricated images of the Decalogue into another realm, the astral gods of foreign peoples. This topic is coordinated with v. 16 as a second "lest" statement. The issue is not images of these heavenly powers, but the worship of heavenly bodies as directly observed in open-air cults (Job 31:26–28). The argument shifts away from what was not seen at Horeb to the contrast between Israel's special standing as the beneficiary of the exodus and religious behaviors assigned to other nations by Yahweh as universal God (cf. Deut 32:8–9). Verse 20 generates this contrast by means of the emphatic position of "you" (note m).

The metaphor of Egypt as a furnace for refining iron (v. 20) communicates the brutality of Israel's experience of slavery by comparing it to the extreme heat of the procedure and the social subjugation and suffering of those enslaved unfortunates who mined and smelted iron (Job 28:2–4). The idea of punishing, testing, or purifying Israel is not part of the image. Rather the furnace of slavery provides the necessary background for Yahweh's acts of taking and bringing out, so that Israel could become "a people of his hereditary possession" (cf. 1 Kgs 8:51; Jer 11:4).[13] "Hereditary possession" (9:26, 29) implies strong personal attachment (cf. Naboth's refusal to part with family land).

[21–24] Moses now explores the disparity between his future fate and that of Israel, already hinted at in vv. 13–14. Verses 20–22 state this contrast distinctly: Yahweh brought *you* out as a *hereditary possession*, but Yahweh was angry with *me* so *I* will not cross into the *hereditary possession—I* am to die in *this land*, but *you* are going to cross into the *good land*. Although these verses may seem to be little more than a random return to the topic of 1:37–38 and 3:23–28, they do relate to the overall argument of chapter 4 in that the punishment of Moses highlights the potential negative consequences of disobedience.

After this topical detour, vv. 23–24 summarize the prohibition of idolatry, returning once more to the language of v. 9 ("forget"), v. 13 ("covenant"), and

---

13. D. Vieweger, "... und führte euch heraus aus dem Eisenschemlzofen aus Ägypten ...": *bwr hbrzl* als Metapher für die Knechtschaft in Ägypten (Dtn 4,20; 1 Kön 8,51 und Jer 11,4)," in *Gottes Recht als Lebensraum* (ed. P. Mommer; Neukirchen-Vluyn: Neukirchener Verlag, 1993), 265–76.

especially vv. 15–16. Now the fire of Horeb is said to be an aspect of Yahweh's very nature (cf. 9:3). The connection between idolatry and Yahweh as "jealous God" (i.e., "passionately intolerant of rivalry or disloyalty") is an allusion to the Decalogue (5:9).

[25–28] Verses 25–28 and then 29–31 move forward into the future and on to new topics, first exile and then restoration. Verses 25–28 do not necessarily presuppose an exilic date, but only an audience familiar with deportation as a feature of Assyrian imperial policy. What Moses foresees as a possible future (idolatry, national destruction, exile into pagan lands) would have been a concrete reality for even the earliest of Deuteronomy's readers, in the shape of the calamity suffered by the northern kingdom.

The verb translated "grown old" in v. 25 (*yšn* nip'al) carries a suggestion of staleness, a loss of initial enthusiasm and engagement (cf. Lev 26:10). Verse 26 ("I call . . . today . . . crossing the Jordan") recalls once more the dramatic premise of Deuteronomy as an address of Moses delivered on the threshold of conquest. The rhetoric of "witness" and the emphatic grammar (*'ābōd tō'bēdûn; hiššāmēd tiššāmēdûn*) stress inevitability. From the perspective of the book as a whole, these catastrophes are the outworking of the concluding curses (cf. 28:36, 62–64). The warning "small number" (v. 27) undermines Yahweh's promise of a large population (cf. 1:11; 6:3; 13:18 [ET 17]). Verse 28 describes the absolute low point of this menacing future as Israel's worship of gods ridiculed as powerless fabrications. Deities that neither see nor hear can pay no attention to one's lament (contrast v. 7). Sacrifice to gods incapable of eating or smelling is pointless. Such inert objects contrast sharply with Yahweh's active power described in vv. 32–34, 37–38. Ironically and appropriately, the crime of idol worship (vv. 16–18, 25) will be punished by idol worship.

[29–31] Readers enduring exile are challenged to repent. In the dominant theology of Deuteronomy, blessing and curse are alternatives that come upon those who either obey or disobey. Here, in contrast, curse and blessing are treated as successive periods of exile and restoration. Correspondence in language and outlook to 30:1–10 make it almost certain that these second-person singular verses are a supplement to the (mostly) plural vv. 25–28.[14]

Nevertheless, redactional elements do connect this section to previous paragraphs. The "covenant" of v. 23 reappears in v. 31, although converted from Decalogue command into patriarchal promise. Verse 31 reverses the pattern of v. 24. "For Yahweh your God . . . is a jealous God" becomes "for a merciful

---

14. H. W. Wolff, "The Kerygma of the Deuteronomic Historical Work" (trans. F. C. Prussner), in W. Brueggemann and Wolff, *The Vitality of Old Testament Traditions* (Atlanta: John Knox, 1975), 83–100; repr. in *Reconsidering Israel and Judah* (ed. G. Knoppers and J. McConville; Winona Lake, Ind.: Eisenbrauns, 2000), 62–78. The initial *kî* of 4:32–34 originally connected to the apostasy of 4:25–28, introducing a call to research history in order to establish Yahweh's uniqueness. The initial *kî* of 4:31 gives the motive for the promise of vv. 29–30.

God is Yahweh your God." The same verse undoes the threat of the verbal root *šht* hip'il in vv. 16, 25 ("act corruptly") by an outright denial of the same root (in its more usual meaning "destroy").

Along with the similar passage 30:1–10, this section sets the whole book of Deuteronomy into a restoration framework. Israel must take the initiative. Alienation from Yahweh and life in an foreign land requires that Israel seek and search in earnest recommitment and obedience (v. 29). However, the possibility of a positive outcome depends ultimately on Yahweh's character as a deity who is not only "jealous" (5:9) but also "merciful" according to the traditional liturgical formula preserved in Exod 34:6; Ps 86:15, and elsewhere. Taken together, vv. 24 and 31 coordinate two divine epithets, *'el qannā'* "jealous God," and *'ēl raḥûm*, "merciful God," each revealing a facet of Yahweh's emotional and relational life. Each verse uses its respective divine title in the context of an explanatory *kî*, "for." "Jealous God" (v. 24) explains why Israel must avoid idols (v. 23) and provides the theological basis for the national catastrophe described in vv. 25–28. The notion of "merciful God" (v. 31) explains why Israel may find it possible to return to Yahweh (vv. 29–30). Yahweh as "merciful God" will neither "desert," "destroy," nor "forget." "Desert" (*rph* hip'il) suggests the context of sacral war (31:6–8; Josh 1:5). Israel may have forgotten the circumstances of the Horeb covenant (vv. 9, 13, 23), but Yahweh will not forget the earlier and different covenant sworn to the patriarchs. Although no return from exile is explicitly mentioned, there is at least a hint of this possibility in the promissory content of Yahweh's covenant with the ancestors.

[32–40] These verses go over ground similar to what has already been covered, but shift the focus away from images to an emphasis on the uniqueness of Yahweh (vv. 35, 39).[15] The text seeks to motivate both faith (v. 39) and obedience (v. 40). Moses turns away from the distant future to recall the past once again, spelling out the consequences of Israel's unique encounters with Yahweh at Horeb and in Egypt. At no other place or time could one find something to compare with these two special experiences—the sound and sights at Horeb that taught discipline (vv. 33, 36), and the exodus and conquest that revealed Yahweh's election and love (vv. 34, 37–38). A proper understanding of what history reveals about Yahweh's unique character should lead to obedience (v.

---

15. For the incipient monotheism of this chapter, see G. Braulik, "Deuteronomy and the Birth of Monotheism," in *Theology of Deuteronomy*, 115–21; trans of "Das Deuteronomium und die Geburt des Monotheismus," in *Studien zur Theologie des Deuteronomiums*, 257–300. A. Rofé, "The Monotheistic Argumentation in Deuteronomy iv 32–40: Contents, Composition and Text," *VT* 35 (1985): 434–45, proposes that the original argument for monotheism here was that in the exodus Yahweh proved able to invade another nation's realm to liberate Israel (v. 34). This showed Yahweh's universal power (v. 39), coupled with a unique relationship to one people (vv. 37–39). The marvel of hearing a divine voice and remaining alive (vv. 33, 36) was added later (cf. 5:21b, 23).

40). This thematic pattern of arguing from history appears also in 7:7–11; 10:12–22; 11:1–8.[16]

The use of "God created" (instead of "Yahweh") in v. 32 may be driven by the vocabulary of the creation tradition (Gen 1:1, 21, 27; 2:3; 5:1). The question of v. 33 may be answered on the basis of vv. 10–13, 15, and points forward to the fears of 5:25–26. The answer to the question of v. 34 is implied in v. 20. Verse 34 lists seven manifestations of Yahweh's power.

The theological conclusion of vv. 35 and 39, a statement very close to monotheism, is based on the realities described in vv. 33–34 and 36–38. Verses 35 and 39 use the same contrastive grammatical pattern, asserting Yahweh's uniqueness and then excluding all other possibilities with the phrase "there is no other" (cf. 1 Kgs 8:60; 18:39; Isa 45:5–6; Joel 2:27; *IBHS* 16.3.3c). Verse 36 stresses the marvel of hearing Yahweh's voice by referencing two alternative traditions about the place of its origin: from fire (as 5:24) and from heaven (as in Exod 20:22).

It is possible to treat vv. 37–40 as a single sentence, with vv. 37–38 as an extended protasis and vv. 39–40 as the apodosis: "Because he loved . . . and chose . . . and brought you out . . . to dispossess[17] . . . , therefore know . . . and keep." "Presence" in v. 37 translates Yahweh's "face," emphasizing personal involvement and the absence of any mediator, and perhaps correcting traditions such as Num 20:16. The logic of "because he loved your ancestors, he chose their descendants" is found also in 10:15; 30:9. The motif of "nations greater" (v. 38) appears in 7:1; 9:1; 11:23. The text temporarily breaks the dramatic frame of Moses' speech with "as is the case today."

"Heaven" and "earth" (v. 39) recall the threat of v. 26, the arenas of Yahweh's uniqueness in v. 32, and the experience cited in v. 36. "Heaven above and earth below," as the all-encompassing sphere of Yahweh's jurisdiction, define Yahweh's exclusive claim to divinity (Josh 2:11; 1 Kgs 8:23; cf. Deut 5:8). Moreover, the word pair "heaven and earth" pulls together many of the themes of this chapter in terms of the transcendence of the heavenly God and the immanence of the one who spoke at Horeb. The accessible divine nearness asserted in v. 7 was literally true in the Horeb experience (vv. 10–11). However, because Horeb involved only hearing, and not seeing a form (v. 12), Israel must avoid the visual and concrete immanence offered by images (vv. 15–18). Instead, Israel experiences divine immanence in the earthly actions of the transcendent Yahweh, who hears lament (v. 7), commands law (vv. 8,

---

16. Braulik, *Die Mittel deuteronomischer Rhetorik*, 63–64, calls this a "schema of the presentation of evidence" (*Schema der Beweisführung*) and isolates as characteristic elements: review of history (vv. 32–34, 36–38), consequence for belief (vv. 35, 39), and practical conclusion (v. 40).

17. The hipʿil of *yāraš* denotes "destroy in order to gain possession" (7:17; 9:3, 4, 5; 11:23; 18:12), while the Qal means "possess by virtue of conquest" (2:12, 21, 22; 9:1; 11:23; 12:2, 29; 18:14; 19:1; 31:3). See N. Lohfink, "*yāraš*," *TDOT* 6:371–76.

34, 37), and bestows land (v. 38). For
ews, for such an accessible "God of
ld be sought and found even in a for-

'—40 by repeating the language and
," most likely is a comforting refer-
ild also apply to the perpetual dura-
es" (cf. 11:1; 14:23; 19:9).

awgiving

Jordan

Mos   the Jordan to the east 42
to fl   ⏤or inadvertently and had
ously   ⏤ could flee to one of these cities and
ive: 43 ⏤ezer in the wilderness on the plateau for the Reuben-
ioth in Gilead for the Gadites, and Golan in Bashan for the
tes.

Introduction to the Law

s is the law that Moses set before the Israelites. 45 These are the pre-
, statutes, and ordinances that Moses spoke to the Israelites when
had come out of Egypt, 46 on the other side of the Jordan in the val-
⏤, opposite Beth-peor, in the land of Sihon king of the Amorites who
ruled at Heshbon, whom Moses and the Israelites struck down when they
came out of Egypt. 47 They took over his land and the land of Og king of
Bashan, the two kings of the Amorites who were on the other side of the
Jordan to the east: 48 from Aroer, which is on the rim of the Wadi Arnon,
as far as Mount Sion,[b] that is, Hermon, 49 and the whole Arabah on the
other side of the Jordan eastward and as far as the Sea of the Arabah,[c]
below the slopes of Pisgah.

a. The pattern 'āz + imperfect, used to indicate a tenuous and approximate chronological connection, often seems to mark an addition (cf. Josh 8:30 and 22:1).
b. This unique designation for Mount Hermon is unrelated to the two names mentioned in 3:9.
c. Follows MT. OG lost mzrḥ[h w'd ym h'rb]h through homoioteleuton.

[41–43] This section fulfills expectations that will be raised by 19:1–13, where Israel is commanded to create cities of refuge to shelter unintentional killers from overhasty vengeance. It also seeks to demonstrate the preeminence of Moses as one who preceded Joshua in designating cities of refuge. This narrative is directly related to the command of 19:3–7 to establish three cities west of the Jordan and tangentially related to the report that Joshua later designated them as part of a total of six (Josh 20).[1] Because chapter 19 does not refer to 4:41–43, these verses must be a late addition, something also indicated by the disjunctive grammar of their introductory words (note a). Although chapter 19 allows for three supplementary cities in addition to the three it commands west of the Jordan, it does not specify where they should be located. Apparently reference to the east Jordan tribes in 3:12–20 triggered this supplement, but the addition was delayed until after Moses had finished speaking. Ramoth in Gilead is located north of the Jabbok, so assigning it to Gad contradicts 3:16.

[44–49] Verse 44 is the second of four headings that partition the final form of the book (cf. 1:1; 28:69 [ET 29:1]; 33:1). A second introduction was apparently felt necessary after the long retrospective narrative that started with 1:6. This paragraph seeks to reorient the reader by restating the content of the address of Moses (v. 45), where he delivered it (v. 46), and the extent of land occupied at this point in the story (vv. 47–49). This goal is accomplished through piling up cross-references to other passages.

Verses 44 and 45 are functional doublets that echo and take up 1:1, 5, in order to reestablish the scene for Moses' proclamation. The pairing of a singular designation for law (v. 44) side by side with a list of synonyms (v. 45) also appears in 5:31; 6:1; 7:11. This stylistic feature is an emphatic rhetorical device that negotiates the interplay between "law" as a comprehensive concept and the individual precepts that constitute it. The term ʿēdwût, "precepts," is used only here and in 6:17, 20, perhaps as a reference to the Ten Commandments.[2]

Verse 46 reviews 2:26–37 and 3:29 (Beth-peor), tying the geography of legal proclamation to that of conquest history. The last words repeat the last words of v. 45, probably a redactional signal that v. 46 is a supplementary addition. Verse 47 focuses on the land of conquest ("took over") and adds Og (3:1–8a) to the story being reviewed. Verses 48–49 retrace the geography of 3:8–17 (specifically vv. 8b–9, 12b, 17). Verse 48 describes a "line of extent" (for these, cf. 2:36; 3:8–10, 16–17; 11:24) that covers the highlands east of the Jordan from south to north. Verse 49 reports on the eastern Jordan valley

---

1. Nelson, *Joshua*, 226–31.
2. B. Couroyer, "'édût: Stipulation de traité ou enseignement?" *RB* 95 (1988): 321–31, suggests the meaning "doctrine" or "teaching." N. Lohfink, "'ed(w)t im Deuteronomium und in den Königsbüchern," in *Studien zum Deuteronomium III*, 167–77, stresses that context determines the choice of either "oath" or "teaching" as a translation.

(Arabah) with a line of extent trending southward. The concluding "Pisgah" (from 3:17) points forward to the concluding panorama seen by Moses before his death (3:27; 34:1).

The Covenant at Horeb
5:1–33

The Ten Commandments

5:1 Moses summoned all Israel and said to them: Hear, O Israel, the statutes and ordinances that I am proclaiming to you today. You shall learn them and be careful to do them. 2 Yahweh our God made a covenant with us at Horeb. 3 Yahweh our God did not make this covenant with our ancestors, but with us, with all of us here alive today.[a] 4 Yahweh spoke with you face to face at the mountain, from the middle of fire 5 (I was standing between Yahweh and you at that time to declare to you the word[b] of Yahweh, because you were afraid because of the fire and did not go up the mountain), saying:

6 "I am Yahweh your God,[c] who brought you out of the land of Egypt, from the house of servitude. 7 Have no other gods beside me.[d]

8 Do not make for yourself an idol of any shape[e] that is in heaven above or on the earth below or in the waters below the earth. 9 Do not bow down to them or serve them,[f] because I, Yahweh your God, am a jealous[g] God, punishing children for the guilt of parents, to the third and fourth generation of those who hate me,[h] 10 but showing loyalty to the thousandth generation[i] of those who love me and keep my commandments.[j]

11 Do not take up the name of Yahweh your God for an empty purpose, for Yahweh will not consider anyone innocent who takes up his name for an empty purpose.[k]

12 Keep the Sabbath day by sanctifying it,[l] just as Yahweh your God commanded you. 13 Six days you may labor and do all your work. 14 But the seventh day[m] is a Sabbath of[n] Yahweh your God. Do not do any work—you, or your son or your daughter, or your male or female slave, or your ox or your donkey or any of your cattle, or the alien resident within your towns, so that your male and female slave may rest as you do. 15 Remember that you were a slave in the land of Egypt, and Yahweh your God brought you out from there with a mighty hand and an outstretched arm. For this reason, Yahweh your God has commanded you to perform the Sabbath day.

16 Honor your father and your mother, just as Yahweh your God commanded you, so that you may enjoy long life and that it may go well with you in the land that Yahweh your God is giving you.

17 Do not commit murder.[o]

18 And do not commit adultery.[p]

19 And do not steal.

20 And do not testify against your neighbor as a lying witness.[q]

21 And do not covet[r] your neighbor's wife. And do not desire your neighbor's house, his field, his male or his female slave, his ox or his donkey, or anything that belongs to your neighbor."

Moses As Intermediary

22 Yahweh spoke these words to your whole assembly at the mountain, from the middle of fire, cloud, and gloom,[s] with a loud voice, and he added nothing more. He wrote them on two stone tablets and gave them to me. 23 As soon as you heard the voice from the middle of the darkness,[t] while the mountain was burning with fire, you[u] approached me, all the heads of your tribes and your elders. 24 You said, "Yahweh our God has now shown us his glory and his greatness,[v] and we have heard his voice from the middle of fire. Today we have seen that God can speak to a human being and yet that one may remain alive. 25 But now, why should we die? Surely this great fire will consume us. If we continue to hear the voice of Yahweh our God, we will die. 26 For who is there of all[w] flesh who has heard the voice of the living God speaking from the middle of fire as we have, and remained alive? 27 You go near and hear everything that Yahweh our God is saying[x] and then you speak to us everything that Yahweh our God speaks to you. Then we will listen and do it."

28 Yahweh heard your words when you spoke to me. Yahweh said to me, "I have heard the words of this people that they have spoken to you. They have spoken correctly in everything they have said. 29 Would that they would be of a mind to fear me and always keep my commandments,[y] so that it might go well with them and with their children forever. 30 Go say to them, 'Return to your tents.' 31 But as for you, stay here with me, and I will speak to you the commandment[z]—the statutes and the ordinances—that you are to teach them, that they may do them in the land that I am giving them to take it over." 32 Be careful to do just as Yahweh your God has commanded you. Do not deviate right or left. 33 Follow the whole way that Yahweh your God has commanded you, so that you may remain alive and that it may go well with you and that you may enjoy long life in the land that you will take over.

a. The word order in MT and Sam. is *ph hywm klnw ḥyym,* "here today all-of-us alive." OG (supported by 4QPhyl A, 4QPhyl B, 4QPhyl J) indicates *ph klnw ḥyym hywm,* "here all-of-us alive today." 4QDeut[n] conflates the two readings into *ph hywm kwlnw ḥyym hywm.* The whole expression is strongly emphatic and contrastive: "indeed with us, us, these here today, all of us alive."

b. Follows MT. Sam. and OG (as well as 4QDeut[n] and Syr., which add "your God" after Yahweh) read *dbry,* "words of," probably to match the "ten words" that follow. Dittography or haplography could have been triggered by the following *y.*

c. Translating as a self-identification formula. Alternate translation taking "your God" as the predicate and emphasizing Yahweh's deed rather than the divine name: "I, Yahweh, am your God, who...."

d. That is, "in addition to me" or "other than me." Alternate translations: "before me," either in the sense of "prior to me, in preference to me" (21:16), or in the sense of "in my presence" as an idol set up at Yahweh's sanctuary; or "over against me" meaning "to my disadvantage." See *HALOT* 3:944.

e. Follows MT *kl-tmwnh* without an initial *waw.* Many witnesses, including 4QDeut[n], Sam., OG, Vulg., Syr., adjust this to the parallel in Exod 20:4: *wkl-tmwnh,* "nor any shape." This translation construes the relative *'ăšer* with *těmûnâ* and treats the relationship between *pesel* and *těmûnâ* as a construct. Alternate translation connecting *'ăšer* to *kol:* "the shape of anything that is in heaven" (as in 4:16, 23, 25). Alternate translation treating *těmûnâ* in apposition with *pesel:* "an idol, any shape." It is also possible (but not natural) to end the sentence at *pesel:* "an idol. Any shape . . . , to them do not bow down."

f. "Serve" is pointed as hop'al: "make yourself servants of," i.e., "allow yourselves to be made participants in their cult." "Them" could refer to the images of v. 8, but if it refers to the gods of v. 7, then prohibition of images is embedded into the first commandment.

g. "Jealous" signifies the intolerant, resentful, and passionate anger of one whose prerogatives have been appropriated by a rival.

h. The preposition *l* in *lěśōn'ay* indicates possession ("of those who hate"), Williams, *Hebrew Syntax,* 270.

i. Translating for better parallelism and in accord with 7:9. Alternate translation: "to thousands."

j. Follows Qere, supported by Sam. and the ancient versions. Kethib *mṣwtw,* "his commandments," originated from a confusion of *y* and *w.*

k. "Take up" in the sense of speaking (Ps 16:4), to bear up on one's mouth. This could occur in the context of an oath ("swear falsely in the name of") or in using the divine name for a worthless purpose in magic or laying a curse. Lying is suggested by the equation of *šawě'* in 5:20 with *šeqer,* "lie," in Exod 20:16 (cf. Hos 4:2; Jer 7:9). "Consider innocent" implies "leave unpunished."

l. The infinitive construct explains the circumstances or manner of the verb "keep," *IBHS* 36.2.3e (cf. 13:19 [ET 18]).

m. Follows MT, Sam., Vulg., Syr.: *wywm.* Other witnesses (OG and 4QDeut[n] among them) harmonize with Exod 20:10: *wbywm,* "on the seventh day."

n. That is, belonging to Yahweh; cf. 15:2.

o. The translation "murder" is too narrow, but "kill" is too broad. All illicit killing of human beings is forbidden: outright murder, death by careless accident, and unauthorized blood vengeance.

p. OG presents vv. 17 and 18 in reverse order (supported by Nash Papyrus, Philo, NT). See R. A. Freund, "Murder, Adultery and Theft?" *SJOT* 2 (1989): 72–80.

q. Accusative of manner: testify as an empty, worthless witness. Contrary to the impression given by many English translations, "witness" denotes someone or something that witnesses, not the content of the testimony (*HALOT* 2:788). The difference from Exod 20:16 (*šāwĕ'*, "emptiness" for *šeqer*, "lie") seems to forbid all misleading evasions, not merely outright lies.

r. The relationship between wish and deed implied in "covet" has been much discussed. Apparently, the verb does not necessarily extend to include actual attempts at appropriation. This conclusion is indicated by the need to add a further verb to describe such attempts (7:25) and by Deuteronomy's equation of "covet" with the verb "desire" in this verse. Nevertheless, Exod 34:24 shows that "covet" can mean more than simple craving. Perhaps the connotation can be captured by "plan to appropriate" or "scheme to acquire."

s. Follows MT. Sam., OG, 4QDeut[n], 4QPhyl B, 4QPhyl J expand this phrase (with slight variations) on the basis of 4:11 (cf. 5:23) into *ḥsk 'nn w'rpl*: "darkness, cloud, and gloom."

t. Follows MT. OG amends to "fire" in order to agree with v. 24.

u. The possibility of a *t*-prefix third-person masculine plural here and at the start of v. 24 is unlikely (*IBHS* p. 497 n. 2, p. 516 n. 48).

v. Follows MT. OG lacks *w't-gdlw*, "and his greatness," lost by a haplography caused by identical initial and final letters: *w't-[gdlw w't-]qlw*).

w. The absence in OG of "all" here and in v. 27a is probably a strategy of translation.

x. Follows MT as shorter. 4QDeut[j], 4QPhyl H, 4QPhyl J, LXX[A], Vulg., Syr. witness a longer text, *'lhynw 'lykh*, "our God [is saying] to you." This expansion may have originated as a dittography, but also duplicates "to you" from later in the verse.

y. Follows Sam. as the shorter text. OG, MT, Vulg., Syr. supplement with *kl*: "*all* my commandments." 4QDeut[k1], 4QPhyl H, and some Hebrew MSS omit both the direct object marker *'t* and *kl*.

z. Follows OG. MT supplemented with *kl*: "the *whole* commandment." This translation construes the pair of words that follow as an apposition to the singular "commandment," as is clearly the case in 6:1 (cf. 7:11) and in the Sam. of all three of these passages. Alternate translation as a series of three items: "the commandment and the statutes and the ordinances."

The Horeb commandments are part of an envelope construction surrounding the whole of Moses' legal proclamation. They are coordinated with the list of twelve curses to be announced at Shechem (27:14–26). Those curses cover some of the same topics: idols, father and mother, the neighbor's life and property.

The Ten Commandments are encased in a narrative of past theophany (vv. 2, 4–5) and continuing revelation (vv. 22–31). By repeating the commandments, Moses locates Deuteronomy in time and space, between Horeb and the passage across the Jordan. The extreme importance of the Decalogue is signaled in the surrounding text (vv. 4 and 22: "Yahweh spoke," "face to face," "fire," "added nothing more"), by their position at the beginning of Moses' legal oration, and by their eventual storage in the ark (10:1–5). The framing narrative sets the dramatic stage for Deuteronomy as a proclamation of law by Moses to the assembly of Israel and assures readers that the law of chapters 12–26 originated from Yahweh at Horeb. This narrative thus serves as an etiology that authorizes the contents of Deuteronomy. What Moses will say in the chapters that follow is the consequence of the people's own request and their promise to obey (v. 27).

Decalogue and Deuteronomic law share the stage. For its part, the Decalogue represents a previous covenant made at Horeb (v. 2), spoken directly to the people from fire and written down by Yahweh (vv. 4, 22). In contrast, the Deuteronomic "statutes and ordinances" are proclaimed by Moses in the book's dramatic "today" (v. 1) and legitimized by a plot involving the people's fear and Moses as intermediary (vv. 5, 23–31). In this way the authority of the Decalogue "voice" (five times in vv. 22–26) is used to validate the "commandment(s)" (vv. 29, 31; 6:1), which are equated with the "statutes and ordinances" of Deuteronomy (vv. 1, 31; 6:1). Verses 32–33 form an admonition to obedience that blends directly into 6:1–3. The text will return to recollection of what happened "on the mountain" in 9:9–10:5.

Chapter 5's double focus on Decalogue and Deuteronomic law reveals that the Ten Commandments were incorporated into the body of Deuteronomy at a relatively late stage. Perhaps the Commandments were included on the model of Exodus, where Decalogue precedes and leads into the Covenant Code that Deuteronomy revises and supplements. The redactional point seems to be that the Commandments are a foundational tradition, normative for the rest of Israel's law, and that what follows them in Deuteronomy should be seen as having the same authoritative status as the earlier Covenant Code.[1]

Deuteronomy establishes its own validity by setting up Moses as an intermediary, a concept perhaps based on earlier tradition (Exod 20:18–21). The

---

1. For the double line of direction in this chapter, see C. Brekelmans, "Deuteronomy 5: Its Place and Function," in *Das Deuteronomium*, ed. Lohfink, 164–73. On the redactional function of ch. 5, see A. D. H. Mayes, "Deuteronomy 5 and the Decalogue," *Proceedings of the Irish Biblical Association* 4 (1980): 68–83. On the relationship between the Decalogue and the compositional development of the law code, see F.-L. Hossfeld, "Der Dekalog als Grundgesetz—ein Problemanzeige," in *Liebe und Gebot: Studien zum Deuteronomium* (ed. R. Kratz and H. Spieckermann; FRLANT 190; Göttingen: Vandenhoeck & Ruprecht, 2000), 46–59. Verse 3 seems to be a later supplement to v. 2 in terms of 28:69 [ET 29:1]. Verse 5 is a parenthetical addition (cf. "at that time"), separating "he said" from the end of v. 4 and promoting the role of Moses as mediator (cf. 34:10). Verse 5 also prepares for and anticipates v. 23–31. Verse 26 is awkward and unnecessary, with a perspective at odds with v. 24, and is usually assumed to be an expansion. Like v. 5, it emphasizes the role of Moses as mediator.

circumstances of the Horeb revelation legitimate both law and lawgiver through a plot of negotiation and the divine approval of a human suggestion (cf. the plots of 1:9–18 and 1:22–23). Both Decalogue and the content of Deuteronomy are revealed at Horeb, the latter being proclaimed a generation later in Moab. The very same divine voice serves as the foundation for both revelations (repeatedly in vv. 22–27). The purpose behind the second revelation is to permit life in the land to flourish (vv. 31, 33). The text motivates obedience through the convincing power of theophany (vv. 23–27), Israel's prior agreement to obey (v. 27), Yahweh's rather wistful-sounding wish in v. 29, and the promise of a good life in the land (vv. 29, 33). Surprisingly, Yahweh's direct revelation does not cause death to those who hear it (v. 24), evidence that Yahweh is a uniquely benevolent God who can claim Israel's exclusive loyalty.

The Commandments themselves begin as a divine speech (vv. 6–10), then shift into speech that refers to Yahweh in the third person (vv. 11–21). Apparently, an older legal list has been partially re-formed into a divine address. Differences from the Exod 20 version reflect the outlook and theology of Deuteronomy. At the same time, the language of Exod 20 itself certainly sounds Deuteronomic in places, perhaps owing to a northern background for the Decalogue.[2] Reading the commandments within the context of Deuteronomy— rather than in their Exodus setting or as an isolated, self-contained entity—gives them special significance. References to "jealous God," "love," "alien resident within your towns," or "the land that Yahweh is giving you" take on a distinctive meaning.

In the final shape of Deuteronomy, the commandments serve as prologue both to the exhortations of chapters 6–11 and to the law code of chapters 12–26. In the dramatic plot of Deuteronomy, they are remembered from Horeb, but restated to Israel at a critical point of transition. They deal with ordinary life, not the milieu of religion, tithes, festivals, and sacrifices. They focus on the commonplace existence of work, sex, property, family life, household images. They also deal with matters of the public square: court testimony, murder and manslaughter, curses and magic. Even the commandments about images, Yahweh's name, and Sabbath are not regulations for priests, but concrete and practical guidance for laypersons. Sabbath, for example, is not a day for pilgrimage or sacrifice; it is simply a pause in ordinary daily labor. In harmony with Deuteronomy, the commandments advance a social morality. One's "neighbor" has a right to rest, respect in old age, life without threat of violence, security in marriage, property, reputation. The negatively formulated commandments stake out a perimeter of outermost behavioral boundaries, inside

---

2. For the case that the Deuteronomic version is a revised form of Exod 20, see A. Graupner, "Zum Verhältnis der beiden Dekalogfassungen Ex 20 und Dtn 5: Ein Gespräch mit Frank-Lothar Hossfeld," *ZAW* 99 (1987): 308–29.

which Israel can live out a rich and free life. The commandments are motivated in the same way as the rest of Deuteronomy, by divine threat (vv. 9, 11) and a promise of favor and life in the land (vv. 10, 16), as well as by human empathy and the memory of the exodus (v. 15). Like Deuteronomy itself, the Decalogue is an ethic inspired by the solidarity of those liberated from Egypt and reverence for the God who freed them.

Some scholars propose that the Decalogue provided an organizing principle for the final order of Deuteronomy's laws. The weak point in this assumption is that it requires a reapplication of the commandment about parents to the topic of public authorities, that is, the officers, judges, king, priests, and prophet of 16:18–18:22. There is no evidence of this analogical interpretation before Philo.[3]

[1–5] The verbal parallel between v. 1 and 29:1 [ET 29:2] associates the covenant assemblies of Horeb and Moab. Use of the vocative and a call to "hear" structure the parenetic section that follows (6:4; 9:1; cf. 10:12).[4] The focus of v.1 is still the law of Deuteronomy, not yet its relationship to the Decalogue introduced in v. 2. Verses 2–3 shift from "you" to "us," transcending the generational gap between the Horeb and Moab audiences (cf. 11:2–7 and 29:13–14 [ET 14–15], which have the same "not . . . but" rhetoric). Horeb and Moab involve the very same audience in a literary and ideological sense that transcends the actual chronology set forth in Deuteronomy. The Horeb covenant, with its direct, unmediated impact (v. 4), is passed on and actualized by the later Moab covenant so that generational boundaries are dissolved. "Ancestors" in v. 3 refers to the previous desert generation, not to the patriarchs.

Taken together, vv. 4–5 reveal the tension between the competing themes of Horeb and Moab. According to v. 4, Yahweh spoke directly ("in person," 2 Kgs 14:8) to the people (4:12, 15, 32–33, 36; 5:22); yet v. 5 insists (in a parenthetical and circumstantial sentence) that Moses served as a go-between, as shown by his spatial positioning. Perhaps v. 5 seeks to keep the

---

3. S. Kaufman "The Structure of the Deuteronomic Law," *Maarav* 1 (1979): 105–58; G. Braulik, "The Sequence of the Laws in Deuteronomy 12–26 and in the Decalogue," in *Song of Power*, ed. Christensen, 313–35; trans. of "Die Abfolge der Gesetze in Deuteronomium 12–26 und der Dekalog," in *Studien zur Theologie des Deuteronomiums*, 231–55; idem, *Die deuteronomischen Gesetze und der Dekalog: Studien zum Aufbau von Deuteronomium 12–26* (SBS 145; Stuttgart: Katholisches Bibelwerk, 1991). On Philo, see Y. Amir, "The Decalogue according to Philo," in *Ten Commandments in History and Tradition* (ed. B. Segal and G. Levi; Jerusalem: Magnes, 1990), 121–60.

4. G. Braulik, *Deuteronomium* (2 vols.; Neue Echter Bibel; Würzburg: Echter, 1986–1992), 1:48, suggests that chs. 5–8 and 9–11 parallel each other. Each section contains three sorts of material: history and narrative (5:1–31 and 9:7–10:11), exhortation (5:32–9:6 and 10:12–11:25), and blessing and curse (contained within the other subsections in 7:12–15; 8:19–20 and 11:13–17, 22–25). As parts of transitional paragraphs, 5:1; 6:1; 9:1; and 10:12 mark off these divisions.

people away from the mountain for reasons of ritual propriety (cf. Exod 19:24; 24:2; 34:3).

[6–7] Yahweh's self-identification as the one who liberated Israel justifies a claim on obedience and encourages exclusive loyalty. It motivates obedience not only to the first commandment but to all the commandments, since each commandment up through the one on parents (vv. 8–16) includes the expression "Yahweh your God." The phrase "brought you out" also reappears in the Sabbath commandment (v. 15). The identification of Yahweh as the God of the exodus is common throughout Deuteronomy (6:12; 7:8; 8:14; 13:6, 11 [ET 5, 10]). The self-identification formula may mirror those that begin royal inscriptions.[5]

Whatever the precise meaning of "beside me" may be (note d), context makes its import clear: my relationship with you must be an exclusive one. From a contextual perspective, the reader of Deuteronomy may be justified in taking this disputed phrase in the sense found in 21:16: "in place of," "in preference to." What it means to "have" a god (i.e., for a god to "be yours," *yihyeh-lĕkā*) is illustrated by Gen 17:7; 28:21. The expression signifies having a distinctive relationship with an individual god. The phrase also relates to the formula of covenant relationship: "I will be your God" (cf. 26:17; 29:12 [ET 13]). This claim of exclusivity implies that Yahweh has and is to have no consort goddess.

[8–10] Verses 8–9a expand v. 7 beyond the theoretical to matters of concrete behavior: "Do not make. . . . Do not bow down . . . or serve [in cultic worship]." Bowing down and serving signify an active relationship with a god involving submission and sacrifice (4:19; 30:17; Exod 23:24). The initial apodictic prohibition ("do not make an idol") suggests at first that this "idol" would be an image of Yahweh, but as the sentence develops, further possibilities unfold. The singular image (*pesel*) develops into multiple potential shapes that, in the context of Deuteronomy, must be understood as idols of heathen deities ("them"). The language generalizes and radicalizes the horizon of prohibition, so that it forbids not only the image of a god, but images of shapes found anywhere.[6] "Shapes in heaven" may refer to birds (in parallel with animals on the earth and sea creatures in the water), but could also be

---

5. *ANET*, 320, 653–56; cf. the oracles to Esarhaddon, *ANET*, 605. Statements of divine self-identification introduce or conclude laws in the Holiness Code (Lev 18:2, 4, etc.).

6. Deuteronomy's "an idol of any shape" (or as an apposition: "an idol, [that is] any shape"; note e) lacks the *waw* of Exod 20:4, "an idol *nor* any shape." Deuteronomy's formulation may be more theologically precise, forbidding only those images that are explicitly idols and thus worshiped. In any case, a close grammatical reading must take "them" in v. 9 as a reference to the "gods" of v. 7, not to the shapes of v. 8. Thus Deuteronomy links the prohibition of images to the commandment demanding exclusivity more tightly than Exod 20 does. At the same time, images of Yahweh are less explicitly forbidden in Deuteronomy than in Exodus.

intended to include images of any sort of celestial being and symbols of sun, moon, and stars (4:19–20).

No philosophical argument is advanced against images. The text simply bases its prohibition on Yahweh's jealous intolerance (cf. 4:24; 6:14–15; 29:19 [E 20]). The supposed guarantee of divine presence and attention offered by images, however, would violate what Deuteronomy confesses about Yahweh. Yahweh is not open to human coercion. Yahweh's promised presence and attention occur only on Yahweh's own terms (e.g., 12:5, 11, 21; 15:9; 20:4; 24:15; 26:15). Images also contradict what Deuteronomy professes about Yahweh's absolutely incomparable nature (6:4). A *těmûnâ* ("shape") is a facsimile that compares the deity with something else in the universe.

The formula of Yahweh's twofold personal character (vv. 9b–10) is a common one (Exod 34:6–7; Num 14:18; Nah 1:2–3; Jer 32:18). "Jealous" comes first in order to motivate the prohibition. The threat against three or four generations of those who repudiate Yahweh stands in some tension with 24:16, which prohibits transgenerational retribution by human authorities. However, the rhetorical emphasis here is not on collective retribution, but on Yahweh's jealous nature. Yahweh's punishment is not open-ended, but directed against the three or four generations alive at any given time, set forth in the familiar rhetorical formula of "x and x plus one." Deuteronomy recognizes elsewhere that apostasy has negative effects on posterity, as illustrated by the problem of intermarriage with pagan foreigners (7:3–4). Deuteronomy's characteristic concern for educating children (6:7, 20–25) also points up the influence of family environment on religious loyalty. In v. 10 Yahweh's covenant loyalty (*ḥesed*), shown to thousands of generations (or individuals, note i), numerically overwhelms the duration of divine punishment. This same relational principle—divine loyalty corresponding to human love and obedience, but divine retribution in response to human rejection—is at work in 7:9–11.

[11] Read in the context of Deuteronomy, this open-ended phrase cannot be restricted to magic or false oaths (note k), but involves all attempts to use the power of Yahweh's name for a worthless purpose. Proper swearing in the divine name is commanded in 6:13 and 10:20, blessing in the name is a Levitical duty (10:8; 21:5), and prophesying in Yahweh's name is regulated by 18:20–22.

[12–15] Deuteronomy's distinctive formulation of the Ten Commandments increases the importance of the Sabbath. The motivation provided by the exodus (v. 15) strengthens the relationship of the Sabbath commandment to v. 6 and the first commandment. At the same time, adding "ox and donkey" to v. 14 has created a linkage to the final commandment. Deuteronomy also groups together the commandments in vv. 17–20 with "and." Joining these last commandments together with conjunctions forms them into a cohesive block and creates a concentric pattern of longer and shorter textual units that places the Sabbath commandment at the center of the pattern.[7] The Sabbath command is given a central, mediating position in another way. Verses 6–11 describe one's duties to Yahweh and vv. 16–21 deal with relationships among humans. By dealing with both these topics simultaneously, the Deuteronomic Sabbath commandment forms a bridge between these two sections. Sabbath is to be sanctified and is "a Sabbath of Yahweh," but at the same time its observance requires human rest that transcends social distinctions.

The initial verb in v. 12 is "keep" rather than "remember" as in Exodus, possibly because Deuteronomy uses the latter verb only to recall historical experience (cf. v. 15). Deuteronomy highlights the rhetorically pleasing bracket of "the Sabbath day" in vv. 12 and 15 through a concentric structure produced by the common word pair šāmar, "keep," and 'āśâ, "perform":

> keep the Sabbath day
> > Yahweh your God commanded you
> > > Yahweh your God
> > > > male or female slave
> > > > male or female slave
> > > Yahweh your God
> > Yahweh your God has commanded you
> perform the Sabbath day[8]

In contrast to Exod 20:11, Deuteronomy always presents "sanctify" as a human action (cf. 15:19; 22:9). On the one hand, Sabbath would seem to be intrinsically "holy" in the sense that it is associated with Yahweh (cf. Israel as a holy people or holy sacrifices, 7:6; 12:26). However, Israel also marks Sabbath off as holy by nonnormal human behavior, that is, by not working. In a similar way, atypical behavior recognizes holiness in 14:1–2 (not engaging in mourning rites), 14:21 (not eating), 23:15 [ET 14] (burying excrement).

"As Yahweh commanded" (vv. 12, 15, 16) communicates awareness that this listing of the Decalogue is a "second delivery" in the dramatic staging of Deuteronomy, a quotation of something already heard in the past. As a "source citation formula" (cf. 4:23; 6:17; 13:6 [ET 5]; 20:17), it signals to the reader that an earlier text is being used. Fittingly, this phrase appears only in the com-

---

7. Long (vv. 6–10), short (v. 11), the long unit on Sabbath (vv. 12–15), short (v. 16), long (vv. 17–21). See N. Lohfink, "The Decalogue in Deuteronomy 5," in *Theology of the Pentateuch*, 256–57; trans. of "Zur Dekalogfassung von Dt 5," in *Studien zum Deuteronomium und zur deuteronomistischen Literatur I*, 193–209. Lohfink insists that this emphasis on Sabbath requires an exilic or postexilic date. Since "rest" is an important theme associated with the land (3:20; 12:10; 25:19), however, an emphasis on Sabbath in Deuteronomy could certainly be preexilic.

8. Lohfink, "Decalogue in Deuteronomy 5," 252–53.

mandments concerning Sabbath and parents, the two that positively "command" (rather than forbid) behaviors. Moreover, since these two commandments are the only ones whose motivations differ from those of Exod 20, "as Yahweh commanded" may stress that the imperatives themselves have been transmitted unchanged, even if the motivations have been expanded.

The Sabbath commandment is addressed to free landowners who own domestic animals and slaves. The "alien resident within your towns" is literally "*your* resident alien," that is, a noncitizen who is in a patron-client relationship with the audience (24:14; 29:10 [ET 11]; 31:12), indicating the elevated social position of the audience. However, Sabbath means that the division between work and leisure is not to be a matter of social class (slave, alien), gender (son or daughter, male or female slave), or even species (domestic animals), but an opportunity for leisure provided to all.[9] Deuteronomy stresses the inclusion of animals by adding "your ox or your donkey or any of" in v. 14 to the "cattle" of Exod 20:10.

Thus it is no surprise that Deuteronomy motivates Sabbath rest by referring to slavery in Egypt (cf. 10:19; 15:15; 16:12; 24:18, 22). The pattern of "remember . . . therefore act" is a standard tactic of Deuteronomic rhetoric (15:15; 16:12; 24:18, 22). Unlike v. 21, where clearly only men are addressed, here the absence of "wife" from the list of those who can rest suggests that she is implicitly included in the addressed "you."

[16] This commandment addresses the situation of adult children living in multigenerational family units under the authority of aged parents. Deuteronomy adds both "as Yahweh commanded you" and "and that it may go well with you" (4:40; 5:29, 33; 6:3, 18; 12:25, 28; 22:7). To "honor" in this context means to submit appropriately to authority (1 Sam 15:30; Ps 86:9). The opposite of such honoring is illustrated by Deut 21:18–21 and 27:16.

[17–21] The collective danger prevented by v. 17 is illustrated by 19:4–6, 10–13, and 21:1–9. Verse 18 prohibits relations between a man and another man's wife or an engaged woman. The focus is the offense against the betrayed husband, either by a woman against her husband or by a man against another man's marriage. The social importance of paternity and inheritance means that adultery is a public and not just a private concern (22:22–27).[10] The language of v. 20 points to the context of legal proceedings rather than lies or slander in general. Deuteronomy provides illustrative background in 19:16–21; 22:13–19.

---

9. P. D. Miller, "The Human Sabbath: A Study in Deuteronomic Theology," *Princeton Seminary Bulletin* 6 (1985): 81–97.

10. There is now consensus that v. 19 is not connected with kidnapping. Contrast A. Alt, "Das Verbot des Diebstahls im Dekalog," *Kleine Schriften zur Geschichte des Volkes Israel*, vol. 1 (Munich: Beck, 1953), 333–40.

The commandments end (v. 21) on a radicalized note, extending their reach beyond outward actions to curb internal attitudes. There is an ongoing debate over the balance in "covet" between inward thoughts and outward action (note r). Nonetheless, the Deuteronomy version unambiguously includes internal thoughts by introducing the verb "desire" as a parallel. Perhaps active coveting implies attempts to alienate family or property by outwardly legal maneuvers or economic pressures, something more subtle than outright theft. Deuteronomy's sequence of "wife" first and then "house" repeats the previous sequence of adultery and theft (vv. 18–19). Some see this change from Exodus as evidence of an increased concern for women and their legal rights as members of the covenant community (cf. 21:10–14, 19; 24:5). Even so, the formulation remains totally androcentric. The focus remains on the male neighbor's rights in regard to his wife. This shift in sequence does make the word "house" less clearly "household" than in the Exodus parallel. Deuteronomy adds "field," perhaps seen as part of a natural word pair with "house" (cf. 2 Kgs 8:3, 5).[11]

[22–31] The "words" of v. 22 are obviously the Decalogue. The Horeb situation means that Israel is functioning as a liturgical "assembly" (*qāhāl*, 9:10; 10:4; 18:16), something it will also become in Moab (31:30). That Yahweh added "nothing more" helps segregate the limited content of Horeb from what Moses would speak in Moab and also highlights the special, "canonical" authority of the Decalogue.[12] Moreover, these words are not just spoken and remembered, but "graven in stone." Both Decalogue and Deuteronomy are delivered orally, then fixed in writing after the people have heard them (v. 22; 31:9, 24).

Those who approach to Moses (v. 23) are appropriately limited to the leadership. Rather than the debilitating terror of Exod 20:18–21, they demonstrate a reasoned and proper caution, approved by Yahweh as appropriate "fear" (v. 29). The people's surprise in v. 24 is patent (picked up by 4:33), but so is their allegiance, as reflected in the repetition of "our God" (vv. 24, 25, 27). Verse 25 gets to the rhetorical point ("but now," *wĕ'attâ*). Taking v. 24 into account ("one may remain alive"), vv. 25–26 must signify, "We have survived so far, but too long an exposure to the divine voice might kill us. Why risk further danger?" "Flesh" in v. 26 implies weakness and underscores the disparity between the human of v. 24 and the "living God" who is powerfully active (cf. Josh 3:10). Verses 27 and 31 clarify and emphasize that Deuteronomy is nothing less than the authoritative voice of Yahweh mediated by Moses. The leaders are surprised

11. On the last commandment, see W. L. Moran, "The Conclusion of the Decalogue (Ex 20;17 = Dt 5;21)," *CBQ* 29 (1967): 543–54. A. Rofé, "The Tenth Commandment in the Light of Four Deuteronomic Laws," in *Ten Commandments in History and Tradition*, ed. Segal and Levi, 45–65, compares it to 19:14; 23:25–26 [ET 24–25]; and 24:10–11.

12. This is similar to 4:2 and 13:1 [ET 12:32]. These expressions reflect scribal formulas. See M. Fishbane, "Varia Deuteronomica," *ZAW* 84 (1972): 349–50.

to have "remained alive" at Horeb (vv. 24, 26), but Israel's long-term option for life is to obey the law in the land (v. 33).

The leaders have spoken to Moses, but it is Yahweh who overhears and approves their request (v. 28). However, Yahweh also points forward to a future of disobedience (v. 29). Returning Israel to its "tents" (v. 30) means to break up the formal assembly (16:7; Josh 22:4). The emphatic personal pronoun "you" in v. 31 emphasizes the separation of Moses and Israel. The people are no longer on the scene, so what they need to hear will be transmitted to them by Moses at a later time.

"Commandment" in the singular (v. 31) refers comprehensively to the whole Deuteronomic law, a unifying concept characteristic of the parenetic chapters (6:1, 25; 7:11; 8:1; 11:8, 22). Deuteronomy 6:1 defines "commandment" appositionally by the "statutes and ordinances" of Deuteronomy's concrete commands, and 5:31 (and 7:11) should probably be understood in the same way (note z). The phrase "statutes and ordinances" in v. 31 forms an inclusive bracket with the same phrase in v. 1.[13]

[32–33] Along with 6:1–3, these two verses make up a transitional section similar to 11:32–12:1. "Be careful to do" creates an artistic bracketing structure with v. 1, marking a conclusion of sorts. There is an abrupt transition back to addressing the audience directly, as Moses returns to the rhetoric of exhortation found in vv. 1–5. A repetition of "Yahweh your God has commanded you" binds vv. 32–33 together. For "right or left," see 17:11, 20; 28:14. A longer than usual list of benefits emphasizes rewards in order to motivate obedience. "The whole way" (cf. 10:12; 11:22) indicates that what is true of the Decalogue is true of Deuteronomy as a whole. Both will lead to long life in the wonderful land (5:16; 33; 6:2–3).

Keep the Law Diligently
6:1–25

The Essence of the Law

6:1 This is the commandment—the statutes and ordinances—that Yahweh your God commanded me to teach you to do in the land into which you are crossing to take it over, 2 so that you may fear Yahweh your God and keep all his statutes and his commandments that I am commanding

---

13. For the use of this word pair in Deuteronomy, see Lohfink, "Die *ḥuqqîm ûmišpāṭîm*," in Studien zum Deuteronomium II, 229–56. He proposes that the interaction between this paired term and "commandment(s)" in 5:28–6:1 incorporates the Decalogue into Deuteronomy and presents the Deuteronomic code as a practical legal extension and elucidation of the commandments (pp. 235–36).

you[a]—you and your child and your grandchild all the days of your life—and so that you may enjoy long life. 3 Hear Israel and be careful to act, that it may go well with you and that you may multiply greatly, just as Yahweh the God of your ancestors promised you—a land[b] flowing[c] with milk and honey.

4 Hear, O Israel. Yahweh is our God, Yahweh alone.[d] 5 You shall love Yahweh your God with all your heart and with all your being and with all your capability.[e] 6 Let these words that I am commanding you today be upon your heart. 7 Recite[f] them to your children and speak about them[g] when you are sitting in your house[h] and when you are walking on the road, when you lie down and when you get up. 8 Tie them as a sign on your hand and let them be like a pendant[i] between your eyes. 9 Write them on the doorposts of your house and on your gates.

Keep the Law in the New Land

10 When Yahweh your God brings you into the land that he swore to your ancestors, to Abraham, to Isaac, and to Jacob, to give you—fine, large cities that you did not build, 11 and houses full of everything good that you did not fill, and hewn-out cisterns that you did not hew, vineyards and olive groves that you did not plant—and you eat your fill, 12 then be careful lest you forget Yahweh, who brought you out of the land of Egypt, from the house of servitude. 13 It is Yahweh your God whom you shall fear and him you shall serve and by his name you shall swear.[j] 14 Do not go after other gods, from among the gods of the peoples who surround you, 15 because Yahweh your God in your midst is a jealous God, lest the wrath of Yahweh your God break out against you and he destroy you from the face of the earth. 16 Do not put Yahweh your God to the test as you did at Massah. 17 Carefully keep the commandments of Yahweh your God, and his precepts and his statutes that he has commanded, 18 and do what is right and good in the opinion of Yahweh, so that it may go well with you and you may enter and take over the good land about which Yahweh swore to your ancestors, 19 to push out all your enemies before you, just as Yahweh has promised.

Answering Your Child's Question

20 When[k] your child asks you in the future, "What is the meaning of the precepts, statutes, and ordinances that Yahweh our God commanded you?" 21 you shall say to your child, "We were Pharaoh's slaves in Egypt, but Yahweh brought us out of Egypt with a mighty hand. 22 And Yahweh performed great and dreadful signs and wonders against Egypt, against

Pharaoh, and against his house[l] in our sight. 23 He brought us out of there to bring us in, to give us the land about which he swore to our ancestors. 24 Then Yahweh commanded us to do all these statutes, to fear Yahweh our God, for our own good always and to keep us alive,[m] as is the case today. 25 Righteousness[n] will be ours if we are careful to do this whole commandment before Yahweh our God, just as he has commanded us."

a. Follows MT as the shorter text. Sam., 8Q3, 4QPhyl J, 4QPhyl M, OG supplement with *hywm*, "today."

b. Follows the elliptical or defective MT. OG and Syr. fill this out with "to give you." NRSV renders this "*in* a land," construing this as an accusative of place. REB treats the phrase as a remote apposition to "land" in v. 1.

c. The participle is in the construct state as a "genitive of mediated object," *IBHS* 9.5.2d. "Honey" denotes a product derived from either fruit or bees.

d. Follows MT. OG and Nash Papyrus preface this verse with a new introductory formula based on 4:45.

e. A unique use of the scalar adverb *mĕ'ōd* as a noun to indicate one's total potential for love: "with all your 'very muchness,'" *IBHS* 39.3.1i.

f. The (resultative) pi'el of *šnn* appears to mean "sharpen up for instruction" (cf. NAB "drill them into your children"). If the verb is construed as a form of *šnh*, the translation would be "repeat constantly for the sake of teaching."

g. Preposition *b* with the object of a verb of speaking: "about them," *IBHS* 11.2.5f.

h. Follows MT *bbytk*. Here and at 11:19, Sam. and OG, supported by 4QPhyl C, 4QPhyl O (and 4QPhyl I at 11:19), read *bbyt*, "in the house."

i. The meaning of this word is uncertain (11:18; Exod 13:16). Alternate translation explaining the metaphor: "emblem, symbol." J. H. Tigay, "On the Meaning of *ṭ(w)ṭpt*," *JBL* 101 (1982): 321–31, suggests "headband" on the basis of Egyptian art. M. Görg, "*T(w)ṭpt*—eine fast vergessene Deutung," *BN* 8 (1979): 11–13, proposes a loanword associated with the serpent emblem worn by the pharaohs. "Between the eyes" indicates the forehead (14:1).

j. All the direct objects are in emphatic position.

k. Follows MT by default. MT and Sam. have *yhwh*, "Yahweh," as the last word of v. 19, but OG lacks this. At the start of v. 20, both Sam. and OG read the graphically similar *whyh*, "and it will be," before the *ky*, "when," that starts v. 20 in MT. Either haplography or dittography involving *yhwh* and/or *whyh* has taken place, but the original text cannot be established.

l. Follows OG. MT supplements with *kl*: "his *whole* house."

m. That is, "to let survive" (20:16; 32:39). Alternate translation: "to maintain us" as a new master would a slave. See N. Lohfink, "Deuteronomy 6:24: *lhytnw* 'To Maintain Us,'" in *"Sha'arei Talmon": Studies in the Bible, Qumran, and the Ancient Near East* (ed. M. Fishbane and E. Tov; Winona Lake, Ind.: Eisenbrauns, 1992), 111–19. *Lṭwb* is the infinitive construct of the verb *ṭwb*.

n. That is, "being in the right," as in a verdict of acquittal, or "being in a right relationship with Yahweh's requirements (24:13)." Some translators connect this with the end of the verse: "It will be our righteousness before Yahweh . . . to do."

A second introduction is needed after the Horeb interlude. Consequently, Moses returns in 6:1 to the language and situation of 5:1, elucidates the meaning of 5:3, and indicates that he is following up on the course of action set forth in 5:27, 31.

Taken together, 5:32–33 and 6:1–3 form a transitional bridge between the Decalogue and the upcoming exhortations to obey Deuteronomic law. Motivational clauses are densely packed together. A concentric structure of verbs surrounds the core admonition of 5:32–33 with "hear" and "do" (5:27; 6:3), "fear," "keep," and "commandments" (5:29; 6:2), and "teach" and "do" (5:31; 6:1).[1] Verses 4–5 move from revelation ("hear") to response ("love") and from Moses' confession ("our God") to his exhortation ("your God"). Verses 4–9 are a single, extended imperative that initiates the exhortation of chapters 6–11 and recommends ways to focus the claim of "these words" (v. 6) on readers' lives.

The remainder of the chapter may be divided into vv. 10–19 and 20–25. Each of these two sections begins with a temporal situation (vv. 10–11, 20) and then continues with what should be thought or done. Verse 25 turns elements of v. 1 around to form a closing bracket: "*This* is the *commandment . . . that Yahweh your God commanded* me to teach you *to do*" is reversed into "if we are careful *to do this* whole *commandment* before *Yahweh our God*, just as he has *commanded* us."

[1–3] The phrase "statues and ordinances" describes and illustrates the content of the "commandment." "Commandment" here could refer to the preceding Decalogue or perhaps, more generally, to Yahweh's basic demand for exclusive loyalty. The phrase "statutes and ordinances," however, clearly refers to the laws of chapters 12–26. The literary effect of piling up these synonyms for law (cf. vv. 2, 17, 20) is to increase urgency and incentive. By repeating the language of 5:31, 6:1 declares that Moses is passing on exactly what Yahweh commanded. Indeed, "commanded me to teach you to do" could serve as a summary statement of purpose for the whole book of Deuteronomy.

Verses 2–3 move from Yahweh's past act of commanding (v. 1) to the present discourse of Moses and on to the extended time and wonderful locale of Israel's obedience. Reference to the land and to future generations forges a rhetorical connection to those reading the book. Because these verses shift to second-person singular address, they may be a later supplement to v. 1, added in the spirit of chapter 4. "Fear" (v. 2) describes a reverence for Yahweh that results in keeping the law. The expanded phrase could mean either "fear in order to keep" or "fear by keeping." Verse 3 uses a traditional description of the land (Exod 3:8 and elsewhere) to inspire attention and obedience (cf. Deut 11:9; 26:9, 15; 27:3; 31:20). Milk and honey are choice foods (Gen 18:8; 43:11), but also represent the sweetness of human love (Cant 4:11; 5:1).

---

1. Lohfink, *Das Hauptgebot*, 66–68, 151.

[4–5] The puzzle of how to translate v. 4 remains unresolved, particularly in regard to the meaning of "one" and the syntax of the sentence.[2] On the one hand, "one" may signify that Yahweh is *unique* in relationship with Israel, alone as Israel's only God. Zechariah 14:9 supports this understanding (cf. 1 Chr 29:1), as does the surrounding context of exclusive relationship ("our God"; "love") and the first commandment. In contemporary terms, Yahweh is to be Israel's "one and only."

On the other hand, "one" may indicate *incomparable* (cf. 2 Sam 7:23), that is, unrivaled and unparalleled by any other god. "Yahweh our God is the one, the only Yahweh." This translation is supported by the general theological outlook of Deuteronomy.

Yet again, "one" may refer to Yahweh's *unitary nature*: singleness, internal oneness, and absence of plurality. Viewed as a matter of character, Yahweh's oneness signifies a personal integrity that allows for no duplicity in promise or intention. In contrast to the capricious gods of mythic narrative, Yahweh's singleness of will and purpose means absolute dependability. Thus Yahweh's corresponding claim on Israel's "one" undivided loyalty is logical and justified.

From the perspective of religious practice, however, the notion of unitary nature may mean that Yahweh does not appear in multiple local manifestations worshiped at different shrines. "Yahweh our God is one Yahweh" with respect to the single appropriate location of Israel's cult. This contrasts with the apparent "poly-Yahwism" of the titles "Yahweh of Samaria" or "Yahweh of Teman" (from Kuntillet 'Ajrud). These epithets seem to refer to distinct Yahweh cults at local shrines.[3] This understanding of "one" fits the ideology of chapter 12. However, Deuteronomy never treats localized poly-Yahwism as a problem or

---

2. *IBHS* 8.4.2g, also 15.2.1c. Recent studies include P. A. H. de Boer, "Some Observations on Deuteronomy VI 4 and 5," in *Selected Studies in Old Testament Exegesis* (ed. C. van Duin; *OtSt* 27; Leiden: Brill, 1991), 203–10; J. G. Janzen, "On the Most Important Word in the Shema (Deuteronomy vi 4–5)," *VT* 37 (1987): 280–300; O. Loretz, "Die Einzigkeit Jahwes (Dtn 6,4) im Licht des ugaritischen Baal-Mythos," in *Vom Alten Orient zum Alten Testament* (ed. M. Dietrich and O. Loretz; AOAT 240; Kevalaer: Butzon & Bercker, 1995), 215–304; R. W. L. Moberly, "Yahweh Is One: The Translation of the Shema," in *Studies in the Pentateuch* (ed. J. Emerton; VTSup 41; Leiden: Brill, 1990), 209–15; E. Nielsen, "Weil Jahwe unser Gott ein Jahwe ist (Dtn 6:4f)," in *Beiträge zur alttestamentlichen Theologie* (ed. H. Donner; Göttingen: Vandenhoeck & Ruprecht, 1977), 288–301; M. Peter, "Dtn 6:4—ein monotheistischer Text?" *BZ* 24 (1980): 252–62. T. Veijola, "Höre Israel! Der Sinn und Hintergrund von Deuteronomium vi 4–9," *VT* 42, (1992): 528–41, construes the verse as two parallel nominal sentences, as does F. Sedlmeier, "Höre, Israel! JHWH: Unser Gott (ist er) . . . ," *Trierer theologische Zeitschrift* 108 (1999): 21–39. V. Orel, "The Words on the Doorpost," *ZAW* 109 (1997): 614–17, interprets the first occurrence of *yhwh* as a verb.

3. P. Höffken, "Eine Bemerkung zum religionsgeschichten Hintergrund von Dtn 6,4," *BZ* 28 (1984): 88–93.

as the reason for centralization, nor does the word "one" play a role in identifying the chosen place (except for 12:14).

Syntactically, "Yahweh" may be the subject and "our God" the predicate: "Yahweh is our God, Yahweh is one" (juxtaposed nominal sentences), or "Yahweh is our God, Yahweh alone" (the option I have chosen). The alternative is to link "Yahweh" and "our God" together in apposition as the grammatical subject: "Yahweh our God is one Yahweh," or (taking the first three words together as subject) "Yahweh our God, Yahweh is one." This approach is supported by the observation that elsewhere in Deuteronomy "Yahweh" and "our God" always stand together in apposition and never function as subject and predicate.

There is probably no way to get beyond this impasse in translation. Instead, the interpreter must try to understand v. 4 in light of the context of the command to love Yahweh in v. 5. The two verses of the Shema shed light on each other, explaining what "our God" (v. 4) and "your God" (v. 5) mean. Grammatically, v. 4 serves as grounding for v. 5.[4] The absolute contrast in nature between Yahweh and any rival gods requires exclusive allegiance. To reverse the equation, the totality of Israel's commitment ("your God"; "all your . . .") is motivated by Yahweh's absolute uniqueness ("our God"; "alone"). The relational connection between unique "oneness" and exclusive "love" also appears in the human contexts of Cant 6:8–9 and Gen 22:2. Yahweh is one in the sense of being the only one Israel loves totally. Thus in light of v. 5, v. 4 really intends to answer the question, Who is our only God? The issue is not really who Yahweh is or what Yahweh is like. And if the question is, Who is our only God? the only possible answer in the context of Deuteronomic theology is the confession: "Our only God is Yahweh."[5] In this way, the Shema unifies the entire proclamation of Deuteronomy into a single statement, narrowing Yahweh's nature to the single point of "oneness" and Israel's obedient response to a single command to "love."

Verse 4 stands out (and indeed is highlighted in the masoretic tradition) as a starting point and nucleus for much future theological elaboration. In the

---

4. That is, the *waw* and perfect verb "and love" continue the force of the imperative "hear": "hear and love." This is the first of seven *waw* perfects with imperative force chained together in vv. 5–9. Another approach would be to construe "love" as an assertion founded on the basis of the nominal sentence of v. 4b (cf. the syntax of Gen 20:11; Ruth 3:9): "Yahweh is one, therefore you should love." However, one would then expect a future rather than imperative force for "love," *IBHS* 32.2.4.

5. "Yahweh is our God" is similar to the confession of faith expressed in Ps 48:15 [ET 14]; 95:7; 99:9, etc. On the Shema as the center of Deuteronomic theology, see P. D. Miller, "The Most Important Word: The Yoke of the Kingdom," *Iliff Review* 41 (1984): 17–29. On its theological impact and history of interpretation, see S. D. McBride, "The Yoke of the Kingdom: An Exposition of Deuteronomy 6:4–5," *Int* 27 (1973): 273–306.

context of Deuteronomy, whose condemnation of the worship of other gods never really denies their sheer existence, one can hardly speak of monotheism. Ultimately, however, the language of the Shema pointed to monotheism and to the universalism of Yahweh's eschatological mission (Zech 14:9). It was not philosophical speculation, but the particularity and distinctiveness of Yahweh's character, action, and demands that eventually led Israel to embrace monotheism.[6]

As a "call to attention," the appeal to "hear" (v. 4) adds a sense of urgency and seeks to evoke both attentiveness and obedient response: hear that you may respond (cf. 20:3–4; 27:9–10). The call to "love" (v. 5) concentrates the personal and relational aspects of Deuteronomy's theology. This theological use of "love" may go back to an old poetic designation for Yahweh's partners in sacral war (Judg 5:31) and to the theology of Hosea. It is also related to the Decalogue (5:10). Such love is not sentimental, but concerns the loyalty and service one owes as a vassal to an overlord or as a child to a parent (cf. 8:5; 14:1). In Deuteronomy, Israel's love shows itself in loyally keeping the law (10:12–13; 11:1, 13; 19:9; 30:16, 20) and is mirrored by Yahweh's love for them (7:8; 10:18; 23:6 [ET 5]).[7] Verse 5 continues with a list of psychological capacities that reinforce the totality and uniqueness of Israel's love (cf. 2 Kgs 23:3). "Heart" is the seat of thought and intention. "Being" (*nepeš*) expresses one's inner self and its desires and emotions and represents the closest possible personal rapport (cf. David and Jonathan, 1 Sam 18:3; 20:17).

[6–9] It is difficult to decide whether "these words" (v. 6) refer narrowly to vv. 4–5 or to v. 4b alone, to the preceding Decalogue (cf. 5:22), or to the entire upcoming parenetic section (cf. 11:18–20). However, the phrase "commanding you today" suggests that the whole of Deuteronomy is intended.[8] A forceful sequence of imperatives moves from the private "heart" outward to the public realm of "gate." "These words" are the content of oral instruction and rumination, but also a written text to be worn and publicized.[9] They are to permeate

6. See Braulik, "Deuteronomy and the Birth of Monotheism," in *Theology of Deuteronomy*, 99–130. Deuteronomy approaches monotheism in 10:14, 17 and nearly achieves it in 4:35, 39.

7. On love in Deuteronomy and the prophets, see K. Zobel, *Prophetie und Deuteronomium* (BZAW 199; Berlin: de Gruyter, 1992), 8–87. For love as treaty language, see W. L. Moran, "The Ancient Near Eastern Background of the Love of God in Deuteronomy," *CBQ* 25 (1963): 77–87 (cf. VTE 24, *ANET*, 537). For an interpretation of the Shema on the basis of love for God, see W. Herrmann, "Jahwe und des Menschen Liebe zu ihm: Zu Dtn. vi 4," *VT* 50 (2000): 47–54.

8. On the relationship between 6:6–9 and 11:18–20 and the supposition that an older poem lies behind them, see J. C. de Moor, "Poetic Fragments in Deuteronomy and the Deuteronomistic History," in *Studies in Deuteronomy in Honour of C. J. Labuschagne* (ed. F. García Martínez et al.; VTSup 53; Leiden: Brill, 1994), 189–91.

9. For the notion that these verses encourage constant vocalized meditation, see G. Fischer and N. Lohfink, "Diese Worte sollst du summen: Dtn 6,7," in *Studien zum Deuteronomium III*, 181–203.

every sphere of life. A double merismus of place and time (v. 7) adds up to "always and everywhere."

The balance between the metaphorical and the literal in these imperatives is hard to weigh. To write on the heart is an image of permanent attentiveness (Prov 3:3; 7:3; Cant 8:6). Exodus 13:9 and 16 are obviously only a metaphor, but later piety obeyed the commands of Deut 6:8–9 in concrete form. On one level, these actions are literary metaphors of constant attention and awareness, but on another level they are based on actual cultural and religious practices. "Upon your heart" (v. 6) suggests texts hung around a learner's neck as an instructional aid (Prov 3:3; 6:21–22) or as an apotropaic amulet (cf. Exod 28:29).[10] With regard to vv. 8–9, the wearing of prized jewelry in the form of arm bangles and frontlets comes to mind. In the religious sphere, objects were worn on the arm to express one's association with a deity, and cultic personnel displayed inscribed headgear (Exod 28:36–38). A silver amulet with the Aaronic benediction has been discovered (Ketef Hinnom, 6th or 7th century). Inscriptions on the inside of the doorpost would be in the brightest part of the room. Gates and their associated chambers were centers of public assembly. Perhaps inscriptions displayed in this way were to serve as alternatives to the placement of apotropaic guardian images at domestic entryways and temple gateways.[11] Whether or not these imperatives were really intended as literal directives, they nevertheless urge devout concentration on "these words" using descriptions related to actual, concrete practices.

[10–19] The affirmative directives of vv. 4–9 shift to cautionary admonitions in vv. 10–19. The introductory *wĕhāyâ kî* ("when") starts a new idea (26:1; 30:1), but also connects to what has come before (cf. 11:26–28 and 29–30; 15:12–15 and 16; 31:19–20 and 21). Three prohibitions are set forth in three contexts: dangerous prosperity (v. 12, "be careful lest you forget"), foreign religion (v. 14, "do not go after"), and doubt about Yahweh's will to punish (v. 16, "do not put to the test"). These are followed by positive admonitions in vv. 17–18. The section is set off by an envelope construction; v. 18 circles back to the ancestral promise of v. 10. It is possible to trace a concentric structure here with v. 15 at the center.[12] Yet v. 18 also represents a change in perspective from v. 10 with the assertion that obedience is a prerequisite for successful conquest.

---

10. B. Couroyer, "La tablette du coeur," *RB* 90 (1983): 416–34; P. D. Miller, "Apotropaic Imagery in Proverbs 6:20–22," *JNES* 29 (1970): 129–30.

11. O. Keel, "Zeichen der Verbundenheit: Zur Vorgeschichte und Bedeutung der Forderungen von Deuteronomium 6,8f und Par.," in *Mélanges Dominique Barthélemy* (ed. P. Caselli et al., OBO 38; Göttingen: Vandenhoeck & Ruprecht, 1981), 183–215. Perhaps the "hand" and "doorpost" of Isa 57:8 refer to pagan realities that Deuteronomy seeks to replace.

12. "Swore to your ancestors" (vv. 10a and 18bβ), the good land (vv. 10b–11 and 18bα), careful obedience (vv. 12–13 and 17–18a), and "do not" (vv. 14 and 16) enclose v. 15 in a chiastic pattern. E. Nielsen, *Deuteronomium* (Handbuch zum Alten Testament 1/6; Tübingen: Mohr, 1995),

This viewpoint represents a distinctive theological strand within Deuteronomy (4:1; 8:1; 11:8–9, 22–23; 16:20).

In vv. 10–11 the three warnings of vv. 12, 14, 16 are introduced by a stereotypical catalog of real estate (cf. Josh 24:13). These verses point to the permanence and richness of settled life (cf. the list of resources in Deut 8:7–9, 12–13). The four "you did not" clauses exhibit poetic balance. The assertion that Israel will not need to expend any effort to gain these good things emphasizes their nature as divine gift and blocks inappropriate pride. Nevertheless, life in the land entails the dangers of forgetting (v. 12) and exposure to pagan ways (v. 14). The repetition of 5:6 by v. 12 and 5:9 by v. 15 signals that these factors particularly imperil obedience to the first commandment. The warning that prosperity is dangerous is characteristic of Deuteronomy (8:12–14; 11:14–16).

"Serve" in v. 13 refers to cultic duties and invites comparison with the "house of servitude" of v. 12. To "swear" suggests an oath of allegiance to Yahweh or the avoidance of swearing by the names of other gods, as one might do in confirming a treaty with a foreign power. Swearing by Yahweh is a mark of true loyalty (cf. 10:20; Ps 63:12 [ET 11]).[13]

In v. 16 the danger of forgetting is countered by remembrance of a tradition readers are expected to know (9:22; Exod 17:1–7; Ps 78:56; 95:8–9). This reference to testing is sharpened by the threat of annihilation in v. 15. At Massah, Israel doubted Yahweh's benevolence, but at this point the danger is instead doubting Yahweh's threat. Verse 16 is the reverse of the way the testing motif is used in 8:2, 16, where it is Yahweh who initiates the test.

Verses 17–18 are logically connected to what precedes. "As he commanded you" refers to 5:31–33; 6:1. The legal designation "precepts" appears also in v. 20 and 4:45. Verse 18 rhetorically balances the duty of doing "good" with the reward of things going "well" (cf. 12:28). Verse 19 is abrupt and concludes with a vague citation formula. It is often considered to be a later addition.

[20–25] The topic of the law (vv. 1, 4–9, 17) returns as the content of a ritual question (Exod 13:14–15; Josh 4:6–7, 21–24).[14] Instead of inquiring about some

---

89–90, traces a chiasm on a larger scale with the prohibition of intermarriage at the center (7:3), surrounded in turn by the admonition not to forget in the context of the good land (6:10–13 and 8:7–13) and the challenge to love and fear (6:4–9 and 10:12, 20–21).

13. This was an important text for early Christianity; see A. Hilhorst, "Deuteronomy's Monotheism and the Christians: The Case of Deut. 6:13 and 10:20," in *Studies in Deuteronomy*, ed. García Martínez et al., 83–91.

14. J. A. Soggin, "Kultätiologische Sagen und Katechese im Hexateuch," *VT* 10 (1960): 341–67. Also M. Caloz, "Exode 13:3–16 et son rapport au Deutéronome," *RB* 75 (1968): 5–62. For the theological implications of this text, see L. Perlitt, "Deuteronomium 6,20–25: Eine Ermutigung zu Bekenntnis und Lehre," in *Deuteronomium-Studien*, 144–56; H. J. Fraas, "Gemeinschaft-Geschichte-Persönlichkeit—Dtn 6,20 als Grundmodell religiöses Sozialisation," in *Von Wittenberg nach Memphis* (ed. W. Homolka and O. Ziegelmeier; Göttingen: Vandenhoeck & Ruprecht, 1989), 21–37.

cultic issue (as in other occurrences of this genre), the questioner asks about the meaning and significance of Deuteronomy as a collection of individual laws (for "precepts, statutes, and ordinances," see 4:45). The child's question is answered with a sort of "historical credo": slavery, deliverance, land, lawgiving, and the outcome of obedience. The law of Deuteronomy is fundamentally about Yahweh's liberation of and goodwill for Israel. It is intended to produce "good," to give "life," and to put Israel "in the right" (note n; cf. 16:20; 24:13).

Israel As a Countercultural Society
7:1–26

Destroy the Nations and Their Religion

7:1 When Yahweh your God brings you into the land that you are going to enter to take it over, he will dislodge[a] many nations before you—the Hittites, the Girgashites, the Amorites, the Canaanites, the Perizzites, the Hivites, and the Jebusites, seven nations more numerous and more powerful than you. 2 When Yahweh your God gives them over to you and you strike them down, devote them completely to destruction. Do not make a covenant with them or show them mercy. 3 Do not intermarry with them. Do not give your daughter to his son. Do not take his daughter for your son. 4 For he would turn your son away from me,[b] and they would serve other gods. Then the wrath of Yahweh would break out against you, and he would quickly destroy you. 5 Instead[c] this is what you shall do to them: you shall demolish their altars, smash their pillars, cut down their asherahpoles, and burn their idols with fire.

Yahweh Has Chosen You

6 For you are a people holy to Yahweh your God. It is you whom Yahweh your God has chosen from all the peoples on the face of the earth to be his treasured[d] people.

7 It was not because[e] you were more numerous than any other people that Yahweh desired[f] you and chose you, for you were the smallest of all peoples. 8 It was because of Yahweh's love for you and his keeping the oath that he swore to your ancestors that Yahweh brought you out with a mighty hand and ransomed you from the house of servitude, from the power of Pharaoh, king of Egypt. 9 Know therefore[g] that Yahweh your God is God indeed, the faithful God who keeps covenant loyalty[h] for

those who love him and keep his commandments,[i] to the thousandth generation,[j] 10 but who repays personally[k] those who hate him by destroying them. He does not hesitate in regard to the one[l] who hates him. He repays that one personally. 11 So keep the commandment—the statutes and the ordinances—that I am commanding you today to do them.

12 Because if you heed these ordinances and keep and do them, Yahweh your God will keep for you the covenant loyalty about which he swore to your ancestors. 13 He will love you and bless you and multiply you. He will bless the fruit of your womb and the fruit of your ground—your grain, your wine, and your oil—the offspring of your cattle and the fertility of your flock, in the land that he swore to your ancestors to give to you. 14 You will be the most blessed of all peoples. Among you or your cattle neither male nor female will be infertile. 15 Yahweh will deflect every illness from you. He will not afflict you with any of the malignant diseases of Egypt[m] that you have known, but he will give them to all who hate you.

Yahweh As Divine Warrior

16 You shall devour all the peoples that Yahweh your God is going to give over to you. Do not look on them with compassion and do not serve their gods, because that would be a snare for you.

17 You may say to yourself, "These nations are more numerous than I. How can I dispossess them?" 18 Do not be afraid of them. Remember instead what Yahweh your God did to Pharaoh and to all Egypt, 19 the great ordeals you witnessed, the signs and wonders, the mighty hand and the outstretched arm by which Yahweh your God brought you out. Yahweh your God will do the same thing to all the peoples of whom you are afraid. 20 Also Yahweh your God will send the hornet[n] against them until the survivors and those who hide from you are destroyed.[o] 21 Do not be alarmed about them, for Yahweh your God is among you, a great and dreadful God. 22 Yahweh your God will dislodge these nations before you little by little. You will not be able to finish them off quickly, lest the wild animals become too numerous for you. 23 Yahweh your God will give them over to you and throw them into a great panic until they are destroyed. 24 He will give their kings into your power and you shall make their name perish from under heaven. No one will withstand you until you have destroyed them.

Eliminate Their Idols

25 The idols of their gods you shall burn with fire. Do not covet the silver or gold on them and take it for yourself, lest you be ensnared by it, for it is something repugnant to Yahweh your God. 26 Do not bring something

repugnant into your house or you will become a devoted object like it.
You must utterly detest and abhor it, for it is a devoted object.

a. The transitive of *nāšal* (also v. 22) is used for loosening and removing shoes; the intransitive is "become detached" (19:5; 28:40).

b. Follows MT to clash with the third-person reference to God in the rest of the verse. REB "from Yahweh" takes the last letter of *m'hry* as an abbreviation for Yahweh. The textual witnesses offer many variations in second person singular and plural in vv. 4–16.

c. *kî-'im* restricts the preceding negatives of vv. 4–5: "rather, instead," *IBHS* 39.3.5d.

d. *Sĕgullâ* (14:2; 26:18; Exod 19:5) refers to a king's treasure or privy purse (Qoh 2:8; 1 Chr 29:3). The owner of a *sĕgullâ* has a special stake in and attachment to it.

e. *Min* is used causally with the infinitive construct here and in v. 8, *IBHS* 36.2.2b.

f. *Ḥāšaq* means "to love passionately, to desire" (cf. 21:11).

g. "Know" implies "keep in mind." The translation reflects both the imperatival and consequent ("so that") implications of the *waw* perfect. The *qṭl* of past divine act followed by *wqṭl* to indicate consequential imperative is typical in Deuteronomy (10:15–16, 17–19; 29:2, 4 leading to v. 8 [ET 29:3, 5, 9]; 30:19), *IBHS* 32.2.3d.

h. Joining *bĕrît* and *ḥesed* as a hendiadys.

i. Follows MT Qere, Sam., and the ancient versions. Kethib: "his commandment."

j. Terminative *l*: "up to the point of," *IBHS* 11.10.2c.

k. Alternate translation for *'el-pānāyw* ("to his face"): "instantly."

l. Follows MT, which presents the participle "who hates him" first as plural (v. 10a), then as singular (v. 10b). The plural comes from a citation of 5:9; the following singular stresses individual responsibility. Sam., OG, Syr., Targ. harmonize the second occurrence into plural.

m. Follows MT. At this point, OG and 5QDeut^corr insert a doublet *'šr r'yt(h)*, "that you have seen," the result of misreading and transposing *yd't*, "you have known," into *r'yt*.

n. Cf. Exod 23:28; Josh 24:12. The translation "hornet" is based on the ancient versions and is a metaphor for panic. Another translation is "pestilence," based on a resemblance to the word for "leprosy." See *HALOT* 3:1056–57.

o. Alternate translation: "those who hide are destroyed before you."

A temporal marker (v. 1a) reminds the reader that the setting of Moses' discourse is the threshold of conquest. Similar temporal markers occur at 12:20; 17:14; 18:9; 19:1; 26:1; 27:2. The topic turns to dangers to faith and obedience inherent in the land and what Israel must do to survive there (cf. 8:1; 9:1). Israel is obliged to remain aloof from the alien peoples of the land, destroying them and their religion. Election and holiness must be protected by rejection and separation. Divine choice calls Israel to be a countercultural society, above all in religious matters, for to reject Canaan's pervasive ("more numerous," vv. 1, 7, 17) culture means to reject its gods. In the context of the upcoming law code, Israel's distinctiveness also implies exceptional social and political structures and special practices in personal and family life.

An overarching, unifying structure for the first part of Moses' parenetic homily (7:1–10:11) is provided by a threefold citation of dangerous, erroneous thoughts that focus the theological hazards of Israel's new situation: fear of the enemy (7:17), false self-sufficiency (8:17), and the idea that the conquest is proof of righteousness (9:4). These three "internal monologues" share the same expression, "say to yourself," literally "say in your heart."[1] They provide topical focal points for three sections of discourse:

> 7:17 focuses 7:1–26 by pointing to Israel's relationship to the nations and its election by Yahweh the Divine Warrior.
> 8:17 points to Yahweh as the true source for Israel's life in the land and focuses 8:1–20.
> 9:4 points to the issue of Israel's righteousness and focuses 9:1–10:11.

Other unifying structures are also present. Chapters 7 and 8 are held together by repeated use of the verbal root *rbb/rbh*, "be many," in various contexts: 7:1 (twice), 7, 13, 17, 22; 8:1; 13 (three times). There is also an envelope structure created by the distinctive phrase *'ēqeb* [*lō'*] *tišmě'ûn*, "because if you heed/because you would not heed," in 7:12 and 8:20.

Still other patterns unify and give structure to chapter 7 itself. First, the topic is emphasized by a range of verbs for destruction: *ḥāram*, "devote to destruction"(v. 2), *śārap*, "burn" (vv. 5, 25), *'ākal*, "devour" (v. 16) *'ābad*, "destroy, perish" (vv. 20, 24), *kālah*, "finish off" (v. 22), *šāmad*, "destroy" (vv. 23, 24). Second, there is a rough concentric structure. Demands to wipe out the nations and their religion bracket the chapter (vv. 1–5 and 25–26). These outer framing sections are highlighted by the root *ḥrm* ("devote to destruction," vv. 2 and 26) and the phrases "do not take for your son/for yourself" (vv. 3 and 25) and "burn with fire" (vv. 5 and 25).

Within this outer framework, two verses launch topical subsections: vv. 6 (election) and 16 (conquest). In the first subsection, v. 6 introduces the topic of election and its consequences. Verses 7–15 then elaborate on this topic in a concentric fashion, centering on the call for obedience in vv. 11–12. Verses 7–10 insist that election grows out of Yahweh's actions and character, leading to an appeal to obey in v. 11. Verse 12 then picks up the issue of obedience and makes it the condition for Yahweh's covenant loyalty, the consequences of which are the blessings of fertility and health articulated in vv. 13–15. In the second subsection, v. 16 reintroduces the command to destroy the nations, and then vv. 17–24 elaborate with instructions about this obligation.[2]

---

1. The internal monologue cites an erroneous thought and then counters it with a list of realities that contradict and correct it. See F. García López, "Analyse littéraire de Deutéronome, V–XI," *RB* 84 (1977): 484, 495–96 and *RB* 85 (1978): 17–19, 21.

2. Lohfink, *Das Hauptgebot*, 171–72, 181–83, proposes that vv. 1–6 and 17–24 are parallel structures involving a protasis containing *yrš* and "nations more numerous" (vv. 1–2a and 17) followed

Portions of this chapter have a convoluted literary relationship to the conclusion of the Covenant Code (Exod 23:20–33). For the most part Deuteronomy exhibits literary dependence on Exodus, but in some places dependence
seems to run the other direction. What in Exodus is a speech of Yahweh appears
in Deuteronomy as a speech of Moses. Deuteronomy eliminates the angel of
Exod 23:20–23a for doctrinal reasons and sharpens the call for expulsion of the
nations by introducing the institution of *ḥērem*. Verses 6–11, 17–19, and 25–26
are unique to Deuteronomy.

The compositional history of this chapter is complicated. Indications of this
complexity include the second-person plural address of vv. 4b-5 and 7–8.
Verses 12–16 and 25–26 each begins in plural and shifts quickly to singular,
although it remains unclear what one should make of this. Some suggest that
two originally separate topics have been combined: the demand to destroy and
remain aloof from the nations (vv. 1–3, 6, 17–24) and the avoidance and obliteration of their religion (vv. 4–5, 7–15, 25–26). Verses 16a and 16b would then
connect the two issues together.[3] Although this may be true, in the present form
of the chapter these two topics have been joined together in a natural way. The
same association of conquest and the destruction of alien cults also appears in
12:2–3, 29–31. What is really most striking about chapter 7 is its strong emphasis on Israel's active role in eliminating the nations (vv. 2, 16, 24; cf. 9:3;
11:23–25; 20:16–17) as a partner with Yahweh the Divine Warrior.

At first sight there would seem to be an irreducible logical tension between
the command to obliterate the nations and the simultaneous prohibition of
social contacts with them. However, this apparent contradiction eases if one
realizes that the text is not really about the long-past conquest, but rather is concerned with the situation of its contemporary readers, for whom conquest is a
distant, legendary memory. The actual issue is that an alien presence and ideology, presumably the Assyrians, currently threaten Israel, and the danger of
assimilation to foreign practices is very real. The text embraces both a demand

---

by two apodosis sections (vv. 2b-4, 5–6 and 18–20, 21–24). He also traces a chiastic structure in
vv. 6–14 that centers on the "ordinances" of vv. 11 and 12. R. H. O'Connell, "Deuteronomy vii
1–26: Asymmetrical Concentricity and the Rhetoric of Conquest," *VT* 42 (1992): 248–65, describes
a pattern that centers on vv. 11–12. He considers vv. 17–24 as an "inset," but one integral to the
chapter. Commands and prohibitions alternate in the main portion and exhortations and admonitions alternate in the inset.

3. G. Seitz, *Redaktionsgeschichtliche Studien zum Deuteronomium* (BWANT 93; Stuttgart;
Kohlhammer, 1971), 74–79. Lohfink, *Das Hauptgebot*, 176–81, 185–87, divides somewhat differently, identifying the two originally separate topics as the call to destroy alien cults and contacts
with the Decalogue. F. García López advances a complex history of composition, "Un peuple con-
sacré: Analyse critique de Deutéronome vii," *VT* 32 (1982): 438–63. He divides the text into four
chronologically distinct units: vv. 1–3, 5–6, 12b, 17–19, 21 (northern kingdom); vv. 8b-11 (also
northern kingdom); vv. 4, 13–16, 20, 22–24 (Judahite monarchy); vv. 7–8a, 25–26 (Josiah).

for total destruction and a simultaneous policy of social separation because both tactics are intended to work together to protect Israel's national identity and its pure and loyal worship. Deuteronomy wants to unify the nation, remove foreign ideologies, and reform religion. Its radical call for a return to sacral war *ḥērem* must be understood as a powerful rhetorical alarm to energize supporters and silence critics of its policies. The cataloged six nations are no more, so by default *ḥērem* annihilation must be turned in the direction of obliterating the paraphernalia of a disloyal cult.[4]

[1–5] The chapter begins with a call for a complete dissociation from the nations. This isolation is a fundamental condition for keeping Israel loyal in an ideologically toxic environment. Any "live and let live" attitude would be an act of national suicide. The standardized list of extinct enemy nations should be understood as rhetorically indicating "all of them." It communicates the overwhelming odds that the power of the Divine Warrior will overcome. These nations represent Israel's paradigmatic enemies, functionally similar to the standardized lists of foes in inscriptions lauding a king's triumphs.[5]

A watertight social separation, expressed by a series of five prohibitions in vv. 2–3, makes any common life or modus vivendi impossible. To make any sort of covenant with these peoples would be to set up a countercovenant to the one with Yahweh and would necessarily entail recognition of alien gods. Intermarriage would form affiliations between families and lead the Israelite partner to worship other gods. Perhaps political alliances sealed by marriage are particularly in mind here, with the problematic policies of Solomon, Ahab, and other kings in view. This prohibition of marriage exists in some tension with 21:10–14, although there the captive woman no longer has any family to constitute a danger. The wording of v. 4 is worth noting: the foreign father-in-law leads the Israelite son astray, and then "they" together engage in improper worship. The Israelite son has merged into the alien "they" of vv. 2–3 and 5.

Because conquest is a victory of the Divine Warrior, it is natural to expect that these peoples would be considered *ḥērem* (v. 2) and thus annihilated. A less

4. Y. Suzuki, "A New Aspect of *ḥrm* in Deuteronomy in View of an Assimilation Policy of King Josiah," *AJBI* 21 (1995): 11–19, connects this annihilation directly to Josianic policies. C. Schäfer-Lichtenberger, "JHWH, Israel und die Völker aus der Perspektive von Dtn 7," *BZ* 40 (1996): 194–218, sees these commands as a way of discouraging contact with foreign culture and religion during the exile. According to Y. Hoffman, "The Deuteronomistic Concept of the *Herem*," *ZAW* 111 (1999): 196–210, the various laws of *ḥērem* belong to a postexilic stratum asserting that *ḥērem* no longer had validity since the Canaanites no longer existed.

5. On these lists see T. Ishida, "The Structure and Historical Implications of the Lists of the Pre-Israelite Nations," *Bib* 60 (1979): 461–90. According to G. Braulik, the text insists that such annihilation is no longer required because the period for such destruction was limited to the conquest ("Die Völkervernichtung und die Rückkehr Israels ins Verheißungsland: Hermeneutische Bemerkungen zum Buch Deuteronomium," in *Deuteronomy and Deuteronomic Literature*, ed. Vervenne and Lust, 3–38).

obvious result, however, is that the images and cult apparatus of their gods are also to be treated as *ḥērem* (v. 5, cf. v. 26). Here *ḥērem* as a traditional aspect of sacral war has been converted into an expression and guarantee of religious loyalty (cf. 13:18 [ET 17]; 20:16–18). That the text moves beyond the total genocide of *ḥērem* to prohibitions of social contact, however, also shows that it recognizes the actual "failure" or nonapplication of the very *ḥērem* policy it demands. Indeed, the call to show no mercy (v. 2) suggests that the text expects its readers to resist taking such brutal action against their neighbors (cf. 7:16; 13:9 [ET 8]; 19:13, 21; 25:12).

Verse 5 is related to Exod 34:13. Deuteronomy has added the distinctive notion of burning the images and replaced the neutral *kārat*, "cut down," with a more intense *gāda'*, "hew down." The second-person plural address seems to result from the plural language of Exod 34:13. A wooden asherah could be cut down, burned (12:3), and, as a stylized tree, "planted" (16:21). Along with the altar and stone pillar, it would have been a standard fixture of a local, open-air shrine (Judg 6:25–30). The asherah pole was associated with the cult of Yahweh, perhaps as a mediator of his fertility blessings. Apparently, an asherah could also be humanoid enough to be considered an image and "dressed" (1 Kgs 15:13; 2 Kgs 23:7).[6] Once again, Deuteronomy is reacting to contemporary dangers under the guise of foreign survivals. This campaign against indigenous asherah poles is similar to Deuteronomy's call to destroy stone pillars (7:5; 12:3), even though Israel's own ancestors had once erected them (Gen 28:18, 22)!

[6–11] The rhetoric of v. 6 is elaborate. There is repetition of "Yahweh your God," alliteration of *b*, *l*, and *m* in v. 6b, and rhyme between *sĕgullâ*, "treasured," and *'ădāmâ*, "earth." This verse is related in some way to Exod 19:5–6. The cultic category of holiness is employed to express a theology of election. As a "holy" people (v. 6), Israel is specially related to Yahweh in the same sense as a holy object or offering would be. That which is holy has an unmediated relationship to Yahweh. This holiness is not a status that Israel needs to achieve, but is a reality that has already been established. That Israel is chosen "from all the peoples" provides a rationale for the countercultural behaviors demanded in vv. 2–5. A similar use of Israel's election distinctiveness to motivate obedient behavior is found in 14:1–2, 21. Like a king's treasury (*sĕgullâ*, note d), Israel is Yahweh's personal and cherished possession.[7]

---

6. J. Day, "Asherah in the Hebrew Bible and Northwest Semitic Literature," *JBL* 105 (1986): 385–408; O. Keel and C. Uehlinger, *God, Goddesses, and Images of God* (trans. T. Trapp; Minneapolis: Fortress Press, 1998), 327–36.

7. On election in Deuteronomy, see R. Rendtorff, "Die Erwählung Israels als Thema der deuteronomischen Theologie," in *Die Botschaft und die Boten* (ed. J. Jeremias and L. Perlitt; Neukirchen-Vluyn: Neukirchener Verlag, 1981), 75–86. Deuteronomy's theology of divine choice applies not only to Israel (4:37; 10:15; 14:2) but also to the place of the central sanctuary and the Levitical priests (18:5; 21:5).

Verses 7–11 emphasize that Israel's election has nothing to do with its own qualities, but rests solely on Yahweh's own actions and character (vv. 7–10). Yahweh has chosen Israel, not because of any special worthiness on its part, but out of a personal attachment based on divine love and the promises made to the ancestors (vv. 7–8). Being the "smallest" of peoples is in some tension with what is said in 10:22, but there the rhetorical context is obviously quite different. Election depends on Yahweh's fidelity to the promise and the relationship established by the exodus (v. 8), but also on Israel's obeying the law in order to concretize its relationship to Yahweh.

The center of this relationship is love—Yahweh's love for Israel made known in the exodus (v. 8) and Israel's love for Yahweh as demonstrated by obedience to the commandments (v. 9). Yahweh's passionate elective love is expressed with the vigorous verb *ḥāšaq*, "desire" (v. 7; cf. 10:15), hinting at sexual craving (cf. 21:11). The more neutral *'āhab*, "love," is more appropriate to describe the divine-human relationship in both its directions (vv. 8, 9, 13; cf. 4:37; 23:6 [ET 5]). Deuteronomy usually expresses Yahweh's love in parental terms (1:31; 8:5; 14:1).

Verses 8–11 use a schematic pattern of argument found elsewhere in the parenesis of Deuteronomy (4:37–40; 8:2–6; 9:4–7a). Verse 8 sets forth Yahweh's historical acts. Verses 9–10 assert the conclusion to be drawn from those acts with a call to "know." Then v. 11 finishes with the implication of this knowing, the necessity to keep the law.[8] That Yahweh "ransomed" (*pādâ*, v. 8) Israel from Egypt is a favorite Deuteronomic expression (9:26; 13:6 [ET 5]; 15:15; 21:8; 24:18) and is especially appropriate in the context of election. Israel, a people once enslaved, but now "bought out" of slavery by Yahweh's action, therefore owes loyalty to the one who "paid out" to liberate it.[9] Here the oath to the ancestors is not about the land (contrast 6:10, 23) but is connected first to the exodus (v. 8) and then to "covenant loyalty" that leads to the continued blessings made possible by obedience (v. 12).

In vv. 9–10 Yahweh's character is expressed through a restatement of the traits described in 5:9b–10. These are set forth in a hymnic, participial style with a confessional echo (*hû' hā'ĕlōhîm*; "Yahweh your God is God"; cf. 4:35, 39; 1 Kgs 18:39). The "jealous God" (*'ēl-qannā'*; 5:9) is replaced by "the faithful God" (*hā'ēl hanne'ĕmān*). The parity in 5:9b–10 between divine punishment and divine covenant loyalty is rebalanced in favor of divine grace. Punishment is moved back to last place, while covenant loyalty applies unambiguously to a thousand generations (5:10 could refer merely to thousands of individuals). Moreover, retribution is directed only on the responsible individual ("to his

---

8. Labeled the "schema of the presentation of evidence" (*Schema der Beweisführung*) by Braulik, *Die Mittel deuteronomischer Rhetorik*, 63–64.

9. For the legal background of this verb, see H. Cazelles, "*pādâ*," *TDOT* 11:484–85.

face"), not upon the children of iniquitous parents (cf. 24:16). Nevertheless, readers are to "know" (i.e., "keep in mind"; note g) that Yahweh's intrinsic nature means they must keep the law, for the integrity of God's character threatens individual retribution upon the apostate (v. 10). The radical alternatives of "love" (v. 9) and "hate" (v. 10) leave no middle ground or room for half measures.

Election thus means that Israel is a people defined by love and obedience. At the center of Israel's election relationship is its obedience of the law (v. 11). In the final form of Deuteronomy, the coordination of "commandment" with the "statues and ordinances" incorporates the Ten Commandments (cf. v. 9 with its reference to 5:10) into a single Mosaic torah.

[12–15] Obedience to Deuteronomy's "ordinances" (v. 12) will keep open the channels of relationship with Yahweh so that the blessings of vv. 13–15 will be granted. That is to say, Israel's obedience gives Yahweh a chance to show love and fidelity. Yahweh's covenant responsibilities and oath to the ancestors (v. 12) go beyond mere possession of the land to the bestowal of rich blessing. At the same time, Yahweh's promise of fruitfulness in family, field, and flock discredits any rival claims of alien gods and rites of fertility. These blessings are more expansive forms of those found in Exod 23:25–26.

Verse 12 links back to v. 8 by means of "oath," to v. 9 through "covenant loyalty," and via "ordinances" to v. 11. Here the concept of "covenant" does not focus on the responsibilities laid on Israel (as in ch. 5), but is associated with a fulfillment of Yahweh's oath made to the ancestors (cf. 4:31; 8:18), the content of which was fertility.

To "bless" (v. 13) means to bestow something concrete and material. The blessing language of vv. 13–15 relates to the blessings and curses of chapter 28 (cf. v. 13 and 28:4, v. 14a and 28:1, v. 14b and 28:11, v. 15 and 28:27–28, 60). The refrain "grain, wine, oil" (v. 13) is standard language for agricultural richness (11:14; 12:17; 14:23; 18:4; 28:51; cf. 6:11; 8:8; Hos 2:10, 24 [ET 8, 22]). The formula refers to these products in a state close to the soil: *dāgān* ("grain in the field," not processed), *tîrōš* ("new wine," just pressed out), *yiṣhār* ("fresh oil," not the product when used). Moreover, under the surface of these common nouns loom the names of rival gods, Dagan and Tyrosh,[10] whose supposed fertility roles and gifts are thus claimed for Yahweh. The formula about cattle and flock in v. 13 also contains a satirical reference to the names of two other rival divinities. Shagar and Ashteroth (Astarte) are mocked and robbed of their claims by their use in the formula "the offspring (*šeger*) of your cattle and the fertility (*'aštĕrōt*) of your flock" (also 28:4, 18, 51). The names of these gods are "demythologized" so that the blessing of the fertility of domestic animals

---

10. *HALOT* 4:1727–28; M. Astour, "Some Divine Names from Ugarit," *Journal of the American Oriental Society* 86 (1966): 277–84 (281).

is dissociated from them and tied to Yahweh. The gods are demoted into merely inanimate powers of blessing that operate under Yahweh's control.[11] Good health (v. 15) is the other side of the plagues used by the Divine Warrior against Israel's enemies (cf. 32:23–24). The diseases endemic to life in Egypt were proverbial (28:27, 60).

[16–24] Verse 16 returns to the topic of destroying the indigenous nations (v. 16a points to vv. 17–24) and their religion (v. 16b points to vv. 25–26). Verse 16a starts as though it were a continuation of the promises of vv. 12b-15, but v. 16b makes clear that the discourse has shifted into an imperative form.

What follows in vv. 17–24 is patterned after the style of a prebattle oration, similar to 1:29–33; 9:1–6; 20:2–4; 31:1–6.[12] As noted above, the argument of this military oration uses the rhetorical form of an internal monologue, the anticipation of an internal mental state of fear or arrogance (cf. 8:17–18; 9:4–7) and an answer to it in the form of a reminder of Israel's experience with Yahweh. Verse 17 raises the rhetorical question ("how can I dispossess them"), and the following battle oration gives the answer ("do not be afraid . . . remember"). "Do not be afraid" is the classic admonition of the sacral war tradition (v. 18; cf. 1:29; 20:1; 31:6). Such fear might seem logical since the enemy's power is overwhelming (vv. 1, 7, 17), but remembering the historical evidence of Yahweh's even greater power counters this apprehension.[13]

An artistic scribal flourish splits the typical Deuteronomic word pair "be afraid" (*yārē'*) and "be alarmed" (*'āraṣ*) (1:29; 20:3; 31:6) between two verses. In v. 18 "do not be afraid" is followed by a rationale involving the past; in v. 21 "do not be alarmed" is followed by one involving the present. The rhetoric of vv. 18–20 assumes that Moses' audience has witnessed the exodus (cf. 4:9, 34; 6:22). For the "hornet" of v. 20, see note n. Insects are sometimes a metaphor

---

11. These two divinities are paired in the Deir Alla text, I 16. "Ashterot of the flock" may be associated with the iconography of the Mistress of the Animals (H.-P. Müller, "*štrt*," *TDOT* 6:423–34; M. Görg, "Die 'Astarte des Kleinviehs,'" *BN* 69 [1993]: 9–10) and of nursing animals (Keel and Uehlinger, *Gods, Goddesses, and Images of God*, 147–49). On implications of this demythologization, see M. Delcor, "Astarté et la fécondité des troupeaux en Deut 7,13 et parallèles," *UF* 6 (1974): 7–14; G. Braulik, "The Rejection of the Goddess Asherah in Israel: Was the Rejection as Late as Deuteronomisitic and Did it Further the Oppression of Women in Israel?" in *Theology of Deuteronomy*, 165–82; trans. of "Die Ablehnung der Göttin Aschera in Israel: War sie erst deuteronomistisch, diente sie der Unterdrückung der Frauen?" in *Studien zum Buch Deuteronomium*, 81–118.; J. M. Hadley, "The Fertility of the Flock? The De-Personalization of Astarte in the Old Testament," in *On Reading Prophetic Texts: Gender-Specific and Related Studies in Memory of Fokkelien van Dijk-Hemmes* (ed. B. Becking and M. Dijkstra; Biblical Interpretation Series 18; Leiden: Brill, 1996), 115–33.

12. Weinfeld, *Deuteronomic School*, 45–51.

13. On memory in Deuteronomy, see E. P. Blair, "An Appeal to Remembrance: The Memory Motif in Deuteronomy," *Int* 15 (1961): 41–47; S. J. De Vries, "Deuteronomy: Exemplar of a Non-Sacerdotal Appropriation of Sacred History," in *Grace upon Grace: Essays in Honor of Lester J. Kuyper* (ed. J. Cook; Grand Rapids: Eerdmans, 1975), 95–105.

for attackers or invaders (1:44; Isa 7:18–19; Ps 118:12). Verse 21 utilizes hymnic language from the Zion tradition about the Divine Warrior who is "in the midst" (1:42; 23:15 [ET 14]; Ps 46:6 [ET 5]) and is "great and dreadful" (Pss 47:3–4 [ET 2–3]; 99:2–3).

Verse 22 gives an answer to the question of why such alien influences should still exist in the readers' own day. The continued existence of the nations is explained in terms of Exod 23:29 (in contrast to Deut 9:3 and the theology of Judg 2:20–23; 3:1–4). As a consequence of such survivals, the present reader is faced by a challenge comparable to that of the conquest.

Verses 23–24 describe a joint sacral war in which Yahweh and Israel work together to destroy the enemy. Panic is the classic weapon of Yahweh as Divine Warrior (v. 23; Judg 7:19–22), but in this sacral war, Yahweh does not act alone. Yahweh is the grammatical subject of most of the conquest verbs, but Israel too will "finish them off," "make their name perish," and "destroy" them (vv. 22, 24). In v. 24 enemy "kings" are the particular targets of destruction (cf. 2:24; 3:2–3; Josh 10:22–26; 11:12; ch. 12). Perhaps this is a way of saying that a free and egalitarian society cannot coexist with oppressive kings. Making "their name perish" no doubt reflects the political practice of excising hated names from monuments, but such action also mirrors Yahweh's own acts of judgment (Deut 9:14; 29:19 [ET 20]).

[25–26] These verses build on the sacral war victories described in vv. 23–24 to call readers to the mission of ruthlessly eliminating contemporary idols and materials associated with them. Verse 5 had proceeded from the practical standpoint that renouncing alien gods meant stopping any worship of them by eliminating their altars and other cult objects (cf. 12:2–3; 16:21–22). However, vv. 25–26 concentrate on eliminating their images.

Verses 25–26 use three repellent cultural categories by which Israel sorted out elements of its world. Whatever is associated with divine images falls under the categories of tôʿēbâ ("repugnant"), ḥērem ("devoted for destruction"), and šeqeṣ ("detestable"; the verb derived from the noun is used).[14] Even precious metals that would have covered these idols as a foil overlay (or perhaps worn by them in the form of jewelry) are assigned to these categories and must be destroyed. Such total eradication must be rigorously applied without any consideration of intrinsic value. Under the terms of sacral war, these things are considered as booty owned by Yahweh, who as Divine Warrior has defeated these gods and now possesses their images. Their destruction is commanded so that Israel will not be contaminated by their contagious quality of ḥērem (Josh 6.18; 7.12). Verse 26 ends on an emphatic and sobering note, reflecting the formula

14. On ḥērem see Nelson, "Ḥerem and the Deuteronomic Social Conscience," in *Deuteronomy and Deuteronomic Literature*, ed. Vervenne and Lust, 41–49. On šeqeṣ see J. Milgrom, *Leviticus 1–16* (AB 3; New York: Doubleday, 1991), 656–59.

of declaration by which priests announced their professional judgments about ritual matters (Lev 13:8, 15, 17; Ezek 18:9; Hag 2:13): *ḥērem hû,* "it is *ḥērem.*"

Remember Yahweh's Saving Deeds
8:1–20

Remember and Obey

8:1 Be careful to do the whole commandment that I am commanding you today, so that you may live and multiply and enter and take over the land that Yahweh swore to your ancestors. 2 Remember the whole way that Yahweh your God has led you[a] in the wilderness, in order to humble you, to test you to know what was in your heart, whether you would keep his commandments[b] or not. 3 He humbled you and made you hungry, then he fed you with manna, about which you did not know[c] nor did your ancestors know,[d] in order to make you know that one lives not only by bread, but one lives by everything that comes from the mouth of Yahweh. 4 Your clothes did not wear out[e] and your feet did not swell these forty years. 5 Know then in your heart[f] that just as one disciplines[g] one's child, so[h] Yahweh your God disciplines you. 6 Keep the commandments of Yahweh your God, walking in his ways and fearing him.

Danger in the Good Land

7 When[i] Yahweh your God brings you into a good[j] land—

> a land with streams full of water, springs, and underground
> waters, which flow out in valley and hill,
> 8 a land of wheat and barley, of vines and fig trees and pome-
> granates,
> a land of olive trees bearing oil, and honey,[k]
> 9 a land where you may eat bread without privation,[l] where
> you will not lack anything,
> a land whose stones are iron ore and from whose hills you
> may dig out copper—

10 and you eat and have enough and bless Yahweh your God for the good land that he has given you,[m] 11 be careful lest you forget Yahweh your God by not keeping his commandments, his ordinances, and his statutes, which I am commanding you today.

12 Lest when you eat and have enough and build good houses and settle down,[n] 13 and when your herds and flocks multiply, and your silver and gold multiply, and all that you have multiplies, 14 your heart then becomes proud and you forget Yahweh your God—

> who brought you out of the land of Egypt, out of the house of servitude;
> 15 who led you in the great and terrible wilderness, with[o] burning snakes[p] and scorpions, a thirsty place where there was no water;
> who made water flow out of the flinty[q] rock for you;
> 16 who fed you manna in the wilderness, about which your ancestors had not known, in order to humble you and to test you, to do you good in the end—

17 and you say to yourself, "My power and the strength of my hand have acquired this wealth for me." 18 But remember Yahweh your God, because he is the one who gives you the power to acquire wealth so that[r] he might establish his covenant that he swore to your ancestors, as is the case today.

19 If you do completely forget Yahweh your God and follow other gods and serve them and bow down to them, I witness against you today that you shall surely perish.

20 Like the nations that Yahweh is destroying before you, so you shall perish, because you would not obey Yahweh your God.

a. Follows OG as the shorter text. MT supplements with the formula *zh 'rb'ym šnh*, "these forty years (cf. v. 4; 2:7).

b. Follows MT Qere with Sam. and ancient versions. Kethib: "his commandment."

c. Follows MT. OG lost "you did not know" by homoioarchton: *l' yd'[t wl' yd']wm*.

d. Perfect with paragogic *nûn* is anomalous, *IBHS*, p. 516 n. 49; cf. v. 16.

e. The preposition *mē'ālêkā* evokes the picture of worn clothing falling off their bodies.

f. The preposition *'im* indicates the locus of psychological interest, *IBHS* 11.2.14b.

g. To instruct and correct in order to shape conduct. Discipline implies a negative approach: rebuking, punishing, correcting. See R. D. Branson, "*yāšar*," *TDOT* 6:129.

h. OG, 4QDeut[j] ease the grammar by inserting *kn*, "thus" or "so," which is only implicit in MT.

i. Taking *kî* as a temporal/conditional "when," parallel to 7:1 and to the pattern of argument in 6:10–12 and 6:20–21. Thus vv. 7–10 are an extended protasis, followed by an apodosis starting with v. 11a: "when Yahweh brings . . . be careful." Alternate translation taking *kî* as causal: "For Yahweh your God is bringing you."

j. Follows MT. Sam., OG, 4QDeut[f], 4QDeut[j], 4QDeut[n] expand with "and wide," similar to Exod 3:8.

k. Context suggests a syrup derived from fruit. This wording is reused in 2 Kgs 18:32.

l. Taking *bĕmiskēnut* as "in poverty," based on the adjective used in Qoh 4:13; 9:15–16 (*HALOT* 2:606).

m. Alternate translation as a temporal/conditional sentence: "When you eat and have enough, bless Yahweh."

n. MT is abrupt: "build good houses and inhabit." OG and 5QDeut^corr expand *wyšbt* with *bm* to read "and inhabit them."

o. "Snake and scorpion" are in apposition with "desert" to further define it.

p. Alternate translation: "poisonous snakes," i.e., with venom that burns. "Burning snakes" hints at mythological creatures, the winged serpents of iconography and Isa 6. Herodotus describes flying snakes in Sinai and Arabia (*Hist.* 2.75; 3.108), as do Assyrian sources (M. Weinfeld, *Deuteronomy 1–11* [AB 5; New York: Doubleday, 1991], 395).

q. "Flinty" communicates that this obdurate rock is an unlikely source of water (cf. 32:13).

r. Follows MT *lm'n*, "so that": it is "wealth" that makes fulfillment of the covenant possible. Sam. and OG read *wlm'n*, "and so that": the gift of "power" brings about both wealth and fulfillment.

s. An "instantaneous perfect," describing a situation occurring at the moment of utterance, *IBHS* 30.5.1d.

The admonitions of chapters 6 and 7 are now carried forward from an internal, "psychological" perspective (vv. 2, 14, 17). Chapter 7 warned of alien dangers lingering in the land; chapter 8 turns to dangers inherent in the land's very goodness, and the topic of the nations and their gods disappears until vv. 19–20. Prosperity might cause Israel to forget its dependence on Yahweh, and dangerous attitudes generated by affluence could result in a failure of loyalty and obedience. The text seeks to counter self-sufficient pride and the disobedience that would result from it by reinvigorating readers' memory of Yahweh's past favors and lessons. This intention operates through verbs that command mental states: "remember" (vv. 2, 18), "know" (v. 5), "fear" (v. 6), do not "forget" (vv. 11, 14, 19).

This chapter repeats much of the argument of 6:10–19, but in a different sequence. (Compare v. 7 to 6:10; v. 10 to 6:11; vv. 11, 14b to 6:12; v. 19 to 6:14.) The overall line of reasoning is clear, although presented in a somewhat tangled way. Verses 1–6 begin and end with a call to obey the law, based on reflections about the wilderness experience. Interpreted in terms of parental instruction, the wilderness is seen as paradigmatic for Israel's whole experience with Yahweh (cf. 29:4–5 [ET 5–6]). It was a tempering of national character and a test of faith and obedience. Manna provided the central lesson: the "necessities of life" are of only relative importance when compared to Yahweh's decrees. Verses 7–18 continue the argument in terms of an opposition between a remembering that results in obedience and a forgetting that would lead to apostasy (vv. 11, 14, 18). A poetic description of the land (vv. 7–10) and the story of economic progress in it (vv. 12–13) illustrate the linked dangers of pride (vv. 14a, 17) and forgetfulness (vv. 11, 19–20). Pride is also undermined by a hymnic recital of Yahweh's saving deeds and discipline in the wilderness (vv. 14b-16). The entire line of reasoning is founded on the opposition of wilderness and land, each depicted in poetic language. The land presents a challenge as dangerous as any threatened by the wilderness, but learning the lessons of the wilderness can prevent catastrophe in the land.

The chapter is structured into sections that come close to being narratives: first vv. 2–6 (the lesson of the wilderness past), then vv. 7–18 (the threat of the future "when Yahweh brings you into the land"). Embedded in this second section are two briefer, supporting story lines: vv. 12–14a, 17 (economic development leads to pride), and vv. 14b–16 (exodus and wilderness).

Various chiastic patterns have been suggested, dividing the text in different ways and putting different topics or phrases in the center. The most compelling concentric structure is a palindromic pattern that centers on the imperative of v. 11:[1]

> v. 1: "today . . . that Yahweh swore to your ancestors"
>   v. 2: "remember"
>   vv. 2–3: "led you in the wilderness in order to humble you, to test you . . . fed you with manna about which . . . nor did your ancestors know"
>   v. 10: "eat . . . have enough . . . good"
>   v. 11: "be careful lest you forget"
>   v. 12: "eat . . . have enough . . . good"
>   vv. 15–16: "led you in the . . . wilderness . . . fed you manna . . . about which your ancestors had not known, in order to humble you and to test you"
>   v. 18: "remember"
> vv. 18–19: "that he swore to your ancestors . . . today"

Another concentric structure, based on topic rather than vocabulary, surrounds the command to remember and obey in v. 11 with past experiences in the wilderness and future possibilities of life in the land. The wilderness was a training ground and a paradigm of life with God. The land, by the very fact of its richness, is potentially a place of spiritual danger:

---

1. Adapted from Lohfink, *Das Hauptgebot*, 189–99. This structure overrides differences between singular and plural address and other suggestions of secondary material. R. H. O'Connell, "Deuteronomy viii 1–20: Asymmetrical Concentricity and the Rhetoric of Providence," *VT* 40 (1990): 437–52, proposes a more complex structure centering on vv. 7b–9.

vv. 2–6: the wilderness ("heart," vv. 2, 5; "bread," v. 3)
vv. 7–10: the land ("water," v. 7; "bread," v. 9; bracketed
by "good land" in vv. 7a and 10b)
   v. 11: the central imperative
vv. 12–13: the land
vv. 14–16: the wilderness ("heart," v. 14; "water," v. 15)

Moses repeatedly challenges his audience to remember and not forget. "Remember" forms an arch between vv. 2 and 18:

Remember the *wilderness* (vv. 2–5).

In the setting of the *land* (vv. 7–10), *do not forget* Yahweh (v. 11).

In the context of the *land* (vv. 12–13, 17), *do not forget* Yahweh (v. 14a), who led you in the *wilderness* (vv. 14b–16).

Indeed, *remember* Yahweh, who empowers you economically in the *land* (v. 18).

Remembering and forgetting are not merely mental activities. One remembers by obeying (vv. 2 and 6) and disobeys out of forgetfulness (v. 11). This same theme continues in a more negative vein in vv. 19–20 ("if you forget").

The text uses several genres to make its argument:

A rhetorical argument from history (vv. 2–6), similar to 4:32–40 and 7:7–11. Here the format consists of three *waw*-consecutive verbs: remember Yahweh's deeds (history, vv. 2–4), know what this means (recognition, v. 5), and therefore apply this knowledge by keeping the commandments (practical conclusion, v. 6).[2]

A poetic description of the natural riches of the land (vv. 7–10). This is similar to 6:10b–11a, where human utilization of the land is the focus. This description is bracketed by "good land" (vv. 7a, 10b). The word "land" is used seven times and seven agricultural products are listed.

A hymn (vv. 14b–16). This poem interrupts the thought connection between vv. 14a and 17. It is similar to retrospective hymns such as Pss 105 and 106.

The rhetorical format of an interior monologue (vv. 17–18) like those found in 7:17–19, 21 and 9:4–7a. There is a

2. Lohfink, *Das Hauptgebot*, 125–31.

three-part schema: introduction (v. 17a), quotation of the
monologue (v. 17b), and the reply: remember Yahweh's
acts in order to counter such improper thoughts (v. 18).[3]

The convoluted nature of this chapter must be the result of a complex history of composition. Although no consensus has been reached about this history, some observations seem fairly evident. The primary line of reasoning
conceives of forgetting Yahweh by proudly taking credit for securing the land
and its prosperity (vv. 7–11a, 12–18). Warnings about this attitude (vv. 11a,
12–14bα, 17–18) incorporate and give structure to the two poetic descriptions
(vv. 7–10, 14bβ-16). However, a secondary line of reasoning associates forgetting directly with a failure to obey the law (vv. 2–6, 11b). This appears to
be a later development of the argument in the direction of legal compliance.
Finally, vv. 1 and 19–20 provide an outer frame concerning obedience to the
"whole commandment" (cf. 5:31; 6:25; 11:8, 22; 15:5; 19:9; 27:1) and the
dire consequences of disloyalty in worship. This framework preaches the
stark alternatives of obedience and blessing, disobedience and catastrophe.
Verse 1 begins in the second person singular, then quickly shifts to plural, and
that the same quick transition takes place between v. 19a and vv. 19b–20.
Overall, then, vv. 7–11a, 12–18 represent the earliest material, vv. 2–6, 11b
are a later expansion from a legal perspective; and vv. 1, 19–20 fashion a
redactional frame.[4]

[1] A list of four verbs describes impending benefits that will follow from
obedience. Verse 1 offers a distinctive theological outlook that makes entrance
into the land dependent on obedience (cf. 6:17–19; 8:1; 11:8–9, 22–23; 16:20).
This perspective is usually understood to be the contribution of an exilic writer.
Here the conditionality of obedience stands in tension with the promise of
divine oath. The notion of oath returns in v. 18, where it is stated in terms of
covenant.

[2–6] "Way" links vv. 2 and 6 and frames the section. Remembering
Yahweh's way (v. 2) and knowing Yahweh's discipline (v. 5) leads to the results
the text seeks to promote: "keep," "walk," "fear" (v. 6). The inner meaning of
wilderness history is exposed. Humbling was imposed in order to test, but also
to train into an attitude of dependence (vv. 2–3; cf. v. 16). Divine testing leads

3. García López, "Analyse littéraire de Deutéronome, V–XI," *RB* 84 (1977): 483–86.
4. One can also analyze vv. 7–11a, 12–18 into earlier and later material. Verses 12–16 separate
v. 11a from its logical continuation in vv. 17–18 ("lest you forget . . . and you say"). At the same
time, vv. 14bβ–16 break into a similar connection between v. 14bα and v. 17 ("you forget Yahweh
your God . . . and you say"). This analysis demonstrates that vv. 7–11, 17–18 constitute the earliest text and were supplemented in turn by vv. 12–14bα (a catalog of progress in the land that continues and replicates the theme of vv. 7–10) and vv. 14bβ–16 (a hymnic story of the wilderness that
contrasts with vv. 12–13).

to knowledge (vv. 3, 5). In fact, "know" serves as the controlling word in a concentric structure that unifies the section:[5]

> v. 2a: "the whole way that Yahweh your God has led you"
> v. 2b: "know . . . heart . . . keep his commandments"
> v. 3: the core lesson repeats "know" three times
> vv. 5–6a: "know in your heart . . . keep the commandments"
> v. 6b" "walking in his ways"

To "test" (*nāsâ*, v. 2) is to bring someone into a critical situation in order to observe reaction and behavior. Testing provokes a decision that proves character and faith. As a result, both Yahweh (v. 2b) and Israel (v. 3b) have learned something. This test involved humbling with hunger and then feeding with manna (v. 3). Manna taught dependence because it came directly from God. In the context of this chapter, such humbling serves to counter pride (vv. 16–17), while feeding corresponds to Yahweh's providence in both wilderness and land (vv. 7–10, 12–13, 15b–16a, 18). Yahweh brings about both satiety and hunger. Israel must remember this lesson when good times bring about inappropriate self-confidence, but also may confidently trust divine providence when bad times threaten despair. Manna is also a foretaste of the land that is the source of Israel's natural sustenance (v. 9). Thus wilderness manna is not presented here as a contrast to the land (contrast Josh 5:12). Rather Yahweh exercises a similar providence in both wilderness and land, and the lesson about total dependence learned in the wilderness also applies directly to life in the land.

Verse 3b is the core of Yahweh's lesson and has attracted much interpretive attention.[6] This maxim stands out from its context because of its universal, almost proverbial, application to the life of *hā'ādām*, humanity in general, and not just to Israel. The experience of manna mirrors Yahweh's normative will for all humankind. It promotes a completely theocentric view of human existence. "Alone" signifies that bread is of course necessary for life, but even more necessary, or the most necessary thing of all, is that which "comes from the mouth of Yahweh." But to what does this celebrated turn of phrase refer?

There are two possibilities. The phrase could signify the whole of Yahweh's creative providence, for the stress on "everything" invites one to interpret the expression in the broadest possible terms. The beneficiary is humankind in general and not just Israel, so "everything" signifies more than just a narrow, national law code. On the contrary, the surrounding literary context, which

---

5. Adapted from T. Veijola, "Das Mensch lebt nicht von Brot allein," in *Bundesdokument und Gesetze: Studien zum Deuteronomium* (ed. G. Braulik; Herders biblische Studien 4; Freiburg: Herder, 1995), 155. The language of v. 2b appears as an expansion to J in Exod 16:4.

6. See L. Perlitt, "Wovon der Mensch lebt (Dtn 8:3b)," in *Deuteronomium-Studien*, 74–96.

speaks of providence, suggests not verbal decrees but divine sustenance. Moreover, in this chapter *môṣā'*, "comes from," refers in a punning way to divine acts of deliverance (v. 14, "brought you out") and providence (v. 15, "made water flow out"). The expression also reminds one of the creative emanation from the divine mouth of Ptah (*ANET*, 5) and Wisdom coming forth from Yahweh's mouth (Sir 24:3). Taken in this broader sense, v. 3b concretizes the lesson of "humbling" from v. 3a: live by providence, not entrepreneurship, not in self-trust, but by reliance on Yahweh's gifts.

However, a more convincing interpretation restricts the reference to the realm of the verbal. Numbers 30:3 [ET 2] makes plain that "everything that comes from the mouth" signifies all that is said. What comes from the mouth usually refers to solemn words of some sort (Judg 11:36; Isa 55:11) and can be a concrete verbal expression of royal will (Esth 7:8). Given the legal context (vv. 1, 2, 6, 11), it is most natural to think here of Yahweh's revelatory words. In Deuteronomy the "mouth of Yahweh" is connected to the notion of a commanding word (1:26, 43; 9:23; 34:5). Indeed, *môṣā'*, "comes from," is not just a wordplay relating to the divine acts of vv. 14 and 15, but may also be understood as a transposition of the consonants of *miṣwâ* ("commandment").[7] Moreover, in v. 3a manna is not used to contrast miraculous providence with ordinary bread, but highlights the similarity of Yahweh's nurturing gifts in both wilderness and land. Continuing this line of thought, v. 3b most likely does not intend to distinguish food from all other aspects of divine providence, but rather contrasts bread with divine "utterance" in the shape of Yahweh's life-giving word. Humanity depends most of all on the saving declarations of Yahweh. This idea corresponds to the theology of 30:15; 32:47: obedience to Yahweh's word leads to life.

Verse 4 reflects a tradition repeated in 29:4 [ET 5] but not found in the Tetrateuch. Verse 5 introduces the theme of Yahweh's parental discipline (cf. Prov 3:11–12; 19:18; 29:17; Hos 7:15; 11:1–2). Just as human discipline takes place through punishment (Deut 21:18; 22:18), divine discipline also operates in terms of suffering, humbling, and testing, but in the end it is for Israel's own good (vv. 2, 3, 16). The section is rounded out as v. 6 repeats the first words of v. 1 in reverse order: *kol-hammiṣwâ . . . tišmĕrûn / wĕšāmartā 'et-miṣwôt* ("the whole commandment . . . be careful" / "keep the commandments").

[7–10] This originally independent poem in praise of the land is similar to 11:9–12.[8] The unit is framed by "good land" (vv. 7a, 10b) and consists of five

7. R. C. Van Leeuwen, "What Comes out of God's Mouth: Theological Wordplay in Deuteronomy 8," *CBQ* 47 (1985): 55–57.

8. Compare Sinuhe's description of the land of Yaa, *ANET*, 19 lines 80–84. In contrast, the descriptions of 6:10–11a and 8:12–13 focus on human artifacts and achievements.

characterizations of the land: vv. 7b, 8a, 8b as genitive expressions and vv. 9a, 9b using the relative pronoun. The encomium begins with abundant water as the requirement for the cultivation of the products that follow. Honey is a proverbial sign of abundance. Metal ores make tools and technology possible. The poem engages in some exaggeration, for the metals mentioned in v. 9 are not common to Palestine. Praise of the land forms an appropriate contrast to the wilderness; in the land there is no need for Yahweh to provide sustenance directly. However, this positive portrayal also points forward to the negative possibilities explored in vv. 11, 12–14a, 17. In Deuteronomy "eat and have enough" (v. 10) is often the precursor of a dangerous attitude (v. 12; cf. 6:11; 11:15; 31:20; 32:13–15).

Because this poem serves as the first part of an extended argument, its initial *kî*, which may have originally denoted "for" or "indeed," must be understood as "when" in its present context (note i). Thus vv. 7–10 serve as the protasis of a line of thought that reaches down through v. 18. The warning of the apodosis begins with v. 11 and continues through "lest when you eat" (v. 12), "and you forget" (v. 14), "and you say" (v. 17), to the contrasting imperative "remember" in v. 18. One might not actually choose to construe vv. 7–18 as a single elongated sentence, but the verses nevertheless present a unified chain of argumentation.

[11] The tests of prosperity replace the tests of wilderness deprivation, but the lesson that was clear in the wilderness will be less obvious in the rich land. The concentric structure discussed above highlights this verse as the central point of the chapter. Indeed, the danger of forgetting permeates the larger parenetic context (4:9, 23; 6:12; 8:14, 19; 9:7; cf. Hos 13:5–6). This warning can be understood as introducing four modes of forgetting: to fail to observe the laws (v. 11b), to be proud and ignore one's dependency on Yahweh (v. 14), to rely on one's own strength (v. 17), and to run after and serve other gods (vv. 19–20).

[12–13] Read in context, this list portrays further developments resulting from the fertility of vv. 7–10: active building (beyond the passive takeover of 6:10–11), an increase in wealth, food beyond immediate needs in the form of livestock, and surplus wealth stored up as silver and gold. The root *rbh*, "multiply," appears three times here (cf. 7:13, 22; 8:1). Possession of the land does not mean just loot but culture, not just daily bread but cattle and money for long-term security. In v. 10 wealth leads to Israel blessing Yahweh, but here it endangers the relationship with Yahweh (v. 14a). In v. 13 the grammatical subjects are the material possessions themselves; they increase as though without human effort. In this way, grammar corresponds to the rhetorical intent of denying pride to Israel. This same line of argument is reflected in 17:17, 20, which associate multiplied wealth with the king's potential for infidelity.

[14–16] The antidote to forgetting is the memory of Israel's foundational past, reviewed in hymnic participle style. Human pride is countered by a catalog of divine saving deeds: exodus, wilderness guidance, water, and manna. This divine pedagogy is the same as that set forth in vv. 2–4, as v. 16b once again connects manna to humility and testing. The section is robustly poetic.[9] Because v. 14bα connects directly to v. 17 ("you forget . . . and you say"), this little wilderness history must once have been an independent piece, appropriated for use in this context.

[17–18] These verses are tied together by a repetition of "power" and "wealth" as gifts of Yahweh that cannot be claimed as personal possessions. Verse 17 states the mechanism by which the forgetting of v. 14a takes place, introducing an attitude that stands in total contrast to the recital of divine acts in vv. 14b-16. Verse 18 contrasts proper thoughts to the improper ones of v. 17. Verse 18a asserts that Yahweh helps with acquisition of wealth, and v. 18b explains why Yahweh may be counted on to do so. The "ancestors" who had not known Yahweh's wonders (vv. 3, 16) now reappear as those to whom a covenant promise has been made (cf. 4:31; 7:12; 9:5). At one level, "as is the case today" means that Yahweh is in the process of fulfilling the promise by events unfolding in Moab (v. 1), but for the readers of Deuteronomy "today" also signifies that their present standard of living is the result of Yahweh's commitment to covenant promises.

[19–20] The theme of going after other gods and perishing falls outside the topic of chapter 8 and returns to the outlook of chapter 7 (cf. 4:25–26; 6:14–15). Perhaps these verses act as a sort of "curse" to balance the blessings highlighted in vv. 7–10, 12–13, and 18. Verse 19 refers to the ideas and language of the Decalogue (5:7, 9): "serve and bow down." "I witness against you" and "surely perish" are paralleled in 4:26; 30:18–19. To "follow" (*hlk* Qal) alien gods would cancel out the leading of Yahweh (*hlk* hitpa'el; vv. 2, 15) and "walking" in the way of Yahweh (*hlk* Qal, v. 6). Verse 20 points forward to the topic of 9:1–6. The good news about Yahweh's obliteration of the nations contains within it the potential bad news of Israel's own destruction.

---

9. Note the numerous *m* sounds throughout the poem, the repetition of *hammôṣî'* in vv. 14b and 15b, and the fourfold repetition of the sequence of *'ayin nun* in v. 16 (*yādĕ'ûn . . . lĕma'an 'annôtĕkā ûlĕma'an*). There is assonance: *miṣrayim*, "Egypt" (v. 14b) and *miṣṣûr*, "from the rock" (v. 15b), *hammôlîkăkā*, "who led you" (v. 15a), and *hammaʾăkilĕkā*, "who fed you" (v. 16a). Verse 15 contrasts *wĕṣimmā'ôn . . . 'ên-māyim*, "a thirsty place . . . no water," with *hammôṣî' . . . mayim*, "who made water flow." The same concepts and similar language are found in Hos 13:4–6.

Complacency, Rebellion, Intercession, and Pardon
9:1–10:11

The Danger of False Assurance

9:1 Hear, O Israel! You are going to cross the Jordan today, to enter and dispossess nations greater and more powerful than you, great cities fortified up to the sky, **2** a people great and tall, the Anakim, about whom you know. You have heard it said, "Who can withstand the Anakim?" **3** Know then today that Yahweh your God is the one who is crossing over before you as a consuming fire. He is the one who will destroy them and subdue them before you, so that you may dispossess[a] and destroy them quickly, just as Yahweh has promised you. **4** Do not say to yourself, when Yahweh your God pushes them out before you, "It is because of[b] my righteousness that Yahweh has brought me in to take over this land." It is because of the wickedness of these nations that Yahweh is dispossessing them before you.[c] **5** It is not because of your righteousness or the uprightness of your heart that you are going in to take over their land, but it is because of the wickedness of these nations that Yahweh[d] is dispossessing them before you and in order to establish the promise that he[e] swore to your ancestors, to Abraham, to Isaac, and to Jacob. **6** Know then that it is not because of your righteousness that Yahweh your God is giving you this good land to take it over, for you are a stubborn people.[f]

Rebellion and Restoration at Horeb

7 Remember, do not forget that you provoked Yahweh your God to anger in the wilderness. From the day you came out[g] of the land[h] of Egypt until you came to this place, you have been rebellious against[i] Yahweh. **8** At Horeb you provoked Yahweh to anger, and Yahweh was angry enough[j] with you to destroy you. **9** When I went up the mountain to receive the stone tablets, the tablets of the covenant that Yahweh made with you, I remained on the mountain forty days and forty nights. I did not eat bread or drink water. **10** Then Yahweh gave me the two stone tablets written by the finger of God. On them were all the words that Yahweh had spoken to you on the mountain.[k] **11** At the end of forty days and forty nights Yahweh gave me the two stone tablets, the tablets of the covenant.

12 Then Yahweh said to me, "Get up, go down quickly from here, because your people whom you brought out of Egypt have acted corruptly. They have turned quickly from the way that I commanded them. They have made themselves a cast image." 13 Then Yahweh said to me, "I have seen this people and they are a stubborn people indeed. 14 Let me alone that I may destroy them and wipe out their name from under heaven, and I will make you into a nation more powerful and more numerous than they."

15 So I turned back and went down from the mountain, while the mountain was burning with fire, and the two tablets[l] were in my two hands. 16 Then I saw that you really had sinned against Yahweh your God. You had made yourselves a cast image.[m] You had turned[n] from the way that Yahweh had commanded you. 17 So I took hold of the two tablets, threw them down from my two hands, and smashed them before your eyes. 18 Then I lay prostrate before Yahweh as before, forty days and forty nights. I did not eat bread or drink water, because of all your sin you had committed, doing what was evil in Yahweh's opinion to offend him.[o] 19 For I was afraid that the wrath and hot anger that Yahweh felt against you would lead him to destroy you. But Yahweh listened to me that time also. 20 Yahweh was angry enough with Aaron to destroy him, but I also prayed on behalf of Aaron at that time. 21 I took the sinful thing you had made, the calf, and burned it with fire and pounded it up, grinding it up thoroughly until it was as fine as dust.[p] I threw its dust into the stream that runs down from the mountain.

22 At Taberah and at Massah and at Kibroth-hattaavah, you provoked Yahweh to anger. 23 And when Yahweh sent you from Kadesh-barnea, saying, "Go up and take over the land that I have given you," you rebelled against the command of Yahweh your God. You did not trust him or obey him. 24 You have been rebellious against Yahweh from the first day I[q] knew you.

25 I lay prostrate before Yahweh forty days and forty nights right where I had fallen, because Yahweh had threatened to destroy you. 26 I prayed to Yahweh and said, "Lord Yahweh, do not destroy your people and your hereditary possession, whom you redeemed in your greatness, whom you brought out of Egypt with a mighty hand.[r] 27 Remember your servants Abraham, Isaac, and Jacob.[s] Do not pay attention to the stubbornness of this people or to its wickedness or its sin, 28 lest the land[t] from which you brought us say, 'Because Yahweh was not able to bring them into the land that he had promised them and because he hates them, he has brought them out to kill them in the wilderness.' 29 But they are your people and your hereditary possession, whom you brought out by your great power and your outstretched arm."

10:1 At that time Yahweh said to me, "Hew out two tablets of stone like the former ones, and come up the mountain to me and make a wooden ark. 2 I will cut onto the tablets the words that had been on the first tablets that you broke and you will put them in the ark." 3 So I made an ark of acacia wood, and I hewed out two tablets of stone like the former ones, and I went up the mountain with the two tablets in my hand. 4 He cut onto the tablets according to the former writing, the ten words that Yahweh had spoken to you on the mountain from the middle of fire.[u] Then Yahweh gave them to me. 5 I turned back and went down from the mountain and put the tablets in the ark that I had made. They are still there, just as Yahweh commanded me.

6 The Israelites marched out from Beeroth-bene-jaakan to Moserah. There Aaron died and there he was buried. Eleazar his son served as priest after him. 7 From there they marched out to Gudgodah and from Gudgodah to Jotbathah, a land with streams full of water.

8 At that time Yahweh set apart the tribe of Levi to carry the ark of the covenant of Yahweh, to stand before Yahweh to serve him[v] and to bless in his name, as is still the case today. 9 Therefore Levi has no share or hereditary possession with their kindred. Yahweh is their hereditary possession, just as he[w] promised them.

10 I took my stand on the mountain,[x] forty days and forty nights. And Yahweh listened to me that time also. Yahweh was not willing to destroy you. 11 Yahweh said to me, "Get up, march out at the head of the people, that they may enter and take over the land that I swore to their ancestors to give them."

a. Follows MT. The absence of *whwrštm*, "dispossess them," in OG was caused either by using one word to translate two verbs or by haplography: *wh[wrštm wh]'bdtm*.

b. The preposition *b* is either causal or circumstantial, *IBHS* 11.2.5e.

c. Verse 4b is a circumstantial sentence expressing background information: you are saying "x" in a situation when "y" is the case (Williams, *Hebrew Syntax*, 219, 494). To indicate that a contrary assertion is being made, translators often insert "it is rather because" or "it is really because." One could also retain the direct discourse to the end of the verse by splitting *mpnyk*, "before you," into *mpny*, "before me," and start v. 5 with *ky*, "because" (Lohfink, *Das Hauptgebot*, p. 201 n. 6). The absence of v. 4b from LXX[B] is a careless error, not a genuine witness to OG.

d. Follows Sam., OG. MT expands with *'lhyk*, "your God."

e. Follows Sam., OG, Syr. MT supplies "Yahweh" as an explicit subject.

f. That is, "stiff-necked" (cf. English "headstrong"). The expression may suggest a refusal to bow one's head to proper authority or the neck of an uncooperative domestic animal. B. Couroyer, "'Avoir la nuque raide': ne pas incliner l'oreille," *RB* 87 (1981): 216–25, suggests a refusal to bend one's neck in order to "incline the ear" in heedful obedience.

g. This verse begins in second person singular and shifts to plural. The difference between MT "you [singular] came out" and the plural read by Sam., OG, Syr. reveals either haplography in MT or dittography in the other witnesses: *ys't[m] m'rṣ*.

h. Follows MT. OG lacks "land of," lost by homoioarchton: *m['rṣ m]ṣrym*.

i. The preposition *'im* in the sense of "dealing with" (cf. v. 24).

j. Infinitive construct with the preposition *l* to indicate degree (cf. v. 20), Williams, *Hebrew Syntax*, 199, 275. Alternate translation of the start of the verse, taking the *waw* as emphatic: "even at Horeb," i.e., even at the supreme moment of revelation.

k. Follows OG. MT expands (possibly on the basis of 10:4 MT; cf. 18:16): *mtwk h'š bywm hqhl*, "from the midst of the fire on the day of the assembly," perhaps a reference to 5:22.

l. Follows OG. MT expands with *hbryt*, "of the covenant" (from 9:9, 11).

m. Follows OG. MT expands into *'gl mskh*, "cast image of a calf" (cf. Exod 32:4, 8 and the identical expansion by Sam. at Deut 9:12).

n. Follows OG and some Sam. evidence. MT expands with *mhr*, "quickly," perhaps from Exod 32:8.

o. Infinitive construct result clause, *IBHS* 36.2.3d.

p. The preposition *l* indicates a comparison, *IBHS* 11.2.10d. The word order emphasizes the direct objects.

q. Follows MT *d'ty* as less expected in context. Sam., OG read *d'tw*, "his knowing," a confusion of *w* and *y*. REB interprets *y* as a misunderstood abbreviation for Yahweh.

r. OG expands this verse at several points (Wevers, *Greek Text*, 171–73).

s. Follows MT. OG expands from Exod 32:13, "to whom you yourself swore," perhaps *'šr nšb't lhm bk*.

t. Follows the striking usage of MT, which has "land" in the singular as the subject of the plural verb. Sam. expands the subject into *'m h'rṣ*, "the people of the land," and the ancient versions follow similar strategies.

u. Follows OG and some Cairo Genizah evidence. MT supplements to achieve the formula it uses in 9:10: *bywm hqhl*, "on the day of the assembly" (cf. 18:16).

v. Follows MT. OG, Vulg. lack the pronominal suffix. This may be a translation strategy, but more likely represents haplography in OG or dittography in MT: *lšrt[w] wlbrk*.

w. Follows OG. MT supplements with the explicit subject *yhwh 'lhyk*, "Yahweh your God."

x. Follows OG. MT supplements with *kymym hr'šnym*, "the same number of days as before," an explanatory cross-reference to 9:18.

Deuteronomy 9:7–10:11: A Later Insertion

Deuteronomy 9:1–6 continues a series of "psychological" dangers presented by victory and life in the land: timidity in 7:17–26, complacency about the law and pride in 8:11–20, and now self-righteousness. These dangers are expressed in the rhetorical form of an internal monologue (7:17; 8:17; 9:4). A discernible break divides the admonitory argument of 9:1–6 (organized by the vocative of 9:1 and picked up again by the vocative of 10:12) from the historical retrospective that begins with 9:7 and is organized by the imperative "remember." Verses 1–6 do not prepare the reader for this retrospective narrative about the wilderness era. In fact, the topic of taking the land in 9:6 does not pick up again until 10:11, where the crossing prepared for in 9:1–2 is finally commanded in the form of a resumptive repetition of 9:5 ("enter," "take over," "swore"). These circumstances indicate that 9:7–10:11 is a parenthetical digression and almost certainly a later insertion.

The link between 9:1–6 and 9:8–10:11 is provided by 9:7, which explores Israel's stubbornness (9:6) by introducing the topic of rebellion in the wilderness. The narrative that follows illustrates and substantiates this general truth. Moses shifts from exhortation to history, relating the past in the first person from his own viewpoint. His narrative buttresses the parenesis into which it has been inserted. In terms of literary effect, this retrospective story introduces suspense and tension. The delay in the argument introduced by "at Horeb" (9:8) is finally relieved by the command to move on in 10:11. It is only then that the two reasons for the conquest advanced in 9:4b, 5b—brought up to counter the erroneous thought of v. 4a—are carried forward by other arguments for Israel's special status: 10:14–15 (election), 17–18 (the character of Yahweh), 21–22 (the deeds of Yahweh).

9:7–10:11: History of Composition

The narrative of 9:7–10:11 is so complex and so chronologically confused that the presence of different literary layers is certain, but for the same reason these are nearly impossible to distinguish. Nevertheless, considerable evidence suggests that an earlier second-person singular narrative has been supplemented by a catalog of place names, a second-person plural narrative, and a few disruptive digressions.

Deuteronomy 9:7a is continued by 9:13–14, 26–29; 10:10bβ–11, verses that form a reasonably coherent *second-person singular narrative*, moving from divine anger through Yahweh's offer to Moses and his prayer in the shape of a communal lament and concluding with divine clemency. Its themes are "stubbornness," "people," and "ancestors" (cf. 9:5, 6). The stone tablets and calf play no explicit role in these verses.

Deuteronomy 9:8, 22–23 consist of a *list of places* where Israel "provoked anger" (cf. 9:7a) and "rebelled" (root *mrh*). The place names (Horeb, Taberah, Massah, Kibroth-hattaavah) are each introduced by *wb* ("and at") and conclude with "from Kadesh-barnea." These incidents are bracketed by a reversed repetition of "from the day" and "you have been rebellious against Yahweh" (9:7b and 24).

Attached to the first item in this list ("at Horeb," 9:8) is a baroque *second-person plural narrative* focusing on the Decalogue tablets and the calf: 9:9–12, 15–19, 21, 25; 10:1–5, 10abα. These verses show literary dependence on texts from Exodus. They also relate to the themes of Deuteronomy 5 (cf. 9:10 and

10:4 with 5:22; "tablets of the covenant" in 9:9, 11 with 5:2–3). The actions of giving, breaking, and remaking the stone tablets organize this plot. The calf image brings about their destruction, and Moses' intercession leads to their being remade. The phrase "forty days and nights" is incessantly repeated as an organizing and connecting element.

Finally, 9:20 and 10:6–7, 8–9 are disruptive *digressions* involving matters of Levitical and priestly interest.[1]

Much of Deut 9:7–10:11 exhibits a literary relationship with texts in Exodus.[2] First, Exod 32:7–14 appears to depend on the *second-person singular narrative* that makes up Deut 9:12–14, 26–29. It is significant that Exod 32:7–10 and 11–13 hold together in a cohesive way what in Deuteronomy is split apart by the second-person plural material about the tablets and the calf. Second, the supplementary *second-person plural narrative* is dependent on various texts in Exodus:

> Deut 9:9–10 on Exod 24:12a; 31:18b
> Deut 9:15–17, 21 on Exod 32:15, 19–20
> Deut 9:18 on Exod 34:28
> Deut 10:1–4 on Exod 34:1–4, 28b.[3]

Structure and Plot

Even though the 9:7–10:11 insertion is clearly a literary composite, a chronologically complex structure emerges from the convolutions of the text. This

---

1. To summarize: (a) the *original text* of a large digression inserted between 9:6 and 10:12: 9:7a, 13–14, 26–29; 10:10bβ–11; (b) a previously existing *place list* with its framework: 9:7b–8, 22–24; (c) a supplementary *calf/tablets narrative* and associated connectors: 9:9–12, 15–19, 21, 25; 10:1–5; 10abα; (d) *expansions*: 9:20; 10:6–9. These conclusions are similar to those of A. D. H. Mayes, *Deuteronomy* (New Century Bible; repr. Grand Rapids: Eerdmans, 1981), 194–96; Seitz, *Redaktionsgeschichtliche Studien*, 51–56, 58–69; and E. Aurelius, *Der Fürbitter Israels* (ConBOT 27; Stockholm: Almqvist & Wiksell, 1988), 44–56.

2. See J. Vermeylen, "Les sections narratives de Deut 5–11 et leur relation à Ex 19–34," in *Das Deuteronomium*, ed. Lohfink, 174–207.

3. At the same time, both the basic second-person singular narrative and the plural narrative about the calf and tablets show relationships to the language and ideology of DH. Compare 9:1–2 with 1:28; 9:3 ("cross before you") with 1:30; 9:7 ("until you came to this place") with 1:31; 9:7, 24 ("rebellious against Yahweh") with 31:27a; 9:23 with 1:21, 26, 32, 43. The address of 9:26 is similar to that of 3:24; 9:24 makes the same assertion as 31:27a. Also compare 9:28 with 1:27 and 10:1–5 ("ark of the covenant") with 31:9, 25, 26. The Levites are those who carry the ark in 10:8 and 31:25. Deuteronomy 9:7–10:11 is assigned to DH by G. Minette de Tillesse, "Sections 'tu' et sections 'vous' dans le Deutéronome," *VT* 12 (1962): 56–63; and by García López, "Analyse littéraire de Deutéronome, V–XI," *RB* 85 (1978): 18–30. B. Peckham, "The Composition of Deuteronomy 9:1–10:11," in *Word and Spirit: Essays in Honor of D. M. Stanley* (ed. J. Plevnik; Willowdale, Ont.: Regis College Press, 1975), 3–59, attributes 9:7–8a, 9, 11–12, 15–17, 21–24 to Dtr I (the Deuteronomist) and 9:8b, 10, 13–14, 18–20, 25–29; 10:1–5, 8–11 to Dtr II (an exilic editor).

structure is based on the repeated mention of "forty days" (9:9, 11, 18, 25; 10:10) and the first-person singular verbs that describe the movement, locale, and position of Moses (9:9, 15, 18, 25; 10:3, 5, 10). The reader can understand the text as describing two separate forty-day periods. Each of these periods involves Moses on the mountain and a set of tablets. The *first* period of forty days is described in 9:9–11 and its aftermath in 9:12–17. This first period encompasses the reception and destruction of the first set of tablets. After this comes a *second* forty-day period in which Moses offers intercession and a second set of tablets is prepared. This second period is presented in a dischronologized manner in that it is revisited four times (9:18–20, 25–29; 10:1–5 ["at that time"], 10–11). The text explicitly indicates this as a subsequent period with "as before" and "that time also" (9:18, 10:10). Deuteronomy 9:18–20 is linked to 9:25–29 by "I lay prostrate before Yahweh forty days and forty nights"; 10:1–5 connects to 9:25–29 by "at that time"; 10:10–11 links to 9:18–20 by "Yahweh listened to me that time also." In addition, Moses' prostration is *kāri'šōnâ* ("as before," 9:18), and the second set of tablets are *kāri'šōnîm* ("like the former ones," 10:1).

Overall, events tend to be reported as doublets: giving the tablets (9:10 and 11), "then Yahweh said to me" (9:12 and 13), intercession (9:18–20 and 25–29), divine hearing (9:19 and 10:10), and clemency (10:1–5 and 10). There are seven references to the first set of tablets and seven more to the second set.

Viewed from a different perspective, the text may be seen as juxtaposing a rebellion theme (9:7–24, framed by the repeated language of vv. 7 and 24) and an intercession theme (9:25–10:11). The rebellion theme is connected with the catalog of places in 9:8 and 22–23. The intercession theme links to a forward-looking itinerary made possible by Yahweh's clemency (10:6–7, 11). Chronologically, the intercession theme takes place in the second forty-day window of time bracketed by Moses' prostration (9:18a = 9:25a) and Yahweh's response (9:19b = 10:10b).

In spite of this complexity, the final form of the text still works as a narrative. The story moves from covenant making (9:9–11), to covenant breaking (9:12–24), and then on to a renewal of the relationship (9:25–10:11). In the end, the provision of new tablets means that Israel's relationship with Yahweh has not been irreparably broken. Moreover, the itinerary of 10:6–7, taken together with the future tasks of the Levites in 10:8–9, means that Israel's story with Yahweh will go on, and does so right up to "today" (10:8). Yahweh forgives (10:10–11) and Israel is again on its way to the land.[4]

---

4. Some of these observations are based on E. Talstra, "Deuteronomy 9 and 10: Synchronic and Diachronic Observations," in *Synchronic or Diachronic? A Debate on Method in Old Testament Exegesis* (ed. J. C. de Moor; OtSt 34; Leiden: Brill, 1995), 187–210. He postulates that an original text that already involved Horeb and the tablets (9:1–6, 7*-17*, 25*-28*; 10:1–5, 10–11)

[1–6] An emphasis on Yahweh's decisive role as Divine Warrior serves to counter Israel's self-important claims. The text seeks to counteract any narcissistic, boastful theology that would collapse the tension between divine grace and human obedience. Such boasting is prevented by a reminder of Yahweh's actual motivations in the conquest (vv. 4b–6a) and of Israel's constant opposition to Yahweh (v. 6b). It may be structurally significant that the root *yrš*, "dispossess, take over," is used seven times. The language is typical of the parenetic chapters and is related to that of chapter 4: "cross the Jordan" (4:21–22, 26; 11:31; 30:18); "people great and tall" (4:38; 7:1; 11:23); "consuming fire" (4:24); "know then" (4:39; 7:9; 8:5). Verses 4–6 echo the language and themes of 6:18–19 ("pushes them out," "take over this land"). The language of vv. 1–2 is similar to that of 1:28 ("great cities fortified up to the sky," "a people great and tall," "Anakim"). Because this language is so closely integrated with the themes of chapter 1, 9:1–2 most likely derives from 1:28. Verse 4b may be a secondary expansion, since it replicates and anticipates v. 5b.

This section begins with a renewed call for attention (v. 1). This formula is expressed without any object indicating content, as is also the case in 6:4 and 20:3 (contrast 5:1 and 6:3). A reminder that Moses is speaking on the threshold of crossing the Jordan launches the topic of conquest. A description of sacral war victory (vv. 1–3) is followed by a warning about false conclusions one might draw from it (vv. 4–6). Verses 1–3 are unified by an inverted structure: "cross / today // today / cross." The dangerous false conclusion "because of my righteousness" (v. 4) is emphatically denied by a twofold "not because of your righteousness" (vv. 5–6).

Two overlapping rhetorical forms are present in vv. 4–7a. On the one hand, these verses present a *schema of evidence from history*. Verses 4–5 present the evidence, v. 6 sets forth the conclusion in the form of what is to be known, and v. 7a the consequences of this lesson as a call to remember.[5] At the same time, the argument uses the rhetorical technique of *internal monologue*. The erroneous monologue (v. 4a) is set up by the situation of Divine Warrior victory (vv. 1–3) and then is followed by a listing of realities that counter this incorrect thought (vv. 4b-6).[6]

Divine Warrior and sacral war notions dominate the argument. Yahweh demonstrates effectiveness as a warrior by the capacity to overcome fortifica-

---

was reorganized and restructured by DH. R. H. O'Connell, "Deuteronomy ix 7–x 7, 10–11: Panelled Structure, Double Rehearsal and the Rhetoric of Covenant Rebuke," *VT* 42 (1992): 492–509, proposes an asymmetrical arrangement that intentionally deviates from expected regularity in order to disturb the reader. The four "panels" are 9:7–8a and 22–24 (Israel provokes Yahweh) and 9:8b–21 and 9:25–10:7, 10–11 (Moses receives the commandments).

5. Lohfink, *Das Hauptgebot*, 125–36. Other examples are 4:37–40; 7:7–11; and 8:2–6.

6. García López, "Analyse littéraire de Deutéronome, V–XI," *RB* 84 (1977): 484, 495–96.

tions and the proverbial Anakim (vv. 1–2) and to do so "quickly" (v. 3). "Who can withstand?" (v. 2) sounds like a proverbial saying (cf. Prov 27:4) and reverses the assurance of 7:24; 11:25. Although the notion of a quick conquest stands in tension with 7:22, the book of Joshua also speaks of rapid initial success followed by a drawn-out period of gradual conquest (Josh 10:40–43; 11:18; 23:4–13). The Divine Warrior will be Israel's vanguard (v. 3, note the emphatic grammar; cf. 1:30). "Devouring fire" is an image of divine jealousy (4:24), but more particularly a weapon of the Divine Warrior (Isa 29:6; 30:27, 30). "As Yahweh has promised" (v. 3) may cite 7:24 or merely allude to Yahweh's promises in general.[7]

Moses begins by imitating the encouraging style of a sacral war sermon (cf. 20:2–4), but turns this genre into a warning. He seeks to counter narcissistic conceit by reviewing the record. Israel dare not take Yahweh's good gifts as evidence of its own righteousness. In place of any fallacious claims of righteousness, there are two bona fide explanations for the conquest: as divine punishment on the indigenous inhabitants and as a fulfillment of Yahweh's oath to the ancestors. Moses seeks to influence attitude; Israel's obedience is to grow out of gratitude for Yahweh's unmerited gift.

The polar opposites of righteous and unrighteous are juridical terms, legal "innocence" or "guilt" (cf. Deut 25:1) as determined by the outcome of battle. Some in Israel would automatically assume that victory belongs to the just and would naturally be tempted to reason that "our victory" means "our righteousness." Moses insists on an opposing logic: "Our victory means enemy wickedness, yes, but also Yahweh's promise to our ancestors. Do not think your victory means that Yahweh has judged you innocent as though in a battle of judicial ordeal. Yes, your foes were guilty and got what they deserved, but you are guilty too. Sacral war victory is not a matter of human righteousness but of Yahweh's judgment and oath." This theology stands in tension with that of 6:18–19 (cf. the shared use of *hădōp*, "push out," in 6:19 and 9:4; cf. Josh 23:5), where Israel's obedience is said to be a prerequisite for conquest (cf. 4:1). Perhaps 9:4 intends to correct any potential misunderstanding of 6:18–19.

The theme of the sins of the land's inhabitants (vv. 4–5) appears often (e.g., 12:31; 18:12; 20:18; cf. Gen 15:16). However, their fate must be understood in light of 8:19–20, which asserts that Israel is just as vulnerable as they were to the judgment of Yahweh. Yahweh's intent to "establish" (*qwm* hip'il) the promise (v. 5) is the same divine purpose as that found in 8:18, where it is expressed as "establish his covenant."

[7–19] Verse 7 marks a shift from exhortation to history and from second-person singular to plural address. The topic "remember/do not forget" links

---

7. D. E. Skweres, *Die Ruckverweise im Buch Deuteronomium* (AnBib 79; Rome: Biblical Institute Press, 1979), 31–34.

back to 7:18; 8:11, 14, 18, 19, but this time the object of memory is a negative experience. Verse 8 functions as a superscription to the narrative of vv. 9–21, which intends to prove the accusation of constant insubordination made in v. 7. The description of 9:9–10 alludes to the revelation of 5:2–22 and stresses the authority of that revelation by spelling out that it was written down by Yahweh personally. Verse 11 recapitulates the direct transfer of the tablets (from v. 10) and concludes the first forty-day period.

A concentric structure brackets the description of apostasy in vv. 12–16:

> "turned quickly from the way that I commanded," v. 12
> > "made themselves a cast image," v. 12
> > "made yourselves a cast image," v. 16
> "turned [MT quickly] from the way that Yahweh had commanded," v. 16

A second, overlapping structure links the obliteration of the calf with this apostasy:

> "down from the mountain" / "with fire," v. 15
> > "sinned" / "you had made" / [MT "calf"], v. 16
> > "sinful thing" / "you had made" / "calf," v. 21
> "with fire" / "down from the mountain," v. 21[8]

In v. 12 Yahweh's alienation is expressed by distancing language: "*your* people whom *you* brought out." "Cast image" emphasizes the metallic makeup of the idol (cf. Exod 32:4). The awkward repetition "Yahweh said to me" that begins v. 13 probably indicates a literary seam, but the distancing language continues: "*this* people." Yahweh agrees with Moses' assessment of Israel's character made in v. 6. In v. 14 Yahweh anticipates and seeks to forestall any intercession on the part of Moses. However, in so doing Yahweh also becomes the first to raise the issue of Moses' prophetic duty to intercede and perhaps even hints that intercession would be the logical next step! In a sense, Yahweh reveals a vulnerability to human appeal. Yet Yahweh also threatens to do to Israel what they are about to do to the nations (cf. 7:23–24; on wiping out names, cf. 25:6; 29:19 [ET 20]).

Verses 15–17 introduce a suspenseful delay after v. 14's teasing hint of intercession (Will Moses pray? What will the outcome be?). Verse 15 recalls the "fire" of 5:23 (4:11), but here fire is a sign of the frightful seriousness of Israel's predicament. This fire makes Yahweh's presence and power as Divine Warrior

---

8. The motif of a stream that flowed down the mountain may have been added to Exod 32:20 for the purpose of creating this scribal structure. The MT tradition recognized these structures and improved upon them (notes m and n).

clearly perceptible, both threatening Israel and removing any excuse for making the idol. The tablets are mentioned expressly as a pointed contrast to the sin Moses is about to observe and to set the stage for smashing them. The start of v. 16 (literally "I looked and behold") reflects the shocked and bewildered perspective of Moses: "I saw to my indignation and horror."[9] Verse 17 implies that his breaking the tablets was intentional, an act done "before your eyes" as a public witness. In Mesopotamia breaking a tablet invalidated a legal document.

"As before" and "that time also" in vv. 18–19 create chronological problems. These expressions cannot refer to any earlier specific episode of intercession and clemency. The reader may choose to assume that "as before" is a generalized reference to the forty days of attendance on Yahweh and fasting described in vv. 9–11 and that "that time also" points in a general way to Yahweh's proven willingness to listen. These phrases could also be indirect references to the incident of 5:23–31 or allude to Israel's general proclivity for apostasy requiring repeated acts of intercession. These references may have originated as intertextual allusions to the two intercessory prayers described in Exod 32:11–14 and 34:8–10, the first of which comes before Moses smashes the tablets. In the Deuteronomy version, Moses waits forty days before destroying the calf, which would place the intercession of 9:18–19 between Exod 32:19 (parallel to Deut 9:17) and Exod 32:20 (parallel to Deut 9:21). In Deuteronomy, Yahweh has already listened favorably before Moses takes action.

[20] Word order foregrounds Aaron as a new subject, referring implicitly to a scandalous role in the calf episode (Exod 32:21–25) that is not mentioned explicitly in Deuteronomy. "At that time" indicates a redactional connection. Interest in Aaron reappears in Deut 10:6.

[21] In the context of Deuteronomy's overall message, the destruction of the golden calf is intended as something for readers to imitate by destroying the idols of their own time. This description depends on Exod 32:20 and presumes that the reader will be familiar with that story. Deuteronomy adds the reference to "sin" (cf. vv. 16, 18, 27) and the refrain word "mountain (vv. 9, 10, 15; 10:1, 4, 5, 10)." The people do not drink the water as in the Exodus parallel. Instead a brook carries it off, removing the danger or guilt from the people and the holy mountain (cf. 21:3–9). Any notion of drinking this sin-laden water as a punishment or an ordeal would be inappropriate in Deuteronomy's view, for Yahweh has already accepted the effective intercession of Moses. Incinerating metal indicates that this description is intended to be more rhetorical than practical. Such language of total obliteration and repudiation, heaping up destructive actions and culminating in a climactic one, is paralleled in other ancient Near Eastern literature (cf. 2 Kgs 23:6, 12, 15).[10]

---

9. *IBHS*, pp. 676–77.
10. Anat's step-by-step obliteration of Mot is often cited (*ANET*, 140). For literary parallels and

[22–24] Verse 22 returns to the geographic catalog begun with "at Horeb" (v. 8) and further illustrates the accusation of v. 7b and v. 24. Again the text counts on the reader's familiarity with tradition. These locations are known from Num 11:1–3, 31–34, and Exod 17:1–7. Their ominous names recall the cautionary tales connected with them: Taberah ("burning"), Massah ("testing"), Kibroth-hattaavah ("graves of craving"). Significantly, these three traditions also involve successful intercessions. The Kadesh story (v. 23) alludes to the tradition of Num 13–14, but also connects to Deut 1:19b-32 (DH) through verbal links to 1:21, 26b, 32.

[25–29] Verse 25 backtracks to the intercessory prayer as a resumptive repetition of v. 18. Repetition of "your people and your hereditary possession" and "you brought out" (vv. 26 and 29) brackets the prayer itself. This frame artistically splits up the standard poetic pair of "mighty hand" (v. 26) and "outstretched arm" (v. 29). Moses prays in the language of communal lament. He begins with the central petition (v. 26), follows with a positive request (v. 27a) and then a negative one (v. 27b), and concludes with motivations (vv. 28–29).[11]

As is often true in biblical narrative, Yahweh is presented as a real character in the story, truly engaged in the plot. Yahweh's threat is real, not a matter of bluffing or playacting. Moses offers motivations that go to the heart of Yahweh's personal priorities: the exodus and redemption of the people, the ancestors, Yahweh's own name and honor. "Your hereditary possession" (vv. 26, 29) evokes the language of family relationships. Moses calls the ancestors "servants," emphasizing their loyalty. Yahweh risks a double-edged slander

---

the relationship of this text to Exod 32:20, see C. T. Begg, "The Destruction of the Calf (Exod. 32,20/Deut 9,21)," in *Das Deuteronomium*, ed. Lohfink, 208–51; idem, "The Destruction of the Golden Calf Revisited," in *Deuteronomy and Deuteronomic Literature*, ed. Vervenne and Lust, 469–79; S. A. Loewenstamm, "The Making and Destruction of the Golden Calf," in *Comparative Studies in Biblical and Ancient Oriental Literature* (AOAT 204; Neukirchen-Vluyn: Neukirchener Verlag, 1980), 236–40. G. J. Venema, "Why Did Moses Destroy 'The Golden Calf'? Four Readings of Deuteronomy 9:21 and Exodus 32:20," in *The Rediscovery of the Hebrew Bible* (ed. J. Dyk et al.; Maastricht: Shaker, 1999), 39–49, focuses on the sequence of burning before crushing and the theological intention of Deuteronomy. M. A. Zipor, "The Deuteronomic Account of the Golden Calf and Its Reverberation in Other Parts of the Book of Deuteronomy," *ZAW* 108 (1996): 20–33, sees the calf as the central subject, introduced in order to disprove the self-righteous thought advanced in 9:4. H.-C. Schmidt, "Die Erzählung vom Goldenen Kalb: Ex. 32* und das Deuteronomistische Geschichtswerk," in *Rethinking the Foundations: Historiography in the Ancient World and in the Bible* (ed. S. L. McKenzie and T. Römer; BZAW 294; Berlin: de Gruyter, 2000), 235–50, seeks to uncover the interrelationships of all relevant texts.

11. Exodus 32:11–13 reuses this text as Moses' first prayer before he goes down the mountain to confront the calf. The expression "people and hereditary possession" has been identified as an expression characteristic of the exilic reviser of DH (4:20; 1 Kgs 8:51, 53; 2 Kgs 21:14); see Nelson, *Double Redaction*, 68–69.

from the court of world opinion (cf. Num 14:16; Josh 7:7–9; Pss 79:9–10; 115:1–2). Some might think that Yahweh was an ineffective God, whose relationship to the people was a deceitful one of hostility under the guise of promise. Moses appeals to Yahweh's own personal integrity as reflected in relational commitment, saying in effect, "Yahweh, to thine own self be true." In v. 26 Moses counters the alienation of v. 12, where Yahweh had labeled Israel as the people of Moses. No, they are *your* people whom *you* brought out, not mine. Then in v. 27 Moses takes over Yahweh's objectification of the people from v. 13 ("this people"), as though to put the relational ball back into Yahweh's court. The "us" of v. 28 communicates Moses' solidarity with Israel over against the offer Yahweh made in v. 14.

[10:1–5] These verses represent Yahweh's first response to Moses' intercession. The provision of new tablets and the ark indicate that Israel's life as Yahweh's people will go on, even before the fact of clemency is explicitly reported (10:10). This section is held together by a repetitive structure of divine command and Mosaic obedience: "hew out two stone tablets as before" (vv. 1aα and 3aβ), "come up the mountain" (vv. 1aβ and 3bα), "make a wooden ark" (vv. 1b and 3aα), "put them in the ark" (vv. 2b and 5aβ). Other unifying factors include Yahweh's forecast of action and its execution (vv. 2a and 4a) and the move of Moses up the mountain in v. 3 and then down in v. 5.

Deuteronomy depends on the more complex story of Exod 34:1–4, but has added the ark to its source text. Deuteronomy views the ark as a chest for deposits, rather than as a war palladium (1 Sam 11:11), throne (Num 10:35–36), or footstool (Ps 132:7). The ark is demythologized into a container, a record box for national archives (Deut 31:9, 25–26; 1 Kgs 8:9).[12] Yahweh commands only "wood" but Moses follows the tradition of "acacia wood," reflected in Exod 25:10 (P) and many of the tabernacle furnishings. Perhaps "acacia" connotes wood that is hard and durable.

"At that time" (v. 1) attaches this material to what has come before and sets up a comparison with the first set of tablets. Moses stresses the total equivalence of what is written on the new tablets and the words spoken at Horeb (v. 4). Yahweh unambiguously writes these second copies (something less clear in Exod 34:1, 27–28). This not only guarantees the text of the Decalogue as found in Deuteronomy, but also restores Israel to the original situation of 5:22. In addition, parallels between 10:4–5 and 31:9 and 26 legitimate Deuteronomy as a whole by associating its transcription and disposition with that of the

---

12. R. E. Clements, "Deuteronomy and the Jerusalem Cult Tradition," *VT* 15 (1965); 300–312; T. E. Fretheim, "The Ark in Deuteronomy," *CBQ* 30 (1968): 1–14; J.-P. Sonnet, *The Book Within the Book: Writing in Deuteronomy* (Biblical Interpretation Series 14; Leiden: Brill, 1997), 61–66. Documents were kept in temples for safety and to indicate the sponsorship of the deity (cf. 1 Sam 10:25; *ANET*, 205). For the unification of ark and law as a Deuteronomic innovation, see O. Loretz, "Die steinernen Gesetzestafeln in der Lade," *UF* 9 (1977): 159–61.

Decalogue.[13] Verse 5 repeats "I turned back and went down from the mountain" from 9:15 to emphasize that the opposite situation now obtains.

[6–7] Word order foregrounds the Israelites as a new subject, now referred to in the third person rather than the second. That Israel's journey continues means that Yahweh has listened. A proper priestly succession carries on in spite of Aaron's death. These supplementary verses relate to the itinerary of Num 33:30–34 (P) and break into the speech of Moses. Names and sequence differ from what is found in Num 33:31, 37–39. For example, Aaron dies at Mount Hor in Num 33:37–38 rather than at Moserah.

[8–9] Legitimate cult and priesthood continue in spite of the calf incident. The addition of these verses (cf. "at that time") seems to have been occasioned by the catchword "ark" in v. 5. They seem to presuppose knowledge of the loyalty of Levites reported in Exod 32:25–29. Perhaps the reference of the citation formula is the promise of Num 18:20 (P).[14] The tribe of Levi engages in priestly tasks: "to stand . . . to serve" (Deut 17:12; 18:5, 7), "to bless" (21:5). Deuteronomy repeatedly stresses that Levi has no territorial entitlement, but instead enjoys the "hereditary possession" of support from the cult (12:12b; 14:27b, 29; 18:1–2). In the context of Deuteronomy, the ark is the ark "of the covenant" because the tablets of the covenant (9:9, 11) are in it (10:2, 5; 31:9, 25, 26).

[10–11] Verse 10a is a resumptive repetition of 9:18 and 25, but changes the verb to 'āmad, "take one's stand, remain." Because the time and place ("the mountain") of 10:10 equal that of 9:18 and 9:25, one might choose to construe the tense as pluperfect: "I had taken my stand." A grammatical emphasis on "I" resumes the speech of Moses by contrasting him with the Levites of vv. 8–9 and introducing him as a new subject. The root šḥt signals the end of the crisis. The pi'el of this verb had described Israel's sin in 9:12 ("act corruptly"); its hip'il depicted the threat of divine destruction in 9:26 ("destroy"), but now in 10:10 "not willing to destroy" communicates the removal of that threat. Verse 11 demonstrates that Israel's story continues into the future. The narrative problem of rebellion has been solved; Israel's special relationship with Yahweh is still in force. The long digression of 9:7–10:11 is now concluded.

---

13. Note the shared vocabulary of kātab, nātan, śîm, and šām. C. T. Begg, "The Tables (Deut 10) and the Lawbook (Deut 31)," VT 33 (1983): 96–97, takes this as evidence that the author of 9:7–10:11 was DH. Also see G. J. Venema, "YHWH or Moses? A Question of Authorship. Exodus 34:28–Deuteronomy 10:4; 31:9,24," in YHWH—Kyrios—Antitheism or the Power of the Word (ed. K. A. Deurloo and B. J. Diebner; DBAT 14; Amsterdam: Selbstverlag der DBAT, 1996), 69–76.

14. Skweres, Ruckverweise, 188–91.

Incentives for Obedience
10:12–11:32

What Yahweh Requires

10:12 And now, O Israel, what is Yahweh your God asking of you? Only to fear Yahweh your God, to walk in all his ways, to love him and to serve Yahweh your God with all your heart and with all your being, 13 to keep the commandments of Yahweh[a] and his statutes that I am commanding you today for your good. 14 Look, to Yahweh your God belong the heaven and the highest heaven,[b] the earth and everything in it, 15 yet Yahweh desired your ancestors, loving them, and chose you, their descendants after them, out of all the peoples, as is the case today. 16 Circumcise the foreskin of your heart and be stubborn no longer, 17 for Yahweh your God is God of gods and Lord of lords,[c] the great God, mighty and terrible, who does not show partiality[d] and will not take a bribe, 18 doing justice for[e] the orphan and widow and loving the resident alien, giving them food and clothing. 19 You too must love the resident alien, for you were resident aliens in the land of Egypt. 20 You must fear Yahweh your God, serve him, and cling to him, and by his name you must swear. 21 He is your renown[f] and he is your God, who has done these great and terrible things for you[g] that your eyes have seen. 22 Your ancestors went down to Egypt as seventy persons, but now Yahweh your God has made you as numerous as the stars of the sky. 11:1 Love Yahweh your God and always keep his charge—and his statutes[h] and his ordinances and his commandments.[i]

Reasons to Obey

2 Consider today (you rather than your children who do not know and have not seen the discipline of Yahweh your God) his greatness, his mighty hand, and his outstretched arm;[j] 3 his signs and his deeds that he did inside Egypt to Pharaoh king of Egypt and to his whole land; 4 and what he did to the army of Egypt, to its horses and chariots, how he made the water of the Red Sea flood back over them when they were pursuing you, so that Yahweh destroyed them as is still the case today; 5 and what he did to[k] you in the wilderness until you came to this place; 6 and what he did to Dathan and Abiram, sons of Eliab son of Reuben, how the earth opened its mouth and swallowed them[l] and their households and their tents and every living thing in their company,[m] in the midst of all Israel. 7 For your eyes have seen every great deed[n] of Yahweh that he has done.[o]

8 Keep the entire commandment that I am commanding you today, so that you may be strong and go in and take over the land to which you are crossing in order to take it over, 9 so that you may enjoy long life in the land that Yahweh swore to your ancestors to give to themP and their descendants, a land flowing with milk and honey.

10 For the land that you are entering to take over is not like the land of Egypt that you left, where you sow your seed and water it with your foot like a vegetable garden. 11 The land to which you are crossing in order to take it over is a land of hills and valleys. It soaks up rainwater from the sky.q 12 It is a land that Yahweh your God cares about.r The eyes of Yahweh your God are continually on it, from the beginning of the year to the end of the year.

13 If you will carefully obey mys commandments that I am commanding you today—to love Yahweh your God and to serve him with all your heart and with all your being—14 then It will give rain for your land in its season, the autumn rain and the spring rain, and you will gather in your grain, your wine, and your oil; 15 and I will give grass in your field for your livestock, and you will eat and have enough. 16 Be careful about yourselves, lest your heart be naive and you turn away and serve other gods and bow down to them. 17 For then the wrath of Yahweh will break out against you and he will shut up the sky so there will be no rain and the land will not give its produce. Then you will perish quickly from the good land that Yahweh is going to give you.

18 Set these words of mine upon your heart and being and tie them as a sign on your hand and let them be like a pendant between your eyes. 19 Teach them to your children, speaking about them when you are sitting in your house and when you are walking on the road, when you lie down and when you get up. 20 Write them on the doorposts of your house and on your gates, 21 so that your days and the days of your children may be multiplied on the land that Yahweh swore to your ancestors to give them, as long as the heavens are over the earth.

22 If you carefullyu keep this entire commandment that I am commanding you by performing it, loving Yahweh your God, walking in all his ways, and clinging to him, 23 then Yahweh will dispossess all these nations before you, and you will dispossess nations greater and more powerful than you. 24 Every place where the sole of your foot steps will belong to you. From the wilderness and the Lebanon, from the river, the Euphrates River, as far as the Western Sea, will be your territory. 25 No one will be able to withstand you. Yahweh your God will put the fear and terror of you upon the whole land on which you step, just as he promised you.

Blessing and Curse

26 See, I am setting before you a blessing and a curse today: 27 the blessing if[v] you obey the commandments of Yahweh your God that I am
commanding you today, 28 and the curse if you do not obey the commandments of Yahweh your God but turn away from the way that I am
commanding you today to go after other gods that you have not known.

29 When Yahweh your God brings you into the land that you are
entering to take over, you shall set the blessing on Mount Gerizim and
the curse on Mount Ebal. 30 (Are they not[w] on the other side of the Jordan—beyond the road to the west[x] in the land of the Canaanites who
live in the Arabah—opposite Gilgal, beside the oak[y] of Moreh?) 31
When you cross the Jordan to enter to take over the land that Yahweh
your God is giving you and you take it over and live in it,[z] 32 you must
be careful to do all the statutes and ordinances that I am setting before
you today.

a. Follows MT. Sam., 8Q3, 8Q4, 4QPhyl A, 4QPhyl K, OG, Syr. supplement with
"your God" to create the expected formula (cf. 4:2; 6:17; 8:6; 11:27, 28; 28:9, 13).

b. Superlative genitive, *IBHS* 14.5d. Alternate translation taking the *waw* as
emphatic: "heaven, indeed the highest heaven."

c. Probably a superlative genitive: "the highest God and the supreme Lord" (*IBHS*
9.5.3j), implying "the true God and true Lord," the concept of God raised to the highest
power. Otherwise, a genitive of comparative relation: "the God over other gods and Lord
over other lords."

d. Literally "to lift up the face" to show favor (cf. 28:50).

e Follows MT. OG and 4QPhyl K complete the usual formula by adding *gr*, "resident alien," at the start of the list. "Orphan" is literally "fatherless."

f. Literally "your praise." Yahweh is either the source of Israel's pride ("your proud
boast") or the recipient of Israel's glorification ("the object of your praise"; cf. Jer 17:14;
Ps 109:1).

g. Understanding *'t* as a preposition of advantage; cf. Deut 1:30.

h. Follows MT and OG *mšmrtw whqtyw*. Sam. reads *mšmrtw hqtyw*, "his charge, his
statutes," indicating a dittography or haplography of *w*.

i. Follows the sequence of MT for the last two nouns. Sam., OG (=LXX[A]), 4QPhyl
P, 4QMez B, 8Q4 have *wmṣwtyw wmšptyw*, "and his commandments and his ordinances." Identical initial and final consonant pairs facilitated transposition.

j. There are three major variables in translation. (1) This translation construes *'et* before
"children" as an emphatic, contrastive particle (*HALOT* 1:101, 4c): "Consider today—*you*
rather than your children who do not know. . . ." Understanding this *'et* as a direct object
marker or preposition would imply that a verb remains unexpressed: "Consider today—
since [I am not speaking? making a covenant?] with your children who do not know. . . ."
(2) If "discipline" is the direct object of "consider" the translation would be: "Consider
today—you rather than your children who do not know and have not seen—the discipline
of. . . ." This is suggested by the masoretic punctuation. Understanding "discipline" as the

direct object of "see" leads to: "Consider today—you rather than your children who do not know and have not seen the discipline of Yahweh your God—his greatness. . . ." (3) "Your children" at the start of v. 2 may form a contrast with "your eyes" at the beginning of v. 7: "Consider today that it was not your children who knew or saw the discipline, . . . but it was your own eyes that saw . . . " (cf. NJPS). Verses 2b–6 would then constitute a long parenthetical catalog of disciplinary lessons.

k. Alternate translation: "for you."

l Follows MT. Sam., 4QPhyl A, 4QPhyl K supplement from Num 16:32: *w't kl h'dm 'šr lqrh,* "and every person that belonged to Korah."

m. Alternate translation: "who followed them."

n. Follows MT (supported by Sam.) in reading the expression as singular. 4QDeut^j, 4QDeut^k1, 4QPhyl K, 8Q4, OG (= LXX^A), Syr., Vulg. read *m'śy/h . . . hgdlym,* "great deeds" in order to conform with v. 3.

o. Follows MT. 4QPhyl A, 4QPhyl K, 8Q4 supplement with *'tkm(h),* "among you." OG also adds "today."

p. Follows MT (supported by OG, Syr., Vulg.). Sam. "corrects" by eliminating "to them and" because the patriarchs themselves did not receive the land.

q. In other words, it depends entirely on rain. The preposition *l* may indicate "according to the rule (or proportion) of rain" (32:8; *IBHS* 11.2.10d, examples 21–22).

r. Alternate translation: "watches over."

s. Follows MT. OG (=LXX^A) levels to the more expected "all his commandments" (cf. 11:8, 22). Syr. drops the problematic pronominal suffix. The *y* ("my") may represent an abbreviation for the divine name: *mṣwt y[hwh],* "commands of Yahweh." See E. Tov, *Textual Criticism of the Hebrew Bible,* (Minneapolis: Fortress Press, 1992), 256–57.

t. Follows MT, which abruptly shifts the speaker from Moses (v. 13) to Yahweh (cf. 28:20; 29:4 [ET 5]). This difficulty is eliminated by Sam., 8Q4, 8QMez, OG by reading *wntn,* "he will give." These witnesses (and 4QPhyl A) display the same modification in v. 15.

u. Follows MT. Instead of *šmr tšmrwn,* OG reflects the verb *šāma':* "hearing you will hear." This harmonizes with the wording of 11:13 so that 11:13–21 and 22–25 become parallel sections. Sam., OG, Syr. expand with *hywm,* "today," after "I am commanding you," again under the influence of v. 13.

v. Conditional *'ăšer,* Williams, *Hebrew Syntax,* 469, 515; *IBHS* 38.2d.

w. Rhetorical question with the force "as you know"; see 3:11b; *IBHS,* p. 684 n. 48.

x. Understanding that it is the *road* that lies in the land of the Canaanites of the Arabah (i.e., the Jordan plain south of Lake Galilee, Josh 11:2; 12:3; NJPS, REB). An alternate translation would place the two *mountains* in the west and in the Arabah: "some distance to the west" (NRSV, NJB).

y. Follows OG and Syr. in reading the singular *'lwn.* This oak is presumably the tree mentioned in Gen 12:26 and Josh 24:26. MT converts to the plural *'lwny* to avoid any suggestion of an unorthodox sacred tree.

z. Taking *kî* followed by the participle as temporal (cf. 18:19). Alternate translations: "For you are going to cross. . . . When you take it over, . . . you must be careful" (cf. NJPS), or "For you are going to cross. . . . Take it over . . . and be careful" (cf. REB).

Rhetorical Development

The previous exhortation (9:1–6) is taken up again by 10:12–11:25, pushed forward by an extended series of imperatives and supported by a rich variety of motivations. Recurring admonitions accumulate with persistent force: 10:12–13, 16, 19–20, and 11:1, 8, 18–20. Deuteronomy 10:12–13 introduces the imperatival theme with a catalog of responses to an initial rhetorical question. Items from this list are picked up and supplemented in turn by the imperatives of 10:20; 11:1, 13. The reader is repeatedly urged to "love" (10:12; 11:1, 13, 22), "fear" and "serve" (10:12, 20), "walk" (10:12; 11:22), "cling" (10:20; 11:22), and "keep" the law (10:13; 11:1, 8, 22; cf. 11:16). The imperatives of 11:18–20 offer a call for an ongoing internal appropriation of the law in every facet of an individual's life. Covenant patterns and theology dominate 10:12–11:30, suggesting that it represents an ideologically unified assemblage of material.[1]

The language of motivation may be divided into hymnic theology (10:14, 17–18, 21a), lessons from history (10:15, 19b, 21b–22; 11:2–7), and references to the land and its conquest (11:8b–9, 10–12, 14–15, 17, 21, 23–25). The historical motivations fall into a rough chronological order: election of the ancestors (10:15), stay in Egypt (10:19b, 21b–22), plagues, Red Sea and wilderness (11:2–7). Some motivations are attached directly to the imperatives: the divine intent for good (10:13), Israel's ability to conquer (11:8), long life in the land (11:9, 21). Others form longer sections interspersed among the imperatives. The argument focuses on Yahweh's character as evidenced in election and redemption (10:14–15, 21–22), Yahweh's greatness as reflected in a concern for the marginalized (10:17–18), Yahweh's discipline in history (11:2–7), the fertility of the well-watered land (11:9–17), and the effortless conquest (11:22–25). Two of the longer motivational sections, 11:13–17 and 22–25, employ parallel examples of conditional rhetoric: if you obey/keep the commandment, then Yahweh will grant you prosperity and victory in connection with the land.[2]

Beginning with 11:13–17, the theme of blessing and curse begins to dominate, as the text prepares for the upcoming law code of chapters 12–26. The reader is urged to make a stark and simple choice (11:26–28). As Moses' introductory discourse concludes, he once more highlights Deuteronomy's dramatic

---

1. T. Veijola, "Bundestheologie in Dtn 10,12–11,30," in *Liebe und Gebot*, ed. Kratz and Spieckermann, 206–21, assigns this to a late layer that reflects treaty traditions.

2. Lohfink, *Das Hauptgebot*, 219–24, maps out successive statements of the "chief command" followed by motivations: 10:12–13 motivated by 14–15; 10:16 and 17–18; 10:20 and 21–22; 11:1 and 2–7; 11:8–9 and 10–12; 11:13a and 13b–17. The last motivation is the blessing and curse of vv. 26–28. Lohfink isolates 10:12–11:32 from its context by observing that this section lacks the language of the Decalogue (pp. 102–3).

setting as an address to those about to enter the land (11:30–31) and appeals to the audience to obey what is being set before them "today" (11:32).

History of Composition

Irregularities suggest a complex history of composition. The most significant are:

> 10:12–13 seem to reach a conclusion, and thus vv. 14–22 may represent a new start.
>
> The second person plural of 10:15b-19 disrupts the singular address that carries on through 11:1. This could represent a plural addition to an earlier text. By contrast, the frequent shift in chapter 11 between second-person singular (vv. 1, 10, 12, 14b–15, 19b–20) and plural address (vv. 2–9, 11, 13–14a, 16–19a, 21) seems to have nothing to do with literary layers.
>
> 10:19 is a disruptive addition, unique except for a later parallel in Lev 19:34. This command with *waw* perfect does not fit the hymnic style of vv. 17–18 and expands on "loving the resident alien" from v. 18.
>
> 10:22 introduces a tangential topic and may be an addition.
>
> The awkward interchange between first and third person in 11:13–15 suggests careless supplementation.
>
> The exhortation of 11:18–21 separates the conditional blessings and curses of vv. 13–17 from the conditional blessing of vv. 22–25. It may be a derivative variant of 6:6–9.

Deuteronomy 10:12–11:32 is related in structure and vocabulary to 4:1–40, which also starts with *wĕ'attâ*.[3] The last verse (11:32) repeats parts of 10:13 to form an inclusive bracket. There are parallels between 4:1–8 and 10:12–22 (commandments, history, the exclusivity of Yahweh); 4:9–14 and 11:1–7 (historical narrative motivating covenant or law); 4:15–24 and 11:8–17 (warning and land); 4:25–31 and 11:18–25 (future obedience and blessing); and 4:32–40 and 11:26–32 (a general exhortation to obedience). Thus chapter 4 and 10:12–11:32 could be seen as forming a large envelope around the parenesis of chapters 5–10. There are also verbal connections between 11:18–21 and 6:6–9. Accordingly, one could understand 11:18–21 and 6:4–9 as another inclusive bracket.

---

3. For the suggestion of a "second layer" that opens with the "and now" of 10:12 and runs to 11:32, see Mayes, "Deuteronomy 4," 39–40.

Structures

Deuteronomy 10:12–11:32 falls naturally into segments:

10:12–11:1 is dominated by imperatives and bracketed by the themes of love and obedience to the commands (10:12–13 and 11:1).

11:2–7 (+ 8–9) reviews the history of what Yahweh has done, bracketed by "the deeds that he did" (11:3 and 7).

11:10–12 and (13)14–17 are descriptions of the land.

11:13–17 and 22–25 are each introduced by a conditional protasis and focus on the land.

11:18–21 links back to 6:6–9.

Although these sections do not exhibit any definitive overarching structure, chapter 11, taken by itself, reveals an internal thematic coherence in the phrases "the land you are entering/crossing to take over" (vv. 8, 10, 29) and "the land that Yahweh swore" (vv. 9, 21). A threefold repetition of "commandment I am commanding [today]" (11:8, 13, 22) emphasizes the source of Deuteronomic law and Deuteronomy's dramatic situation. In addition, 11:2–9 ties structurally and topically to 11:10–21. Verses 2–9 begin with the new generation of children and trace an educational discipline that ends in the land. Inversely, vv. 10–21 start with the land and conclude with the education of children. The classroom of the past was Egypt and the wilderness; the classroom for the new generation will be life in the land.[4]

Deuteronomy 11:26–32 forms an organized unit bracketed by the formula "I am setting before you today." The three parts of 11:26–32 conclude the parenetic complex of chapters 6–11 and form nesting envelopes around the following law code:

in Moab before the conquest—11:26–28 and chapters 28–29
in the land at Shechem—11:29–30 and chapter 27
"be careful to do statutes and ordinances"—11:31–32 and 26:16

Deuteronomy 11:26–28 (second person plural) unfolds blessings and curses in the same fashion as chapter 28. Deuteronomy 11:29–30 shifts to singular address and presents blessings and curses in the ritual terms of 27:11–13. The detailed geographic concern is jarring and suggests that v. 29 (and v. 30) is a

---

4. Nielsen, *Deuteronomium*, 125–26. Seitz, *Redaktionsgeschichtliche Studien*, 82–87, proposes a covenant format: 11:2–7 as historical prologue, vv. 8–9 as stipulations, vv. 10–12 as the description of the land grant, and vv. 13–17 as blessing and curse. He understands the chapter as Deuteronomistic (secondary to Deuteronomy proper), with vv. 18–21, 26–30 being even later additions.

redactional insertion intended to lay the groundwork for chapter 27. Deuteronomy 11:31–32 (plural address) forms a small concentric structure with 12:1 that concludes the parenesis and sets the scene for the law to follow.

[10:12–11:1] The strong section marker "And now" in 10:12 (cf. 4:1) refers generally to what has gone before and begins a summary list of admonitions. "And now" marks a turn from the historical survey of 9:7–10:11 to its implications for behavior and loyalty. It also effects a transition from Israel's relationship to Yahweh considered in general terms to a concern for Israel's obedience to a concrete law code. An elevated prose style features a sequence of matching phrases in vv. 12, 17, 20 and parallelism in vv. 14, 16, 18. There are alliterated *alephs* in v. 17 (*'elōhê hā'ĕlōhîm wa'ădōnê hā'ădōnîm hā'ēl*) and *beths* in v. 20b (*ûbô tidbāq ûbišmô tiššābēa'*), as well as rhyme in vv. 18a and 18b (*wĕ'almānâ; wĕśimlâ*). At places the language is similar to that of the Psalms (cf. v. 14 with Pss 24:1; 96:11; 97:9; 148:4; v. 17 with Ps 136:2–3; and v. 21 with Ps 22:4, 26 [ET 3, 25]). Verses 14, 17–18 associate Yahweh's divine authority and Yahweh's social concern is a way similar to Ps 146:6–9.

Verses 12–13 propound a basic thesis—Yahweh desires obedience—that is expanded and motivated in the verses that follow. The rhetorical schema of question and response implies that Yahweh's requirements are not complicated or obscure, but clear and simple; there can be no excuse for disobedience. What Yahweh commands is well within Israel's capabilities (cf. 30:11–14). A list of infinitives from earlier in Moses' speech (especially chs. 5 and 6) is taken up as the admonition unfolds: "fear" (5:29; 6:2,13, 24), "walk" (5:33), "love" (6:5), "serve" (6:13) with heart and being (6:5). Yahweh's requirement is further defined as "to keep" the law (cf. 5:29; 6:2, 17). The purpose of law is Israel's well-being. This imperatival catalog is paralleled in 10:20.

Verses 14–16 and 17–19 exhibit a repeated pattern of topically linked verses. Hymnic descriptions of Yahweh's cosmic eminence (vv. 14, 17) and loving, just character (vv. 15, 18) support imperatives based on those same characteristics (vv. 16, 19). Verses 14–16 are theocentric (a cosmic God who loved the ancestors and calls for unhindered obedience), while vv. 17–19 focus more on the human, social world (a God who shows justice and love to the unfortunate and evokes Israel's love for aliens).

Verse 14 begins with an attention-getting particle and uses hymnic language to proclaim Yahweh's role as divine overlord. The "yet" (*raq*) of v. 15 sets forth a contrasting or unexpected point, "in spite of this." The contrast is between Yahweh's greatness and the election of the ancestors, an election based on love and "desire." "In spite of this" and "desire" express Yahweh's sovereign freedom in election (cf. 7:6–8). Israel's election results from the free choice of a universal, cosmic God, not merely preferential treatment by an ethnically restricted god. Yahweh's past act of election also applies to the present audience: "as is now the case."

Verse 16 returns to the problem of Israel's stubbornness (9:6, 13, 27). Perhaps the topic of "circumcision" was triggered by the reference to the ancestors in the previous verse. Metaphorically, "circumcise" implies "cut away the thickening about your hearts" (NJPS) in order to remove impediments or blockages to obedience. "Circumcise your heart" means free yourselves from all hindrances in thought and will and make yourselves open to obedience (cf. Exod 6:12, 30; Jer 6:10). The verses that follow imply that an uncircumcised heart would show itself in unfair partiality and a failure to love the vulnerable. In contrast to this imperative, Deut 30:6 speaks of circumcision of the heart as something that would be done by Yahweh in order to restore Israel.

The initial "for" (*kî*) of v. 17 links back to the previous imperative "circumcise." Hymnic language sets forth the ideology of divine kingship (Pss 24:8, 47:3 [ET 2]; 95:3; 136:2–3). Yahweh is "mighty" in the sense of being a warrior who inspires numinous terror. Yahweh is described here as El, the ruling God and divine warrior (*hā'ēl haggādōl haggibbōr*; cf. 7:21). "Partiality" in association with "bribe" indicates forbidden favoritism toward the rich and powerful. Its opposite is set forth in v. 18 as "justice" for the poor. Thus v. 18 illustrates v. 17, echoing both the social ethics of the law code that follows (16:19; 27:25) and the behavior expected of a human king.[5] Yahweh's own character establishes the emphasis on social justice in Deuteronomy (most directly, 24:17–22). Divine justice and divine love are not opposites. In v. 19 Deuteronomy's ethics move beyond the "do not oppress aliens" of Exod 22:20 [ET 21] or 23:9 to a more radical call to "love" them (cf. Lev 19:18, 34). This is unusual not only because the beneficiaries of this love are non-Israelites, but because elsewhere Deuteronomy commands love for Yahweh, but not for other humans.[6]

Verse 20 picks up "fear" and "serve" from the list of vv. 12–13, then repeats or cites the command of 6:13, adding the idea of *dābaq*, "cling," from the realm of human love (Gen 2:24; 34:3; 1 Kgs 11:2) and loyal attachment to a leader (2 Sam 20:2). To swear in a god's name would be to acknowledge the power and overlordship of that god (Jer 5:7). This admonition would have limited Israel's capacity to participate in international treaties. Verse 21 takes up v. 17; Yahweh is "great and terrible" because of the great and terrible deeds Israel has witnessed. This assertion prepares for the argument of 11:2–7. The affirmation

---

5. For example, the epilog to the Code of Hammurabi, *ANET*, 177–80.

6. This move beyond material support of resident aliens to fraternal acceptance of them suggests a postexilic controversy to J. E. Ramírez Kidd, *Alterity and Identity in Israel* (BZAW 283; Berlin: de Gruyter, 1999), 78–84. On the role of love in Deuteronomy, see L. E. Toombs, "Love and Justice in Deuteronomy: A Third Approach to the Law," *Int* 19 (1965): 399–411; B. Greenberg, "Deuteronomy 1–34. Hear, O Israel: Law and Love in Deuteronomy," in *Preaching Biblical Texts: Expositions by Jewish and Christian Scholars* (ed. F. Holmgren and H. Schaalman; Grand Rapids: Eerdmans, 1995), 149–58.

that Yahweh is Israel's "renown" and Israel's God again reflects hymnic language (Ps 22:4, 26 [ET 3, 25]). The word order of v. 22 emphasizes "seventy persons," a tradition with the patriarchal promise as its background (Gen 46:27; Exod 1:5).

In 11:1 four synonyms for law are piled up together along with "always" in order to summarize the legal contents of Deuteronomy and to express the totality of Yahweh's requirements. "Love" and "keep" link back to the list of 10:12–13.

[11:2–9] Verses 2–7 form a section that is bracketed by "children who have not seen" (v. 2) and "your eyes have seen" (v. 7), along with "deeds that he did" (vv. 3, 7). It is possible to construe vv. 2–7 as one long sentence consisting of the imperative "consider" and an extended list of phrases as grammatical objects describing what is to be considered. There is a persistent rhythm of *ʾăšer ʿāśâ*, "what/that he did" (vv. 3, 4, 5, 6; cf. 10:21). This pattern of listing Yahweh's deeds is similar to that of 8:14b–16. A key word is *mûsār*, "discipline" (v. 2), a concept derived from the sphere of wisdom. The theme of Yahweh as cosmic God (cf. 10:14) emerges from the traditions that are cited: Yahweh controls both the sea that overwhelms (v. 4) and the underworld that swallows up (v. 6). The paired formulas at the ends of vv. 4 and 5 indicate validity up to the time and place of the audience. The formula that concludes v. 4 implies "once and for all" or "with lasting effect" and may reflect an awareness that Egypt has lost its former supremacy. The expression "came to this place" in v. 5 indicates the wilderness period by designating its spatial end point (cf. 1:31; 9:7; 26:9; 29:6 [ET 7]). The description of Dathan and Abiram (v. 6) depends on Num 16:32 (J; thus without Korah, who is P). "In the midst of all Israel" emphasizes that the rest survived in safety and thus could serve as eyewitnesses in v. 7.

Verses 8–9 articulate the purpose of and motivation for this lesson from history, arguing on the basis of a causal relationship between Israel's obedience and the fulfillment of Yahweh's promise (cf. 7:12–13). Obedience is required in order for a successful conquest to take place (cf. 4:1; 6:18–19; 8:1; 16:20; 11:22–23).[7] "Entire commandment" in the singular views the diverse laws of Deuteronomy as a unified expression of divine will (5:31; 6:1, 25; 7:11; 8:1). The formula "milk and honey" (v. 9) leads into (and may have triggered the addition of) the following description of vv. 10–12, which in turn points forward to the conditional paragraph about rain in vv. 13–17.

[11:10–12] Verses 10–12 praise the land from the perspective of its water. It is a land of special divine providence. This description is similar in spirit to 6:10–11 and 8:7–9. These verses confess Yahweh as a God of fertility, but one

7. For the suggestion that this perspective reflects the exilic aspiration of return to the land, see N. Lohfink, "Kerygmata des deuteronomistischen Geschichtswerks," in *Studien zum Deuteronomium II*, 125–42.

who functions as such specifically in the topography, hydrology, and climate of one special land. The central theme is the contrast to Egypt: ease versus hard labor, divine providence versus human effort. The reference to watering by one's feet (v. 10) has provoked much discussion. Possibilities include use of a foot-operated apparatus, digging channels with feet, or carrying water to the fields "on foot."[8] The point is that Egypt has to be artificially irrigated by human effort, something one does in Palestine only with gardens. The hills and valleys of this land generate the movement of water (v. 11; cf. 8:7). Dependence on rain means that the constant attention ("eyes"; cf. Prov 15:3; Amos 9:8) of Yahweh always remains critical (v. 12). Yahweh remains attentive throughout the year; there is no mythic cycle of divine death or absence. This land is open to the providence of Yahweh, but vv. 13–17 point out that this fact also means that it is particularly vulnerable to the effects of disobedience.

[11:13–17] These verses use the land's dependence on rain as a motivation to keep the law, modifying the promise of vv. 10–12 into a conditional blessing and curse.[9] Verse 13 starts the same way as vv. 22–25, recapitulating the topic of obedience from v. 8 (although the plural "commandments" is used in contrast to vv. 8 and 22). There are also echoes of 6:4–5. The "I" of Moses and the "I" of Yahweh fuse as v. 13 moves into vv. 14–15. Whatever the origin of this anomaly, the literary effect is to interlock the words of Moses and those of Yahweh. The autumn ("early") rain starts in October/November; the spring ("late") rain falls in March/April. "Grain, wine, oil" are a formulaic expression for the agricultural products of the land (7:13; 28:51, etc.).

In Deuteronomy, however, satiation (v. 15) usually brings with it the danger of apostasy (6:11–12; 8:10–11, 12–17; 31:20). Moreover, the subject of rain and fertility seems to lead naturally to the topic of "other gods," to whose power these good things might be credited (v. 16). Such apostasy is characterized as gullibility, openness to deception (*pātâ*; cf. Job 31:27; Hos 7:11). Drought and poor yields are the ecological consequences of disobedience (v. 17). Thus this special land does not provide Israel assured security, but rather serves as an open-ended motivation for and challenge to constant obedience.

[11:18–21] Verses 18–20 reiterate the images of 6:6–9. Perhaps this repetition represents a redactional framing of the parenetic chapters by the brackets of 6:6–9 and 11:18–21. What was written by God (5:22; 10:4), taught by Moses (5:31; 6:1), and "put" (*nātan*) into archival storage in the ark (10:2, 5) now is

---

8. L. Eslinger, "Watering Egypt (Deut. xi 10–11)," *VT* 37 (1987): 85–90, proposes that this is a sarcastic slur portraying watering with urine (cf. 2 Kgs 18:27 Qere). G. G. Nichol, "Watering Egypt (Deuteronomy xi 10–11) Again," *VT* 38 (1988): 347–48, agrees and suggests that the image points to the tiny slave plots in Egypt as small as vegetable gardens.

9. For the idea that dependence on rain makes a land vulnerable to divine displeasure, see Herodotus, *Hist.* 2.13 and *ANET*, 257. For blessings and curses with this theme, see 28:12, 23–24, and VTE 63–64, *ANET*, 539.

to be publicly written and taught by Israel itself (11:19–20) and "set" (*nātan*) into the heart (11:18). Verse 18 is an individual admonition, while the admonitions of vv. 19–20 are communal and pedagogic. The educational methodology of v. 19 is that of oral instruction; the parent teaches by reciting aloud. This emphasis on the education of children responds to the challenge presented by the division of generations raised in 11:2 and looks forward to the long life of those same children in the land of promise (v. 21).

[**11:22–25**] Once again, attention turns to the land: its conquest (vv. 22–25), the role blessing and curse will play in it (vv. 26–30), and obedience to the law there (vv. 31–32). The content and rhetoric of vv. 22–25 associate this section with the military orations of 1:29–30; 2:24–25; 3:21–22; 7:17–24; 20:2–4; 31:1–6.[10] Verse 22 begins the way v. 13 does, picking up the imperatives of 10:12 and 20 to initiate a conditional situation. As in vv. 8–9, the reward for current obedience will be a trouble-free conquest of the fullest extent of promised territory. In v. 23 the warlike actions of Yahweh and Israel are coordinated by the use of the same verbal root (*yrš* hip'il and Qal); this same synergy of divine and human action is expressed in v. 25. Verse 24 functions like a transfer deed, describing the territory to be acquired. "The sole of your foot" suggests the practice of walking over land to make a legal claim to it (Gen 13:17; Josh 14:9).[11] The citation formula of v. 25 may refer to the promise of Exod 23:26–31 or Deut 7:19–24. Similar sacral war language is found in 2:25 and Exod 15:15.

[**11:26–30**] The parenetic section constituting chapters 5–11 ends with reference to blessings and curses, just as the upcoming legal section of chapters 12–28 does. Blessings and curses have the rhetorical effect of targeting the decision for obedience directly at the audience. To "set before" indicates that choice is called for (v. 26; cf. 4:8; 30:1, 19). What must be chosen is obedience to Deuteronomy itself as "the commandments of Yahweh" and "the way" (cf. 9:12, 16; 13:6 [ET 5]). "Gods you have not known" (cf. 13:3, 7, 14 [ET 2, 6, 13]; Hos 13:4) are gods not "experienced," who have not "proved themselves."

Verse 29 is singular in a plural context, and its content is discursive. Perhaps the verse is an addition triggered by the mention of blessing and curse in the previous verses. In any case, v. 29 now functions in conjunction with chapter 27 to bracket the law code of chapters 12–26. Blessing and curse are to be fixed upon (*nātan 'al*; cf. Exod 32:29) the two mountains, appropriately

10. Weinfeld, *Deuteronomic School*, 45–51.

11. Three "lines of extent" are drawn out "as far as the Western Sea": (1) from the wilderness (in the south?), (2) [from] the Lebanon, and (3) from the Euphrates. For a different approach, see J. C. de Moor, "Poetic Fragments in Deuteronomy and the Deuteronomistic History," in *Studies in Deuteronomy*, ed. García Martínez et al., 191–93. This geographical description resembles Deut 1:7 and is quoted (with modifications) by Josh 1:3–4 (Nelson, *Joshua*, 33).

directing the blessing toward the south (right) and the curse toward the north (left).[12]

The geographic gloss of v. 30 (perhaps needed by readers from Judah; cf. Judg 21:19) fits with the book's dramatic setting in that the people have not yet entered the land and so require directions. The "road to the west" (note x) is probably the west-east road from the ford at Adam (Josh 3:16) running through the Shechem pass. Alternatively, it may refer to the road running up the west side of the Arabah, that is, in the valley of the Jordan (Josh 11:2; 12:3). The expression 'aḥărê derek could signify that the mountains are "beyond" or "west of" or even "down along" this road.

Things become more puzzling when v. 30b goes on to locate the mountains "opposite" or "over against" Gilgal. Perhaps the author is thinking on a large scale, imagining a lengthy line of travel running from Moab through Gilgal to Shechem. However, this is most likely an attempt to (re)locate Gerizim and Ebal and the ceremony associated with them into the neighborhood of Gilgal. Verse 30b invites a rereading of v. 30a to understand it as situating the *mountains* themselves (rather than the "road to the west") in the Jordan Arabah. This redactional move indicates that Joshua could obey this command immediately, just as soon as Israel set foot across the Jordan (cf. 27:2–3, "on the day you cross").[13] The "oak" (note y) seems to be the oracular tree referred to in Gen 12:6; Josh 24:26; and Judg 9:37.

[**11:31–32**] These second-person plural verses both conclude the parenesis of chapters 6–11 and set the scene for the law code that follows. The introductory *kî* (v. 31) can hardly be construed as causal, but must be taken as "when," stating the time and place for obedience to the Deuteronomic law. The connection between parenesis and law code is made through a chiastic, connecting structure that includes 12:1:

> 11:31: "when you cross the Jordan to enter"
> "to take over"
> "the land that Yahweh is giving you"
> 11:32: "you must be careful to do"
> "all the statutes and ordinances"
> "I am setting before you today"
> 12:1: "these are the statutes and ordinances"

---

12. The possible existence of earlier traditions behind such a Shechem ceremony is a complex and disputed question. For a summary of the theory of competing Shechem and Gilgal traditions, see J. H. Tigay, *Deuteronomy* (JPS Torah Commentary; Philadelphia: Jewish Publication Society, 1996), 486–87.

13. For this tendency, see Nelson, *Joshua*, 116–17; and E. Noort, "The Traditions of Ebal and Gerizim: Theological Positions in the Book of Joshua," in *Deuteronomy and Deuteronomic Literature*, ed. Vervenne and Lust, 161–80.

"you must be careful to do"
"in the land that Yahweh has given you"
"to take over"
"for all the days that you live."[14]

Centralization and Fidelity
12:1–31

Destroy Their Places, Sacrifice at Yahweh's Place

12:1 These are the statutes and ordinances that you must be careful to do in the land that Yahweh the God of your ancestors has given to you[a] to take over, for all the days that you live on the earth. 2 Completely destroy all the places where the nations that you are going to dispossess served their gods, on the high mountains, on the hills, and under every[b] leafy tree. 3 Demolish their altars, smash their pillars, burn their asherah poles with fire, and cut down the idols of their gods, and thus make their name perish from that place.

4 Do not act in that way toward Yahweh your God. 5 Instead you shall seek out the place that Yahweh your God will choose out of all your tribes to put his name there to make it dwell,[c] and go there.[d] 6 Bring there your burnt offerings and your sacrifices, your tithes and your voluntary contributions,[e] your votive gifts, your freewill offerings, and the firstborn of your herds and flocks. 7 And you shall eat there in the presence of Yahweh your God and rejoice in every undertaking of yours, both you and your households, as[f] Yahweh your God has blessed you.

When You Live in the Land

8 Do not do as we are doing here today, each doing what is right according to personal opinion, 9 for you have not yet come into the rest and the hereditary possession that Yahweh your God is giving you. 10 When you cross the Jordan and live in the land that Yahweh your God is causing you to inherit and he gives you rest from your surrounding enemies and you live in safety, 11 then the place that Yahweh your God will choose to make his name dwell[g] will be in existence. To there you shall bring everything that I command you, your burnt offerings and your sacrifices, your tithes

14. Seitz, *Redaktionsgeschichtliche Studien,* 39–40.

and your voluntary contributions,[h] and all your choicest votive gifts that you vow to Yahweh. 12 And you shall rejoice before Yahweh your God, you and your sons and your daughters, and your male and female slaves, and the Levite resident within your towns, because he has no share or hereditary possession along with you.

Only at the Place Yahweh Will Choose

13 Be careful lest you offer your burnt offerings at just any place you see, 14 but [offer them] only at the place that Yahweh will choose in one of your tribes. There you shall offer your burnt offerings and there you shall do everything that I command you. 15 However,[i] whenever you wish you may slaughter and eat as much meat as the blessing of Yahweh your God provides you, within[j] any of your towns. The unclean and the clean[k] may eat of it, as though it were a gazelle or deer. 16 Only do not eat the blood. You shall pour it out on the ground like water. 17 You dare not eat[l] within your towns the tithe of your grain, your wine, or your oil, the firstborn of your herds and your flocks, any of your votive gifts that you vow, your freewill offerings, or your voluntary contributions. 18 Instead, you shall eat them in the presence of Yahweh your God at the place that Yahweh your God will choose, you and your son and your daughter, and your male and female slaves, and the Levite resident within your towns. You shall rejoice in the presence of Yahweh your God in every undertaking of yours. 19 Be careful lest you neglect the Levite as long as you live in your land.

When Yahweh Enlarges Your Territory

20 When Yahweh your God enlarges your territory, just as he promised you, and you say, "I would like to[m] eat meat," because you wish to eat meat, you may eat meat whenever you wish. 21 If the place where Yahweh your God will choose to put his name is too far from you, you may slaughter from your herd or flock that Yahweh has given you, just as I have commanded you, and you may eat within your towns when[n] you wish. 22 Indeed, just as the gazelle or deer[o] is eaten, so you may eat it. The unclean[p] and the clean may eat it together. 23 Only remain firm in not eating the blood, because it is the blood that is the life, and do not eat the life with the meat. 24 Do not eat it. You shall pour it out on the ground like water. 25 Do not eat it, so that it may go well with you and your children after you, because you will be doing what is right in the opinion of Yahweh. 26 However, the holy things that you may have, and your votive gifts, you shall take along when you come to the place that Yahweh will

choose. 27 You shall perform your burnt offerings, both the meat and the blood,[q] on the altar of Yahweh your God. The blood of your sacrifices shall be poured out beside[r] the altar of Yahweh your God, but the meat you may eat. 28 Be careful to obey[s] all the words[t] that I command you,[u] so that it may go well with you and with your children[v] forever, for you will be doing what is good and right in the opinion of Yahweh your God.

Resist the Lure of Alien Religion

29 When Yahweh your God has cut off before you the nations that you are going in to dispossess, and you have dispossessed them and live in their land, 30 be careful lest you be ensnared into following them,[w] after they have been destroyed before you, and lest you inquire about their gods, saying, "How did these nations serve their gods? I too will do the same thing!" 31 Do not act in that way toward Yahweh your God, because they have performed for their gods every[x] act repugnant to Yahweh that he hates. They even[y] used to burn their sons and their daughters with fire for their gods.

a. The perfect tense either implies the certainty of the divine promise or adopts the perspective of later readers.

b. Follows MT and the standard formula (2 Kgs 16:4; Jer 2:20). OG lacks *kl*, "every," possibly considering it an exaggeration.

c. Vocalizing *lšknw* as a pi'el infinitive (GKC 61b) and associating it with the first half of the verse. This difficult phrase combines two standard sanctuary election formulas, one using *śym*, "to put" (v. 21; 14:24), and the other *škn* pi'el, "cause to dwell" (v. 11; 14:23; 16:2, 6, 11; 26:2). The two infinitives in this expression may be the result of a conflated doublet reading. The masoretic punctuation and vocalization as an otherwise unattested noun ("his habitation," perhaps Sir 14:25) represent an exegetical attempt to clarify matters: "to put his name there; his habitation you shall seek" (cf. NJPS). N. Lohfink suggests that this expression can be resolved into "you shall seek the place that Yahweh put his name, and to his dwelling place you shall come" ("Zur deuteronomischen Zentralisationsformel," in *Studien zum Deuteronomium II*, 147–77).

d. The second person singular of MT is abrupt and is leveled to plural by Sam., OG, Syr. Although Vulg. suggests that MT may represent a dittography involving the beginning of v. 6 (*wb't šmh*, "and go there," doubling *whb'tm šmh*, "and bring there"), I have retained MT because Vulg. often paraphrases.

e. Follows MT and Syr.: *trwmt ydkm*, literally "the contributions of your hand" (vv. 11, 17). Sam. lost a *d*: *trwmtykm*, "your contributions." The absence of "your tithes" and "hand" in OG (*BHS* notes b, c) is the result of translating two Hebrew expressions by a single Greek word (Wevers, *Greek Text*, 209–10). The idea seems to be "portion lifted off" with reference to the separation of a part from the whole in order to set it aside. *HALOT* 4:1788–90: "something handed over once and for all."

f. Accusative of specification (cf. 15:14; Williams, *Hebrew Syntax*, 492).

g. Factitive pi'el: "to make the name dwell, to settle the name, to see to it that the name dwells." See E. Jenni, *Das hebräische Pi'el* (Zurich: EVZ Verlag, 1968), 92–93. The meaning of the infinitive here (and in vv. 5, 21) is unclear. It could range from purpose ("in order to") through result ("so that") to a simple gerundive ("in that" or "in so far as").

h. Follows MT. Sam. supplements with an item from v. 6, *wtrmtykm* (as in v. 6 Sam.) *wndbtykm*, "and your contributions and your freewill offerings." OG apparently supports Sam., translating the second expression as at 23:23 (Wevers, *Greek Text*, 213). The decision for the shorter text witnessed by MT remains uncertain, given the possibility of haplography caused by the repeated pronominal suffixes.

i. Restrictive *raq*: "however [only burnt offerings are so limited, but] whenever," *IBHS* 39.3.5c.

j. *IBHS* 11.2.5b.

k. Follows MT. OG spells out that this impurity refers to the people who eat and not to the animals eaten, using its translation of v. 22: "the unclean among you and the clean together." See note p.

l. Prohibition strengthened by *lō'-tûkal* (16:5; 17:15; 22:3).

m. Cohortative seeking permission, *IBHS* 34.5.1a.

n. Follows OG, which lacks *kl*. MT harmonizes with the standard formula of vv. 15, 20; 18:6: "whenever you wish."

o. The subjects of the nip'al verb are marked with *'et*, *IBHS* 23.2.2e.

p. To make clear that this impurity does not refer to the animals eaten, Sam. and OG expand with *bk*, "among you." Cf. OG at 15:22 and 11QTemple 53:7–8.

q. Follows MT. OG omitted *whdm*, "and the blood," because this seemed to contradict the rest of the verse.

r. Alternate translation: "upon the altar." The text follows MT. OG changed the verb to "sprinkle" and altered "beside the altar" to "at the base of the altar" in order to approximate the standard formula of Leviticus (cf. Lev 7:2). See P.-E. Dion, "Early Evidence for the Ritual Significance of the 'Base of the Altar,'" *JBL* 106 (1987): 487–90.

s. Follows MT. Sam. and OG expand with *w'śyt*, "and do it."

t. Follows OG. MT expands with *h'lh*, "*these* words."

u. Follows MT and OG (see Wevers, *Greek Text*, 222). Sam. and Syr. supplement with *hywm*, "today."

v. Follows OG. MT fills out the formula from v. 25 (cf. 4:40) by adding *'hryk*, "after you."

w. Alternate translations of *'aḥărêhem*: "the way they were" or "after their practices."

x. Follows MT. OG lost "every" by haplography triggered by the previous word: *ky* [*kl*].

y. The grammar is emphatic: *kî gam* followed by the direct object in emphatic first position. The absence of *gam* in OG is most likely a strategy of translation.

Centralization As Reform

The centralization of sacrifice is the focal point of Deuteronomy's reform program. The dramatic scene has been set (chs. 1–3), the commandments of Horeb recalled (ch. 5), and the groundwork of exhortation thoroughly laid (chs. 4,

6–11). Now the long-awaited "statutes and ordinances" (5:1; 6:1; 11:32) begin with the core requirement that every sacrifice be brought to a single "place" (vv. 5–6, 11, 13–14, 17–18, 26–27). This order of presentation follows a legal tradition of beginning legal codes with altar laws (Exod 20:24–26 for the Covenant Code, Lev 17:1–9 for the Holiness Code). Although Deuteronomy contains various streams of theology and instruction, the centralization of sacrifice represents the most fundamental of these. It has an effect on many other primary concepts in Deuteronomy, most clearly the joy and inclusivity of the worship assembly, the insistence on correct worship as essential for exclusive loyalty to Yahweh, and the desacralization of substantial portions of life. Many of the regulations that follow represent modifications of law and custom made necessary by centralization or devised to promote it: the laws about tithes and firstborn animals (14:22–29; 15:19–23; 26:1–15), jurisprudence (17:8–13), the festal calendar (16:1–17), priesthood (18:1–8), cities of asylum (19:1–13), and the prescriptions of 16:21 and 31:11. More generally, the impulse to centralize national life limited the legal powers of fathers, husbands, and local elders, while modifying the situation of women.

Deuteronomy's program of centralization combines a characteristically utopian flavor with pragmatic considerations. Deuteronomy urges centralization on its readers as a radical cure for religious apostasy. Yet it also depicts central sacrifice as an occasion for solidarity with one's household and the marginalized of society. One of the economic and social purposes of sacrifice was to make animal protein available to the population as a whole. Centralization meant that the important food distribution system of local sacrifice had to be replaced. Thus Deuteronomy not only permits local, nonsacral slaughter, but also emphasizes the collective joy of the sacrificial feast, a meal that includes women, slaves, and Levites (vv. 12, 18–19).

The motivations offered to the reader are typical of Deuteronomy: Yahweh's blessing, the security of the land, and general welfare (vv. 7, 9–10, 25, 28). Also typical is the author's limited concern for the details of ritual practice. What is important is not technical precision, but rather the joy of Yahweh's assembled people (vv. 7, 12, 18). Deuteronomy thus addresses this law to the citizenry, not to the priests, and seeks to describe its effects on practical concerns and daily life: What offerings must I bring? How may we eat meat in our home communities? In fact, the text's impact is more rhetorical than legal. Its legal format is neither apodictic nor casuistic in the strict sense, but a sort of blurred "apodictic style" (vv. 4, 8, 16, 24, 25), supplemented by the distinctively Deuteronomic "if-you" casuistic form (vv. 20, 21).

Deuteronomy promotes centralization in order to safeguard the exclusive "Yahweh alone" worship demanded by the first commandment. It implicitly views multiple worship sites as an inherently pagan or polytheistic practice. Centralization was a radical, potentially unpopular program, advocating an astonishing desacralization of the landscape and the rejection of venerable traditions. From what we know of the premises of sacrifice, the demand for centralization seems puzzling. Why would the earthly "launch point" of sacrifice to a God located in heaven matter? Yet Deuteronomy does not really justify its radical demand, and ultimately Yahweh's choice is simply a fait accompli. Even the apparently oldest part of this chapter (vv. 13–19) simply presumes Yahweh's election of an exclusive place and deals only with ensuing matters of practice.

The Roots of Centralization

The historical origins of centralization remain obscure. Some seek its foundation in the eighth-century prophets. Hosea and Amos witness to apostasy practiced at local holy places (Hos 4:12–15; Amos 2:8). Hosea 8:11–14 disparages the multiplication of shrines and their associated sacrificial meals. Yet this prophetic criticism never went so far as to advocate closing ancient shrines. It may be that centralization sought to combat popular notions of multiple "Yahwehs" associated with individual shrines. People spoke of the God of Dan and the deities of Samaria and Beer-sheba (Amos 8:14), as well as of the Yahweh of Teman and the Yahweh of Samaria (Kuntillet 'Ajrud inscription).[1] Hosea's references to multiple "baals" and the "names of the baals" (2:15, 19 [ET 13, 17]) may reflect a conceptual differentiation between divine manifestations worshiped at different places, such as Baal of Peor (Num 25:3), Baal of Hermon (Judg 3:3), Baal-tamar (Judg 20:33), Baal of Perazim (2 Sam 5:20), or Baal-berith at Shechem (Judg 8:33). Admittedly, however, Deuteronomy itself makes no explicit connection between its demand for centralized sacrifice and the concept of Yahweh's unity or singularity, so famously set forth in 6:4.

The book of Kings associates centralization with royal power and the policies of Hezekiah and Josiah.[2] As royal policy it may be seen as a strategy for control and supervision and as a plan favorable to the economic and political interests of the king, the royal court, and priests of the central sanctuary. Consolidating sacrifices at one place would seem to be a functional parallel to gathering taxes into a central treasury. The concept of tithe encompassed a royal tax as well as cultic duty (1 Sam 8:15, 17). Centralization thus extended typical

1. P. K. McCarter, "The Religion of the Israelite Monarchy," in *Ancient Israelite Religion* (ed. P. D. Miller et al.; Philadelphia: Fortress Press, 1987), 139–42.

2. For a defense of the historicity of 2 Kgs 22–23, see N. Lohfink, "The Cult Reform of Josiah of Judah: 2 Kings 22–23 as a Source for the History of Religion," in *Ancient Israelite Religion*, ed. Miller, 459–76; idem, "Recent Discussion on 2 Kings 22–23: The State of the Question," in *Song of Power*, ed. Christensen, 36–61; trans. of "Zur neuren Diskussion über 2 Kön 22–23," in *Studien zum Deuteronomium II*, 179–207.

royal patterns of central supervision and resource concentration into the cultic sphere.[3]

Centralization could have developed as a deliberate increase of the inherent prestige and governmental supervision of a nationally significant royal sanctuary like Bethel ("a royal sanctuary and a temple of the kingdom," Amos 7:13) or Jerusalem. The authorities could more easily monitor ritual behavior and public expressions of religious opinion (cf. Amos and Jeremiah) at a single location. The idea that Yahweh had chosen a single sanctuary may rest on the tradition of Davidic election, widening Yahweh's exclusive choice of a certain royal family into a choice of the cult site under its control. Both the Ark Story (1 Sam 4–6; 2 Sam 6) and 2 Sam 24 witness to an old ideological connection between Yahweh's choice of the Davidic kingship and that of a sacred place. The concept of a sequence of chosen sanctuaries is present in the Ark Story and in the tradition behind Jeremiah's "Shiloh to Jerusalem" schema (Jer 7:12). The verb "choose" (*bāḥar*) plays a significant role in the ideology of Yahweh's relationship to Jerusalem (Pss 78:60, 67–71; 132:13).

In spite of sporadic scholarly protestations to the contrary, the only natural way to read Deut 12 is that Yahweh has chosen only one, single, exclusive place of sacrifice. The verb *bāḥar* entails the selection of one possibility among many, as in the case of the exclusive election of Israel or Levi by Yahweh or of a king by the people (7:6–7; 17:15; 18:5).

The most likely place to seek the historical roots of centralization is the reign of Hezekiah. An economic and ideological strengthening of Jerusalem would have helped him achieve the national unification needed to meet the Assyrian threat. Centralization would have also served the cause of national unification by undermining the prestige of Bethel, which apparently continued as an active shrine after the fall of the northern kingdom (2 Kgs 17:27–28; 23:15–16). The devastation of Sennacherib's invasion must have ruined many local sanctuaries, while the consequent loss of Judahite territory to the west would have cut off others. As a result, there would have been a natural increase in religious traffic to Jerusalem, as sacrifices formerly taken to alienated or discredited shrines were offered there instead. Perhaps the territorial shrinkage of Judah under Hezekiah also meant that the former tax system was no longer adequate and needed to be supplemented by temple revenue sources. On the other hand, a smaller Judah could more easily bear the logistical burdens that centralization would bring. Moreover, the circumstance that Jerusalem had been spared a suc-

---

3. W. E. Clayburn, "The Fiscal Basis of Josiah's Reform," *JBL* 92 (1973): 11–22; M. Weinfeld, "Cult Centralisation in Israel in the Light of a Neo-Babylonian Analogy," *JNES* 23 (1964): 202–12; N. Steinberg, "The Deuteronomic Law Code and the Politics of State Centralization," in *The Bible and Liberation: Political and Social Hermeneutics* (ed. N. Gottwald and R. Horsley; Maryknoll, N.Y.: Orbis, 1993), 365–75. Royal taxation practices are reflected in Solomon's district system (1 Kgs 4:7–19) and that of Judah (Josh 15:20–62; 18:21–28).

cessful Assyrian assault would have enhanced its prestige and revitalized traditional notions of divine choice, helping to extend the concept of election of king and people to that of a sacred place.[4]

However, we cannot simply equate centralization with Zion theology or the self-interested policies of Judah's kings. Deuteronomy cites no mythic connections of the central "place" to king or city. Rather, centralization springs from a characteristically Deuteronomic theological perspective. What is significant for Deuteronomy is the people's assembly "before Yahweh," not a building to localize Yahweh's presence. There is no mention of the ark, any temple building, or indeed the "high places" so important to the book of Kings. The chosen "place" is described in terms of human actions rather than defined by the numinous holiness of sacred space, and sacrifice there is concerned more with bringing and eating than in transferring what is offered into the sphere of God's ownership.[5]

Thus centralization was not simply a royal or priestly power grab. In its present form, at least, Deuteronomy insists on a corresponding weakening of the royal center, expressed in the law of king (17:14–20) and the restoration of the nonmonarchic (or premonarchic?) practice of sacral war (20:1–20; 23:10–15 [ET 9–14]; 24:5). Although centralization in worship is matched by a concentration of jurisprudence in a central court (17:8–13) and a reduction in the legal authority of the extended family, local elders and parents continue to play an important legal role in the Deuteronomic law code. Certain proceedings with important economic consequences remain dispersed, notably the storage and distribution of the tithe of the third year for the poor (14:28–29; 26:12–15) and the practice of domestic butchering. In Deuteronomy priests lose many benefits from tithes and the offering of firstfruits and many of their traditional sacrificial portions. Nonsacral slaughter must have radically reduced the total number of sacrifices, so that worshipers would now bring sacrifices only at special times and for special reasons.

Moreover, Deuteronomy does not present centralization as a strategy for royal political control, but as a way to eliminate apostasy. At least part of the motivating context is a need to control disloyal religious behavior in cities outside the central place (13:13–19 [ET 12–18]). Deuteronomy explicitly advocates centralization as a way of disrupting popular but problematic religious

---

4. For the alternative view that centralization resulted from exilic realities, making a "virtue out of a necessity," see R. E. Clements, "Law of Centralisation and the Catastrophe of 587 B.C.E.," in *After the Exile: Essays in Honour of Rex Mason* (ed. J. Barton and D. Reimer; Macon, Ga.: Mercer University Press, 1996), 5–25. His thesis is that, in light of a loss of Davidic prestige, ark, and temple, centralization sought to avoid the transfer of loyalty to some other, unscathed place of sacrifice.

5. On the "logic of sacrifice," see R. D. Nelson, *Raising Up a Faithful Priest: Community and Priesthood in Biblical Theology* (Louisville, Ky.: Westminster John Knox, 1993), 55–82.

practices (12:2–4, 29–31), making supervision by an orthodox, central authority possible. This may have been a power play, but it was a theological power play, intended to eliminate religious behaviors viewed as unorthodox.[6]

Structures

Chapter 12 is integrated with what precedes and follows through the chiastic structure of 11:31–12:1 (see the commentary on ch. 11) and by a bridging structure in 12:30–13:1 [ET 12:32]. A more extensive link, framing the whole of chapters 12–26, is created by the repetition of "statutes and ordinances . . . be careful . . . do" in both 12:1 and 26:16. Chapters 12 and 26 bracket the rest of the law code with a focus on bringing offerings to the central place. Internal structuring elements create links between vv. 1 and 28 ("be careful"), between vv. 8 and 25, 28 (literally "doing what is right in his / Yahweh's eyes"), and between vv. 13, 19 and 30: "be careful lest you. . . ."

Verses 2–4 and 29–31 frame chapter 12 with a concern for the religious installations and practices of the dispossessed nations. "When Yahweh your God enlarges" (v. 20) links to "when Yahweh your God has cut off" (v. 29). These correspondences point to a rough chiastic pattern that holds together the final form of the text:

> vv. 2–7—polemic purification
>> vv. 8–12—temporal conditions for centralization
>>> vv. 13–19—centralization and secular slaughter
>> vv. 20–28—geographic conditions for secular slaughter
> vv. 29–31—polemic purification[7]

Rhetorical Flow

As is typical of Deuteronomy, this chapter is both composite in origin and cohesive in its final form. The redundancy of the chapter and its shift from second-person plural (vv. 2–12) to singular language (vv. 13–31) witness to a complex history of composition, although there is no consensus on historical-critical issues.[8] Most scholars identify vv. 13–19 (second person singular) as the oldest block of material, with the occurrence of plural address suggesting that vv.

6. See E. W. Nicholson, "The Centralisation of the Cult in Deuteronomy," *VT* 13 (1963): 380–89; Weinfeld, *Deuteronomic School*, 210–24; idem, "The Emergence of the Deuteronomic Movement," in *Das Deuteronomium*, ed. Lohfink, 85–86.

7. Adapted from Braulik, *Die deuteronomischen Gesetze*, 23–30.

8. Studies include B. Halpern, "The Centralization Formula in Deuteronomy," *VT* 31 (1981): 20–38; B. M. Levinson, *Deuteronomy and the Hermeneutics of Legal Innovation* (New York: Oxford University Press, 1997), 23–50; N. Lohfink, "Zur deuteronomischen Zentralisationsformel,"

2–12 were added later. The chapter's redundancy, however, also functions successfully as an emphatic and didactic tool. Repetition accentuates importance, embraces a wide range of possibilities, and fixes these instructions in readers' minds.

Contrast drives the rhetoric: *not* as the nations (v. 4), *not* as today (v. 8), *not* in every place (v. 13), *not* in your towns (v. 17), *not* like nonsacral slaughter (v. 26). In addition, a rhetoric of lists itemizes sacrifices and participants (vv. 6–7, 11–12, 17–18). The center of gravity is the repeated formulaic assertion of Yahweh's selection of the "place" (vv. 5, 11, 14, 18, 26), and out of this flow descriptions of the anticipated human responses to Yahweh's choice: "destroy," "bring," "eat," "rejoice," and so on.

Chapter 12 is artfully structured as four repetitive sections. Three of these (vv. 2–7, 8–12, and 13–19) follow an identical outline:

> prohibition (vv. 4, 8–9, 13)
> requirement for centralization (vv. 5–6, 10–11, 14)
> summons to eat and rejoice (vv. 7, 12, 18)

In addition, the elements of vv. 13–19 that give permission for nonsacral slaughter are duplicated by vv. 20–28:

> permission—vv. 15 and 20–22
> prohibition—vv. 16–17 and 23–25
> directive—vv. 18 and 26–27
> persuasion—vv. 19 and 28

These four sections unfold in a logical order: where to sacrifice (vv. 2–7), when to centralize (vv. 8–12), necessary changes in former practice (vv. 13–19), and finally limits on the new practice (vv. 20–28). Verses 2–7 (second person plural) operate in the context of cultural limits and alien sanctuaries.

---

in *Studien zum Deuteronomium II*, 357–85; E. Reuter, *Kultzentralisation: Entstehung und Theologie von Dtn 12* (BBB 87; Frankfurt: Anton Hain, 1993); A. Rofé, "The Strata of the Law about the Centralization of Worship in Deuteronomy and the History of the Deuteronomic Movement," in *Congress Volume: Uppsala 1971* (ed. H. Nyberg et al.; VTSup 21; Leiden: Brill, 1972), 221–26; Y. Suzuki, "'The Place Which Yahweh Your God Will Choose' in Deuteronomy," in *Problems in Biblical Theology: Essays in Honor of Rolf Knierim* (ed. H. Sun and K. Eades; Grand Rapids: Eerdmans, 1997), 338–52; H. Weippert, "'Der Ort, den Jhwh erwählen wird, um dort seinen Namen wohnen zu lassen': Die Geschichte einer alttestamentlichen Formel," *BZ* 24 (1980): 76–94. For arguments that vv. 13–19 are the oldest material, see R. P. Merendino, *Das deuteronomischer Gesetz: Eine literarkritische, gattungs- und überlieferungsgeschichtliche Untersuchung zu Dt 12–26* (BBB 31; Bonn: Hanstein, 1969), 12–60; M. Rose, *Der Ausschliesslichkeitsanspruch Jahwes: Deuteronomische Schultheologie und die Volksfrömmigkeit in der spätern Königszeit* (BWANT 106; Stuttgart: Kohlhammer, 1975), 59–76.

Verses 8–12 (also second person plural) are governed by the "before and after" pattern of entry into the land of rest. Verses 13–19 (second person singular) contrast mere human perception of sacred places with divine choice and explore the practical considerations of nonsacral slaughter. Verses 20–28 go on to regulate this slaughter. In addition to their common overall structure, these four sections share a great deal of vocabulary and ideology.

The Centralization Formula

The chapter encompasses several variations on the centralization formula ("the place that Yahweh will choose"; vv. 5, 11, 14, 18, 21, 26). This formula appears in several formats in Deuteronomy:

> the short form without any further elaboration (vv. 18, 26; 14:25; 15:20; 16:7, 15, 16; 17:8, 10; 18:6; 31:11)
> with "out of all your tribes" (v. 5) or "in one of your tribes" (v. 14)
> with "to put his name there" (vv. 5, 21; 14:24)
> with "to make his name dwell there" (vv. 5, 11; 14:23; 16:2, 6, 11; 26:2)

Thus v. 5 represents a composite, inclusive formula that pulls together all of the longer forms. Designations of offerings range from the simple "burnt offerings" of vv. 13–14 to more elaborate lists in vv. 6, 11, 17, and 26–27. The cumulative effect of these different lists communicates that every conceivable sort of offering is to be included.

The longer centralization formulas emphasize Yahweh's name (vv. 5, 11, 21; 14:23, 24; 16:2, 6, 11; 26:2). However, one should not read into those expressions any notion of an abstract "name theology" that insists that only Yahweh's name, and not Yahweh's actual presence, resides in the temple.[9] On the basis of the centralization formula itself, the personal dwelling of Yahweh at the holy place can neither be asserted nor excluded. "To make his name dwell" (*šākan*) and "to put his name" (*śîm*) are equivalent expressions and do not imply anything about Yahweh's presence or absence at the place where the name has been

---

9. For example, G. von Rad, *Studies in Deuteronomy* (trans. D. Stalker; SBT 1/9; Chicago: Henry Regnery, 1953), 37–44; R. E. Clements, "Deuteronomy and the Jerusalem Cult Tradition," *VT* 15 (1965): 300–12; Weinfeld, *Deuteronomic School*, 191–209. This misunderstanding is strongly criticized by Ian Wilson, *Out of the Midst of Fire: Divine Presence in Deuteronomy* (SBLDS 151; Atlanta: Scholars Press, 1995), who finds that interest in Yahweh's earthly presence is actually heightened in Deuteronomy. In contrast to Deuteronomy, DH does use the placement of Yahweh's name to insist that Yahweh cannot be localized in the temple (1 Kgs 8:29–30). Also see A. S. van der Woude, "Gibt es eine Theologie des Jahwe-Namens in Deuteronomium?" in D. Barthélemy et al., *Übersetzung und Deutung* (Nijkerk: Callenbach, 1977), 204–9.

situated. Indeed, any concept of Yahweh's "real absence" seems to be excluded by Deuteronomy's repeated references to the performance of sacral acts "before Yahweh," that is, in Yahweh's presence (e.g., vv. 7, 12, 18). It is significant that the formula using the verb *šākan* ("make his name dwell") dominates the festival calendar (16:2, 6, 11), which concludes with the call for appearance "before Yahweh" (16:16). This same connection appears in 14:23 and 26:2, 5.

The concept of "putting one's name on" or "making one's name dwell" reflects the practice of kings immortalizing their names on memorials and monuments in order to demonstrate possession and sovereignty (cf. 2 Sam 12:28).[10] The centralization formulas thus assert that the election of the central place is a matter of extrinsic divine choice, not the result of some "natural" holiness implicit in the site itself or based on older cult traditions. The name of the chosen place does not even have to be mentioned, for it is only Yahweh's name that is important. Hence Yahweh's name distinguishes the central sanctuary as the place with which Yahweh has chosen to identify. It is not a symbol of divine transcendence but an expression of decisive choice. The basic concern of these formulas is to affirm Yahweh's real and effective connection to the central sanctuary.

Perspectives on Centralization

This chapter expresses three different perspectives on centralization (vv. 2–7 plus 29–31, vv. 8–12, and vv. 13–14) associated with two perspectives on non-sacral slaughter (vv. 15–19 and 20–28). Verses 13–19 encompass both these topics and manifestly represent the original text on which the other perspectives of the chapter offer comment. Verses 8–12 emphasize the difference in appropriate behavior before and after settlement in the land. Verses 2–7 and 29–31 explore centralization in terms of the avoidance and elimination of alien religion. Verses 20–27 regulate the practice of secular slaughter permitted by vv. 15–16 and contrast bona fide sacrifice to that procedure.

The perspective of vv. 13–19 contrasts a merely human perception of sacred places with divine choice and explores some practical considerations of nonsacral slaughter. This is not simply a centralization law; rather it deals with the consequences of Yahweh's choice of one place. The basic structure contrasts what is to be done at the sanctuary (vv. 13–14 and 18–19) with what

---

10. R. de Vaux, "Le lieu que Yahvé a choisi pour y établir son nom," in *Das ferne und nahe Wort* (ed. F. Maass; BZAW 105; Berlin: Töpelmann, 1967), 219–28. An Amarna letter is often quoted in this regard: "has set his name in the land of Jerusalem forever" (287: 60–61, *ANET*, 488; cf. 288: 5–6). Perhaps a proclamation of the divine name by Yahweh over the cult site is implied, as suggested by Akkadian parallels (A. S. van der Woude, "*šēm*," *Theological Lexicon of the Old Testament* [ed. E. Jenni and C. Westermann; trans. M. Biddle; 3 vols.; Peabody, Mass.: Hendrickson, 1997], 3:1361).

is permitted and forbidden locally (vv. 15–17). A chiastic arrangement seems
to be present:

> v. 13 "be careful lest"
>> v. 14 "but only—(*kî 'im*) at the place . . . you shall offer"
>>> v. 15 "slaughter and eat within your towns"
>>>> v. 16 "do not eat the blood"
>>> v. 17 "you dare not eat within your towns"
>> v. 18 "instead (*kî 'im*) . . . you shall eat . . . at the place"
> v. 19 "be careful lest"[11]

Verses 13–14 reformulate the older altar law of the Covenant Code, Exod
20:24–26. This redrafted law takes over some of the content of the older text
(Yahweh's selection of places for sacrifice and burnt offerings), but v. 13 is a
direct contradiction of the Covenant Code's authorization to sacrifice "in every
place" (*bĕkol-hammāqôm*).

The point of view of vv. 13–19 has two central themes: first the careful distinction of appropriate place ("at the place" over against "within your towns"),
and second, the joyful sharing of Yahweh's material blessings. Ritual concerns
remain in the background or are present only in service of these two central
themes. For example, there is no interest in distinguishing various types of sacrifice. At first, the text mentions only burnt offerings (vv. 13–14, in contrast to
vv. 6, 11, and 27). Because "burnt offerings" are not eaten, they introduce by
contrast the following meals of nonsacral slaughter (v. 15a). Ritual cleanness is
treated as immaterial so that a large social circle can share in Yahweh's blessing by eating this meat (v. 15b). Blood is treated with the respect it deserves,
but is not utilized ritually or connected with the altar (v. 16, in contrast to v. 27).
This powerful blood is simply disposed of in a nonsacral manner, dumped out
like ritually neutral water. The offhand use of the verb *zābah* (meaning both
"sacrifice" and "butcher") for this nonsacral slaughter (v. 15; also v. 21) again
shows a lack of cultic perspective and precision. This nonchalant usage would
seem to be open to misunderstanding in that the corresponding noun is used in
reference to bona fide sacrifice in vv. 6, 11, 27. In fact, it is only with v. 15b that
the reader understands that v. 15 is not contrasting the burnt offerings of vv.
13–14 with sacrificial slaughter (*zābah,* verb) leading to a sacrificial meal
(*zebah,* noun). The highly generalized "everything I command" (v. 14) again
shows no interest in ritual details. Contrast v. 11, where this phrase leads into a
list of sacrifice types.

The first theme of vv. 13–18 is the clear distinction between centralized
offerings and local meals outside the ritual frame. The verb *zābah* is converted

11. Adapted from Seitz, *Redaktionsgeschitliche Studien,* 211.

from "kill for sacrifice" (as in Exod 20:24) into "slaughter" and the resulting meat is changed from sacrifice to ordinary food. Because game animals are not part of the sacrificial system, they can provide the template for this novel practice. The expression "eat meat" robs the event of its sacral character, as does the unimportance of cleanliness (cf. 15:22). Perhaps Deuteronomy already knew of nonsacrificial banquets as a social practice and was not concocting something completely new. Householders may have supervised nonpriestly sacrifices performed without altars, something that was probably the case with the pre-Deuteronomic Passover meal.[12]

Emphasis on the chosen place remains relatively low-key in vv. 13–19. *Māqôm* is used indiscriminately for "holy place," whether illegitimate (v. 13) or divinely chosen (v. 14). "Any place you *see*" (v. 13) seems to polemicize against the idea that a place becomes holy because a deity appears there (to Jacob at Bethel, Gen. 28:13, 16; to David at Araunah's threshing floor, 2 Sam 24:16–17). The restrictive expression "in one of your tribes" (v. 14) is added to the most common and nonspecific form of the centralization formula in order to draw a sharp contrast with "any place" in the previous verse.

The second major theme is the enjoyment of Yahweh's benefits, whether within or outside the ritual frame.[13] To "rejoice" (v. 18) at a sacrificial banquet was not a new thought, but something basic to the sharing of sacrificial food. Hannah's sadness at a sacrificial banquet is something unexpected, and joy is an element in Absalom's sheep shearing (1 Sam 1:7–8; 2 Sam 13:28). The voluntary freedom of "whenever you wish" (v. 15) contrasts with the "command" of v. 14, and is more generalized and open-ended than the temporally limited v. 20 ("when Yahweh . . . enlarges"). The list of sacrifices in v. 17 is not intended to provide a liturgically complete catalog, but rather explores various manifestations of "the blessing of Yahweh" introduced in v. 15. The language of "grain, wine, oil, herds, flocks" is indicative of Yahweh's blessings (7:13; 11:14–15; 14:23; 28:51). These good things from Yahweh are for the benefit of the people as a whole and are to be brought to the chosen place. Verse 18 (cf. v. 12; contrast the simple "household" of v. 7) lists those who participate in the joyous

---

12. H. Seebass, "Vorschlag zur Vereinfachung literarischer Analysen im dtn Gesetz," *BN* 58 (1991): 83–98, suggests that profane slaughter was an older, formerly acceptable practice in sacral war when a proper altar was not available (cf. 1 Sam 14:32–35).

13. "Rejoice" occurs in seven centralization laws (12:7, 12, 18; 14:26; 16:11, 14; 26:11). On this theme see G. Braulik, "The Joy of the Feast: The Conception of the Cult in Deuteronomy, the Oldest Biblical Festival Theory," in *Theology of Deuteronomy*, 27–65; trans. of "Die Freude des Festes: Das Kultverständnis des Deuteronomium—die älteste biblische Festtheorie," in *Studien zur Theologie des Deuteronomiums*, 161–218. He points out that this emphasis on joy would have counteracted the attractions of popular religion. Also T. M. Willis, "'Eat and Rejoice Before the Lord': The Optimism of Worship in the Deuteronomic Code," in *Worship and the Hebrew Bible* (ed. M. P. Graham et al.; JSOTSup 284; Sheffield: Sheffield Academic Press, 1999), 276–94.

banquet, including the socially explosive category of slaves. This list is reminiscent of the Sabbath commandment (5:14) and is repeated later in 16:11, 14. Scholars have supposed that the "you" in v. 18 must include the participation of wives, a conclusion based on common sense and 1 Sam 1.

The *perspective of vv. 8–12* is temporal, concentrating on the times before and after entry into the land of rest. This section focuses on salvation history. The contrast is between "then" (vv. 8–9) and "now" (vv. 10–11), namely between the unstructured practices of the Mosaic period and the later practice of sacrifice exclusively at the chosen sanctuary. When there was no "rest" or "hereditary possession" (v. 9) west of the Jordan, things were done that would be inappropriate once Israel entered the land. The human sight involved in mere personal preference (literally "in the eyes of," v. 8) seems to comment on and intensify the criticism of choice based on what one sees found in v. 13.

In the dramatic setting of Deuteronomy, rest from enemies has not yet been won, but lies in the near future (3:20). However, there may be ambiguity about what time period is meant in v. 9. DH (2 Sam 7:1, 11; 1 Kgs 8:56) conceives of rest as first occurring in the time of David and Solomon and connects it to the erection of the Jerusalem temple. According to DH, the requirement of centralization took effect only in the early monarchy (cf. 1 Kgs 3:2). Some scholars suggest that Deuteronomy refers in v. 9 to rest in the period of Solomon in order to indicate that centralization would not be obligatory until then.[14] However, v. 10 explicitly associates rest with entry into and ownership of the "hereditary possession," namely the land west of the Jordan, and with security from enemies. Thus "rest" alludes to the success of the conquest (Josh 21:43–45), in harmony with the most natural understanding of Deut 25:19. Centralization was to be in effect *whenever* Israel lived in the land. Of course, this is a matter of generalized theology that ignores historical reality. Nevertheless, knowledge that the temple came only later would directly affect how a reader would understand these verses. Territorial growth under the monarchy seems to lie behind the issues of expansion and distance addressed in vv. 20–28.

Verse 11 uses a long form of the centralization formula, one that includes an infinitive of *škn* pi'el with Yahweh's name as its object. Jeremiah 7:12 uses this particular formula for Shiloh in order to say that Yahweh was once as fully engaged with Shiloh as Yahweh now is with Jerusalem. Verse 12 emphasizes that centralized worship is to be socially inclusive and beneficial to all. In contrast to the mere "households" of v. 7, v. 12 parallels v. 18 in specifying a more expansive list. Proper support for the Levites also receives special emphasis (v. 12; cf. v. 19).

14. G. Braulik, "Some Remarks on the Deuteronomistic Conception of Freedom and Peace," in *Theology of Deuteronomy*, 87–98; trans. of "Zur deuteronomistischen Konzeption von Freiheit und Frieden," in *Studien zur Theologie des Deuteronomiums*, 219–30.

The *perspective of vv. 2–7 and 29–31* commands the demolition of other worship sites, adding this requirement to that of central sacrifice. These verses surround the centralization law with a concern for the religious behavior of the dispossessed nations, how they "served their gods" (vv. 2–4 and 29–31). There also is a bracketing inversion between "be careful to do" + examples of pagan worship + "do not act in that way toward Yahweh" (vv. 1–2, 4) and "do not act in that way toward Yahweh" + example of pagan worship + "be careful to do" (12:31; 13:1 [ET 12:32]). A quasi-chiastic repetition of language also structures these framing verses:

> be careful to do—v. 1; 13:1 [ET 12:32]
> nations that you dispossess—vv. 2, 29
> burn with fire—vv. 3, 31
> do not act in that way toward Yahweh—vv. 4, 31
> you seek/inquire—vv. 5, 30

"Be careful" (*šāmar*, vv. 1, 30) echoes the introduction to vv. 13 and 19, but expands the horizon of obedience to include the entire legal presentation of Deuteronomy ("statutes and ordinances," v. 1) and any potential imitation of alien ways (v. 30). The perspective is one of orthodox militancy and a general sense of threat and danger. Verse 4 reveals that what vv. 2–3 identify as purely foreign dangers could also be religious possibilities indigenous to Israel. The overall perspective is the same as that of chapter 7. One can compare vv. 1–4 to 7:1–5 ("destroy"), vv. 5–7 to 7:6–7 (Yahweh's choice), and vv. 29–31 to 7:17, 25–26 (internal thoughts, the snare of repugnant alien religion). The catalog of v. 3a mirrors that of 7:5.

This call for destruction (vv. 2–3) reflects the tradition and wording of Exod 23:23–24 and 34:11–14. The targets are not buildings, but open-air sites (cf. Hos 4:13; Isa 1:29) and their associated cult objects (Jer 17:2–3; Ezek 6:13; 1 Kgs 14:23). The identification of asherah poles as alien cultic items is tendentious, for 16:21 makes clear they also could be a feature of Yahwistic worship. Deuteronomy is really vilifying traditional Israelite practices as being survivals of a foreign religon in order to motivate their elimination. To destroy the equipment of these gods is to destroy their "name," a reversal of the act of election by the placement of Yahweh's name stressed in v. 5 (and vv. 11, 21). The "names" of these gods could refer literally to inscriptions at holy places and allude to the practice of obliterating royal and divine names from monuments. On the other hand, the text may be advocating an obliteration of the names of the alien nations rather than those of their gods (cf. 7:24; 25:19; 29:19 [ET 20]). In either case, the basic idea seems to be that if a name is not spoken or written, the existence of the one who is named will fade away.

Verse 5 proclaims centralization in explicit contrast to the alien "places" mentioned in v. 2. There is an emphasis on pilgrimage ("seek out," "go there"; cf. Amos 5:5). Verse 5 combines the divergent name election formulas of v. 11 ("make his name dwell") and v. 21 ("put his name") into a single robust and insistent statement of faith ("put his name there to make it dwell"). The forceful phrase "out of all your tribes" (rather than the less exclusive "in one of your tribes" of v. 14) strengthens the singularity of the central sanctuary. In the final form of the text, this is the first occurrence of the centralization formula, so that its comprehensive and uncompromising perspective shapes the reader's interpretation of the shorter forms that follow (vv. 11, 14, 18, 21, 26).

Verse 6 sets forth a comprehensive list in order to emphasize that every single type of sacrifice is to be centralized. The social welfare perspective appears only in a reduced way in that the more extensive lists of vv. 12 and 18 are reduced to "your households" (v. 7). The theme of divine blessing is present only awkwardly, as though as an afterthought (contrast v. 7b with 15a).

The verbal correlation between v. 31a and v. 4 shows that this same perspective continues in vv. 29–31. The indication of time ("when Yahweh has cut off," v. 29) reappears in 19:1 to refer to asylum cities. The question of v. 30 would be a reasonable one from an ancient viewpoint. Taking "their land" (v. 29) might logically lead one to worship "their gods" (v. 30)! Second Kings 17:25–28 provides an example of this way of thinking. The topic of apostate behavior dominates these verses, and the text takes advantage of the rhetorical shock value of child sacrifice to motivate compliance to its demands.

The perspective of vv. 20–28 centers on issues of distance (v. 21) created by an enlargement of territory (v. 20). There is a focus on liturgical correctness and a certain narrowing or limitation of the nonsacral slaughter permitted by vv. 15–16. The temporal horizon points to future developments and to generations yet to come. This section duplicates the structural pattern of vv. 15–18: what you may do at home (vv. 15, 20–22); what you must not do at home (vv. 16–17, 23–25); what you must do at the sanctuary (vv. 18, 26–27). Verses 23–25 describe the nonsacral slaughter of v. 16 more precisely, and vv. 26–27 do the same for centralized sacrifice. Overall, vv. 20–28 modify the viewpoint of vv. 15–16 into one closer to the perspective of Lev 17:3–5, 14.

Verses 20 and 21 are almost doublets. The topic of territorial enlargement in v. 20a introduces the issue of distance in v. 21a. In a way similar to 7:1; 12:29; and 19:1, v. 20 indicates a future act of Yahweh as the prelude for Israel to perform an act in response. Territorial extension also plays a role in modifications to the asylum city law by 19:8–9. Perhaps the historical reference is to a recovery of territory lost to Assyria, either as a matter of anticipation or of recent fulfillment. Verse 21 limits the permission for desacralized slaughter to places "too far" from the central place. The blanket permission of v. 15 ("within any of your towns") is restricted in regard to areas closer to the central place. This same redactional procedure is used in 19:8–9 and 14:24, where distance provides the justification for a modification in procedure, and in the war law of 20:15–18, where introducing the topic of distance justifies a new severity. This section also focuses on liturgical correctness. Thus vv. 22–24 repeat the admonition of vv. 15–16, but underscore the blood prohibition with a motivation identical to that of Lev 17:14. A repeated admonition to do right in the opinion of Yahweh (vv. 25, 28; cf. 13:18–19 [ET 17–18]) surrounds a concern for propriety in sacrifice. Verses 26–27 carefully highlight the differences between permitted nonsacral slaughter and required centralized sacrifices. The treatment of burnt offerings and the cataloging of other offerings are presented with sensitivity to cultic concerns. The text designates offerings other than vowed gifts (what would include tithes, firstfruits, and firstlings) with the more technical term "holy things" (v. 26; cf. 26:13). Both the meat and the blood of burnt offerings must be handled properly with respect to the altar, and the blood of other sacrifices must be separated from the meat and disposed of beside the altar (v. 27). Such liturgical precision contrasts sharply with the nonchalance of vv. 13–19. For example, v. 16 concerns itself only with the consumption of blood, which was more of a cultural than a ritual issue, and the neutral disposal of nonsacrificial blood (as in v. 24). Although the perspective of vv. 20–28 is ritually oriented, it is still not that of the Priestly Writing. For example, neither the important fat and kidneys (Lev 7:22–27; 1 Sam 2:15–16) nor the topic of sin and guilt offerings appears here.

[1] The expression "statutes and ordinances" stands isolated in four framing verses: 5:1 and 11:32 bracket chapters 5–11, and 12:1 and 26:16 enclose chapters 12–26. The phrase functions as an inclusive term for the whole law found in chapters 5–26.

Lohfink has suggested that v. 1 is exilic, intending to restrict the law's application to the geography of Palestine and to the time when Israel is there.[15] However, the more natural meaning is that living in the land makes obedience possible. Verse 1 may perform a structural function, "in the land" pointing to the issues of geographic location in 12:2–14:21 and "all the days" to the calendar of 14:22–16:17.

[2–7] Verse 3 interrupts the semantic connection between vv. 2 and 4 and unfolds the prohibitions of v. 2 in five concrete commands related to 7:5. "Do not act in that way" (v. 4; *kēn* pointing back to v. 2) indicates that multiple worship sites are an inherently pagan phenomenon. In contrast to v. 2, worshiping at multiple shrines would not be to "serve" Yahweh at all. The same verbal relationship between "serve" and "act in that way" occurs in vv. 30–31. "Instead"

---

15. N. Lohfink, "Die *ḥûqqîm ûmišpāṭîm* im Buch Deuteronium und ihre Neubegrenzung durch Dtn 12,1," in *Studien zum Deuteronomium II*, 229–56; idem, "Dtn 12,1 und Gen 15,18: Das dem Samen Abrahams geschenkte Land als der Geltungsbereich der deuteronomischen Gesetze," in *Studien zum Deuteronomium II*, 257–85. G. Braulik more plausibly insists that "statutes and ordinances" here refers to the whole of chs. 5–26, i.e., law code and parenesis together ("Die Ausdrücke für 'Gesetz' im Buch Deuteronomium," in *Studien zur Theologie des Deuteronomiums*, 11–38).

(kî-ʾim) in v. 5 sets up an antithesis to the "places" of v. 2. This conflated centralization formula (note c) uses a typically Deuteronomic infinitive chain (cf. 6:1, 24) to assert the fact of election with added urgency. Verse 6 exhaustively lists sacrifices as three paired terms, followed by firstlings. Deuteronomy will discuss tithes further in 14:22–29, firstlings in 15:19–23, and vows in 23:22–24 [21–23]. "Undertaking" in v. 7 (literally "the putting forth of your hand," v. 18; 15:10; 23:21 [ET 20]; 28:8, 20) incorporates both effort and the results and benefits of that effort (cf. Isa 11:14). The awkward concluding clause guards against any thought of human achievement independent of Yahweh.

[8–12] Parts of v. 9 are repeated nearly verbatim in 25:19. Verses 10a and 10b synchronize what Israel will do in the conquest with what Yahweh will do.

[13–19] Of course, no ancient worshiper would do what v. 13 suggests, sacrificing carelessly at just any location whatsoever, with no concern for tradition or sacredness! This is an easily refutable straw-man argument intended to undermine the old law of Exod 20:24 by exploiting the potential ambiguity of its phrase běkol-māqôm ʾăšer, "in every place where." By the same token, "place" means both a simple "location" (v. 13) and a "sanctuary" (v. 14).[16] That v. 14 refers to an exclusive place is made clear by the contrasting use of "any" (kol) in the surrounding vv. 13 and 15. The citation formula of v. 14 ("that I command/have commanded you") again refers to Exod 20:24, reversing its elements "burnt offerings" and "in the place." Verse 15 also echoes Exod 20:24, picking up the verb zābaḥ and the concept of "blessing." This creates a redefinition of zābaḥ from "sacrifice" in Exod 20:24 to "slaughter" here.[17]

Verse 15 insists that Yahweh's blessing remains local, even if the act of sacrifice must be distant. "Joy" at the sanctuary (v. 18) is balanced by local blessing (v. 15). Both the local community and the centralized sanctuary are valid realms of religious meaning, and centralization does not mean that Yahweh has become distant from life on the local level. It is not so much that what once was sacred has become secularized, but rather that much of daily life has now been placed into Yahweh's realm.[18] Verse 17—with its sharp language of prohibition (lōʾ-tûkal; cf. 16:5; 17:15; 21:16; 22:3, 19)—and v. 18 work together to oppose forbidden local sacrifice. Verse 19 introduces a concern for the Levite (14:27–29; 18:6–8).

[20–28] Verse 20 and in turn v. 21 attach conditions to the permission for nonsacral slaughter: territorial enlargement and the resulting situation of dis-

16. *HALOT* 2:626–27, comparing sections 2–5 and 6.

17. Levinson, *Deuteronomy and Hermeneutics*, 33–36. The recycled elements of Exod 20:24 are A, "you shall sacrifice," B, "your burnt offerings," C, "in every place where," and D, "bless." Deuteronomy 12:13 uses B and C; v. 14 reverses this to C and B; v. 15 uses A and D.

18. N. Lohfink, "Opfer und Säkularisierung im Deuteronomium," in *Studien zu Opfer und Kult im Alten Testament* (ed. A. Schenker; FAT 3; Tübingen: Mohr, 1992), 15–43, counters the view that Deuteronomy advocates secularization by tracing a "pilgrimage schema" describing cultic action at the central sanctuary and travel there.

tance. Each limitation is introduced with *kî* ("when"/"if"). The two verses engage in reversing wordplay with elements of v. 15 ("when[ever] you wish" and "eat meat").

The verb *śîm*, "put," in the centralization formula of v. 21 (also 14:24) offers a more common equivalent for the unusual *šākan*, "make dwell," of v. 11 and perhaps puts more emphasis on the original act of election. *śym* is the verb used by DH (1 Kgs 9:3; 11:36; 14:21; 2 Kgs 21:4, 7) and appears to be a later clarification of the more obscure formula using *škn*. The citation formula of v. 21 is a puzzle. "Just as I have commanded" probably refers to the permission (but not really command) of v. 15.[19]

Verse 22 emphasizes the nonsacrality of the nonsacrificial meal. Clean and unclean may eat it "together," that is, side by side in the same company (cf. Judg 19:6; Jer 41:1). In contrast, v. 23 vigorously forbids eating blood (for "remain firm," cf. Josh 23:6). Verse 27 views the meal from the perspective of a layperson, describing in the passive voice the priest's duty involving blood and passing over the issue of priestly dues, later picked up in 18:3. Verse 27 takes "on/beside the altar" (*'al-mizbaḥ*) from Exod 20:24 (*ālāyw*) and uses it twice. The expression "perform (*'āśâ*) burnt offerings" sounds similar to 16:1, 10, 13: "perform the Passover," etc. Verse 28 concludes with a motivation parallel to that of v. 25 and a reminder of the dramatic situation of Moses' speech.

[29–31] This transitional and introductory paragraph forms a bridge between sections (cf. 11:31–12:1 and 5:32–6:3). Verse 30 picks up "be careful" from vv. 13 and 19. The question cited in v. 30 about how to "serve . . . gods" points directly to the three situations described in the next chapter (13:3, 7, 14 [ET 2, 6, 13]). Verse 31 repeats the whole of v. 4 and subtly previews primary vocabulary for ch. 13: "repugnant" (13:15 [ET 14]), "burn with fire" (13:17 [ET 16], and "sons and daughters" (13:7 [ET 6]). Verse 31 employs the rhetorical shock value of child sacrifice, the most appalling "repugnant thing" conceivable, to motivate the elimination of pagan worship. Child sacrifice provides a concrete, particular example of the sort of religion Yahweh hates. It also motivates the repudiation of other "repugnant things" in the chapters to follow (13:15 [ET 14]; 14:3; 17:1, 4, etc.).[20]

---

19. Skweres, *Ruckverweise*, 71–72. Other suggestions: (1) reference to the prescription to slit the animal's throat (J. Milgrom, "Profane Slaughter and a Formulaic Key to the Composition of Deuteronomy," *HUCA* 47 [1976]: 1–17); (2) a "pseudo-ascription" to harmonize nonsacral slaughter with Lev 17:1–9 (M. Fishbane, *Biblical Interpretation in Ancient Israel* [Oxford: Clarendon, 1985], 534); (3) a pseudo-citation of part of Exod 20:24 that actually negates it (Levinson, *Deuteronomy and Hermeneutics*, 42–43).

20. Prophetic rhetoric makes clear that not only was child sacrifice practiced in Judah, but it was considered by some to be part of Yahwistic religion (Jer 7:31; 19:5; 32:35; Ezek 16:20–21; 20:26, 31; 23:37, 39). This expression refers clearly to a lethal sacrifice, in contrast to the more ambiguous "pass through fire" of 18:10, which may denote a nonlethal ritual of dedication by fire.

Eradicate Treason against Yahweh
13:1–19 [ET 12:32–13:18]

Admonition

13:1 [ET 12:32] You must be careful to do everything that I command you. Do not add to it or subtract[a] from it.

A Prophet

2 [1] If a prophet or a dreamer of dreams should arise among you and offer you a sign or a wonder, 3 [2] and the sign or wonder that he promised you comes true, and he says, "Let us follow[b] other gods, which you have never known, that we may serve them,"[c] 4 [3] do not listen to the words of that prophet or that dreamer of dreams, for Yahweh your God is testing you, to discover whether you really love[d] Yahweh your God with all your heart and with all your being. 5 [4] You shall follow Yahweh your God, and he is the one whom you shall fear. It is his commandments that you shall keep, and he is the one you shall obey. He is the one you shall serve, and to him you shall cling.[e] 6 [5] But that prophet or that dreamer of dreams shall be put to death, for he has spoken treason[f] against Yahweh your God—who brought you out of the land of Egypt and redeemed you from the house[g] of servitude—to lead you astray from the way in which Yahweh your God commanded you to walk. You shall sweep out the evil from among you.

Family or Friend

7 [6] If your brother entices you, the son of your mother,[h] or your own son or daughter, or your beloved wife, or your intimate friend, saying in secret, "Let us go and serve other gods," which you and your ancestors have never known, 8 [7] from among the gods of the peoples who surround you, whether near you or far from you, from one end of the earth to the other, 9 [8] do not accede to him or listen to him. Do not look with compassion on him or feel pity for him or conceal him.[i] 10 [9] No![j] You shall certainly kill him![k] Your hand shall be the first raised against him to put him to death, and then afterward the hand of the whole people. 11 [10] Stone him with stones until he dies, because he sought to lead you astray from Yahweh your God, who brought you out of the land of Egypt, out of the house of servitude. 12 [11] Then all Israel shall hear and be afraid, and never again[l] do such a wicked thing among you.

A City

13 [12] If you hear about one of the cities[m] that Yahweh your God is giving you to live in, 14 [13] that scoundrels[n] from among you have gone out and led astray the inhabitants[o] of their city, saying, "Let us go and serve other gods," which you have never known, 15 [14] then you shall inquire and investigate and ask[p] carefully. If the matter is established as true that this repugnant thing was done among you,[q] 16 [15] you shall surely strike down the inhabitants of that city with the edge of the sword, devoting it and everything in it to destruction, and its cattle with the edge of the sword.[r] 17 [16] You shall gather all its booty into the middle of its public square and burn the city and all its booty with fire, like a whole burnt offering[s] to Yahweh your God. It shall be a permanently deserted mound. It shall never be rebuilt. 18 [17] Do not let anything of what is devoted to destruction cling to your hand, so that Yahweh may turn from his fierce anger and show you compassion and be compassionate to you and multiply you, just as he swore to your ancestors, 19 [18] if you obey Yahweh your God by keeping all his commandments that I am commanding you today, doing what is upright in the opinion of Yahweh your God.

a. Appropriately, "trim off" (Jer 48:37), as a scribe might do with a papyrus or leather document.

b. Cohortative expressing mutual encouragement, *IBHS* 34.5.1a.

c. The anomalous masoretic vocalization as hop'al is theologically motivated: "allow oneself to be brought to serve" (cf. 5:9).

d. Grammatically this is set up as a question: "to know 'do you love . . . ?'" The participle emphasizes the durative quality of this love.

e. A series of six imperatival imperfects. Word order emphasizes the direct objects.

f. The translation is based on Assyrian parallels (*dibber-sārâ* reproducing Akkadian *dabab surrāte*); see Weinfeld, *Deuteronomic School*, 99. For a complete discussion see E. Jenni, "Dtn 16,19: *sarā* 'Falschheit,'" in *Mélanges bibliques et orientaux en l'honneur de M. Henri Cazelles* (ed. A. Caquot and M. Delcor; AOAT 212; Kevelaer: Butzon & Bercker, 1981), 201–11, who points to Deut 19:16; Jer 28:16; 29:32 and maintains that this malicious falsehood is the bogus claim that Yahweh authorized such worship.

g. Follows MT. OG lacks *mbyt*, "from the house of," for translational reasons (Wevers, *Greek Text*, 230).

h. Follows the shorter text of MT. Sam. and OG preface this phrase with *bn 'byk 'w*, "the son of your father or" (cf. 27:22). Although this could have been lost by homoioarchton helped by a potential confusion between *b* and *m* (*bn 'byk* and *bn 'mk*), it is more likely an addition based on a desire for symmetry and the misunderstanding of a social norm. In a polygamous family, the son of one's mother would be the closest brother. Thus MT represents a rhetorical step up from a generalized "brother," who could be a half-brother, to a more intimate full brother. VTE speaks several times of "his brothers, sons of his mother" (e.g., VTE 8, *ANET*, 535).

i. Literally "cover him over." The translation is based on Pss 32:5; 40:11 [ET 10], and OG. OG, however, seems to have been influenced by a false contrast with its secondary reading "report him" in the next verse. For an alternate translation as "condone him," based on Prov 10:12 and Neh 3:37 [ET 4:5], see B. M. Levinson, "Recovering the Lost Original Meaning of *wl'tksh 'lyw* (Deuteronomy 13:9)," *JBL* 115 (1996): 601–20. Conceal or condone "it" (rather than "him") is unsustainable because all the other pronouns refer to the offender.

j. Adversative *kî* after a negative, Williams, *Hebrew Syntax*, 447, 555. The asyndetic construction suggests that this "no" is intended to counter the whole of v. 9, not just the previous phrase "do not conceal."

k. Follows MT *hrg thrgnw*. OG harmonizes with the procedures of 17:2–7, offering a reading derived from a confusion of *d* for *r* combined with a reversal of letters: *hgd tgydnw*, "you shall surely report him." This reading may have seemed to lead more easily into the procedures of vv. 10b-11. An Assyrian parallel confirms MT (see commentary). For a defense of OG, see A. Aejmelaeus, "Die Septuaginta des Deuteronomiums," in *Das Deuteronomium und seine Querbeziehungen,* ed. Veijola, 19–21, who argues that it eliminates a double mention of execution, its rare use of *ngd* hip'il for "denounce" is the more difficult reading, and it explains the initial adversative *kî*: "do not conceal, but instead report."

l. Follows MT. Sam., OG, Vulg. strengthen the statement by expanding with *'wd,* "once more."

m. Alternate translation: "hear [while you are] in one of your cities."

n. Literally "sons of *bĕlîya'al*," antisocial types and wrongdoers of various sorts whose behavior undermines the stability of society and abets chaos (cf. 15:9); see B. Otzen, "*bᵉliyya'al*," *TDOT* 2:131–36.

o. Follows MT. OG (and 11QTemple) expands to "all the inhabitants" here and in v. 16 in order to assert that all those to be killed are guilty without exception.

p. The *BHS* note is misleading. OG (= LXX^A) has the same verbs as MT, but the second and third are reversed.

q. *Hinnēh* introduces the conditional result of investigation as in 17:4; 19:18. The subject of the sentence is *haddābār,* and the noun clause *ne'eśtâ hattô'ēbâ hazzō't* is in apposition with it, *IBHS* 38.8 and p. 644 n. 35. For *'ĕmet nākôn* as "factual truth," cf. 17:4.

r. Follows MT in spite of variants offering shorter texts. Cairo Genizah evidence lacks "and its cattle." Vulg. does not have the second "with the edge of the sword," perhaps omitted as repetitious. OG lacks both phrases, perhaps omitting them as superfluous.

s. This is not an actual sacrifice but a metaphor: "like a *kālîl*- sacrifice to Yahweh." There can be no real sacrifice apart from an altar (cf. 33:10). Moreover, these items already belong to Yahweh because they are in a state of *ḥērem* and cannot be transferred to him by sacrifice. An alternate translation is "totality" (cf. Judg 20:40), following the ancient versions. This suggests a wordplay on the concept of "all," important to the ideology of *ḥērem*. See A. Kapelrud, "*kālîl*," *TDOT* 7:182–85.

Themes

The framing verses 12:2–4, 29–31 situated the core demand for centralization into a context of religious loyalty in opposition to alien worship, in line with the warnings about "other gods" set forth in the previous parenetic material (7:4; 8:19; 11:16, 28). This same context governs chapter 13. The chapter thus promotes obedience to the first commandment (5:8–10), urging drastic action to counteract apostasy. It does so by offering three potential cases, each focusing on a tempting refrain advocating worship of "other gods" (vv. 3, 7, 14 [ET 2, 6, 13]). Here danger does not threaten from outside, but results from deeds done "among you" (vv. 6, 12, 15 [ET 5, 11, 14]).

These three scenarios were not just theoretical dangers for readers, but reflect actual experience. International situations in which Yahweh seemed unable to protect the nation from danger must have led to calls for less exclusive religious behavior (cf. 2 Kgs 16:18; 18:22; Jer 44:16–18). Prophets making such appeals would be especially tempting if they could perform authorizing signs (cf. Deut 18:22). Situations of intermarriage with foreigners would also offer syncretistic temptations, something certainly experienced in the royal family (Solomon, Ahab). Formerly Canaanite cities assimilated into the monarchical state would naturally continue aspects of their native religion. More generally, the traditional practices and loyalties of the people as a whole fell short of the orthodoxy expected by the authors of Deuteronomy.

Over against these very real temptations, the text is uncompromising. Loyalty to Yahweh must take precedence over all other considerations. Cast the first stone even at your own kinfolk as a salutary public lesson (vv. 10–12 [ET 9–11])! Prosecute sacral war and *ḥērem* ruthlessly against renegade cities (vv. 16–18 [ET 15–17])! The motivations offered are potent. These situations are divine tests (v. 4 [ET 3]). Such behaviors are "wicked" and "repugnant" (vv. 6, 12, 15 [ET 5, 11, 14]). You have an exodus history with Yahweh, but not with those other gods, whom you have "never known" (vv. 6, 11 [ET 5, 10] over against vv. 3, 7, 14 [ET 2, 6, 13]; cf. 11:28; 28:64; 29:25 [ET 26]; 32:17). To "serve" those gods would contradict the appropriate result of your "servitude" in Egypt, which should be to "serve" Yahweh (vv. 3, 5–6 [ET 2, 4–5]). Ruthless extermination will lead to blessing (v. 18 [ET 17]). Above all, the unalterable authority of Moses' all-inclusive revelation backs up this uncompromising demand (v. 1 [ET 12:32]).

Context and Composition

Structurally, chapter 13 is linked to the preceding chapter by 12:29–13:1 [ET 12:32], which provides a transition from the demand to worship only in the ways commanded in chapter 12 to the concerns of chapter 13. The question asked in 12:30 points to the service of "their gods," which is the theme of chapter 13. The verb "serve" in 12:2, 30 connects to 13:3, 5, 7, 14 [ET 2, 4, 6, 13]. In a skillful scribal flourish, words from 12:31 are recycled in the presentation of the third case: "sons" (v. 14 [ET 13], part of the expression "scoundrels"), "repugnant thing done" (v. 15 [ET 14]) and "burn with fire to" (v. 17 [ET 16]). Verses 1 and 19 [ET 12:32 and 13:18] enclose chapter 13 with shared language: "everything that I command you." Verse 1 refers back to 12:1, 29 with "be careful to," while v. 19 [ET 18] alludes to 12:25, 28 by means of "do what is upright in the opinion of Yahweh." Thus the frame formed by vv. 1 and 19 [ET 12:32 and 13:18] connects to the one formed by 12:1 and 28–31.

Yet there is also a topical shift, signaled by the abrupt placement of 13:1 [ET 12:32] and its reminder of the dramatic situation ("I command you"). The theme widens from the indigenous cult of the land and Israel's potential imitation of it in service to Yahweh (12:29–31) to the broader topic of other gods. That is, the focus shifts from liturgical forms and sacred places borrowed from the worshipers of alien gods to those gods themselves.

There are indications of literary growth. For example, the sign of vv. 2b–3a [ET 1b–2a] creates an awkward distance between v. 2a [ET 1a] (the instigator who speaks) and v. 3b [ET 2b] (what is said). The plural address of vv. 4b–5 [ET 3b–4] in a singular context suggests that this explanation of why the sign has come true is a later addition. As a theological reflection, related to 18:20–22, v. 4b [ET 3b] seeks to counter potential resistance from readers who might otherwise respect such confirmatory prophetic signs. Because they do not deal with a prophetic word, the other two cases do not need to speculate about such matters. Further traces of compositional growth are redundant double references to the sword in v. 16 [ET 15] and to divine compassion in v. 18 [ET 17]. Verse 8 [ET 7] is sometimes thought to be a discursive addition. Chapter 13 has an indisputable relationship to 17:2–7.

Three Parallel Scenarios

Three quasi-casuistic laws describe three situations, each insisting on exclusive loyalty to Yahweh.[1] They are shaped by Deuteronomy's typical "if . . . you" form of casuistic law. The protasis sections are full of ideological rhetoric (vv. 2–3, 7–8, 13–14 [ET 1–2, 6–7, 12–13]). The apodosis verses first admonish "do not listen" (vv. 4, 9 [ET 3, 8]) before referring to any sort of legal action. These cases are exemplary, extreme, boundary situations illustrating conspiracy, agitation, and apostasy. They are described in order to define the problem and illustrate a demand for total, uncompromising loyalty. Neither prophetic authority backed up by signs, familial intimacy, and affection, nor ethnic solidarity is to stand in the way of the pitiless eradication of religious treason.

---

1. For a detailed analysis of this chapter, see P.-E. Dion, "Deuteronomy 13: The Suppression of Alien Religious Practices in Israel during the Late Monarchical Era," in *Law and Ideology in Monarchic Israel* (ed. B. Halpern and D. Hobson; JSOTSup 124; Sheffield: Sheffield Academic Press, 1991), 147–216.

These three cases are arranged by the social situation of their perpetrators. The first (vv. 2–6 [ET 1–5]) describes the public enticement of a prophet who successfully backs up prophetic authority with a sign. The second (vv. 7–12 [ET 6–11]) concerns secret temptation by a relative or friend. In the third (vv. 13–19 [ET 12–18]), a rebellious element leads a whole city into disloyal worship. Each step is a rhetorical boost: not just a prophet but a relative, not just individuals but an entire city, not just enticement but actual apostasy. The punishments also ratchet up from "put to death" to a stoning begun by friends or relatives to the total annihilation of a city.

Shared language and structure hold the three cases together, inviting the reader to weigh one against the other. The structure and vocabulary of the first two sections match tightly; the third tends to go its own way:

> protasis
> > perpetrators (vv. 2–3, 7a, 13–14a [ET 1–2, 6a, 12–13a])
> > quoted enticement (vv. 3, 7b, 14b [ET 2, 6b, 13b])
> apodosis
> > warning: "do not listen" (vv. 4–5, 9 [ET 3–4, 8])
> > violent elimination (vv. 6a, 10–11, 16–18a [ET 5a, 9–10, 15–17a])
> > motivation and outcome (vv. 6b, 12, 18b–19 [ET 5b, 11, 17b–18])

The cases are linked together in other ways as well. The emotional relationship involving *nepeš* tested by Yahweh in v. 4 [ET 3] (where *nepeš* is translated as "being") connects to the beloved family and friends of v. 7 [ET 6] (*nepeš* translated as "intimate"). "All Israel shall hear" in v. 12 [ET 11] leads to hearing the report in v. 13 [ET 12]. The cases share a motivational argument based on Yahweh's graciousness, referring to the exodus in vv. 6 and 11 [ET 5, 10] and to the gift of cities in v. 13 [ET 12]. The first and second cases are bound together by characteristic motive clauses in vv. 6 and 12 [ET 5, 11] (which always occur together in this same order in Deuteronomy: 17:12–13; 19:19–20; 21:21). All three cases share a context of speaking (vv. 3, 6, 7, 13, 14 [ET 2, 5, 6, 12, 13]) and hearing ("do not listen," vv. 4, 9 [ET 3, 8]; also vv. 12, 13, 19 [ET 11, 12, 18]).

Procedural issues appear in the second two cases (vv. 10–11, 15 [ET 9–10, 14]), but in the first case the public nature and sheer facticity of the offense obviates any need for an investigation or a description of the execution procedure. In the third case, there is no warning about consenting to the blandishment, for it is not addressed to those tempted, but to those who have heard about the wrongdoing of others. It is only in the third case that inquiry about what has been heard is required, for in the first two cases there can be no possible doubt.

Genre and Rhetoric

This chapter breathes the atmosphere of Assyrian treaty documents, parallel-ing the requirements for loyalty found in them. In the Vassal Treaties of Esarhaddon (VTE), prophets or mantics, along with relatives in the form of brothers, sons, and daughters, serve as potential instigators, and their sup-posed words are quoted. The similarities between this chapter and VTE are so close that a deliberate imitation of Assyrian forms is nearly certain. Deuteronomy has thus converted the requirement of total loyalty to the Assyr-ian king into a demand for loyalty to Yahweh. The book draws an analogy between political treachery and a sort of religious high treason and mandates the same ruthless response. Conspiracies against Yahweh are to be decisively suppressed.[2]

Each case is a little hypothetical drama. The "if . . . you" style intends to cre-ate personal involvement on the part of the reader. In fact, in the second case the addressee is at the same time the object of the seduction attempt. The rep-etition of "among you" (concerning the instigator in vv. 2 and 14 [ET 1, 13], the crime in v. 15 [ET 14], and the motive for punishment in vv. 6 and 12 [ET 5, 11]) also aims at personal involvement on the part of the reader. The first two cases emphasize how hard such temptations would be to resist. In the first, an indisputable sign backs up prophetic authority; in the second the instigator's relationship to the addressee is personal and intimate. The last drama is cli-mactic, a mass defection followed by a mass action of punishment and decon-tamination. The attractiveness of these temptations and their strong effect is underscored by use of the verb *ndḥ* hip'il (vv. 6, 11, 14 [ET 5, 10, 13]). This denotes "seduce, lead astray" (cf. Prov 7:21), but also implies a more forceful "thrusting away" from Yahweh or his way.[3]

In its quotation of the proposals to commit apostasy, the text discloses its own negative evaluation: "other gods, which you have never known." By merging its own perspective with that of the apostate, the text expresses a negative judgment while ostensibly summing up the traitor's argument. Because the prophet addresses the whole nation and the relative entices an

2. Compare VTE 10, *ANET*, 535. See also the Zakutu Treaty, lines 18–27, in S. Parpola and K. Wanatabe, *Neo-Assyrian Treaties and Loyalty Oaths* (State Archives of Assyria 2; Helsinki: Helsinki University Press, 1988), 64. For further examples see Weinfeld, *Deuteronomic School*, 91–100; and Dion, "Suppression," 199–204. E. Otto, "Treueid und Gesetz: Die Ursprünge des Deuteronomiums im Horizont neuassyrischen Vertragsrechts," *ZABR* 2 (1996): 1–52, dates this use of Assyrian treaty terminology to the time of Josiah. For the opposing opinion that this treaty influ-ence should be traced to the polemics of the exilic period, see T. Veijola, "Wahrheit und Intoleranz nach Deuteronomium 13," *ZTK* 92 (1995): 300–301, 308. M. Nissinen, "Falsche Prophetie in neuassyrischer und deuteronomistischer Darstellung," in *Das Deuteronomium*, ed. Lohfink, 172–95, compares the criteria of judgment used in these treaties with those of Deuteronomy.

3. *HALOT* 2:673; T. Kronholm, "*nādaḥ*," *TDOT* 9:235–41.

individual, the first two cases use second-person singular language. In the third case, however, the addressee of the temptation shifts, and the scoundrels of v. 14 [ET 13] use the plural to speak to the city's inhabitants as a group.

A rhetoric of emotional language seeks to convince the reader, as though much resistance to these harsh demands is expected. "Love" (v. 4 [ET 3]) is invoked as something stronger than prophetic authority. Yahweh's "compassion" is assured for those who obey, in contrast to "fierce anger" (v. 18 [ET 17]). The absence of any prior relationship to these alien gods ("never known"; vv. 3, 7, 14 [ET 2, 6, 13]) is contrasted to Yahweh's past gracious acts (vv. 6, 11, 13, 18 [ET 5, 10, 12, 17]). Obedience is promoted with the language of relationship: "follow," "cling" (v. 5 [ET 4]).

The theology is that of the first commandment and an uncompromising "Yahweh alone" dogma. The concerns of the first commandment are clear: the exodus and other gods (5:6), divine anger and mercy (5:9–10; 13:18–19 [ET 17–18]). The "love formula" of 13:4 [ET 3] echoes 5:10 (cf. 6:5; 10:12; 11:13; 30:6). The unyielding harshness of this chapter reflects an orthodox narrowing of Israel's earlier, more multifaceted religious practices. It points to a sociological revolution brought about when the concerns of a cohesive monarchical state suppressed elements of Israel's traditional religion as idolatrous. This is the only Old Testament law against those who proselytize for other gods. However, it is not mere inward opinion that is punished here, but public deeds of enticement.[4]

[1] (ET 12:32) This command is often misconstrued as a "canonical formula" intended to protect the text of Deuteronomy. If that were the purpose of this verse, however, one would expect it to appear at the end of law code. Instead, both occurrences of this formula (4:2 and 13:1 [ET 12:32]) appear in the context of a polemic against alien gods. The expression highlights the importance of obeying what has come before and what will follow in the text. Adding and subtracting do not refer to accurate textual transmission, but to the commands one is to "be careful to do." The intent of this formula, then, is to encourage careful, exact compliance with everything Moses has decreed. Nevertheless, the scribal culture from which Deuteronomy emerged would have used phrases similar to this one to encourage care for

---

4. For a description of this social phenomena, which leads to ascribing certain traditional religious practices to what he calls "indigenous outsiders," see L. Stulman, "Encroachment in Deuteronomy: An Analysis of the Social World of the D Code," *JBL* 109 (1990): 613–32. On the problem that this text offends modern tolerant attitudes, see J. M. Hamilton, "How to Read an Abhorrent Text: Deuteronomy 13 and the Nature of Authority," *Horizons in Biblical Theology* 20 (1998): 12–32; and B. Lang, "George Orwell im gelobten Land: Das Buch Deuteronomium und der Geistkirchlicher Kontrolle," in *Kirche und Visitation* (ed. E. Zeeden and P. Lang; Spätmittelalter und Frühe Neuzeit 14; Stuttgart: Klett Cotta, 1984), 21–35.

a transmitted text.[5] Thus Deuteronomy reuses a formulaic prohibition on eliminating items when copying a text to inspire obedience to the positive commands of centralization (ch. 12) and the punishment of disloyalty (ch. 13). At the same time, the prohibition of adding to a text is used to prevent the adoption of novel religious practices, even at the instigation of a prophet. Possibly the formula appears here specifically to counter any claims that human sacrifice (12:31) had been commanded by Yahweh (cf. Ezek 20:25–26).

[2–6 (ET 1–5)] On the face of it, such a prophet should be believed, and the test (v. 4 [ET 3]) arises because the corroborating sign has come true (18:21–22). The noun "sign" (v. 3 [ET 2]) seems to highlight confirmation (Exod 3:12; Judg 6:17), whereas "wonder" emphasizes the miraculous quality of a prophetic deed (Exod 4:21; 1 Kgs 13:3, 5).[6] "Never known" means "not experienced," "having had no close relationship to." It describes the polar opposite of the God known through the exodus. "Follow" (*hālak 'aḥărê*) reflects the language of relational and wifely fidelity (Ruth 3:10; Jer 2:2, 5; Hos 2:7; 15 [E 5, 13]) and the expected military role of a subordinate (Judg 9:4, 49; 1 Sam 17:13–14).

The countercommand of v. 5 [ET 4] picks up the language of the temptation of v. 3 [ET 2]: "follow," "serve." To speak of following Yahweh is unique here in Deuteronomy, as opposed to references to alien gods. "Serve" in this context implies that true service to Yahweh consists not so much in particular cultic practices as in obedience to divine commands. The series of six imperatival verbs in v. 5 [ET 4] follows a common and effective rhetorical format for parenesis, one found also in 6:13; 10:12b–13; 10:20 (cf. 30:20; Josh 22:5; 1 Sam. 12:14). The phrases form a concentric pattern based on their predicates:

> prepositional phrase (*'aḥărê yhwh*, "after Yahweh")
> personal object pronoun (*'ōtô*, "him")
> nonpersonal object (*miṣwotāyw*, "his commandments")
> nonpersonal object (*qōlô*, "his voice")
> personal object pronoun (*'ōtô*, "him")
> prepositional phrase (*bô*, "to him")

5. An example is in the conclusion to the Code of Hammurabi 26, *ANET*, 178–79. For other comparative material, see M. Fishbane, "Varia Deuteronomica," 349–52; and C. Dohmen and M. Oeming, *Biblischer Kanon, warum und wozu?* (Quaestiones disputatae 137; Freiburg: Herder, 1992), 68–89. For the relationship of this formula to the duties of a scribe, see E. Reuter, "'Nimm nichts davon weg und füge nichts hinzu': Dtn 13,1, seine alttestamentlichen Parallelen und seine altorientalischen Vorbilder," *BN* 47 (1989): 107–14.

6. Narrative examples of the prophetic sign are found in 1 Kgs 13:3, 5; 2 Kgs 20:8–11. For the verb *bô* to describe a sign coming to pass, see 1 Sam 10:7, 9; Deut 18:22. For prophetic dreams, see Jer 23:25–32.

The verbs are similar to those used by Assyrian kings to demand loyalty from their vassals.[7]

"He has spoken treason" (v. 6 [ET 5]) motivates the death sentence and again reflects the language of Assyrian loyalty oaths.[8] The text's demand is further underscored by the motivational formula "sweep out the evil." Tolerating such rebellion would lead to communal guilt, so there must be a communal response to eradicate it from the body politic. "Evil" refers to deeds that contaminate society and damage its relationship to Yahweh. Such "evil" is an objective, almost material danger, the object of an act of sweeping away as though it were excrement (cf. 1 Kgs 14:10). Deuteronomy commonly supplements laws protecting the social order and family with this expression (17:7, 12; 19:19; 21:21; 22:21, 22, 24; 24:7), most often employing it to counteract feelings of compassion when capital punishment is called for.[9]

Deuteronomy will have more to say about prophets and their confirming signs in 18:15–22. Deuteronomy 13:2 [ET 1] establishes a verbal relationship to 18:15 and 22 (a prophet "arises" and the confirmation "comes true"). The successful sign suggests that this prophet is not simply a "false prophet." Rather Yahweh's overall control of events implies that this must be a divine test (v. 4 [ET 3]; cf. 1 Kgs 22:19–23).

[7–12 (ET 6–11)] The text directly addresses the male family head with wife and children, who has the power both to "cover up" and to initiate an execution. Yet this individualized address stands in tension with the overarching collective address of the section (cf. v. 8 [ET 7], "peoples who surround you"; v. 12 [ET 11], "among you"). With "in secret" (v. 7 [ET 6]), the text moves into possibilities for a private, underground, alternative cult. In an embryonic drama of intimacy and secrecy, the instigators move from the closest (full brother) outward. The "beloved wife" (literally "wife of your bosom") underscores physical affection and closeness. One's "intimate friend" is as close and as valued "as one's very self" (the literal translation of *kĕnapšĕkā*; cf. 1 Sam 18:1, 3; Lev 19:18b). Every social and familial instinct demands that the addressee should go along with or at least protect these who are his nearest and dearest. This most powerful of temptations is rhetorically countered by a demand for the most absolute loyalty (vv. 10–11 [ET 9–10]) as the text explores the dilemma of emotional attachment and conflicting loyalties.

---

7. Weinfeld, *Deuteronomic School*, 83–84.

8. See note f; VTE 57, line 502, *ANET*, 539.

9. On this formula see U. Rüterswörden, "Das Böse in der deuteronomischen Schultheologie," in *Das Deuteronomium und seine Querbeziehungen*, ed. Veijola, 223–41. This is a pre-Deuteronomic expression (2 Sam 4:11) with a background in surrounding cultures. See P.-E. Dion, "Tu feras disparaître le mal du milieu de toi," *RB* 87 (1980): 321–49. The wide range of legal topics motivated by this formula makes it unlikely that it indicates an earlier law collection, as was suggested by J. L'Hour, "Une législation criminelle dans le Deutéronome," *Bib* 44 (1963): 1–28.

Verse 8 [ET 7] expands the perspective beyond indigenous gods to those of neighboring peoples. Assyrian gods such as the Queen of Heaven, Tammuz, and astral deities may be in view. Verse 9 [ET 8] increases the level of warning from that of v. 4 [ET 3] ("do not listen") by adding another verb, "do not accede . . . or listen."[10] The instigator's close relationship in v. 7 [ET 6] logically suggests the topic of potential compassion and pity in v. 9 [ET 8]. A temptation to cover up would be natural, given that this is an enticement "in secret" (v. 7 [ET 6]). A list of five prohibitions (v. 9 [ET 8]) counterbalances the five intimates mentioned in v. 7 [ET 6]. The first four prohibitions come in two pairs. The initial pair seeks to block acquiescence to the persuasion. The second pair seeks to overcome the immobilizing effects of emotion and kinship. The language forbidding compassion reflects 7:16; 19:13, 21; 25:12. The final prohibition refers either to shielding or condoning (note i).

The sharp adversative that begins v. 10 [ET 9] demands the polar opposite of normal human feelings and cultural loyalties in the shape of hands-on involvement in an immediate, summary execution. This ruthless demand seems to be at odds with the legal due process outlined in vv. 13–19 [ET 12–18] (fair investigation) and 17:2–7 (two witnesses). However, the comparable demands of Assyrian vassal treaties, in situations when the life of the heir to the throne was threatened by treason, suggest that instant execution is precisely what is intended here (note k). The "clear and present danger" of apostasy requires radical measures, for Yahweh is owed absolute and instant loyalty. The story told in Exod 32:25–29 illustrates just such a situation. Mere enticement is enough to trigger punishment; no actual apostasy is required. Moreover, if enticement to apostasy is done in secret (v. 7 [ET 6]), the legal nicety of a trial with two witnesses would be impossible. Insistence on a proper trial procedure would be fatal to the relationship with Yahweh.[11]

As the sole witness to the otherwise secret enticement, the one addressed is to take the lead in the execution (vv. 10–11 [ET 9–10]; cf. 17:7). Stoning (prescribed in 17:2–7; 21:18–21; 22:20–21, 23–24) seems to have been a social mechanism for acting out mass anger and revulsion (Exod 17:4; Num 14:10; 1 Sam 30:6; 1 Kgs 12:18). At the same time, stoning demonstrates the community's noninvolvement in and disapproval of a criminal act and eliminates the danger of a collective guilt that threatened the safety of the whole community. In v. 12 [ET 11] execution is motivated by a uniquely Deuteronomic formula

---

10. "*abhah* denotes the first beginnings of a positive reaction, whereas *shama'* indicates complete obedience" (B. Johnson, "*ābhāh*," *TDOT* 1:25).

11. See VTE 12 and 26, *ANET*, 535–37; B. M. Levinson, "'But You Shall Surely Kill Him!' The Text-Critical and Neo-Assyrian Evidence for MT Deuteronomy 13:10," in *Bundesdokument und Gesetz*, ed. Braulik, 37–63. For a critique see H. Seebass, "Noch einmal zu Dtn 13,10 in Dtn 13,7–12," *ZABR* 5 (1999): 189–92.

of deterrence (17:13; 19:20; 21:21). This crime is linked to that of the first case by being termed "a wicked thing among you" (similar to "evil from among you" in v. 6 [ET 5]; cf. 17:5; 19:20).

[13–19 (ET 12–18)] The third case begins with the mechanism of its discovery as news or rumor (cf. 17:4). Passing mention of Yahweh's gift (v. 13 [ET 12]) underscores the depravity of the crime. The "you" addressed is not an individual as in the second case, but the whole nation (cf. "one of your cities"). As the rebellion is described, however, what was "your city" in v. 13 [ET 12] becomes "their city" in v. 14 [ET 13]. The triple repetition of verbs in v. 15a [ET 14a] underscores careful investigation. Although no mechanism or public forum for this is described, context indicates that *dāraš* ("inquire") is being used in a legal sense, not an oracular one (17:4; 19:18; cf. 18:11). In v. 15b [ET 14b] the roots *'mn* ("true") and *kwn* ("established") point to an assured verdict.

Verse 16 moves away from capital punishment (vv. 6 and 10–11 [ET 5, 9–10]) to sacral war, since this case no longer deals with an individual malefactor but an entire community capable of resistance. The language of political treaty appears once more.[12] The apostate town becomes the object of sacral war, dealt with as though it were an element of the pagan nations of the land (7:1, 25–26; 20:16–18). Judges 20 reflects a similar internal sacral war against Israelites who have violated fundamental community norms.

The demand to treat the city as *ḥērem* relates to Exod 22:19 [ET 20], although the ban is applied collectively to the guilty community rather than to an apostate individual. When something was categorized as being in a state of *ḥērem*, it became Yahweh's exclusive property and all human use was prohibited. Treating a city as *ḥērem* meant exterminating its entire human population. In this particular case, however, everything else in the city, including its cattle, was also to be made unavailable for human use or consumption. Verse 16 [ET 15] deals with living beings treated as *ḥērem*, and vv. 17–18a [ET 16–17a] with inanimate objects. The effects of *ḥērem* even continue into the future, so that the city can never be lived in again (cf. Josh 6:26; 8:28). The prohibition of v. 18 [ET 17] is founded on the concept that the state of being *ḥērem* is contagious if one seeks to benefit from it (cf. Josh 6:18; 7:10–26). The possibility that some of the city's population may be innocent or the caveat of Deut 24:16 is not raised, because this annihilation is not precisely a punishment. Rather it is the expected result of the city falling into the status of *ḥērem* because it is booty captured in sacral war.[13]

In this third case, Yahweh's blazing anger has already broken out against Israel (v. 18 [ET 17]), for the apostasy is presented as a fait accompli, not just

---

12. "If it is a city, you must slay it with the sword," Sefire III, 12–13, *ANET*, 661.

13. On the category of *ḥērem*, see Nelson, *Joshua*, 19–20, 101–2. Perhaps the cultural category of *tô'ēbâ*, "repugnant thing" (v. 15 [ET 14]; cf. 17:4), was thought to connect to the category of *ḥērem* (7:26).

as a proposal as in the other cases. Yahweh's anger is directed against the "you" of the whole community of Israel. Any attempt to avoid the costly consequences of *ḥērem* would keep this anger in effect. Yahweh may relent, however, if Israel will "obey" (v. 19 [ET 18]; literally "listen to the voice of") Yahweh rather than listening to these apostate persuaders (cf. vv. 4, 9 [ET 3, 8]). The text's move from anger to divine favor is bridged by alliteration (v. 18 [ET 18]): *mēḥārôn . . . raḥămîm wĕriḥamĕkā wĕhirbekā,* "from anger . . . compassion and be compassionate to you and multiply you." The motivation of population increase intends to counteract any potential distress over the loss of a whole city. Israel need not be reluctant on this account.

Act As Yahweh's Holy People
14:1–21

Abstain from Mourning Customs

14:1 You are children of Yahweh your God. Do not gash yourselves or shave your foreheads bald[a] for the dead. 2 For you are a people holy to Yahweh your God. It is you whom Yahweh has chosen from of all the peoples on earth to be his treasured people.

Permitted and Forbidden Foods

3 Do not eat any repugnant thing.[b] 4 These are the animals that you may eat: the ox, the sheep, the goat, 5 the fallow deer, the gazelle, the roe deer, the wild goat, the aurochs,[c] the oryx, and the mountain-sheep. 6 Any animal that grows a hoof and exhibits a cleft through the two hooves,[d] bringing up a cud among the animals, you may eat. 7 But do not eat these from those that bring up a cud and that grow a split hoof: the camel, the hare, and the rock badger, because they bring up a cud but do not grow a hoof. They are unclean for you. 8 And the pig, because it grows a hoof but not a cud.[e] It is unclean for you. Do not eat their meat and do not touch their carcasses.

9 These you may eat of any that are in water: any that have fins and scales you may eat. 10 But whatever does not have fins and scales do not eat. It is unclean for you.

11 You may eat any clean bird. 12 But these are ones you must not eat: the eagle, the vulture, the osprey, 13 the buzzard, any kind of kite,[f] 14 every kind of raven, 15 the ostrich,[g] the nighthawk, the sea gull, any kind of hawk, 16 the little owl[h] and the great owl, the water hen, 17 and the desert

owl,[i] thecarrion vulture and the cormorant, 18 the stork, any kind of heron, the hoopoe, and the bat. 19 All winged swarmers are unclean for you. They shall not be eaten.[j] 20 You may eat any clean winged creature.[k] 21 Do not eat any carrion. You may give it to the alien resident within your towns and he may eat it, or you may sell it to a foreigner. For you are a people holy to Yahweh your God. Do not boil a kid in its mother's milk.[l]

a. Literally "make baldness between your eyes." The expression denotes removing hair without reference to method.

b. MT puts this section heading in singular address. Other witnesses level it to the plural that follows (Sam., OG, Syr., Vulg.).

c. The old-world bison, from Akkadian *ditanu*, *HALOT* 1:221. Alternate translation: "ibex" or "antelope."

d. This translation takes *prs* hip‘il as denominative ("have/grow a hoof") and the corresponding noun as simply "hoof" rather than "cloven hoof." Cf. Exod 10:26; Isa 5:28.

e. Follows MT, which is starkly elliptical: *wl' grh*, "and not a cud." To clarify this, Sam. and OG supplement from Lev 11:7: *wšs‘ šs‘ prsh whw' grh l' ygwr*, "and it has a split hoof but it does not chew a cud." Although MT is the earliest recoverable text, one wonders if it represents a reversed haplography of an original *wgrh l' [yg(w)r]*, "and a cud it does not chew."

f. Follows Sam. and OG (and Lev 11:14) in reading only two birds: *d'h*, "buzzard," and *'yh*, "kite." Apparently MT suffered a corruption of *d'h* into *r'h* (*r* for *d* confusion; a "seeing bird"?), then incorporated a correction of this (as *dyh*; cf. Isa 34:15) as a third bird. This third bird is not present in some Hebrew mss.

g. This is how the ancient versions translated what is literally "the daughter of the desert."

h. Sam. moved *šlk*, "cormorant," from v. 17 to here in order to reproduce the order of Lev 11:17. The place of "cormorant" is the only deviation in the order of items between Deuteronomy and Leviticus. OG has the same order as MT in Deuteronomy.

i. As suggested by Isa 34:11; Zeph 2:14; Ps 102:7 [ET 6]. The ancient versions took this as "pelican," probably a folk etymology based on the notion that pelicans vomit (root *qy'*) to feed their young.

j. Follows the MT third-person nip‘al imperfect as less expected in this context. Sam. and OG (with some support from 4QpaleoDeut[r]) level to the pattern of v. 12 (cf. vv. 20, 21) with the Qal second person plural: *l' t'klw mhm*, "you shall not eat of them."

k. *'wp* must refer to insects in the broad sense of "other things that fly." Clean birds have already been dealt with in v. 11 under the term *zippôr*, and the Lev 11:21 parallel speaks of hopping insects at this point.

l. Alternate vocalization of *ḥlb* as *ḥēleb*, "fat": "cook a kid in its mother's fat."

Using as its basis several traditional apodictic prohibitions (vv. 1, 3, 21), the text seeks to make readers' diet, customs of mourning, and cooking consistent with their identity as Yahweh's elect and holy people. This section works together with the rest of the law code to revitalize a national identity threatened by the Assyrian Empire. It intends to construct and reconstruct endangered boundaries around Israel's peoplehood. Election affects not just public affairs as in chapters 12–13, but also private, domestic behavior. These admonitions are tailored for a lay audience and are made user friendly by means of easy-to-follow rules of thumb (vv. 6, 9–10, 19–20) and traditional lists (vv. 4–5, 12–18). Deuteronomy is more concise than the parallel text, Lev 11, and more practically oriented.

Although the arena of obedience has shifted, this section does not mark a sharp break from chapters 12–13. The idea held in common is that Israel is different from other peoples. Israel is not to use their worship places (12:2–4), follow their religious customs (12:30–31), or serve their gods (ch. 13). Similarly, chapter 14 goes on to assert that Israel is to follow its own distinctive standards of daily life. This topical connection is strengthened by the shared concept of things and behaviors that are "repugnant" (*tôʿēbâ*, 12:31; 13:15 [ET 14]; 14:3). More narrowly, 14:3–20 deals with a question naturally raised by the nonsacral slaughter permitted in chapter 12. Besides domestic animals, what can one eat? General rules and positive and negative lists seek to answer this question. Nor is this section out of harmony with the succeeding laws that aspire to establish societal unity through the tithe (14:22–15:18). The thematic word "eat" ties together chapters 12, 14–15 (cf. 14:23, 26, 29; 15:20, 22, 23). More narrowly, the repeated "do not eat" of 14:3–21 forms a contrasting connection to the positive "you shall eat" of vv. 23 and 26, while v. 21 ties dietary law to social concern through mention of the resident alien (cf. 14:29) and foreigner (cf. 15:3).[1]

This section is framed by the theological motivation of Israel's identity as a "holy people" (vv. 2, 21; cf. 7:6). In contrast to the theology of the Priestly Writer or the Holiness Code, in Deuteronomy Israel is already a holy people by virtue of divine election. It does not have to achieve holy status by obedience or effort. Holiness is not to be accomplished but protected. Israel's special status is the reason for its special behavior, not the other way around. As a holy people Israel avoids what is repugnant and unclean, in contrast to the behavior of other nations. By forbidding these customs and foods, Deuteronomy seeks to distinguish Israel from other peoples, defining chosen peoplehood in terms of cultural behavior. Nonfood animals are unclean explicitly "for you" (vv. 7, 8, 10, 19). Three overlapping identities underscore Israel's distinctiveness. They are children of Yahweh, a "holy people," and the metaphorical equivalent of a ruler's treasured possession (v. 2; *sĕgullâ*). Israel is explicitly contrasted with the alien and foreigner in v. 21.

1. In contrast, A. D. H. Mayes, "Deuteronomy 14 and the Deuteronomic World View," in *Studies in Deuteronomy*, ed. García Martínez et al., 165–81, judges that the dietary laws are secondary because they are not harmonious with Deuteronomy's overall purpose.

After the heading of v. 1a, the dietary regulations are enclosed in an artful concentric frame:

"do not gash" (v. 1b)
  "you are a people holy to Yahweh" (v. 2)
    "do not eat any repugnant thing" (v. 3)
    "do not eat carrion" (v. 21aα)
  "you are a people holy to Yahweh" (v. 21aβ)
"do not boil" (v. 21b)

Food and nonfood animals are presented according to the three realms in which they live: land (vv. 4–8), water (vv. 9–10), and air (vv. 11–20). The realms of land and water divide into what is permitted (vv. 4–6, 9) and what is forbidden (vv. 7–8, 10). In the realm of the air, what is prohibited (vv. 12–19) is enclosed by parallel permission sentences (vv. 11 and 20). The repeated motif is "do not eat" (vv. 7, 8, 10, 12, 21).

Shifts in address are evidence for a composite history of composition. The food law section is in plural address, doubtlessly because it was taken from a source related in some way to Lev 11. This is enclosed by singular address in vv. 2–3 and all but the first words of v. 21. The whole section is introduced by second person plural in v. 1. Although these shifts most likely point to different levels of redaction, they also illustrate the characteristic use of plural address to particularize commands for individual application and singular address to emphasize collective matters of election and communal behavior.

We can trace three terse apodictic prohibitions taken from older legal tradition in vv. 1, 3, and 21. These stand out as having a normal verb + object order, in contrast to the solemn style of the other proscriptions, which put the object first (vv. 6, 8, 10, 11, 19, 20) or use the demonstrative pronoun as a replacement object before the verb (vv. 4–5, 7, 9, 12). The traditional genre of priestly declaration is used three times to underscore the prohibitions: "they are/it is unclean for you" (vv. 7, 8, 10). Priests used these fixed formulas to express their judgments on ritual matters (cf. Lev 11:38; 13:11; Hag 2:14).

A similar list of clean and unclean animals is given in fuller and more characteristically priestly form in Lev 11:2–23. Moran has decisively explicated the relationship between the two unclean bird lists. The Deuteronomic version originally had only ten unclean birds, those without the direct object marker before them. These paralleled the ten clean animals (also without the sign of the direct object). As a harmonizing move, ten more unclean birds were transferred from Leviticus, where there are twenty. These additional ten were taken up with their direct object markers and the phrase "after its/their kind" (in the translation: "any kind of"). These are the "kite" of v.

13, all five birds in vv. 14–15, the first two of v. 16, and finally the last two of v. 17.[2]

Israel's purity system categorized persons, objects, and foods. It had nothing to do with modern notions of hygiene. Those who ate unclean food became ritually unclean and were excluded from the worship assembly until their impurity was removed. The fundamental principle was that it was dangerous and inappropriate to bring something unclean (such as dead people, nonfood animals, or an animal that has died by itself) into connection with that which is holy. If such a combination were to occur, the holy entity could be drained of its holiness (profaned) or Yahweh's dangerous wrath could break out. The obligation to avoid any such catastrophic association is the central idea behind this section. Israel as a holy people must keep away from what is unclean.

Food laws are best understood and conceptualized from an anthropological perspective. A culture's food preferences and avoidances arise from economic and environmental circumstances. Food laws define boundaries and establish distinctiveness and self-identity for ethnic or vocational groups (cf. Gen 43:32, Egyptians; Jer 35:5–7, Rechabites). Dividing animals into clean and unclean expresses the natural human drive to categorize the world. Confusion in categories is uncomfortable and threatening to psychological and social order and therefore must be held at bay. Ambiguity or category confusion is unclean. Thus this list of food and nonfood animals takes as the norm the locomotion equipment (feet) and chewing patterns of domestic animals. Animals that do not conform to this template are unclean. Conventional water creatures look a certain way and move with fins; what deviates is to be avoided. Most winged insects behave in a repulsive, disorderly fashion. They are "swarmers," small creatures appearing in teeming numbers.[3]

[1–2] Israel's special relationship with Yahweh motivates obedience. The "sonship" of Israel reflects a long-standing election tradition (Exod 4:22–23; Hos 2:1 [ET 1:10]; 11:1) that emphasizes the relational aspects of Israel's status with Yahweh. It is found elsewhere in Deuteronomy (8:5; 32:5, 19, 20). The other two images of identity appear as a literal repetition of 7:6. Being a "holy

---

2. W. L. Moran, "Literary Connection between Lev 11:13–19 and Deut 14:12–18," *CBQ* 28 (1966): 271–77.

3. The most recent study on dietary law is W. Houston, *Purity and Monotheism: Clean and Unclean Animals in Biblical Law* (JSOTSup 140; Sheffield: JSOT Press, 1993). Also see E. B. Firmage, "The Biblical Dietary Laws and the Concept of Holiness," in *Studies in the Pentateuch* (ed. J. A. Emerton; VT Sup 41; Leiden: Brill, 1990), 177–208. On the system of holiness and impurity in general, see Nelson, *Raising Up a Faithful Priest*, 17–38. For a non-Western theological perspective, see K. Chan, "You Shall Not Eat These Abominable Things: An Examination of Different Interpretations on Deuteronomy 14:3–20," *East Asia Journal of Theology* 3 (1985): 88–106. Attempts to understand dietary laws as expressions of good hygiene or through the application of Eurocentric notions of cultural loathing are unhelpful.

people" means that everything repugnant (*tô'ēbâ*) and unclean must be avoided. This notion probably arose from the practice of group sanctification for those preparing for ritual (Exod 19:10, 14; 1 Sam 16:5) or military action (Deut 23:15 [ET 14]). Election as Yahweh's "treasured people," in contrast to all other nations, evokes the image of a king's treasury (1 Chr 29:3; Qoh 2:8). In Deut 26:17–19 the reciprocal proclamation of covenant is the context for Israel's standing as a holy and treasured people.

Gashing and making bald spots are mourning practices known from comparative sources and the prophets (Amos 8:10; Isa 15:2; 22:12; Jer 16:5–6; 41:5; 47:5; Ezek 7:18). Such actions expressed the strong emotions of bereavement and also seem to have been practiced to honor one's ancestors and (perhaps) keep their ghosts at bay. Such rites were forbidden to priests as part of their vocation of holiness (Lev 19:27–28), and here the ban is extended to the lay populace as a holy people. Israel considered the sphere of the dead to be an unclean realm incompatible with holiness, under the sway of powers outside the arena of Yahweh's rule. What is more, mourning activities were part of the cult of other gods (Baal: 1 Kgs 18:28; Hos 7:14; Tammuz: Ezek 8:14). Motivating this prohibition on the basis of Israel's "sonship" is especially appropriate for a custom so profoundly involved with kinship concerns. Note the emphatic order that starts v. 1: "children you are of Yahweh."

[3–20] The food laws are formatted as instruction, rather than priestly lore. For example, instead of the technical priestly category of *šeqeṣ* found in Leviticus, Deuteronomy uses the more ordinary term "unclean." Avoiding the complexities of the priestly system, "unclean" (*ṭāmē'*) is defined in purely functional terms as that which is forbidden as food "for you," while "clean" (*ṭāhôr*) is what is edible.

The section begins with an apodictic principle (v. 3), which is then explained by means of lists and more general principles. This is a sort of handbook intended to make obedience to the demand of v. 3 possible. Verse 3 makes clear that the concept of "repugnant" (*tô'ēbâ*) is not just a matter of psychological or social revulsion, but a cultural category analogous to "holy" or "unclean." It is a quality that defiles and breaks one's relationship with Yahweh, sometimes because of an association with non-Yahwistic religion (7:25; 12:31; 13:15 [ET 14]). *Tô'ēbâ* is a broad category in Deuteronomy, extending beyond religious practice even to matters of business ethics (25:16). The concept did not need to be explained; it was culturally self-evident to readers.

A list of permitted domestic and game animals (vv. 4–5) is followed by a rationalized template based on domestic food animals (v. 6). The identities of the fourth, sixth, and seventh animals in v. 5 are highly uncertain. In v. 7 a short illustrative list of animals falling outside the template is summarized by a priestly declaration: "they are unclean for you" (v. 7). The pattern is concentric: list (vv. 4–5), rule (v. 6) / rule (v. 7a), list (v. 7b). The three prohibited animals appear in the order of their distance from civilized life. This catalog is hardly complete. For example, the unclean ass is missing (Exod 34:20). Rather it gives representative examples to show the reader how to apply the template of v. 6.

The pig is the subject of a special instruction based on the template and rounded out by another priestly declaration (v. 8). In fact, the double-barreled template seems to have been devised specifically to exclude the pig, since camels, hares, and rock badgers do not have hooves. The special precaution of not touching dead swine, more at home in Leviticus (Lev 11:8; cf. vv. 24–39), suggests that the prohibition of pork needed an extra measure of stress. The proscription of the pig has generated much controversy. Because they require a large amount of water, swine are unlikely to be popular in a dry climate. Because they are not herded or pastured, swine are incompatible with herding flocks. Moreover, pigs seem to have been associated with alien cultic contexts. Pig offerings are scorned as secret and revolting rites performed at graves (Isa 65:4; 66:3, 17).[4] Even if the pig was sometimes a pagan sacrificial animal, however, its impurity in this text is firmly based on the rationale of the hoof and cud template and nothing else.

[11–20] In contrast to animals or fish, there is no principle or template for birds, only a list of twenty unclean examples. Its extreme length suggests rhetorical emphasis more than practical application. The identities of these birds are generally obscure, but it seems clear that most are scavengers or carnivorous and would involve the prohibition on eating blood or carrion at one remove. Some may be unclean because they live far from orderly human existence (the ostrich; Isa 43:20) or frequent abandoned places (the little owl, great owl, and desert owl; Ps 102:7 [ET 6]; Isa 34:11). The hoopoe may just be utterly revolting in that it smells bad and uses rubbish to build its nest. The featherless bat is certainly nontypical and flies in an abnormal way with its hands (cf. Lev 11:27). The repeated phrase "any kind of" is intended to broaden the prohibitions to closely related types.[5] Verse 19 forbids winged swarmers, namely insects that teem and proliferate in a disturbing way. Verse 20 is elliptical and can only be understood in light of Lev 11:20–23, where it is clear that edible insects (locusts) are meant.

[21] Verses 19–21 form an inverted construction that connects v. 21 with the rest of the section: "shall not be eaten" / "you may eat" / "do not eat." The prohibition of carrion again rests on the danger of eating blood. This law reflects

---

4. On the issue see F. Stendebach, "Das Schweinopfer im alten Orient," *BZ* 18 (1974): 263–71; U. Hübner, "Schweine, Schweineknochen und ein Speiseverbot im alten Israel," *VT* 39 (1989): 225–36.

5. For identifications see Nielsen, *Deuteronomium*, 152–54; R. Bulmer, "The Uncleanness of the Birds of Leviticus and Deuteronomy," *Man* 24 (1989): 304–21.

the same concern as Exod 22:30 [ET 31] but the emphasis here is on the carcass and possibilities for its advantageous disposal. Unlike the body of the unclean pig that may not be touched (v. 8), the carcass of a food animal may be exploited. Because impurity does not matter outside the "holy people" of the worshiping community, one may donate this meat to the (often poor) resident alien within one's town, or it may be sold to a foreigner. Here Deuteronomy manages to blend its humane social ethics with its insistence on a sharp ethnic boundary.[6]

The kid cooked in its mother's milk is a problematic matter and has been the focus of massive debate. It was formerly thought to refer to a Canaanite ritual practice, but the previously cited parallel text has proven irrelevant and there is no evidence of any such ritual practice.[7] Although the verse appears to sit loosely in its context, so that translations tend to isolate it typographically, it most likely is to be read as an implication or extension of the assertion of Israel's holiness in v. 21a. Of the numerous explanations offered, only two now seem cogent. Laws such as Exod 22:29 [ET 30]; Lev 22:27–28; and Deut 22:6–7 suggest a certain feeling of moral impropriety about violations of the maternal relationship. Mother birds and nestlings are not to be killed together. Baby animals are not to be sacrificed younger than eight days, nor are mothers and their young to be sacrificed on the same day. In keeping with this ethos, cooking a young animal in its own mother's milk would be ethically revolting, a denial of the tenderness and love of the maternal relationship and the life force expressed by it. This cultural value seems to be illustrated by the conventional iconography of mother animals nursing their offspring.[8] Perhaps such a practice would also have been seen as an unnatural mixing of the realms of life and death.[9]

Another possible approach begins with the observation that when this same law appears in Exod 23:19 and 34:26, its context is not dietary regulation, but the pilgrimage festival calendar. Perhaps the law's original reference was to an abuse connected with festival celebrations. Rather than being some aberrant sacrifice, a kid cooked up in soured milk may have been a favorite gourmet delicacy. Because goats were the standard milk animal, the law restricts its

---

6. On the relationship of this law to the Leviticus parallel, see M. Cohen, "Ségrégationnisme et intégrationnisme comme mobiles sous-jacents à l'antinomie de Dt 14,21 et Lv 17,15–16," *Revue d'histoire et de philosophie religieuses* 73 (1993): 113–29. On its relationship to other laws about corpses, see K. Sparks, "A Comparative Study of the Biblical *nblh* Laws," *ZAW* 110 (1998): 594–600, who translates *nĕbēlâ* as a "clean animal not properly slaughtered."

7. R. Ratner and B. Zuckerman, "'A Kid in Milk'?" *HUCA* 57 (1986): 15–60.

8. O. Keel, *Das Böcklein in der Milch seiner Mutter und Verwandtes* (OBO 33; Freiburg: Universitätsverlag, 1980), 46–144.

9. If fat (*ḥēleb*) rather than milk (*ḥālāb*) is intended (note 1), then this culinary process would involve the simultaneous death of mother and offspring.

reference to them. Revulsion over this practice became an ethnic marker over against other groups who continued to practice it.[10] A further extension of this line of thinking suggests that the baby goats in question were being taken to the sanctuary as firstlings, and their mothers were taken along to nurse them. These firstlings were so young (eight days, Exod 22:29 [ET 30]) that the mother animal was still giving colostrum in her milk. This substance makes milk reddish, which would cause anxiety over the danger of consuming blood. Understood in this way, the law is consistent with the content of the rest of vv. 3–21. Because firstlings were offered when older in Deuteronomy (15:19), the prohibition was dissociated from its festival context and came to refer solely to abstinence from a favorite gastronomic indulgence.[11] In any case, Deuteronomy uses the prohibition in its struggle to assert and maintain Israel's special identity. A holy people would never do such an abhorrent thing.

Set Apart a Tenth
14:22–29

Every Year

14:22 You shall surely set apart a tithe of all the yield of your seed that comes out from the field[a] each year.[b] 23 You shall eat—in the presence of Yahweh your God, in the place that he will choose to make his name dwell there—the tithe of your grain, your wine, and your oil, and the firstborn of your herd and your flock, so that you may learn to fear Yahweh your God always. 24 But if the road is too long for you so you cannot carry it—because the place where Yahweh your God will choose to put his name is too far away from you, because Yahweh your God will bless you—25 then you may turn it into money. Wrap up the money in your hand and go to the place that Yahweh your God will choose. 26 Spend the money on anything you wish—on cattle, sheep, wine, strong drink, or anything you want. You shall eat there in the presence of Yahweh your God and rejoice, you and your household. 27 Do not abandon[c] the Levite

---

10. M. Haran, "Seething a Kid in Its Mother's Milk," *JJS* 30 (1979): 23–35; idem, "Das Böcklein in der Milch seiner Mutter und das säugende Muttertier," *TZ* 41 (1985): 135–59; E. Knauf, "Zur Herkunft und Sozialgeschichte Israels: 'Das Böckchen in der Milch seiner Mutter,'" *Bib* 69 (1988): 153–69.

11. C. J. Labuschagne, "You Shall Not Boil a Kid in Its Mother's Milk: A New Proposal for the Origin of the Prohibition," in *The Scriptures and the Scrolls* (ed. F. García Martínez et al.; VTSup 49; Leiden: Brill, 1992), 6–17.

within your towns, because that one has no share or hereditary possession along with you.

Every Third Year

28 At the end of every three years you shall bring out the entire tithe of your yield for that year and deposit it in your towns. 29 The Levite may come, because he has no share or hereditary possession along with you, and the resident alien, the orphan, and the widow who are in your towns, and they may eat and have enough, so that Yahweh your God may bless you in any task that you undertake.

a. Accusative of the place from which departure takes place, *IBHS* 10.2.2b; p. 170 n. 17.

b. There is no preposition *b* with this expression (contrast 15:20), perhaps suggesting "on an annual basis" rather than a distributive "year by year." The former translation prepares better for the exception of v. 28. An alternate translation would connect this time expression with the main verb: "Each year you shall set apart."

c. Follows MT as the more difficult text. OG (and Kennicott 69) drops *l't'zbnw*, "you shall not abandon," and joins the remainder to the previous verse, so that the Levite is included in the celebration of v. 26: "you and your household and the Levite. . . ." "You shall not abandon" awkwardly separates the Levite from the following explanatory clause (contrast the beginning of v. 29), so that OG represents a grammatical smoothing of the text.

Centralization and the development of a monetary economy called for changes in traditional practices. Deuteronomy 14:22–15:23 seeks to reshape the system of tithes and firstlings and to promote a periodic remission of debts and release of slaves. As is usual in Deuteronomy, religious and social practices are integrally related. Tithes become opportunities for social assistance, and the long-standing practice of leaving the land fallow becomes the foundation for giving the poor and enslaved recurring opportunities for a new start. These regulations reflect an economically stratified society. As is the case with Deuteronomy as a whole, they address free, landowning citizens, not the beneficiaries of social aid or other family members, and certainly not priests or royal officials. It is as though the context of state and temple does not even exist. These laws concerning the tithe have a conservative flavor, placing the burden of social support entirely on the farmer, while ignoring artisans, merchants, and officials.

The influence of centralization on the system of firstlings and tithes had been touched on in 12:17. Now the text turns to give more careful attention to two sorts of tithes (14:22–27 and 28–29). The second of these, the poor tithe, leads on naturally to the humanitarian laws of chapter 15. The text only then circles back to the topic of firstlings (15:19–23). The overall structure of 14:22–15:23

is one of temporal rhythm: "each year," "every three years," "every seven years" (14:22, 28; 15:1, 9, 12, 20). A second structuring factor is an organization by different social groups, something typical of ancient law codes: "you and your household [and Levite]" (14:22–27; cf. v. 26); the four distressed groups (14:28–29); the poor kindred (15:1–6, 7–11); the enslaved kindred (15:12–18); and then again "you and your household" (15:19–23; cf. v. 20). The topic of support for underprivileged groups permeates the whole section.

These laws represent a development in the concept of the tithe.[1] Most texts indicate that one paid tithes to the king or to a temple. First Samuel 8:15 and 17 label tithes as harsh royal impositions, but in Amos 4:4–5 they appear as voluntary sacrificial gifts. According to Lev 27:30–33, tithes were "holy" and presumably given for the support of the sanctuary, while in Num 18:21–32 they went to Levites, who in turn tithed them to priests. Tithes were originally brought to local sanctuaries (Gen 28:22; 1 Sam 1:21 LXX), but also to the state shrines of Bethel (Gen 28:22; Amos 4:4) and Jerusalem (Gen 14:20). The Covenant Code has no specific law of the tithe, but Exod 22:28 [ET 29] urges some sort of transfer of part of the crop. It is only in Deuteronomy that religious tithes are clearly obligatory. The background of tithe as a type of tax surfaces in the third and sixth year when it is to be handed over to some local entity. It is unclear just how mathematically exact the idea of a "tenth" was supposed to be. The assertive insistence on "all the yield" (v. 22) and an "entire tithe" (v. 28), however, suggests there must have been some degree of personal judgment in determining the amount. Even though the tithe in Deuteronomy is no longer given over to a shrine, it is still called a *qōdeš* ("holy portion") in 26:13–14, and one had to be ritually clean in order to set it aside.

Centralization is used as an opportunity to restructure the people's religious experience, and the revenue provided by the custom of tithing is reused to promote joyful worship and social security. Textual connections to chapter 12 indicate that the text is working out the implications of centralization. Verses 26–27 clearly reflect 12:7, 12, 20. Eating tithes in one's hometown ("within your gates") was expressly forbidden by 12:17, suggesting that it would not be eaten at the local shrine either.

Deuteronomy's law of the tithe grows out of an older "seed tithe" law, visible behind v. 22, which is converted into an opportunity for joyful familial and social fellowship at the central sanctuary. This is followed by details of obedience in vv. 23–27. The geographic distance entailed by centralization is overcome by means of money. The poor tithe of vv. 28–29 is then presented as an exception to the general centralization requirement. Tithes of the third and sixth

---

1. See E. M. Gitlin, "The Tithes in Deuteronomy," *Religion and Life* 32 (1963): 574–85; and more generally, H. Jagersma, "The Tithes in the Old Testament," in B. Albrektson et al., *Remembering All the Way . . . (OtSt* 21; Leiden: Brill, 1981), 116–28.

year of a seven-year cycle (cf. 15:1) constitute a sort of "food bank" or "community chest" for society's marginal members. The two laws (vv. 22–27 and 28–29) share the same basic outline: command to tithe and when to do it (vv. 22, 28), eating (v. 23, 29aβ), Yahweh's blessing (vv. 24, 29b), and participants (vv. 27, 29aα). The first law fleshes out this bare outline with lists underscoring the richness of the menu (vv. 23, 26) and with repeated references to centralization (vv. 23, 24, 25). The second law emphasizes its underprivileged beneficiaries. These two tithe laws correlate important theological themes: the central shrine, joyful celebration, desacralization of offerings, social solidarity, and Yahweh's blessing through the fertility of the land. Deuteronomy's theology of freedom, based on the experience of exodus, and egalitarian ideology, has transformed tithes that once were royal taxes or priestly requirements into sources of community joy and solidarity.

It is generally agreed that the animal firstlings in v. 23aβ are out of place and represent a disturbing addition. The third *kî* clause of v. 24 may also be an addition; it confuses the notion of distance by presenting the reason for one's inability to bring the tithe as due to the rich extent of Yahweh's blessing. The parenthetic list of v. 26 also seems to represent an expansion.

Yahweh's promised blessing serves as both motivation and assurance (vv. 24, 29). Blessing also functions as a key theme in the larger calendar and offerings section of 14:22–16:17 (cf. 14:29; 15:4, 6, 10, 14, 18; 16:10, 15). The joyful banquet at the central sanctuary is promoted as a lesson in dependence on divine bounty and a proper fear of Yahweh (v. 23). Obedient reverence thus develops in the context of joy and community solidarity. The motivational clause, "learn to fear," reappears in 17:19 as a consequence of the king's reading the law and contrasts sharply with the disloyal learning warned against in 18:9; 20:18.[2]

Although some sort of relationship between tithes and firstfruits is suggested by 26:1–15, in 18:4 firstfruits are clearly a perquisite of the priests. By their very nature, tithes and firstfruits are different sorts of offerings. Tithes are obviously offered after the harvest is finished and can be measured. A tithe is a calculated amount and is relatively sizable. In contrast, one offers firstfruits as the harvest begins, and they are small enough to fit in a basket (26:2, 4). Firstling animals are also linked with tithes (v. 23aβ; cf. 15:19–20) in some way. It is best to understand the reference to firstlings in v. 23 not as something equivalent to the tithe, but as an illustrative example of a related offering also taken to the central sanctuary (as in the list in 12:6).

---

2. On this theme, see G. Braulik, "Deuteronomy and the Commemorative Culture of Israel," in *Theology of Deuteronomy*, 183–98; trans. of "Das Deuteronomium und die Gedächtniskultur Israels: Redaktionsgeschichtliche Beobachtungen zur Verwendung von *lmd*," in *Studien zum Buch Deuteronomium*, 119–46.

There is a utopian flavor to these laws. Is it reasonable or even possible to eat more than a month's supply of food all at once? For this reason, some have suggested that in an earlier form of this law only part of the tithe was consumed (cf. the wording of v. 23, which could be understood as "eat of the tithe" (cf. Lev 19:25, 22:10). In this case, the bulk of the tithe would continue to support the sanctuary, but a family meal would be supplied from a portion of it. The impression that the tithe was to be consumed completely rests largely on the menu lists of vv. 23a and 26a, which could conceivably be additions to the original text. The calendar system of 14:22–15:18 appears to be a synthetic arrangement, exploiting the tithes of years three and six of a seven-year cycle for a new purpose. Is the reader to assume that the seventh year involves no tithe at all, or is that year's tithe to be treated like those of the first, second, fourth, and fifth years? The tithes are not specifically tied to the upcoming liturgical calendar of chapter 16, although "at the end" in v. 28 seems to suggest the Feast of Booths.

[22–27] Verse 22 vigorously sets forth an older "seed tithe" law (cf. the wording of Lev 27:30; 1 Sam 8:15), grammatically strengthened by an infinitive absolute. The *waw* perfect of v. 23 then links together gift and meal. There is some tension between v. 22, which concerns only grain, and the more wide-ranging instructions that follow. The tithe is described in terms of produce close to the field. *Tîrōš* is juice in the winepress (Hos 9:2), and *yiṣhār* is freshly pressed oil. Along with grain, these form the three traditional hallmarks of agricultural prosperity (Deut 7:13; 11:14; 18:4; Hos 2:10, 24 [ET 8, 22]). Verses 24–26 form a casuistic "if . . . you" instruction, with the apodosis starting at v. 25. In the protasis, the wording is repetitious and overfull, mixing the competing ideas of distance (v. 24a) and blessing (v. 24b). The issue of territorial size relates back to 12:20–21 and forward to 19:8–10. The point of "wrap up in your hand" (v. 25) is to secure and isolate the money to spend it only in the central place. Now that they are part of the banquet, the grain and juice that were described in terms close to their harvested state in v. 23 are portrayed in v. 26 in their processed state as "wine and strong drink" (the latter perhaps barley beer).

An explicit reference to local Levites may seek to cushion the negative economic effect of centralization on this group, in that the former use of the tithe to support the local sanctuary had been eliminated (cf. 12:12). These particular Levites are specifically those with whom the householder has a neighborly relationship ("within your towns").

[28–29] The tithes of years three and six of a seven-year cycle are stored for distribution over time, conceivably during the whole three- or four-year period until the next assistance tithe. When Deut 26:12–15 addresses the centralized aspect of this tithe, however, the phrase "year of the tithe" is used (26:12), perhaps because distribution was restricted to that year. The Hebrew of v. 28 suggests that the food is to be stored within the town gateway edifice ("deposit it in your gates"). Keeping this tithe under local control seems to preserve an element of the earlier practice of tithing to the neighborhood sanctuary. Some suggest that this represents an additional second tenth rather than a different use of the same single tithe (cf. the understanding of Tob 1:6–8). Although this is possible, given the utopian flavor of these laws, the most natural reading suggests otherwise: "the *entire* tithe of your yield for *that year*" (v. 28).

The social background is that of an agricultural community with some marginal members who do not have a direct right of access to the crop. As in v. 27, the standard triad of those threatened by exploitation (10:18–19; 27:19) is supplemented by the Levite. Characteristically, Deuteronomy pays no attention to administrative problems. What institution is responsible for storage and distribution? Is there a regular, periodic distribution? There is no bureaucracy or state interference; this is a purely local social program. On the other hand, storage at the gate and the statement that distributed amounts are to be sufficient to ensure satiety imply some measure of public control. The tithe is intended to be a standardized and dependable social support program, rather than something ad hoc and voluntary. The text emphasizes "the entire tithe." There is to be an openhanded response with no skimping!

Every Seventh Year
15:1–23

Perform a Debt Remission

15:1 At the end of every seventh year you shall perform a debt remission. 2 This is the manner of the debt remission. Let every creditor remit his claim that he holds against his neighbor.[a] Let him not press his claim against his kindred,[b] because the remission of Yahweh has been proclaimed.[c] 3 You may[d] press your claim against a foreigner, but you must remit[e] whatever is owed you by your kindred. 4 Nevertheless, there will not be any poor among you, because Yahweh will surely bless you in the land that Yahweh your God is going to give you as a hereditary possession to take it over, 5 if only[f] you will obey Yahweh your God, being careful to do this whole commandment that I am commanding you today. 6 When Yahweh your God has blessed you, just as he promised you, you will lend to many nations, but you will not borrow;[g] and you will rule over many nations, but they will not rule over you.

Do Not Harden Your Heart

7 If there is anyone poor among you, one of your kindred[h] in one of your cities in your land that Yahweh your God is going to give you, do not harden your heart or shut your hand against your poor kindred. 8 Instead you should open your hand wide to him. You should surely lend him enough for his need that he needs. 9 Be careful lest there be a worthless thought in your heart,[i] thinking, "The seventh year, the year of debt remission, is near," and you are ungenerous to your poor kindred and do not give anything to him, and he cries out against you to Yahweh and it be a sin against you. 10 Give freely to him[j] and do not let your heart be ungenerous when you give to him, because on account of this thing Yahweh your God will bless you in all your work and in every undertaking of your hand. 11 Since the poor will never cease to exist in the land,[k] for this reason I command you, "Open your hand wide to the needy and poor kindred in your land."

Free Slaves after Seven Years

12 If your kindred, a Hebrew man or a Hebrew woman, is sold[l] to you and serves you six years, in the seventh year you shall set him free. 13 And when you set him free, do not send him out empty-handed. 14 Load him down[m] with things from your flock, your threshing floor, and your winepress. Just as[n] Yahweh your God has blessed you, you shall give to him. 15 Remember that you were a slave in the land of Egypt, and Yahweh your God redeemed you. For this reason I am commanding you this thing.[o] 16 But if he says to you, "I do not want to leave you," because he loves you and your household, because it goes well for him with you, 17 then you shall take an awl and put it through his ear into the door, and he shall be your permanent slave.[p] You shall do the same thing with your female slave. 18 Do not consider it a hard thing when you send him out free, because he has served you six years, worth the wages of a hired hand,[q] and Yahweh your God will bless you in everything that you do.

Firstborn Male Animals

19 Every firstborn male in your herd and flock you shall consecrate to Yahweh your God. Do not put your firstborn ox to work[r] or shear the firstborn of your flock. 20 You shall eat it in the presence of Yahweh your God year by year at the place that Yahweh will choose—you and your household. 21 But if there is a blemish, it being lame or blind—any serious blemish—do not sacrifice it to Yahweh your God. 22 You may eat it within any

of your towns, the unclean[s] and the clean together, like a gazelle or deer.
23 Only do not eat its blood. You shall pour it out on the ground like water.

a. The infinitive absolute as a legislative jussive, *IBHS* 35.5.1a. This translation takes *ba'al* alone as the subject ("creditor"), and *maššeh yādô* ("his claim," i.e., "the claim of his hand") as a direct object further explained by the *'ăšer* clause ("that he holds against his neighbor"). This corresponds with "your hand" as the object of *tašmēṭ* in v. 3b and the wording of Neh 10:32 [ET 31]. The grammar would be less abrupt if one were to insert a second *maššeh* and direct object marker (see *BHS*): *kol-ba'al maššeh 'et maššeh yādô*: "let every holder of a claim remit the claim he holds." Masoretic punctuation construes the entire phrase *ba'al maššeh yādô* as the subject and the *'ăšer* clause as the direct object: "let every holder of a claim of his hand remit what he has lent to his neighbor." One could also understand the subject as *kol-ba'al maššeh* and the direct object as *yādô*: "Let every holder of a claim release his hand in regard to what he holds." Or one could construe the imperative without a direct object: "let every holder of a claim of his hand who lends to his neighbor, grant remission." It is even possible to understand the *'ăšer* clause as the subject of the following sentence: "he who lends to his neighbor shall not press his claim against his kindred." The verb *nāšā'* denotes: "to enter into a relationship centered on a pledge, to grant a loan that entails a pledge," and the preposition *b* expresses the personal obligation of the debtor (cf. 24:11). See F. Hossfeld and E. Reuter, "*nāšā'* II," *TDOT* 10:55–59.

b. Follows OG, which reflects a single direct object *before* the verb: *w't 'hyw l' ygś ky qr'*, "and his kindred let him not press because [remission] has been proclaimed." (OG converts this to second person, however.) 4QDeut[c] also reads *l' ygś ky qr'* and has room for a single direct object on the previous line. MT (Sam., Syr., Vulg.) has *two* direct objects coming *after* the verb: *l' ygs' 't r'hw (w)'t 'hyw ky qr'*, "let him not press his neighbor (and) his kindred because [remission] has been proclaimed." OG (4QDeut[c]) is preferable because it preserves the object-first parallel structure of vv. 2–3 (kindred, foreigner, kindred) and because it is shorter, avoiding what looks like a doublet or expansion in MT. The verb *ngś* denotes the assertion of a right to seize the property or person of the debtor; see E. Lipiński, "*nāgaś*," *TDOT* 9:213–15.

c. Taking the expression as impersonal, "one has proclaimed." The remission is *lyhwh*, i.e., it "derives from Yahweh" or is "in honor of Yahweh." Alternate translation: "for he [the debtor] has appealed to Yahweh for remission."

d. Modal permission, *IBHS* 31.4d.

e. That is, "you must make your hand let go of whatever is owed," a causative hip'il with two objects. Alternate translation taking "your hand" as the subject: "your hand must release."

f. Emphatic use of *raq*, Williams, *Hebrew Syntax*, 393.

g. Here the hip'il of *'ābaṭ* denotes "loan against a pledge to someone" (see v. 8), and the Qal "borrow against a pledge." K.-M. Beyse, "*ābaṭ*," *TDOT* 10:405–6.

h. Follows the awkward MT *m'ḥd 'ḥyk*, "from one of your kindred" (cf. 18:6). Syr. and Tg. offer the easier "one from your kindred," while OG fails to reproduce "one" at all, reading simply "from your kindred." These are probably attempts to produce a clear translation of MT.

i. Follows MT. OG has "secret" before "in your heart," so *BHS* suggests inserting the Hebrew equivalent as *msttr*. However, OG represents a conflated doublet translation: first freely as "secret" and then literally as "in your heart."

j. Follows MT. OG avoids the notion of an outright handout by repeating "and you shall surely lend him enough for his need" from v. 8b.

k. Not "earth." See J. M. Hamilton, "*Hā'āreṣ* in the Shemitta Law," *VT* 42 (1992): 214–22.

l. That is, by his or her parent. Alternate translation as reflexive: "sells himself."

m. Literally "put a necklace on his neck" (Ps 73:6), thus "adorn," "deck out," implying honor and dignity (cf. Judg 8:26; Prov 1:9).

n. Follows Sam. and OG in reading the expected *k'šr* (cf. 16:10). MT ("with that which") lost a *k* by haplography: *wmyqbk [k]'šr*.

o. Follows OG. MT expands with *hywm*, "today." OG, 1QDeut[b], Tg. Ps.-J. supplement with *l'śwt*, "to do," after "commanding you."

p. *'ebed 'ôlām* is a technical term (1 Sam 27:12; Job 40:28 [E 41:4]).

q. Translations of this cost-benefit analysis vary. Some take *mišneh* as "twice," thus "at half the cost of a hired servant" (no wages needed, only support) or "worked twice as hard as a hired servant" (being on call night and day). I understand *mišneh* as "equivalent," thus "services worth the wages of a hired servant [but without cost to you]." This is advocated by M. Tsevat, "The Hebrew Slave According to Deuteronomy 15:12–18: His Lot and the Value of His Work, with Special Attention to the Meaning of *mšnh*," *JBL* 113 (1994): 587–95, responding to J. M. Lindenberger, "How Much for a Hebrew Slave? The Meaning of *Mišneh* in Deut 15:18," *JBL* 110 (1991): 479–82.

r. Alternate translation reflecting the preposition *b* before "ox": "do work with."

s. OG adds "among you" to avoid the impression that unclean animals are meant; cf. 12:15, 22.

Deuteronomy seeks to reform social and economic practices so that Israel may achieve the life envisioned for it in the land. Formerly independent citizens have become victims of an emerging monetary economy and a concurrent breakdown of Israel's traditional communitarian ethos. Borrowing to survive, many have become dependent on or enslaved to more affluent fellow Israelites. Deuteronomy intends to prevent the perpetuation of a permanent underclass of poor and enslaved fellow Israelites. Although the solutions advanced may sound idealistic to modern ears, they are similar to reform efforts in the Mesopotamian legal tradition. If this is a "utopia," it is one of the here and now, not the Greek model of a distant, mythic arrangement. These laws seek to rob debt of its tyrannical power, to limit human misery, and to avoid a paralysis of economic life that would stunt the blessings of productivity.[1]

1. For general background, see N. P. Lemche, "The Hebrew Slave," *VT* 25 (1975): 129–44; idem, "The Manumission of Slaves—the Fallow Year—the Sabbatical Year—the Jobel Year," *VT* 26 (1976): 38–59; S. A. Kaufman, "A Reconstruction of the Social Welfare Systems of Ancient Israel," in *The Shelter of Elyon: Essays in Ancient Palestinian Life and Literature in Honor of G. W. Ahlström* (ed. W. Barrick and J. Spencer; JSOTSup 31; Sheffield: JSOT Press, 1984), 277–86;

Characteristically, Deuteronomy addresses its reforming challenge to the propertied class, those who could lend money and own slaves. It expands an older tradition of letting the land lie fallow into a way out of the worst effects of these social and economic inequities. Deuteronomy also rewrites the old slave release law of the Covenant Code, expanding a description of a male slave's legal rights into the imposition of a moral duty on the slave holder. Traditionally, the clan or family had shielded the individual from poverty and exploitation. Now Deuteronomy expands this familial obligation to the metaphorical "kindred" (literally "brother," vv. 2, 3, 7, 9, 11, 12) who is one's enslaved or less affluent fellow citizen. Motivations involving the memory of slavery in Egypt and the material blessing of Yahweh seek to overcome an expected resistance to these new responsibilities. The extension of the slave release law to women is also typical of Deuteronomy (cf. 21:10–17).

These reform laws are set into a larger text complex organized by time, 14:22–16:17. This section is structured first by yearly intervals (14:22, 28; 15:1, 12, 20) and then by the festival calendar (16:1–17). If one supposes that the laws of Deuteronomy follow the order of the Decalogue, this emphasis on chronological cycles would seem to connect 14:22–16:17 to the Sabbath commandment. An even broader context is the topic of social support made available through open participation in the centralized cult (12:12, 18–19; 14:27, 29; 16:11, 14). The laws about tithes and firstlings (14:22–29; 15:19–23) serve as brackets for the social provisions of 15:1–18, connecting back to the centralized sanctuary law and joining the central shrine and the needy into a single web.

The motivation of Yahweh's blessing as something that results from obedience also links this material together (14:29; 15:10, 18; 16:15; cf. 23:21 [ET 20] and 24:19). A similar rhetorical movement from basic law to divine blessing is visible between 14:28 and 29b; 15:1 and 10b; and 15:12 and 18b. Deuteronomy thus envisions a circle of generosity empowered by blessing. To obey is to generate the blessing of prosperity, and in turn this divine blessing makes it possible to obey the command to serve those in need (15:4–6, 14; cf. 14:24; 16:10). The welfare of the poor and enslaved depends on the prosperity of landowners, which in turn depends on Yahweh's blessing, which in turn depends on obedience. In fact, the promise of blessing as well as prayer for it encloses the entire legal corpus (12:7; 26:15). Deuteronomy has thus transferred the notion of blessing, traditionally connected to a proper observance of cultic rhythms and rituals, into the realm of social laws.

M. J. Oosthuizen, "Deuteronomy 15:1–18 in Socio-Rhetorical Perspective," *ZABR* 3 (1997): 64–91. On ethical implications, see W. Houston, 'You Shall Open Your Hand to Your Needy Brother': Ideology and Moral Formation in Deut 15:1–18," in *The Bible in Ethics: The Second Sheffield Colloquium* (ed. J. Rogerson et al.; JSOTSup 207; Sheffield: Sheffield Academic Press, 1995), 296–314.

The two social laws are bound together by the key expression "seventh year" (vv. 1, 9, 12) and by the topical connection of the injurious effect of debt. The overall pattern is one of law (vv. 1–3, 12–14, 16–17) followed by exhortation about attitude (vv. 7–11, 15, 18). The potential stinginess of creditors in vv. 7 and 10 corresponds to the slaveowner's attitude in v. 18. In fact, the wording of vv. 10 and 18b is almost identical. Internal unity is also provided by repeated references to "kindred" (vv. 2, 3, 7, 9, 11, 12) and Yahweh's blessing (vv. 4, 6, 10, 14, 18). The divine warrant for obedience to the first law ("remission of Yahweh," v. 2) corresponds to Yahweh's exodus redemption that motivates the second (v. 15). Both laws refer to the command of Moses (v. 5, 15). They also share a rhetoric of contrast in that the expectations set up by the idealistic vision of vv. 4–6 and the manumission of 12–15 are each modified by reflection on potential consequences in the form of resistance to liberal lending (vv. 7–11) and a slave's refusal to depart (vv. 16–18). The law about firstborn animals is loosely tied to the first two laws by the catchword "serve" (vv. 12, 18, 19 [translated "work"]) and the phrase "year by year" (v. 20), which in turn leads on to the calendar that follows in chapter 16.

These two social laws, along with those of 24:10–15, share a different focus from that of Deuteronomy's standard concern with the marginalized widow, fatherless, and alien. Those particular marginalized groups lacked the standing to have legitimate access to the economy, so that the social welfare laws concerning them refer primarily to their participation in the joyous cultic assembly. In contrast, the disadvantaged in these texts have legitimate ways to support themselves (as small farmers or daily wage earners) and could break out of poverty if given a chance. However, they find themselves trapped in the debt system. Their poverty is not a permanent feature of the social system, but the result of bad harvests or individual hard luck. The goal of these laws, therefore, is not the long-term charity provided to the widow, fatherless, and alien, in the shape of the third-year tithe, admission to the cultic assembly, and gleaning (14:28–29; 16:11, 14; 24:19–20). Rather these laws seek to break the cycle of debt and enslavement and to reintegrate these poor into the economy as independent, productive members. These poor are not lumped together into a social classification like the widow or alien, but spoken of as individual "kindred" (i.e., "brothers"). Moreover, these individuals could complain directly to Yahweh. Consequently, failure to help in their economic recovery would count as sin (15:9; 24:15).[2]

[1–11] Sporadic debt remissions are known from the ancient Near East.[3]

---

2. On these issues, see N. Lohfink, "Das deuteronomische Gesetz in der Endgestalt—Entwurf einer Gesellschaft ohne marginale Gruppen," in *Studien zum Deuteronomium III*, 205–18.

3. *ANET*, 526–28. For parallels, see J. M. Hamilton, *Social Justice and Deuteronomy: The Case of Deuteronomy 15* (SBLDS 136; Atlanta: Scholars Press, 1992), 45–72; M. Weinfeld, "Freedom

Deuteronomy seeks to put such erratic attempts to restore the economic balance of society onto a predictable basis. What elsewhere was the function of the king is here the responsibility of all citizens under the command and authorization of Yahweh.

Metaphorical body language or somatic imagery unifies this first law. "Hand" represents the power to hold or release a claim against one's neighbor and "kindred" (vv. 2–3), as well as the economic power to refuse or grant loans (vv. 7, 8, 11). The internal volition to withhold or grant help is expressed by a hard and ungenerous heart, the repository of worthless thoughts (vv. 7, 9, 10). An "evil eye" that looks fiercely and discloses a jealous demeanor (v. 9) indicates a grudging attitude.[4] The actions of opening and closing the hand, the inner will of the heart, and the visible glance of the jealous eye combine to express a unity of action and attitude. Further unity is provided by the verb *qārā'*, "call," which connects the proclamation of the remission in v. 2 and the cry of the poor in v. 9.

Verse 1 is an earlier, pre-Deuteronomic law requiring an otherwise undefined remission. This ambiguity is explained through a formula of juridical explanation ("this is the manner of"; cf. 18:3; Lev 6:7–11 [ET 14–18]) linking the second person of v. 1 to the third person of the rest of v. 2. The use of "neighbor" as well as the Deuteronomic "kindred" (v. 2) is a further indication that earlier material is present.[5] Verses 4–6 may represent later supplementary motivations and considerations. Because the law addresses the existence of poor people, vv. 4–6 create tension, especially with v. 11. These verses seem to be related to the blessing of 28:11–13. Nevertheless, the text in its present form does make sense. Verses 4–6 portray the world as it should be, a society without poverty, while v. 11 admits to how things really are. Verse 4 is the expected norm; v. 11 the temporary exception. The recurring problem of poverty is not due to some systemic fault in Yahweh's blessing or bestowed land, but is episodic and implicitly assumes a lack of full obedience to laws such as this one. The reality of poverty provides an opportunity for

Proclamations in Egypt and in the Ancient Near East," in *Pharaonic Egypt: The Bible and Christianity* (ed. S. Israelit-Groll; Jerusalem: Magnes, 1985), 317–27; idem, "Sabbatical Year and Jubilee in the Pentateuchal Laws and Their Ancient Near Eastern Background," in *The Law in the Bible and in Its Environment* (ed. T. Veijola; Suomen Eksegeettisen Seuren Julkaisuja 51; Göttingen: Vandenhoeck & Ruprecht, 1990), 39–62.

4. For the "evil eye" as an expression of the tension and suspicion generated by legally ambiguous situations, see J. E. Elliott, "The Evil Eye in the First Testament: The Ecology and Culture of a Pervasive Belief," in *The Bible and the Politics of Exegesis: Essays in Honor of Norman K. Gottwald* (ed. D. Jobling et al; Cleveland: Pilgrim, 1991), 147–59. It is the polar opposite of social solidarity in an economically tight situation (cf. 28:54, 56).

5. For further detail, see W. S. Morrow, "The Composition of Deut 15:1–3," *Hebrew Annual Review* 12 (1990): 115–31.

obedient generosity, but does not undermine the sufficiency and goodness of
Yahweh's gifts.

A traditional, positive apodictic law is cited in v. 1 and reinterpreted for a
new situation by v. 2. "Remission" ("an act of letting drop") originally referred
to the practice of leaving the land fallow, as can be seen by the use of the verbal root in Exod 23:10–11. This custom already reflected social concern in that
whatever the unsown land produced was available for the poor. Verse 2 alters
this into a remission on claims of pledged property (and persons?). The "letting
go" of the field's harvest becomes a "letting go" of debt claims and the economic dependence inevitably connected to them. Nehemiah 10:32 [ET 31] also
coordinates the agricultural fallow year and debt remission. Deuteronomy
31:10–11 synchronizes the year of remission with the year of reading the law
at the Festival of Booths.

In vv. 2–3 a concentric structure focuses attention on Yahweh's right to
expect obedience:

> Let every creditor remit his claim ("the claim of his hand")
> that (*ăšer*) he holds against his neighbor.
> Let him not press his claim
> against his kindred
> because the remission of Yahweh has been
> proclaimed.
> Against a foreigner
> you may press your claim,
> but whatever (*ăšer*) is owed you by your kindred
> you must remit ("release your hand").[6]

These were loans of desperation, not efforts to accumulate investment capital.
Those poor enough to need to borrow could pledge nothing but the bare necessities of life (one's primary garment, the household millstone) or perhaps one's
ancestral land. Nehemiah 5:2–5 and 11 describe the social trap of pledge for-
feiture and debt dependency and envision a voluntary remission. It remains
unclear whether a movable pledge was handed over to the creditor at the start
of the loan, or was only seized in the case of default or to pressure repayment,
although the latter seems more likely. Nothing suggests that the debtor's dependents served as loan pledges in Israel. This was unlike the situation in
Mesopotamia, where a creditor would gain the work of such a person, "dis-
trained" or held hostage in servitude, until the debt was paid.[7] The pledges mentioned in Deuteronomy are all inanimate (24:6, 10–13).

---

6. Adapted from Seitz, *Redaktionsgeschichtliche Studien*, 168.
7. Code of Hammurabi, 114–16, *ANET*, 170.

"At the end of" (v. 1; cf. 14:28) indicates "after a term of." Given uncertainty over the meaning of *maššeh* ("debt" or "pledge"), it is not immediately clear whether v. 2 intends an actual forgiveness of the debt or merely a release of what was pledged against the debt. In any case, vv. 7–11 do make clear that the practical result was that the whole debt became permanently uncollectible. My translation "claim" for *maššeh* intends to communicate that the concept of a debt and the pledged collateral held for it cannot be separated. The standing claim against the pledge put the defaulted borrower into a relation of personal attachment with and dependence on the creditor. The meaning of v. 2 is that the creditor who controls an item of collateral should release it to the indebted person. Remission means the renunciation of any claim over the pledge. The "hand" in the expression *maššeh yādô* is not that of the borrower but denotes the power of the creditor (as is clear from Neh 10:32 [ET 31]). The creditor is to "let drop" or "let go" the claim in his hand (v. 3), that is, the pledge over which he has control. Although not a direct forgiveness of the money owed, this release means that the debt could no longer be collected. The ruthless connotation of *nāgaś*, "press a claim against," is indicated by 2 Kgs 23:35.

Proclamation of "the remission of Yahweh" implies a public declaration as a religious occasion (Lev 25:10; Isa 62:1). Verse 3 comments on vv. 1–2, allowing legal action against foreigners, but preventing it against compatriots. The contrast between foreigner and "kindred" is a characteristic concern of Deuteronomy (14:21a; 17:15; 23:21 [ET 20]) and strengthens the motivation. This foreigner (*noqrî*) is not a poor brother or disadvantaged resident alien, but most likely a merchant. The relationship would be commercial, not familial or neighborly.

Verses 4–6 move in the direction of motivation and attitude. There need not be any poor because Yahweh will richly bless (v. 4), but only if you obey (v. 5)—then Yahweh's blessing occurs (v. 6). Full obedience would bring about a state of affairs in which this particular law would actually not be needed. In light of this promise of blessing, there is no need to worry about any deleterious economic consequences from obedience. The prospect of becoming a "creditor nation" further motivates obedience (cf. 28:12, 44).[8] The poetic parallel of "borrow" and "rule" in v. 6 is instructive: a loan relationship unavoidably entails dependency in either the personal or political realm.

Verses 7–11 seek to counter attitudes that would undermine the intention of debt remission. The temporary nature of loans must not lead to a "tightfisted" suspension of lending (note the opposition between closed and open hands in vv. 7 and 8). Lending is not to be a commercial transaction with the goal of

---

8. See R. Kessler, *"Gôjim* in Dtn 15:6; 28:12: 'Volker' oder 'Heiden'"? in *Dort ziehen Schiffe dahin* . . . (ed. M. Augustin and K.-D. Schunck; BEATAJ 28; XIV IOSOT Congress, Paris; Frankfurt: Lang, 1996), 85–89.

gaining power over the person or labor of the debtor, but an institution of social benevolence intended to help the poor "kindred." The train of thought leads away from the mere possibility of poverty (v. 7) to the state of constant poverty (v. 11). The section is held together by an alternation of negative (vv. 7b, 9) and positive (vv. 8, 10–11) admonitions, each coordinated with negative and positive consequences (vv. 9b and 10b). The vocabulary of v. 9 ties back to the core law of vv. 1–2. A concentric structure is evident, enveloping the imperatives with a concern for the "poor":[9]

> poor in the land . . . surely open your hand (vv. 7–8a)
> *dābār* (translated as "thought"; v. 9aα)
> evil eye (translated as "ungenerous"; v. 9aβ)
> do not give to him (v. 9aγ)
> give freely to him (v. 10aα)
> evil heart (translated as "ungenerous"; v. 10aβ)
> *dābār* (translated as "thing"; v. 10b)
> poor in the land . . . open your hand (v. 11)

In a way typical of Deuteronomy, vv. 7–11 move away from the sphere of public legality into the realm of inner motivation. The motive for lending is not economic advantage, but the plight of one's "kindred." Legal stipulations alone cannot inspire generosity, so the text stresses the potential reaction of Yahweh to lament (cf. 24:14–15; Exod 22:26 [ET 27])[10] and uses the relational language of "your kindred," "your cities," "your land" (vv. 7, 9, 11). This welfare program is intended to build community, not create alienation.

[12–18] This law extends the principle of "remission" (vv. 1–2) to those who have lost their freedom because of debt and poverty.[11] Heavy taxation, the breakdown in kinship structures and loyalties, and astronomically high interest rates meant that debt was an inescapable trap for many (Amos 2:6–8; 8:4–6). All too often, these loans of desperation must have resulted in debt slavery for the debtor's dependents (cf. 2 Kgs 4:1; Neh 5:1–6). Naturally, the head of a household, upon whose economic viability the whole family's survival depended, would first sell off his dependents rather than himself. It is generally

---

9. Adapted from Seitz, *Redaktionsgeschichtliche Studien*, 169–70.

10. R. Kessler, "Die Rolle des Armen für Gerechtigkeit und Sünde des Reichen: Hintergrund und Bedeutung von Dtn 15,9; 24,13.15," in *Was ist der Mensch ...? Beiträge zur Anthropologie des Alten Testaments* (ed. F. Crüsemann et al.; Munich: Kaiser, 1992), 153–63.

11. On debt slavery, see G. C. Chirichigno, *Debt-Slavery in Israel and the Ancient Near East* (JSOTSup 141; Sheffield: Sheffield Academic Press, 1993); W. W. Hallo, "Slave Release in the Biblical World in Light of a New Text," in *Solving Riddles and Untying Knots* (ed. Z. Zevit et al.; Winona Lake, Ind.: Eisenbrauns, 1995), 79–94. On the rhetoric of this law, see G. Lasserre, "Lutter contre la paupérisation et ses conséquences: Lecture rhétorique de Dt 15,12–18," *Etudes théologiques et religieuses* 70 (1995): 481–92.

agreed that this law refers to such debt slaves, not to foreign or chattel slaves owned outright as property. Nevertheless, the same Hebrew word covered both categories, and certainly both are referred to as participants in the joyful celebration (12:12, 18; 16:11, 14), although debt slaves might have joined their own families on such occasions. A similar manumission of debt slaves sold to pay a debt or surrendered to the creditor upon default (rather than chattel slaves or those held as "distraints" to secure a loan), is the topic of the Code of Hammurabi, 117–19 (*ANET*, 170–71), with §117 offering a close parallel. One difference is that the term of service in Deuteronomy is twice that of the three years of Hammurabi's law. There is probably an unstated assumption that a debt slave could be redeemed early by paying off the overdue debt.

This law represents a radical rewriting of the manumission law in the Covenant Code (Exod 21:2–6).[12] The differences are telling. Although Deuteronomy retains the main case of manumission and the subcase regarding one who wishes to stay, it adds an entirely new requirement to provide a grubstake for the released slave. Exodus operates from the point of view of the buyer and owner. Deuteronomy emphasizes the desperate perspective of the enslaved kindred. Deuteronomy shifts from the predominantly third-person reference to the slave found in Exodus and directs the responsibility straight at the "you" of the slaveowning audience. In Deuteronomy, "Hebrew" clearly refers to a fellow Israelite "brother" in an egalitarian way. In Exodus the term might indicate membership in a subgroup with low social status. Where Exodus speaks of the slave being permitted to leave, Deuteronomy obligates the owner actively to send him or her out (*šālaḥ*, vv. 12, 13, 18). Deuteronomy changes the entire tone by imposing on the owner the obligation of a liberal gift to give the slave a new start in honor and dignity.

The relational focus between slave and owner shifts so that the slave who chooses to remain does so exclusively because of a positive relationship with the owner and the owner's family. In contrast, Exodus includes as part of the slave's motivation his love for wife and children, who are clearly intended to be left behind as property of the master. However, because the obligation to manumit is absolute, Deuteronomy does not deal with the marital status and

---

12. Literary dependence on Exod 21:2–6 seems certain. Dissent from this broad consensus is offered by J. Van Seters, "The Law of the Hebrew Slave," *ZAW* 108 (1996): 534–46. N. Lohfink, "Fortschreibung? Zur Technik von Reschtsrevisionen im deuteronomistischen Bereich, erörtert an Deuteronomium 12, Ex 21:2–11 und Dtn 15,12–18," in *Das Deuteronomium und seine Querbeziehungen*, ed. Veijola, 149–64, uses this text to demonstrate the impossibility of recovering the texts of earlier laws used by Deuteronomy. On the comparative dating of these laws, see S. A. Kaufman, "Deuteronomy 15 and Recent Research on the Dating of P," in *Das Deuteronomium*, ed. Lohfink, 273–76; over against S. Japhet, "The Relationship between the Legal Corpora in the Pentateuch in Light of Manumission Laws," in *Studies in Bible* (ed. S. Japhet; ScrHier 31; Jerusalem: Magnes, 1986), 63–84.

rights of the debt slave. As a fellow citizen, the slave's family is his own business and the matter of affection toward wife and children is not an issue. Because the topic of the interaction between slavery and marriage (present in Exod 21:2–6 and 7–11) is not of interest to Deuteronomy, the wife and children of the slave are beside the point and eliminated. It is significant that Deuteronomy completely avoids the term "master," replacing it with " you," and does not even use the word "slave" until v. 17. Deuteronomy's special interests dominate: social responsibility and generosity (vv. 13–14), the exodus as motivation (v. 15a), and the situation of Mosaic command (v. 15b; cf. vv. 5 and 11).[13] The ceremonial conversion to permanent slave status is a desacralized version of Exod 21:5–6 that takes centralization into account (v. 17a).

Deuteronomy also extends the manumission law to the "Hebrew woman" slave (v. 12). She is also a "kindred" [literally "brother"] to be released. The concubine slave law that follows in Exod 21:7–11 is simply dropped and replaced by an abrupt v. 17b. The inclusion of women slaves is appropriate since women sometimes owned property (2 Kgs 8:3) and they certainly could be sold for family debts. Even though Deuteronomy no longer speaks of giving freedom to a wife brought into bondage along with her husband (as in Exod 21:3), this silence should probably not be taken as an abrogation of that legal obligation.

The law is enclosed by "serve you six years" (vv. 12, 18) and attached to the previous law by "seventh year" (vv. 1 and 12). The text shifts from the seven-year remission cycle to the start of the seventh year of an individual slave's service. Even though Jer 34:8–14 conflates vv. 1 and 12 in regard to a mass release of slaves, Deuteronomy itself does not intend that manumission take place at the same time as the debt remission. The wording of v. 12 and the motivating timetable of v. 18 make this clear. Structurally, the basic shape consists of three "if/when . . . you" casuistic formulations: vv. 12, 13–15, and 16–17. Verses 13–15 are a further consequence of v. 12, while vv. 16–17 serve as a subcase, marked by a grammatically subordinate form (wĕhāyâ kî). The main case is brought to a close by the formula of v. 15 and motivated by v. 18. Although the abrupt transition between v. 17 and v. 18 has been taken to indicate that vv. 16–17 represent a later addition, these verses continue to depend on the Exodus base text. It is better to understand v. 18 as a return to the main topic of release after the tangential subcase of vv. 16–17.

In the Exodus parallel the designation "Hebrew" may indicate an underclass highly likely to suffer enslavement, whereas in Deuteronomy the term is used as an emotionally laden indication of shared relationship (v. 12). The term "Hebrew" develops solidarity between master and slave in the same way that the memory of Egyptian slavery (v. 15) or the use of the word "brother" ("kin-

13. On this promulgation formula, see S. De Vries, "The Development of the Deuteronomic Promulgation Formula," *Bib* 55 (1974): 301–16.

dred") does. The social categories of "brother Hebrew" and "slave" are understood as simply incompatible in the long run. Verse 12 also implies that foreign chattel slaves, that is, those who are not "Hebrew," are to remain permanent slaves.

The expression *ḥopšî* (vv. 12, 13, 18) may be a technical term for a special social status as "freedman" or "emancipated slave." The cuneiform cognate suggests a member of a lower social class, so that the meaning "dependent client" may be appropriate in Exod 21:2, 5, and Jer 34:9–16. In Deuteronomy, however, the provision of a generous endowment means that any continued dependency is explicitly discouraged.[14]

The introductory *kî* of v. 13 does not indicate a special subcase (as in v. 16), but a further description of the basic situation. The adverb *rêqām*, "empty-handed," occurs in a similar context in Gen 31:42 (Jacob's release from service) and Exod 3:21 (Israel's escape from slavery), suggesting a natural association with the topic of slavery. The generous gift of v. 14 is intended to break the cycle of poverty and prevent a recurrence of servitude. It comprises not only the immediate necessities of bread and wine, but also animals to provide milk and textiles over the long term and to start a new herd or strengthen an existing one. References in v. 15 to slavery in Egypt and to Yahweh's act of "buying out" (*pādâ*, "redeem") provide exceptionally appropriate incentives to obey this particular law (cf. 7:8; 9:26; 13:6 [ET 5]; 21:8; 24:18).

The *kî* of v. 16 introduces a particular subcase intended to be the only possible exception to the law of release. The law intends that all should go out; only the refusal of the slave can block this universal principle. Verse 17 describes a ritual or symbolic action marking passage from the status of debt slave into the status of a permanent slave, perhaps a technical legal term (note p). The version of this ear-piercing ceremony in Exod 21:6 takes place at a doorway "before God," either at a local sanctuary or a household shrine of some sort. In Deuteronomy the slave's ear is explicitly nailed *to* the door and the locale is apparently the home, another desacralizing by-product of centralization. Ear piercing may have had a metaphoric implication, representing heedful obedience, or perhaps it was a practical provision for an earring or tag to indicate permanent slave status. Although the hole would presumably heal otherwise, the public doorway performance would continue to serve as a memorable sign of the slave's decision (cf. the shoe and spitting of 25:9). No questions about status could arise in the future. The slave has now been "nailed down" to that house.[15]

---

14. Lemche, "Hebrew Slave," 139–42; N. Lohfink, "*ḥopšî*," *TDOT* 5:114–18.

15. For further observations, see V. Hurowitz, "'His Master Shall Pierce His Ear with an Awl' (Exodus 21:6): Making Slaves in the Bible in Light of Akkadian Sources," *American Academy for Jewish Research* 58 (1992): 47–77.

Verse 18 returns to the main topic of manumission and seeks to counter attitudes that might hinder obedience. The motivation is twofold: you will really lose nothing financially in the arrangement, and Yahweh's blessing will make up any possible loss anyway.

[19–23] This is a reformed version of the traditional requirement to reserve firstborn male animals (cf. Exod 22:28–29 [ET 29–30]). The structure is that of a general law (vv. 19–20) followed by a special case (vv. 21–23). The text cites a basic apodictic law in v. 19a and another in v. 19b, then modifies v. 19a in the direction of centralized sacrifice. Note the shift from *bāqār*, "herd," to *šôr*, "ox," between vv. 19a and 19b. The blemish law of v. 21 must also be an earlier traditional regulation. The awkward v. 21aβ may be a supplementary gloss. Structurally, vv. 19–23 are held together by the repetition of "eat" in vv. 20, 22, 23, and the opposition of "place" and "towns" (vv. 20, 22).

The basic principle is that no secular or economic benefit may be derived from the firstling animal because it belongs to God. The animal is to be put into a holy state or declared to be holy (taking the verb "consecrate" as a delocative hip'il). This act indicates that its holiness is not simply automatic. It must be eaten as a meal sacrifice at the central sanctuary or, if unsuitable for sacrifice, as a desacralized local banquet. The gauge of secularity ("unclean and clean together") is repeated from 12:15–16, 20–25, and the concern about blood reflects 12:16. There is no parenesis or motivation here, only law.

The topic of firstlings has already been raised by Deut 12:6, 17; 14:23. Like the firstfruits of the crops, such animals were ritually special simply through the fact of being "first." Setting them apart had the correlative effect of putting the rest of the crop or animals in to a common, usable state. Perhaps they were also seen as a sort of tribute to Yahweh as overlord of the land. The expression "year by year" (v. 20) suggests an unspecified time, notably different from the precise requirement of Exod 22:29 [ET 30] to sacrifice them eight days after birth. Centralization would have naturally required a more flexible schedule than this, and Deuteronomy implies sacrifice during one of the annual pilgrimages. This delay and the greater potential age of firstling animals made Deuteronomy's rules about working and shearing necessary. It is unclear whether the priests of the sanctuary are to share in this sacrifice (cf. 18:4; Num 18:15–18). There is nothing here about redeeming blemished animals or the whole topic of firstborn sons (cf. Exod 13:13–15). Instead, the subcase of v. 21 prohibiting the sacrifice of a blemished animal becomes an opportunity for a common banquet (vv. 22–23). The formulation of v. 21 is similar to that of 17:1. "Lame and blind" represent a fixed word pair (2 Sam 5:6, 8; Mal 1:8).

Festival Calendar
16:1–17

Passover

16:1 Observe the month[a] of Abib and perform the Passover for Yahweh your God, for in the month of Abib Yahweh your God brought you out of Egypt by night. 2 You shall sacrifice the Passover for Yahweh your God from flock and herd at the place that Yahweh will choose to make his name dwell. 3 Do not eat any leavened bread with it. For seven days you shall eat unleavened bread with it—the bread of affliction—because in fearful haste[b] you went out of the land of[c] Egypt, so that you may remember the day you went out from the land of Egypt all the days of your life. 4 No leaven[d] shall be seen associated with you in your whole territory for seven days; and none of the meat that you sacrifice on the evening of the first day shall remain until[e] morning. 5 You dare not sacrifice the Passover within any of your towns that Yahweh your God is going to give you. 6 But at the place that Yahweh your God will choose to make his name dwell,[f] there you shall sacrifice the Passover in the evening at sunset, the time when you went out from Egypt. 7 You shall boil it and eat it at the place that Yahweh your God will choose. In the morning you shall go back to your tents. 8 Six days you shall eat unleavened bread, and on the seventh day there shall be a solemn assembly[g] for Yahweh your God. Do not do work.[h]

Feast of Weeks

9 You shall count seven weeks. From when the sickle is first put[i] to the standing grain you shall begin to count seven weeks. 10 Then you shall perform the Feast of Weeks for Yahweh your God, the voluntary gift that you give being in proportion to how Yahweh your God blesses you.[j] 11 You shall rejoice before Yahweh your God—you and your son and your daughter, your male and female slave, the Levite within your towns, and the resident alien, the fatherless, and the widow who are among you—at the place that Yahweh your God will choose to make his name dwell. 12 Remember that you were a slave in Egypt, and keep and do these statutes.

Feast of Booths

13 You shall perform the Feast of Booths for seven days, when you gather in the produce from your threshing floor and your wine press. 14 Rejoice

during your feast, you and your son and your daughter, your male and female slave, and the Levite, the resident alien, the fatherless, and the widow within your towns. 15 Seven days you shall celebrate a feast for Yahweh your God at the place that Yahweh will choose; for Yahweh your God will bless you in all your yield and in all the work of your hands. You shall surely be joyful.

Appear before Yahweh

16 Three times a year every male among you shall appear[k] before Yahweh your God at the place that he will choose: at the Feast of Unleavened Bread, at the Feast of Weeks, and at the Feast of Booths. Let no one appear before Yahweh empty-handed, 17 but each with a gift in hand[l] in proportion to the blessing of Yahweh your God that he has given you.

a. Alternate translation: "new moon." "Abib" may be treated as a common noun: "month of newly ripe grain" or "milky grain" (Lev 2:14).

b. The noun implies panic and hasty flight (Exod 12:11, 39); see G. André, "*ḥāpaz*," *TDOT* 5:90–91.

c. Follows MT. OG does not reflect "land of" at this point and may have lost it through homoioarchton: *m['rṣ m]ṣrym*.

d. *Śĕʾōr* ("leaven") is the sourdough that works to create *ḥamēṣ* ("leavened bread").

e. Temporal use of the preposition *l* as a terminative; *IBHS* 11.2.10c.

f. Follows the text and punctuation of MT. Sam. levels into a less abrupt formula that probably originated as a dittography: *šmw šm šm*, "his name there, there. . . ." However, the identical Greek reading cited by *BHS* is secondary and arose independently on the basis of 12:11. 4QDeut[a] supplements with *bw*, "in it," before *lškn*, apparently also derived from 12:11. Ignoring the masoretic accent division would associate *šm*, "there," with the centralization formula: "make his name dwell there. You shall . . ." (cf. 14:23, 24; 16:2, 11).

g. Follows MT. Sam. has the more common *ḥg*, "feast," and OG conflates these two readings. The translation "solemn assembly" is suggested by 2 Kgs 10:20–21; Jer 9:1 [ET 2]. Alternate translations are "work-free day," "closing ceremony" (Lev 23:36–37), or "taboo day" (cf. 1 Sam 21:6, 8 [ET 5, 7]).

h. Follows the rather abrupt MT. To soften MT, Sam. expands with *kl*, "any work" (cf. 5:14), while OG and 4QDeut[c] add *bw kl*, "any work on it." In addition, Sam. adds a word to harmonize with Lev 23:7–8, and OG adds several words to harmonize with Exod 12:16.

i. Follows MT *mhḥl* (hipʿil infinitive construet), literally "from the beginning of the sickle in the standing grain." Sam., OG, Syr. assimilate to the context of second-person verbs: *mhḥlk*, "from your beginning."

j. Follows MT with the imperfect as in v. 15. Sam. and OG have the perfect as in 15:14. The translation "being in proportion" understands *missat* as "measure" (*HALOT* 2:604–5). Alternate translation deriving the word from *mas*, "forced labor": "tribute of a voluntary gift."

k. The masoretic pointing as nip'al ("appear") here and in v. 16b preserves a tradition of vocalization at least as old as the Greek translation. *BHS* supposes that this is a pious correction of an original Qal ("see the face of Yahweh"), a more naive way of describing a ritual audience with Yahweh (cf. 2 Sam 3:13; 14:28, etc.). This would account for the direct object markers. The nip'al pointing requires that these be construed as markers of the adverbial accusative, *IBHS* 10.3.1c. A related situation occurs at 31:11.

l. Alternate translation understanding *yādô*, "his hand," as "according to his power": "a gift as he is able."

Deuteronomy reworks Israel's traditional liturgical timetable (found in Exod 23:14–17; 34:18–23) in order to convert celebrations formerly held at local shrines into pilgrimages to the central sanctuary "before Yahweh" (vv. 11, 16). The themes are entirely typical: the place chosen (vv. 2, 11, 15, 16), support for marginalized classes (vv. 11, 14), the opportunities and motivation provided by divine blessing (vv. 11, 14–15, 17), and the memory of exodus and slavery (vv. 1, 3, 6, 12). Deuteronomy's liturgical reformulation is driven by a theology that sees traditional local and private celebrations as dangerous subversions of Israel's relationship to Yahweh. In order to honor and obey Yahweh's election of a central place, Deuteronomy converts localized observances into national assemblies and merges the Passover sacrifice formerly celebrated within the household with the Feast of Unleavened Bread. At the same time, these observances are deritualized to some extent and humanized. Their meaning and effects are to be found in the realm of Israel's memory of past deliverance and in a festival joy that transcends social distinctions. From a polemic standpoint, these three festivals with agricultural connections counter the fertility claims of rival cults. As usual in Deuteronomy, command leads into motivational homiletic and is integrated with it.[1]

The structure of a three-part calendar followed by a summary replicates the format of Exod 23:14–17, almost certainly the source used by Deuteronomy. In the Covenant Code the three festivals are related directly to the rhythm of agriculture, but Abib is also specified as the month of exodus. Deuteronomy configures this inherited structure with the repeated command, "you shall perform," for each observance (root *ʿśh*; vv. 1, 10, 13). For Passover this "performing" is further defined by the verbs "sacrifice" (vv. 2, 5–6), "boil," and "eat" (v. 7). For the other two festivals the operative verb is "rejoice" (vv. 11, 14, 15). Verse 16 sums up this range of commands with the verb "appear." Each

---

1. On the theological implications of this chapter, see G. Braulik, "Commemoration of Passion and Feast of Joy: Popular Liturgy According to the Festival Calendar of the Book of Deuteronomy (Deut. 16:1–17)," in *Theology of Deuteronomy*, 67–85; trans. of "Leidensgedächtnisfeir und Freudenfest: 'Volkliturgie' nach dem deuteronomischen Festkalendar (Dtn 16, 1–17)," in *Studien zum Buch Deuteronomium*, 95–121.

of the three sections begins with a statement about when the celebration should take place: the month of Abib, counting weeks, gathering harvest (vv. 1, 9, 13). Each observance is executed "for Yahweh" (*lĕyhwh*; vv. 1, 2, 8, 10, 15), perhaps meaning "in honor of Yahweh" (cf. 5:14; 12:4, 31). There is a repeated pattern of positive second-person commands (vv. 2, 3aβ, 6–8, 10, 13) restricted by apodictic negatives (vv. 3, 4, 8bβ, 16b). It is probably no accident that the word "seven" is used seven times.

The section about Passover and Unleavened Bread (vv. 1–8) stands out over against the less complex presentations of Weeks and Booths (vv. 9–15). The mood of Passover is not one of joy but affliction and fearful haste, and there is a heavier emphasis on the central sanctuary as the place where one is to sacrifice, cook, and eat. In contrast to its stress on Passover and Unleavened Bread, Deuteronomy flattens out the distinctive character of the other two festivals. Weeks and Booths exhibit a relatively uncomplicated format of law (vv. 9–10a and 13–14a) followed by theological elaboration (vv. 10b–12 and 14b–15). The focus is on joy and community rather than on liturgical details. The list of celebrating participants is emphasized by repetition (vv. 11, 14). Yet no duration is given for Weeks and no mention is made of dwelling in shelters for Booths. Each festival reflects the agricultural schedule, but their prescribed offerings remain undefined as to type or quantity and vary with the situation of the worshiper (vv. 10, 17). The offering for Weeks is a vague voluntary gift; the offering for Booths is mentioned only in the concluding summary section. In short, these two feasts are liturgically thin, deritualized and humanized into joyful responses to a prosperous harvest.

This section's history of composition, especially that of vv. 1–8, is disputed, and opinions are closely bound up with various theories about the development of Israel's worship life.[2] There are obvious irregularities. Unleavened Bread (vv. 3aβ–4a) abruptly interrupts Passover. The six days of eating and the solemn assembly (v. 8) stand in some tension with eating for seven days (v. 3a) and the return to tents (v. 7). The difficult double use of '*ālāyw*, "with it," in v. 3 is strong evidence for some sort of editorial development. Three reconstructions

---

2. On the composition of this passage, see J. Halbe, "Passa-Massot im deuteronomischen Festkalender: Komposition, Entstehung und Programme von Dtn 16:1–8," *ZAW* 87 (1975): 147–68; J. C. Gertz, "Die Passa-Massot-Ordnung im deuteronomischen Festkalender," in *Das Deuteronomium und seine Querbeziehungen*, ed. Veijola, 56–80; T. Veijola, "The History of Passover in the Light of Deuteronomy 16, 1–8," *ZABR* 2 (1996): 53–75; P. Weimar, "Pascha und Massot: Anmerkungen zu Dtn 16;1–8," in *Recht und Ethos im Alten Testament* (ed. S. Beyerle et al.; Neukirchen-Vluyn: Neukirchener Verlag, 1999), 61–72. Concerning the chapter's implied attitude toward kingship, see J. G. McConville, "Deuteronomy's Unification of Passover and Massot: A Response to Bernard M. Levinson," *JBL* 119 (2000): 47–58; and B. M. Levinson, "The Hermeneutics of Tradition in Deuteronomy: A Reply to J. G. McConville," *JBL* 119 (2000): 269–86.

have been suggested: (1) Unleavened Bread is primary. A pre-Deuteronomic Unleavened Bread law consisting of vv. 1a, 3aβb-4a, and 8 was combined with Passover legislation by the Deuteronomic author in order to create a new sanctuary-based festival.[3] (2) Passover is primary. Verses 3aβb-4a and 8 are later supplements that modify a total replacement of Unleavened Bread by Passover in an earlier form of the text.[4] (3) Both are primary. Deuteronomy interrelated two originally independent pre-Deuteronomic laws, one about Unleavened Bread (Exod 23:15; 34:18) and one about Passover (Exod 23:18; 34:25).[5]

It is unlikely that critical scholarship will achieve any convincing solution to this impasse, but it is at least clear that the final text combines two originally separate observances, although not without some confusion. Passover seems to provide the base text of Deuteronomy from a literary-critical perspective, yet Unleavened Bread is more fundamental to the traditional agricultural calendar. Unleavened Bread as an observance independent of Passover appears both in Deuteronomy's source text, Exod 23:14–17, and in Deuteronomy's own summary in v. 16. Yet Passover dominates vv. 1–8 as Deuteronomy's main interest because as a sacrifice it was more radically affected by centralization. Most likely, many of the text's internal anomalies represent ideological stresses within the Deuteronomic movement itself, similar to those visible in the multiple perspectives on centralization in chapter 12. Combining the two observances made Passover the opening day of a seven-day Unleavened Bread observance (vv. 4, 8).

The text also exhibits unmistakable redactional contacts to the Ten Commandments:

> Not just a departure (*yṣ* 'Qal, vv. 3, 6) but a divine "bringing out (*yṣ* 'hip'il) in v. 1 and 5:6
> "Observe" (*šāmôr*) in v. 1 and 5:12
> The phrasing and six/seven pattern shared by v. 8 and 5:13–14
> "Remember you were slaves" in v. 12 and 5:15 (cf. 15:15; 24:18, 22)

[1–8] The preponderance of evidence suggests that Deuteronomy crafted this section on the basis of Exod 23:14–18, perhaps with input from other

---

3. Merendino, *Das deuteronomische Gesetz*, 125–49.

4. Seitz, *Redaktionsgeschichtliche Studien*, 196–98; F. Horst, *Das Privilegrecht Jahves: Rechtsgeschichtliche Untersuchungen zum Deuteronomium* (FRLANT 45; Göttingen, Vandenhoeck & Ruprecht, 1930), 106–19; A. Cholewiński, *Heiligkeitsgesetz und Deuteronomium: Eine vergleichende Studie* (AnBib 66; Rome: Biblical Institute Press, 1976), 178–81.

5. For arguments that Exod 23:18 (and 34:25) refers specifically to the Passover sacrifice, see M. Haran, *Temples and Temple-Service in Ancient Israel* (Oxford: Oxford University Press, 1978), 327–41.

source texts.[6] In the process, vocabulary used in Exodus for Unleavened Bread was reapplied to Passover. Examples of this reuse of earlier texts include:

> Verse 1 uses elements of Exod 23:15 to bracket mention of Passover with a repetitive resumption involving "the month of Abib."
>
> Verses 3–4 surround Unleavened Bread (vv. 3aβ–4a; cf. Exod 23:15) with Passover (vv. 3aα and 4b), using a repetitive resumption of "seven days." This procedure led to a double occurrence of *ʿālāyw*, "with it," in v. 3 (see below).
>
> The notion of sacrifice (*zābaḥ*; vv. 2, 4, 6) and its association with unleavened bread (v. 3) comes from Exod 23:18a.
>
> Verse 4 picks up "remain until morning" from Exod 23:18b.
>
> Verse 6 uses *mô'ēd* from Exod 23:15, converting it from "appointed time" into a reference to the evening of exodus.[7]

A concentric topical pattern holds together Deuteronomy's fusion of Passover and Unleavened Bread, putting the memory of exodus at the center:

> Passover—v. 3aα
> Unleavened Bread—v. 3aβ
> Exodus—v. 3b
> Unleavened Bread—v. 4a
> Passover—v. 4b[8]

Another concentric pattern based on grammatical features unifies the entire section:

> An outer chronological frame in vv. 1aα and 8
> An inner Passover frame in vv. 1aβ–2 and 7 (*wqṭl* commands)
> A syntactically patterned central section merging Passover and Unleavened Bread in vv. 3–6 (*yqṭl* sentences):
> v. 3—prohibition/command about Unleavened Bread
> v. 4—prohibition/prohibition about both Unleavened Bread and Passover
> vv. 5–6—prohibition/command about Passover

6. For an instructive analysis, see Levinson, *Deuteronomy and Hermeneutics*, 53–97.

7. Generally, Exod 34:18–23, 25 occupies a mediating position between Exod 23:14–17 and Deut 16:1–8. There is also a textual relationship between Deut 16:1, 3, 4, 8, and Exod 13:4, 6–7, but the direction of dependence is much less certain. The relationship to Exod 12:21–22 is also unclear.

8. Halbe, "Passa-Massot," 150, 153–54.

This sophisticated scribal design explains the delayed position of the ritual operations described in v. 7, since they correspond in the pattern to what is commanded in v. 2.[9]

Rather than simply reporting on an updated practice, Deuteronomy is being theologically proactive in merging the two observances. It is more concerned with attitude and memory than with ritual details. Israel should remember that Passover takes place on the very same month, day, and hour as the exodus did (vv. 1, 3, 6). The tradition that the exodus happened "by night" (vv. 1, 6) is unique to Deuteronomy (unless this is intended as an oblique reference to the death of the firstborn). "By night" also establishes the ceremony's chronological skeleton: evening sacrifice (v. 6), morning conclusion (v. 4), and a return "to tents" the next day (v. 7).

Deuteronomy brings the celebration of Passover into line with centralization. What had been a local affair is transformed into a pilgrimage to the central sanctuary so that the sacrifice will be performed at the proper place. The centralization formula appears three times (vv. 2, 6, 7). The domestic and neighborhood nature of Passover is abolished by the restriction of v. 5. A common date is set by naming the month as Abib, thus making possible a coordinated, nationwide gathering ("your whole territory," v. 4). No longer a household slaughter without altar (*šāḥaṭ*; Exod 12:6, 21), killing and eating are described unambiguously in terms of sacrifice (*zābaḥ*, vv. 2, 4, 6). Deuteronomy moves Passover in the direction of a normal sacrifice by widening the choice of victim to include cattle and not just a lamb or a young goat (v. 2; contrast Exod 12:3–5, 21) and by describing the cooking method as sacrificial boiling (*bšl* pi'el, "cook in a container," 1 Sam 2:13–15; contrast Exod 12:8–9). Permitting the sacrifice of cattle also fits the requirements of the larger groups associated with centralization better than the small household companies that celebrated the earlier, noncentralized ritual. Perhaps cattle are also intended to function as a sign of prosperity (cf. 7:13).

Although Unleavened Bread keeps its label as a *ḥag*, "feast" (v. 16; Exod 23:15), it has lost much of its zest through its connection with (and subordination to) Passover. In contrast to the other two feasts, there is no rejoicing. Israel eats unleavened bread not in delight, but as food of affliction and haste in order to remember the exodus (v. 3). Deuteronomy seems to compromise at this point, describing the practice of eating unleavened bread as simultaneously local and centralized. According to v. 3, unleavened bread is to be eaten specifically "with it" (the Passover sacrifice) for seven days, yet leaven is to be removed not just from the region of the central sanctuary but from *all* of Israel's territory (v. 4). Apparently one is to eat unleavened bread at the central shrine, yet the return to "tents" (v. 8) suggests that eating unleavened bread was also to be practiced on the way back and at home.

---

9. Adopted from E. Otto, "*pāsaḥ*," *ThWAT* 6:674–75.

The month name "Abib" (v. 1) denotes barley still in the ear and not totally ripe, but milky when crushed (Exod 9:31; Lev 2:14). This growth stage would be too early for a harvest festival or for making new bread from the grain.[10] Unless the text specifically refers to the night of the new moon (note a), the actual date of Passover is not given. This indicates that Deuteronomy's reforming interest is narrowly focused on the location of the Passover celebration and its nature as a sacrifice, rather than on other liturgical matters.

The double occurrence of *ʿālāyw*, "with it" (v. 3), reflects the scribal procedure used to unite Passover and Unleavened Bread. In both occurrences, "it" must refer to the Passover. The first instance refers to the Passover victim narrowly and seems to have been taken up from Exod 23:18a (cf. Exod 34:25). It reflects technical terminology for food eaten "with" a sacrifice (Exod 12:8; Num 9:11) and the general rule that this should be unleavened bread (cf. Lev 2:11; 6:9, 10 [ET 16, 17]). In this way, the nonspecific unleavened bread of general sacrificial procedure has been combined with the special food of the Unleavened Bread festival. The second *ʿālāyw* completes the fusion of Passover and Unleavened Bread, although here "it" refers to the whole ceremony of Passover (rather than just the sacrificial meat) and "with" implies a more general association. Otherwise, the clash between the "seven days" of eating bread (v. 3) and the single night of finishing the sacrifice (v. 4) would be unbearable. Unleavened bread was not just a complement to sacrifice, but also the bread of the campfire, of sudden hospitality, of urgency. As the "bread of affliction," it draws the exodus story into the connection between Passover and Unleavened Bread, recalling the emergency, pressure, and stress of a quick departure. Perhaps "affliction" also reflects the tradition behind Exod 3:7.

The reworking of Exod 23:18 into Deut 16:4 joins the topic of leaven with the Passover even more tightly. Mention of what is expressly a *"first* day" incorporates the sacrificial meal into the seven-day timetable of Unleavened Bread.

There are two ways to understand the "tents" of v. 7. Return to tents sometimes denotes a departure for home, suggesting that vv. 7–8 intend for the people to go back home after the Passover sacrifice in order to eat unleavened bread (cf. v. 4a) and observe the final day of rest from work there. Indeed, forbidding work while away from one's daily tasks at the central sanctuary would not make much sense. On the other hand, Deuteronomy always presumes that Israel will enjoy a settled existence in houses (cf. 20:5–8 with Josh 22:4, 8; 2 Sam 20:1). This would indicate that "tents" signifies temporary residence in pilgrim encampments (cf. Hos 12:10 [ET 9]). Remaining at the central location would fit the commonly accepted translation of "solemn assembly" (v. 8; note g) and

---

10. Therefore Unleavened Bread cannot be understood as an old Canaanite harvest festival, nor can it be equated with the beginning of the barley harvest. See J. Halbe, "Erwägungen zu Ursprung und Wesen des Massotfestes," *ZAW* 87 (1975); 325–38.

the evidence of Exod 23:15 that Unleavened Bread involved "appearing before" Yahweh. Both returning home or going to an off-site encampment imply some sort of a departure from the central "place" of exclusive sacrifice, and either could have been used by Deuteronomy as a workable strategy to accommodate Unleavened Bread into the practice of centralization. There is no real contradiction between the "six days" of v. 8 and the "seven days" of v. 3. Verse 8 first highlights the initial six of the total seven days of eating unleavened bread, then lays special emphasis on the seventh.

[9–12] This section depends on Exod 23:16 (34:22), the "feast of harvest" being renamed "Weeks." This act of renaming indicates that a special emphasis of this observance is a deliberate counting of days from the start of harvest. There is no indication in Deuteronomy that this start date is coupled in any way with Passover and Unleavened Bread. In fact, its association of Abib with pre-harvest "milky grain" makes Unleavened Bread too early to mark the start of the harvest. In contrast to the sophisticated astronomical calculations of ritual specialists, the practice of counting to set a ritual date is an activity appropriate for ordinary people. Indeed, vv. 1–17 lack the character of a true "calendar" in the sense of providing dates for those who schedule observances, but rather offer general information of the sort needed by nonspecialists. The period of seven weeks is a countdown to the hoped-for success of a finished harvest. Deuteronomy focuses not so much on a set date, but on the goal of the garnered crop. Although the first act of cutting with the sickle would take place on different days in different parts of the country, this diversity would have made no difference when Weeks was a localized festival. In the context of a centralized observance, however, this sounds like a utopian feature, unless some sort of designated single sickle is envisioned to set the date for the whole nation. Perhaps, however, Deuteronomy envisions pilgrimages by individual families or regions at different times, rather than a coordinated mass celebration on a given date. A concentric structure unifies v. 9: "seven" / "count" / "first put" (*hll* hip'il) . . . "begin" (*hll* hip'il) / "count" / "seven." There is no mention of any role for firstfruits in Weeks at this point (contrast Exod 23:16; 34:22). This issue is put off until chapter 26. Perhaps Deuteronomy's emphasis on joy seeks to counteract the attraction of competing fertility rites.

[13–15] Judges 9:27 and 21:19–21 describe an earlier manifestation of Booths as a local celebration of the vintage. Again, Deuteronomy establishes no definite date, only the time of gathering and storing grain and grape. The timing of this event would be different for different areas, and again the possibility of unsynchronized pilgrimages at somewhat different times cannot be excluded. This would only be a problem when the situation of reading the law to a nationwide assembly, as envisioned in 31:10–11, comes into view. Deuteronomy uses the name Booths for what Exod 23:16b (cf. 34:22b) calls Ingathering. Weeks celebrates the grain harvest; Booths commemorates the act of putting the processed grain and pressed grapes into storage (note the contrast implied between Exod 23:16a and 16b). The verb distinctive to Booths is *ḥāgag*, "celebrate a feast," picked up from Exod 23:14. Deuteronomy did not specify the duration of the Feast of Weeks; at the Feast of Booths pilgrims can remain at the central sanctuary for seven days because the entire crop would be completely harvested. The theological rhetoric in vv. 14–15 is forceful: "*your* feast," Yahweh's blessing "in all . . . and in all," "surely be joyful."

[16–17] This summary is a scribal construction based on Exod 23:15–17 (34:20b, 23), created by an artistically reversed citation and an interpolation of the centralization formula into it.

> Verse 16aα takes over Exod 23:17, adding centralization
> Verse 16aβ uses Exod 23:16, making two name changes
> Verse 16b duplicates the last part of Exod 23:15 so that it
> refers to all three observances

The distinctive verb is "to appear," which links back to the "shall not be seen" of v. 4. At this point Deuteronomy refers to the combined spring observance simply as Unleavened Bread. The minimum legal requirement derived from the source text applies only to "males," but Deuteronomy of course envisions the wider participation described in vv. 11 and 14.

Constitutional Proposals
16:18–17:20

Maintain Fair Justice

16:18 You shall appoint judges and officers for your tribes, in all your towns that Yahweh your God is going to give you, and they shall judge the people with true justice. 19 Do not pervert justice, do not show partiality, and do not take a bribe,[a] for a bribe blinds the eyes of the wise and twists the words of the righteous.[b] 20 Justice, justice[c] alone shall be your goal, so that you may live and take over the land that Yahweh your God is going to give you.

21 Do not plant an asherah pole, any sort of tree,[d] beside the altar of Yahweh that you build. 22 And do not set up a stone pillar, something that Yahweh your God hates. 17:1 Do not sacrifice to Yahweh your God an ox or a sheep that has a blemish, any serious defect, for it is something repugnant to Yahweh your God.

2 If there is found among you, in one of your towns that Yahweh your

God is going to give you, a man or woman who does what is evil in the opinion of Yahweh your God, transgressing his covenant, 3 and goes and serves other gods and bows down to them, or[e] to the sun or the moon or any of the host of heaven, something I have not commanded,[f] 4 and it is reported to you or you hear of it,[g] then inquire carefully. If[h] the matter is established as true that this repugnant thing has been done in Israel, 5 you shall bring that man or that woman who has done this wicked thing out to your gates,[i] the man or the woman,[j] and you shall stone them to death. 6 On the testimony of two or three witnesses shall the condemned be executed. No one shall be executed on the testimony of a single witness. 7 The hand of the witnesses shall be the first raised against him to execute him, and afterward the hand of the whole people; so you shall sweep out the evil from among you.

8 If a case for judgment is too difficult for you between different kinds of homicide, different kinds of legal claims, or different kinds of assault[k]—legal cases in your towns[l]—then you must immediately go up to the place that Yahweh your God will choose. 9 Go to the Levitical priests[m] and[n] to the judge who is in office in those days. Inquire[o] and they will tell you the decision. 10 Perform exactly the decision they tell you from the place that Yahweh will choose. Be careful to do everything that they teach you. 11 Perform exactly the law[p] and the ruling that they announce to you. Do not turn aside from the decision that they tell you, either to the right or the left. 12 Anyone who acts in arrogance to disobey the priest who stands to minister there[q] to Yahweh your God, or the judge, must be put to death; so you shall sweep out the evil from Israel. 13 All the people will hear and be afraid, and will not act arrogantly again.

You May Appoint a King

14 When you have come into the land that Yahweh your God is going to give you, and have taken it over and settled down in it, and you say, "I will set a king over me like all the nations that surround me," 15 you may certainly set a king over yourself, one whom Yahweh your God chooses. You may set as king over you someone from your own kindred.[r] Do not dare put a foreigner over you, who is not your kindred. 16 Only he shall not acquire numerous horses for himself, nor return the people to Egypt in order to acquire more horses,[s] since Yahweh has said to you, "Do not return[t] that way again." 17 And he shall not acquire numerous wives for himself, lest his heart turn aside, nor shall he acquire much silver and gold for himself. 18 As soon as he sits on the throne of his kingdom, he shall write for himself a copy of this law in a book in the presence of[u] the Levitical priests. 19 It shall be beside him and he shall read in it all the days of

his life, so that he may learn to fear Yahweh his God, by observing all the words of this law[v] and these statutes to do them. 20 Thus he will not think himself higher than his kindred nor turn aside from the commandment, either to the right or the left, so that he and his sons may enjoy a long reign in Israel over his kingdom.

a. Follows MT. OG converted these prohibitions to third person plural to harmonize with context. A *šōḥad*, "bribe," is a gift on the basis of which something is expected and by which a relationship is established. It can be tribute (1 Kgs 15:19) or range from a court fee (Mic 3:11) to a payoff (Deut 27:25).

b. That is, it makes even a just person give a crooked answer when in the role of judge or witness. Alternate translation, construing the "righteous" as the innocent party: "subverts the cause of those in the right."

c. Emphatic repetition: "perfect justice, justice alone." Cf. the syntax of 2:27.

d. *Kol-'ēṣ* is in apposition to "asherah." As an indication of material (*IBHS* 12.3c, "an asherah made of any kind of wood") this would be beside the point. It is better to take this as an extension of "asherah pole," widening the prohibition to "any sort of tree or treelike object."

e. Follows MT, taking the *waw* as "or." It could also be explicative: "that is." OG, Vulg. read no conjunction, implying a complete equation of pagan gods with astral bodies. Lest the text be read to suggest that apostates are required to worship *both* pagan gods and astral bodies or that *all* pagan gods can be equated with astral bodies, 11QTemple reads unambiguously '*w*, "or," as does a secondary LXX reading. See L. H. Schiffman, "The Septuagint and the Temple Scroll: Shared Halakhic Variants," in *Septuagint, Scrolls, and Cognate Writings* (ed. G. J. Brooke and B. Lindars; SBLSCS 33; Atlanta: Scholars Press, 1992), 285–87.

f. Follows MT and OG. Sam. *ṣwytyw*, "I commanded him," resulted from a dittography of the following *w*. Both "I commanded you" and "he commanded" (LXX[B]) are later developments within the LXX tradition. Alternate translation as a sort of litotes: "something I have forbidden."

g. Follows MT. OG probably dropped "and/or you hear of it" as a redundancy.

h. *Hinnēh* serves as a logical bridge, "and as a result," *IBHS* 40.2.1e.

i. The plural of "gates" may indicate one of several choices, "to any one of your various gates," *IBHS*, p. 122 n. 15.

j. OG (= LXX[B]) has a long gap (from after "that woman" as far as "the woman"), abbreviating unnecessary or problematic material (Wevers, *Greek Text*, 280–81). Vulg. engages in a less sweeping abbreviation, omitting "the man or the woman."

k. Literally "between bloodshed and bloodshed, between claim and claim, and between blow and blow." OG has a fourth case: *byn ryb lryb*, "between different kinds of lawsuits," a scrambled dittography of *dbry rybt*, "legal cases."

l. Alternate translation taking "gates" as the location of jurisprudence: "in your courts."

m. Follows MT and OG. LXX[B] omits "the Levitical priests" through an inner-Greek homoioteleuton from *pros* to *pros*. Syr. understands the priests and Levites as separate groups.

n. Alternate translation: "or" (cf. v. 12).

o. Follows MT; the person bringing the case asks the court's opinion. Sam., OG "they shall inquire" understands this as a judicial investigation. However, the context is very different from that of 19:18. It is not the facts but the difficulty of the case that is the problem here.

p. Follows OG. MT repeats *'šr ywrwk*, "that they teach you," from the end of v. 10.

q. Follows MT *šm 't-yhwh*, "there to Yahweh." OG reverses to *'t-šm yhwh*, "to the name of Yahweh," a formula similar to 18:5, 7. The context of juridical activity in contrast to liturgical service favors MT.

r. Alternate translation, less permissive and more directive: "You surely must set over yourself a king whom Yahweh your God chooses. You must set as king over you someone from your own kindred."

s. That is, either "to buy horses" or "in exchange for horses."

t. Alternate translation as a promise: "you will never return."

u. The nuance of *mlpny* is in doubt. Is it the book itself that is "from before" the priests ("from [the copy] in the charge of, in the custody of") or is it the act of writing ("under the supervision of"; cf. 1 Sam 3:1)? Less likely alternate translations: "in a book at the dictation of" or (taking the verb *ktb* as indirect action) "written for him in a book by."

v. Follows MT. OG "all these words" levels to a common formula (see J. W. Wevers, *Text History of the Greek Deuteronomy* [Mitteilungen des Septuaginta Unternehmens 13; Göttingen: Vandenhoeck & Ruprecht, 1978], 92).

A Constitutional Proposal

Deuteronomy 16:18–18:22 is a self-contained section dealing with state and religious officials, the local court and its process (16:18–20; 17:2–7), the central court (17:8–13), the king (17:14–20), and—in chapter 18—the priest and prophet. These chapters offer a sort of constitutional proposal with definite concepts about the judge, king, priest, and prophet. Interest focuses on how these officeholders are to be selected, their functions, the obedience owed to them, and mechanisms of succession. The appointment of judges is commanded, the choice of a king is allowed, priests are already in place but are to be centralized, while the prophet is promised by Yahweh. Judges are a human choice, priest and prophet are divinely endorsed, while the king is designated by both Yahweh and Israel. This "constitution" conceives of Israel as a unitary realm with centralized institutions and state power to enforce obedience. It explores the effects of centralization (on jurisprudence and priests) and the interaction between local leaders and national ones (local and central court, local priests and the central sanctuary).

While the concerns are practical, the proposal gives the impression of being a utopian, theoretical construct, "Israel as it ought to be." The result is a coherent constitutional system directed by the notion of checks and balances. Its guiding principle is the distribution of power so that it is not concentrated in the king and in the priestly class. Kings and priests are downgraded in favor of judges and prophets. Power does not flow downward from a hierarchy; rather governing elements operate alongside one another in a parallel fashion.[1]

All this in harmony with Deuteronomy's general political ethic, in which there in no state control of tithes or harvest, no special rights for the king in the war laws of chapter 20, no royal role in the choice of the sacral place or in any construction of a "house" there (contrast the role of David and Solomon in temple building). The king is no longer the supreme arbiter of justice, but gives way to a central court. The government is subordinate to the law: the king studies it and the priests are its custodian. Law is written in a book and yet also emanates from the central court (17:11).

Themes and Structure

There is a consistency of purpose between 12:1–16:17 (reform of the cult) and 16:18–18:22. Both major blocks involve centralization and revisions to the Covenant Code. The constitutional proposal exhibits the same tensions between centralized and local issues as does chapter 12. The national unity sought in cult centralization is paralleled in a central court. The sacral aspects of law enforcement no longer take place locally, resulting in changes in the roles of elders, judges, priests, and the king. Restricting ritual to a central sanctuary desacralizes local jurisprudence and creates a need to fill the resulting vacuum. The threat of monolithic tyranny inherent in centralization is anticipated and countered by retaining local, citizen-based jurisprudence, restraining royal power, limiting the role of priests, and facilitating the expansion of those who serve at the central sanctuary. An egalitarian ethic of "brotherhood" limits the potential domination by a centralized aristocracy. In spite of its social and economic diversity, Israel is addressed with the collective singular "you." This "you" signifies the fraternal citizenry that appoints judges, takes responsibility for jurisprudence, and installs the divinely chosen king.

The repetition of *kî* unifies this constitutional proposal: 17:2, 8 (casuistic

---

1. N. Lohfink, "Distribution of the Functions of Power: The Laws Concerning Public Offices in Deuteronomy 16:18–22," in *Song of Power*, ed. Christensen, 336–52; trans. of "Die Sicherung der Wirksamkeit des Gotteswortes durch das Prinzip der Schriftlichkeit der Tora und durch das Prinzip der Gewaltenteilung nach den Ämtergesetzen des Buches Deuteronomium (Dt 16,18–18,22)," in *Studien zum Deuteronomium I*, 305–23; C. Schäfer-Lichtenberger, "Der deuteronomische Verfassungsentwurf: Theologische Vorgaben als Gestaltungsprinzipien sozialer Realität," in *Bundesdokument und Gesetz*, ed. Braulik, 105–18; E. Otto, "Von der Gerichtsordnung zum Verfassungsentwurf: Deuteronomische Gestaltung und deuteronomistische Interpretation im 'Ämtergesetz,' Dtn 16, 18–18, 22," in *Wer ist wie du, HERR, unter den Göttern?* (ed. I. Kottsieper et al.; Göttingen: Vandenhoeck & Ruprecht, 1994), 142–55.

"if"), 17:14, and 18:9 ("when you have come into the land"). "The land Yahweh your God is going to give" connects 16:20 and 17:14. Those who find the Decalogue as an organizing pattern connect this section to the commandment concerning parents. Topical paragraphs are apparent:

16:18–20. A provision for local judges downgrades the traditional role of elders and complements (or replaces) them by appointed officials. Significantly, the king does not appoint these judges. "Justice" is the ultimate goal for the law as a whole, as in 6:25 (cf. 24:13). Instructions to these judges lead to subsequent sections on the process for achieving such "justice."

17:2–7. Centralization affects local, secular (i.e., nonritual) justice, the sort dispensed at the city gate. Cases with witnesses and without technical complications remain local ones, something true even of the ultimate crime of apostasy. In such a case, two factors trigger legal action: the occurrence of apostasy and hearing a report of it.

17:8–13. Centralization also affects ritual justice, the sort brought into play when no witnesses are available. These cases are "too wonderful," beyond secular jurisprudence. Procedures involving oaths, ordeals, lots, and oracles are transferred to the central sanctuary. The present form of the text also centralizes cases involving difficult legal interpretations. This central court holds in balance the offices of secular judge and priest. However, the traditional role of the king in jurisprudence (2 Sam 12:1–14; 14:1–24; 15:2–4; 1 Kgs 3:16–28; 7:7; Ps 72:1) remains significantly unmentioned.

17:14–20. The constitutional proposal degrades the traditional roles and prerogatives of the king. The king is relegated to the middle of the list. Officeholders are installed not by the king, but by the citizenry ("you"). Other offices are hereditary (priests) or appointed directly by Yahweh (prophet). The appointment of the first king is handled in a shared manner by both the populace ("you") and Yahweh. The king is no longer in charge of war (horses), no longer symbolizes the power and prosperity of the state (wives, possessions), is no longer at the center of international contacts (no trade or treaties sealed by marriage). Instead the king serves as the model Israelite.

History of Composition

The unified internal sequence of this "constitutional proposal" and its connection to previous sections raise questions of compositional history and original order. Deuteronomy 16:21–17:1 and 17:2–7 separate the material about courts in 16:18–20 from that in 17:8–13. At the same time, there are strong connections between 16:21–17:1 and 12:29–31 and between chapter 13 and 17:2–7. This has led to attempts to reorder the text of Deuteronomy.

Some suggest that the original sequence was 12:29–13:1 [ET 12:32] + 16:21–17:1 + 17:2–7 + 13:2–19 [ET 1–18], and that 16:21–17:7 was moved farther back and interpolated between 16:18–20 and 17:8–13.[2] Another possi-bility is that chapter 13 and 17:2–13 originally appeared together as a sequence of five hypothetical cases and that chapter 13 was moved forward to follow chapter 12 in order to connect its concerns related to the first commandment with centralization. The bracketing verses 12:29–31; 13:1, 19 [ET 12:32; 13:18] reveal this redactional intent.

Another way of approaching the possibility of displacement is to ask why 16:21–17:1 does not come immediately after the other ritual materials that con-clude with 16:17. Perhaps these prohibitions were originally part of an inde-pendent apodictic series consisting of 16:19–17:1 that was inserted between 16:18 and 17:2 as a continuation of the topic "true justice" in 16:18.

The "block model," favored by Norbert Lohfink and Georg Braulik, sup-poses that Deuteronomy originally stopped at 16:17 and that the following con-stitutional proposal (16:18–18:22) was added during the exile. Because justice involves sacral matters, cult and justice were interwoven at the start of this block: justice (16:18–20)/cult (16:21–17:1)/justice (17:2–7 + 8–13). This pat-tern of interspersing elements of the "constitution" into the cultic prohibitions of 16:21–17:1 was intended to present government as a system for securing reli-gious purity. It is thus no accident that the sample case of 17:2–7 is specifically about apostasy. Moreover, a further redactional connection to chapter 19 (cities of refuge) is suggested by a framing pattern of unifying apodictic prohibitions: 16:19, 21, 22; 17:1, then 18:1, then 19:14, 15, 21. The entire constitutional pro-posal is thus enclosed by the topic of the "judicial system," with local and national courts coming at the beginning and cities of refuge at the end.[3]

Later additions are visible in 17:10b–11 (which is superfluous after vv. 9b–10a), v. 3b (astral worship), the repetitious relative clause in v. 5a, v. 8aβ ("legal cases in your towns"), and v. 16b (plural address). The topic of law (vv. 18–19, 20aβb) seems to have been added later to the original law of the king.

From a form-critical perspective, there are seven second-person apodictic prohibitions: three in 16:19 with a positive opposite in v. 20, three in

2. See the review of arguments in Levinson, *Deuteronomy and Hermeneutics*, 104–9. Con-ceivably, 16:21–17:7 could have originally attached directly to 14:2.

3. For details, see Braulik, *Die deuteronomischen Gesetze und der Dekalog*, 46–61. Lohfink postulates an original text 16:18–17:13 and 19:1–21 centered around the offices of judge, priest, and elder. The other material was attracted by topical similarity and redacted into a comprehensive system at the start of the exile ("Distribution of the Functions of Power," 344–46). Braulik empha-sizes the unity and independence of this section as an exilic text, "The Sequence of the Laws in Deuteronomy 12–26 and in the Decalogue" (trans. L. Maloney), in *Song of Power*, ed. Christensen, 313–35. In contrast, Mayes, *Deuteronomy*, 263–64, explains this section as a piecemeal accretion, with a pre-Deuteronomic 16:19, 21–17:1a as the core and 16:19 as the attachment point for an inser-tion of the material on courts. The comprehensive study of U. Rüterswörden, *Von der politischen Gemeinschaft zur Gemeinde: Studien zu Dt 16, 18–18, 22* (BBB 65; Frankfurt: Athenäum, 1987), traces a preexilic original text in 16:18–19, 21–22; 17:8–10, 12–16a, 17, 20; 18:1, 3–15.

16:21–17:1 with supplements, and one in 17:11b. There is a third-person prohibition in 17:6b and a sequence of them in 17:16–17. Two positive commands involve coming into land: 16:18a and 17:15a. Finally there are casuistic formulations in second person singular addressed to the people in 17:2–7 and to local judges in 17:8–13.

[16:18–20] The citizenry is to appoint an independent judiciary answerable to lofty principles of justice. This section is organized as a positive command (v. 18), followed by three prohibitions (v. 19a) and a proverbial statement about bribes (v. 19b). It concludes with a rhetorically charged, oathlike command to the people (v. 20).[4] The context is local, "in all your towns," literally "in all your gates," perhaps echoing the practice of judging at the gate. The "you" of the community makes these appointments, not the king.[5] This same citizen "you" is given similar authority to act in 17:15 (king) and 19:2 (cities of refuge).

Those who are "wise" in performing justice are not the king (contrast Solomon, 1 Kgs 3:12, 16–28) but the appointees of the people. It is unclear to what office *šōṭĕrîm*, "officers," refers in this context, perhaps some sort of recorder or scribal administrator. The Akkadian cognate is connected with the task of writing (*HALOT* 4:1475–76). Such "officers" also appear in the sacral war legislation, where they undermine the expected military leadership of the king (20:5–9).[6]

The provision of v. 18 would have diminished the traditional roles of local elders. It remains uncertain whether these judges are intended to replace the elders completely or only take over a part of their customary responsibilities. Local elders still have a role in 21:19; 22:15; 25:7, and the judges have tasks that are more supervisory than adjudicatory in 21:2; 25:2.[7]

---

4. The model for this may be the juridical system of Jerusalem (cf. Isa 1:26; 3:2; Zeph 3:3); see J. C. Gertz, *Die Gerichtsorganisation Israels im deuteronomischen Gesetz* (FRLANT 165; Göttingen: Vandenhoeck & Ruprecht, 1994), 89–92. Gertz concludes that these verses were influenced by Deut 1:13–17, which also speaks of "tribes," the "wise," "officers," and "partiality," and that 16:19 was based on Exod 23:8 (pp. 38–41). In contrast, Rüterswörden, *Von der politischen Gemeinschaft*, 21–22, describes v. 19 as being independent of Exod 23:8 and considers Deut 1:13, 15, 17 dependent on 16:18–19.

5. Y. Suzuki, "Deuteronomic Reformation in View of the Centralization of the Administration of Justice," *AJBI* 13 (1987): 22–58, suggests that this represents an actual reform of Josiah.

6. Rüterswörden, *Von der politischen Gemeinschaft*, 109–11.

7. Appointed judges coexisted with traditional elders according to E. Otto, "Soziale Verantwortung und Reinheit des Landes: Zur Redaktion der kasuistischen Rechtssätze in Deuteronomium 19–25," in *Prophetie und geschichtliche Wirklichkeit im alten Israel* (ed. R. Liwak and S. Wagner; Stuttgart: Kohlhammer, 1991), 290–306. Gertz, *Gerichtsorganization*, 173–225, concluded that judges were original to Deuteronomy and that the elders were an exilic addition. See also J. Milgrom, "The Ideological Importance of the Office of the Judge in Deuteronomy," in *Isaac Leo Seeligmann Volume* (ed. Y. Zakovitch and A. Rofé; 3 vols.; Jerusalem: Rubenstein, 1983) 3:129–39.

Verse 19 is apparently addressed not only to judges, but to the "you" of the whole citizenry, making justice a communal responsibility. Although the three coordinated prohibitions may reflect a pre-Deuteronomic "model for judges" (*Richterspiegel*), it is more likely that two of them derive from Exod 23:6, 8. Verse 19 picks up from Exod 23:1–8 only what applies to "judges and officials." The Deuteronomy version widens the narrower focus on the poor (Exod 23:6) into a demand for justice in general (but cf. Deut 24:17). Verse 19b is obviously a proverb or wisdom saying parallel to that used in Exod 23:8, but it replaces the rare *piqhîm* ("clear-sighted"?) of Exodus by the more predictable *ḥăkāmîm*, "wise." For this proverbial style, compare Qoh 7:7. The "partiality" of v. 19 is defined in Lev 19:15; Prov 24:23b; 28:21. Yahweh, too, is impartial (Deut 10:17).

Verse 20 uses the rhetoric of emphatic doubling (cf. Isa 51:9, 17; 52:1, 11). The theology of Deut 6:18–19; 8:1; 11:8, 22–25 is reflected here in that Israel's acquisition of the land depends on achieving justice. This is often thought to reflect hope for the restoration of the land in the exilic period.[8] Again the "you" of Israel as a whole is being addressed, bringing together the accountability of appointed judges and the entire citizenry.

[16:21–17:1] This short sequence of cult-oriented prohibitions is only minimally related to its context. There is assonance between 16:19, "do not pervert" (*lō'-taṭṭeh*), and v. 21, "do not plant" (*lō'-tiṭṭa'*). The "ox or sheep" of 17:1 reappears in 18:3, and the notion of "repugnant" occurs in 17:1 and 18:12. More broadly, 17:1 seems to be a shorter and secondary form of 15:21–23 in that it replicates 15:21 in reversed form and universalizes the more narrow topic of firstlings into all sacrifices. These prohibitions move beyond the demand to destroy the cult objects of the previous inhabitants (7:5; 12:2–4) to prevent Israel itself from installing such things. The scope is expansive: "any tree," "any defect." Perhaps 12:2–3, 29–31, and 16:21–17:1 are intended to form a frame around the primary ritual laws of chapters 12–16.

An asherah (v. 21) was a wooden artifact "made" and "set up." However, an asherah was also intended to be a stylized tree and was represented as such in iconography. "Plant" enriches the notion of an artificial pole "put into the ground" with that of a literal tree. Living trees were sometimes present at sanctuaries (Gen 21:33; Josh 24:26; metaphorically in Pss 52:10 [ET 8]; 92:14 [ET 13]) just as an asherah pole could be (Judg 6:25–26; 2 Kgs 21:7; 23:4, 6, 15). However, Jer 17:2 indicates that the two sorts of cult objects were in reality separate items. Verse 21 expressly forbids only an asherah beside the central sanctuary altar. Such an object would be a specifically Yahwistic asherah, in contrast to the (supposedly) indigenous, pagan ones to be destroyed in 7:5;

8. N. Lohfink, "Kerygmata des deuteronomistischen Geschichtswerks," in *Studien zu Deuteronomium II*, 125–42.

12:2–3. Perhaps the asherah was understood as a symbol or hypostasis of Yawheh's power of fertility.[9] The "stone pillar" (*maṣṣēbâ*, v. 22) was also a traditional Yahwistic religious object (Gen 28:18; Josh 24:26; cf. Hos 3:4; 10:1–2), but one connected with Baal (2 Kgs 3:2; 10:26–27) and perhaps funerary rituals (Gen 35:19–21; 2 Sam 18:18). In contrast to the asherah pole, the prohibition of pillars is not restricted to the neighborhood of the central altar, but applicable everywhere. The comment of v. 22b may refer to both asherah and pillar.

The law of 17:1 is not a technical rule defining "blemish" for priests, but a guideline for laypersons akin to the parallel 15:21, where lameness and blindness are defects obvious to all (cf. Mal 1:8). The motivation clause uses the category *tô'ēbâ* ("repugnant") in its ritual or cultic sense (cf. 7:5; Lev 18:22).

[17:2–7] A sample case of someone who worships "other gods" illustrates judicial procedures that are both fair and rigorous. However, the admonitory, "if . . . you" casuistic format means that the interest here is more than purely legal. This section is nicely bracketed by "among you" (vv. 2 and 7). The case links back to 16:18–20 in that "in your towns" connects 17:2 to 16:18 (skipping over 16:21–7:1). At the same time, v. 6 points forward to 19:15–21. This can be seen as a relaxation of the harsher *ḥērem* law of Exod 22:19 in that here only the lawbreaker is punished; *ḥērem* implies the destruction of one's entire household (Josh 7:24–26).

Deuteronomy 17:2–7, 12–13 replicate the subject, shape, and vocabulary of 13:2–15 [ET 1–14]. Beginning as an "if . . . you" casuistic form like those of chapter 13 (13:2 [ET 1] and 17:2: "if . . . among you"), the case repeatedly parallels the formulaic language of chapter 13:

> 17:3 and 13:3, 7, 14 [ET 2, 6, 13] ("goes and serves")
> 17:4 and 13:13, 15 [ET 12, 14] ("you hear," "inquire care-
> fully. If the matter is established as true," etc.)
> 17:7, 12 and 13:6 [ET 5] ("sweep out the evil")
> 17:13 and 13:12 [ET 11] ("hear and be afraid and will not")[10]

Deuteronomy 17:5b and 7 repeat 13:10–11b [ET 9–10b] in reverse order ("stone to death" and "first raised against him . . . and afterward the hand of"). This calls

9. In addition to being a cult object (Isa 17:8; 27:9; Mic 5:13 [ET 14]), Asherah was also a separate goddess in her own right, at least in Deuteronomistic texts (Judg 3:7; 1 Kgs 15:13; 18:19; 2 Kgs 21:7; 23:4, 7). For the asherah and associated problems, see P. D. Miller, *The Religion of Ancient Israel* (Louisville, Ky.: Westminster John Knox, 2000), 29–40.

10. For charts, see Seitz, *Redaktionsgeschichtliche Studien*, 154; and Levinson, *Deuteronomy and Hermeneutics*, 103. Most understand ch. 17 as dependent on ch. 13: Rüterswörden, *Von der politischen Gemeinschaft*, 32–38; Dion, "Suppression" *in Law and Ideology,* ed. Halpern and Hobson," 147–216; Gertz, *Gerichtsorganisation*, 45–52. Otto instead postulates a common Deuteronomic core with divergent Deuteronomistic additions, "Von der Gerichtsordnung," 149, 153.

attention to the relationship with chapter 13 and highlights the topic of witnesses by putting it in the middle of this reversal (17:6).

In the more generalized situation of chapter 17, the witnesses begin the execution, not the accuser as in chapter 13. The death sentence is carried out according to due process, in contrast to the summary execution of 13:10 [ET 9]. After all, witnesses to the secret conspiracy of 13:7–12 [ET 6–11] would presumably be unavailable. The procedural sequence of 17:2–7 is discovery (vv. 2–3), inquiry to establish guilt (v. 4), execution (vv. 5, 7a), and motive clause (v. 7b). This order of presentation clearly fits the situation of chapter 13 (discovering and uncovering religious sedition) better than the topic of juridical fairness and due process that is the theme of 17:1–7. These verses insist that, if a case is dependent on witnesses, one must use the local courts, even if it concerns the exceedingly repugnant crime of apostasy.

Verses 2–3 introduce the offense in a generalized, comprehensive fashion ("man or woman," "transgress the covenant"). "Found" indicates the existence of appropriate eyewitness evidence.[11] The equal responsibility of women is emphasized by a triple use of the double formula (vv. 2, 5; cf. 13:7 [ET 6]). Perhaps this explicit and emphatic inclusion of women offenders reflects a greater prevalence of inappropriate worship among women (cf. Jer 7:17–18; 44:15–25; Ezek 8:14). In any case, this is an example of Deuteronomy's distinctive concern with women's place in society (13:7 [ET 6]; 15:12; 22:22). The generalizing phrase "transgress the covenant" is used only here in Deuteronomy, although it is a feature of the language of DH (Josh 7:11, 15; 23:16; Judg 2:20; 2 Kgs 18:12; cf. Hos 6:7; 8:1). Transgression of "the covenant" seems to refer to a violation of the first commandment (cf. 4:23; 17:2; 29:24; 31:16, 20).[12] "I have not commanded" merges the lawgiving authority of Yahweh and Moses. Perhaps "not command" simply means "forbid" (note f). However, this phrase probably seeks to rebut any claim by polytheistic Yahwists that their practices have been authorized by divine revelation.

Verse 4 states that this is a public case, which has come to light either by direct report or indirect rumor, but which still must be proven. Execution occurs in the open (v. 5), in the public space of the gate, in order to deter similar crimes (cf. 21:21). Verse 6 returns to the question of "established as true" from v. 4, citing the principle of two witnesses (in a reversed form of 19:15). The third witness may refer to the plaintiff or accuser. Witnesses cast the first stones in order to affirm the truth of their testimony (v. 7; John 8:7; Acts 7:58) and to

---

11. S. Dempster, "The Deuteronomic Formula *KÎ YIMMĀṢĒ'* in the Light of Biblical and Ancient Near Eastern Law," *RB* 91 (1984): 188–211.

12. Braulik, "Ausdrücke für Gesetz," in *Studien zur Theologie*, 15–16. "Serve" and "bow down" seem to be a reversed allusion to 5:9.

emphasize their responsibility for not bearing false witness (19:18–19). A singular "hand" is used with the plural noun; each person uses one hand.

[17:8–13] This central court is not a court of appeal for the accused but a resource for local judges. Previously, local jurisprudence would have turned to the priests of the local sanctuary to help decide cases lacking eyewitnesses or clear-cut evidence. Such cases would be "too difficult" (literally "too wonderful"). Such "wonderful" cases are beyond human knowledge (Job 42:3; Ps 131:1; Prov 30:18; cf. Gen 18:14) and would require priestly intervention.[13] To discover the truth, the priests of the central court would engage in ritual procedures at the central sanctuary. These might include oaths of innocence or ordeals imposed on the parties (Exod 22:7, 10 [ET 8, 11]; Num 5:11–31; 1 Kgs 8:31–32), as well as divination by lots (Exod 28:29–30) or direct priestly oracle. The text firmly emphasizes that the priests involved are located at the central shrine (vv. 9, 12).

The present form of the text also, somewhat awkwardly, includes a "judge" in this central court (vv. 9, 12). The singular "judge" is odd; in 19:17 there are several judges. The inclusion of a judge suggests that appealed cases could also include ones involving difficult legal distinctions that would require special legal expertise. The distinctions of v. 8 would then be matters of legal nicety. Apparently, the text combines two different realms of judicial tradition. The result is a civil and priestly mix that gives the central courts a double function, providing both priestly rituals and legal know-how. This may stem from a commonsense recognition that legal knowledge as well as ritual competence could help adjudicate "wonderful" cases. Perhaps this judge was intended to be a substitute for the king, whose appellate role in the judicial system has been eliminated.

The transfer of location in v. 8—from "your gates" (vv. 2, 5) to the chosen "place"—signals a change in topic. For ritual judgments, those who are to appear would be the contending parties (cf. 19:17); for difficult legal issues this might also include the local judges. The "case definitions" seem to refer to distinctions between intentional and unintentional deaths and injuries. Was the homicide (literally "between blood and blood") or assault ("between blow and blow") intentional or accidental? Issues of careful legal distinctions in such case are illustrated by Exod 21:18–25. Distinctions in "legal claims" (*dîn*) may refer to conflicting legal rights or to contradictory testimony.

"In those days" (v. 9) points forward into the time of Deuteronomy's readers. "In office" parallels the situation of 26:3 and suggests that, of the numerous priests and judges, only one group or individual is authorized to perform this task. "Inquire" (*dāraš*) could refer either to ritual inquiry or to posing legal

---

13. Rütersworden, *Von der politischen Gemeinschaft*, 40, 44–45. What is "wonderful" can refer to matters beyond human achievement (2 Sam 13:2; Deut 30:11; Prov 30:18).

questions to the authorities. Verse 11 distinguishes between "exactly the law" (*pî hattôrâ*) and "the ruling" (*hammišpāṭ*), referring to different areas of competence. "Law" (*tôrâ*) would be the priestly answer based on priestly lore or oracle; "ruling" (*mišpāṭ*; cf. 16:18–19) would be the decision of a judge based on precedent or accepted legal standards. Yet at the same time the text emphasizes that the two declare the decision jointly ("they"; vv. 9, 10, 11). The death sanction (v. 12) makes sense because any decision made on the basis of ritual would actually originate from Yahweh. The priest's job description is the same as that of 10:8 (cf. 18:5). Standard motivational formulas promote compliance: "do not turn aside" (v. 20; 5:32), "sweep out the evil" (v. 7; related to 13:6 [ET 5]; also 19:19; 21:21; 22:21, 22, 24; 24:7), "hear and be afraid" (related to 13:12 [ET 11]; also 19:20; 21:21).

[**17:14–20**] The king is to be an obedient constitutional monarch on the same level with ordinary citizens and under the control of the law.[14] Regulations for all subsequent kings are included in the description of the appointment of the first one. Traditional royal powers are limited if not abrogated. The text's chief interest is in what the king ought not do, so that the positive aspects of kingship fall into the shadows. Here the flavor of utopian idealism is strong. The king becomes the ideal citizen, a model Israelite, more a student of the law than a ruler. In a way analogous to what all are to do in 6:4–9 and 11:18–21, he is to be engaged in writing and verbalizing the law, keeping it close at hand. He is to embrace the law just as any Israelite should, to "observe," "do," "learn to fear" (14:23); "not think himself higher" (8:14) or "turn aside" (5:32; 17:11).

Nevertheless, the text recognizes that there will be a king. It does not forbid characteristic royal activities, but rather thoroughly limits them. The king has a ruling position "over you" and sits on "the throne of his kingdom" (cf. 2 Sam 7:13; 1 Kgs 9:5). He can have military forces, wives, and a treasury, but he is not to "multiply" them, that is, not acquire too many or too much.[15] This viewpoint runs directly counter to the royal theology found in Ps 2:7–9; Ps 72, or the figure of the activist David and Josiah approved of in DH. Yet like DH, Deuteronomy understands Israel's kingship as the result of historical choice rather than the product of some mythic event. The story of kingship is set in motion not by divine initiative, but with Israel's urge to imitate the nations. Nevertheless, Yahweh's act of choice legitimates the king whom Israel is to appoint. Unquestionably, this text must have been the product of some interest

14. For an overview of research and an analytical study, see F. García López, "Le roi d'Israel: Dt 17, 14–20," in *Das Deuteronomium*, ed. Lohfink, 277–97. He describes the original material as vv. 16a–17 and later supplements in the reference to kinship and vv. 18–19. B. Gosse, "Deutéronome 17,18–19 et la restauration de la royauté au retour de l'exile," *Bibbia e oriente* 181 (1994): 129–38, suggests that vv. 18–19 represent a postexilic proposal to reform and reestablish the monarchy in a power-sharing arrangement with the priesthood.

15. "To acquire a great deal for someone," *HALOT* 3:1177.

group outside the mainstream of the Jerusalem royal court, perhaps elite factions whose power was threatened by royal activism.

Sometimes the law of the king is understood as an exilic or postexilic text looking forward to the restoration of an idealized, limited kingship. Yet the text shows no concern about whether there will be a king again, but rather seeks to limit an office all too prone to despotism. Its guarded opinion of kingship gives the impression of being based on grim experience. A similar perspective is found in the critiques of Isa 2:6–9 and in Jer 22:13–17, which attack the king's selfish luxury and exploitation. It is sometimes thought that this law may preserve a pre-Deuteronomic "model for the king" (*Königspiegel*), as a parallel to 16:19 concerning the judge. Both texts set forth triple limitations.[16] Perhaps it also relates to an old antimonarchic ideology represented in texts such as 1 Sam 8:11–18; 10:25. On the other hand, the text's ideology of choice by Yahweh is harmonious with both Judah's notion of divine dynastic promise and the prophetic designation stories told about northern kingdom monarchs (1 Sam 10:20–24; 1 Kgs 11:26–39; 2 Kgs 9:1–13; cf. Hos 8:4).

This is a unified section held together by prepositions with third masculine singular suffixes: the triple "acquire for himself" (vv. 16–17, *lô*), carried forward by "write for himself" (v. 18, *lô*), "beside him" (v. 19, *'immô*), and "read in it" (v. 19, *bô*). Another unifying pattern is the threefold "who" (*'ăšer*) in vv. 14–15 (two positives and a negative), the threefold limitation of vv. 16–17 (horses, wives, treasure), and then the threefold instruction in vv. 18–20 (two positives and a negative).

The law of the king shares a distinctive historical introduction (v. 14; cf. 26:1 and the analogous 12:29 and 19:1) with the law about the prophet (18:9–22). The two preliminary requisites for kinship are a completed conquest and a wish to have a king. The initial *kî* is both temporal and conditional: "when" you enter and "if" these conditions are met. A rhetorical format of statement and quoted reaction strengthens the identification between text and addressee. The grammar of v. 15 is permissive (cf. 12:20; 18:6–8). However, this permission is limited by the requirements of divine choice and ethnic kinship, the latter issue being sharply accentuated by "do not dare" (*lō' tûkal*; 12:17; cf. 16:5, 22:3). This expression connotes something dishonorable or contrary to duty (Gen 37:4; Lam 4:14). The restriction to an ethnic Israelite (literally "brother") designated by Yahweh may reflect historical experiences such as the potential imposition of Tabeel (Isa 7:6) or the story of Abimelech.[17]

---

16. For the threefold prohibitions of the original law, see E. Gerstenberger, *Wesen und Herkunft des apodiktischen Rechts* (WMANT 20; Neukirchen-Vluyn: Neukirchener Verlag, 1965), 67–68.

17. D. Daube, "One from among Your Brethren Shall You Set King over You," *JBL* 90 (1971): 480–81. One or more of the usurpers in the northern kingdom may have been foreign mercenary commanders.

Verse 16 continues the theme of limitation with "only" (*raq*; cf. 12:23, 26), and attention shifts from "you" to "he" as the party to whom this part of the law applies. The ideology of choice by Yahweh immediately raises the specter of despotism on the part of kings who could claim this divine mandate. The actions prohibited are all characterized by the phrase "for himself" and thus relate to the goal of "not think himself higher" in v. 20. The psychology is the same as that of 8:12–14. The king is not to be a symbol of national glory or prosperity. Perhaps warhorses are forbidden as something counter to the ideology of the divine warrior. Isaiah 2:7 and Mic 5:10, at least, mention them in a context of infidelity. Verse 16b legitimates the unusual constraint of v. 16a. It is uncertain whether this intends to disallow simple commercial transactions or is thinking of trading mercenaries to Egypt for horses. If the latter is the case, perhaps some actual event is in view, such as Manasseh's participation in Ashurbanipal's campaign in Egypt (*ANET*, 294), a possible Judahite mercenary colony under Psammetichus I (Herodotus, *Hist.* 2.152, 154; *Let. Aris.* 13), or other alliances or understandings with Egypt. On the other hand, perhaps this is a metaphorical reference to a reversal of the exodus. In is even unclear whether these words are intended to be a prohibition or a promise (note t). Promise is suggested by the curse in Deut 28:68. Perhaps one could say that this is a promise that, by its very nature, implies a command.[18]

Limiting the royal harem (v. 17) would have both external and internal effects. Characteristically, the explicit reason given is the destructive effect such marriages would have on the king's religious loyalty, pointing to the dangers of political alliances. (The reader would certainly think of Solomon's wives and Jezebel.) Although this is similar to the preventive ideology of 7:3–4, it is not actually foreign wives who are forbidden, but too many wives of any sort. Royal marriages were also important within Israel as a way of consolidating political power. A large number of such marriages would increase the influence of those families so favored at the expense of others. Numerous wives would also flaunt the conspicuous wealth required to support them. Moreover, wisdom tradition warned kings in particular of the distractions presented by women (Prov 31:3).[19]

Verses 18–19 move away from negative limits to a king's positive duties and from the general circumstances of his rule to the specific situation of his accession. The production of a copy of the law book is to be an integral part of his enthronement. The king is to gain an intensive knowledge of the law. This is the

18. The source of the citation is uncertain. Lohfink proposes Hos 11:5, "Hos XI 5 als Bezuugstext von Dtn. XVII 9," in *Studien zum Deuteronomium II*, 143–46. Exodus 14:13 is suggested by Skweres, *Ruckverweise*, 193–94. On this verse, see D. Reimer, "Concerning Return to Egypt: Deuteronomy xvii 16 and xxviii 68 Reconsidered," in *Studies in the Pentateuch*, ed. Emerton, 217–29.

19. For examples outside Israel, see W. G. Lambert, *Babylonian Wisdom Literature* (Oxford: Clarendon, 1960), 110–17; E. Reiner, "The Babylonian Fürstenspiegel in Practice," in *Societies and Languages of the Ancient Near East* (Warminster: Aris and Phillips, 1982), 320–26.

same spirit of careful attention and study as that required in 6:6–9; consequently the king is the ideal Israelite. Behind this requirement is the cultural concept of documents specially written for royal instruction (such as *ANET*, 414–20), but here the king in fact studies the same law as everyone else. The notion of making a "copy" implies an authoritative prototype (cf. 31:9, 24–26). The totality of Deuteronomic law is emphasized by a variety of terms: "this law," "all the words," "these statutes." The first "it" in v. 19 is a feminine pronoun and refers to the law. "Read in it" uses the masculine pronoun and refers to the book.

Verses 18–19 contain the only references to "this law" and "book" in chapters 5–26. In referring to itself as written law in the midst of its original oral delivery, Deuteronomy here reflects a perspective that transcends that of Moses in his speech to Israel. In calling itself a "book," Deuteronomy sees itself as a self-contained unity. It has become a protocanonical book, a reforming and controlling agent safeguarded by priestly oversight. If one thinks in political terms, Deuteronomy claims a constitutional status as a written legal document, to which even the king is subject.

Verse 20 describes first negative, then positive goals for this legislation. It may have originally followed v. 17 directly, suggesting that vv. 18–19 represent a later supplement. The ideal citizen king shows solidarity with his "kindred" (cf. v. 15). Perhaps "the commandment" refers narrowly to v. 19 or to vv. 16–19, but more likely designates the whole law (cf. 8:1; 11:8). The king's dynasty ("his sons") has the potential to be long-lasting (but not expressly eternal), contingent on obedience. Perhaps this suggests some sort of reflection on the more ephemeral dynasties of the northern kingdom. The royal dynasty reigns "over" the kingdom, but still "in [literally 'in the midst of' (*bĕqereb*)] Israel."

Thus the ideals of national solidarity are integrated with the blunt realities of monarchy, and the sovereignty of Yahweh is protected from royal pretensions. In practical terms, however, the elite classes would be especially well served by this limitation on royal power and wealth. Reigning in royal authority would permit other traditional power groups to operate more freely. An unrestrained royal chariot force could be used to enforce tyranny and would be extremely costly to taxpayers. It would also promote an elite military class. Royal marriages would affect the status of elite families in internal politics. Centralization would compound such problems by directing greater resources into the royal treasury to the detriment of other economic interests, especially those outside Jerusalem. This law of the king would also reduce the potential for conflict with Assyria in that there could be no alliances or contacts with Assyria's rival, Egypt.[20]

---

20. I owe these observations to P. Dutcher-Walls, "Deuteronomistic Royal Ideology: Sociological Perspectives" (paper presented at the annual SBL meeting, Nashville, November 22, 1999). The installation of Josiah and then Jehoahaz by "the people of the land" (2 Kgs 21:24; 23:30) represent attempts by the upper classes to regulate royal policy.

Constitutional Proposals Continued
18:1–22

The Levitical Priests

18:1 The Levitical priests, the whole tribe of Levi, shall have no share or hereditary possession within Israel. They shall eat the offerings by fire[a] of Yahweh that are his[b] hereditary possession. 2 But he[c] shall have no hereditary possession among his kindred; Yahweh is his hereditary possession, as he promised him.

3 But this shall be the prerogative[d] of the priests from the people, from those offering sacrifice, whether an ox or a sheep: he shall give to the priest the shoulder, the two cheeks, and the stomach. 4 The firstfruits of your grain, your wine, and your oil, and the first of the fleece of your sheep, you shall give him. 5 For Yahweh[e] has chosen him out of all your tribes, to stand and serve in the name of Yahweh,[f] him and his sons for all time.

6 If a Levite comes from one of your towns, from wherever in all Israel he has been residing, and comes whenever he wishes[g] to the place that Yahweh will choose, 7 and serves[h] in the name of Yahweh his God, like all his kindred Levites who stand there before Yahweh, 8 then they shall eat equal shares, without regard to any income from his sale of an ancestral estate.[i]

Soothsayers and Diviners

9 When you come into the land that Yahweh your God is going to give you, do not learn to perform the repugnant acts of those nations. 10 Let no one be found among you who makes his son or daughter pass through fire, any diviner, soothsayer, or fortune-teller, or sorcerer, 11 or anyone who casts spells, or consults ghosts or spirits, or seeks oracles from the dead. 12 For everyone who does these things is repugnant to Yahweh.[j] It is because of these repugnant things that Yahweh your God is dispossessing them before you. 13 You shall be blameless before Yahweh your God. 14 For these nations that you will dispossess listen to soothsayers and diviners, but as for you, Yahweh your God does not permit you to do this.

The Prophet

15 Yahweh will raise up for you a prophet[k] like me from among you, from your own kindred.[l] It is to him you must listen. 16 This is exactly what

you asked of Yahweh your God at Horeb on the day of the assembly when you said, "Let me no longer hear the voice of Yahweh my God nor see this great fire again, or I shall die." 17 Then Yahweh said to me, "They are right in what[m] they have said. 18 I will raise up for them a prophet like you from among their own kindred. I will put my words in his mouth, and he shall speak to them everything[n] that I command him. 19 Anyone who does not listen to my words[o] that he speaks[p] in my name, I myself will call to account. 20 But any prophet who acts arrogantly to speak in my name a word that I have not commanded him to speak or who speaks in the name of other gods—that prophet shall be put to death." 21 What if you say to yourself, "How may we[q] recognize a word that Yahweh has not spoken?"[r] 22 When a prophet speaks in the name of Yahweh but the thing does not happen or come true, it is a word that Yahweh has not spoken. The prophet has spoken it in arrogance. Do not fear him.[s]

a. The association of this kind of offering (1 Sam 2:28; Num 15:10 = wine) with "fire" may be a folk etymology. The root may be '*wš* with the meaning "gift" (Ugaritic; *HALOT* 1:26). According to J. Hoftijzer, "Das sogenannte Feueropfer," in *Hebräische Wortforschung* (ed. B. Hartmann et al.; VTSup 16; Leiden: Brill, 1967), 114–34, the word denotes edible parts of the offering that were sometimes burned and sometimes eaten by priests, rather than a type of sacrifice.

b. The pronominal suffix could refer to either Yahweh or Levi (cf. 10:9). The awkwardness suggests that this word is a gloss or redactional addition connecting to v. 2.

c. The antecedent is either "Levi" or "the tribe of Levi." In v. 5 "he and his sons" must refer to Levi.

d. For *mišpāṭ* in this sense, see 1 Sam 8:11; cf. 1 Sam 2:13.

e. Follows OG (= LXX[B] and 848; Wevers, *Text History*, 76–77). MT expands with '*lhyk*, "your God."

f. Follows MT *lšrt bšm-yhwh*. In place of this, Sam. and OG have a long expansion taken from 10:8 and 21:5: *lpny yhwh 'lhyk (w)lšrt(w) wlbrk bšmw*, "before Yahweh your God (and) to minister (to him) and to bless in his name." This longer text is also reflected in 11QTemple 60.

g. For this translation, cf. 12:15. Alternate translation: "in the eagerness of his desire," perhaps intending to discourage casual claims.

h. This translation continues the protasis from v. 6 and begins the apodosis at v. 8, thus focusing on the Levite's right to an equal portion: if he comes and serves, then they may eat (cf. REB). The Levite's right to come to the central shrine is simply assumed. An alternate translation would begin the apodosis at v. 7: "if a Levite comes . . . then he may serve . . . and they shall eat equal shares" (cf. NRSV, LXX). This translation assures or legislates the right of any Levite to join the staff of the central sanctuary. However, that the shift from protasis to apodosis takes place between vv. 7 and 8 is indicated by the break in the *waw* perfect pattern at that point (cf. 17:14–15). Moreover, the word order of v. 8, which emphasizes "equal shares," indicates that the point of the sentence is equitable support, not any extension of the rights of Levites. The predominant topic throughout vv. 1–8 is the support of personnel in cultic service. See R. K. Duke, "The Portion of the Levite: Another Reading of Deuteronomy 18:6–8," *JBL* 106 (1987): 193–201.

i. This translation is uncertain. Masoretic vocalization indicates the noun *mimkār*, "sale." However, the preceding preposition *lĕbad* would seem to require the presence of *min*, "from," giving rise to the conjecture followed here: *mimmekārāyw*, "from his sale." Second Kings 12:6, 8 suggest the noun *makkār* instead, thus *mimmakkārāyw*, "from his acquaintances" (i.e., "from personal gifts over and above ['al*, HALOT*, 2:826, §6b] inheritances from their fathers"). N. Airoldi, *"lbd mmkrjw 'l-h'bwt* (Dtn 18, 8b)", *BZ* 18 (1974): 96–101, construes the noun as *meker*, "goods" (Num 20:19; Prov 31:10; Neh 13:16). It is also uncertain that the last word refers to patrimony; cf. T. E. Ranck, "Patrimony in Deuteronomy 18:8—A Possible Explanation," in *The Answers Lie Below: Essays in Honor of Lawrence Edward Toombs* (ed. H. Thompson; Lanham, Md.: University Press of America, 1984), 281–85. L. S. Wright, *"MKR* in 2 Kings xii:5–17 and Deuteronomy xviii:8," *VT* 39 (1989): 438–48, suggests "things sold according to ancient custom," i.e., proceeds from marketing the meat of sacrifices.

j. Follows MT. Sam., OG, Syr. expand with *'lhyk*, "your God."

k. Alternate translation here and in v. 18: "[a succession of] prophets."

l. Follows MT as an unusual and difficult combination. Sam. and OG have a more standard *mqrb 'hyk*, "from among your kindred" (cf. v. 18; 17:15).

m. Follows MT. OG, Syr., Vulg. supplement with *kl*; "in *everything* they had said."

n. Follows MT. The absence of *kl*, "everything," in OG should be understood as a strategy of translation.

o. Follows MT. Sam. OG (= LXX^A) *dbryw*, "his words," adjust to the following "that he shall speak."

p. Alternate translation: "when he speaks."

q. Follows MT supported by OG. Syr. and Vulg. "how may I recognize" is an adjustment to the singular context. Sam. solves the difficulty with a nip'al passive: "how may it be recognized?"

r. Literally "that is not his word" (also in v. 22).

s. Alternate translation: "afraid of it" (i.e., the word).

The constitutional proposal continues from chapter 17, focusing in turn on the offices of priest and prophet. Elements found in the previous sections on jurisprudence and kingship continue: a focus on obedient listening to authorized functionaries (17:12; 18:15, 19), repugnant behavior "found" (17:2, 4; 18:9–10, 12), "Levitical priests" (17:9, 18; 18:1), arrogance (17:12–13; 18:20, 22), "kindred" (17:15; 18:7, 15), selection for office (16:18; 17:15; 18:5, 15), succession (17:20; 18:5), and the parallel introductions of 17:14 and 18:9.

[1–8] This section focuses on the rights of priests with Levitical credentials to share in the consumption of sacrifices at the central sanctuary (vv. 1, 3–4). Service at the sanctuary qualifies someone with the proper Levitical genealogy to a fair share of the offerings. The text envisions that some Levites from outlying areas will choose to come to the central altar to share in this service (vv. 6–8). Priestly entitlement is justified by divine election (v. 5) and their exclusion from the standard patterns of land ownership (v. 2). Other sorts of assets should not impede their receiving a fair share (v. 8). Verses 1–2 set forth the core principle: priests have no inherited land, but instead have a right to sacrificial offerings. Verses 3–4 detail the proper portion for priests. Verses 6–8 secure an equal share for the kindred ("brother") Levite who arrives and engages in service at the central shrine. Taken at face value, the import of vv. 6–8 seems clear. The Levite who voluntarily chooses to relocate to the central sanctuary and functions there may share in the sacrifices. It is not clear whether such transfers into priestly positions are intended to be a normal procedure or something envisioned as happening only occasionally.

A scribal pattern of linked vocabulary unifies the final form of the text:

> v. 1: no *share* or *hereditary possession*
> v. 2: no *hereditary possession* among his *kindred*
> v. 7: his *kindred* Levites
> v. 8: then they shall eat equal *shares*

Beneath the surface of this integrated text, however, there is evidence that an earlier law assuring Levitical priests their rightful share of sacrifices was modified to emphasize the special privileges of all Levites. In 18:1 a coherent third-person plural sentence, "the Levitical priests . . . shall have no share . . . they shall eat," has been disrupted by singular elements that advance a "pan-Levi" point of view: "whole tribe . . . his hereditary possession" (note b). Verse 1 is the only passage in Deuteronomy that unambiguously equates Levitical priests with the "whole tribe of Levi." This pan-Levi concern is carried forward in v. 2 ("as he promised him") and then in v. 5 ("chosen him out of all your tribes"). Moreover, this same redactional interest in the special privileges of all those with Levite descent is evident in the secondary addition 10:8–9. This passage also focuses on the "tribe of Levi" as a whole (10:8; cf. 18:1), the cultic functions "serve" and "stand before" (10:8; cf. 18:5), and Yahweh as a "hereditary possession as he promised" (10:9; cf. 18:2).

Whether vv. 6–8, which speak of Levites generally, should also be assigned to this pan-Levi redactional concern must remain an open question. It is not necessary to do so, however, if the protasis of the conditional sentence is understood to be vv. 6–7 and the apodosis as v. 8 (note h). Those Levites who voluntarily relocate to the central sanctuary and serve there in priestly functions are to receive priestly benefits. Such relocation is not described as a universal phenomenon, however, nor is the acceptance of such hopeful job seekers mandated or necessarily automatic.[1]

---

1. U. Dahmen, *Leviten und Priester im Deuteronomium. Literarkritische und redaktions-geschichtliche Studien* (BBB 110; Frankfurt: Athenäum, 1996), distinguishes four layers about priests and Levites in Deuteronomy, three of which are present in ch. 18. A monarchic original text (vv. 1, 3–5) asserts rights to sacrifice for priests, who are otherwise undefined. Later an exilic

Verses 1–2 set forth two basic principles: priests have no inheritance, but do have access to sacrificial offerings for their primary support. The second principle is developed by the list of vv. 3–4. Then the first principle is expounded by references to "reside" (verb *gwr*, "dwell as an outsider without an inheritance of land") in v. 6 and "ancestral estate" in v. 8.

Verse 3 begins with a disjunctive *waw*, which turns the focus onto the priests' portions, in implied contrast to whatever might be claimed by laypersons. The phrase "those offering sacrifice" (literally "slaughter the sacrificial victim") indicates that killing the animal remained the prerogative of the layperson bringing the offering. The list of vv. 3–4 does not use the language of the Priestly Writer (contrast Lev 7:32–34). As an example of the genre "catalog of offerings," this list is similar to the Punic Marseilles Tariff (*ANET*, 656–57). In preamble and function it parallels the description of a standard priestly prerogative (*mišpāṭ*) embedded in 1 Sam 2:13–14.[2] The lay addressee of the text is highlighted by the appearance of "you" in v. 4. Verse 5 stresses that the priest, like the king (17:15), is divinely elected.

Beginning a new idea, again marked by an initial *waw* (cf. v. 3), vv. 6–8 turn to a casuistic situation that shifts away from the divine initiative of v. 5 to human initiative and desire. However, the overall topic remains the right to receive provisions from the sacrificial system. Here the basic principle is the just correspondence between equivalent service (*kĕkol-'ehāyw*, "like all his kindred," v. 7) and equivalent compensation (*hēleq kĕhēleq*, "equal shares," v. 8).

Four things are said about this Levite. First, he starts off "from one of your towns (literally "gates"), which identifies him with the local Levites for whom those addressed by the law have special responsibilities. Second, as one who "resides" (verb *gwr*, "live with the status of an alien"), he is landless and not included in local clan structure (cf. 12:12; 14:27, 29, etc.). Third, his transfer grows out of personal desire and choice. "Whenever he wishes" is the language used for desiring to eat meat (12:20) and enjoying the tithe (14:26). Fourth— in reference to v. 5—he "serves in the name" like those others who "stand before Yahweh." Although the first of these phrases does not necessarily refer to tasks performed exclusively by priests, usage elsewhere in Deuteronomy strongly implies that priestly duties are meant (10:8; 17:12; 21:5). This conclusion is supported by the basic logic of the argument: equal support implies

---

Deuteronomist added the "Levitical priests" formula of v. 1 to emphasize the proper genealogical background for priests. Finally a postexilic pro-Levitical writer claimed extensive priestly rights for Levites (cf. 10:8–9) by adding "the whole tribe of Levi" to v. 1, "out of all your tribes" to v. 5, along with vv. 2, 6–8. Rüterswörden, *Von der politischen Gemeinschaft*, 67–75, largely agrees about what is secondary to the original text in vv. 1–2, 5, but considers vv. 6–8 as original rather than secondary.

2. This parallel is obscured by a textual error in 1 Sam 2:13 MT (*'t* for *m't*; cf. OG).

equivalent "service" (vv. 5, 7). The second phrase is an unambiguous description of unique priestly access to the altar (Ezek 44:15).[3] Characteristically, the
motivation offered for obedience is "brotherly" solidarity ("kindred Levites").
A number of critical questions remain. First, does this provision seek to
cushion the economic effects of centralization on members of the tribe of Levi
who had formerly enjoyed economic rights at local sanctuaries? The text is not
explicit about this. The right of those who do serve as priests to share in the sacrifices is stressed, but the privilege of functioning as a priest is not necessarily
affirmed for all Levites. Moreover, the social situation of the Levites in
Deuteronomy is not presented as one of powerlessness or poverty (contrast
10:18; 24:17, 19–20). This text argues not on the basis of the poverty of Levites,
but from their situation with respect to "inheritance," fairness given Yahweh's
promise and choice, and "brotherhood."

Second, does Deuteronomy draw a distinction between "Levitical priests"
(v. 1) and other members of the tribe of Levi? The answer would seem to be
yes, but not in the same sharp way that Ezekiel and the Priestly Writer do. In
Deuteronomy the noun "Levite" is a collective singular referring to a group
who are members of the addressees' extended social family and participate as
such in cultic events. "Levitical priests" are distinguished from the "Levite" not
by genealogy, but by function and office. They have clearly defined juridical
and sacrificial roles at the central sanctuary. The phrase "Levitical priests" (literally "the priests, the Levites") is not meant to equate all Levites with priests.
It does not seek to identify the priests and Levites as a single group, but rather
emphasizes that the priests in question are properly Levitical in their ancestral
background. Grammatically, the word pair is not presented as a nominal sentence (as though *hakkōhănîm lĕwîyim*, "the priests are Levites"). Rather it is an
apposition, *hakkōhănîm halĕwîyim*, "the *Levitical* priests," as opposed to any
putative non-Levitical ones.[4]

---

3. Nelson, *Raising Up a Faithful Priest*, 59–62.
4. For this grammar of explanatory apposition, cf. 17:1; 23:20 [ET 19]; 25:16. This is not an
Identitätsformel that seeks to equate Levites and priests (as suggested by A. H. J. Gunneweg,
*Leviten und Priester: Hauplinen der Traditionsbildung und Geschichte des israelitisch-jüdischen
Kultpersonals* [FRLANT 89; Göttingen: Vandenhoeck & Ruprecht, 1965], 126–32). The relationship between the Levitical priests and the Levites in Deuteronomy is fiercely disputed. Some insist
that the two groups are simply equated (J. A. Emerton, "Priests and Levites in Deuteronomy," *VT*
12 [1962]: 129–38). Others trace a functional distinction between priests who served at altars and
Levites who did not (R. Abba, "Priests and Levites in Deuteronomy," *VT* 27 [1977]: 257–67). On
the basis of the terminology in Deuteronomy, J. Lindblom distinguished four Levitical categories,
including two types of noncultic rural Levites (*Erwägungen zur Herkunft der josianischen Tem-
pelurkunde* [Lund: Gleerup, 1971], 22–41, 44). Rüterswörden, *Von der politischen Gemeinschaft*,
74, concludes that Deuteronomy makes no distinction between priest and Levite in the cultic service they could potentially perform, but does distinguish them in status. There is a clear distinction
between the Levitical priest and Levite in 26:3 and 11.

Third, how does this text relate to Josiah's reform program, if at all? It can hardly be a retrospective reflection on Josiah's resettlement of priests to Jerusalem. These verses describe a spontaneous, apparently occasional, and voluntary movement of Levites to serve at the central sanctuary. This situation seems to have little to do with Josiah's forced settlement of non-Jerusalem priests (and not Levites in general!) described in 2 Kgs 23:8–9. Conversely, it seems completely unlikely that Josiah would have thought he was violating Deut 18:6–8 in denying priestly office to priests who had perpetrated scandalous sacrifice at Judahite high places. Properly translated, 18:6–8 takes for granted that some Levites would assume priestly office, but does not require that every single Levite be permitted to do so.[5]

[9–14] This is a transitional section, setting up a negative foil to the upcoming admonition about prophets. It also alludes to the previous topic, however, since priests were responsible for oracles and legitimate divination. These verses seek to restrict attempts to learn about the divine will, the future, and hidden mysteries. They also serve as a rhetorical prelude to the command to listen to the divinely chosen prophet (v. 15). Israel should rely on true prophets and not utilize other sources of information. This prohibition is in line with other laws (especially Exod 22:17 [ET 18]; also Lev 19:31; 20:6, 27), but seems to run counter to what was commonly practiced (1 Sam 28:6–19; Isa 3:2–3; 29:4; Jer 27:9; Mic 3:7).[6]

The office of the prophet is introduced in nearly the same way as that of the king, although the participle *bā'*, "come," in v. 9a suggests a more immediate situation than that envisioned by 17:14. Verses 9 and 12–14 form a motivational bracket ("repugnant," "nations") around a list of eight participants in divination (vv. 10–11). These behaviors are treated as markers of the ethnic boundary between the doomed "nations" and "you." Divinatory practices and those who do them are tightly bracketed by the category of *tô'ēbâ*, "repugnant" (vv. 9b and 12a) and as such would undermine Israel's relationship with Yahweh. Learning from the contagious practices of the dispossessed nations is also prohibited in 12:29–31; 20:18, and is the opposite of the positive learning advocated by 14:23; 17:19.

The catalog of persons involved in divination appears within a "not found" apodictic prohibition (v. 10a; cf. 16:4 and Exod 12:19). The list intends to be

5. For the way in which DH read Deut 18:6–8, see R. D. Nelson, "The Role of the Priesthood in the Deuteronomistic History," in *Congress Volume, Leuven 1989* (ed. J. A. Emerton; VTSup 43; Leiden: Brill, 1991), 141–44.

6. For the importance of divination and its association with prophecy in Israelite and neighboring societies, as well as Deuteronomy's redefinition of prophecy in terms of the law, see H. L. Bosman, "Redefined Prophecy as Deuteronomic Alternative to Divination in Deut 18:9–22," *Acta Theologica* 16 (1996): 1–23. On the relation of divination to the cult of the dead, see J. Blenkinsopp, "Deuteronomy and the Politics of Post-Mortem Existence," *VT* 45 (1995): 1–16.

exhaustive in order to emphasize a complete prohibition of every conceivable sort of such practices.

The context suggests that passing one's child through fire (v. 10) was a divinatory practice rather than a sacrifice to turn away a divinity's wrath or as part of the cult of the dead. Perhaps the survival or death of the child indicated a yes or no answer. The practice is also mentioned in a divinatory context by 2 Kgs 17:17; 21:6.[7]

The second person on the list (root *qsm*) may be someone who shoots or manipulates arrows as lots (Ezek 21:21–22), but the meaning of the verb probably extends to divination in general (1 Sam 15:23; Mic 3:7). Because the third item lacks a conjunction, it could be intended as a clarification of the second. The root *'nn* (as a Polel participle) suggests someone who observes clouds or other meteorological phenomena, but an Arabic cognate implies "one who causes something to make an appearance," perhaps a necromancer (*HALOT* 2:857). In spite of its verbal root *nḥš*, the fourth practice apparently has nothing to do with snakes (*HALOT* 2:690; see also *lḥš*, *HALOT* 2:503). The LXX understood this as a reference to one who takes portents from birds, but Gen 44:5 and 15 point to divination by reading the surface of oil or water in a cup. The fifth person (the last word of v. 10) is a "magician" (Akkadian cognate *kaššapu*, *HALOT* 2:503). The female practitioner of this art is guilty of a capital crime according to Exod 22:17 [ET 18].

The root *ḥbr* lying behind the sixth item (beginning v. 11) suggests "joining, weaving" and thus the casting of spells. In Ps 58:6 [ET 5] it means to keep a snake at bay with magic words or sounds. The seventh item is someone who inquires of spectral sources described by the standard word pair *'ôb* and *yiddĕ'ōnî* (Isa 8:19–20). The first word implies a ghost or the pit utilized to communicate with one. The second term only appears in connection with *'ôb*. The root *yd'* suggests either consulting one "known," that is, a "familiar spirit" or dead relative, or consulting one who "knows" the desired information.[8] The eighth expression explains the previous item in less technical language.

Verse 12 motivates the prohibition of these practices with an explicit warning based on their nature as *tô'ēbâ* ("repugnant"). The verse offers an implicit threat based on what happened to the dispossessed nations. Verse 13 commands the positive opposite of the crimes of vv. 10–11 (cf. the rhetoric of 16:20). The subject pronoun "you" in v. 14 is emphatic and stresses the opposition between

---

7. The ancient versions (LXX, Vulg.), on the other hand, thought of this as a purification rite (cf. Num 31:23). The extent and purpose of child sacrifice is a matter of dispute. See G. C. Heider, "Molech," *ABD* 4:895–98.

8. LXX translated *'ôb* as "ventriloquist," perhaps a skeptical exposé of the necromancer's actual methodology. LXX connected *yiddĕ'ōnî* with the observation of portentous monstrous births. For another view of these two terms, see J. Lust, "On Wizards and Prophets," in *Studies on Prophecy* (VTSup 26; Leiden: Brill, 1974), 133–42.

Israel and the nations. The second and third items from the list (v. 10) are
repeated and inverted. To seek out these channels would be to deny that Yahweh
has provided a sufficient way to find out such information through the legitimate prophet and to assert that there are effective powers outside the sphere of
Yahweh's activity, especially in the realm of the dead. "Listen" builds a topical
bridge to v. 15: the listening that the nations do is the opposite of Israel's obedient listening to the authorized prophet (vv. 15, 19).

[15–22] This section deals with three issues or problems involving
prophecy. First, it provides an etiology for the institution of prophecy. Second,
it seeks to motivate obedience to authentic prophets. Third, it strives to eliminate the danger of false prophets.[9]

Through a word order that emphasizes "prophet" and "to him," v. 15 connects to v. 14 as a contrasting response to what Yahweh does not permit. One
could translate the first words: "Instead it is a prophet that Yahweh will raise
up." This introduces a retrospective dialogue highlighting the speech of
Yahweh (vv. 16–20), followed by a likely objection triggered by internal ques-
tioning (vv. 21–22; cf. 7:17), and concluded by a succinct apodictic prohibition
(v. 22bβ). Verses 16–18 take the reader back to the event at Horeb as reported
in 5:5, 23–31. Verse 18a employs a resumptive repetition of v. 15a to hold
together vv. 15–18. Verses 20 and 22 echo and reverse some of the vocabulary
of 17:12–13: "acts arrogantly . . . put to death . . . in arrogance," drawing a parallel between the obedience required of the prophet and that owed to the centralized court.

In providing *an etiology for prophecy* that connects it to Moses, Deuteronomy is not merely raising questions of historical interest. From the viewpoint
of the book's dramatic staging in Moab, the audience listening to Moses would
naturally be concerned about how Yahweh will communicate after his death.
The validity of prophecy would also be a vital concern for the readers of
Deuteronomy, given conflicts between competing prophets and the failure of
widely accepted oracles. In spite of the literal singularity of "a prophet" (v. 15,
note k), it seems obvious that a series of prophets is meant (cf. 17:14–15, where

---

9. On the theology of the prophets in Deuteronomy, see H. M. Barstad, "The Understanding of
the Prophets in Deuteronomy," *SJOT* 8 (1994): 236–51 (Deuteronomy has a negative view and
understands the "like Moses" successor as Joshua); K. Jeppesen, "Is Deuteronomy Hostile Towards
Prophets?" *SJOT* 8 (1994): 252–56 (not negative overall); E. Otto, "'Das Deuteronomium krönt
die Arbeit der Propheten.' Gesetz und Prophetie im Deuteronomium," in *Ich bewirke das Heil und
erschaffe das Unheil (Jesaja 45,7)* (Forschung zur Bibel 88; Würzburg: Echter, 1998), 277–309
(Deuteronomy does away with prophecy's legitimacy). For the relationship of these verses to other
texts, see W. H. Schmidt, "Das Prophetengesetz Dtn 18,9–22 im Kontext erzählender Literatur," in
Deuteronomy and Deuteronomic Literature, ed. Vervenne and Lust, 55–69; and M. Köckert, "Zum
literargeschichtlichen Ort des Prophetengesetzes Dtn 18 zwischen dem Jeremiabuch und Dtn 13,"
in *Liebe und Gebot*, ed. Kratz and Spieckermann, 80–100.

more than one king is undeniably in view). The suitability of prophetic mediation is illustrated by the classic example of revelation at Horeb (v. 16), and Yahweh's response to the people's fear there supports prophetic authority (vv. 17–18). Indeed, the etiology of the prophet parallels that of the Deuteronomic law itself (5:25–31). Although v. 16 quotes only the first part of the people's request (5:25), their appeal for an intermediary (5:27) is obviously implied as well.

"Like Moses" (vv. 15, 18) certainly does not mean "equal to Moses" (so that 34:10 represents no real contradiction), but indicates that this prophet will have the same relationship to the people and to Yahweh's word as Moses did. A prophet "like Moses" describes a certain kind of prophet among other possibilities. He will be an authorized mediator, an intercessor (cf. 9:18–20, 25–29), and a teacher of the law. This evaluation of prophecy cuts across the categories important to modern scholarship: prophet of salvation or doom, independent or cult prophet, ecstatic prophet or not. Like the king of 17:15, the legitimate prophet will be "from among you, from your own kindred" (vv. 15, 18), a fellow Israelite who stands in solidarity with the people.

This etiology for prophecy works in service of the text's second purpose of *motivating obedience to prophets*. The focus is not so much on what prophets are to do as on what their hearers are to do. The line of reasoning is: you yourself asked for this and Yahweh agreed, so heed the prophet! "Raise up" (vv. 15, 18) emphasizes the initiative of Yahweh (Amos 2:11; Jer 29:15), something prophets repeatedly claimed in call narratives and messenger formulas. "Put my words in his mouth" (v. 18) is the language of Jer 1:9 (cf. Exod 4:15; Jer 5:14). Yahweh commands the prophet, so what this prophet speaks is unequivocally Yahweh's word in its entirety. The first word of v. 19 (*wĕhāyâ*) introduces another sort of incentive for listening based on threat. First Kings 20:35–36 offers a narrative illustration of "call to account" (*dāraš*; cf. Ps 10:13).

The third purpose is to *eliminate the danger of false prophets*. These are to be eliminated by execution (v. 20; for this language, see 17:12; 24:7). The notion of "my name" connects vv. 20–22 to v. 19. Prophetic oracles spoken on the authority of other gods would present no particular difficulty, but a pragmatic rule is needed for those who claim to be prophets of Yahweh (cf. the two types in Jer 23:13 and 21–22). Perhaps Deuteronomy has in mind some particular contemporary group of prophets with a rival viewpoint. The critical importance of the predictable question of v. 21 is reflected in prophetic call narratives and reports of prophetic disputations. Fundamentally the issue is: Whom do we fear and whom do we put to death? "Fear" refers to threats of national or individual judgment, but also to a reverent obedience of prophetic commands (cf. Lev 19:3; Josh 4:14). In the context of Deuteronomy, this natural concern is intensified by the threat of prophetic treason set forth in 13:2–6 [ET 1–5], where the apostate content of the message leads to its automatic rejection.

The advice of v. 22 is subtler. Time will tell, for the true prophetic word inexorably sets impending events into motion (1 Sam 3:19–20; Amos 1:2; Jer 1:9–10). Moreover, a true prophet may back up oracles by predicting accompanying signs (cf. 1 Sam 10:1–7; 2 Kgs 20:8–11). According to 13:2–3 [ET 1–2], however, even signs that come to pass are to be ignored if the content of the prophetic message encourages disloyalty. This "wait and see" principle obviously points to an evaluation of long-term performance and general reputation rather than to any specific oracle about which judgment must be made immediately. Deuteronomy proposes this test only in its negative form for presumptuous prophets speaking words not authorized by Yahweh. It is not intended to undermine the command to listen to the prophet "like Moses" (vv. 15, 19) or to cast any doubt on that prophet's legitimacy.

As an element of Deuteronomy's "constitutional proposal" (16:18–18:22), prophets function as a divinely authorized counterweight to the potent institutions of public justice, kingship, and cult. Highlighting the prophetic office implies a corresponding reduction in the importance of priestly divination and oracle. Yet prophets also remain subservient to the constraints of the law (13:2–6 [ET 1–5]) and the will of Yahweh. Deuteronomy emphasizes Yahweh's initiative and activity in prophecy ("raise up," "put my words in his mouth," "I command," "in my name"), in opposition to the human initiative involved in forbidden acts of divination (vv. 9–12). The prophet is "charismatic" in the sense of being impelled by Yahweh, rather than being the occupant of a routinized office. Genuine prophets follow the pattern of being "like Moses," the profile for which is set forth throughout the book of Deuteronomy: accurate transmission of Yahweh's word, utilization of effective rhetoric, intercession in crisis, promotion of public and private ethics, and concern for the plight of the distressed.

Fairness in the Practice of Justice
19:1–21

Cities of Refuge

19:1 When Yahweh your God has cut off the nations whose land Yahweh[a] your God is going to give you, and you have dispossessed them and settled in their cities and in their houses, 2 you must set apart three cities within your land that Yahweh your God is giving you.[b] 3 You must arrange the routes[c] and divide into three the territory of your land that Yahweh your God will cause you to inherit, so that anyone who kills can flee there.

4 Here is an example of[d] a killer who might flee there and live, someone who has struck down his neighbor inadvertently without previously being hostile to him. 5 Suppose[e] someone goes into the forest with his neighbor to cut wood and swings the ax to cut down a tree, and the ax head separates from the handle[f] and hits his neighbor, who then dies. He may flee to one of these cities and live. 6 Otherwise the blood avenger would pursue the killer in hot anger[g] and might overtake him because the distance was too great, and strike him dead, although there should be no death sentence for him since he had not previously been hostile to him. 7 That is why I am commanding you to set apart three cities.

8 If Yahweh your God enlarges your territory, just as he swore to your ancestors, and gives you all the land that he promised your ancestors he would give[h]—9 if you are careful to do this whole commandment that I am commanding you today, to love Yahweh your God and walk in his ways always—then you shall add three more cities to these three. 10 Thus innocent blood will not be shed within the land that Yahweh your God is going to give you as a hereditary possession and bloodguilt fall upon you.

11 But if there is someone who is hostile to his neighbor and lies in wait for him and attacks him and strikes him dead, and then flees into one of these cities, 12 then the elders of his city must send to fetch him from there and hand him over[i] to the blood avenger, that he may die. 13 Do not look upon him with compassion. You shall sweep out the blood of the innocent person[j] from Israel, that it may go well with you.

Boundary Markers

14 Do not move your neighbor's boundary marker, located by those of an earlier time in your hereditary possession that you will inherit in the land that Yahweh your God is going to give you to take over.

A Vicious Witness

15 A single witness shall not stand up against a person concerning any crime or any sin in regard to any fault that he may have committed. Only on the testimony of two witnesses or the testimony of three witnesses shall a case stand.[k] 16 If a vicious witness[l] stands up to accuse someone of apostasy,[m] 17 then[n] the two parties in the dispute shall appear before Yahweh, before the priests and the judges then in office. 18 The judges shall investigate thoroughly. If the witness is a false witness and has falsely accused his kindred, 19 then you shall treat[o] him just as he had planned to treat his kindred. So you shall sweep out the evil from among you. 20 The rest shall hear and be afraid and never again do such a wicked

thing among you. 21 Do not look with compassion: life for life, eye for eye, tooth for tooth, hand for hand, foot for foot.

a. Follows MT. OG skips over the second "Yahweh" to avoid repetition.

b. Follows OG in not reading *Iršth*, "to take over." OG consistently translates this elsewhere (5:31; 15:4; 19:14; 21:1).

c. Alternate translations: "prepare the roads" (1 Kgs 6:19) or "calculate the distances." MT *tākîn* (root *kwn*) is translated by OG as "estimate," as though *takkēn* (*tkn* pi'el), "measure" in engineering operations. See P.-E. Dion, "Deuteronomy 19:3: Prepare the Way, or Estimate the Distance?" *Eglise et théologie* 25 (1994): 333–41. The context of dividing into three suggests the issue is an even distribution of the cities, and v. 6 points to a concern for fair distances. In contrast, better roads would benefit both pursuer and pursued.

d. "Here is an example" translates *wĕzeh dĕbar*, expressing a course of action or events (15:2; Siloam Inscription, line 1 [*ANET*, 321]). Alternate translation: "this is the procedure for."

e. Explicative *waw*, *IBHS* 39.2.1b.

f. Alternate translation seeking consistency in the meaning of *'ēṣ*: "glances off the tree." For the meaning of the verb *nāšal* as "separate from," cf. 28:40.

g. Literally "because his heart is hot." Alternate translation (cf. Ps 39:4 [ET 3]): "eagerly."

h. Alternate translation: "promised to give your ancestors."

i. Alternate translation: "and have him handed over."

j. Follows MT *dm-hnqy* (noun + noun). Sam., OG, Syr. harmonize with 19:10 and 21:8–9 by reading *hdm hnqy* (noun + adjective), "innocent blood."

k. The first occurrence of the verb *qwm* in this verse denotes "stand up" in the sense of "appear as a witness." The second means "endure as valid." Some translations extend the notion of validity or sufficiency to the first occurrence as well (NRSV: "a single witness shall not suffice"). For *dābār* as "case," cf. 17:9.

l. Literally "a witness of violence," suggesting a witness whose goal is violence against the defendant (cf. Exod 23:1; Ps 35:11; also Ps 27:12).

m. For *sārâ* as apostasy, cf. Deut 13:6 [ET 5]. E. Jenni, "Dtn 19, 16: *sara* 'Falschheit,'" in *Mélanges bibliques et orientaux en l'honneur de M. Henri Cazelles* (ed. A. Caquot and M. Delcor; AOAT 212; Kevelaer: Butzon & Bercker, 1981), 201–11.

n. Mention of the central sanctuary ("before Yahweh") suggests that the apodosis begins at this point. One might instead continue the protasis through v. 17 and begin the apodosis with v. 18 (cf. 13:13–16 [ET 12–15] and 17:2–5, where the apodosis starts with the investigation).

o. Follows MT and OG (= LXX^B). The passive reading of LXX^A (*BHS* note a) resulted from an inner-Greek corruption.

Deuteronomy now moves from the issues of centralization (12:1–16:17) and officeholders (16:18–18:22) to laws promoting justice in both the public and private spheres (chs. 19–25). Because the law concerning cities of refuge (19:1–13) is needed lest centralization increase the potential for injustice, it serves as an appropriate transition to the topics that follow. The response to the problem of an unsupported malicious witness (vv. 15–21) continues the concern for systemic fairness in law enforcement from both 16:18–17:13 and 19:1–13. The genres in this chapter are mixed: third-person casuistic law (vv. 4–5, 11–12, 16–19 moving to second person in the punishment), second-person casuistic (vv. 1–3, 7, and 8–10), apodictic prohibition ("you" in v. 14; third person in v. 15), and characteristic parenetic expansions (vv. 13, 19b–21).

[1–13] This law replaces the ancient custom of seeking asylum at local altars by the designation of nonsacral urban safety zones. It eliminates reliance on local sanctuaries and restricts the retributive power of the extended family. The basic reform law (vv. 1–3) is followed by a case illustrative of the distinction between murder and accident (vv. 4–7). The increased distances implicit in future expansion (cf. 12:20) are to be met by designating three more cities (vv. 8–10). Finally, the problem of illegitimate claims for asylum is explored by a contrasting representative case. The rationale and motivation for this reform is that any fatal miscarriage of justice would endanger the nation and subvert the gift of the land (vv. 10, 13).[1]

This section is related to its context in several ways. The issue of juridical procedure has already been raised by 16:18–20 and 17:8–13. The positive law of v. 2 is similar to arrangements for officeholders such as 16:18; 17:15. The presence of elders relates to other laws describing their function in local and family law (21:1–9, 18–21; 22:13–19; 25:5–10). In addition, the refuge law shares a common concern for the guilt of shedding innocent blood with the upcoming unsolved murder law of 21:1–9 (cf. 19:13 and 21:9). "When Yahweh your God cuts off" (v. 1) points forward to the situation of sacral war that introduces chapter 20.

A characteristic "you" address (vv. 1–3, 7, 13) directs this law at the reader. The introduction to vv. 4–6 signals an illustrative example in that v. 4 repeats "killer" and "flees there" from v. 3. Verse 6 comments on the issue raised by v. 3. Verse 7 is a resumptive repetition that closes this illustration and returns attention to the main topic of v. 2. The anticipated developments of vv. 8–10 are introduced as a condition, while the introductory phrase *wĕkî yihyeh* establishes vv. 11–12 as a countercase to vv. 4–6 (cf. 15:21). These two mirror-image cases share the same impersonal casuistic style and exhibit parallel structure and vocabulary ("strike down," "neighbor," "being hostile," "so he dies," "flee into one of these cities," "the blood avenger"). The sharp contrast between the two illustrations is highlighted by the last words of vv. 5 and 12: "live" versus "die."

Deuteronomy adapts Exod 21:12–14, which denied asylum to the intentional killer, in order to take centralization into account. Although asylum

---

1. On this law, see A. Rofé, "A History of the Cities of Refuge in Biblical Law," in *Studies in Bible*, ed. Japhet, 205–39.

seems narrowly restricted to the altar itself in 1 Kgs 1:50–53; 2:28–34, Exodus refers more broadly to a "place," that is, a holy place. In addition to an overall similarity of conception, Deuteronomy shares parallel language with its source: "strike down so he dies," "flee there," "neighbor," and "take from" (which in v. 12 I translated "fetch"). In Deuteronomy the encouragement for execution is moderated by a concern to prevent unjust results (v. 6) and the shedding of innocent blood (v. 10). The manslaughter case is no longer an "act of God" (Exod 21:13), but an accident explained "naturally" (v. 5).

Deuteronomy's striking silence about the central sanctuary as a site of asylum requires some explanation. Perhaps this is evidence that, in addition to Exod 21:12–14, Deuteronomy reused an earlier, precentralization law about refuge cities. Or perhaps asylum at the central shrine is simply assumed on the basis of the continuing validity of Exod 21:13–14 with its reference to "place" and "altar." The older law is thus revised but not replaced.

The summaries of vv. 7 (cf. 15:11) and 13 are clearly Deuteronomic. The law about territorial expansion and its motivation (vv. 8–10) is also Deuteronomic in both style and ideology, but may be a later addition to the original text. These verses are different in character from the surrounding legal interpretations of vv. 4–6 and 11–12 and go beyond the issue of distinguishing murder from manslaughter to introduce a broader temporal horizon (cf. 12:20). The addition of this supplement seems to have been triggered by "set apart three cities" in v. 7. The intrusive and awkward vv. 8b–9a appear to be an even later addition.[2]

Cities of refuge balance the interests of family honor and reprisal with communal interest in fairness. An entire city, and not just an altar, constitutes the safe place. These cities are important only because of their location; nothing is suggested about any special sacrality. They offer physical and social protection and provide a fair chance for the elders of the city of the accused to act (or not act) based on a determination of guilt (v. 12). No mechanism for making this determination is suggested, unless it rests with these city elders. If a pre-Deuteronomic refuge city law lies behind this text, it would be difficult determine a date for it. The pattern of three (or six) cities ignores tribal structuring in favor of the perspective of central authority, but the functioning of this law would seem to usurp royal prerogatives. The absence of any names for these cities is appropriate to Deuteronomy's dramatic situation before entry into the land, but makes the existence of a pre-Deuteronomic law more doubtful.

---

2. E. Otto, "Von der Programmschrift einer Rechtsreform zum Verfassungsentwurf des Neuen Israel: Die Stellung des Deuteronomiums in der Rechtsgeschichte Israels," in *Bundesdokument und Gesetz*, ed. Braulik, 93–104, understands most of vv. 2–6, 10–13 as a Deuteronomic revision of Exod 21:12–14; vv. 7–8, 9b as a postexilic Deuteronomist; and v. 9a as a second Deuteronomist influenced by the Decalogue (cf. 5:9–10).

Although presumably this text thinks of the three primary cities as being located west of the Jordan, a supplement in 4:41–43 reports on Moses designating cities east of the Jordan first.[3]

Verse 1 parallels 12:29. Mention of cities and houses introduces this law in an apt manner. The cities are "set apart" (*bdl* hip'il) just like the tribe of Levi (10:8). Verses 4a and 5b form a unifying bracket: "flee . . . and live." The actions of a blood avenger (v. 6) are illustrated by 2 Sam 14:6–7, 11. The root *g'l* (as well as the emotional involvement of "hot anger") undoubtedly indicates that this is a close relative who is authorized and obliged to perform this act of vindication. The concern for distance depends totally on the desacralization of local shrines caused by centralization (cf. 14:24–25). There are to be several cities in order to prevent excessive distance (v. 7, "that is why").

The enlargement envisioned by vv. 8–10 may be related to the notion of a gradual conquest of the land—as suggested by 7:22—or to imperialistic aspirations (cf. 1:7; 11:22–24). Both 11:22 and 19:9 also make future territorial expansion conditional on obedience. In 19:8–10, however, the concept of expansion is more a way of emphasizing and illustrating the principle of nearness than a definite prediction of future enlargement. The motivation for designating new cities is expressly to protect the people from collective culpability for the "innocent blood" of the killer (v. 10; cf. v. 13 and 21:8–9). For a narrative example of what this could entail, see 2 Sam 21:1–6.

The period of refuge for an "innocent" killer is left open in Deuteronomy (contrast to Num 35:25, 28; Josh 20:6), but a procedure is provided for the killer guilty of murder (vv. 11–13). Hometown elders take this responsibility, perhaps because of their role in family law (21:19–20; 22:15–18; 25:8–9) and their responsibility for localized bloodguilt (21:3–4). The murderer's fate corresponds literally to the crime itself (*wāmēt*, "so he dies," at the end of vv. 11a and 12). The formulaic motivation (v. 13) is that of 13:6, 9 [ET 5, 8]. Perhaps this implies that one may not substitute the payment of blood money for execution (cf. Num 35:31).

[14] This apodictic prohibition is loosely related to the preceding occurrence of "neighbor" in vv. 4, 11; *gĕbûl* ("boundary marker" or "territory") in vv. 3, 8; and *naḥălâ* ("hereditary possession") in v. 10. Another explanation of the abrupt appearance of v. 14 could be that chapter 19 follows the order of the Decalogue: kill (vv. 1–13), steal (v. 14), and then false witness (vv. 15–21); or that it is related to the curse list of chapter 27: 27:24 (murder), 27:17 (neighbor's landmark), 27:25 (bribe). Or perhaps v. 14 had been previously joined to v. 15 in a list of apodictic prohibitions and was drawn along with that verse when the topic of witnesses was attached to that of refuge cities. A clandestine

---

3. For intertextual relationships between Deut 4:41–43; 19:1–7; and the MT and LXX of Josh 20:1–9, see Nelson, *Joshua*, 226–31.

relocation of landmarks is only part of what this law prohibits, for long-standing property rights could be also be compromised through economic pressure against poor landowners (Prov 22:28; 23:10; Isa 5:8; Mic 2:2; 1 Kgs 21; Instruction of Amen-em-opet, chapter 6, *ANET*, 422). Ancestral lands are gifts from Yahweh and not to be lost to the family. Mention of the first settlers as "those of an earlier time" creates tension with the book's dramatic premise and suggests that v. 14a is a pre-Deuteronomic law. The motivational clause of v. 14b is worded in Deuteronomic language and relates back to v. 3.

[**15–21**] The subject of devious testimony is connected to that of refuge cities by the topic of dangers inherent in the justice system. A second connection is that witnesses would be needed to make the distinctions described in vv. 4–6 and 11–12. A scribal arrangement coordinates this law with previous ones on similar topics:

> 17:2–7—two witnesses
> 17:8–13—central court, not decided by witnesses
> 19:15—two witnesses
> 19:16–21—central court, not decided by witnesses

This law recognizes that cases based principally on personal testimony are open to abuse. The general principle of v. 15 expands the requirement for multiple witnesses beyond capital cases (17:6; Num 35:30) to all misdeeds. The option of "three" witnesses suggests that one of these might be the victim or the accuser.

The situation of a single malicious witness offers a case that goes beyond this general principle. Such a witness could not simply be ignored, however, because this sort of testimony raises the possibility of rancorous falsehood and perhaps a lying oath. All cases were initiated by private accusation, so a solitary witness would also be the accuser. In the text's presentation, this witness is assumed to be a liar, although the other participants in the case do not yet know this. Both complainant and defendant must come "before Yahweh" (at the central shrine) and before the centralized court described in 17:8–13. This is a "too difficult" case in terms of 17:8 in that there is no obvious way to determine if the witness is indeed lying.

The apodictic style of v. 15 and the impersonal casuistic style of vv. 16–18 suggest that an older law has been molded in a Deuteronomic direction in accordance with 17:6 and 17:8–9. Certainly the present form of v. 15a is overloaded. The use of *sārâ* to refer to apostasy (v. 16; cf. 13:6 [ET 5]) and the use of "kindred" (v. 18) is characteristic of Deuteronomy. The characteristic language of Deuteronomic motivation is unmistakable in 19:19–21: "sweep out" (v. 19b; 13:6 [ET 5]; 17:7, 12), "hear and be afraid" (v. 20a; 13:12 [ET 11]; 17:13; 21:21), and the demand to show no "compassion" (v. 21; cf. 7:16; 13:9 [ET 8]; 19:13).

Perhaps the pre-Deuteronomic law spoke only of priestly cultic inquiry "before Yahweh," but Deuteronomy's addition of judges converts this venue into the central court mentioned previously. It is now the judges who "investigate thoroughly," although the presence of priests makes it likely that both secular inquiry and ritual methods (ordeal, oath, divination) are intended (cf. the investigations of 13:15 [ET 14] and 17:4). The issue would be whether the testimony in question could be proved or disproved on other grounds. Oddly, the single judge of 17:9 appears in the plural here as "judges." The concluding formula of balanced retribution (cf. Exod 21:23–25) uses the principle of restoring equilibrium to discourage leniency.[4] "Life for life" is not an exact fit, but the death of the accused would be the likely outcome if malicious testimony were accepted as true.

When You Go to War
20:1–20

Preparing for Battle

20:1 When you go out to battle against your enemies and see horses and chariots,[a] an army larger than yours, do not be afraid of them; for Yahweh your God is with you, the one who brought you up from the land of Egypt. **2** As soon as you draw near them in battle, the priest shall approach and speak to the army. **3** He shall say to them, "Hear, O Israel! Today you are drawing near to battle against you enemies. Do not be fainthearted. Do not be afraid or alarmed[b] or frightened by them. **4** For Yahweh your God is going with you to fight for you against your enemies to give you victory."

5 Then the officers shall speak to the army saying, "Is there anyone[c] who has built a new house but not dedicated it?[d] Let him go back to his house, lest he die in the battle and someone else dedicate it. **6** Is there anyone who has planted a vineyard but not yet enjoyed its fruit?[e] Let him go back to his house, lest he die in the battle and someone else enjoy its fruit. **7** Is there anyone who has become engaged to a woman but not yet taken her in marriage? Let him go back to his house, lest he die in the battle and someone else take her in marriage." **8** The officers shall continue to speak to the army and say, "Is there anyone who is afraid or fainthearted? Let him go back to his house, so that the heart of his kindred does not melt[f]

---

4. For balanced retribution in Mesopotamian law, see *ANET*, 175–76, 184–85.

like his heart." 9 As soon as the officers have finished speaking to the army, the military commanders shall take command^g at the head of the army.

The Conduct of War

10 When you draw near to a city to fight against it, you shall proclaim to it an offer of peace.^{h} 11 If it accepts your offer of peace and opens to you, then all the people found in it shall become forced labor for you and serve you. 12 If it does not submit^i to you but makes war with you, then you shall besiege it; 13 and when Yahweh your God gives it into your power, you shall strike down all its males with the edge of the sword. 14 But the women, the children, the cattle, and everything else in the city, all its booty, you may plunder for yourself. You may consume the booty of your enemies, which Yahweh your God has given you.

15 That is how you shall treat all the cities that are very far from you, which are not among the cities of these nations right here. 16 But from the cities of these peoples that Yahweh your God is going to give you as a hereditary possession, do not let anything that breathes live. 17 You shall devote them to destruction completely—the Hittites and the Amorites, the Canaanites and the Perizzites, the Hivites and the Jebusites^j—just as Yahweh your God has commanded you, 18 so that they may not teach you to imitate all their repugnant acts that they perform for their gods, and you sin against Yahweh your God.

A Limit on Total War

19 If you besiege a city many days, fighting against it in order to seize it, you shall not destroy its trees by wielding an ax against them. You may eat from them, but do not cut them down. Is a tree of the field a human being, to come under siege by you?^{k} 20 You may destroy only the trees that you know do not yield food. These you may destroy and cut down and construct siegeworks against the city that makes war with you, until it falls.

a. This pair of singular nouns represents a conventional collective (Josh 11:4; 1 Kgs 20:1; 2 Kgs 6:15); see *IBHS* 7.2.1c.

b. The verb implies panicked flight.

c. *Mî* as an indefinite pronoun, *IBHS* 18.2e.

d. Alternate translation: "use for the first time" as implied by 28:30. Probably no actual dedication ceremony or "housewarming" (cf. NAB) is in view. The only dedication ceremonies known in the Old Testament are for public structures. See S. C. Reif, "Dedicated to *ḥnk*," *VT* 22 (1972): 495–501.

e. Literally "to make profane use of," i.e., to desacralize after a sacral period and use the fruit for the first time (Lev 19:23–25; Jer 31:5).

f. Follows MT with *yms* vocalized as nip'al "to melt" (intransitive; cf. NJPS "lest courage flag"). The object marker is used with nip'al to indicate "the participant in the verbal situation that is most directly affected" (*IBHS* 23.1b). Sam. eases the atypical grammar by using the hip'il *ymys*, "cause to melt" (cf. 1:28).

g. That is, "inspect, muster." Alternate translation construing "they" as an impersonal expression for the passive: "commanders shall be appointed." Or taking "officers" as the subject and the verb as transitive (Num 3:10): "they shall appoint officers at the head of the army."

h. Taking *lĕšalôm* as the content of the proclamation (cf. Judg 21:13; Jer 28:9; Mic 3:5). Alternate translation: "peacefully demand a surrender of the city." This construes *lesalôm* as an adverbial modifier of the main verb, "proclaim in a peaceable way" (Gen 37:4; 1 Kgs 20:18; *IBHS* 11.2.10d and p. 206 n. 66.) In either case, context makes clear that this is a diplomatic call for submission. E. Otto, "Die keilschriftlichen Parallelen der Vindikationsformel in Dtn 20,10," *ZAW* 102 (1990): 94–96, sees this as a juridical vindication formula with Akkadian parallels.

i. "To make peace" (*šlm* hip'il) in this context has nothing to do with resolving differences in a nonviolent manner. It means "to submit" in the face of a threat of violence (cf. Josh 10:1, 4; 11:19–20).

j. Follows MT with a list of six nations. There are usually seven, so Sam. and OG add "Girgashites," but in different places.

k. Modern translations regard the initial *h* of *haʾādām* as an interrogative. The ancient versions were of the same opinion, presenting the question in a negative format: "a tree is not a human, is it?" Verse 19bβ means "to retreat into a state of siege on your account" (2 Kgs 24:10). The point is either that trees cannot go into the besieged city to protect themselves or that they are not the real human enemies who need to withdraw in such a way. A clearer translation would be, "Do not cut them down (with the thought that) the trees are humans themselves, so that they must be besieged by you." If one takes the *h* of *hāʾādām* as a definite article, however, then the idea may be that the life-giving products of the trees are the equivalent of the enemy humans they would otherwise be sustaining: "for the tree of the field is [worth] a human life."

Themes and Structures

War is an important topic in Deuteronomy. These laws echo the ideology of war found in the sermons of 7:1–2, 17–26; 9:1–3; 31:3–8. In the final form of the book, they also play out against the background of the conquest stories of chapters 1–3 and the mythic portrayal of the Divine Warrior in chapter 32.[1] Deuteronomy describes war as it thinks it ought to be waged, depicting the

---

1. On the Deuteronomic war laws in general, see A. Rofé, "The Laws of Warfare in the Book of Deuteronomy: Their Origins, Intent and Positivity," *JSOT* 32 (1985): 23–44. On this chapter, see E. Noort, "Das Kapitulationsangebot im Kriegsgesetz Dtn 20:10ff. und in den Kriegserzählungen," in *Studies in Deuteronomy*, ed. García Martínez et al., 197–222.

proper role of the "citizen soldier" in a restored and reformed practice of sacral war. This concern for war is not just about the distant past, for these laws go beyond the conquest tradition to comment on the policies and difficulties of the late monarchy. They reflect the technology of siege warfare, the political horizon of forced labor, and the problems of a nonprofessional army facing a technologically superior foe. The citizen soldiers who attack distant cities are not landless invaders, but a settled population with houses and vineyards.

Topically, the chapter falls naturally into three divisions: vv. 1–9, preparations; vv. 10–18, treatment of the enemy; vv. 19–20, restrictions on cutting trees. The overall order is more thematic than chronological, since the siege (vv. 19–20) comes *after* the defeat of enemy cities. Likewise, the priestly speech urging confidence (vv. 2–4) sounds odd coming *before* the discharge of elements of the army (vv. 5–8).

The three divisions are segmented by a casuistic "when/if . . . you" format (vv. 1–9, 10–14 [15–18], 19–20). These introductory clauses are comparable to ones that begin other sacral war laws (21:10–14; 23:10–15 [ET 9–14]), suggesting a larger unity or an inherited topical collection. Each of these war laws first describes the stage of military operation under consideration (20:1, 10, 19; 21:10; 23:10 [ET 9]), then gives instructions for that specific state of affairs. A larger structure consists of two successive units of four laws each (20:1–21:9 and 21:10–23), both headed by "when you go out to battle against your enemies" and concluding with a law about a body.[2]

Internal unity is promoted by verbal links:

> "to battle against your enemies," vv. 1, 3
> "draw near," vv. 2, 3, 10
> "speak to the army," vv. 2, 5
> "peace," vv. 10, 11, 12
> "makes war with you," vv. 12, 20
> "Yahweh your God has given/is going to give," vv. 14, 16
> "the cities of these nations/peoples," vv. 15, 16

Compositional History

A topical connection between vv. 10–14 and 19–20 suggests that vv. 15–18 are a secondary insertion between them. Verses 19–20 urge leaving intact the very

---

2. R. Westerbrook: "Riddles in Deuteronomic Law," in *Bundesdokument und Gesetz*, ed. Braulik, 171–72, suggests that the "pierced" (*ḥālāl*, 21:1) body discovered in an open field is connected to the warfare theme as a consequence of the banditry connected to the disorder of war (cf. Judg 9:25). Much less likely is a suggestion that the law of the captured wife (Deut 21:10–14) is topically associated with the following two laws (21:15–21) in that such family problems would be characteristic of such a mixed marriage. See Y. Suzuki, "A New Aspect of *ḥrm* in Deuteronomy in View of an Assimilation Policy of King Josiah," *AJBI* 21 (1995): 20–21.

infrastructure that is the goal of the campaign of vv. 10–14. The topic of eating plunder also connects v. 14 with vv. 19b–20a. There is even a unifying concentric structure:

> v. 12a—makes war with you
> v. 12b—you shall besiege it
> v. 19a—you besiege a city
> v. 20b—makes war with you[3]

For these reasons, it is widely accepted that vv. 15–18 represent a later and harsher rethinking of the earlier and more moderate stance of vv. 10–14. In vv. 15–18 the perspective of the conquest of the land takes the place of the theme of general rules for war. Apprehension over the temptations of foreign worship replaces the issues of a political covenant and the economic value of a conquered population. In place of an offer permitting the enemy at least to live, or allowing the survival of noncombatants, the total extermination of *ḥērem* comes into play. The concerns of vv. 15–18 are similar to the xenophobic and uncompromising viewpoint found in chapter 7 and 13:13–19 [ET 12–18]. "Repugnant" apostasy (cf. *tôʿēbâ* in 7:25–26; 13:15 [ET 14]) must be exterminated through the application of *ḥērem* (7:2, 26; 13:16, 18 [ET 15, 17]). It may be significant that the order of the six-nation list of 20:17 is the same as that of the seven-item list in 7:1. The change to second person plural in v. 18 rhetorically emphasizes the danger of contaminating imitation, something also stressed in 12:29–31. The assumptions behind Josh 9:1–27 and 11:19–20 suggest that Deut 20:15–18 was already present in the form of Deuteronomy known to DH.

Other irregularities provide further evidence for the existence of varied perspectives and literary growth. There is some tension between the straightforward confidence of v. 1 and the potential for death in battle that lies behind vv. 5–7. The speeches of vv. 2–4 and 5–7 form a sort of doublet and come in an odd order. Verses 2–4 are in second person plural, and the priest who speaks these words appears and disappears abruptly. Verse 8 adds a new and typically Deuteronomic concern to vv. 5–7, suggesting that those three verses preserve older, pre-Deuteronomic formulas.

---

3. Braulik, *Die deuteronomischen Gesetze und der Dekalog*, 67. Nielsen, *Deuteronomium*, 200, points out another scribal pattern that is aba´b´ in form, but abb´a´ in regard to the topic of annihilating and sparing:

> (v. 13) you shall strike down . . . you may consume (eat)
> (v. 14) but (*raq*) the women . . . you can plunder
> (v. 19a) you shall not destroy . . . you may eat
> (v. 20a) only (*raq*) the trees . . . you may destroy.

Theologies of Warfare

Deuteronomy 20:1–14 deals with war in a realistic and practical light, in contrast to the more ideological outlook of vv. 15–18. War is described as an offensive operation involving aggressive attacks on enemy cities. From a historical standpoint, this perspective does not correspond very well with the defensive efforts of Hezekiah or the participation of Manasseh as a vassal in Assyrian military campaigns. It would fit better with the expansionistic policies (or dreams) associated with the revival of nationalism under Josiah.

Israel's wars are to be consonant with its nature as a people liberated by the exodus. They are to be carried out in a manner that appreciates the value of material blessings gained with the aid of Yahweh the Divine Warrior. The standard themes of sacral war are present. In the face of the classic alternative between the might of Yahweh or that of chariots (Isa 31:1–3), faith that Yahweh is "with you" makes courage possible (vv. 1, 4). The exodus is the basis for faithful confidence (v. 1), which is traditionally the requirement for victory in sacral war (vv. 3, 8). Courage is the norm for Israel; panic properly belongs to the enemy (v. 8). A reduced army is no problem (vv. 5–8; cf. Gideon). No doubt, this rhetoric of sacral war was intended in part to counter the terror of Assyrian propaganda and policies (2 Kgs 18:19–36; 19:10–13).

The propriety of wars fought to subjugate others and enjoy what can be plundered from them is simply accepted as a given fact of public life. The fruits of such victories, including the slave labor of conquered peoples, are understood to be gifts of Yahweh (v. 14). For this very reason, the dangers of war are not to undermine one's enjoyment of life's sweetest blessings (vv. 6–7). Respect for noncombatants (vv. 11, 14) and the necessities of life (vv. 19–20) prohibit the atrocities all too common in the prosecution of warfare (2 Kgs 8:12; 15:16; Hos 10:14; 14:1 [ET 13:16]; Amos 1:13; Isa 13:16; Nah 3:10; Ps 137:8–9). If the spoils of war can be enjoyed without bloodshed, peaceful submission is preferable (vv. 10–11); if not, the onus for choosing violence lies squarely upon the enemy (cf. "makes war with you," v. 12).

It is noteworthy that these are not wars of the king, but wars of the citizenry ("you go out," "you draw near") under the guidance of team leadership (vv. 5, 8). Šōtĕrîm ("officers," vv. 5, 8) are officeholders with clerical duties (cf. 1:15). The "military commanders" ("śārîm of the host," v. 9) were a feature of royal military organization (1 Kgs 2:5), but here the plural seems to indicate a more democratized council of war. Israel's wars are wars of Yahweh (vv. 4, 15), not of the king. They are wars that engender widespread faith and popular support rather than fear, and material gain for the citizenry ("you," v. 14) rather than personal loss (vv. 5–7).

In contrast, vv. 15–18 use the theology of sacral war for a very different theological purpose. The moderate rules of vv. 10–14 are relegated to behavior for campaigns "far from you," and the focus shifts to "homeland security," to the "nations right here" (v. 15). Although the classic period of the conquest is evoked, the list of v. 17 catalogs nations that no longer exist. This is not really about past conquest, but about present internal threats to Israel's self-identity and authentic religion. As in chapter 7, the peoples once conquered in Israel's tradition are resurrected to represent contemporary alien cult practices and non-Yahwistic temptations "right here" (v. 15). Because dangerous apostasy is understood to be an imitation of foreign models, Israel must be put into a state of theological quarantine. As a result, the long obsolete concept of *ḥērem* in warfare is revived to undermine other cult traditions and to exterminate dangers to Yahwism close at hand. This threat (if not the actual practice) of annihilation is used in the service of national religious purity and unification. Moreover, the terror of *ḥērem* could counteract the terror engendered by Assyrian psychological warfare.

The modern reader may properly object that this chapter authenticates violence used to subjugate other peoples and to steal their wealth. The supposedly humane treatment of enemy populations (vv. 10–14) is only humane if one accepts the legitimacy of aggressive war in the first place. The supposedly sensitive treatment of fruit trees has its real motive in what the victor may consume from them (v. 19). Even the discharges from military service that are offered (vv. 5–7) participate in the same acquisitive philosophy, the fear that another may get to enjoy one's house, fruit, or woman and that the aggrandizing intention of war would thus be undermined.[4]

[1–4] Verses 1–9 are framed by the topic of fear (vv. 1, 3, 8). Using language typical of sacral war, first Moses and then a priest, who appears unexpectedly, urge courage and faith. Priests played a role in the traditional practice of war by delivering oracles (Judg 18:5–6; 20:26–28; 1 Sam 23:9–12; 30:7–8; 2 Sam 5:23–24), but here the priest speaks a didactic sermon along the lines of Deut 7:17–21; 9:1–3 (cf. 1:20–21, 29–31; 31:3–8). Yet the language of sacral war oracle may still be traced in the assurance of Yahweh's activity and the admonition not to fear (Judg 18:6; 20:28; Isa 7:4; cf. the Stele of Zakir, lines 13–15, *ANET*, 655). The language about the exodus in v. 1 ("brought you up," *ʿālâ* hip'il, rather than "brought you out," using *yṣ'* hip'il) is not the usual Deuteronomic formula. The direction "up" points to the land Yahweh has given.[5]

---

4. See H. C. Washington, "'Lest He Die in the Battle and Another Man Take Her': Violence and the Construction of Gender in the Laws of Deuteronomy 20–22," in *Gender and Law in the Hebrew Bible and the Ancient Near East* (ed. V. Matthews, et al; JSOTSup 262; Sheffield: Sheffield Academic Press, 1998), 195–202. He points to the female image of the city who "opens" to her besieger and is violently "seized" (vv. 11, 19; cf. the usage of *tāpaś* in 22:28).

5. Scholars have connected this formula with the northern kingdom, with an old creedal formula, and with the sacral war tradition. See H. F. Fuhs, "*ʿālâ*," *TDOT* 11:85–89.

[5–8] The four exemptions from service are formatted in a special casuistic shape using "who" questions. The parallel language of vv. 5a and 9a brackets them. The practice of granting deferments from battle was common in the ancient world, as evidenced by the Gilgamesh Epic and the Legend of Keret.[6] Originally, such exemptions were based on the notion that persons in certain liminal or threshold states would present a special danger if they took part in a sacral enterprise. Each of the first three cases requires two things: entry into a brand-new liminal situation and the noncompletion of the dynamics of that situation. A new act of construction or planting or betrothal has not yet been transformed into the corresponding normal situation by a transitional event (dedication, profanation [note e], marriage). Although scholars have sometimes spoken of a humane ethic at this point, or the protection of family life, it is really an understanding of the genre of "futility curse" that opens the door for proper interpretation. Futility curses are found in ancient treaties and in 28:30–34. Deuteronomy 28:30 closely parallels 20:5–7 in language and outlook. Like the operation of a futility curse, "premature" death in battle would break the natural relationship between an initial act and its expected consequence, the anticipated next step in continuity with the first step. This sort of "futility" undermines the natural and expected order of the cosmos. The prosecution of war must not be permitted to endanger the proper sequence of events or to undercut someone's rights to enjoy the completion of what has been started. These regulations are intended to prevent Israel from coming under the influence of the curse of futility and to permit enjoyment of the good things given by Yahweh.[7] The discharge questions are powered by a rhetoric of opposition. The subject matter is formulaic and general (cf. Jer 29:5–6) and has as its theme the enjoyment of the basic good things of a full life. Discharge because of betrothal is topically related to the law of Deut 24:5.

Verse 8 is of a different character than vv. 5–7 and returns to the topic of v. 1. Here the issue is not the private rights of an individual, but the psychological effect of panic on one's "kindred." Such an exemption, which may have roots in the traditional practice of sacral war (cf. Judg 7:2–7), flies in the face of all state compulsion in the management of warfare.

[10–14] These verses, taken by themselves without vv. 15–18, could be understood to refer to all wars, local ones as well as campaigns outside the land of promise. In fact, forced labor was imposed on local Canaanite peoples (Judg

---

6. *ANET*, 48, lines 50–53; 143–44, lines 96–103, 184–91.

7. W. M. de Bruin, "Die Freistellung vom Militärdienst in Deut. xx 5–7: Die Gattung der Wirkungslosigkeitssprüche als Schlüssel zum Verstehen eines alten Brauches," *VT* 49 (1999): 21–33. For another view on the theology of v. 5, see Y. Guillemette, "'Pour vivre heureux dans le pays': À propos de deux lois du Deutéronome, in *"Où demeures-tu?" (Jn 1,38)* (ed. J.-C. Petit et al.; Paris: Fides, 1994), 123–37.

1:28, 33, 35; 1 Kgs 9:20–21) and seems incompatible with the geographical situation of a "far off" city. Moreover, the elimination of bellicose males sounds like a tactic for avoiding future problems at the local level.

Verse 10 is not so much a diplomatic proposal of "peace" as a nonnegotiable demand for submission. There are only two possible alternative consequences: capitulation or siege.[8] The offer of peace in 2:26, 30 is something quite different. Verse 11 lays out the consequence of surrender as subjection to levies of forced labor gangs for public projects. This does not refer to the enslavement of individuals, but rather to an imposition of tributary responsibilities on the entire subjugated community. Refusal of these terms leads to an aggressive four-step process: "besiege," "strike down," "plunder," "consume" (vv. 12b–14). In this case, the personal capture of individuals as slaves is in view, the situation reflected in the law of 21:10–14.

[15–18] Verse 15 forms a bridge between the practical guidelines of vv. 10–14 and the supplementary ideology of total extermination in vv. 16–18. It converts the wars of vv. 10–14 into distant campaigns and turns readers' attention to local affairs. A geographic distinction between "far" and "near" is introduced to separate imperialistic wars from the struggle against the domestic danger of contemporary apostasy, presented under the guise of the conquest. The generic "enemies" of v. 14 are narrowed into the "nations" and "peoples" that make up the stock catalog of v. 17.

"Anything that breathes" in v. 16 was understood by DH to refer to the human population only, sparing the cattle as booty (2:34–35; 3:4–7; Josh 10:40; 11:11, 14; cf. Gen 7:22; 1 Kgs 15:29). This interpretation is probably correct because the list of nations in v. 17 stands in apposition to the pronoun "them" and thus describes those nations as the object of *ḥērem*. This list functions as a typical "*ḥērem* inventory," detailing what is to be destroyed (cf. 2:34; 3:6; Josh 6:21; Judg 21:10; 1 Sam 15:3). The citation formula in v. 17 is most naturally understood as a reference to Moses' directive in 7:1–2, although another possibility might be Exod 23:23, 32–33 (34:11–12, 15).[9]

This policy of annihilation is driven by reasons of religious purity, not military logic (v. 18; cf. ch. 7; 8:19–20; 11:16–17; 13:13–19 [ET 12–18]). At one level, the tradition of a conquest *ḥērem* functioned to explain the supposed "disappearance" of the land's previous inhabitants. However, the assumption here is that the baneful influence of these nations survived to infect Israel's later generations. Therefore, this law is not really about the distant past of conquest, but about present menaces such as the situation described in 13:13–19 [ET 12–18]. These alien "nations" of the past stand for contemporary Israelite apostasy and

8. For general background see D. J. Wiseman, " 'Is It Peace?' Covenant and Diplomacy," *VT* 32 (1982): 311–26.

9. Skweres, *Ruckverweise*, 43–47.

for those whose present disloyal behavior must be eliminated. Their "repugnant acts" (*tôʿēbōt*; cf. 12:31; 18:9–14) pose a clear and immediate threat to national well-being that requires drastic action.

[19–20] This law seeks to limit the practice of total war, as described, for example, in 2 Kgs 3:19, 25. Until the reader reaches v. 20, the law seems to refer to trees in general, suggesting that an earlier comprehensive ban on cutting trees has been restricted to one limited to food trees. Thus v. 20 sounds like a redefinition of v. 19, but even in this verse, the cutting permitted is limited to the purpose of building a counterwall. Fruit trees cannot be cut down as an act of vandalism or psychological warfare. "Many days" would add to the psychological pressure on the besiegers to take drastic action, and the need for wood would increase as the campaign dragged on.

The reader is offered a double motivation to obey: the importance of food to the besieging army and what sounds like sympathy for the trees themselves. The first motivation is similar to v. 14 ("you may eat"), and indeed, v. 19 sounds like a limitation or control on the general permission to plunder given by v. 14. The second, anthropomorphizing, "environmental" argument is based on the impropriety of breaking the natural connection between the act (planting a tree) and its consequence (fruit), between intention and result. This way of thinking is similar to the desire to avoid "futility" in vv. 5–7, particularly in regard to fruit (v. 6), and to the concern for the future productivity of the mother bird found in 22:6–7.

In the Land Yahweh Is Going to Give You
21:1–23

A Body in an Open Field

21:1 If a slain body is found on the land that Yahweh your God is going to give you to take over, fallen in the open country, and it is not known who struck him down, 2 then your elders and your judges[a] shall come out and measure the distances to the cities that surround the slain body 3 and determine the city nearest the slain body. The elders of that city shall take a young cow[b] that has never been put to work, one that has never pulled in a yoke. 4 The elders of that city shall bring the young cow down to a wadi constantly running with water,[c] which is not tilled or sown, and break the young cow's neck there in the wadi. 5 Then the priests, the sons of Levi, shall approach, because Yahweh your God has chosen them to minister to him and to bless in the name of Yahweh, and every dispute and assault is to be settled by their decision. 6 All the elders of that city nearest the slain body shall wash their hands over[d] the young cow whose neck was broken in the wadi, 7 and solemnly declare: "Our hands did not shed[e] this blood, and our eyes have seen nothing. 8 Absolve your people Israel, whom you redeemed O Yahweh. Do not bring the guilt of innocent blood among your people Israel." Then the bloodguilt will be absolved for them.[f] 9 So you yourself shall sweep out the guilt of innocent blood from among you, because you must do what is right in the opinion of Yahweh.[g]

A Captive Wife

10 When you go out to battle against your enemies and Yahweh your God gives them into your power and you take captives, 11 and you see among the captives a beautiful woman and you desire her and would take[h] her in marriage, 12 and you bring her into your house,[i] then she shall shave her head, pare her nails, 13 and lay aside her captive's clothing and live in your house. She shall weep for her father and mother for a full month. After that you may go into her and act as a husband with her, and she shall be your wife. 14 Then if you no longer find her pleasing, you shall let her go freely, but you surely shall not sell her for money. Do not treat her as a commodity, since you have had sex with her.[j]

The True Firstborn Son

15 If a man has two wives, one of them loved and the other unloved,[k] and if both the loved and the unloved have borne him sons, but the firstborn son is of the unloved one, 16 then on the day when he bequeaths his property to his sons, he dare not proclaim as firstborn[l] the son of the loved one in place of the son of the unloved one, who is the true firstborn. 17 Instead, he must acknowledge the true firstborn, the son of the unloved one, giving him a double share[m] of all that he has; since he is the first product of his procreative power, the right of the firstborn is his.

A Rebellious Son

18 If someone has a stubborn and rebellious son who does not obey his father and mother, and even when they discipline him, does not listen to them, 19 then his father and his mother shall take hold of him and bring him out to the elders of his city, to the gate of his hometown. 20 They shall say to the elders of his city, "Our son here is stubborn and rebellious. He does not obey us. He is a glutton and a drunkard." 21 Then all[n] the men of his city shall stone him to death. So you shall sweep out the evil from among you and all Israel will hear and be afraid.

A Hanging Corpse

22 When someone is guilty of a capital crime and is put to death, and you hang him from a tree,[o] 23 his corpse shall not remain on the tree. Instead, you shall surely bury him that same day, for the one who is hung[p] is accursed by God.[q] Do not defile the land that Yahweh your God is going to give you as a hereditary possession.

a. Follows MT. Sam. *wštryk*, "officers," is an error of transcription, perhaps nurtured by 16:18.

b. The traditional translation "heifer" is misleading; an *'eglâ* could be as much as three years old and give milk (Gen 15:9; Isa 7:21–22).

c. Some contexts for *'êtān* suggest "enduring, unchanging, " others "strongly flowing." A ravine that never runs dry but is not cultivated would seem to be too rare a phenomenon for widespread use, but the procedure clearly demands readily available water.

d. OG (and 11QTemple) adds "over the head of" as though this were a transfer of guilt to a sacrificial victim. See P.-E. Dion, "The Greek Version of Deut. 21:1–9 and Its Variants: A Record of Early Exegesis," in *De Septuaginta: Studies in Honor of John William Wevers* (ed. A. Pietersma and C. Cox; Mississauga, Ont.: Benben, 1984), 151–60.

e. Qere (and Sam., OG, Tg., 4QDeut[f]) corrects to a plural verb to agree with "our hands." Kethib (and Syr.) is singular.

f. Alternate translation continuing the quotation: "and let the bloodguilt be absolved for them."

g. The relation of v. 9b to 9a is obscure. Is doing the right thing the *means* for sweeping out evil (REB, NJPS)? Or is it the *goal* of the sweeping out (NRSV, NJB)?

h. A modal translation is required by the reference to ensuing marriage in v. 13. This verb must be construed either as a statement of intention (as here) or permissive: "you may take." Sam., OG, Syr. fill out the expected suffix lacking in MT to read explicitly: "take *her*."

i. This translation begins the apodosis with the change in grammatical subject. Alternate translations: starting the apodosis earlier, "then you shall bring her . . . and she shall shave"; or as a statement of permission, "then you may bring her."

j. The verb translated "treat as a commodity" denotes "exercise one's power of commercial disposal" (cf. 24:7; *HALOT* 2:849). Its relation to the root "grain" shows its origin in the language of commerce and connects it to grain trading (A. Alt, "Zur *Hit'ammer*," *VT* 2 [1952]: 153–59). The OG translation "break faith with her" ("oppress" in 24:7) was based on context. "Treat as a slave" (NRSV) goes back to Josephus (*Ant.* 4. 259) and Philo (*Virt.* 115). "Let her go" (*šlḥ* pi'el) may hint at manumission or divorce (15:12–13; 22:19, 29), but *lĕnapšāh*, "freely," suggests she is an unbound, free woman (Jer 34:16). The verb *'nh* pi'el, "had sex with," usually indicates humiliation through forced or adulterous sex, but here and in 22:24 it is neutral (cf. Exod 21:10, where the root denotes a wife's sexual rights).

k. Thus "loved" and "hated" in the sense of Gen 29:30–31: "preferred" and "disliked."

l. Taking the verb *bkr* pi'el as delocative. Alternate translation: "treat as firstborn."

m. 2 Kgs 2:9; MAL B 1, *ANET*, 185. The meaning "two-thirds" in Zech 13:8 developed out of the basic idea of "two parts."

n. Follows MT and Sam. The absence of *kl*, "all," from OG and Vulg. resulted from the harmonistic reading of "men" instead of "elders" in v. 20 (Sam. and OG). Once the group of v. 21 was considered to be the same as that in v. 20, the word "all" lost its function and was dropped or not translated.

o. Or "on a pole." Alternate translation reflecting Assyrian practice: "impale him on a stake." However, this law refers to exposure *after* execution (Gen 40:19), not hanging or impalement as a method of execution.

p. Follows MT. The longer reading of OG is a clarification that harmonizes with v. 22: *tlwy 'l-'ṣ*, "who is hung *on a tree*" (cf. Gal 3:13).

q. This translation understands God as the subject who curses (subjective genitive). Alternate translation construing as an objective genitive: "is an affront to God." Or perhaps *'ělōhîm* is being used as a superlative adjective: "a most appalling curse" (D. Winton Thomas, "A Consideration of Some Unusual Ways of Expressing the Superlative in Hebrew," *VT* 3 [1953]: 209–24). This might even refer to the *'ělōhîm* of the dead person and imply potential problems with a ghost.

The disparate laws in this chapter are enclosed by the phrase "the land that Yahweh your God is going to give you" (vv. 1 and 21). The logic of organization seems to be more associative than systematic. The first two laws point back to the war laws of chapter 20. This is obvious in the case of 21:10–14, both in content and in the way it begins (cf. 20:1 with 21:10). However, 21:1–9 also seems to relate to the unsettled social conditions prevalent in wartime. The law about the captive bride then leads on to two elements of family law involving inheritance and the punishment of sons (vv. 15–17, 18–21). Then vv. 22–23 attach to vv. 18–21 through the topic of execution. Each of the last three laws begins with variations on the phrase *kî yihyeh lě'îš* [*bě'îš*], literally "if there is to a man" or "in a man" (vv. 15, 18, 22). If one sees a connection involving sacral war between chapters 20 and 21, it is possible to speak of two sets of four laws—20:1–21:9 and 21:10–23—each beginning with the same formulaic introduction and each ending with a dead body. Finally, 21:1–9 connects to 20:19–20 by the catchword *śādeh*, "countryside/field," while 21:22–23 links back to the same law through the word "tree."[1]

---

1. Those who conjecture a structure corresponding to the Ten Commandments connect chs. 19–21 to "do not kill." The proposal of C. M. Carmichael, "A Common Element in Five Supposedly Disparate Laws," *VT* 29 (1979): 129–42, that the chapter follows the theme of setting life apart from death seems unhelpfully broad. His proposal (*Laws of Deuteronomy* [Ithaca: Cornell University Press, 1974], 68–254; and "Uncovering a Major Source of Mosaic Law: The Evidence of Deut 21:15–22:5," *JBL* 101 [1982]: 505–20) that the order of these laws relates to the narratives of the Pentateuch and that vv. 15–17 specifically connect to Leah and Rachel and to Gen 49:3 has met with a general lack of agreement.

[1–9] Behind this law is the concept of objective communal responsibility for criminal homicide, "the guilt of innocent blood" (cf. 19:10).[2] Such violence was thought to bring uncleanness on the land (Num 35:33–34), requiring some sort of ritual to block or undo such a catastrophic outcome.[3]

Once responsibility has been determined, the elders of the indicated city engage in a nonsacrificial ritual of atonement. Breaking the cow's neck signals (twice, vv. 4 and 6) that this ritual is not intended to be a sacrifice (cf. Exod 13:13; 34:20; Isa 66:3). Priests appear, supposedly because of their vocation to minister, bless, and judge (v. 5), but they do not actually perform any of those tasks. Perhaps priests are needed to hear or administer the oath of innocence spoken by the elders. These priests might also solemnly declare the effectiveness of the atonement at the close of the ceremony. The judges represent the interests of central authority to prevent friction between cities. Thus it is they who supervise the measurement to make sure that the right city is identified. Judges from the central court would guarantee impartiality.[4] The elders are primarily responsible for the removal of guilt involving their city. Hence they are the main actors, who break the cow's neck, wash their hands, make the declaration of innocence, and pray.

Deuteronomic style in vv. 1 and 9 frames the whole procedure. Some scholars consider the priests in v. 5 to be a late addition (connecting to 17:9 and using the wording of 31:9). The climactic prayer in v. 8 is in Deuteronomic style and exhibits a wider horizon of interest, speaking of the whole people and not merely the affected city. Evidence of an earlier, pre-Deuteronomic, third-person casuistic law appears in vv. 1aα, 1b, 3–4, 6–8. The protasis of v. 1 is followed by a long row of verbs that make up the apodosis. Then there is a new start in v. 6 (wĕkol + subject + verb) that introduces the succession of clauses in vv. 6–8. In the present form of the text, the prayer (v. 8) is the real, climactic center of interest. Deuteronomy has turned an older atonement ritual into an occasion for a prayer that itself becomes the actual medium for atonement. The vestigial ritual details are simply left unexplained, possibly even purged of their original significance. The text in its present form emphasizes prayer as the key to atonement and that, in the last analysis, it is actually Yahweh as the God of the exodus who performs the atonement.

---

2. For legislation about regional public liability for lost property or life, see LH 23, 24 (*ANET*, 167). A Hittite law involving death discovered in open land between villages requires measuring to a nearby village, which must bear financial responsibility (*ANET*, 189, law 6). See also A. Jirku, "Drei Fälle von Haftpflicht im altorientalischen Palästina-Syrien und Deuteronomium cap 21," *ZAW* 79 (1967): 359–60.

3. T. Frymer-Kensky, "Pollution, Purification, and Purgation in Biblical Israel," in *The Word of the Lord Shall Go Forth* (ed. C. Meyers and M. O'Connor; Winona Lake, Ind.: Eisenbrauns, 1983), 399–414.

4. Perhaps judges were added later to vv. 2 and 5 in order to forge a link with the laws of 16:18–17:13.

The "slain" one (v. 1) has not died naturally but is literally "pierced, wounded." Murder in the open country, away from witnesses, would likely remain unsolved. Verse 2 introduces "your elders," either some centralized official group or the elders of the nearby towns (16:18). That these are indicated as "your" elders and "your" judges signals that this localized problem is actually a concern for the whole nation. Although the "nearest" city (v. 3) might have been thought of as the most likely residence of the perpetrator, the real issue is an objective, impersonal bloodguilt that would most endanger the closest town and for which that town would be considered the most responsible. What is untouched and pristine is advantageous in ritual (cf. the unworked cows and new cart of 1 Sam 6:7; cf. 2 Sam 6:3; the red heifer, Num 19:2; firstlings, Deut 15:19), and this special quality is required of both the cow and the wadi. The absence of cultivation also indicates that this potentially dangerous ritual operation can take place at a safe distance from human residence.

Hand washing (v. 6) is a public act that declares and illustrates innocence (cf. Isa 1:15–16; Pss 26:6; 73:13). It is interpreted as such by the words of the oath that accompany it (v. 7). The prayer that follows (v. 8a) also suggests that this hand washing is meant to be an act of atonement. Although it could be understood as merely symbolic, here hand washing seems to be intended as a ritual of transfer that "concentrates" the "free-floating" bloodguilt onto the cow. Through the means of flowing water, the elders transfer onto the animal's carcass whatever measure of guilt that geographical nearness has brought their city. This "constantly running" water may also be understood as transporting the guilt away (cf. 9:21). Perhaps the animal is slaughtered in order to keep such transferred guilt from returning, as in the elimination rite involving a bird in Lev 14:1–7 or the scapegoat. In that case, however, it might seem more logical to kill the cow *after* the transfer of guilt rather than before. Perhaps this slaughter is intended as a dramatic reenactment of the murder, for according to the elders it is specifically "this blood" of which they are innocent (v. 7). Other suggestions are that the killing of the cow is a vicarious or symbolic execution of the unknown murderer or a dramatic act representing what would happen to these oath-taking elders if they are lying.[5]

With the washing of hands comes a solemn declaration of innocence (v. 7; cf. the fixed word pair also found in 25:9; 26:5; 27:14, 15: "answer and say," translated "solemnly declare"). If they had seen anything, they would be taking suitable retributive action. "This blood" refers to the violence done to the

---

5. For a survey and evaluation of explanations, consult D. P. Wright, "Deuteronomy 21:1–9 as a Rite of Elimination," *CBQ* 49 (1987): 387–403, who argues that this is a rite of guilt transfer and elimination. Z. Zevit, "The *'eglâ* Ritual of Deuteronomy 21:1–9," *JBL* 95 (1976): 377–90, traces three developing stages in the understanding of the ritual. P.-E. Dion, "Deutéronome 21,1–9: Miroir du développement légal et religieux d'Israël," *Studies in Religion* 11 (1982): 13–22, proposes a combination of an old casuistic law (vv. 1, 2, 7) and a ritual law (vv. 3b-4, 6, 8b).

victim, represented by the violence done to the cow. The elders go on to speak
not only for themselves and their city, but for the whole nation (v. 8). Now the
people as a whole become the focus for atonement, no longer one town only or
even the land that v. 1 emphasized. Deuteronomy's theology of Israel as the
"people of Yahweh" comes to the fore (cf. 7:1–6). As such Israel is a
"redeemed" people, that is, one liberated from Egypt. Deuteronomy uses this
verb *pādâ* as a sort of concentrated, miniature creed (7:8; 9:26; 13:6 [ET 5];
15:15; 24:18). To "absolve, atone for" is to remove or cover over a barrier or
obstacle to the relationship with Yahweh. The elders' prayer makes clear that it
is really Yahweh who works this atonement, not the ceremony by itself. Both
the oath of innocence and the history of redemption provide impetus for
Yahweh to act. Deuteronomy also prescribes a prayer during the ritual of
26:3b–10a, 13–15. Strict observance of this law is motivated by language similar to the formulas of 13:6, 18 [ET 5, 17]; 19:13.

[10–14] The original pre-Deuteronomic law is most clearly visible in what
the woman does to prepare for her marriage in vv. 12b–13a. This contrasts with
the casuistic second person singular of the remainder, which is the pattern of
Deuteronomy's other laws about sacral war (20:1, 10–14, 15–18, 19–20). The
main case (vv. 11–13) is followed by a subcase (v. 14) that ends in a positive
command and a double prohibition. The main case of this law validates marriage to a captive woman. In such a case, normal contractual arrangements
between families would be impossible and the female captive would have no
legally competent relative to defend her interests (cf. Judg 21:8–12). The subcase protects her from a reduction to slave status in case of a later divorce. Their
sexual relationship establishes the husband's obligation. A proper understanding of the main case depends on understanding that the apodosis begins with v.
12b (note i).

The law envisions a situation in which a captive is taken to a man's house in
order to be married, but it does not overtly prohibit battlefield rape (Judg 5:30).
Nor does it explicitly exclude the practice of enslaving her and then having sexual relations with her outside marriage. Marriage is in the picture in this particular case only because of the man's choice. If the male captor *does* choose to
enter into a marriage, however, then this law restricts his power over his captive
bride. To marry her he must be willing to forfeit his claim to her potential value
as a slave, because sexual relations under these conditions create a relationship
of marital responsibility. The law does give her some legal protection in the case
of any subsequent divorce in that she must be treated as a free woman, not as a
slave. She is also given time to adjust to her new situation and has full status as
a wife. Before consummation of the marriage can take place, she is to be integrated into her new family through what is in effect a rite of passage.

The case statement (v. 12) envisions that she has been brought "in the midst
of" the man's house, implying that she has been incorporated within the struc-

ture of the household (cf. 22:2; 1 Kgs 11:20). The acts required of her are ritually symbolic of her change of status. Her month-long seclusion ("live in your house") is a classic example of the liminal state, characteristic of rites of passage that separate a person from a previous status and incorporate him or her into a new one. It is also likely that this month gives her time to have her menstrual period in order to demonstrate that she is not pregnant by a previous husband or other man. She sheds her former life and captive status, represented by her clothes, hair, and nails. Changing clothes (Gen 35:2) and shaving (Lev 14:8–9; Num 6:9) were part of the transition rituals of purification (cf. Joseph's transition from prison to freedom, Gen 41:14). A woman's shaved head would be a sign of humiliation (Isa 3:24), something also characteristic of rites of passage. Since there is no reason to think that captives wore any special garb, she is simply removing the clothes of her former life. The wife-to-be is shedding bits of her former selfhood.[6]

It is unclear whether these acts are also to be understood as part of her mourning routine (v. 13aβ). Structurally, the repetition of "your house" in vv. 12 and 13aα may form an inclusio that effectively separates the actions of her transition in status from the statement about her mourning. A month would be an unusually long mourning period, stretching to the length of that for Moses himself (34:8), and her acts are not similar to the mourning rituals forbidden in 14:1. Even if her parents are not dead, in her new life they are as good as dead to her (cf. the admonition of Ps 45:11 [ET 10]). She explicitly mourns her parents, but not any former husband. Yet this does not necessarily imply that she had been unmarried, for according to 20:14 the wives of slain foes were subject to capture. Apparently the question of any husband or children is simply beside the point. The double marriage formula of v. 13b emphasizes that the couple enter into a standard, full marriage. As a result, the husband must deal with her as he would any Israelite wife, giving her a proper divorce and treating her as a free woman. The language of v. 14 implies she is comparable to the Israelite "kindred" (literally "brother") of 24:7. The motivating reason for her status is the sexual intercourse that has been imposed on her by forced marriage.

This law is notable more for what it envisions than for what it requires. The only case offered is one in which the captive woman is desired for marriage and brought home—as though saying implicitly this is or should be the norm. Of course, to read this law as much of a positive gain for captive women requires the reader to adopt its androcentric perspective. The law is hardly the humanitarian breakthrough in gender relations that some interpreters have imagined it

---

6. Hair and garment fringes were thought of as extensions of one's person. Thus at Mari fingernails and fringes were used to validate contracts in the absence of a proper seal or to identify a person who suffered from illness or reported an ominous dream (*ANET*, 623–25, 629–32).

to be. It assumes the victorious male's right to capture for the purpose of marriage. The woman's consent or lack of consent to this arrangement is completely beside the point. The issue of her attachment to any former husband or children is simply bypassed. Moreover, what real protection is provided by her release as a "free" woman into a patriarchal society without any protective family structure or even the support that was provided to a freed Hebrew slave (15:14)?[7] Yet v. 11 also implies that a pretty appearance is not the whole story, but that marriage is properly founded on desirous love, analogous to the love that Yahweh has for Israel (7:7; 10:15; cf. Gen 34:8).

Here there is no ethnocentric hesitancy about intermarriage, so this law is in some tension with the more rigorous 7:3, which forbids intermarriage with the land's indigenous inhabitants. In this case, however, there would be no family to entangle Israel into pagan practices. Moreover, the introduction "go forth" parallels 20:1 and suggests that what is meant here is war outside the land, as described in 20:10–14. As one "far from you" (20:15) she may be taken captive rather that liquidated as *ḥērem* according to the rule of 20:16–18.

[15–17] The practice of giving the oldest son a larger inheritance cannot be set aside because of favoritism. The situation of the "unloved" wife is topically associated with "no longer find her pleasing" in the previous law of the captive wife. The stories of Rachel and Leah or Hannah and Peninnah are narrative reflections of the social situation behind this law, and 22:13–21 and 24:1–4 are legal responses to similar marital realities. The unstated presupposition here is that a second wife with a son born later would normally be younger and more appealing. The focus of this third-person casuistic law is "the day" (v. 16) on which the father either announces the details of the division he has determined or actually distributes his estate so that his sons could go forth to establish their own households. The law seeks to limit a father's freedom to set traditional inheritance patterns aside. Perhaps to "proclaim" (v. 17) the firstborn was a formal and legal act (cf. 33:9). The motivation (v. 17b) is almost biological, appealing to the "natural superiority" of the first issue of the father's sexual potency (cf. Gen 49:3; Pss. 78:51; 105:36). The law deals only with the status and portion of the firstborn and says nothing about what should be done in regard to other sons and the rest of the property.[8]

[18–21] A Deuteronomic motivation clause (v. 21aβb) has been added at the

---

7. For a balanced view of these implications, see C. Pressler, *The View of Women in the Deuteronomic Family Laws* (BZAW 216; Berlin: de Gruyter, 1993), 9–15.

8. For similar laws: LH 165–70 (*ANET*, 173). For background, see E. W. Davies, "Inheritance Rights and the Hebrew Levirate Marriage," *VT* 31 (1981): 257–68. In support of understanding the firstborn's portion as two-thirds, see B. J. Beitzel, "The Right of the Firstborn (*pî snayim*) in the Old Testament (Deut. 21:15–17)," in *A Tribute to Gleason Archer* (ed. W. Kaiser Jr. and R. Youngblood; Chicago: Moody Press, 1986), 179–90.

end of a casuistic third-person law (case in v. 18, judicial process in vv. 19–20, punishment in v. 21a). This law is associated with the previous one by the topic of "son" and as a similar limitation on a father's rights. It seeks to halt a breakdown in traditional family life under the pressures of social change (cf. 5:16; 27:16; also Prov 19:26; 28:24; 30:17), while at the same limiting a father's power over his family. This law is one of several in which Deuteronomy introduces local elders into family affairs. Intergenerational conflict is to be resolved in the public arena, where the influence of the elders can modify an unrestrained paternal authority that might lead either to excessive harshness or to inappropriate laxity. One notes that elders and legal process played no role in the earlier apodictic laws of Exod 21:15, 17.

The central thrust of this law is that, if the burden of proof is met, the son's offense is gravely serious. Thus the core law requires stoning, and the motivation puts his transgression on the same level as bloodguilt and sedition (13:6, 12 [ET 5, 11]; 17:12–13; 19:13, 19–20; 21:9). This is an offense against community stability that must be sharply deterred and eradicated. Disrespect for *both* father and mother is the issue, and both parents are to take action together. The verbs "take hold," "bring," and "say" are all in the plural. Emphasizing the role of the mother seems to be a further way of limiting the father's exclusive authority. The phrase "his city" (v. 19) treats the son as a responsible adult. A rigorous burden of proof must be met in order to reduce the likelihood of execution: refusal to respond to discipline (most likely corporal punishment, 22:18) along with a solemn assertion by both parents of habitual and repeated impertinence (for the word pair, see Ps 78:8; Jer 5:23), disobedience, and proverbially dissolute behavior. Proverbs 23:20–22 connects the son's lifestyle as a "glutton and drunkard" to disobedience of and disrespect for parents. The accusation is made in the public gate so that the whole citizenry can exercise a measure of social control. In the end, it is the citizens who carry out the execution, apparently without the assistance of the parents. The theologically sensitized reader will draw a parallel to Israel as Yahweh's rebellious son (Deut 8:5; 9:23–24; 32:19; cf. Isa 1:2).[9]

[22–23] This law is topically connected to the occurrence of the death penalty in the previous one. The concluding words of v. 23, "the land that Yahweh your God is going to give you," form an enclosing frame with v. 1 (and

---

9. See further E. Bellefontaine, "Deuteronomy 21:18–21: Reviewing the Case of the Rebellious Son," *JSOT* 13 (1979): 13–31 who distinguishes two laws combined into one; P. R. Callaway, "Deut 21:18–21: Proverbial Wisdom and Law," *JBL* 103 (1984): 341–52, who theorizes that wisdom concepts are being used secondarily in a legal context; P.-E. Dion, "La procédure d'élimination du fils rebelle (Deut 21,18–21): Sens littéral et signes de développement juridique," in *Biblische Theologie und gesellschaftlicher Wandel: Für Norbert Lohfink SJ* (ed. G. Braulik et al.; Freiburg: Herder, 1993), 73–82. A. C. Hagedorn, "Guarding the Parent's Honor—Deuteronomy 21:18–21," *JSOT* 88 (2000): 101–21, proposes that this law offers guidelines to encourage parents in proper child rearing and stresses the risk to family honor if they fail.

with 19:2). The extended exposure of a hanged body must be prevented, for this would put the land into a state of ritual impurity. Exposure after execution was intended as degrading and would serve as a public warning (Gen 40:19; 1 Sam 31:10; 2 Sam 4:12). Permanent denial of burial would be an even more serious affront (2 Sam 21:8–14; Jer 22:18–19). The format is mixed, shifting twice from impersonal casuistic to second person. There are two coordinated motivations: "accursed by God" and the ban on polluting the land (cf. Deut 24:4) with an unclean dead body. The mechanism of curse remains unclear (note q). Is the body accursed due to the fact that it is hanging and thus a public example to be reviled, or is it hanging exposed because of its accursed state as the corpse of a criminal? Joshua scrupulously obeys this law in Josh 8:29; 10:26–27.[10]

Property Laws and Family Laws
22:1–29

A Kindred's Animals

22:1 Do not observe your kindred's ox or sheep straying off and be indifferent[a] about them; you must surely take them back to your kindred. 2 If your kindred is not near you or[b] you do not know who he is, bring it inside[c] your house, and it shall remain with you until your kindred asks after it. Then return it to him. 3 Do the same with his donkey, do the same with his garment, and do the same with anything that your kindred loses and you find. You dare not remain indifferent. 4 Do not observe your kindred's donkey or ox fallen on the way and be indifferent about them. You must surely help lift it up.

Threats and Mixtures

5 A woman must not wear man's apparel,[d] nor may a man put on a woman's garment; for whoever does these things is repugnant to Yahweh your God.
     6 If you come upon a bird's nest on your way, in any tree or on the

---

10. In the Roman period this passage was sometimes read in terms of crucifixion (Gal 3:13; 4QpNah 3–4 i 6–8; 11QTemple 64.7–12). On the interpretive divide between Christians and Jews, see J. M. Lieu, "Reading in Canon and Community: Deuteronomy 21.22–23, A Test Case for Dialogue," in *The Bible in Human Society: Essays in Honour of John Rogerson* (ed. M. Daniel Carroll R. et al.; JSOTSup 200; Sheffield: Sheffield Academic Press, 1995), 317–34.

ground, with young birds or eggs, and the mother is sitting on the young birds or eggs, do not take the mother along with the young. 7 You must surely let the mother go and take only the young for yourself, in order that it may go well with you and you may enjoy long life.

8 When you build a new house, make a parapet for your roof, so that do not bring bloodguilt on your house if someone should fall from it.

9 Do not sow your vineyard with a second kind[e] of seed, lest the total yield come into a state of holiness[f]—the crop of the seed that you have sown and the produce of the vineyard. 10 Do not plow with an ox and a donkey together. 11 Do not wear mixed fabric,[g] wool and linen together. 12 You are to make twists[h] on the four corners of your garment that you wrap around yourself.

Sex and Family

13 If a man takes a woman as wife and has sex with her, but then comes to dislike her,[i] 14 and makes shameful charges[j] against her and defames her saying, "I took this woman as wife, but when I first had intercourse with her, I did not find her to be a virgin,"[k] 15 then the father of the young woman[l] and her mother shall take out the evidence of the young woman's virginity[m] to the elders of the city[n] at the gate. 16 The father of the young woman shall say to the elders: "I gave my daughter as wife to this man, but he came to dislike her. 17 Now he has made shameful charges[o] saying, 'I did not find your daughter to be a virgin.' But here is the evidence of my daughter's virginity." Then they shall spread out the cloth before the elders of the city. 18 The elders of that city shall take the man and punish him.[p] 19 They shall fine him one hundred [shekels] of silver and give it the father of the young woman, because he has defamed a virgin of Israel. She shall remain his wife; he dare not divorce her as long as he lives. 20 But if this charge proves true, evidence of virginity in regard to the young woman not being found, 21 then they shall bring the young woman out to the entrance of her father's house, and the men of her city shall stone her to death, because she committed an outrage in Israel, having illicit intercourse[q] while in her father's house. So you shall sweep out the evil from among you.

22 If a man is found lying with a woman married to another man, both of them shall die, the man who lay with the woman and the woman as well. So you shall sweep out the evil from Israel.

23 If there is a young woman, a virgin engaged[r] to a man, and a man comes upon her in the city and lies with her, 24 you shall bring both of them to the gate of that city and stone them to death, the young woman because she did not cry out in the city and the man because he had sex

with his neighbor's wife. So you shall sweep out the evil from among you.

25 But if the man comes upon the engaged young woman in the open country, and the man seizes her and lies with her, then only the man who lay with her shall die. 26 Do not do anything to the young woman. She is not guilty of a capital crime, because this case is like that of someone who attacks and murders his neighbor. 27 Because he came upon her in the open country, the engaged woman may have cried out, but there was no one to rescue her.

28 If a man comes upon a virgin who is not engaged, and seizes her and lies with her, and they are discovered,[s] 29 the man who lay with her shall give the father of the young woman fifty [shekels] of silver, and she shall become his wife. Because he violated[t] her he dare not divorce her[u] as long as he lives.

a. The hitpaʻel reflexive, literally "hide yourself from it," "dodge responsibility."

b. Alternate translation: "and"; in other words, because this is not a neighbor, you are not acquainted.

c. The animal is stabled in the house with the rest of one's livestock; cf. 1 Sam 28:24.

d. Alternate translation: "an article appropriate to a man," such as a weapon or tool. An artificial phallus has also been suggested.

e. Literally "two kinds." Either one sort of seed sown among the grapevines ("a second kind of seed") or two different seed types in addition to the grapes ("two kinds of seed"). The conclusion in v. 9b supports the former alternative. This refers to the practice of "intercropping" common to subsistence agriculture (cf. perhaps Isa 28:25).

f. Follows MT (supported by OG). Sam. has the hipʻil *tqdyš*, "you make holy."

g. The technical term *šaʻaṭnēz* (cf. Lev 19:19) is explained for the lay reader by an apposition.

h. Or "braids" (*HALOT* 1:180), perhaps a less technical word than the "tassels" of Num 15:37–41. For what is meant see *ANEP*, nos. 6, 7, 45, 48, 52.

i. Literally, he now "hates" her (cf. 2 Sam 13:15).

j. Construing as "a wanton act involving [his] words" or "wanton acts that are [nothing but] words," i.e., a baseless accusation on his part, which fits the situation of v. 17. Alternate translation: "wantonness of deeds," i.e., shameful conduct on *her* part (not clearly false at this point). Another possibility is "wanton acts that cause words [gossip]." The text explains this difficult expression with "puts out a bad name about her," i.e., makes a public accusation (as in v. 19).

k. In this verse his claim involves the "state of virginity" (cf. Lev 21:13), supposedly based on his experience of intercourse ("I did not find"). In v. 15 the word *bĕtûlîm* refers to the "physical evidence of virginity," the bloodstained sheet on which the marriage was consummated.

l. Throughout vv. 15–29 the Kethib *nʻr* is clarified as *nʻrh*, "young woman," by the Qere.

Property Laws and Family Laws

m. For the suggestion that this was the distinctive garment worn by a virgin (2 Sam 13:18–19; Ps. 45:14–15 [ET 13–14]), and given up by her when she was married in good faith, see R. I. Vasholz, "'A Legal Brief' on Deuteronomy 22:13–21," *Presbyterian* 17 (1991): 62.

n. OG has "elders" in this verse (as does MT in v. 16), while MT has "elders of the city" here and in vv. 17, 18. Harmonization has taken place in one direction or the other.

o. Follows MT. OG, Syr., Vulg. (*śm lh*), and Sam. (*lh śm*) supplement with an explicit "against her" taken from the start of v. 14. In fact, the accuser has attacked the reputation of the parents: "your daughter."

p. Corporal punishment is implied (cf. 21:18); the verb "take" points to something more physical than just a fine.

q. Follows MT in reading Qal (= "commit fornication"). Sam. and OG read hip'il so that "father's house" is taken as the direct object rather than as an accusative of place: "prostituting her father's house." Alternate translations emphasizing "father's house" as a familial unit: "while under her father's authority" or "bringing disgrace on her father's family."

r. G. J. Wenham, "*Bᵉtûlāh*: 'A Girl of Marriageable Age,'" *VT* 22 (1972): 326–48, suggests that *bĕtûlâ* here and in v. 28 signifies "young woman of marriageable status" rather than virgin. This is refuted by C. Pressler, *View of Women*, 25–28. In legal material, "virgin" indicates a young woman who has not had sexual relations, even in situations where this fact does not directly matter. The culture simply assumed that all unmarried young women were virgins. "Engaged" means that a bride-price has been paid (2 Sam 3:14), leading to a not-yet-consummated relationship often termed "inchoate marriage."

s. Follows MT in reading a plural verb *wnmṣ'w*. OG reads the singular *wnmṣ'*,"he is discovered," perhaps a haplography triggered by the initial *waw* of the next verse and buttressed by the ensuing focus on the man.

t. Translation depends on whether one understands v. 28 as rape. The verb *'nh* pi'el ranges from a neutral reference to intercourse (cf. v. 24 and 21:14) to forcible violation (Gen 34:2; Judg 19:24; 2 Sam 13:12). Alternate punctuation: "she shall become his wife because he violated her. He dare not divorce her."

u. The absence of *l* before the infinitive construct is unusual. Here and in v. 19 (where Sam. lacks *l* in the same phrase), there is a possibility of haplography or dittography caused by the preceding word: *ywkl [l]šlḥh*.

The laws of chapter 22 divide into a mostly apodictic cluster (vv. 1–12) and a casuistic cluster about marriage and sex (vv. 13–29). This second group is bracketed by a scribal maneuver in 22:12 and 23:1 involving covering and uncovering and *kānāp* ("wing" or "skirt"). The internal organizations of these two blocks have been elucidated in various ways.

In the apodictic cluster, vv. 5 and 9–11 are mixture taboos, with vv. 9–11 exhibiting a parallel in content to Lev 19:19. Verse 12 attaches to v. 11 (and 5) by the topic of clothing. Several unifying patterns suggest overlapping (or highly sophisticated) scribal activity:

"Donkey or ox fallen on the way" (v. 4) . . . "on your way"
(v. 6) . . . "fall" (v. 8) . . . "ox and donkey" (v. 10).

"House" in vv. 2 and 8, "garment" in vv. 3 and 5, "not wear"
in vv. 5 and 11.

A thematic unit of "what to do with property" sequenced as
vv. 1–5 (other people's property), vv. 6–7 (ownerless
property), vv. 8–12 (one's own property of house, land,
animals, clothing).[1]

The family laws of vv. 13–29 represent another thematic unit, similar to
Mesopotamian laws that are grouped by type of person or station in life. They
all deal with women, most often designated as a na'ărâ, "young woman"
(except in v. 22). The women appear in a sequence determined by social status,
in reverse chronological order from being married (vv. 13–22), to engaged (vv.
23–27), to unengaged (vv. 28–29). Further unity is provided by the repeated
verb māṣā', "find" (vv. 14, 17, 20, 22, 23, 25, 27, 28), and the expression šākab
'im, "lie with," in vv. 22–29. Four of the laws are paired together as case and
countercase (vv. 13–19 and 20–21; vv. 23–24 and 25–27). A concentric structure emerges when the penalties are considered: vv. 19 and 29 involve payments
and no future divorce, vv. 21 and 25 involve execution of the one guilty party,
and vv. 22 and 24 require the execution of both parties. Another way to conceive of the structure of vv. 22–29 is to see vv. 22 and 28–29 as opposites. The
first law is a public capital case involving a married woman, the last a matter
of private remedy involving an unbetrothed young woman. The first protects
the married man, the last the girl's father. In between are intermediate cases that
fall between the opposed states of "married" and "unbetrothed" and between
the clear-cut situations of consensual adultery and rape.[2]

The hypothesis of a redactional shaping in accordance with the Decalogue
understands this material as a juncture between sections relating to two commandments, with killing represented by 19:1–21:23 and adultery by 22:13–23:15
[ET 14]. Verses 22:1–12 supposedly represent an interleaved transitional section.
Verses 1–3, 4, 6–7, 8 are laws that preserve life. Verses 5, 9–11, 12 are laws for-

---

1. The first two patterns are described by Braulik, *Deuteronomium*, 2:160–63. For the third, see
R. Westbrook, "Riddles in Deuteronomic Law," in *Bundesdokument und Gesetz*, ed. Braulik,
166–68.

2. E. Otto, "Das Eherecht im Mittelassyrischen Kodex und im Deuteronomium: Tradition und
Redaktion in den Paragraphen 12–16 der Tafel A des Mittelassyrischen Kodex und in Dtn
22,22–29," in *Mesopotamica—Ugaritica—Biblica* (ed. M. Dietrich and O. Loretz; AOAT 232;
Kevelaer: Butzon & Bercker, 1993), 259–81, uses this pattern to suggest the text's history of composition. This redactional structure finds a parallel in MAL A 12–16, *ANET*, 181. G. J. Wenham
and J. G. McConville, "Drafting Techniques in Some Deuteronomic Laws," *VT* 30 (1980): 248–52,
structure this as a chiasm created by the changing location of the cases.

bidding mixing (symbolic of adultery) and involve topics suggestive of sex such as seeds and vineyards (vv. 9–11) and covering oneself (v. 12).[3]

Pre-Deuteronomic legal content is undoubtedly present here. There are parallels to Exod 23:4–5 (vv. 1, 4), Lev 19:19 (vv. 9–11), and Exod 22:15–16 [ET 16–17] (vv. 28–29). Deuteronomic contributions to the apodictic cluster (vv. 1–12) are visible in the "kindred" (literally "brother") ethic in vv. 1–4 and the typical "casuistic you" format in vv. 6–8. Almost all of the marriage cluster (vv. 13–29) sounds like inherited traditional material except for the "sweep out evil" formulas and the second-person address of vv. 24–26. The harsh provisions of vv. 20–21 are sometimes thought to be a later, more severe addition.

[1–4] Verses 1 and 4 are clearly related to the second-person casuistic laws of Exod 23:4–5. However, the law in Deuteronomy is more or less apodictic in format, although an underlying casuistic thought pattern remains: "if you observe . . . you must." The expanded Deuteronomic form uses "kindred" ("brother") five times rather than the "enemy" found in Exodus. An awareness of psychology is suggested by "observe" ("see"; cf. 20:1; 21:11) and "be indifferent." Verses 2–3 expand the core law of v. 1 with answers to natural questions: What if I cannot bring it back? What about other sorts of property? One's responsibility is expanded to include caring for the animal until found, and the scope of the law is expanded to include every Israelite, distant or unknown, and every sort of property. These laws seek to address a perceived breakdown in social order. The possibility of not knowing your fellow Israelite suggests social alienation resulting from a transition from small local communities to urban anonymity. In response, Deuteronomy extends the scope of "brotherhood" to those who are nonlocal and personally unknown.

Deuteronomy's "ox or sheep" (v. 1) also appears in 17:1 and 18:3. The range of lost property in v. 3 seems to come from Exod 22:8 [ET 9]. The legal attachment formula *wĕkēn ta'ăśeh*, "do the same" (Exod 26:4; Lev 16:16), is used three times to broaden the scope of what is to be returned not only to other domestic animals, but to inanimate property as well. The point is that lost property of any sort must be restored. Exodus 23:5 indicates a laden pack animal; in v. 4 the situation is more general, although the static "lying" of Exodus is strengthened to a more dramatic "fallen, collapsed" (*nāpal*). Deuteronomy's concern is not just about property rights, but about the care of animals, something in line with its ethic of interconnectedness with the natural world (cf. vv. 6–7; 20:19–20).[4]

[5] Mixtures seen as violating or blurring natural or social boundaries were thought to generate ritual impurity (Lev 19:19). Here failing to differentiate

---

3. Braulik, "The Sequence of the Laws in Deuteronomy 12–26 and in the Decalogue," in *Song of Power,* ed. Christensen, 322–26.

4. This law ignores the danger of being accused of theft; cf. LH 7, *ANET,* 166.

gender boundaries is forbidden as something *tôʿēbâ*, "repugnant." Although in Deuteronomy the category of *tôʿēbâ* usually appears as a motivational element in nonritual moral, civic, or loyalty contexts (as in Proverbs), this is one of several times where the word echoes its more technical connotation as a particular sort of impurity (cf. 14:3; 17:1; 18:12; 23:18–19 [ET 17–18]; 24:14). Structurally, the third-person apodictic double formation of this law finds parallels in 23:18 [ET 17] and 24:16. Although this is usually translated as an uncomplicated matter of cross-dressing, the enigmatic *kĕlî-geber* suggests something even more particularly gender sensitive (note d). In what realm of life this transvestite behavior was expected to occur remains uncertain. Although commentators tend to think immediately of non-Yahwistic religious ritual, cultural anthropology reports that cross-dressing takes place in many different contexts in human society.[5]

[6–7] This law proscribes an act seen as proverbially callous. The phrase "the mothers with the children [young]" seems to have been a proverbial expression for a reprehensible act of complete extermination, as in total warfare (Gen 32:12 [ET 11]; Hos 10:14). The format is: situation (v. 6a), prohibition (v. 6b), then contrasting positive command in emphatic grammar (v. 7a), and motivation (v. 7b). Verbal pairs create a pleasing poetic design: tree/ground, young birds/eggs, let the mother go/take the young, go well/enjoy long life.

This inclination to include the nonhuman world in the circle of decent behavior is also reflected in 14:21b; 20:19–20; 21:1–4; and 25:4. Some commentators also suggest a sort of protoecological concern for renewable resources; the freed mother can produce new young. There may be a sort of cross-reference here to 5:16 in that v. 7b is a reversed form of the motivation clause for the "honor your parents" commandment.

[8] Although the topic seems narrow, perhaps this is a paradigm law, one that illustrates and establishes a wider principle deterring negligence in other areas of life. Exodus 21:33–34 sets forth the same principle in a similar way.[6]

[9–11] These three laws may be connected to v. 8 by a common association of ideas: house, vineyard, field (cf. 20:5–7; 28:30). They also link up to v. 5 in both topic and negative apodictic form. Verses 9–10 may be understood as a pre-Deuteronomic "farmer's code of conduct."[7] Sowing other crops in a vine-

---

5. For Mesopotamian ritual parallels, see W. H. Ph. Römer, "Randbemerkungen zur Travestie von Deut. 22,5," in *Travels in the World of the Old Testament* (ed. M. Heerma van Voss et al; Assen: Van Gorcum, 1974), 217–22. To apply classical parallels such as Lucian, *De Dea Syria* 15, 26, 51, and suggest that this prohibition has something to do with "Canaanite" worship stretches the evidence.

6. See LH 229–30, *ANET*, 176.

7. For the implausible hypothesis that these laws allude to the Genesis narratives about Jacob and his sons, see C. M. Carmichael, "Forbidden Mixtures," *VT* 32 (1982): 394–415; idem "Forbidden Mixtures in Deuteronomy XII 9–11 and Leviticus IX 19," *VT* 45 (1995): 433–48. The

yard (note e) produces a situation of mixing or boundary violation.[8] As a result, the entire crop falls into a state of holiness. That is, it is transferred out of the normal profane state and thus become unavailable for common use. This way of thinking relates to the concept that the fruit of a vineyard is not "profaned" for common use until a given time period has passed (20:6; cf. Lev 19:23–25). The translation "forfeited" (NRSV) and the even more interpretive "forfeited to the sanctuary" (RSV) go well beyond what the text actually says. The impropriety involved and the results this would entail were apparently obvious to the reader and no further explanation is given. Verse 10 regulates a second agricultural practice. Perhaps a concern for the safety of the draft animals (cf. 25:4) overlays an older issue of ritual purity.

Verse 11 actually forbids only the wearing of such fabric and not the mixing itself. This particular combination, blending animal and vegetable products, was seen as generating ritual or numinous power and so it was used for priestly vestments (Exod 39:29; cf. 26:1).

[12] The requirement for tassels attaches to v. 11 by the topic of clothing. No explanation is given for this stark command, in contrast to Num 15:37–41, which speaks of memory (cf. Deut 6:8–9). Perhaps these are functional rather than symbolic, intended to weigh down the cloak and to permit it to be tied under the body to prevent indecent exposure. In a tour de force of scribal technique, *kānāp* (literally "wing," here "corner") reappears in 23:1 [ET 22:30] (as "skirt") to produce an envelope bracketing the four intervening laws about sexual offenses. In 22:12 the action referred to is "covering" (root *ksh*, translated "wrap around"); 23:1 [ET 22:30] refers to "uncovering" (root *glh*).

[13–21] The local elders witness a procedure that limits a husband's behavior concerning a disliked wife (cf. their role in 21:18–21). The law seeks to protect the woman and her family of origin from slander and her father from financial loss. The format is: case (vv. 13–14 as a single conditional sentence), procedure (vv. 15–17), outcome (vv. 18–19), countercase (v. 20), and its outcome (v. 21). The repetition of the key issue under dispute, first by the narrator and then by a party in the case, is also a feature of 21:18–21 and 25:5–10.[9]

From our uninformed perspective, it is hard to understand what is going on. The pursuit of a simple divorce would normally be uncomplicated. After all,

---

briefer and more tightly constructed parallel text Lev 19:19 seems older than the version in Deuteronomy. Deuteronomy is more reader friendly, adding an explanatory result clause to the prohibition of mixed crops and explaining the difficult technical term about fabric with "wool and linen." Deuteronomy seems to limit a comprehensive ban on mixed seeds to the narrower situation of a vineyard. The most striking difference is that where Deuteronomy speaks of plowing, Leviticus speaks of mating.

8. C. Houtman, "Another Look at Forbidden Mixtures," *VT* 34 (1984): 226–28.

9. See MAL A 5, 22, 24, 45, 47, *ANET*, 180–84.

the husband "dislikes" her, that is, "hates" her, which is the technical language that permits him to send her away (24:1–4). Is the husband trying to get out of the marriage without forfeiting the bride-price back to his father-in-law? Is he trying to negotiate a reduction in bride-price after the fact? Or is this just a classic case of malice engendered by marital stress? The law itself seems entirely unworkable. If the husband knows or suspects that this evidence exists and is in the hands of her parents, why would he bring the charge in the first place? Indeed, how hard could it have been to mock up some fake evidence? Does the law assume there would be witnesses to the authenticity of this cloth? Moreover, it is well known (to moderns at least) that the absence of blood on the occasion of first intercourse proves nothing about virginity. Perhaps the intended effect of this law was to encourage parents to obtain and preserve the "evidence of virginity" and to discourage husbands from raising such a socially destructive charge.[10]

The husband's punishment most likely includes a beating (note p; cf. 25:1–3). Yet in light of what is supposed to happen to a malicious witness (19:18–19), he seems to get off lightly, possibly because he has not actually offered formal testimony or because it would be unimaginable that his testimony could be contradicted by two witnesses. The specification of a hundred shekels seems significant; it is double the amount of vv. 28–29, which is often assumed to be a standardized bride-price (cf. Exod 22:15–16 [E 16–17]). The fine would thus represent twice the amount he was attempting to extract.[11] On the other hand, perhaps this represents a fine for the slander broadcast against the bride and her father (note o). Verse 19 understands his crime as one that transcends the interest of the families involved. The husband has defamed the whole people; it is not just a private matter. This observation shifts the focus of the law to the reputation of the woman and away from the rights of her husband or father. The strong proscription formula *lō' yûkal*, "he dare not," is used in similar contexts involving family law in 21:16; 22:29; and 24:4. The prohibition on divorce protects the woman and the heritage of any sons she would bear (v. 29), but also relieves her father of any future responsibility to support her.

The subcase (vv. 20–21) is introduced by *wĕ'im*, "and if" (cf. 19:8; 22:2; 24:12; etc.). However, it is really more of a countercase than a subcase.[12] It abruptly takes a harsher, more rigid approach. The presentation is much more compact, and this scenario is really not allowed for by the statement of the main

---

10. The problems are extremely complex and the reader is referred to C. Locher, *Die Ehre einer Frau in Israel: Exegetische und rechtsvergleichende Studien zu Deuteronomium 22:13–21* (OBO 70; Fribourg: Universitätsverlag, 1986); and idem; "Deuteronomium 22,13–21: Vom Prozeßprotokoll zum kasuistischen Gesetz," in *Das Deuteronomium*, ed. Lohfink, 298–303.

11. For double restoration, see Exod 22:6 [ET 7]; and LH 160, *ANET*, 173.

12. LH 142–43, *ANET*, 172, is a double law. In MAL A 55–56, the second law does not fit the situation of the first.

case (vv. 13–14). The ground shifts away from the issue of divorce and slander to a capital offense. No juridical process is provided; the woman's guilt is simply asserted to be "true" on the basis of the absence of exculpatory evidence. The penalty is ruthless, moving beyond physical discipline and financial loss to a highly public, shaming death.[13] This law is also more severe than the other laws in this context. The betrothed woman discovered in extenuating circumstances is given the benefit of the doubt (v. 26), and the unbetrothed virgin who has been compromised becomes a wife (vv. 28–29; cf. Exod 22:15–16 [ET 16–17]). In the subcase of vv. 20–21, however, neither circumstances that might affect her culpability nor the question of betrothal plays any role.

The critical difference seems to be that her offense here goes beyond mere illicit intercourse. It is in reality marriage under a false pretense of virginity. On the one hand, as in vv. 22 and 24, the woman is treated as a fully responsible person who must bear the consequences of her act, stoned by the men of "her city" (cf. 21:19); on the other hand her previous male partner (seducer? even rapist?) makes no appearance. The central issue seems to be less her earlier sexual behavior per se than its outcome in a marriage under false pretenses, shaming both father and husband. The husband's crime of defamation in the main case pales before the rhetoric that condemns her. Her crime is nothing less than "an outrage in Israel."[14] It is "fornication" (note q). It is "evil" to be swept out. The tight link between proven charge and death echoes the serious treasons of 13:15–16 [ET 14–15] and 17:4–5.

Like the insubordinate son (21:19, 21), she is "brought out" and then stoned by the male citizens of her town. That 21:18–21 offers such a close parallel may provide the key to understanding why this is such a sensitive issue. It is a matter of family honor and social integrity. She is executed at her father's house because her offense shames her extended family, the *bêt-'āb*. She engaged in sex before marriage while still under her father's authority, while resident "in" the building that localizes the family unit. Perhaps her execution takes place specifically at the entrance of the house because her behavior has both literally and symbolically breached what should have been the impenetrable boundary of her own body and that of her family's integrity. Perhaps her execution is also a shaming, punitive measure against her father. He did not control her as he should, or has even knowingly perpetrated a fraudulent marriage. This is a rigorous, dare one say reactionary, law intended to ensure the virginity of brides and perhaps to halt the threat of a laxity seen as a dangerous trend.

13. For the role of shame in this law, see V. H. Matthews, "Honor and Shame in Gender-Related Legal Situations in the Hebrew Bible," in *Gender and Law in the Hebrew Bible*, ed. Matthews et al., 97–112.

14. A crime that violates an important shared value and destroys a basic relationship (Gen 34:7; Judg 20:6–10; 2 Sam 13:12). See A. Phillips, "*Nebalah*—A Term for Serious Disorderly and Unruly Conduct," *VT* 25 (1975): 237–42.

[22–29] These four laws make up a connected sequence: illicit sex involving a married woman, illicit sex involving a betrothed virgin, and illicit sex involving a virgin not betrothed.

In v. 22 a prima facie case (they are "found" and she is another man's wife) leads to the statement of capital punishment (cf. Lev 20:10), followed by a motivation clause. The requirement that they be caught in the act is a protection against unfounded accusations. Because she is fully married, it is only in this law that the woman is not designated as na'ărâ, "young woman." The wording makes clear that the offense consists in the violation of the husband's rights in that only the woman needs to be described as married. Less rigorous practices are suggested by Prov 6:32–35 (compensation) and Hos 2:4 [ET 2] and Jer 3:8 (divorce).[15]

The case and countercase concerning the engaged virgin (vv. 23–27) are more complicated. Here public "discovery" is not part of the situation and would not fit at all with the second case. The central issue is the woman's consent, confirmed by circumstances in the first case, but unproven in the second. She is presumed innocent unless there is circumstantial evidence to the contrary. The wording of v. 23 leaves the potential for her consent open, although the man is described as the grammatical subject who actively "comes upon her" (literally "finds her"). That is, mutual assignation is not in the picture. The wording of v. 25 also lessens the potential for her responsibility: he "seizes her" (see the next paragraph). The countercase is introduced by wĕ-'im as in v. 20 and followed by supplementary implications in vv. 26–27 that underscore her innocence. The point of the murder analogy in v. 26 is that she is an innocent, passive victim and the man is the violent, intentional perpetrator. Perhaps these somewhat narrow laws should be seen as "paradigm laws," establishing principles for a variety of actual cases involving consent and force and questions about the guilt or innocence of an involved woman.[16]

I have rendered the man's action in v. 25 as "seize" (hzq hip'il; in v. 28 a different verb is used). Does this verb indicate forceful rape or merely an embrace ("take hold of") in the course of seduction? Nonviolent seduction is possible and is suggested by Prov 7:13. Yet the suggested parallel to murder hints at a degree of force. In a patriarchal culture, however, one wonders whether much difference in a man's culpability would be perceived between seducing an inexperienced young woman and forcing her. In any case, neither this law nor the one to follow centers on the issue of rape. The real issue concerns the rights of husbands or fathers. The woman's consent plays a role only if she is engaged, and even then her consent or lack of it is immaterial to the gravity of the offense

---

15. See LH 129 (ANET, 171) and MAL A 13–14 (ANET, 181).
16. Parallels: Hittite Laws 197 (ANET, 196) and MAL A 12–16 (ANET, 181).

or any interest as to whether it was rape or seduction. Her consent only affects her own innocence or guilt, but the crime itself is equally serious because it is not so much an offense against her but against the male who has rights over her.[17]

In the case of the virgin who is not engaged (vv. 28–29), there is no question of a capital offense because no marriage or betrothal has been compromised. The issue rather is the loss or reduction in value of her bride-price, and it is the father who is the injured party. Because they have been "discovered" (literally "found"), the matter has become public and must be resolved. The overall effect of this law would be to prevent vendettas (as over Dinah, Gen 34) and to discourage infringement of fathers' rights over their daughters' marriages. Again one is faced with the question of rape versus seduction. Certainly the parallel law in Exod 22:15–16 [ET 16–17] is about seduction, but matters are less clear here (note t). That "they" are discovered (contrast v. 22) might suggest some responsibility on her part. In regard to v. 28, some suggest that *tāpaś,* "seize," could be understood simply as "hold" as in Amos 2:15. When used with people as its object, however, *tāpaś* always means "hold by force" (cf. Num 5:13). If something less than forcible rape had been intended, why not employ the weaker verb used in v. 25? Nevertheless, as in the preceding law, the question of rape has nothing essential to do with the crucial point of the offense, which is the diminution of the father's financial stake in his daughter.

In comparison with Exod 22:15–16 [ET 17–18], however, Deuteronomy does seem somewhat more concerned with the young woman's security. Marriage without divorce is the only option offered, and the father's right to block this marriage is not mentioned. Of course, requiring marriage would also protect the father, who need not support her or try to find her another husband under these dubious circumstances. The father is to accept a fixed, nonnegotiable settlement in place of the flexible bride-price mentioned in the Exodus version. Modern readers' revulsion over her being required to marry her attacker falls outside the horizon of this law; the woman's feelings are not relevant to its purpose.[18]

17. C. Pressler, "Sexual Violence and Deuteronomic Law," in *A Feminist Companion to Exodus to Deuteronomy* (ed. A. Brenner; Feminist Companion to the Bible 6; Sheffield: Sheffield Academic Press, 1994), 102–12.

18. Parallels are Laws of Eshnunna 26 (*ANET,* 162), LH 130 (*ANET,* 171), MAL A 55–56 (*ANET,* 185). On the history of interpretation, see R. J. V. Hiebert, "Deuteronomy 22:28–29 and Its Premishnaic Interpretations," *CBQ* 56 (1994): 203–20.

Ritual and Social Boundaries
23:1–26 [ET 22:30–23:25]

One's Father's Wife

23:1 [ET 22:30] A man must not take his father's wife; he must not uncover the skirt of his father.[a]

Exclusion and Inclusion

2 [1] No one whose testicles are crushed or whose penis is cut off shall enter the assembly of Yahweh. 3 [2] No one misbegotten[b] shall enter the assembly of Yahweh. Even to the tenth generation, none of his descendants shall enter the assembly of Yahweh.[c] 4 [3] No Ammonite or Moabite shall enter the assembly of Yahweh. Even to the tenth generation, none of their descendants shall enter the assembly of Yahweh forever, 5 [4] because they did not meet you with food and water on your journey from Egypt, and because Moab[d] hired against you Balaam son of Beor from[e] Aram-naharaim to curse you. 6 [5] Yahweh your God refused to listen to Balaam, and Yahweh your God turned the curse into a blessing for you,[f] because Yahweh your God loves you. 7 [6] Do not ever seek their welfare or their prosperity[g] as long as you live.

8 [7] Do not abhor an Edomite, for he is your kindred. Do not abhor an Egyptian, because you were a resident alien in his land. 9 [8] As to children born to them, the third generation may enter the assembly of Yahweh.[h]

The Sacral War Camp

10 [9] When you go out as a war camp against your enemies, you must guard against any evil thing. 11 [10] If one of you is not clean because of a nocturnal emission,[i] he must go outside the camp; he must not come back into the camp. 12 [11] Toward evening he shall wash with water, and when the sun sets he may come back into the camp.[j] 13 [12] There shall be a designated area[k] for you outside the camp and you shall go there outside. 14 [13] You shall have a digging stick with your equipment.[l] When you squat down outside, you shall dig a hole with it and turn around and cover up your excrement. 15 [14] Because Yahweh your God journeys along with your camp[m] to rescue you and to give your enemies over to you, your camp[n] is to be holy, so that he may not see any indecent thing[o] among you and turn away from you.

Fugitive Slaves

16 [15] Do not turn over to his master a slave who has escaped to you from his master. 17 [16] He may settle among you in any place he chooses in any one of your towns, where he pleases;[p] do not oppress him.

Holy Persons and Forbidden Vows

18 [17] None of the daughters of Israel shall be a consecrated woman; none of the sons of Israel shall be a consecrated man.[q] 19 [18] Do not bring the fee of a prostitute or the recompense for a dog into the house of Yahweh your God in payment for any vow, for both of them are repugnant to Yahweh your God.

Loans at Interest

20 [19] Do not loan at interest to your kindred, interest on money, interest on food, interest on anything for which one may charge interest.[r] 21 [20] To a foreigner you may loan at interest, but to your kindred you must not loan at interest, so that Yahweh your God may bless you in all your undertakings in the land that you are going to enter to take over.

Vows

22 [21] If you make a vow to Yahweh your God, do not delay fulfilling it, for Yahweh your God will surely require it of you, and you will be guilty of a sin. 23 [22] But if you refrain from vowing, you will not be guilty of a sin. 24 [23] What proceeds from your lips[s] you must observe and do—exactly what you voluntarily vowed to Yahweh your God, what you promised with your own mouth.

Vineyard and Field

25 [24] If you go into your neighbor's vineyard, you may eat as many grapes as you wish until satisfied, but do not put any in a container. 26 [25] If you go into your neighbor's standing grain, you may pluck ears[t] with your hand, but do not put a sickle to your neighbor's standing grain.[u]

a. Understood on the basis of 27:20. Such uncovering would negate the protective claim his father once made in regard to that wife (Ruth 3:9; Ezek 16:8) and invade the privacy of the marital relationship.

b. Context indicates that a *mamzēr* is the issue of a prohibited union, perhaps like the one described in v. 1, the circumstances that gave rise to Ammon and Moab (v. 4), or interethnic marriage (Zech 9:6).

c. OG lost all of v. 3b by homoioteleuton from *bqhl yhwh* to *bqhl yhwh*.

d. Literally "he." This could refer to the king of Moab.

e. Follows OG, which does not have "Pethor," the name of Balaam's city. MT added this from Num 22:5 (*ptwr*; Sam. *ptrh*).

f. Follows MT. OG lost *lk*, "for you," by homoioteleuton: *'lhy[k l]k*.

g. No political or economic relationships are permitted. The cognates for "welfare" and "prosperity" were used in Akkadian for friendly international relations; see D. R. Hillers, "Notes on Some Treaty Terminology in the Old Testament," *BASOR* 176 (1964): 46–47; W. L. Moran, "Notes on the Treaty Terminology of the Sefire Stelas," *JNES* 22 (1963): 173–76; cf. Ezra 9:12.

h. Moving the *athnah* back to *lāhem*. Masoretic punctuation: "Children born to them of the third generation may enter."

i. Literally "what happens at night," understood on the basis of Lev 15:16.

j. Sam. gives the content in a different form, harmonizing with the language of Leviticus (cf. 15:16; 16:26): "except when he washes his flesh with water and the sun sets and afterward he may come back into the camp."

k. Literally "hand." This word is sometimes translated as "marker, sign" (cf. its use as "monument") and sometimes as "bordered area" (Jer 6:3 LXX). The translation tries to capture both concepts.

l. This translation of *'āzēn* follows the lead of Aramaic, *'āzênā,'* "weapon" (*HALOT* 1:28). The LXX and Vulg. translation "belt" comes from reading the root *'zr* (*r* for *n*).

m. This translation fits the whole phrase and reflects the concept of 20:4. Alternate translation: "moves about within your camp."

n. "Camps" in MT. The textual tradition predictably flattens this out to singular.

o. *'erwat dābār*, literally "the nakedness of a thing."

p. Follows MT with reservations. OG witnesses to something like *'mk yšb bqrbkm yšb bkl-mqwm 'šr btwb lw*, "he may settle among you, in your midst he may settle in any place, where he pleases." This repeats the verb "settle" and lacks *ybhr b'hd š'ryk*, "he chooses in any one of your towns." This omission by OG suggests that MT represents a conflated doublet: *'šr ybhr b'hd š'ryk*, "wherever he chooses in one of your towns," alongside *'šr btwb lw*, "wherever he pleases." The former alternative may have been considered too close to the centralization formula (cf. 12:14); the latter alternative is part of the OG text, but is suspiciously inoffensive.

q. OG has a doublet translation of this verse, pointing first to "prostitute" and then to "person with a sacral duty." This anticipates contemporary debates. Modern translations almost invariably opt for "cult prostitute" and "male cult prostitute."

r. For *nāšak* ("bite," "charge interest"), see S. A. Loewenstamm, "*Nšk* and *m/trbyt*," *JBL* 88 (1969): 78–80; E. Lipiński, "*Nešek* and *Tarbīt* in the Light of Epigraphic Evidence, *OLP* 10 (1979): 133–41; A. Kapelrud, "*nāšak*," *TDOT* 10:61–65. Alternate translation referring to "something bitten off" in the form of a prepaid discount: "deduct interest."

s. An idiom for a solemn promise (Num 30:13; Ps 89:35 [ET 34]).

t. Soft ears that can be rubbed with the hands (from the root *mll*, "rub"), as illustrated by Mark 2:23.

u. OG transposes v. 25 [ET 24] (vineyard) and v. 26 [ET 25] (standing grain), presumably by accident.

It is difficult to uncover any strategy of arrangement in this chapter. The clearest linkages are of a catchword nature: "(not) enter" in vv. 2–4, 8, and [ET 1–3, 7, 10] 11, the root *yšb* in vv. 14 and 17 [ET 13, 16], the root *nṣl* in vv. 15 and 16 [ET 14, 15], "holy" in vv. 15 and 18 [ET 14, 17], "vow" in vv. 19 and 22–23 [ET 18, 21–22]. Verses 16–26 [ET 15–25] fall into a pattern that alternates relationships in the human realm with duties associated with Yahweh. Thus vv. 16–17, 20–21, and 25–26 [ET 15–16, 19–20, 24–25] affirm or deny various claims involving a series of persons: slave, kindred ("brother"), foreigner, neighbor. The laws concerning one's relationship to Yahweh (vv. 18–19, 22–24 [ET 17–18, 21–23]) involve vows.[1] The theory that Deuteronomy has been ordered on the model of the Decalogue assigns vv. 1–15 [ET 22:30–23:14] to the adultery commandment, but sees vv. 16–26 [ET 15–25] as part of a transition section that interleaves sex (vv. 18–19 [ET 17–18]) and theft (vv. 16–17, 20–26 [ET 15–16, 19–25]). The presence of pre-Deuteronomic traditional laws is widely recognized in vv. 2–4, 10–15, 18, 19 [ET 1–3, 9–14, 17, 18], and there is general agreement that "forever" in v. 4 [ET 3], the repetitive v. 24bβ [ET 23bβ], and the awkward "until satisfied" of v. 25 [ET 24] are later glosses.[2]

[1 (ET 22:30)] This verse forms a bracket with 22:12, surrounding the marriage laws of 22:13–29 with the noun *kānāp* ("corner," "skirt") in the context of covering (22:12) and uncovering (23:1 [ET 22:30]). A curse on having sex with a stepmother appears in 27:20, but the law here refers to marriage after one's father has died or a divorce has occurred. That is, this is not an incest law (as in Lev 18:8; cf. Gen 49:4), but a marriage law. This law protects the integrity of the extended family in a polygamous context by blocking a son's inheritance of his father's wives. Given the young age at which women married, a son of an earlier wife could easily be about the same age as his father's later wives (cf. Gen 35:22).[3]

[2–9 (ET 1–8)] This section of four laws about inclusion and exclusion consists of three-third person apodictic laws distinguished by the phrase *lō' yābō'*, "shall not enter" (vv. 2, 3, 4–7 [ET 1, 2, 3–6]). These are followed by a second-person exemption (vv. 8–9 [ET 7–8]). This "shall not enter" refrain also pro-

---

1. Braulik, *Die deuteronomischen Gesetze*, 94–96. Carmichael, *Laws of Deuteronomy*, 169–201, relates the laws in this chapter to the Genesis stories of Reuben and his father's concubine (v. 1 [ET 22:30]), the birth of Ammon and Moab (v. 3 [ET 2]); Jacob's camp (vv. 10–15 [ET 9–14]) and flight from Laban (vv. 16–17 [ET 15–16]).

2. The relationship of some of these laws to the Holiness Code is disputed. Parallels to 22:22 and 23:1 [ET 22:30] appear together in Lev 20:10–11, and Deut 23:20–21 [ET 19–20] correlates with Lev 25:35–38. See Cholewiński, *Heiligkeitsgesetz und Deuteronomium*, 297–98, 301–2; G. Braulik, "Weitere Beobachtungen zur Beziehung zwischen dem Heiligkeitsgesetz und Deuteronomium 19–25," in *Das Deuteronomium und seine Querbeziehungen*, ed. Veijola, 23–55.

3. See LH 158, *ANET*, 172–73. For the suggestion that this law prohibits homosexual contact between son and father (Hittite Laws 189, *ANET*, 196), see A. Phillips, "Uncovering the Father's Skirt," *VT* 30 (1980):38–43.

vides a catchword to which the following law was attached (vv. 10–15 [ET 9–14]; cf. v. 11 [ET 10]). The text is a product of successive growth. Three older negative laws in vv. 2, 3a, and 4a [ET 1, 2a, 3a] have been supplemented by a positive admonition in v. 8 [ET 7]. These four laws have been expanded from various perspectives: temporal in vv. 3b, 4b, 9 [ET 2b, 3b, 8]; historical in vv. 5 and 6 [ET 4, 5]; intensifying in v. 7 [ET 6]. The *qāhāl*, "assembly," refers to participation in corporate worship, sacral war, and civil gatherings. In Deuteronomy, however, this religious assembly has been generalized into a synonym for the national community as a whole.

The classic study is that of Galling, who connected these admission laws to different sanctuaries. The ban of v. 4 [ET 3] and the acceptance of v. 8 [ET 7] represent the differing perspectives of two border sanctuaries, the latter on the southern periphery. In contrast, vv. 2–3a [ET 1–2a] originally referred to the matter of entry into a shrine in the interior of the country.[4] The proscriptions of vv. 2–4 [ET 1–3] have been dated as late as Nehemiah (Neh 3:35 [ET 4:3]), and the open attitude toward Edomites and Egyptians in vv. 8–9 [ET 7–8] as late as John Hyrcanus. However, a premonarchic date for these laws is completely reasonable. Anything so friendly to Edom must certainly be pre-586 B.C.E., and anti-Moabite and anti-Ammonite attitudes could fit anywhere in a wide time frame—from the Jephthah narratives in Judges through Omri and Ahab in the northern kingdom to the shifting political situation of the Assyrian period. Perhaps the more positive attitudes toward eunuchs found in the postexilic Isa 56:3–5 supports a preexilic date for the more rigorous stance of v. 2 [ET 1].

The thinking behind v. 2 [ET 1] may be related to sacral requirements for worship and warfare (cf. Lev 21:18–20; 22:24), respect for male procreative power, or, possibly, castration as a cult practice. If we understand the *qāhāl* as a periodic sacral assembly for landowners (cf. Mic 2:5), then issues of inheritance may help explain this ban on those who could not father children. The exclusions of vv. 3 and 4 [ET 2, 3] have been strengthened by the addition of the tenth generation, essentially the equivalent of "always" (at least 250 years!), and the last words of v. 4 [ET 3] ("forever") make this explicit. The otherwise lost tradition behind v. 5 [ET 4] is at odds with that reported in 2:28–29, 37. Successive explanatory expansions have created a complex text. Verse 5a [ET 4a] is second person plural and refers to Moab as "they"; vv. 5b-6 [ET 4b–5] are phrased in second person singular and refer to Moab in the singular.[5] That Yahweh "loves" Israel is typically Deuteronomic (7:13), as is the appeal to historical remembrance (cf. 24:9; 25:17–19).

---

4. K. Galling, "Das Gemeindegesetz in Deuteronomium 23," in *Festschrift Alfred Bertholet zum 80. Geburtstag* (ed. W. Baumgartner; Tübingen: Mohr, 1950), 176–91.

5. Because Balaam did not actually "curse" Israel according to Num 22–24, this suggests the existence of an alternate tradition. See D. Frankel, "The Deuteronomic Portrayal of Balaam," *VT* 46 (1996): 30–42.

In v. 8 the topic shifts from admission into the worshiping community to a more general attitude of acceptance toward resident foreigners. The statement that Israel was a *gēr* ("resident alien") in Egypt is paralleled in 10:19b and gives a comparatively positive view of that experience (contrast 6, 11 [ET 5, 10] and elsewhere). This may be a reference to the Joseph story or traditions about the patriarchs. This particular motivation is used elsewhere to support laws protecting resident aliens of undefined nationality (10:19; Exod 22:20 [ET 21]; 23:9; Lev 19:34).[6] Verse 9 [ET 8] counts inclusively, denoting the grandchildren of the first immigrants. This seems to be a later corrective comment on the exclusion of ten generations demanded by vv. 3b and 4b [ET 3b and 4b].

[**10–15 (ET 9–14)**] Sacral war required a special sanctity on the part of participants (1 Sam 21:5–6 [ET 4–5]; 2 Sam 11:11). Because Yahweh is present as divine warrior in the war camp (cf. 7:21; 20:1, 4), he can be expected to perform a liberating, saving act of sacral war victory (v. 15 [ET 14]). This means that ritual impurity must be prohibited, lest Yahweh be driven away and defeat result.

"When you go out . . . against your enemies" also introduces other sacral war laws (see 20:1–14 and 21:10–14). The general concept of war camp sacrality is illustrated by two possible violations, one contrary to the purity of one's body, one against the purity of sacral space. Verses 11–12 [ET 10–11] are a third-person casuistic law (except for the transitory "you" in v. 11 [ET 10] that ties in to v. 10 [ET 9]). Verses 13–14 [ET 12–13] are a positive command in the second person. These two laws are bracketed by reversed expressions describing what must be avoided: *dābār rā'*, "any evil thing" (v. 10 [ET 9]), . . . *'erwat dābār*, "any indecent thing" (v. 15 [ET 14]).

The nonspecific notion of an "evil thing" (v. 10 [ET 9]; *dābār rā'*; in 17:1 an animal disallowed for sacrifice) is illustrated by two possibilities. "What happens at night" (v. 11 [ET 10]) is usually understood as a nocturnal emission on the analogy of Lev 15:16, but perhaps a more general range of improprieties that could occur under the cover of darkness is intended. The second illustrative violation reflects the strict impurity attitude of Ezek 4:12–15. Excrement must both remain outside and be covered up. An *'erwat dābār* (v. 15 [ET 14]; literally "nakedness of a thing") refers broadly to a shameful matter or behavior and is associated with sexuality through the notion of "nakedness." The "nakedness of the land" refers to its vulnerability, something better left unseen (Gen 42:9, 12). Because it is characteristic of nakedness that it ought not be seen (Gen 9:22; Lev 20:17; Ezek 16:37; Lam 1:8), such a danger is naturally countered by "covering" (v. 14 [ET 13]). In fact, "cover" and "nakedness" often occur together (Gen 9:23; Exod 28:42; Ezek 16:8; Hos 2:11 [ET 9]). A

6. See J. E. Ramírez Kidd, *Alterity and Identity in Israel: The gēr in the Old Testament* (BZAW 283; Berlin: de Gruyter, 1999), 86–90.

generalized and unexplained *'erwat dābār* on a wife's part can lead to divorce (Deut 24:1); here it would lead to Yahweh "turning away."

Redactional ordering suggests an identification of this war camp with the whole community, the *qāhāl* of the previous section. Deuteronomy may cite this law for the larger purpose of linking obedience to success in a more general way. Yet one should not assume that Deuteronomy is entirely uninterested in matters of purity and sacrality, as is demonstrated by the inclusion of laws such as 14:3–21; 15:21; and 17:1.[7]

[16–17 (ET 15–16)] This law is related to v. 15 [ET 14] through the verbal root *nṣl* (hip'il "rescue"; nip'al "escape") and the phrase "among you" (vv. 15, 17 [ET 14, 16]). The prohibition of v. 16 [ET 15] is developed by a positive command in v. 17a [ET 16a] and a further prohibition in v. 17b [ET 16b]. The phrase "settle among you" almost certainly means that this law in its present form refers to slaves from foreign countries, but v. 16 [ET 15] alone could originally have been a general slave law that also applied to slaves held by Israelites. International treaties often required the return of fugitive slaves.[8] Such refugees would include not only literal slaves, but also renegade servants and underlings of a higher class (cf. 1 Kgs 11:17, 23, 26). Perhaps "oppress" (v. 17 [ET 16]) implies "reduce to slavery" again; the verb may be borrowed from Exod 22:20 [ET 21]. The rhetoric is intensely theological in that the slave is permitted to imitate Yahweh in the free choice of a "place" (as in the centralization law) and lives fully integrated in Israel's midst ("among you") just as Yahweh does (Deut 6:15; 7:21).[9]

[18–19 (ET 17–18)] Verse 18 is commonly understood in terms of cult prostitution and v. 19 [ET 18] in terms of female and male commercial sex workers. These views require modification.

It is unlikely that anything like cult prostitution was practiced in Israel, and the linkage of the *qĕdēšâ*, "consecrated woman," and *qādēš*, "consecrated man," with such an institution is unproven. That these words denote some sort of cult personnel is undeniable. At Ugarit, "consecrated women" were ritual specialists associated with temples, but the texts do not explain what they did. A similar situation obtains with the *qadištu* in Mesopotamian sources, although they had a reputation for engaging in (apparently profane) sexual activity. The Hebrew Bible associates "consecrated women" obliquely with prostitutes, perhaps because they were women whose public roles released them from the strictures of a patriarchal household and who had a proclivity for (or at least a

---

7. On the role of Deut 23:10–15 [ET 9–14] at Qumran and in developing Judaism, see B. M. Bokser, "Approaching Sacred Space," *HTR* 78 (1985): 279–99.

8. *ANET*, 200–201, 203, 204, 531 (§ 5), 532 (§ 2), 660 (Sefire III); cf. LH 15–20, *ANET*, 166–67.

9. Hamilton, *Social Justice and Deuteronomy*, 117–21.

reputation for) notorious sexual behavior. Genesis 38:21–22 describes a *qĕdēšâ* as a woman who could be expected to be on the roadside and receive an animal (for sacrifice?). The use of this word there seems to be part of a cover story to avoid searching openly for a public prostitute (*zônâ*; Gen 38:15). In Hos 4:14 the *qĕdēšâ* is directly connected to offering sacrifice, an apostate act put in poetic parallelism with going off with a *zônâ*. "Consecrated men" were also cult functionaries at Ugarit and appear in what seems to be the same role in 1 Kgs 14:24; 15:12; 22:47 [ET 46]; and 2 Kgs 23:7, most likely in connection with the worship of Yahweh. The questionable translation "male cult prostitute" is based solely on the parallel with *qĕdēšâ*. One should note that v. 18 [ET 17] does not speak of the elimination of such cultic staff positions, but does forbid Israelites from serving in them.[10]

The link between v. 18 [ET 17] and v. 19 [ET 18] is accomplished by the shared topic of temple affairs and a similar twofold gendered format. The first forbidden item in 19a [ET 18a] is clear enough. Proverbs 7:10–20 seems to describe a woman without other resources (v. 20) who pays her sacrificial vows (v. 14) with money earned through prostitution (v. 10). The indecency of such a procedure is reflected in the insult against Samaria in Mic 1:7.[11] The second item is more problematic. "The earnings of a dog" is traditionally interpreted as the fee of a (presumably) homosexual male prostitute, largely based on the poetic parallelism of this verse. However, no ancient Near Eastern text suggests that "dog" could mean male prostitute, and *mĕḥîr* certainly denotes "price in exchange for" or "equivalent value" (*HALOT* 2:568–69) rather than "wages." "Dog" could refer to a "devoted follower" (cf. *ANET*, 322) in the service of a pagan god.[12] The payment forbidden here might even involve a real dog, either fulfilling a vow with money acquired from selling a dog or an attempt to substitute a monetary equivalent or another animal to satisfy a vow promising a dog to the temple, since a canine could not itself be sacrificed.[13] Since a dog was a pariah animal (cf. the phrases in 1 Sam 24:14; 2 Sam 3:8; Qoh 9:4) and an urban carnivore (1 Kgs 22:38; 2 Kgs 9:36), the attempt to pay a vow with money derived from a dog would presumably be *tôʿēbâ* ("repugnant") in the technical, ritual sense of the term. This evaluation as *tôʿēbâ* and a similar twofold gendered format link v. 19 [ET 18] to 22:5 (crossdressing). This is the only direct reference to the temple in Deuteronomy.

---

10. M. I. Gruber, "Hebrew *qĕdēšāh* and Her Canaanite and Akkadian Cognates," *UF* 18 (1986): 133–48.

11. K. van der Toorn, "Female Prostitution in Payment of Vows in Ancient Israel," *JBL* 108 (1989): 193–205.

12. D. Winton Thomas, "*Kelebh* 'Dog': Its Origin and Some Usages of It in the Old Testament," *VT* 10 (1960): 424–26; M. A. Zipor, "What Were the *kᵉlābîm* in Fact?" *ZAW* 99 (1987): 425–26.

13. E. A. Goodfriend, "Could *keleb* in Deuteronomy 23:19 Actually Refer to a Canine?" in *Pomegranates and Golden Bells* (ed. D. P. Wright et al.; Winona Lake, Ind.: Eisenbrauns, 1995), 381–97. The ritual implications of the Ashkelon dog burial site are intriguing.

[20–21 (ET 19–20)] Perhaps "dog" provided a catchword connection for the topic of loans at interest (literally "biting"). This prohibition must be understood against the background of 15:1–11 and the requirements of an agrarian economy. Loans were made to the poor for their survival, not to be used as commercial capital. They were a response to crisis, like contemporary public loans made to victims of floods or farm emergencies. Lending to the poor was a public virtue (Pss 15:5; 37:26; 112:5). Deuteronomy has revised Exod 22:24 [ET 25], incorporating its own characteristic "kindred" ethic and expanding the list of what should be lent (cf. Lev 25:35–37). One is to loan without interest to any Israelite, not just to poor ones, and not just food or money but anything. The dictates of a changing economy involving caravans and trading colonies (1 Kgs 20:34) lead Deuteronomy to add permission to make interest-bearing loans to foreigners (v. 21 [ET 20]). The motivation clause promising blessing in the land is characteristically Deuteronomic (14:29; 24:19). The structure is concentric: "do not loan to your kindred . . . to a foreigner you may loan . . . to your kindred you must not loan." The root *nšk* (verb: "loan at interest," noun: "interest") occurs seven times.

[22–24 (ET 21–23)] The word "vow" provides a catchword connection to v. 19 [E 18]. A vow was a sacrifice or gift promised when petitioning the deity for help. As a promise of a future expression of gratitude and as a gift, it was intended to establish and strengthen one's relationship with the divine (12:6; Num 30:3). These verses sound more like a wisdom saying than a law; Qoh 5:3–5 [ET 4–6] offers similar advice on avoiding vows. The motivation of v. 22 [ET 21] is typical of Deuteronomy. Yahweh will "require" it (cf. 18:19) and it would be a "sin" (cf. 15:9). The format is approximately concentric:

> if you make a vow to Yahweh your God
> > do not delay fulfilling it
> > > you will be guilty of a sin
> > > you will not be guilty of a sin
> > what proceeds from your lips you must observe and do
> what you vowed to Yahweh your God
> > what you promised with your own mouth

[25–26 (ET 24–25)] Landowners are protected from unfair exploitation by the community, who were permitted to gather food from vineyard and field. Related laws are found in 24:19–22; 25:4; cf. 14:28–29. Each of these two laws gives a permission and then declares a limitation. It is not the poor who addressed here, but the more wide-ranging "you" of the whole community. Hence these laws deal with a general custom of communal sharing, not merely with an institution to support the poor.[14]

14. A. Rofé, "The Tenth Commandment in the Light of Four Deuteronomic Laws," in *Ten Commandments in History and Tradition*, ed. Segal and Levi, 45–65.

Marriage and Community Welfare
24:1–22

Remarriage to a Former Husband

24:1 If someone takes a woman as wife and acts as husband with her,[a] but she does not please him because he finds something indecent about her, and he writes her a certificate of divorce and puts it in her hand and sends her from his house, 2 and she leaves his house and goes[b] to become the wife of another; 3 and then the second man dislikes her[c] and writes her a certificate of divorce and puts it in her hand and sends her from his house, or if the second man who took her as wife dies—4 then her first husband who sent her away dare not take her again to be his wife after she has been made unclean,[d] for that would be something repugnant[e] to Yahweh. Do not bring sin on the land that Yahweh your God is going to give you as a hereditary possession.

Deferral from Service

5 If a man has newly taken a woman as wife, he shall not go out with the army or serve in any public duty.[f] He shall be exempt at home[g] one year, to give happiness[h] to his wife whom he has taken.

Community Welfare

6 No one[i] shall seize a handmill or an upper millstone in pledge,[j] for that is seizing a life in pledge.

7 If someone is found to have kidnapped a person, one of[k] his kindred from the Israelites, and treated him as a commodity[l] or sold him, then that kidnapper shall die. So you shall sweep out the evil from among you.

8 Be on guard[m] in an outbreak of leprosy to be very careful to do whatever the Levitical priests teach you. You must be careful to do just as I have commanded them. 9 Remember[n] what Yahweh your God did to Miriam on the journey when you left Egypt.

10 When you make your neighbor any sort of contractual loan, do not go into his house to take possession[o] of his collateral deposit. 11 Stand outside, while the person to whom you are making the loan brings the collateral deposit to you outside. 12 If the person is poor, do not sleep in his collateral deposit. 13 You shall surely return the collateral deposit to him by sundown, so that he may sleep in his cloak and bless you, and it will

be a righteous deed for you before Yahweh your God.

14 Do not exploit[p] a poor and needy wage laborer,[q] whether one of your kindred or one of your resident aliens who are in your land[r] within your towns. 15 You must give him his wages each day before the sun goes down, because he is poor and his life depends on it; otherwise he may cry out to Yahweh against you, and it would be a sin against you.

16 Parents must not be put to death[s] for children, and children must not be put to death for parents; each person must be put to death[t] only for his own crime.

17 Do not subvert justice for a resident alien or[u] orphan. Do not seize the garment of a widow[v] in pledge. 18 Remember that you were a slave in Egypt and Yahweh your God redeemed you from there.[w] Therefore I am commanding you to do this thing.

19 When you reap your harvest in your field and forget a bundle of grain in the field, do not go back to get it. It shall be for the resident alien, the orphan, and the widow, in order that Yahweh your God may bless you in all your undertakings. 20 When you beat your olive trees, do not go through the branches afterward.[x] It shall be for the resident alien, the orphan, and the widow. 21 When you harvest your vineyard, do not pick it over again.[y] It shall be for the resident alien, the orphan, and the widow. 22 Remember that you were a slave in the land of Egypt. Therefore I am commanding you to do this thing.

a. Follows MT. Sam. prefaces with *wb''lyh*, "and goes into her," either a dittography of MT *wb'lh* or a conflation of alternate readings. OG *synoikein* could translate either expression.

b. Follows MT (supported by Sam., 4QDeut[k2], Tg., Syr.). OG lacks two words. *BHS* wrongly suggests the omission as *mbytw whlkh*, "from his house and goes," which could only be a stylistic abbreviation to avoid repetition. However, 4QDeut[a] shows that OG (and Vulg.) actually omits the last word of v. 1 and the first word of v. 2 through haplography: *wšlh[h mbytw wyṣ']h mbytw*. That *aperchesthai* is the usual OG translation for *hlk* in Deuteronomy supports this conclusion.

c. Literally "hate," i.e., "no longer love" (Judg 15:2). This does not necessarily imply divorce for purely subjective reasons.

d. *Huṭṭammā'â* is supposedly hotpaʿal (*IBHS* 26.3b; GKC 54h; *HALOT* 1:376), thus passive or reflexive: "she has been caused to be unclean" by this chain of circumstances. Her "defilement" applies exclusively to their relationship: "for him she has become unclean" (REB). She is out of bounds for him. To be defiled literally or absolutely would require the piʿel or hitpaʿel. J. H. Walton, "The Place of the *Hutqattēl* within the D-Stem Group and Its Implications in Deuteronomy 24:4," *Hebrew Studies* 32 (1991): 7–17, construes this as a delocative reflexive passive: "she has been made to declare herself unclean."

e. Alternate translation: "*she* would be repugnant."

f. His exemption is apparently not just from the military, but also from all compulsory public service (cf. Isa 40:2 for *ṣābā'* as "forced labor"). Verse 5aβ is obscure and paraphrased here. Understanding the subject as an indefinite reference to his potential obligation: "it shall not pass over upon him with regard to anything [i.e., for any purpose]." Taking the exempted groom as subject: "he shall not enter into it" (cf. *'br 'l* in 29:11 [ET 12]; Exod 30:13).

g. Alternate translation: "for the sake of his household."

h. Follows masoretic tradition and the LXX translator in taking the verb as pi'el "make glad." This might reflect Deuteronomy's concern for women. Other translators (Syr., Vulg., Tg. Ps.-J., Aquila, Symmachus) understood it as Qal: "rejoice with his wife."

i. Follows the impersonal third person singular of MT. OG, Vulg., Syr. level to the more expected second person: "do not" (cf. v. 17).

j. The *rēḥayim*, "handmill," is the set of two stones, the base and a smaller one rubbed over it. The "upper millstone" (*rekeb*, literally "rider") is mentioned separately as a portable pledge without which no grinding could take place. *ḥābal*, "seize in pledge" (also v. 17), means "impound," "seize collateral for a defaulted loan," "take in distraint." See S. M. Paul, *Amos* (Hermeneia; Minneapolis: Fortress Press, 1991), 84–85.

k. The translation takes the preposition *min* as partitive. Alternate translation understanding the object of *min* as the one stolen from (cf. Gen 44:8; Exod 22:11 [ET 12]): "kidnapped a person away from his kindred."

l. See 21:14 note j.

m. Cf. *šmr* with *b* in 2 Sam 20:10; 2 Kgs 9:14; Neh 11:19.

n. Deuteronomy uses the infinitive absolute "remember" to warn (9:7), encourage (7:18), instruct (8:2), and provoke (25:17).

o. Here the verb is *'ābaṭ* (not *ḥābal* as in vv. 6 and 17). The Qal denotes "obtain a deposit as collateral," and the hip'il (15:6, 8) means "make a loan against a deposit of collateral" (*HALOT* 2:777–78). The situation of vv. 10–13 involves the lender collecting and holding collateral handed over by the borrower to secure a loan.

p. The verb *'āšaq* is associated with robbery and fraud (Lev 19:13; 1 Sam 12:4–5). It appears in the curses of Deut 28:29, 33.

q. Follows MT and Sam. *śkyr* as grammatically more awkward. Although weakly attested in the Hebrew evidence (including 1QDeut^b), *śkr*, "wages," may lie behind OG, Vulg., Syr. "wages of the poor and needy" (cf. REB). Malachi 3:5 reflects this usage as *śkr śkyr*, "wages of the wage earner," which equals Tg. Ps.-J. (cf. Deut 15:18) and is probably a conflated doublet.

r. Follows MT. OG and Syr. lost "in your land" by homoioarchton: *b['rṣk b]'š'ryk*.

s. MT has *mwt* as hop'al three times in this verse: "be put to death." OG, Syr., Tg. Onq. read Qal "die" in all three places, a matter of transposition (*ymwtw* for *ywmtw*). I follow the MT passive as more difficult than the familiar active voice formula (Lev 19:20; Deut 17:6).

t. Follows the plural of MT (hop'al; quoted by 2 Chr 25:4 as Qal plural) as more difficult in light of the singular subject. Sam. reads hop'al singular, and the singular is also supported by 1QDeut^b, OG, Vulg., Syr., Tg. Neof. (as Qal), and the quotation by 2 Kgs 14:6 (Kethib Qal; Qere hop'al).

u. MT lacks a conjunction, a difficulty eased by the insertion of "and" in OG, Vulg., Syr., Tg. Ps.-J. "Justice" is in a construct relationship with both "resident alien" and "orphan" (10:18; 27:19; *IBHS* 9.3b). OG fills out the usual formula with "and the widow."

v. The "garment of a widow" may be a distinctive sign of her status and identity (Gen 38:14, 19).

w. Follows MT. Sam. lacks *mšm*, "from there."

x. Olives were harvested by hitting the branches with poles, and some would fail to drop off (Isa 17:6; 24:13). *p'r* pi'el is denominative of *pō'râ*, "branches," thus "go through the branches" to knock down the remaining olives with a stick.

y. Perhaps means picking what was not yet ripe the first time.

Verses 1–5 deal with marriage and vv. 6–22 with matters of communal welfare. Those who support the theory that the Decalogue lies behind the present structure of Deuteronomy's laws assign 24:1–5 to the adultery commandment and vv. 6–7, 19–22 to the theft commandment as parts of an overlapping transition, while vv. 8–18 are said to begin a juridical section related to the false witness commandment.[1]

A concentric arrangement involving vv. 8–9 and v. 18 brackets vv. 10–17, while the repetition of v. 18 by v. 22 brackets vv. 19–21. Taken together, this bracketed material (vv. 10–17 and 19–21) forms a cohesive "social torah." A shared notion of one's day-by-day moral status before Yahweh (vv. 13, 15) links vv. 10–13 (loan collateral) to vv. 14–15 (daily wages). In a similar way, focus on the triad of alien, fatherless, and widow, together with the motif of Egyptian slavery, unifies the laws in vv. 17–22. This "social torah" seems to be related to the genre of the torah liturgy that lies in the background of Ezek 18:5–9 (cf. Ps 15 and 24). The content of these laws in Deuteronomy overlaps at points with the catalog in Ezekiel, and a priestly declaration of righteousness like that proclaimed in Ezek 18:9 seems to lie behind Deut 24:13b.[2]

[1–4] This law limits a man's legal rights regarding the established custom of divorce. It is not a general law permitting divorce or setting forth grounds for it, but simply takes the practice of divorce for granted. Verses 1–3 are the protasis, describing a case of successive marriages that have terminated. In unfolding this highly specific case, however, the law incidentally reveals information on divorce procedures in general. Verse 4 consists of the apodosis, followed by a sequence of motivations.[3] Behind this law lies some sort of

---

1. Braulik, *Die deuteronomischen Gesetze*, 89–107.

2. Braulik, *Die deuteronomischen Gesetze*, 102–5; W. Zimmerli, *Ezekiel 1* (trans. R. E. Clements; Hermeneia; Philadelphia: Fortress Press, 1979), 374–77.

3. A. Warren, "Did Moses Permit Divorce? Modal *wĕqāṭal* as Key to New Testament Readings of Deuteronomy 24:1–4," *Tyndale Bulletin* 49 (1998): 39–56, proposes that v. 1b is an initial apodosis: "then he may/should write." As evidence for this, he points to the repetition of "from his house" in vv. 1b and 2a as a divider between a first and second set of protasis/apodosis sentences.

pre-Deuteronomic taboo against such a remarriage as something that would involve or generate ritual impurity. The characteristic ideology of Deuteronomy is visible only in the motivation of "repugnant (*tôʻēbâ*) to Yahweh" and in the description of the land.[4]

The grounds for the first divorce are generalized and comprehensive. She is simply not pleasing (beautiful, charming, gracious?) because of an unspecified "something indecent," an *ʻerwat dābār* (v. 1). This somewhat baffling expression is part of the protasis setting up the circumstances of the case; it is not anything prescribed or proposed as grounds for divorce. Rather the phrase seems to be intended to cover the whole range of customary reasons for divorce. To "find" implies a later discovery of something not originally realized by the husband. To some interpreters, the occurrence of this expression in 23:15 [ET 14] suggest that 24:1 refers to obnoxious bodily emissions or an indecent, immodest, or improper act on the woman's part. Other suggestions include a physical defect, infertility, a long-term state of ritual impurity, an unverifiable suspicion of adultery, some personality trait, or simply annoying behavior. Whatever the character of her *ʻerwat dābār*, however, it does not prevent remarriage (v. 2). In her second divorce (v. 3), the grounds are even more open-ended; the feeling of love is absent (note c). The divorce certificate protects her by clarifying her status as a free woman. As such, it is to be a written document (not merely an oral declaration) and must be delivered to her personally, emphatically "put in her hand." The text carefully describes this procedure twice to make clear that these consecutive divorces are proper in every way. What is forbidden by v. 4 is expressed in the strong language of *lōʼyûkal*, "he dare not" (21:16; 22:19, 29).

Because scholars tend to think of Deuteronomy as uninterested in ritual purity, they have searched for motives for the inclusion and purpose of this law that go beyond the explicit ones of becoming "unclean," the category of *tôʻēbâ* (in the technical ritual sense of 14:3; 17:1; 22:5; 23:19 (ET 18]), and bringing "sin on the land" (cf. 21:23). One theory is based on ancient Near Eastern parallels and suggests that this law is intended to prevent the financial exploitation of the woman, who would lose her bride-price in the first divorce because it was considered to be her fault.[5] The bride-price, held in trust by her father, would have had to be paid over to her first husband. If her first husband could then take her back after an intervening marriage, however, he would be able profit twice, now having control of both her forfeited bride-price and the bride-price she

---

4. This legal principle is used as a theological metaphor in Isa 50:1; Jer 3:1–5. T. R. Hobbs, "Jeremiah 3:1–5 and Deuteronomy 24:1–4," *ZAW* 86 (1974): 23–29, sees the divergent viewpoints of Jeremiah and Deuteronomy as separate developments of an earlier law.

5. Interpreting *ʻerwat dābār*, "something indecent," as a sexual offense and relying on LH 141, 142, *ANET*, 172; MAL A 29, *ANET*, 182; *m. Ketub.* 7:6. The legal situation of the bride-price is helpfully summarized by E. Lipiński, "*mōhar*," *TDOT* 8:142–49.

would bring from her second marriage.[6] Another view suggests that this law would protect the new, second marriage from any pressure on the part of her former husband for the woman to return to him or any desire on her part to do so.[7] Yet another approach proposes that death was not the only possible disposition of a case of a wife's adultery (as in 22:22). In the case of a sexual offense on her part (described as an *'erwat dābār*), a husband would have the right under civil law to dispose of the case by a divorce involving the shameful public exposure of his delinquent wife (Hos 2:4–5 [ET 2–3]). This law, however, restricts a husband's free capacity to make such a noncriminal resolution of his wife's sexual transgression. For if he chooses to take the route of a private sanction through divorce, he may not subsequently try to undo this by seeking to take her back and repair the marriage.[8] Another hypothesis points out that this law would discourage husbands from hasty divorce and enable a divorced woman to marry more easily.[9] At the very least, one imagines that it would enhance family stability by preventing an open-ended, back-and-forth shuttling between former spouses; there would be a least some irreversible consequences to divorce.

The nature and implications of the woman's status as "unclean" in regard to her first husband are also unclear. If her supposed *'erwat dābār* refers to something that makes her ritually unclean and the first husband has declared that he has "found" such impurity in her, is he now thought to be irretrievably bound by what he has proclaimed? Would he by guilty of the *tô'ēbâ* of hypocrisy by remarrying her?[10] Or is her latent relationship to her first husband viewed in familial terms so that to return to him would be viewed as a matter of incest?[11]

6. R. Westbrook, "The Prohibition on Restoration of Marriage in Deuteronomy 24:1–4," in *Studies in Bible*, ed. Japhet, 387–406. This interpretation depends on a restricted understanding of *'erwat dābār* and setting aside the evidence of Jer 3:1–5, which speaks only of impurity and not of financial justice.

7. R. Yaron, "The Restoration of Marriage," *Journal of Semitic Studies* 17 (1966): 1–11. But why prohibit remarriage upon the second husband's death?

8. E. Otto, "Das Verbot der Wiederherstellung einer geschiedenen Ehe: Deuteronomium 24,1–4 im Kontext des israelitischen und judäischen Eherechts," *UF* 24 (1992): 301–10. He cites MAL A 13 and 15 (*ANET*, 181) as contrasting cases under criminal and civil law. Yet another approach considers the first marriage an "inchoate" one in which the pair are betrothed and the woman lives in the man's house, but they are not yet fully married (cf. 21:10–14). If the man decides not to complete the inchoate marriage by consummating it, he may not reestablish the inchoate marriage even if a second period of betrothal intervenes. This requires translating v. 1 as "wants to take a woman as wife in order to act as husband with her," which is hardly the most natural reading. See D. Volgger, "Dtn 24,1–4—Ein Verbot von Wiederverheiratung?" *BN* 92 (1998): 85–95.

9. D. I. Brewer, "Deuteronomy 24:1–4 and the Origin of the Jewish Divorce Certificate," *JJS* 49 (1998): 230–43.

10. Westbrook, "Prohibition on Restoration," 404–5.

11. G. J. Wenham, "The Restoration of Marriage Reconsidered," *JJS* 30 (1979): 36–40. The language of defilement and "sin on the land" is indeed used for incest; cf. Lev 18:25, 27. But why is remarriage forbidden only after an intervening marriage?

Would a return to her first marriage retroactively convert her second one into an adulterous relationship?[12]

[5] This law is linked to the previous one by topic and a nearly identical introduction. For the thinking behind this law, see the commentary at 20:7. Enjoyment of a new marriage takes precedence over obligations for military conscription, forced labor, or other government service (note f; 1 Sam 8:11–13). The groom is *nāqî*, "exempt" (cf. 1 Kgs 15:22). In part this notion rests on the sacral character of any situation that is "new," but Deuteronomy characteristically speaks here in terms of social and personal benefits. The new husband is to be "at home" (note g) to provide pleasure for his bride (or perhaps enjoy himself with her; note h). This certainly refers to sexual activity (Prov 5:19), but also to delight in a more general sense (Qoh 9:9). That this state of affairs lasts for a year suggests that this delight may also involve the joy of becoming a parent (Jer 20:14–15).

[6] This law shares the topic of loans with vv. 10–13 and 17. It may be connected to the previous law through an association of the sound of the mill with the joys of homelife (Jer 25:10) or a cruder association of intercourse with grinding (Job 31:10). A collateral "pledge" of this sort was not taken when the loan was made, but subsequent default would permit the creditor to seize something (note j; cf. v. 17; the "collateral deposit" of vv. 10–13 is a different matter). It is unclear whether this item would be agreed on ahead of time or was left up to the choice of the creditor. Taking a poor person's hand mill or more portable millstone would be a forceful way of pressuring repayment. However, this is censured as the equivalent of seizing "a life" in that one's household mill was a indispensable requirement for existence (cf. Job 24:3). A millstone was made of a special type of stone not always locally available and thus expensive to replace. The principle is that human survival takes precedence over a creditor's rights (cf. Deut 15:1–11 and 23:20–21 [ET 19–20]).[13]

[7] *Nepeš*, "life," provides a catchword connection to v. 6. The expression translated "kidnap" is literally "steal a life from his brothers," emphasizing that this crime is a sort of "social murder" and a violation Deuteronomy's "brotherhood" ethic. This is a restatement of Exod 21:16, which mentions nothing about nationality or selling and does not use the evocative term "life."[14]

[8–9] In the Hebrew Bible, "leprosy" (better: "repulsive skin disease") refers to a wide range of dermatological problems. Verse 8 is overfull, with v. 8a in second person singular and v. 8b in plural address. It is likely that the mention of priests in their teaching role was appended somewhat later to the original

---

12. This is the opinion of Pressler, *Deuteronomic Family Laws*, 45–62, who provides a helpful review and critique of several of the theories addressed only briefly here.

13. For limits on seizing pledges, see LH 113, 241, *ANET*, 170, 176.

14. For the same penalty, LH 14, *ANET* 166.

warning. These verses form a concentric bracket with v. 18 to surround and highlight vv. 10–17 as a topical unit: "command . . . to do" / "remember" / "remember" / "command . . . to do." Verse 8 clearly presents a lay view on leprosy in contrast to the technical prescriptions of Leviticus 13–14.

An insistent repetition of the verb *šmr* reinforces the warning, literally: "be on guard [careful] . . . be careful to do . . . be careful to do." The citation formula in v. 8b points to some unspecified command directed by Yahweh to the priests, although perhaps this is just a generalized use of the formula involving no specific text. The point of the reference to Miriam (cf. Num 12:10–15) is apparently that such a calamity could happen to anyone, or perhaps it is intended to encourage keeping lepers apart from society as was done with Miriam. "When you left Egypt" unobtrusively recalls Yahweh's deliverance and looks back to 23:5 [ET 4] and forward to 25:17. Memory of the tradition motivates obedience.

[10–13] To borrow was automatically to be in economic and legal peril, for it put one's creditors in a position of great power. This law severely limits the pressure a lender could use to collect outstanding loans. It seeks to ensure that the borrower remains a dignified actor in the situation, one who hands over the required collateral deposit without overt compulsion, whose domestic threshold is a boundary that is not to be transgressed, and who is not to suffer excessively. Concrete, storylike situations illustrate this ideal, and Yahweh monitors societal justice by being the ultimate target of the gratitude or complaint of the needy. Verses 10–11 represent the main case about any neighbor; a subcase specifically concerning the poor continues in vv. 12–13. The main case concerns the integrity of the debtor's house; the subcase the return of essential pledges. In contrast to vv. 6 and 17, here the borrower hands the pledge over immediately as part of the loan agreement (note o).

Verses 10–18 as a whole are a restatement of Exod 22:20–23, 25–26 [ET 21–24, 26–27]. The main case about entering the debtor's house (vv. 10–11) is not present in Exodus, although the term "neighbor" derives from Exod 22:25 [ET 26]. However, the subcase in vv. 12–13 about the poor person plainly reflects Exod 22:25–26 [ET 26–27]: "you shall restore," "the sun goes down." The neighbor's negative cry in Exodus becomes the poor person's blessing, while the rhetorical question about the debtor sleeping in his or her cloak is converted into an outright prohibition of the creditor doing so. The concern that the sun not go down on this situation may reflect a deep-seated perception that things should be returned to a proper balance before the dark powers of chaos emerge (cf. Deut 21:23).

The law envisions the narrowly localized economic horizon of a single village or city. Verse 11 emphasizes the creditor's proper distance by repeating "outside" at the start and finish of the sentence. It remains unclear which party specifies what the pledge is to be. Verses 12–13 exhibit respect for human dignity and the needs of the debtor class. This person is undeniably "poor," at the lowest point of having to pledge something as basic as a cloak, something needed day and night. This item of collateral is labeled a "cloak" for the first time only in v. 13; v. 12 assumes the reader knows a standard association between the pledge of the poor and "cloak" and thus can fill in the blank (Amos 2:8; Prov 20:16; 27:13; Job 22:6). Presumably, "sleep in" was not meant literally, but as a powerful piece of rhetoric, perhaps reminding the reader that the well-off creditor has no real need for this garment.

The homiletical, emphatic style ("surely return," v. 13) hints that there is a real danger that this law will be ignored.[15] Probably for this same reason, the motivation offered is strongly theological. A "righteous deed" (*ṣĕdāqâ*) before Yahweh would be the opposite of the "sin" of 15:9 and 24:15. No doubt this is a reflex of the cultic formula by which a priest would declare a person righteous (cf. Gen 15:6; Ezek 18:9). Through their spoken blessings, the poor thus have an active role in determining the moral state of the propertied class (cf. Job 29:12–13; Prov 11:26; 22:9).[16] For the weak to be in a position to bless the powerful makes sense only if Yahweh is part of the equation. The importance of righteousness and the role of keeping the law as the path to it are also emphasized in Deut 6:25 and 16:20.

[14–15] These verses are integrally related to the previous law by means of the motifs of the sun going down and the appeal of the oppressed to Yahweh. Because hired workers were landless, temporarily employed, and not members of the employer's household, they were open to exploitation. In contrast, working conditions are to be fair and not abusive. The motivational language appeals to commonality: "your kindred," "your resident aliens" (cf. 5:14; 29:10 [ET 11]; 31:12), "your land," "your towns." The law starts with a brief, probably pre-Deuteronomic apodictic: "do not exploit a wage laborer." The word *śākîr*, "wage laborer," suggests a literary relationship of some sort to Lev 19:13b. Moreover, Mal 3:5 seems to allude to this law. The awkward phrase "poor and needy" gives the impression of being a secondary addition, perhaps suggested by the language of lament in v. 15 ("his life depends on it" is literally "he lifts up his soul on it"; cf. Pss 25:1; 86:4; 143:8). Verse 15 gives a concrete example of the more generalized v. 14. There is a double motivation. The first ("he is poor and his life depends on it"; cf. v. 6) appeals to human compassion. The second reverses the situation of v. 13 and reflects Exod 22:26b [ET 27b]. The cries of the oppressed would find concrete expression in the practice of lament, in which the distressed would call down imprecations on

15. Compare the Yabneh-yam letter, *ANET*, 568.
16. On the tradition history behind these notions, see R. Kessler, "Die Rolle des Armen für Gerechtigkeit und Sünde des Reichen: Hintergrund und Bedeutung von Dtn 15,9; 24,13.15," in *Was ist der Mensch . . . ?* (ed. F. Crüsemann et al.; Munich: Kaiser, 1992), 153–63.

their enemies (Pss 31:18–19 [ET 17–18]; 55:16 [ET 15]; 109:28–29; Jer 18:18–23).

[16] There is a catchword connection to *ḥēṭ'*, "sin," in v. 15. What is meant here, however, is a legal offense or "crime," not "sin" in a theological sense. This is a law of judicial procedure (cf. 17:8–11; 19:15; 25:1–3). The thrice-repeated passive formula denotes authorized, formal execution. Putting family members of a malefactor to death could stem from notions of collective guilt or as the punishment of a vicarious substitute for the actual offender.[17] In Deuteronomy intergenerational collective responsibility does not apply in jurisprudence, although it is still assumed to operate in the wider realm of divine-human relationships (5:9; 7:10). This law is cited and obeyed in 2 Kgs 14:6.

[17–18] These verses were inspired by Exod 22:20–21 [ET 21–22]. "Subvert justice" means to judge unfairly (see 16:19), something likely to result from prejudice against foreigners and the lack of economic influence on the part of the fatherless and widows. This triad of widows, fatherless, and resident aliens is the standard Deuteronomic catalog of marginalized people (10:18; 14:29; 16:11, 14). Providing justice for these groups was a recognized duty of kings and judges and was a frequent preoccupation of sages (Ps 72:1–4, 12–14; Exod 23:6; Prov 22:22), but in Deuteronomy it is something incumbent on every citizen addressed by the pronoun "you" (cf. 27:19). The topic of debt collateral continues from vv. 6, 10–13, but is applied specifically to the widow (v. 17). Although one might impound the garments of other debtors, that of a widow is to be exempt (cf. Job 24:3 for a widow's ox). Verse 18 may been seen as a general motivation for the entire "social torah" that falls between the brackets formed by vv. 8b–9 and v. 18. Israel's own experience with slavery is to be paradigmatic for its empathy for distressed groups (cf. v. 22). In Deuteronomy the expression "Yahweh redeemed you" (*pādâ*, "bought you free") is virtually a miniature creed with powerful social justice implications (cf. 7:8; 9:26; 13:6 [ET 5]; 15:15; 21:8).

[19–22] These laws are directly related to vv. 17–18 by the reappearance of the "marginal triad." An old custom of leaving agricultural produce behind is restated as a provision for social welfare. There are similar laws in Exod 23:10–11; Lev 19:9–10; 23:22. The three laws in vv. 19–22 are held together by a common structure: "when you . . . do not . . . it shall be for. . . ." They may have originally been connected as part of an earlier apodictic "farmer's code of conduct" along with 22:9–10 ("do not sow," "do not plow") and 25:4 ("do not muzzle"). Perhaps at an earlier period the unharvested bundle was customarily "forgotten" as tribute to some divinity or power.

---

17. For collective family punishment in Hittite law, see *ANET*, 207–8. LH 230, *ANET*, 176, provides that a builder's son be executed as a reckoning for a collapsed building.

These laws reflect the fundamental social division between landowners and the landless classes: aliens, the fatherless, and widows, along with daily wage earners (vv. 14–15). As a sort of "workfare," this practice would prevent the need for handouts or begging and preserve the dignity of the poor, as is evident from Ruth 2. "It shall be for" could be translated "it belongs to." This is not voluntary almsgiving; the poor have a legal right to access the three most important products of the land: grain, oil, and wine. This section should be read in concert with the laws of 23:25–26 [ET 24–25] that limit the communal right to eat from ripe vineyards and fields. Taken together, these two legal clusters strike a balance between the dissimilar perspectives of eater and owner, the general rights of all citizens over against the special rights of the needy, and the difference between harvestable produce and what is left over after harvesting. The motivation offered in v. 19 asserts that what is "forgotten" is no loss to the landowner, but rather a sort of "investment" leading to prosperity in future undertakings (cf. similar motivational arguments in 14:29 about the third-year tithe and 23:21 [ET 20] concerning loans). The motivational language of v. 22 is nearly equivalent to that of v. 18, forming a bracket around vv. 19–21.

Personal and Social Integrity
25:1–19

Corporal Punishment

25:1 If there is a dispute between persons and they present themselves for judgment, and they give them a judgment and declare[a] the one in the right to be right and the one in the wrong to be wrong, 2 and if the one in the wrong is to be flogged,[b] the judge shall make him lie down and be flogged in his presence, by number according to his offense.[c] 3 One may give him forty blows, but not more, lest in going on to flog him with more blows than these, your kindred be degraded in your sight.

The Threshing Ox

4 Do not muzzle an ox[d] while it is threshing.

Levirate Law

5 When brothers live together, and one of them dies and has no son, the wife of the dead man is not to marry outside with a stranger. Her husband's brother is to have intercourse with her and take her as wife and perform

the duty of a husband's brother for her. 6 The firstborn[e] that she bears shall perpetuate the name of his dead brother, that his name may not be wiped out from Israel. 7 But if the man does not desire to take his brother's widow as wife, then his brother's widow must go up to the elders at the gate and say, "My husband's brother refuses to perpetuate his brother's name in Israel. He is not willing to perform the duty of a husband's brother for me." 8 Then the elders of his city shall summon him and speak to him.[f] If he stands firm, saying, "I do not desire to take her as wife," 9 then his brother's widow shall approach[g] in the sight of the elders, pull his sandal off his foot, spit in his face,[h] and declare,[i] "This is what is done to a man who does not build up his brother's house." 10 In Israel his family name will be called "the house of one whose sandal was pulled off."

Immodest Intervention

11 If men quarrel together, man to man,[j] and the wife of one moves in to rescue her husband from the one hitting him and reaches out and seizes hold of his genitals,[k] 12 then you shall cut off her hand. Do not look with compassion.[l]

Commercial Honesty

13 Do not have in your bag alternate weights, one large and one small. 14 Do not have in your house alternate ephah measures, one large and one small. 15 You must have a full and accurate weight; you must have a full and accurate ephah measure,[m] so that you may enjoy long life in the land that Yahweh your God is going to give you. 16 For anyone who does these things, anyone who performs injustice, is repugnant to Yahweh.[n]

Remember Amalek

17 Remember what the nation of Amalek did to you on the way when you left[o] Egypt, 18 how it came upon you on the way and destroyed your rear guard,[p] all[q] who straggled behind you,[r] when you were exhausted and weary. It did not fear God. 19 When Yahweh your God has given you rest from all the enemies that surround you in the land that Yahweh your God is going to give you as a hereditary possession to take it over, you shall wipe out the memory of Amalek from under the sky. Do not forget!

a. The hip'il verbs describe "delocative" states based on a declaration, *IBHS* 24.2f, g.
b. Literally "a son of flogging" (cf. 1 Sam 20:31; 2 Sam 12:5).
c. The translation understands "by number" as the number of strokes appropriate for

the level of guilt. Alternate translation interpreting "by number" as describing the method of flogging: "flogged by count in his presence according to his offense." For contextual and exegetical reasons, the Greek translator adjusted this to "and you shall make him lie down in the presence of the judges and they shall flog him in their presence according to his offense. By number. . . ." Details in Wevers, *Greek Text*, 389–90.

d. The noun indicates an individual bovid without defining sex (*HALOT* 4:1452; cf. the plow animal in 22:10).

e. Follws MT *hbkwr*. OG offers *to paidion*, which according to the translators's practice equals *hbn*, "the son." Sam. (supported by a Byzantine LXX variant) conflates these two readings into *hbn hbkwr*, "the firstborn son." MT is preferable because the issue is not merely bearing offspring but producing an heir (cf. 21:15–17), while OG may be harmonizing to the "son" of v. 5.

f. "Speak to" in the directive sense of Gen 12:4; Exod 1:17; 23:22.

g. Follows OG (= LXX[B] 848) in not reading *'lyw*. MT supplements in order to clarify who is present for the following scene: "approach *him* in the sight of." "Approach" (*nāgaš*) indicates a formal legal procedure as in 25:1 (cf. Exod 21:6).

h. Alternate translation: "spit before him."

i. To "answer and say" is to make a solemn declaration (26:5; 27:14).

j. Literally "a man and his brother."

k. Follows Sam. *bbśrw*, literally "by his flesh" (cf. Exod 28:42). MT *bmbšyw*, "by his instruments of shame," is a euphemism. This is no accident. She "sends out her hand" and "grabs hold hard."

l. Follows MT (cf. 19:21). OG, Vulg., Syr. fill out with *'lyh*, "on her."

m. The balanced direct objects are in emphatic position so that vv. 13–15 form a satisfying poetic pattern.

n. Follows OG (= 848, OL, Philo). MT supplements with *'lhyk*, "your God."

o. OG and Vulg. have second person singular in agreement with the immediate context, and one is tempted to consider the plural of MT as a dittography of the following *m: bṣ 'tk[m] mmṣrym*. However, this particular expression seems to be standardized as plural (23:5 [ET 4]; 24:9; Josh 2:10).

p. That is, "attacked your tail"; cf. Josh 10:19.

q. Follows MT. The absence of *kl*, "all," in OG is probably a deliberate translational strategy.

r. Nip'al participle of *hšl*, a hapax legomenon. The meaning "stragglers" is suggested by an Arabic parallel (*HALOT* 1:362). In the Aramaic of Dan 2:40 the root means "crushed." Could this be a transposition of the root *hls*, "defeat," "weaken," used in Exod 17:13?

This seems to be a thoroughly miscellaneous concatenation of laws, although they generally embody the theme of integrity (as regards self-respect, the agricultural cycle, inheritance, sexual privacy and potency, commercial relations, and ethnic honor). Nevertheless, there are some indications of organization by topic and structural signals. Thus the importance of honor and shame as a motivation for proper behavior and a means for social control permeates vv. 1–3, 7–10, and 11–12. A unifying redactional pattern is visible in the parts of the body implied by successive laws: back in vv. 1–3, face in v. 4, face and foot in vv. 5–10, hand in vv. 11–12, perhaps testicles in the "stones" of vv. 13–16, and finally tail in vv. 17–19.[1] Another unifying pattern is bounded by the wordplay between *lō'-tahsōm*, "do not muzzle" (v. 4), and *lō'tāhôs*, "do not look with compassion" (v. 12). These verses bracket a concentric pattern: vv. 5 and 11 ("brothers together"; note j), vv. 6 and 10 (one's "name" in "Israel"), and vv. 7–9 in the center (intricately repeating "to take," "his brother's widow," "elders").[2] According to the theory that Deuteronomy has been edited to correspond to the order of the Decalogue, vv. 1–4 connect to false witness, vv. 5–12 to coveting another's wife, and vv. 13–16 to the last commandment.[3]

[1–3] This is a law of legal procedure like 19:15–21. It establishes a proper, equitable process for corporal punishment and protection from possible excesses. Flogging takes place after a proper hearing and is performed under the supervision of a local judge (cf. 16:18–20). It is to be appropriate to the offense and strictly limited.

The catchword *mišpāt*, "justice, judgment," links back to 24:17. There may also be a subtle allusion to the practice of beating olive trees (24:20), although a different verb is used. Two older casuistic laws seem to have been merged into one. At first glance, the structure seems to be that of a main case with protasis and apodosis (v. 1) followed by a subcase (v. 2). The main case would have required that true justice be given (cf. Amos 5:7; 6:12), without reference to punishment. In Deuteronomy's presentation, however, the main case is no longer of independent interest and exists only to introduce the topic of flogging. The "if . . . then" of v. 1 has become an "if . . . and," so that vv. 1–2a now function as a protasis for vv. 2b–3. This case starts as a private "dispute" (*rîb*) that has been taken into the juridical realm when the parties "present themselves" (*nāgaš*, "draw near"; note g). A plurality of adjudicators ("they") renders the verdict, but only one judge supervises the punishment. The makeup of the decision panel is unspecified because the important point is that a correct judgment has been given, not who has given it. The number forty is not intended as a fixed norm for all sentences, but rather the absolute maximum (i.e., "up to forty"). The motive clause urging moderation comes at the end of v. 3: the criminal is still your "kindred" ("brother") and is not to be shamed.

1. Westbrook, "Riddles in Deuteronomic Law," 173–74.

2. L. E. Eslinger, "More Drafting Techniques in Deuteronomic Laws," *VT* 34 (1984): 222–23. The levirate marriage law exhibits a lexical pattern using the same root seven times. The sequence *yābām* + the verb *ybm* pi'el + *yĕbāmâ* occurs in vv. 5–7a and again in vv. 7b-9, with a further occurrence of *yĕbāmâ* in the center of the pattern at the beginning of v. 7b. See G. Braulik, ""Die Funktion von Siebenergruppierungen im Endtext des Deuteronomiums," in *Studien zum Buch Deuteronomium*, 66–67.

3. Braulik, *Die deuteronomischen Gesetze*, 94–111.

[4] "Threshing" (i.e., "stamping on") may be a clever reference to flogging in vv. 1–3 and beating olive trees in 24:20. Perhaps this was originally part of a "farmer's code of conduct" mirroring the agricultural calendar: 22:9–10 (sowing, plowing), 24:19–21 (reaping), 25:4 (threshing). The law reflects an ethical principle of wisdom (Prov 12:10) and may be included at this point to inculcate a merciful stance toward the offender of vv. 1–3.[4] Another possibility is that it foreshadows the following levirate law as a denial of a rightful and appropriate benefit, or even as a wordplay involving "thresh" ("tread") and the sexual intercourse denied to the widow there.[5] This law should be understood in connection with other laws protecting the structures of life (14:21b; 20:19–20; 22:6–7) through which the natural world remains in proper balance. This draft animal (note d) that is now treading on the stalks or pulling a threshing sledge had earlier done the plowing for this grain (Prov 14:4), and the connection between goal-oriented act and its consequence is not to be frustrated (cf. Deut 20:5–7).[6]

[5–10] Deuteronomy's version of the levirate law diverges from the patterns reflected in Gen 38 and Ruth 2. In part this is because Deuteronomy is a reform law (rather than a folktale) and deals with a narrowly defined situation. The most important difference is that in Deuteronomy the surviving brother's responsibility is not mandatory, and public humiliation is the only penalty available to encourage compliance. This may reveal a breakdown in earlier, traditional family customs.

The primary effect of this law would be to preserve justice in the form of land tenure for the deceased husband. His "name" and "house" (family) are the primary considerations. His "name" appears three times (vv. 6–7) and is mirrored in the "countername" of v. 10; his "house" (v. 9) is highlighted over against the negative "house" of v. 10. More broadly, this law intends to stabilize the relationship of families with their ancestral property. Preserving family land tenure rights would also have the secondary effect of providing economic security and social status for the affected widow. The law upholds her opportunity to bear a son through surrogate fatherhood and thus gain access to the economic value of her former husband's patrimony.[7] However, it is important to note that the law makes no direct mention of inheritance, economic matters,

---

4. E. Nielsen, "You Shall Not Muzzle an Ox While It Is Treading out the Corn," in *Law, History, and Tradition*, 94–105.

5. C. M. Carmichael, "'Threshing' in the Book of Ruth," *ZAW* 92 (1980): 249–53.

6. For the premise that the laws in this chapter reflect narratives in the Pentateuch, specifically that this verse relates to Onan, see J. T. Noonan, "The Muzzled Ox," *Jewish Quarterly Review* 70 (1980): 172–75.

7. For confirmation that a childless widow could exercise control of an inheritance, see P. Bordreuil et al., "Deux ostraca paléo-Hébreux de la Collection Sh. Moussaïeff," *Semitica* 46 (1997): 49–76. That she could actually inherit it remains doubtful.

or the protection of the widow. It deals explicitly only with the future "rights" of the deceased to a lasting "name" and a secure "house." Whatever benefits the widow may receive are not mentioned.[8]

The main case is presented in vv. 5–6, followed by a subcase of refusal in vv. 7–10. The conclusions of each case share vocabulary: "his name," "his brother", "Israel." The law uses technical legal language:

> The *'îš zār*, "stranger" (v. 5), is a man outside the family circle of the "father's house" (Job 19:15).
> The noun *yābām*, "husband's brother," denotes "a brother-in-law with levirate responsibilities." As such he is in a position to carry out the associated denominative verb *ybm* pi'el (vv. 5, 7): "perform the duty of a husband's brother," "consummate a marriage as a *yābām*." Verse 5 defines this verb with two others: "have intercourse" (literally "come upon her," as in Gen 19:31 in a similar situation) and "take her as wife."
> The feminine form of the noun, *yĕbāmâ*, "brother's widow," indicates the woman who could be the direct object of the verb *ybm*.

"Perpetuate the name" (v. 6) is literally "stand up upon the name," perhaps implying "establish" or "represent" it, or even "succeed to" it. This may imply that the levirate practice was thought to benefit the dead man and his ancestors through Israel's cult of the dead.[9] Given the orthodox and reformist tendencies of Deuteronomy, however, it is better to understand what is meant in light of similar phrases in Ruth 4:5, 10, and Gen 48:6, which involve questions of inheritance. Thus "name" implies legal status in regard to inheritance, and loss of the inheritance entails loss of the "name" (Num 27:4). That the heir is explicitly a "son" (v. 5) means that the possibility of inheritance by daughters (Num 27:1–11; ch. 36) is not part of this law's horizon.

The main case (vv. 5–6) limits the application of the levirate to situations in which the brothers live "together," that is, as joint tenants of the whole of an as

---

8. Helpful studies include E. W. Davies, "Inheritance Rights and the Hebrew Levirate Marriage, Part 2," *VT* 31 (1981): 261–63; D. A. Leggett, *The Levirate and Goel Institutions in the Old Testament* (Cherry Hill, N.J.: Mack Publishing, 1974), 55–62; A. Viberg, *Symbols of Law: A Contextual Analysis of Legal Symbolic Acts in the Old Testament* (ConBOT 34; Lund: Almquist & Wiksell, 1992), 145–65. On Ruth, see J. A. Loader, "Of Barley, Bulls, Land and Levirate," in *Studies in Deuteronomy*, ed. García Martínez et al., 123–38. MAL A 30, 31, 33, 43, *ANET*, 182, may refer to institutions somewhat parallel to the levirate.

9. For background, see T. J. Lewis, *Cults of the Dead in Ancient Israel and Judah* (HSM 39; Atlanta: Scholars Press, 1989).

yet undivided property.[10] The implications of this situation are not completely clear. Could the living brother continue to control or even inherit the whole of the undivided property? It would seem that the deceased has no absolute right of inheritance to part of it and that his widow is particularly vulnerable. The surviving brother is free from any absolute duty to divide the property at some future point, for his deceased brother has no son. By refusing to engender such a son, he can remain in control of the whole inheritance. This law seeks to harness public opinion to restrain such an abuse, insisting that it would have negative implications "in Israel" (v. 10; cf. 22:19, 21).

In the subcase (vv. 7–10), the surviving brother refuses to do his customary duty. Levirate marriage must have been an unattractive option (cf. Ruth 4:6). It would eventually divide an inheritance that the surviving brother could otherwise control alone, requiring that he expend years of effort on property that another would ultimately inherit. The widow is to take two successive steps. First, she appeals publicly ("at the gate") to the elders and to public opinion. She appears on her own initiative as a legally competent plaintiff before the elders whose task it is to apply family law (19:12; 21:20; 22:15–18). She "goes up," as to a higher authority (Gen 46:31; Judg 4:5), and makes a double declaration. From the standpoint of her deceased husband, she asserts the surviving brother's unwillingness to perpetuate his name. Then from her own standpoint she declares in effect, "My *yābām* . . . is not willing to '*yābām*-ize' me." The language of the facts in v. 7a is nicely mirrored by her charge (v. 7b) and his response v. 8b: "not desire to take as wife . . . not willing to perform . . . not desire to take as wife." His resistance in v. 8 suggests that the elders are trying to talk him over (note f).

If this first effort fails, she "approaches" (*nāgaš*) her delinquent brother-in-law and performs a juridical act and solemn declaration with the elders as witnesses (vv. 9–10). The import of her removal of his sandal is open to several interpretations. (The scene in Ruth 4:7–8 in which one of the opposing male parties removes a sandal is very different and its relationship to what is going on here is obscure.) In part her act seems to be intended to humiliate him publicly. To be barefoot could be a sign of humiliation (2 Sam 15:30; Isa 20:2), and spitting is an act of dishonor (Num 12:14; Isa 50:6). Her statement unmistakably disgraces him as one who refuses to produce children for the family (for "build up a house," cf. Gen 16:2; 30:3; Ruth 4:11). What is more, this disgrace is to be enduring, for this man's family will have to bear the derisive nickname "the house of the unsandaled one."

Yet some sort of formal legal procedure also seems to be taking place.

---

10. This situation is in evidence in MAL B 2, 3, *ANET*, 185, and Laws of Eshnunna 16, *ANET*, 162. For the important difference between undivided and divided property, see MAL A 25 and 26, *ANET*, 182. A less likely interpretation is that they simply live near each other (Gen 13:6; 36:7).

Because stepping on ground can indicate a legal claim (Gen 13:17; Josh 1:3), this loss of a shoe could point to a negation of the man's claim to control his brother's property and a confirmation of the widow's right to enjoy the use of it, perhaps until she marries or dies. Another possibility is that this is an act of release. In pulling off the sandal, the widow may be releasing herself from any obligation to her husband's house and from her ongoing status as a potential levirate bride. Like the sandal, she is "untied" from her brother-in-law, and can now marry outside that family to a "stranger" (v. 5). Then again, the shoe could serve as a emblem of trampling, that is, of his marital domination over her (Pss 60:10 [ET 8]; 108:10 [ET 9]), and its removal would indicate the termination of his potential marital rights. Conversely, viewed from the man's perspective, this act can be seen as his release from any lingering obligation to marry her. Some interpreters suggest a concrete sexual symbolism involving his "foot" as a euphemism for his penis in her receptive sandal and consider the spitting symbolic of semen.[11] Although the ceremony itself remains ambiguous, her accompanying verbal declaration makes it perfectly and publicly clear that he has not had intercourse with her and does not intend to do his duty.

[11–12] The link to the previous law is verbal ("together," "brother" [note j], "wife") and topical (a woman disgracing a man not her husband). Similar concerns about redressing the effects of fighting are reflected in Exod 21:18–19, 22–25. A characteristic Deuteronomic concern emerges in that the combatants are called "brothers." As in the levirate law, the woman here is a legally recognized person whose motives are of interest and who is subject to retributive "mirror punishment." This loyal wife's motivations are completely honorable. She intends to rescue her husband "from the hand of" his opponent by sending out "her hand" (both *yad*). In recompense her "hand" (*kap*) is cut off. Her praiseworthy motive provides no justification; indeed the very circumstance that her admirable intentions simply do not matter underscores the inexcusable gravity of her offense. It is usual to understand laws with such a narrow focus as demonstrations of more general principles. The central theme seems to be that *any* case of assault by a woman on a man's genitals, no matter what the circumstances, must be punished without compassion.

Although common in surrounding cultures, this is the only mutilation punishment prescribed in the Hebrew Bible (apart from the nonspecific *lex talio-*

---

11. As a symbolic humiliating exposure of his genitals, this could then tie up to the following law. C. M. Carmichael, "Ceremonial Crux: Removing a Man's Sandal As a Female Gesture of Contempt," *JBL* 96 (1977): 321–36, proposes that the episode about Onan and Tamar shapes this law and that the muzzled ox of v. 4 connects to its motif of semen (seed). A more persuasive argument is made by P. A. Kruger, "The Removal of the Sandal in Deuteronomy XXV 9: 'A Rite of Passage'?" *VT* 46 (1996): 534–39, who understands this ceremony as a dissolution of a latent marriage by the man's performative statement in v. 8 and the woman's act in v. 9 that effects her transition to a new status as a free, marriageable woman.

nis formula). The severity of her punishment assails the sensibilities of the modern reader. However, this loyal wife has committed a grave boundary violation, trespassing into a zone of deep psychological anxiety on the part of the males who developed and enforced public law. Has her immodest act humiliated him? Has she endangered his capacity to procreate? By terming his genitals "that which provokes shame" (note k), the masoretic tradition interprets her offense as shaming him.[12] Because literal retribution (19:21) is impossible, she must suffer retribution by a removal of the offending body part. Perhaps this is a "mirror punishment by analogy" in that *yad*, "hand," can refer to male genitals (*HALOT* 2:387, §1e).[13] The text anticipates sympathetic resistance to this cruel procedure and adds a formulaic demand to show no pity (7:16; 13:9 [ET 8]; 19:13, 21).

[13–16] Weights and measures must be the same for buying and selling, and the mere possession of dishonest ones is an offense. Archeology shows that weights and measures were uneven and established by custom rather than government decree. Weights were kept in a pouch (Mic 6:11; Prov 16:11). Weighing out payment was a feature of the money economy that was encroaching on Israel's traditional modes of commerce, so it is not surprising that *kîs*, "weight pouch," is a loanword (*HALOT* 2:472) or that the prophets would condemn the potential for dishonesty in the procedure (Hos 12:8 [ET 7]; Amos 8:5; Mic 6:11). The heavier weight would be used to weigh the silver received when selling, and the lighter one to weigh what one would pay out when buying. The ephah volume measure would be the corresponding means of fraud in selling and buying grain.

Two traditional apodictic prohibitions (vv. 13–14) have been strengthened by a positive command (v. 15a) and motivations characteristic of Deuteronomy (vv. 15b–16). This is not just a law for merchants, for these prohibitions are addressed to all ("you"). The motivation is twofold: long life and the avoidance of becoming *tô'ēbâ* ("repugnant") to Yahweh. Verse 16a (literally "for repugnant to Yahweh is anyone who does these things") does not attach to the positive admonitions of v. 15, but rather to the apodictic negatives of vv.

12. For the role of shame in this law, see P. E. Wilson, "Deuteronomy xxv 11–12—One for the Books," *VT* 47 (1997): 220–35; V. H. Matthews, "Honor and Shame in Gender-Related Legal Situations in the Hebrew Bible," in *Gender and Law in the Hebrew Bible*, ed. Matthews et al., 100–102.

13. The body part that caused injury is the object of punishment in LH 195, *ANET*, 175. See MAL A 8, *ANET*, 181, for analogous retributions upon a woman who damages testicles in a fight: a finger for one, something worse for both, possibly her eyes or breasts. See S. M. Paul, "Biblical Analogies to Middle Assyrian Law," in *Religion and Law: Biblical-Judaic and Islamic Perspectives* (ed. E. Firmage et al.; Winona Lake, Ind.: Eisenbrauns, 1990), 335–39. For the suggestion that severing her *kap*, "hand," refers to a mutilation of her genitals (on the basis of Cant 5:5; Gen 32:26, 33 [ET 25, 32]) see K. Eslinger, "The Case of an Immodest Lady Wrestler in Deuteronomy 25:11–12," *VT* 31 (1981): 269–81.

13–14. This suggests that v. 15 represents a somewhat later supplement and that the awkward v. 16b ("anyone who performs injustice") was added to restore clarity. The implements of commerce are to be *šělēmâ* ("perfect, full") and *ṣedeq*, "righteous," that is, appropriate both to the system of weights and measures and to the requirements of social justice.[14] Proverbial wisdom also taught that unfair weights were *tô'ēbâ* ("repugnant") to Yahweh, for regulating them was something beyond the capacity of human authority (Prov 11:1; 16:11; 20:10, 23).[15]

[17–19] This call for permanent enmity against Amalek moves beyond the realm of community law to an apparently unconnected topic. These verses are often taken to be a later addition. Nevertheless, from a structural perspective this passage functions as a bracket along with 23:4–7 [ET 3–6] to enclose the various laws of chapters 23–25. Moreover, v. 19 repeats the theme and vocabulary of 12:9–10 concerning what Israel is to do when it experiences "rest from all the enemies that surround you." This repetition can be understood as forming a frame around the entire body of cultic and social laws in chapters 12–25.

The paired imperatives "remember" and "do not forget" bracket the passage as the first word of v. 17 and the last phrase of v. 19. Verse 18 picks up *badderek*, "on the way," from v. 17 and explains what happened. The rhetoric of v. 19 is striking: wipe out all memory of them, but always remember! For "wipe out," see 9:14; 25:6; 29:19 [ET 20] and the parallel verse Exod 17:14.

The call to remember and not to forget is characteristic of Deuteronomy (cf. 9:7). Israel has "unfinished business" with Amalek. Amalek is Israel's archetypal, traditional enemy, the desert raiders of Judg 6:33; 7:12; and 1 Sam 30, against whom the *ḥērem* must be practiced (1 Sam 15; cf. Esth 3:1; Ps 83:8 [ET 7]). Israel is to remember the tradition of a paradigmatic battle similar to, but not exactly equivalent to, the one narrated in Exod 17:8–16. The ethical horizon is universal, transcending narrow ethnic rivalries. Amalek committed a "war crime," a violation of universally accepted principles of war. In so doing, Amalek failed to exhibit that "fear of God" that is the common morality expected of all nations (Gen 20:11; Exod 1:17, 21; 18:21). For this reason, their memory is to be blotted out everywhere "under the sky."[16]

---

14. Overlapping systems are implied by the royal weight (2 Sam 14:26) and the sanctuary weight (Exod 30:13).

15. For a parallel, see Instructions of Amen-em-opet, chapter 16, *ANET*, 423. There may be a connection to the previous law through an association of weights (literally "stones") with testicles. There is some sort of literary relationship to Lev 19:35–36.

16. For interpretive implications, see M. Severin-Kaiser, "Gedenke dessen, was dir Amalek antat . . . : Auslegungen zu Ex 17,8–16 und Dtn 25,17–19," in *(Anti-)Rassistische Irritationen* (ed. S. Wagner et al.; Berlin: Alektor, 1994), 151–66.

Firstfruits and Tithes
26:1–19

Presenting Firstfruits

26:1 When you have come into the land that Yahweh your God is going to give you as a hereditary possession and you take it over and settle in it, 2 you must take some of the first of the fruit[a] of the ground, which you harvest[b] from your land[c] that Yahweh your God is going to give you, and put it in a basket and go to the place that Yahweh your God will choose to make his name dwell. 3 Go to the priest who is on duty at that time and say to him, "I proclaim today to Yahweh my God[d] that I have come into the land that Yahweh swore to our ancestors to give us." 4 The priest will take the basket from your hand and set it before the altar of Yahweh your God. 5 You must declare[e] before Yahweh your God: "My ancestor was a wandering Aramean.[f] He went down to Egypt and resided there as an alien, few in number.[g] There he became a great, powerful[h] and numerous nation. 6 The Egyptians treated us harshly and afflicted us and imposed hard labor on us. 7 Then we cried out to Yahweh, the God of our ancestors. Yahweh heard our voice and saw our affliction, our toil, and our oppression. 8 Then Yahweh brought us out of Egypt with a mighty hand and with an outstretched arm and great terror, and with signs and wonders. 9 He brought us into this place and gave us this land, a land flowing with milk and honey. 10 So now I bring the firstfruit of the ground that you have given me, O Yahweh." You are to set it[i] before Yahweh your God and bow down before Yahweh your God. 11 Then you are to rejoice over all the bounty that Yahweh your God has given you and your house, you[j] and the Levite and the resident alien who is among you.

Completing the Third-Year Tithe

12 When you have completed tithing the whole tithe of your produce in the third year, the year[k] of the tithe, and given it to the Levite, the resident alien, the orphan, and the widow, so that they may eat within your towns and have enough, 13 then you must say before Yahweh your God: "I have removed[l] the holy portion from the house and have given it to the Levite, the resident alien, the orphan, and the widow, according to your entire commandment that you commanded me. I have not transgressed or neglected any of your commandments: 14 I have not eaten any of it while in mourning. I have not

removed any of it while I was unclean. I have not offered any of it to the dead.[m] I have obeyed Yahweh my God. I have done just as[n] you commanded me. 15 Look down[o] from your holy dwelling place, from heaven, and bless your people Israel and the ground that you have given us, as you swore to our ancestors—a land flowing with milk and honey."

Conclusion to the Law

16 Today Yahweh your God is commanding you to perform these statutes and ordinances, so be careful to do them with all your heart and with all your being. 17 You have caused Yahweh to agree[p] today to be your God; and [for you] to walk in his ways, to keep his statutes, his commandments,[q] and his ordinances, and to obey him. 18 And Yahweh has caused you to agree today to be his treasured people, just as he promised you, and to keep his commandments; 19 to set you high above all the nations that he has made, in fame and renown and honor;[r] and for you to be a people holy to Yahweh your God, just as he promised.

a. Follows Sam. and OG (cf. v. 10). MT supplements with *kl* to read "every fruit."

b. For "bring" as "harvest" cf. 2 Sam 9:10; Hag 1:6. Alternate translation: "you bring" (to the sanctuary); cf. v. 10; 12:6, 11; 23:19 [ET 18].

c. Follows MT. OG lost *'šr tby' m'rṣk*, "which you harvest from your land," by homoioarchton from *'šr* to *'šr*. Or perhaps there was a very early inner-Greek haplography by homoioteleuton: *tēs [gēs sou (= hā'ădāmâ) apo tēs] gēs sou (= mē'arṣĕkā)*.

d. Follows OG *'lhy*, understanding that this personal offering to God entails a personal relationship (cf. v. 14). MT (supported by Sam., Vulg., Syr.) reads the more common "your God" by dittography: *'lhy[k] ky*.

e. To "answer and say" is to make a solemn declaration (21:7; 25:9; 27:14, 15).

f. The expression displays pleasing assonance, but is ambiguous. Was the ancestor "wandering, gone astray," or "about to perish, close to destruction"? The first option would refer to an unsettled or sojourner existence, a reference to a homeless way of life perhaps typified by an Aramean, something like our "gypsy." This is implied by the "fugitive Aramean" of an Assyrian royal inscription (*HALOT* 1:2). Otherwise it could refer to Jacob's travels in Aram (Hos 12:13 [ET 12]) or to the patriarchs' purported Aramean genealogy (Gen 24:4, 10; 25:20). In any case, "wandering" would coordinate with Jacob's dispossessed existence in Genesis and to the context of the promise and gift of land. "Perishing," in contrast, implies that Israel came to Egypt to avoid famine. The OG and Vulg. translations go their own ways, understanding the expression as a reflection of the historical hostility between Israel and Aram. S. Norin, "Ein Aramäer, dem Umkommen Nahe—ein Kerntext der Forschung und Tradition," *SJOT* 8 (1994): 87–104, considers the transitive understanding of the ancient versions as original: "an Aramean [= Laban] wanted to destroy my father [Jacob]."

g. The preposition *b* indicates identity (the *beth essentiae*), "being but a few"; cf. 28:62.

h. Not surprisingly, several witnesses add a supplementary "and": *w'ṣwm*, including OG. *BHS* note 5b is misleading. OG translated *gdwl* with *mega*, *w'ṣwm* with *kai plēthos* (*poly?*) and *wrb* with (*poly?*) *kai mega*. It was *kai mega* (= *wrb*) that was omitted by LXX[B] and the Byzantine tradition in order to avoid a repetition of *mega* (Wevers, *Greek Text*, 404–5).

i. "It" is a remote reference to the basket of vv. 2 and 4. The worshiper paradoxically replicates the priest's action of v. 4, using the same verb. Although this may be evidence of a merger of two forms of the ceremony in the growth of the text, the present form may be understood as a similar action performed twice.

j. Follows MT; all these formulaic "rejoice" lists begin with "you." OG does not witness *'th* "you," possibly the casualty of a very early inner-Greek haplography: *oikia sou*, [*sy*] *kai ho leuitēs*. NAB "you and your family . . . shall make merry" (*'th wbytk* instead of *lbytk 'th*) follows the majority tradition of LXX[B], but this is a secondary development and not the true OG (= LXX[A*]).

k. Follows MT, which vocalizes as *šĕnat*, "year of [tithing and given]." OG understands this as *šēnît* and does not have "and" before the verb, thus: "the second tithe you shall give." This resulted from an exegesis that sought to avoid the notion of a third tithe (E. Tov, *The Text-Critical Use of the Septuagint in Biblical Research* (Jerusalem Biblical Studies 3; Jerusalem: Simor, 1981), 77.

l. There may be wordplay between *b'rty*, "I have removed," and *'brty*, "I have transgressed," in v. 13b.

m. The translation implies food offerings to dead relatives (Ps 106:28; Tob 4:17). Alternate translation: "for a dead person," i.e., to furnish a meal in a house of mourning.

n. Follows OG and Syr. *'šr*. MT supplements (under the influence of v. 13?): *kkl 'šr*, "according to all."

o. "Look down here from above," i.e., spoken from the viewpoint of a lower perspective. The causative verb stem and the relation to derived words for "window frame" (1 Kgs 6:4; 7:4–5) imply "show yourself from your dwelling," "appear in the window frame" (2 Kgs 9:30) as in a theophany (cf. the theme in iconography, *ANEP*, no. 131). See *HALOT* 4:1645–46.

p. *BHS* suggests that vv. 17–19 are scrambled, but there is no evidence to support this. My translation takes the hip'il as causative in the sense of "induce someone to say" or less actively, "let stand/accept what someone says." One might translate "you have agreed to the declaration of Yahweh that" or "obtained Yahweh's agreement" (cf. NRSV). See T. C. Vriezen, "Das hip'il von *āmar* in Deut. 26, 17.18," *Jaarbericht van het Voorziatische-Egyptisch Gezelschap Ex oriente lux* 17 (1964): 207–10. Yahweh is the direct object in v. 17 and thus the one who pledges. The reverse is true in v. 18. A less complex alternate translation takes the verb stem as intensive: "you have proclaimed/affirmed" or "you have recognized Yahweh as" (REB; cf. NJPS, RSV). This would make the content of v. 17 the pronouncement of Israel and vv. 18–19 the declaration of Yahweh.

q. Follows MT. OG lost the second word of the list, skipping either *ḥq[yw wmṣwt]yw* or *wm[ṣwtyw wm]špṭyw*. Sam. dropped the third word by a similar process: *wmṣwt[yw wmšpt]yw*.

r. Follows MT in the order of these three items (supported by Sam., Vulg., Syr.). 4QDeut[c] and OG reverse the first and second terms. This translation applies these advantages to Israel (cf. 4:6–8). Alternate translation taking these as divine predications (cf. 10:21; Jer 13:11; 33:9): "to bring him praise and renown and honor."

Moses' promulgation of law ends as it began in chapter 12, with worship at the central sanctuary. Verses 1–11 and 12–15 establish two liturgical events, each with a declaration that reveals the significance of the ceremony it accompanies. These two units take the form of "ritual instruction": an introductory temporal clause (vv. 1 and 12) followed by instruction using the *waw* perfect. The first declaration uses the *waw* imperfects of narrative; the second uses perfects to indicate completed acts and avoidances. However, the real connection between the two ceremonies is not so much ritual similarity, but their use of liturgical oration to promote Deuteronomic theology. Both declarations take place "before Yahweh" and speak of the land of "milk and honey" as Yahweh's gift. Both advocate centralization. Even though firstfruits are to be given over to priests (cf. 18:4), they still must go to the central altar. Even though the third-year tithe supports the local poor, the declaration about it must still be made at the central sanctuary. The two ceremonies are also held together by the same chronological pattern as that of 14:22–27 (yearly) followed by 14:28–29 (third-year tithe).[1] In vv. 16–19 Moses returns to the "today" of his address and summarizes the character of the covenantal relationship being established.

[1–11] The firstfruits ceremony ties together important Deuteronomic themes: exodus, the gift of the land, the central altar, and social concern. It is introduced by a chronological marker like that of 17:14, which along with 19:1 and 12:29 section the law into four subdivisions.

At first sight, these harvest offerings appear to be identical with the annual tithe brought to the central sanctuary along with firstling animals and enjoyed by all (12:17–18; 14:22–27). Yet firstfruits, which are the earliest and best of the crop and a matter of personal selection (Hos 9:10), cannot be equated with tithes, which consist of a fixed percentage. These latter were associated with state taxation (1 Sam 8:17) and also paid to principal sanctuaries (Amos 4:4; Gen 14:20; 28:22). Firstfruits focus on the beginning of the harvest. Tithes focus on the end of the harvest, when the percentage can be calculated. Certainly only a fraction of a ten-percent tithe could have fit into a presentation basket. Moreover, the tithe of a crop is supposed to be eaten along with the animal firstlings, not relinquished to the sanctuary. In contrast, the firstfruits are the prerogative of the priests according to 18:4. This whole issue is further complicated by the freewill offering prescribed for Weeks (16:9–12), a ceremony connected with the firstfruits of grain elsewhere in the Pentateuch (Exod 23:16;

---

1. If one incorporates the seventh year of 31:9–13 into this pattern as the "today" of 26:16–19, the parallel chronological structure would also extend to the seventh year of 15:1–11; see Nielsen, *Deuteronomium*, 237–38.

34:22; Num 28:26). The use of a basket (and not just sheaves) suggests grapes and fruits are being offered, not just grain alone.

To cut through this impasse, the interpreter must recognize that Deuteronomy was more interested in promoting theology than in establishing a coherent liturgical system. Because theology took precedence, a certain amount of liturgical imprecision was acceptable. The text explicitly describes a "foundation" ceremony, undertaken at the time of the first harvest after entry. The primary goal is not to establish a recurring ceremonial obligation, but to convey the creedal declaration to the reader. For this purpose, firstfruits offered at the sanctuary would be a much more appropriate vehicle for the author than tithes consumed by the donor's household. Here firstfruits are explicitly the initial products of the newly given land (note the repetition of "of the ground" and "from your land" in v. 2), not simply the first or best of a variety of products (as in 18:4). Firstfruits may also appear here because the author had at hand an embryonic traditional declaration formula, which could then be expanded (specifically vv. 5 and 10a).

However, even though the firstfruits ceremony is explicitly described as an initial, foundational requirement, the most natural reading of the text must also assume the institution of an annual observance. This ceremony is built into the pilgrimage festival pattern by the wording of v. 2 (cf. 14:25; 15:20; 16:2, 11, 15) and into Deuteronomy's repeated communal celebrations by the wording of v. 11 (cf. 12:18; 16:11, 14). The previous use of the temporal formula of v. 1 in 17:14 also introduces an act that initiates a permanent institution. The contrast between the continuing rite of firstfruits and the clearly unique ceremony of chapter 27 is obvious (cf. "on the day you cross," 27:2). Contextually, then, one must understand this offering as a portion of firstfruits taken to the central place along with the annual tithe (or its monetary equivalent; 14:22–27) and brought to the sanctuary. One goal of the text is to underscore the exclusivity of the central sanctuary. Firstfruits may no longer be handed over locally at the start of harvest, but must be saved to become part of the tithe pilgrimage to the central sanctuary. The text seeks to clarify that the practice commanded in 18:4 is to be understood as a centralized procedure.

Structurally, two declarations (v. 3 and vv. 5–10) are each followed by an act of conveyance to Yahweh, first through the agency of the priest (v. 4) and then by the landowner directly (v. 10). Although some see vv. 3–4 as a later "correction" of the lay activity of v. 10 in accord with 18:4, in its present form the text uses these two actions as brackets for the creedal declaration, along with the repetition of "before Yahweh your God" (vv. 5a, 10b). The reader can make sense of the verbal doublet as two related actions. The priest "deposits" the offering as a gift near the altar; the donor "leaves it behind," stressing that it is not consumed in the celebration that follows. The first act shows a concern for limiting to priests any approach to the altar; the second closely associates the offering with the giver, who sets it "before Yahweh" and bows down "before Yahweh."

Before the first act of conveyance, the donor in v. 3 speaks to the priest "in office" (cf. 17:9; 19:17), and in so doing "proclaims to Yahweh" (root *ngd*, "overtly acknowledges") the fact of entry into the land. The creedal discourse that follows (vv. 5–10a) abounds in Deuteronomic expressions and seems to be a literary epitome similar to those of 6:20–25 and 11:2–7. Nevertheless, within this unmistakably Deuteronomic construct, a skeleton of older material remains visible in the "I" portions, that is, vv. 5a and 10a.[2] This is clearest in the alliterated "wandering Aramean" phrase of v. 5,[3] for by Deuteronomic times such an expression would have been derogatory.[4] This core of inherited material provided the basic plot movement of the declaration, moving from a precarious existence in v. 5a to the enjoyment of the fertile land in v. 10a. This embryonic plot has been filled out with elements of the national story from Num 20:15–16 (see below), enriched with Deuteronomic language. The result is that Israel's reversal in circumstances takes place explicitly because of the actions of Yahweh. What is included is only what fits this central contrast between "then" and "now": residence as aliens, oppression, exodus, the gift of the land. There would be no point in including the Red Sea, Sinai, or the wilderness in such a

2. L. Rost, "Das kleine geschichtliche Credo," in *Das kleine Credo und andere Studien zum Alten Testament* (Heidelberg: Quelle & Meyer, 1965), 11–25. It is widely agreed that von Rad's influential thesis of an ancient creedal outline cannot be sustained; see von Rad, "The Form-Critical Problem of the Hexateuch," in *The Problem of the Hexateuch and Other Essays* (trans. E. W. Trueman Dicken; London: SCM, 1984), 1–78. It is still possible to speak of a "short historical credo," but only as a Deuteronomic theological summary. H. F. Fuhs, "Aus der Befreiung Leben: Erwägungen zum geschichtlichen Credo in Dtn 26,1–11," in *Schrift und Tradition: Festschrift für Josef Ernst* (ed. K. Backhaus and F. Untergaßmair; Vienna: Schöningh, 1996), 3–18, proposes an exilic author who sets a recollection of an older cultic ritual into a family-oriented framework, later supplemented by vv. 2–4 in order to return the text to cultic usage. J. C. Gertz, "Die Stellung des kleinen geschichtlichen Credos in der Redaktionsgeschichte von Deuteronomium und Pentateuch," in *Liebe und Gebot*, ed. Kraft and Spieckermann, 30–45, concludes that the author is a later Deuteronomist who knew and sought to correct the P source. D. R. Daniels, "The Creed of Deuteronomy xxvi Revisited," in *Studies in the Pentateuch*, ed. Emerton, 231–42, follows von Rad in finding a premonarchic creed behind the present text. For a similar position, see G. Wassermann, "Das kleine geschichtliche Credo (Deut 26,5ff.) und seine deuteronomische Übermalung," *Theologische Versuche* 2 (1970): 27–46.

3. The literature on the "wandering" or "perishing Aramean" (note f) is extensive. For the primary issues, see M. A. Beek, "Das Problem des aramäischen Stammvaters: Dt 26,5," *OtSt* 8 (1950): 193–212; and E. Lipiński, "Mon Père était un Araméen errant: l'histoire, carrefour des sciences bibliques et orientales," *OLP* 20 (1989): 23–47. J. G. Janzen, "The 'Wandering Aramean' Reconsidered," *VT* 44 (1994): 359–75, opts for "perishing from hunger."

4. Cf. Amos 1:3; A. R. Millard, "A Wandering Aramean," *JNES* 39 (1980): 153–55. C. M. Carmichael, "A New View of the Origin of the Deuteronomic Credo," *VT* 19 (1969): 273–89, explains "Aramean" with reference to Num 20:14–16. N. Krausz, "*Arami oved avi*: Deuteronomy 26:5," *Jewish Bible Quarterly* 25 (1997): 31–34, proposes that Abraham is meant.

portrayal. The basic format is that of the lament and thanksgiving Psalms: past predicament (vv. 5–6), cry (v. 7a), hearing (v. 7b), and deliverance (vv. 8–9).

This creedal thanksgiving prayer moves from national history to the farmer's present situation, linking current agricultural prosperity to Yahweh's past acts of deliverance. The individual "I" of the present (vv. 5 and 10) surrounds the communal "we" of the past (vv. 6–9). The contrast between then and now is pointed. The nameless ancestor's insecure state as a landless resident alien with a small household makes him a paradigm of someone without prospects or opportunity. Yet in spite of that, he becomes numerous and powerful (7:1; 9:14). Our oppressive slavery was a dead end; all we could do was cry out. Yet in spite of that, Yahweh liberated us and brought us to the land. God makes no appearance in the negative episodes of vv. 5–6, but after an appeal is made in v. 7, Yahweh becomes the verbal subject and the overriding actor in a history of salvation. The repeated key words are *nātan*, "give," and *bô'*, "come in/bring." Yahweh has made all the difference with "hand" and "arm" (4:34; 5:15; 7:19; 11:2), "great terror" (4:34; 34:12; Exod 14:24; 15:14–16), and "signs and wonders" (Deut 6:22; 28:46; Exod 4:21).

The text provides a pleasing rhetoric of threes. There are three initial *alephs* in the identification of the ancestor in v. 5a, followed by three verbs describing what he did and three adjectives for the sort of nation he became. In v. 6 the Egyptians do three things. In v. 7 the three verbs "cried," "heard," and "saw" are followed by three direct objects with first-person plural possessive suffixes. In vv. 8–9 Yahweh "brought out," "brought," and "gave" by means of "hand and arm," "terror," and "signs and wonders." Verses 9–10 cohere nicely through "he brought . . . he gave . . . land" and "I bring . . . ground . . . you have given." The writer almost certainly used Num 20:15–16 (E?) as a model for vv. 5–8. The same six verbs occur in the same sequence, expanded in Deuteronomy at points to make up a rhythm of threes. Deuteronomy characteristically leaves out the angel of Num 20:16.[5]

In v. 5 language typical of Abraham (cf. Gen 12:10; 18:18, both J) expands the Aramean Jacob so that he grows into a collective representative of all the patriarchs. "Place," *māqôm*, in v. 9 is open to two interpretations. Is this the sanctuary where the speaker stands (the standard usage in Deuteronomy)? Or does this refer to the land as a whole (cf. the "place of the Canaanites" in Exod 3:8)? The latter understanding seems to fit better with context and purpose. The "resident alien" of v. 11 appears as a reflex of Israel's history in v. 5.

5. N. Lohfink, "The Small Credo of Deuteronomy 26:5–9, in *Theology of the Pentateuch*, 265–89; trans. of "Zum 'kleinen geschichtlichen Credo,' Deut. 26,5–9," in *Studien zum Deuteronomium I*, 263–90. For theological analysis, see idem, "Dtn 26:5–9: Ein Beispiel altisraelitischer Geschichtstheologie," in *Studien zum Deuteronomium I*, 211–62; and S. Kreuzer, "Die Exodustradition im Deuteronomium," in *Das Deuteronomium und seine Querbeziehungen*, ed. Veijola, 99–101.

The text intends to unify the events of national history in terms of Yahweh's saving action and to concretize them in the fertility of the land. The farmer offers physical evidence of what has been proclaimed, a "bringing" (v. 10) that confesses Yahweh's "bringing in" (v. 9). Fertility is centered firmly on Israel's history with Yahweh, perhaps as a way of devaluing competing, problematic ceremonies or ideologies of fertility. As in its presentation of Passover and Weeks, Deuteronomy turns the focus away from the fecundity of agricultural seasons and processes to the sphere of history (16:1–8, 12).

[12–15] The tithe of the third year reiterates the themes of rich land and social concern from vv. 1–11 and adds to this the theme of obedience to the law. This centralized declaration would provide some measure of central control over practices involved with the local tithe for the poor. Although the third-year tithe (14:28–29) was not taken to the sanctuary, it was still something holy. It had to be kept apart from unclean persons and forbidden activities. Deuteronomy uses an older tithe declaration in vv. 13–14 to integrate the third-year tithe with the central sanctuary and the fertility of the land.

The declaration is made after the separation and distribution of the tithe of various crops harvested at different times have been finished (v. 12). The explanatory phrase, "the year of the tithe," may be intended to clarify that years three and six of the cycle are intended. From a social and communal perspective, these would be the years most impacted by the practice of tithing. The list of beneficiaries is identical to that of 14:29. "Within your towns" emphasizes that the tithes themselves remain at home. In the context of Deuteronomy, "before Yahweh" (v. 13) can only mean at the central sanctuary. The one who pays the tithe is personally involved in both separation and distribution as an active "I" and the "me" whom Yahweh has directly commanded. Repetition stresses the importance of total obedience. "Entire command" refers back to 14:28–29 and links to the comprehensive compliance of "you have completed" in v. 12 and the summary of the declaration in v. 14b.

A pre-Deuteronomic affirmation of ritual innocence (cf. 21:7; Ps 26:4–5) can be traced in the verbal chain and partitive *min* prepositions within vv. 13–14: "I have removed from . . . I have not transgressed any of . . . I have not eaten any of it . . . I have not removed any of it . . . I have not offered any of it." These concerns point to potential misuses of the tithe that transcend Deuteronomy's horizon of social benefit and deal instead with issues of proper ritual behavior. The tithe had to be "removed" from one's house because it was a holy thing and not for personal use (cf. 22:9). "Transgress" is probably part of the old formula because of its wordplay (note l). Touching such holy food while involved with a dead body during mourning or while in some other unclean state was illicit. Offering it to dead ancestors (see note m) or using it as a meal in a house of mourning (Hos 9:4; Jer 16:5–9) would also bring the holy tithe into contact with ritual impurity. Verse 15 concludes the declaration with an appeal for a beneficent theophany from Yahweh's heavenly observation post (note o; Ps 102:20 [ET 19]) and for a fertility blessing implicitly connected to heavenly rain. The notion is similar to that of 11:11–12, 14–15. For Deuteronomy it is Yahweh's oath and Israel's obedience to social welfare legislation that brings fertility, not the ritual concerns hinted at in v. 14. This blessing falls not only on the "ground," but upon Yahweh's "people," a key word that connects forward to the next paragraph.

[16–19] This paragraph is a framing device that links Deut 6–11 and 12–26 with chapter 28. These verses conclude the law begun in chapter 12, forming a frame with 11:32–12:1 ("today," "statutes and ordinances," " be careful to do"). "Today" restates the dramatic setting of Moses' address that, along with the concept of covenant, points forward into chapters 27–30. The language also shows a return to the concerns of the parenetic chapters 6–11. Thus v. 16 speaks of "heart and being" (4:29; 6:5; 10:12; 11:13). Verse 17 offers "walk in his ways" (8:6; 10:12; 11:22) and the threefold designation of the law (5:31; 6:1; 7:11; 8:11; 11:1). Verses 18–19 utilize the image of a treasured and holy people, which image appears in 7:6 (and 14:2, 21). At the same time, the language of "careful to do" and "obey" (vv. 16–17) points forward to the framing verses of chapter 28 (cf. 28:1, 2, 13, 15, 45). This is also true of "set high above all the nations" and "holy people" (v. 19 and 28:1, 9).

The nucleus of this complex pattern of reciprocal commitment and mutual interrelationship is the so-called covenant formulary as set forth in 29:12 [ET 13] and Hos 2:23 [ET 21].[6] The word "covenant," however, is not used. That notion will emerge explicitly only in Deut 28:69 [ET 29:1]). Characteristically, Deuteronomy expands this relationship formula in the direction of keeping the law.

Each party has made a solemn declaration of the covenant relationship. At the heart of this mutual declaration is the relationship between Yahweh as Israel's "God" and Israel as Yahweh's "people." This basic formula has been filled out into a double declaration that is both poetic and intricately reciprocal. Both partners are fully involved in the language of both declarations. Each party induces the other to make a commitment or (less strongly) accepts the verbal commitment of the other (note p). In each declaration the subject of the first infinitive is the speaker, but then the subjects of the succeeding infinitives shift around (cf. Exod 5:21; Deut 6:1, 24). Perhaps this grammatically recursive usage is intended to reflect the role of Moses as mediator between the parties.

6. R. Rendtorff, *The Covenant Formula: An Exegetical and Theological Investigation* (trans. M. Kohl; Edinburgh: T. & T. Clark, 1998), 5–14, 22–26; trans. of *Die Bundesformel: Eine exegetisch-theologische Untersuchung* (SBS 160; Stuttgart: Katholisches Bibelwerk, 1995), 9–20, 27–31. Such reciprocal relational declarations probably derive from the sphere of adoption and marriage (2 Sam 7:14; Jer 31:9; Hos 2:4 [ET 2]).

The agreement formula is bilateral, but the partners' relationship is inherently that of nonequals: God and the people of that God. The responsibilities of each party are interwoven with those of the other. Each party asserts its own role and the responsibilities connected to that role, but also the effect of this agreement on the other party. In v. 17 the main action is that of Yahweh, who agrees to be Israel's God, but the consequent actions are those of Israel. The status of having Yahweh as God means obedience. In vv. 18–19 the focal point is the agreement of Israel, yet election and promise are acts of Yahweh. Yahweh's role of having a people involves keeping promises and raising Israel to international eminence. Israel's status—both as a treasured people and as a holy people—rests on Yahweh's promise (*kaʾăšer dibber* repeated in v. 18 and v. 19; is the reference Exod 19:5–6?). The verb "to be" is explicit in both assertions: Yahweh exists as "God for you"; Israel exists as "people for him." Taking the two declarations together, Yahweh commits to bring about and maintain the relationship of God and people ("treasured," "promised," "set high," "holy") and Israel commits itself to obey the law ("walk," "keep," "obey").[7]

A Ceremony of Commitment at Shechem
27:1–26

Moses and the Elders Commanded

27:1 Then Moses and the elders of Israel commanded the people[a] saying: Keep[b] the entire commandment that I am commanding you today. 2 On the day you cross the Jordan into the land that Yahweh your God is going to give you, you are to set up large stones and coat them with plaster. 3 You must write on them all the words of this law, when you have crossed over in order to go[c] into the land that Yahweh your God is going to give you, a land flowing with milk and honey, just as Yahweh the God of your ancestors promised you.[d] 4 When you have crossed the Jordan, you must set up these stones, about which I am commanding you today, on Mount Ebal,[e] and you shall coat them with plaster. 5 You shall build an altar there to Yahweh your God, an altar of stones on which you have not wielded an iron tool. 6 You must build the altar of Yahweh your God with unhewn stones[f] and offer on it burnt offerings to Yahweh your God, 7 and sacrifice peace offerings and eat them there and rejoice before Yahweh your God. 8 You shall write on the stones all this law,[g] making it thoroughly plain.[h]

7. N. Lohfink, "Dt 26,17–19 und die 'Bundesformel,'" in *Studien zum Deuteronomium I*, 211–62.

Moses and the Priests Spoke

9 Moses and the Levitical priests spoke to all Israel, saying: Be silent and hear, O Israel! Today you have become[i] the people of Yahweh your God. 10 Obey Yahweh your God and perform his commandments[j] and his statutes that I am commanding you today.

Moses Commanded

11 Moses commanded the people that day, saying: 12 These shall stand for blessing the people[k] on Mount Gerizim when you have crossed the Jordan: Simeon, Levi, Judah, Issachar, Joseph, and Benjamin. 13 And these shall stand for the curse on Mount Ebal: Reuben, Gad, Asher, Zebulun, Dan, and Naphtali.

14 Then the Levites must solemnly declare[l] to all Israel[m] in a loud voice:

15 'Cursed be anyone who makes an idol or cast image, something repugnant to Yahweh, the handiwork of an artisan, and sets it up in secret.' And all the people are to say, 'Amen!'

16 'Cursed be one who treats his father or mother with contempt.' And all the people are to say,[n] 'Amen!'

17 'Cursed be one who displaces his neighbor's boundary marker.' And all the people are to say, 'Amen!'

18 'Cursed be one who leads astray a blind person on the road.' And all the people are to say, 'Amen!'

19 'Cursed be one who perverts justice for the resident alien, the orphan, and the widow.' And all the people are to say, 'Amen!'

20 'Cursed be one who lies with his father's wife, because he has uncovered the skirt of his father.'[o] And all the people are to say, 'Amen!'

21 'Cursed be one who lies with any animal.' And all the people are to say, 'Amen!'

22 'Cursed be one who lies with his sister, the daughter of his father or the daughter of his mother.'[p] And all the people are to say, 'Amen!'

23 'Cursed be one who lies with his mother-in-law.'[q] And all the people are to say, 'Amen!'

24 'Cursed be one who strikes down[r] his neighbor in secret.' And all the people are to say, 'Amen!'

25 'Cursed be one who takes a bribe to strike down a life, innocent blood.'[s] And all the people are to say, 'Amen!'

26 'Cursed be that one who does not uphold the words[t] of this law to do them.' And all the people are to say, 'Amen!'

a. Follows MT. OG lacks 't-h'm, "the people." However, the absolute use of the verb "command" is very rare, and the phrase "Moses commanded [direct object], saying," serves as a structuring formula in these last chapters (27:11; 31:10, 25).

b. The infinitive absolute used as an imperative could appropriately be translated as a plural (as OG, Vulg., Syr.). Sam. does read a plural imperative, but the singular of MT is preferable as more difficult. 4QDeut^c and OG expand what follows into "*this* entire commandment."

c. This translation treats entering the land as a consequence of crossing over. An alternate translation, understanding entrance as a result of obediently writing the law: "When you have crossed over, write all the words . . . in order to go into the land" (cf. NAB). This is supported by the masoretic punctuation, which signals a sharp break between "when you have crossed over" and "in order to." Yet another possibility is to end the sentence at "this law" and start a new one with "When you have crossed over" (cf. NJPS).

d. OG expands this verse with formulaic language at several points: "write on *the stones . . .* crossed over *the Jordan . . .* Yahweh the God *of your ancestors* is going to give. . . ."

e. Follows MT and Josh 8:30. The Samaritan tradition substitutes "Gerizim." Samaritan texts show strong sectarian tendencies (E. Tov, *Textual Criticism of the Hebrew Bible* [Minneapolis: Fortress Press, 1992], 94–95), while such influences in MT are minimal. Thus it is unlikely that "Ebal" is an anti-Samaritan reading as suggested by *BHS*.

f. A double accusative: the object made preceded by an "accusative of material," *IBHS* 10.2.3c. There is wordplay between these *šĕlēmôt*, "unhewn [stones]," and *šĕlāmîm*, "peace offerings," in v. 7.

g. Follows OG, which does not reflect *dbry*, "words of," although it translates this phrase fully elsewhere in Deuteronomy (except 17:19). MT has expanded to match 27:3 (31:24) and the standard formula.

h. The two infinitives absolute are used as adverbs, the second intensifying the first (*GKC* 113k): "clearly and carefully."

i. *Hāyâ* with the preposition *l* can mean to enter into a stated relationship with someone (cf. 26: 17, 18; 29:12 [ET 13]). The nip'al with *l* is found only here in the Hebrew Bible, perhaps implying "you were caused to become" or "you have let yourself become."

j. Follows the plural of the Qere along with Sam. and the ancient versions. Kethib: "his commandment."

k. The relationship of the two tribal groups to the two actions is unclear. (1) Does each group *proclaim* either a blessing or curse? This alternative is supported by the natural reading of *lĕbārēk* (v. 12a) as an infinitive of purpose, "to bless the people," and the circumstance that *'āmad 'al* (v. 13a) can mean "stand to supervise" the curse (Num 7:2; 1 Sam 19:20; cf. *'al* as "with regard to," Gen 41:32; Ruth 4:7). (2) Or are the two groups recipients or audiences for blessing and curse pronounced by others? This would take *lĕbārēk* as "for the blessing of the people" and v. 13a as "stand for the curse." This alternative corresponds better to vv. 14–25 and to the staging of this event in Josh 8:33. The phrase about the curse may be less explicit because it is a euphemistic circumlocution.

l. That is, "answer and say" (cf. 21:7).

m. The phrase *'îš yiśrā'ēl* is a collective expression for the assembled nation (Josh 9:6, 7; Judg 8:22; 20:11; 21:1; 1 Sam 11:8).

n. Sam. and OG present this verb as plural in vv. 16–25 (cf. v. 15 MT). 4QDeut^c has the plural in v. 26.

o. That is, invade the father's marital privacy and compromise the protection he has provided his wife in marriage (cf. 23:1 [ET 22:30]; Ruth 3:9; Ezek 16:8).

p. Follows both MT and OG (= LXX^A). The Greek translation *ek patros ē mētros* renders MT correctly and elegantly, even though it does not expressly reproduce either occurrence of *bt*, "daughter." LXX^B secondarily dropped the prepositions, ending up with "sister of father or mother" = "aunt," which is the reading cited by *BHS*.

q. The feminine participle of *ḥātan*: "she who has taken him as son-in-law."

r. Perhaps stronger: "slay" (21:1; Exod 21:12).

s. This curse condemns accepting a payment or gift that leads to the murder of an innocent person. Alternate translation assuming a bribe in a juridical setting: "in the case of the murder of an innocent person."

t. Follows MT. Sam. and OG supplement with *kl*, "all," to fill out the usual formula: *'t-kl-dbry*, "all the words of." *BHS* note 26b is incorrect and should read G $^{-min}$.

It is widely agreed that this chapter intrudes between chapters 26 and 28. The focus shifts abruptly to a different time ("the day you cross" rather than the "today" of 26:16, 18, and 28:1) and place (Shechem, not Moab). The speech of Moses is interrupted by a temporary return to narrative (vv. 1, 9, 11), something that is ignored when Moses begins to speak again in 28:1. Deuteronomy's sequence of covenants (previously at Horeb, today at Moab) is complicated by the appearance of Shechem out of chronological order as a third locale. Moreover, the constituent pieces of chapter 27 fit together poorly. The transitions are abrupt between the installation of stones at Shechem in vv. 1–8, the admonition of vv. 9–10, the division of the tribes (back at Shechem!) in vv. 11–13, and the responsive liturgy of vv. 14–26. Only vv. 9–10 carry on the theme of 26:16–19 directly.

Nevertheless, chapter 27 is redactionally associated with previous material. The speech of Moses and the elders concerning obedience (vv. 1–8) is connected to the declaration of the covenant made in 26:17 ("today," "keep the covenant," 27:1). The speech delivered by Moses and the priests about becoming Yahweh's committed people (vv. 9–10) alludes to the declaration of 26:18–19 ("today," "people of Yahweh"; also "obey" from 26:17). Probably the first supplementary material added to the end of chapter 26 was vv. 9–10. Later vv. 1–8 were also added, with v. 1 serving to anchor this speech to 26:17. Verses 11–13 were added in order to provide an explicit fulfillment of 11:29–30. Finally the twelve curses of vv. 14–29 became attached to vv. 11–13 by the associative notions of "twelve tribes" and "curse."[1]

1. A. E. Hill, "The Ebal Ceremony as Hebrew Land Grant?" *Journal of the Evangelical Theological Society* 31 (1988): 399–406, proposes that the chapter is a unified text, constructed on the model of a royal land grant ceremony (Babylonian *kudurru*).

These directives to erect stones and to bless and curse at Shechem reflect the topic and wording of 11:29–30 to form a bracket for the whole of chapters 12–26. Deuteronomy 27:1–8, 11–13, and 14–26 each seeks to unpack what is required in 11:29–30, but do so according to three different "scripts." Verses 1–8 focus on inscribing the law, vv. 11–13 on setting the blessing and curse, and vv. 14–26 on the content of the curse.

There has been much speculation that an older ceremony performed at Shechem stands in the background of this chapter (cf. Gen 33:18–20; 35:2–4).[2] This Shechem tradition was supposedly in competition with a similar ceremony practiced at Gilgal, with the consequences of their competition visible in the literary history of this chapter. The Gilgal tradition is thought to appear in vv. 2–3, 8, which focus on what is to be done immediately upon crossing the Jordan (cf. Josh 4–5). The competing Shechem tradition would then be represented by the altar and sacrifices on Mount Ebal in vv. 4–7 (cf. Josh 8:30–35; Josh 24). Certainly confusion (or competition) between the respective roles of Shechem and Gilgal is visible in the geographical ambiguity of 11:29–30. Shechem and Gilgal were obviously important cult centers, but there is no solid evidence for the existence of competing traditions centered at these shrines.

This chapter presents (in a disjointed way) a ceremony intended to found a new society. A parallel may be found in ceremonies that marked the founding of Greek colonies.[3] The central theme is continuity in transition. Even though Moses will not cross the Jordan River, the words of the law will (vv. 3, 8). The law will continue, in written form, to guide Israel's new existence. Elders (v. 1) and priests (vv. 9, 14) will replace Moses. Israel will renew in the new land ("on the day," v. 2; "when you have crossed," v. 4) its covenant decision for obedience made "today" in Moab (vv. 1, 9, 10; cf. v. 11).

[1–8] This is obviously a composite text. Moses gives what is essentially the same command twice, first in vv. 2–3 and then redundantly in vv. 4, 8: "when you cross the Jordan . . . set up stones . . . coat . . . write." The first instance (vv. 2–3) is more Deuteronomic in language and the stones are set up on the very day of crossing. This might suggest a site somewhere near the Jordan rather than Shechem. The second formulation (vv. 4, 8) mentions Mount Ebal explicitly, a site too far from the Jordan to reach "on the day you cross."[4] This suggests a later revision interested in pinpointing the locale of this action at Shechem. Finally, a

---

2. Notably E. Nielsen, *Shechem: A Traditio-Historical Investigation* (Copenhagen: Gad, 1959), 86–141; idem, *Deuteronmium*, 245–46. In my opinion, Josh 8:30–35 is completely dependent on the present form of Deut 11:26–29 and 27:1–13. In addition, Josh 24 is a theological and literary construction rather than a remnant of an old liturgical script; see Nelson, *Joshua*, 117–19, 265–73.

3. M. Weinfeld, "The Emergence of the Deuteronomic Movement: The Historical Antecedents," in *Das Deuteronomium*, ed. Lohfink, 76–98.

4. This inconsistency has influenced the text transmission of Josh 8:30–35; see Nelson, *Joshua*, 116–17.

third element, the requirement for an altar and sacrifice set forth in vv. 5–7, interrupts this second command regarding stones, creating some confusion about which stones are to be inscribed (cf. Josh 8:32). The insertion of vv. 5–7 seems to reflect a melding of separate traditions, one involving a stele and one an altar.[5]

The phrase "entire commandment" (v. 1) refers not only to all of chapters 12–26, but also to what Moses is about to say. As Israel's new future without Moses comes into view, "elders" now appear at key moments (29:9 [ET 10]; 31:9, 28; cf. 5:23). Inscribed steles were a standard way of permanently publicizing a text, but the use of plaster outdoors would seem to undermine durability. Use of this technique may intend to communicate that the Shechem arrangement was to be temporary. Plaster may also imply easy readability ("thoroughly plain") or speed of execution ("on the day"). The erection of stones was also a way of marking entrance into new territory (Gen 28:18, 22; 35:14, 20; Josh 4). That the stele and altar are erected on what v. 13 will identify as the mountain for the curse (cf. 11:29) is not an issue for v. 4 (note e).

Verses 5–7 are similar to the "altar law" of Exod 20:24–25, but use Deuteronomic language: "altar of Yahweh" (12:27), "offer on it burnt offerings" (12:13–14), "eat there" (e.g., 12:7), "rejoice before Yahweh" (e.g., 12:18). These verses are secondary to their current context, connected to the previous verse by the ambiguous "there" of v. 5 (Ebal? across the Jordan?). Use of explicitly Deuteronomic language creates tension between this altar at Shechem and the central altar promoted in the rest of Deuteronomy. Is it possible that the addition of vv. 5–7 was intended to promote Shechem as the central sanctuary or to undermine the axiom of a single sanctuary? In any case, Josh 8:30–35 (DH) shows that a very early reader had no trouble interpreting this altar as a transitory pre-Shiloh (cf. 1 Kgs 2:27) arrangement, one that did not undercut the principle of centralization. Deuteronomy 12:10–11 makes clear that centralization at the designated place was to follow achievement of "rest" in the land, not merely passage across the Jordan.[6]

Verse 8 generates some confusion with its reference to "stones." These can hardly be the altar stones of vv. 5–7, but must point back past those intervening verses to the standing stones of vv. 2–4. In the final form of the text, v. 8

---

5. For the interlocking geographical and critical problems of this text, 11:29–30, and Josh 8:30–35, see E. Noort, "The Traditions of Ebal and Gerizim: Theological Positions in the Book of Joshua," in *Deuteronomy and Deuteronomic Literature*, ed. Vervenne and Lust, 161–80. He judges vv. 4, 8 (placing the event at Ebal) to be the oldest text, with vv. 5–7 inserted later. He sees vv. 2–3 as an even later transfer of the ceremony to the time and place of the crossing at Gilgal (cf. 11:30). R. P. Merendino, "Dt 27:1–8: Eine literarkritische und überlieferungsgeschichtliche Untersuchung," *BZ* 24 (1980): 194–207, finds the original text (from the time of Hezekiah) in vv. 1a, 3b, 5a, 7, a subsequent addition in vv. 5b-6; a Josianic rewrite in vv. 2b-3a, 8; another addition in v. 4; and finally a "Deuteronomist" in v. 1b and a few other places.

6. N. Naʾaman, "The Law of the Altar in Deuteronomy and the Cultic Site Near Shechem," in *Rethinking the Foundations: Historiography in the Ancient World and in the Bible* (ed. S. McKenzie and T. Römer; BZAW 294; Berlin: de Gruyter, 2000), 141–61, proposes that the Shechem altar

brackets together the two topics of standing stones and stone altar by means of a resumptive repetition of vv. 2b–3a ("stones . . . write . . . law" repeated as "write . . . stones . . . law"). Verse 8 may have originated as a summary recapitulation of vv. 2–4 composed to facilitate the insertion of vv. 5–7 or as part of a connected earlier whole consisting of vv. 4 and 8, broken in half by the interpolation of vv. 5–7. In addition, v. 8 may seek to correct any potential misunderstanding caused by the introduction of an altar into the Shechem ceremony. The standing stones are not to be considered the sort of pillars (*maṣṣēbôt*) one builds beside an altar, which are prohibited by 16:21–22.[7] "Make plain" translates the same verb that describes the task of Moses in 1:5.

[9–10] These verses form a rhetorical bridge between 26:16–19 and 28:1, following the same repetitive technique visible in 5:32–6:1 and 11:31–12:1. "Today," "people of Yahweh," and "perform" in 27:9–10 repeat the language of 26:16–19, while 27:10 parallels the use of "obey Yahweh your God . . . perform his commandments . . . that I am commanding you today" in 28:1. At the same time, as an appeal for attention these verses provide an introduction for the two ceremonies that immediately follow.

In the midst of a portrayal of the future ceremonies that are to take place at Shechem, the reader is reminded of the "today" of Moab. That looming future will lack Moses, but the Levitical priests join him as an element of continuity (cf. the elders of v. 1; 31:9). Here the priests are labeled in the usual Deuteronomic way (17:9, 18; 18:1; 24:8; contrast v. 14). A call for silence sets up an expectation for a liturgical event (Hab 2:20; Zech 2:13), one that eventually leads into the proclamation of blessings and curses in chapter 28. However, first vv. 11–13 and 14–26 intervene with further instructions about the future.

[11–13] Moses again speaks about "when you have crossed the Jordan" (cf. vv. 2, 4), commanding the roster and position of the tribes for blessing and curse. These commands give more concrete detail to the indefinite directive of 11:29. Verses 11–13 are more likely to be a scribal construction composed for this context than a genuine ceremony derived from earlier tradition. The connection between vv. 11–13 and vv. 14–26 is oblique. The latter verses offer only curses (without blessings) and portray the entire people responding as a unity to what the Levites declare. In v. 12 the tribe of Levi is simply one tribe among the twelve; in v. 13 the Levites occupy center stage.

---

represents an attempt by exilic scribes to replace Jerusalem as the central sanctuary. The requirement that the altar stones be "unhewn" (literally "complete") is based on the notion that any alteration that compromised completeness would profane what had to be holy. See S. M. Olyan, "Why an Altar of Unfinished Stones? Some Thoughts on Ex 20,25 and Dtn 27,5–6," *ZAW* 108 (1996): 161–71.

7. M. A. Fishbane, *Biblical Interpretation in Ancient Israel* (Oxford: Oxford University Press, 1985), 161–62.

The greener Mount Gerizim on the south (right) makes sense as a locus of blessing; the more barren Ebal is on the inauspicious north (left). It is not entirely clear why the tribes are split as they are. The Gerizim group consists of the central tribes of Judah and the hill country of the northern kingdom; the ones on Ebal are the peripheral Galilee and east-of-Jordan tribes.[8] In 11:29 the blessings and curses are "set on," that is, directed upon (Gen 28:4; Josh 15:19) the two mountains. Here the groups take their stand on the mountains, but the nature of their assigned task is unclear (note k). Verses 12 and 13 are asymmetrical in a way that emphasizes the blessing. Only blessing has an expressed direct object; an abstract noun expresses the curse rather than the more dynamic infinitive verb used for the blessing.

[14–26] The Levites—in the absence of Moses—will lead the ceremony on the other side of the Jordan. This responsive liturgy provides the entire people with an opportunity to agree to obedience (cf. v. 26). In addition, the liturgy gives specific content to the "curse on Mount Ebal" (v. 13). These curses intend to discourage misdeeds through the threat of divine sanction. Similar curses used to dissuade behavior within the community occur in Judg 21:18 and 1 Sam 14:24. In effect, the responsive "amens" convert these twelve imprecations into self-curses (cf. Num 5:22; Neh 5:13). Essentially they function as a series of apodictic prohibitions.[9] They proscribe behaviors that would bring about an accursed state, and as such differ from the curses of chapter 28, which describe the consequences that would result from disobedience.[10]

Most of this list deals with infractions that would be hard for the community to discover or to control with legal punishments. The prohibited deeds are explicitly "secret" (vv. 15, 24) or the sort of behavior carried out in private (vv. 16, 17, 20–23, 25). The perpetrator of v. 18 would be hard to discover. On the other hand, there seems to be nothing particularly surreptitious about v. 19. Most of these offenses are dealt with elsewhere in the legal corpus as prohibitions, often as capital crimes.[11] By affirming these curses with an "amen," the community separates itself from these behaviors and thus protects itself from

8. H. Seebass, "Garizim und Ebal als Symbole von Segen und Fluch," *Bib* 63 (1982): 22–31, proposes that the blessing group represents the tribes incorporated into Josiah's expanded kingdom, while the curse tribes were considered "lost."

9. G. Wallis, "Der Vollbürgereid in Deuteronomium 27:15–26," *HUCA* 45 (1974): 47–63, proposes the original setting as an oath taken when young men become full citizens. A Hittite "Soldiers' Oath" (*ANET*, 353–54) offers a functional parallel.

10. For this distinction, see P. Buis, "Deutéronome 27:15–26: Malédictions ou exigences de l'alliance?" *VT* 17 (1967): 478–79, who points out that these are not the sort of curses expected from v. 13 but really a proclamation about the requirements of the covenant with a catechetical purpose.

11. E. Bellefontaine, "The Curses of Deuteronomy 27: Their Relationship to the Prohibitives," in *Song of Power*, 256–68. Also H. Schulz, *Das Todesrecht im Alten Testament* (BZAW 114; Berlin: Töpelmann, 1969), 61–71.

the consequences of transgressions it cannot control or even discover. Retribution is fixed squarely and exclusively on the unknown perpetrator so that the power of curse does not endanger the people as a whole. The law of 21:1–9 illustrates this same concern over undiscovered transgression. A liturgy of self-cursing would also have the effect of deterring any hypocritical agreement to the obligations of Deuteronomy by those harboring secret reservations (cf. 29:17–18 [ET 18–19]). From a theological perspective, this list of curses means that Yahweh's will extends even into the hidden places of life. From a redactional standpoint, it provides a balancing companion piece for the Decalogue, so that the two lists bracket the parenesis and law code of chapters 6–26.

The first and last curses (vv. 15, 26) appear to be secondary to an older core list of ten. These bracketing curses use the relative pronoun and imperfect; the inner ten use the participle format instead. Moreover, v. 26 is unmistakably a summary. It is possible to trace five pairs in the ten central curses: family and inheritance (vv. 16–17), social welfare (vv. 18–19), sexuality (vv. 20–21 and 22–23), and "strike down" (vv. 24–25).[12] Perhaps there is also a concentric structure, with the relationship to Yahweh (vv. 15, 26) framing social relationships (vv. 2–5 and 10–11), and sexual relationships occupying the central position (vv. 6–9). This ten-item list consists of older, inherited material. Although v. 19 sounds typically Deuteronomic, the oppressed triad of alien, orphan, and widow already appears in the Covenant Code (Exod 22:20–21 [ET 21–22]).[13]

The topic of idolatry (v. 15) is stressed by being in first position and by an emphatic grammatical format (*'îš 'ăšer*; "anyone who"). The bare curse is supplemented by commentary. Such an idol is "something repugnant (*tô'ēbâ*) to Yahweh," like child sacrifice (12:31; cf. 7:25–26). Moreover, it is simply a manufactured object. The "treat with contempt" of v. 16 (*qlh*) is the opposite of the honor (*kbd*) of 5:16 and is illustrated by 21:18–21. The topic of v. 17 appears in prohibitive form in 19:14 (cf. Prov 23:10; Instruction of Amen-em-opet, ch. 6, *ANET*, 422). Such encroachments could be effected by legal chicanery, not just by clandestine relocation. For the concern of v. 18, see Lev 19:14; the blind could not witness such an offense. The need for vv. 20, 22–23 would have been occasioned by the temptations of a multigenerational, polygamous family. An apostate worship practice may lie behind v. 21. The parallel text, Exod 22:18 [ET 19], is the only sexual offense in the Covenant Code and is set in a context of apostasy. The "in secret" of v. 24 could refer to an undiscovered assailant (21:1–9), to deliberate murder misjudged as an accident, or to a stealthy ambush

---

12. H. Gese, "Der Dekalog als Ganzheit betrachtet," *ZTK* 64 (1967): 129–30.

13. For the classic attempt to restore an older list see A. Alt, "The Origins of Israelite Law," in *Essays on Old Testament History and Religion* (trans. R. A. Wilson; Garden City, N.Y.: Doubleday, 1966), 147–48; trans. of "Die Ursprünge des israelitischen Rechts," *Kleine Schriften I* (Munich: Beck, 1953), 313–14.

(Ps 10:8–9). The recipient of the bribe in v. 25 is also undefined: a judge (16:19), a false witness, or a hired assassin? For "innocent blood," see 19:10; 21:8. Verse 26 along with v. 3 form an inclusio ("the words of this law") unifying the whole Shechem event and connecting it to the law code of Deuteronomy in its entirety. Although "words of this law" could refer merely to the words engraved on the plastered stones (as in v. 8 MT), elsewhere this is an all-inclusive reference to the whole Deuteronomic law (17:19; 28:58; 29:28 [ET 29]; 31:12, 24; 32:46). For "uphold the words" (literally "cause to stand up") see 1 Sam 15:11; Neh 5:13 (cf. 2 Kgs 23:3, 24).

Blessings and Curses
28:1–68

Blessings If You Obey

28:1 If you obey completely Yahweh your God, being careful to do all his commandments that I am commanding you today, Yahweh your God will set you high above all the nations of the earth. **2** All these blessings will come upon you and overtake you, if you obey Yahweh your God: **3** You will be blessed in the city and you will be blessed in the field.

4 Blessed will be the fruit of your womb, the fruit of your ground, and the fruit of your cattle,[a] the offspring of your herd, and the fertility of your flock. **5** Blessed will be your basket and your kneading bowl. **6** You will be blessed when you come in and you will be blessed when you go out.

7 Yahweh will cause your enemies that attack you to be routed before you; they will come out against you one way, but by seven ways flee before you. **8** Yahweh will command blessing for you in your barns and in all your undertakings, and he will bless you in the land that Yahweh your God is going to give you. **9** Yahweh will establish you as his holy people, just as he swore to you, if you keep the commandments of Yahweh your God and walk in his ways. **10** All the peoples of the earth will see that the name of Yahweh has been pronounced over you, and they will be afraid of you. **11** Yahweh will cause you to abound in prosperity, in the fruit of your womb, in the fruit of your cattle, and in the fruit of your ground in the land that Yahweh swore to your ancestors to give you. **12** Yahweh will open for you his rich storehouse, the heavens, to give rain for your land in its season and to bless all your undertakings. You will lend to many nations, but you will not borrow. **13** Yahweh will make you the head, and not the tail. You will only be at the top, and not at the bottom, if you obey the commandments of Yahweh your God that I am commanding you today, being careful to do them, 14 and if you do not deviate right or left from all the words that I am commanding you today, by following other gods to serve them.

Curses If You Do Not Obey

15 But if you do not obey Yahweh your God by being careful to do all his commandments and his decrees that I am commanding you today, then all these curses will come upon you and overtake you: 16 You will be cursed in the city and you will be cursed in the field. 17 Cursed will be your basket and your kneading bowl. 18 Cursed will be the fruit of your womb and the fruit of your ground, the offspring of your herd and the fertility of your flock. 19 You will be cursed when you come in and you will be cursed when you go out.

20 Yahweh will send upon you cursing, panic, and rebuke[b] in all your undertakings that you do, until you are destroyed and quickly perish,[c] because of the wickedness of your deeds in forsaking me. 21 Yahweh will cause pestilence to cling to you until it[d] has exterminated you from the land that you are going in to take over. 22 Yahweh will strike you with consumption, inflammation, and fever, with feverish heat and drought,[e] with desiccation and yellow mildew. They will pursue you until you perish.[f] 23 The sky over your head will be bronze, and the earth under you iron. 24 Yahweh will make the rain of your land into powder and dust; it will come down on you from the sky until you are destroyed.[g] 25 Yahweh will cause you to be routed before your enemies; you will go out against them one way but by seven ways flee before them. You will become an object of horror to all the kingdoms of the earth. 26 Your corpses will become food for the birds[h] of the air and the animals of the earth, with no one to frighten them off.

27 Yahweh will strike you with the boils of Egypt, with swellings,[i] festering eruptions, and itch, from which you cannot be healed. 28 Yahweh will strike you with madness, blindness, and confusion of mind. 29 You will be groping[j] around at noon as the blind grope about in darkness, and you will not succeed in finding your way, but be exploited and robbed constantly, with no one to rescue. 30 You will become engaged to a woman, but another man will have sex with her.[k] You will build a house, but not live in it. You will plant a vineyard, but not make use of it. 31 Your ox will be slaughtered[l] in your sight, but you will not eat of it. Your donkey will be stolen in front of you, but not be returned to you. Your flock will be given to your enemies, with no one to rescue you. 32 Your sons and daughters will be given to another people while you look on. Your

eyes will wear out[m] looking for them all day long, but you will be help-
less.[n] 33 A people whom you do not know will eat up the fruit of your
ground and all the product of your labor. You will be exclusively and constantly exploited and ground down. 34 You will be driven mad by the
sights your eyes will see.

35 Yahweh will strike you with severe boils on the knees and on the
legs from which you cannot be healed, from the sole of your foot to the
crown of your head. 36 Yahweh will remove you and your king whom you
set over you to a nation that neither you nor your ancestors have known.
There you will serve other gods of wood and stone. 37 You will become
an object of horror,[o] a proverb, and a word of taunt among all the peoples
to which Yahweh will lead you. 38 You will take much seed out into the
field but gather little in, for the locust will consume it. 39 You will plant
vineyards and cultivate them, but you will not drink wine nor gather in,[p]
for the worm will eat it. 40 You will have olive trees throughout all your
territory, but you will not anoint yourself with oil, for your olives will
drop off. 41 You will have sons and daughters, but they will not remain
yours, for they will go into captivity. 42 Crickets will take over all your
trees and the fruit of your ground. 43 The resident alien among you will
rise above you higher and higher, while you sink lower and lower. 44 He
will lend to you but you will not lend to him. He will be the head and you
will be the tail.

Because You Did Not Obey

45 All these curses will come upon you, pursue you, and overtake you
until you are destroyed, because you did not obey Yahweh your God, to
keep his commandments and his decrees that he commanded you. 46 They
will be a sign and a portent against you[q] and your descendants forever.

47 Because you did not serve Yahweh your God in joy and gladness of
heart for the abundance of everything, 48 you will serve your enemies
whom Yahweh will send against you in hunger and thirst, in nakedness
and in lack of everything.[r] He will put an iron yoke on your neck until he
has destroyed you. 49 Yahweh will raise up against you a nation from far
away, from the end of the earth, just as an eagle swoops down—a nation
whose language you do not understand, 50 a stern-faced[s] nation who have
no respect for the old or pity for the young. 51 It will eat up the fruit of
your cattle and the fruit of your ground until you are destroyed. It will not
leave you grain, new wine, or fresh oil, the offspring of your cattle or the
fertility of your flock, until it has caused you to perish. 52 It will besiege
you in all your towns until your high and fortified walls come down, in
which you trusted in your whole land. It will besiege you in all your

towns in your whole land[t] that Yahweh your God has given you. 53 You
will eat the fruit of your womb, the flesh of your sons and daughters
whom Yahweh[u] has given you, in the siege and pressure that your enemy
has pressed on you.[v] 54 The most sensitive and pampered man among you
will look coldly on his brother, his dear wife, and the last of his children
who remain, 55 not giving to any of them some of the flesh of his children
that he is eating, because he has nothing else left in the siege and pressure that your enemy has pressed on you in your towns. 56 She who is the
most sensitive and pampered among you, so pampered and sensitive that
she would not venture to set[w] the sole of her foot on the ground, will look
coldly on her dear husband, her son, and her daughter, 57 and on her after-
birth that comes out from between her legs, and her children that she
bears, because she is eating them in secret in total deprivation, in the siege
and pressure that your enemy has pressed on you in your towns.

Plagues and Exile

58 If you are not careful to do all the words of this law that are written in
this book, to fear this glorious and awesome name: "Yahweh your God,"
59 then Yahweh will inflict astonishing plagues on you and your offspring,
severe and long-lasting plagues and malignant and long-lasting diseases.
60 He will bring back upon you every disease[x] of Egypt of which you were
afraid, and they will cling to you. 61 Also every other disease and plague
that are not written in the book of this law Yahweh will bring upon you
until you are destroyed. 62 You will be left few in number instead of being
as many as the stars of the sky, because you did not obey Yahweh your
God. 63 And just as Yahweh took delight in making you prosperous and
numerous, so Yahweh will take delight in causing you to perish and
destroying you. You will be torn out of the land that you are going in to
take over. 64 Yahweh will scatter you among all peoples, from one end of
the earth to the other, and there you will serve other gods that neither you
nor your ancestors have known, gods of wood and stone. 65 Among those
nations you will not find repose and there will not be a resting place for
the sole of your foot. There Yahweh will give you a trembling heart, failing eyes, and a despondent spirit.[y] 66 Your life will be hanging before you;
you will be in dread night and day, and you will not be assured of your
life. 67 In the morning you will say, "If only[z] it were evening!" and at
evening you will say, "If only it were morning!"—because of the dread
of your heart that you will feel and the sights of your eyes that you will
see. 68 Yahweh will bring you back to Egypt in ships by a route that I had
said to you you would not see again; and there you will offer yourselves for
sale to your enemies as male and female slaves, but there will be no buyer.

a. Follows MT. OG lost "the fruit of your cattle" by homoioteleuton: *'dm[tk wpry bhm]tk.*

b. Three general expressions introduce the concrete calamities that follow, "sent" by Yahweh as one might send an agent. "Panic" refers to the confusion sent by the Divine Warrior (7:23; 1 Sam 5:9, 11; Isa 22:5). "Rebuke" implies the concrete effects of Yahweh's angry shout (see A. Caquot, "*gā'ar*," *TDOT* 3:49–53). For the generic article with these abstractions (and in vv. 21–22), see *IBHS* 3.5.1g.

c. In the masoretic tradition, "destroy" and "perish" are nip'al and Qal infinitives construct with pronomial suffixes. Sam. instead has third-person active perfects with God as the actor: "he destroys you" and "he causes you to perish." OG translated both verbs in accordance with Sam., as did Syr. and Vulg., but this does not necessarily indicate a text different from MT. Sam. uses active forms at v. 22 (*'bd*) and vv. 24, 45, 51, 61 (*šmd*), and the Greek translator follows the same strategy at those points (translated with a doublet in v. 24; not present in v. 51).

d. Alternate translation: "he."

e. Masoretic tradition vocalizes *ḥrb* as "sword" (followed by OG "slaughter"). Probably *ḥōreb*, "drought," is intended (Vulg.).

f. Follows MT in reading as an infinitive construct with pronomial suffix. Sam., OG, Syr. reflect a finite verb, "until they destroy you."

g. This respects the masoretic punctuation. Alternate translation: "powder, and dust will come down on you from the sky."

h. Follows Sam., OG, Syr. MT expands with *kl*: "every bird."

i. The Kethib is preferable: *'plym* ("bumps," "swellings"). Qere *ṭḥrym* is explanatory, characterizing more specifically as "anal tumors, hemorrhoids," as in 1 Sam 6:11, 17. See *HALOT* 2:374, 861. OG takes up the Qere tradition with "Egyptian boils in the seats."

j. The participle indicates a future progressive, *IBHS* 37.7.1b. The blind person gropes in the darkness of his or her disability, not in the actual absence of light. The "way" is metaphorical: you will not have success (Josh 1:8; Judg 18:5).

k. The Kethib is preferable: *yšglnh*, "violate, ravish her" (supported by 4QDeut^c, OG, Syr.). Considered obscene, it is always softened by the Qere *yškbnh*, "lie with her," supported by Sam. (*yškb 'mh*), Vulg., Targ. Ps.-J.

l. Participles of imminent future, *IBHS* 37.6f.

m. As in Lev 26:16. Alternate translation: "You will cry your eyes out," i.e., "your eyes will run out [of tears]"; cf. Lam 2:11. Cf. v. 65.

n. Literally "the deity [i.e., power] of your hand will not be"; cf. Gen 31:29; Mic 2:1.

o. Follows MT *lšmh*. Sam. gives as *lšm*, "as a [notorious] name." OG *ekei* is not a dittography (as *BHS* suggests) but a double translation of the last word in the verse intended to link back to the previous verse.

p. Alternate translation: "store it up." The Greek translator failed to understand this rare word and translated contextually with a reflection back to wine: "you will not be merry from it."

q. Alternate translation: "among you."

r. Verses 47 and 48a are nicely balanced: "serve Yahweh . . . in joy . . . abundance of everything" versus "serve your enemies . . . in hunger . . . lack of everything." This correlation indicates that *taḥat 'ăšer* at the start of v. 47 is primarily intended to point forward to give the reason for what v. 48 threatens. However, *taḥat 'ăšer* may also simultaneously point backward as the reason for v. 46. For the meaning "because," cf. 21:14; 22:29. Alternate translation of the beginning of v. 47: "Instead of serving" (cf. v. 62; *HALOT* 4:1723). Perhaps one should translate the end of v. 47 as "by reason of the abundance."

s. Literally "harsh of face." This is explained by a proverbial formula in v. 50b (cf. Isa 13:18b) and links up nicely with "have respect for," which is literally "lift up the face of."

t. Follows MT. OG skipped over "your whole land": *bkl-š'ry[k bkl-'rṣ]k*. Could v. 52b be a dittography or alternate reading for parts of v. 52a? In any case, v. 52b now functions as a flashback, repeating events before the conclusion of the siege reported in v. 52a in order to introduce vv. 53–57.

u. Follows OG (see Wevers, *Text History*, 55). MT adds "your "God." In these curses, the divine name occurs without further modifier whenever Yahweh is the actor; see J. W. Wevers, "Yahweh and Its Appositives in LXX Deuteronomium," in *Studies in Deuteronomy*, ed. García Martínez et al., 269–80. Sam. omits the explicit subject entirely.

v. There is wordplay involving *māṣôr*, "siege," and *māṣôq*, "pressure," with the root of the latter word continued by the verb "press" (*ṣwq*; cf. vv. 55, 57). This same refrain occurs in Jer 19:9.

w. The infinitive *haṣṣēg* serves as a complement to or the object of the verb "venture" (*nsh* pi'el; *IBHS* 35.5.4b; Williams, *Syntax*, 203).

x. The preferred, more difficult text is MT and OG: the singular *mdwh* taken as a collective (cf. "they will cling"). The plural *mdwy*, "diseases" (Sam., Vulg., Syr., Targ., with substantial support from Hebrew MSS), is a secondary clarification.

y. Alternate translation: "dry throat": M. I. Gruber, "Hebrew *da'ăbôn nepeš* 'Dryness of Throat,'" *VT* 37 (1987); 365–69. On "eyes," cf. v. 32, note m.

z. A fixed expression (5:29) for a wish; see Williams, *Syntax*, §547.

Moses recounts the consequences of obedience and, especially, disobedience in excruciating detail, ranging thematically from narrow household concerns to national annihilation. Curses (and to a lesser extent blessings) as a motivational element were common to both ancient law codes and treaties. Deuteronomy 28 exhibits parallels to the epilog of the Laws of Hammurabi (*ANET*, 177–80) and the Sefire treaty (*ANET*, 659–60). The remarkable correspondence in sequence between vv. 26–33 and VTE 39–42, the combination of motifs shared by vv. 23–24 and VTE 63–64, and the thematic order common to vv. 20–44 and VTE 56 make it certain that Deuteronomy depends here on Assyrian treaty documents.[1] The disorder, doublets, and "internal conclu-

1. This offers nearly conclusive evidence that a form of Deuteronomy that included most of ch. 28 emerged in the period of Assyrian ascendancy over Judah. See R. Frankena, "The Vassal-Treaties of Esarhaddon and the Dating of Deuteronomy," *OtSt* 14 (1965): 122–54; H. U. Steymans, "Eine assyrische Vorlage für Deuteronomium 28:20–44," in *Bundesdokument und Gesetz*, ed. Braulik, 119–41; idem, *Deuteronomium 28 und die Adê zur Thronfolgeregelung Asarhaddons: Segen und Fluch im Alten Orient und in Israel* (OBO 145; Freiburg: Universitätsverlag, 1995). VTE is readily accessible in *ANET*, 534–41. The standard edition is S. Parpola and K. Watanabe, *Neo-Assyrian Treaties and Loyalty Oaths* (State Archives of Assyria 2; Helsinki: Helsinki University Press, 1988), 28–58.

sions" of these parallel documents should discourage overly detailed attempts to reconstruct the literary history of Deut 28. Nevertheless, it is likely that duplications in both Assyrian and Israelite examples arose from the reuse of earlier texts.[2]

Much of the content of Deut 28 is thoroughly Yahwistic (vv. 9, 36, 60, 64, 68), so chapter 28 should be seen as a scribal reworking of borrowed political curse material for theological purposes. As was the case with blessings and curses in treaties and law codes, this catalog intends to motivate obedience. Curses and threats outnumber blessings because deterring infractions was the primary goal. Blessings are also brief or nonexistent in comparative ancient texts.[3] Repetition is not necessarily a sign of compositional growth, but was intended to reinforce the rhetorical impact. The sequence of the individual items seems to be almost entirely arbitrary. Threats of defeat and exile are not necessarily evidence of exilic composition, but represent a customary theme in comparative curse literature. The narrative preparation for this list occurs in 27:9–10. At the same time, there is also a redactional connection between vv. 1b-2 and 26:16–19.[4]

This extended catalog of blessings and curses is a self-conscious scribal production and the result of a complex process of growth. The blessings of vv. 1–14 have been coordinated with the much longer list of curses in vv. 15–68 by the opposition of the similarly worded vv. 1–2 and 15. "If (*'im*) you obey" (v. 1) stands over against "if (*'im*) you do not obey" (v. 15; cf. v. 58). The positive condition of v. 1 is carried forward by "if (*kî*) you obey/keep" in vv. 2, 9, and 13. The negative conditions of vv. 15 and 58 are continued by "because (*kî*) you did not obey" in vv. 45 and 62. Verses 1–2, 15, 45, and 58 function as turning points that restate the circumstances and purpose of the lists. The first three turning points match in language ("obey," "come upon you," "overtake you," "commandments"); v. 58 has a somewhat different perspective involving Deuteronomy as a "book" and the divine "name." Verse 45 simultaneously performs both a concluding and introducing function (see below). Thus the chapter may be divided into the following sections: vv. 1–14, 15–44, 45–57, and

---

2. For "internal conclusions," compare v. 45 with VTE 56, lines 472–75, and the concluding VTE 57 with the new start in 58 (*ANET*, 539).

3. For example, *ANET*, 532–41, 659–61.

4. For a proposal that ch. 28 continues the Levites' speech from 27:12–26, so that Moses speaks the same words in Moab that will later be spoken by the Levites at Shechem, see N. Lohfink, "Moab oder Sichem—wo wurde Dtn 28 nach der Fabel des Deuteronomiums proklamiert?" in *Studies in Deuteronomy*, ed. García Martínez et al., 139–54; repr. in *Studien zum Deuteronomium IV*, 205–18. J.-P. Sonnet, *The Book within the Book: Writing in Deuteronomy* Biblical Interpretation Series 14; (Leiden: Brill, 1997), 97–103, suggests that the "book" in vv. 58 and 61 refers to the inscribed stones of ch. 27. Thus ch. 28 would be part of the Shechem event, while 28:69 [ET 29:1] draws attention back to Moab.

58–68. These repeated headings remind readers that the point of this long catalog is to motivate obedience.

Subsidiary structures occur within this larger overall structure, suggesting a step-by-step history of development. To reduce confusion, I have labeled text units as follows (B = blessing; C = curse):

> B1 (vv. 1–6)
> B2 (vv. 7–14)
> C1 (vv. 15–19)
> C2 (vv. 20–44 [45])
> C3 (vv. 45–57)
> C4 (vv. 58–68)

B1 (vv. 1–6) and *C1* (vv. 15–19) constitute the earliest nucleus of chapter 28. These two sections oppose the language of *bārûk* and *ārûr* ("blessed" and "cursed") and present a balanced reversal of vv. 3–6 by 16–19.

B2 (vv. 7–14) and *C2* (vv. 20–44) were added to this nucleus somewhat later. These two sections are coordinated by the reversal of v. 7 by v. 25a and of vv. 12b–13a by vv. 43–44. B2 elaborates the core blessings of B1 through promises (vv. 3 and 5 by vv. 8 and 12a ["undertakings"], v. 4 by v. 11, v. 6 by v. 7). Then C2 balances the promises of B2 with threats, exhibiting many verbal contacts. The "futility threats" (vv. 30–33, 38–41) and the "strike" series (vv. 22, 27, 28, 35) represent thematic unities within C2. To some degree the sequence of C2 depends on an Assyrian source (see below). *C1* and *C2* taken as a whole (vv. 15–44) are bracketed by "all these curses" in vv. 15 and 45.

Later still, the curses of *C3* (vv. 45–57) and *C4* (vv. 58–68) were successively added to the redactional stage represented by vv. 1–44 (*B1* + *B2* + *C1* + *C2*). The curse sequences within *C3* and *C4* are storylike in that *C3* describes the progress of an enemy attack and *C4* the effects of plagues and exile. *C3* was attached by means of a redactional hinge at vv. 45–46 and emphasizes the inevitability of defeat and foreign domination ("because"). *C4*, focused on the harsh realities of exile, is generally recognized as the latest material. With its references to "this book" (vv. 58, 61), *C4* is conscious that it is a component of a larger literary entity.

There is a distinction in genre between blessing/curse on the one hand and promise/threat on the other. Verses 3–6 and 16–19 are *blessings* and *curses* in the proper sense in that they have a declaratory shape, utilize a participial verbal form, and lack any mention of Yahweh. Verses 3–6 sound like liturgical priestly blessings (cf. 1 Sam 2:20; Ps 118:26) and concentrate on agriculture and fertility. The curses of vv. 16–19 were probably modeled on the blessings of vv. 3–6.[5] In contrast, *promises* and *threats* use finite verbs. They appear in

---

5. Seitz, *Redaktionsgeschichtliche Studien*, 268–73.

two forms. Some invoke Yahweh as cause: vv. 7–9, 11–13aα, 20–22, 24–25a, 27–28, 35–36. The direct object may be a noun (e.g., vv. 8, 20) or the pronoun "you" (e.g., vv. 11, 22). A second type describes events without reference to divine causation (vv. 10, 13aβ, 23, 25b, 29, 34, 37).

A rhetoric of opposition and contrast dominates chapter 28 (vv. 7 and 25, 12b-13a and 44). Catastrophe threatens but there will be no deliverance (vv. 26–27, 29, 31–32, 35). The same vocabulary may be used first in a positive and then in a negative way (vv. 47–48, 63), or there may be opposing word pairs (v. 62). "Futility threats" are rhythmic antithetical parallels in which potential projects and benefits are initiated, but then success or reward is thwarted (vv. 30–33a, 38–41).

Poetic parallelism is evident in v. 23. The three disasters of v. 20 are alliterated (*mĕ'ērâ, mĕhûmâ, mig'eret*); the three in v. 28 use rhyme (*šiggā'ôn, 'iwwārôn, timhôn*). Rhyming word pairs occur in vv. 24, 29, 33, 48, and in the refrain repeated in vv. 53, 55, and 57. Verbal patterns reappear: Yahweh will act "until" ruin takes place (vv. 20, 21, 22, 24, 48b; cf. 51–52); "Yahweh will strike" (vv. 22, 27, 28, 35); what "your eyes will see" (vv. 34, 67); the reaction of others (vv. 10, 25, 37). The roots *šmd*, "destroy," and *'bd*, "perish," recur unremittingly, clustering in vv. 20 and 24; 45, 48, and 51; 61 and 63.

[1–14] Demands for obedience in vv. 1–2 and 13b–14 bracket this section of blessings and promises. The six blessings of vv. 3–6 are reflected by the promises of vv. 7–13a in a roughly concentric structure: commercial and agricultural prosperity in vv. 3 and 12–13a; fruit of womb, ground, and cattle in vv. 4 and 11; food in vv. 5 and 8; and military affairs in vv. 6 and 7. The promises of vv. 7–13a interpret the blessings of vv. 3–6. Thus the generalized expression "go out and come in" v. 6 is taken to mean military expeditions by v. 7, and the urban/rural pair of v. 3 is expanded into agricultural and financial enterprises by vv. 12a and 12b–13a.

"Today" in v. 1 refers to Deuteronomy's dramatic setting in Moab and to the covenantal challenge of 26:16–19. "If you obey Yahweh" brackets vv. 1–2, restating 26:19 in conditional terms. In this way a language of conditionality, reminiscent of 15:5, modifies the language of careful obedience taken up from 26:16–17 (cf. 27:10). Verse 2 treats blessing as an objective entity that can be the grammatical subject of active verbs of motion (cf. vv. 15, 22, 45). Verses 3 and 6 communicate a total panorama of blessing with a merismus of place and activity using the format "blessed are you." Verses 4–5 offer fertility and food lists in the format "blessed is your [noun]." The curses of vv. 16–19 mirror the blessings of vv. 3–6, although with a reversal of the middle items. These initial blessings and curses deal with the daily concerns of individuals rather than the national and historical horizon that will open up as the chapter unfolds.

"Offspring" and "fertility" (*šeger* and *'aštĕrôt*; vv. 4, 18, 51) also occur in

7:13, where the word pair hints at the names of deities (*HALOT* 4:1416).[6] The "basket" and "kneading bowl" of v. 5 are a synecdoche (describing the whole by referring to one part) for the harvest in general. Verse 6 (taken alone without the interpretive v. 7) uses the phrase "come and go" for the activities of daily life (Ps 121:8), that is, going out to the fields in the morning and returning home at evening.

Up until v. 7 the blessings are anonymous, but the promises that follow identify Yahweh as their grammatical subject. At the same time, the language becomes more Deuteronomic and theological (vv. 8b–10). Verse 7 interprets v. 6 in military terms through the ideology of the Divine Warrior. Yahweh disperses orderly, focused enemy attacks ("one way"), converting them into panicked fugitives ("seven ways"). In v. 8 Yahweh gives orders to "blessing" as though it were a personified underling. The word translated "barns" occurs again only in Prov 3:10. For Yahweh to swear about something (v. 9) without reference to the ancestors is unique in Deuteronomy. This verse seems to refer to 26:18–19. To pronounce one's name over something (v. 10) is to proclaim one's ownership and protection (2 Sam 12:28; Amos 9:12). The language of v. 11 (and v. 4) will reappear in 30:9. For the heavens as Yahweh's storehouse (v. 12) see Job 38:22. The formula about the importance of timely rain occurs in 11:11, 14 as well. Verse 12b refers to individual Israelites lending to individual non-Israelites.[7] The promise of vv. 12b–13 also appears in 15:6.

[15–19] The conditional heading of v. 15 introduces three pairs of primary curses that balance the primary blessings of vv. 3–6. The reversal of the order of vv. 4–5 by vv. 17–18 may intend a rhetorical boost in intensity—from material things to living creatures.

[20–44] It is possible to divide this section into three cycles, each starting with diseases: vv. 21–26, 27–34, and 35–44. At the same time, one may discern a concentric shape in vv. 23–42:

> vv. 23–24 and 38–42—agricultural disaster
> vv. 25–26 and 36–37—an object of horror to others
> vv. 27 and 35—boils from which you cannot be healed
> vv. 28–29a and 34—madness involving blindness and what is seen
> vv. 29b and 33b—constantly exploited
> vv. 30–33a—futility threats at the center

Verses 43–44 reverse the promises of 12b—13a.

---

6. J. M. Hadley, "The Fertility of the Flock? The De-Personalization of Astarte in the Old Testament," in *On Reading Prophetic Texts* (ed. B. Becking and M. Dijkstra; Biblical Interpretation Series 18; Leiden: Brill, 1996), 115–33. *Šeger* denotes "what is dropped in birthing, newborn animals."

7. R. Kessler, "*Gôjim* in Dtn 15;6; 28;12: 'Volker' oder 'Heiden'? in *"Dort ziehen Schiffe dahin . . ."* (ed. M. Augustin and H.-D. Schunck; BEATAJ 28; Frankfurt: Lang, 1996), 85–89.

Verse 20 functions as an introductory synopsis of what is to follow. Yahweh dispatches three adversities. This reverses the similar image in v. 8 ("command blessing"), which also uses *bĕkol-mišlaḥ yadĕkā*, "in all your undertakings." The anomalous "me" clearly refers to Yahweh. The proverbial triad of pestilence, hunger, and sword (cf. 32:23–25; Jer 14:12) are grouped together in vv. 21–26.[8]

The seven harrying disasters of v. 22 are held together by the general notion of heat, but raise many lexical issues. The first three are diseases. Items four and five, usually understood in terms of weather, could be construed as symptoms of disease ("fever," "dehydration"). The last two items, which always occur as a lexical pair, seem to be crop problems, but could also refer to human illness ("scorching" of grain by the east wind[9] or of humans by fever; "yellowness" as a crop disease or a symptom of jaundice). Comparisons with Amos 4:6–11 and Lev 26:16–39 show that such lists of sevenfold calamities represent a conventional literary format. These seven entities depict active, hostile forces; they "pursue" (cf. v. 45).

The images of vv. 24–25 are paralleled in the same order in VTE 63–64 (*ANET*, 539). Impenetrable hardness of sky prevents rain (contrast v. 12a) and that of earth blocks cultivation (or perhaps the upwelling of springs). Verse 25 reverses v. 7. Instead of being an object of worldwide fear (v. 10), Israel will become an object of international revulsion. Second Samuel 21:10 illustrates the cultural horror of lying unburied (v. 26).

Verses 27–34 begin a second cycle of threats, starting from disease and moving into invasion. The second part is unified by the similar language of vv. 29 and 33 and the contrasting visual images of vv. 29 and 34.[10] The order of vv. 27, 28–29, and 30–33 replicates the sequence of VTE 39–42 (*ANET*, 538), reflecting the spheres of power of the gods Sin, Shamash, and Venus in turn. Verses 27–28 present a second grouping of seven disasters (cf. v. 22) depicting four outward dermatological afflictions followed by three inner sensory and psychological ones (for the latter, cf. Zech 12:4). "Boils" reappear in v. 35; their connection to Egypt is reflected in Exod 9:8–12. The "futility threat" of v. 30 appears in another form in the law of military deferment (20:5–7). "Make use of" in v. 30 is literally "profane" it, referring to using the fruit for the first time as common food.

A third cycle (vv. 35–44) begins again with disease and then moves into exile and futility in agriculture and family. The boils of v. 35 express full-blown misery (cf. Job 2:7). The threat of exile in v. 36 is infused with the language of

---

8. For this triad, see H. Weipert, *Die Prosareden des Jeremiabuches* (BZAW 132; Berlin: de Gruyter, 1973), 148–91.

9. Compare LXX "wind damage."

10. Braulik, *Deuteronomium II*, 206, points to a chiastic structure: boils in vv. 27 and 35, madness in vv. 28 and 34, exploitation in vv. 29 and 33b, with the antithetic futility threats of vv. 30–33a at the center.

Deuteronomy: "king whom you set" (17:15), "gods of wood and stone" (4:28; 29:16 [ET 17]). In the background of vv. 38–40 is the standardized triad of "grain, wine, and oil" (7:13; Hos 2:10 [ET 8]). Verses 43–44 describe threats of social reversal, overturning the "proper" subservient social and economic role of the resident alien.

[45–46] Structurally, v. 45 serves a dual purpose. On the one hand, it concludes vv. 15–44 in that vv. 44–45 repeat the language and themes of v. 13 and thus bracket the material in between. At the same time, v. 45 introduces a new section with an altered perspective. Now transgression and punishment are no longer only possibilities, but sound like foregone conclusions. The threats attack Israel like an enemy in warfare. Verse 46 attaches to v. 45 with a conjunction and a reference to its "curses" as "they" (wĕhāyû), and v. 47 may offer the reason for what is described in v. 46 (note r). The idea that the curses will remain permanently active as signs and portents (v. 46) stands in logical tension with the portrayal of Israel's complete annihilation in v. 45 (cf. vv. 20, 24, 51, 61).

[47–57] These calamities seem to be a foregone conclusion (v. 47: "*because you did not*"). The organizing concept for this inventory of threats is the catastrophe of serving one's enemies rather than Yahweh (vv. 47–48; cf. serving alien gods in vv. 14, 36). Verses 49–57 come close to being a narrative about an invasion and siege initiated by the action of Yahweh. The comprehensive catalog of v. 51 reverses and cancels out the list of blessings in v. 4. However, v. 51 is alarmingly silent about the "fruit of your womb" appearing in v. 4 (and vv. 11, 18). Instead this expression is picked up by v. 53 to convey the horrors of siege warfare.[11] A patterned refrain (vv. 53b, 55b, 57b; note v) and the phrase "look coldly" (or "eye grudgingly," vv. 54 and 56) unite this gruesome description. The rhetorical power of these vignettes rests in their emphasis on selfishness, as though to say that mere cannibalism of one's children is no longer viewed as much of a problem! Moreover, it is not brutal people who do this, but "the sensitive and pampered." Even a woman accustomed to walking on carpets or being carried in a litter eats these horrific objects, and does so "in secret" lest she have to share.

[58–68] Verse 58 launches the theme for a new section. The perspective shifts once more, showing an awareness of being part of a larger "book" (v. 61; cf. 31:9) and promoting fear of the "awesome" name (cf. Pss 99:3; 111:9). After the apparently inevitable and inescapable threats of vv. 47–57 (v. 47: "because you did not"), an outlook of conditionality returns as v. 58 repeats the language of v. 15 ("if you are not careful to do all").

Verse 60 implies a reversal of the exodus in its reference to Egyptian disease (undoing the exodus is stated unambiguously in v. 68). To "bring back"

---

11. The topic is paralleled in VTE 47, 69–72, 75, *ANET*, 538–40. Cf. 2 Kgs 6:28; Lam 2:20.

(*šwb* hip'il) every disease (cf. v. 27) might refer to a lost tradition of illnesses suffered by Israel in Egypt, but more likely means "cause to turn against you." This threat reverses the promise of 7:15, while "cling" cross-references 28:21.

Verses 62–63bα are composed using second-person plural language and effect a transition between the unmitigated destruction of vv. 58–61 and the national dispersion depicted in vv. 63bβ–68. Not all will be destroyed; a "few" will survive to be exiled. From "many" to "few" reverses the positive trend of 10:22; 26:5 (and the promise of Gen 15:5, 18). Perhaps "be determined to" is a better translation of v. 63 than "delight in," which may be too emotive (cf. 30:9).

The scattering of these few and their service of fabricated gods (v. 64; cf. v. 36) is reminiscent of 4:27–28. Verse 65 cancels out Yahweh's gift of a "resting place" (12:9–10). The image of v. 66 appears to be that of something precariously suspended as though by a thread; "heart" and "eyes" point forward to v. 67. Verses 66–67 cohere cleverly: "dread night and day . . . morning/evening . . . evening/morning . . . dread." With v. 68 Israel hits rock bottom. Yahweh's declaration in 17:16 is undone. These enigmatic "ships" may refer to galleys transporting the international slave trade (Amos 1:9; Joel 4:6 [ET 3:6]). One could also construe this noun—otherwise translated as "ships"—as an abstract plural of *ŏnîyâ*, "sorrowing" (cf. REB).[12] Israel has fallen to the level of commercially traded slaves. Yet they prove to be an unmarketable commodity, suggesting either they are now worth nothing or that their fate has made them an object of revulsion to potential purchasers.

The Covenant Made in Moab 28:69–29:28 [ET 29:1–29]

Heading

28:69 [ET 29:1] These are the words of the covenant that Yahweh commanded Moses to make with the Israelites in the land of Moab, in addition to the covenant that he had made with them at Horeb.

---

12. D. J. Reimer, "Concerning Return to Egypt: Deuteronomy xvii 16 and xxviii 68 Reconsidered," in *Studies in the Pentateuch*, ed. Emerton, 217–29. D. G. Schley, "'Yahweh Will Cause You to Return to Egypt in Ships' (Deuteronomy xxviii 68)," *VT* 35 (1985): 369–71, understands this reference against the background of Ashurbanipal's use of naval allies in his campaign against Egypt.

History: "You Have Seen"

29:1 [2] Moses summoned all Israel and said to them: You have seen all that
Yahweh did before your eyes in the land of Egypt, to Pharaoh and to his
servants[a] and to all his land, 2 [3] the great ordeals that your eyes saw, the
signs, and those great wonders. 3 [4] But Yahweh has not given you a mind
to understand or eyes to see, or ears to hear up until this day. 4 [5] I[b] have
led you forty years in the wilderness. Your clothes[c] did not wear out from
upon you and your sandal did not wear out from upon your foot.[d] 5 [6]
Bread was not what you ate nor was wine or strong drink what you
drank,[e] so that you might know that I am Yahweh your God. 6 [7] When
you came to this place, Sihon king of Heshbon and Og king of Bashan
came out against us to encounter us in battle, but we struck them down.
7 [8] We took their land and gave it as a hereditary possession to the
Reubenites, the Gadites, and the half-tribe of Manasseh. 8 [9] Keep the
words of this covenant and do them, in order that you may succeed in
everything you do.

Identity: "You Stand Today"

9 [10] You all stand[f] today before Yahweh you God—your heads, your
tribal chiefs,[g] your elders, and your officers, all Israel,[h] 10 [11] your small
children, your women, and the resident aliens who are within your
camps,[i] from those who hew your wood to those who draw your water—
11 [12] to enter into the covenant of Yahweh your God, and into its curse,[j]
which Yahweh your God is making with you today 12 [13] in order that he
may establish you[k] as his people and be your God, just as he promised
you and just as he swore to your ancestors, to Abraham, to Isaac, and to
Jacob. 13 [14] It is not only with you that I am making this covenant and
this curse, 14 [15] but also with those who are standing[l] here with us today
before Yahweh our God and those who are not standing here with us
today.

Curses: "You Know Well"

15 [16] You know well[m] that we lived in the land of Egypt, and that we
passed through the midst of the nations through which you passed, 16 [17]
and you saw their detestable things[n] and their idols of wood and stone, of
silver and gold, which were among them. 17 [18] Beware lest there be[o]
among you a man or woman or a clan or tribe whose heart is turning[p]
away from Yahweh our God to go and serve the gods of those nations.
Beware lest there be among you a root sprouting a poisonous plant and

wormwood. 18 [19] When such a one hears the words of this curse and thinks himself blessed,[q] saying in his heart, "I have security even if I walk in the stubbornness of my own heart" (thus sweeping away moist and dry alike),[r] 19 [20] Yahweh will not be willing to pardon him, for then Yahweh's wrath and jealousy will smoke[s] against him. The whole curse written in this book will settle down[t] on him, and Yahweh will wipe out his name from under heaven. 20 [21] Yahweh will single him out from all the tribes of Israel for calamity, according to all the curses of the covenant written[u] in this[v] book of the law.

21 [22] The next generation will say (your children who rise up after you and the foreigner who comes from a distant land will see the plagues of that land and the sicknesses that Yahweh made break out[w] in it, 22 [23] all its land scorched with sulfur and salt, not sown, not made to sprout, no vegetation growing in it, like the overthrow of Sodom and Gomorrah, Admah and Zeboiim, which Yahweh overthrew in his wrath and hot anger)[x] 23 [24] and all the nations will say, "Why did Yahweh treat this land in such a way? Why this great burning of wrath?" 24 [25] And they will say,[y] "It is because they forsook the covenant of Yahweh the God of their ancestors, which he made with them when he brought them out of the land of Egypt. 25 [26] They went and served other gods and bowed down to them, gods that they had not known and that he had not allotted to them. 26 [27] So the wrath of Yahweh burned against that land to bring on it every curse written in this book. 27 [28] Yahweh uprooted them from their land in wrath, hot anger, and great fury, and cast them into another land, as is the case today."

28 [29] The secret things belong to Yahweh our God, but the revealed things belong to us and to our children forever, to do all the words of this law.[z]

a. Follows OG (LXX[B], 848, 963) *wl'bdyw*. MT supplements with *kl*: "to *all* his servants."

b. Follows MT with reference to Yahweh. To avoid confusion with Moses, OG, Vulg., Syr. read (or translated as) "he led." OG modified its translation of v. 5 toward the same end.

c. MT *śalmâ* and Sam. *śimlâ* are a commonly transposed pair of synonyms (8:4; 24:13). OG lost "from upon you" by homoioteleuton: *ślmt[ykm m'l]ykm*.

d. The compound preposition *mē'al* describes these worn-out items falling off the wearer.

e. Word order emphasizes bread and wine.

f. "Stand" (*nṣb* nip'al) in the sense of "present yourselves before," "take your stand" (Exod 19:17; Josh 24:1).

g. Follows MT *r'śykm šbṭykm* (supported by Sam. and Vulg.) and translates the second word as an old designation for leader (2 Sam 7:7; cf. the parallelism of Deut 33:5).

See C. J. Begg, "The Reading *šbty(km)* in Deut. 29:9 and 2 Sam 7:7," *ETL* 58 (1982): 87–105. Syr. and Targ. Ps.-J. reflect an easier *r'šy šbtykm*, "the heads of your tribes" (cf. 5:23). Because it is unclear whether *archiphyloi* translates one word ("heads") or two ("heads" and "tribes"), the retroversion of OG is uncertain. OG adds *šptykm* ("your judges") to the list between *zqnykm* ("your elders") and *štrykm* ("your officers"). Joshua 23:2; 24:1 have *r'šykm šbtykm*, "your heads, your judges," in this context. Cf. Deut 31:28 for a similar problem.

h. *'îš yiśrā'ēl* is a collective for the whole military or cultic levy (27:14; Judg 7:23; 1 Sam 17:19).

i. Follows MT. The plural was leveled to singular by Sam., OG, Syr. (cf. 23:15 [ET 14]).

j. *Běrît* and *'ālâ* (also v. 13 [ET 14]) may be a hendiadys meaning "a covenant guarded by or including a curse" or "a sworn covenant." One swears allegiance to a covenant by invoking a self-curse. "Covenant" is used alone in 29:8 [ET 9] and "curse" alone in 29:18 [ET 19]; 30:7. Translating *'ālâ* as "oath" fails to communicate the connotation of threat. See J. Scharbert, "*'ālāh*," *TDOT* 1:261–66.

k. Follows OG. MT supplements with *hywm*, "today."

l. Follows MT. 1QDeut^b and OG lost "standing" due to its similarity with the preceding "with us": *'mnw* [*'md*].

m. Emphatic *kî*.

n. *Šiqqûṣ* usually categorizes disgusting, repellent foods; this is the rhetoric of the gag reflex. "Wood and stone" signifies that these images are inanimate, inert (4:28; 28:36, 64).

o. *Pen yēš* is used elliptically; cf. Isa 36:18; Williams, *Hebrew Syntax*, 461.

p. Follows OG. MT (supported by 1QDeut^b) supplements with *hywm*, "today."

q. That is, blessed rather than cursed; hitpa'el as an estimative-declarative reflexive, *IBHS* 28.2f. Alternate translation: "bless himself in his heart saying, 'May I be secure'" as a sort of counterblessing to offset the curse.

r. The metaphor is open to various interpretations. (1) It may describe a comprehensive catastrophe. "Moist and dry" could be a merismus incorporating the whole people, or "moist [fruitful soil]" may refer to the innocent and "dry [unproductive soil]" to the guilty who suffer together (LXX; Ps 1:3; Jer 17:6–8). (2) The merismus could indicate that the whole life of the reprobate will be subject to punishment. (3) The idea could be part of the reprobate's own inner thoughts: "[Yahweh cannot punish me, else he might] sweep away the innocent and the guilty [indiscriminately]." Verses 19–20 [ET 20–21] contradict this line of thinking by insisting that punishment will come individually. (4) The metaphor could refer to the speaker's expectation that the fidelity of the larger community would cover over or make up for any single individual's fault: "The irrigated moist land [of the righteous] will water the dry land [of my own stubbornness]" ("water" is based on an Arabic cognate meaning "quench thirst," *HALOT* 2:763–64). (5) NJB offers "much water drives away thirst" as the continued speech of the apostate, meaning "in order to satisfy my thirst [desire]" or perhaps "[nothing will happen to me, for in the long run] watering brings drought to an end." (6) Based on v. 22 [ET 23] and contacts between vv. 17–18 [ET 18–19] and Jer 23:14–15, 17, the phrase might refer to the fate of the previously well-watered (Gen 13:10) Sodom and Gomorrah (cf. *sāpâ* in Gen 18:23; 19:15–17).

s. Follows MT in using the uncommon verb '*āšan*. Sam. and OG have the more usual *ḥārâ*, "burn."

t. Follows MT and Sam. in using the striking verb *rābaṣ*, which almost always refers to the lying down of an animal. The curse "crouches" on him like a stretching carnivore (cf. Gen 4:7). 4QDeut^c, OG, Tg. soften this startling image by substituting *dābaq*, "cling to," which could have originated through misreading *d* for *r* (and perhaps *q* for *ṣ*).

u. Follows MT and understands *hktwbh* as a collective abstract (cf. 30:10) referring to the curses. The feminine singular form *hktwbh* might signify that it is the *covenant* that is written. However, because context indicates that the *curses* are written (vv. 19, 27 [E 20, 28]), Sam., OG, Syr. harmonize by reading the masculine plural *hktwbym*. The agreement of LXX^A with MT is coincidental, resulting from an inner-Greek process of case attraction (Wevers, *Greek Text*, 473).

v. Follows MT in reading "this book" (30:10; 31:26). OG, Vulg., Syr. reflect "the book of this law" instead (28:61; 28:58 has both).

w. A factitive pi'el: causation that produces a state of being, *IBHS* 24.2.

x. The long excursus in parentheses describes the questioners and the sight that motivates their query. This breaks into the compound subject and verb that appear as the first words of vv. 21 and 23 [ET 22, 24] ("the next generation will say . . . and all the nations will say"). "Your children" picks up the first group and "the foreigner" describes the second (v. 21 [ET 22]). An alternate translation strategy would take v. 22 [ET 23] as the content of what the next generation of v. 21 [ET 22] says (cf. NJB). The Kethib and Qere are variants of the same place name.

y. Either the response of others to the question ("the answer will be") or their own deduction ("they themselves will conclude").

z. Cf. NAB: "Both what is still hidden and what has already been revealed concern us and our descendants forever." This translation stems from eliminating *lyhwh 'lhynw*, "to Yahweh our God," as an erroneous substitute for the words marked by *puncta extraordinaria*: *lnw wlbnynw*, "to us and to our children." There is no other textual support for such a move. Moreover, these enigmatic dots are usually thought to suggest the omission of the *marked* words (Tov, *Textual Criticism*, 55–57). Alternate translation based on rabbinic tradition: "concealed acts . . . overt acts" (cf. NJPS).

This chapter motivates obedience to the law Moses has promulgated. Three topical sections are addressed to assembled Israel, each beginning with the emphatic personal pronoun "you": *history* ("you have seen," vv. 1b-8 [ET 2b–9]), *identity* of the covenant partners ("you stand," vv. 9–14 [ET 10–15]), and fulfillment of the *curse* ("you know," vv. 15–28 [ET 16–29]). At the end of each section, the "you" plural address changes into first-person plural "we" (vv. 6b–7, 14, 28 [ET 7b–8, 15, 29]), expressing solidarity between speaker and audience. The third section is further subdivided into two topical units. The first part deals with elements in the community who may have accepted the covenant with secret reservations (vv. 15–20 [ET 16–21]). The second part concerns the impending destruction and exile that threaten the community as a whole (vv. 21–28 [ET 22–29]). These last verses draw attention to their literary context as part of a "book" that proclaims covenant curses (vv. 19, 20, 26 [ET 20, 21, 27]; cf. 30:10).[1]

[28:69 (ET 29:1)] Deuteronomy 28:69 [ET 29:1] restates the place and circumstances of Moses' address, making clear that a covenant relationship is its expected outcome. The verse calls on the reader to pay attention, giving notice that a challenge for decision is impending. It separates the two covenants of Horeb and Moab in time and place, but also coordinates them ("in addition to"), thus giving the Horeb Decalogue and Deuteronomic law equal standing as expressions of Yahweh's will. The reader is reminded yet again of the dramatic staging of Deuteronomy as an address delivered on the verge of entry into the land.

Scholars dispute whether this verse is a subscription or summary of what has gone before or a superscription introducing a new section. In the final form of Deuteronomy, it is certainly a superscription, one of the four major headings that configure the book as a narrative describing the speech acts of Moses: 1:1–5 ("the words"), 4:45–49 ("the law"), 28:69 [ET 29:1] ("words of the covenant"), and 33:1 ("the blessing"). However, what was the role of 28:69 [ET 29:1] before this pattern of four headings was introduced?

The argument that this verse was originally a retrospective summary or *subscription* centers on the semantic field of "words of the covenant" as something that can be obeyed and disobeyed as well as written down. "Words of the covenant" in this sense matches the content of chapters 12–28 as a covenant text made up of stipulations followed by blessings and curses. In other words, 28:69 [ET 29:1] recapitulates what has been said about Horeb and Moab, that is, chapters 5–28 construed as a covenant by 26:17–19; 27:1, 8, and the blessings and curses of chapter 28. In contrast, "words of the covenant" is a poor description of the admonitory material that follows. The following chapters may follow the outline of a covenant ceremony, but lack any cited stipulations, blessings, or curses, that is, anything one could point to as "words of the covenant." Insofar as 28:69 [ET 29:1] is a subscription or summary, it forms

---

1. Some discern a covenant or treaty format in chs. 29–30; N. Lohfink, "Der Bundesschluss im Lande Moab: Redaktionsgeschichtliches zu Dt 28,69 bis 32,47," in *Studien zum Deuteronomium I*, 58–61; idem, "Bund als Vertrag in Deuteronmium," *ZAW* 107 (1995): 215–39; A. Rofé, "The Covenant in the Land of Moab (Dt 28,69–30,20): Historico-literary, Comparative, and Form-Critical Considerations," in *Das Deuteronomium*, ed. Lohfink, 317–18; repr. in *Song of Power*, ed. Christensen, 277–79. It is possible to speak of a historical prologue in vv. 1–7, curses in vv. 20–27, and blessings, curses, and witnesses in 30:15–20. A. Cholewiński, "Zur theologischen Deutung des Moabbundes," *Bib* 66 (1985): 96–111, interprets this chapter as a concrete example of the prophetic "new covenant," intended to convince readers of such a possibility. E. Talstra, "Texts and Their Readers: On Reading the Old Testament in the Context of Theology," in *The Rediscovery of the Hebrew Bible* (ed. J. Dyke et al.; Maastricht: Shaker, 1999), 101–19, offers a theological interpretation based on reader-response theory.

an inclusio with 1:1–5, describing the "words that Moses spoke" (1:1) in terms of a covenant.[2]

The argument that this verse looks forward as a *superscription* rests on its character as a framing and structuring verse. Chapters 29–30 contain elements of covenant and decision making, introduced by 28:69 [ET 29:1] and concluded by 30:20. Moreover, 4:44–5:1 and 28:69–29:1 [ET 29:1–2] are parallel texts ("these are . . . the Israelites . . . in the land of . . . Moses summoned all Israel and said to them"). Deuteronomy 4:44–5:1 obviously points forward as a superscription; therefore, 28:69–29:1 [ET 29:1–2] must do so as well. Furthermore, 29:8 [ET 9] explicitly refers to "the words of the covenant," and 29:11–13 [ET 12–14] alludes to covenant making in the context of a "today" that clearly refers to Moab. In fact, chapter 29 uses "covenant" five times. Finally, in dissociating Horeb from Moab ("in addition to"), 28:69 [ET 29:1] prepares for the content of chapters 29–30 as an event taking place "today" (29:9—14 [ET 10–15]; 30:8, 11, 15–16, 17–18), as opposed to something done in the past. Since the reader has most recently encountered proceedings located at Shechem (ch. 27), 28:69 [ET 29:1] is required to redirect attention to Moab.[3]

It is best to conclude that in the final form of Deuteronomy this verse looks both ways, referring to previous material and summarizing it, while simultaneously pointing forward and initiating what follows. The phrase "words of the covenant" looks back to the laws, blessings, and curses cited previously. "Covenant . . . in the land of Moab" describes the *entire* task of Moses, certainly in exhortation (chs. 6–11) and legal promulgation (chs. 12–28), but also his upcoming act of covenant mediation (chs. 29–30). One might say that the covenant *text* ("words") is found in the previous chapters, while the *ritual* of covenant making is reflected (although not actually described) in chapters 29–30.

[1–8 (ET 2–9)] This section is formulated primarily in second person plural, with two shifts to singular in verbs that describe Israel's experience (vv. 2 and 4 [ET 3, 5]). Verses 1–8 [ET 2–9] are shaped as the literary, rhetorical format of an "argument from history" (cf. 4:35–40; 7:7–11; 8:2–6). *Remember* what Yahweh has done (vv. 1–2, 4, 6b–7 [ET 2–3, 5, 7b–8]), *know* what this implies (vv. 3 and 5 [ET 4, 6]), and then *apply* this by keeping the commandments (v. 8 [ET 9]). Verses 1–3 and 4–6a [ET 2–4, 5–7a] have similar structures, each starting with the past and ending with the present ("this day," "this place").

---

2. H. F. Van Rooy, "Deuteronomy 28:69—Superscript or Subscript?" *Journal of Northwest Semitic Languages* 14 (1988): 215–22.

3. Most of these arguments are presented by N. Lohfink, "Dtn 28:69—Überschrift oder Kolophon?" in *Studien zum Deuteronomium III*, 279–91. Insofar as this verse is a superscription, one must ask what block of text it designates. The natural referent would seem to be 29:1 [ET 2] –30:20. However, Lohfink proposes that the heading introduces a unit of text that runs up to 32:47. This ignores the most natural reading of 31:1 as a conclusion.

Within this shift from past to present comes a declaration of what Israel could not know or was to know from their experiences. The generations merge: all are addressed as having experienced the past from Egypt to the victories over Sihon and Og. All are challenged to obey the covenant.[4]

The summons of the people is startling, since Moses has never dismissed them after 5:1, but the call to (re)assemble signifies that an important communal occasion is about to be described. It also indicates that a new section of the book, just as important as that begun by 4:45–5:1, is about to commence. The verbal relationship to 5:1–5 is strong (v. 1 [ET 2] and 5:1; vv. 13–14 [ET 14–15] and 5:3), pointing to a redactional effort to communicate that the summons and assembly of chapter 5 and of chapters 29–30 are to be thought of as a single event.[5]

The appeal for obedience based on personal experience is reminiscent of 11:1–9. The change to singular address in v. 2 [ET 3] may involve a citation of 7:19. Verse 3 [ET 4] builds on vv. 1–2 [ET 2–3]. In the past, Israel may have had eyes to witness, but it could not perceive deeper meanings. The last words of v. 3 [ET 4] might suggest that even now Yahweh has not granted the capacity for insight (cf. NRSV, NJPS). However, the logic of the argument demands that we interpret these verses to mean that now Israel is indeed able to understand. Now that Moses has promulgated the law and encouraged obedience to it, the implications of older memories can finally be grasped. Israel's past inadequacies are behind it; now it can obey the covenant (v. 8 [ET 9]).

In vv. 4–5 [ET 5–6] Yahweh speaks directly through Moses ('I'; cf. 7:4; 28:20) and expresses the same idea as 8:2–4. Israel did not consume bread and wine, the standard products of human endeavor, thus implying that Israel survived on Yahweh's direct providence (8:3, 16). As a result, Israel could acknowledge the formula: "I am Yahweh your God" (cf. Exod 6:7; 10:2; 16:12).[6] Verse 6 [ET 7] localizes the setting of this assembly unambiguously in Moab. Verse 8 [ET 9] offers the lesson of success that history teaches (cf. 8:6 and DH in Josh 1:7–8; 1 Kgs 2:3; 2 Kgs 18:7). "Covenant" functions as a catchword that bridges into vv. 9–14 [ET 10–15].

[9–14 (ET 10–15)] The decisive encounter in Moab gathers up the past of patriarchal promise and Horeb assembly into a new act of covenant making, and then applies this covenant relationship to future generations. There is a

---

4. These observations are based on Lohfink, *Das Hauptgebot*, 125–28; idem, "Bundesschluss," 59–61.

5. This is the basis of Lohfink's thesis that all of Deut 1–32 is dramatically envisioned as occurring on a single day ("Zur Fabel des Deuteronomiums," in *Bundesdokument und Gesetz*, ed. Braulik, 65–78).

6. C. H. Begg, "'Bread, Wine, and Strong Drink' in Deut 29:5a" *Bijdragen* 41 (1980): 266–75, proposes that by denying Israel alcohol with its potential for obscuring clear perception, Yahweh made it possible for Israel to attain proper discernment.

pleasing chiastic pattern. "Stand today before Yahweh" (vv. 9 and 14 [ET 10–15]) and "making covenant and curse" (vv. 11 and 13 [ET 12, 14]) form nesting brackets around the relational formula about "his people" and "your God" in v. 12 [ET 13].[7] The community is positioned "before Yahweh" as a liturgical assembly (*'îš yiśrā'ēl*, note h) to engage in a ceremonial act. Those incorporated into this covenantal relationship are an inclusive congregation, both socially (vv. 9–10 [ET 10–11]) and temporally (vv. 13–14 [ET 14–15]). Deuteronomy's liturgical assemblies typically involve full participation (12:12, 18; 16:11, 14). This all-encompassing gathering mirrors the one that will assemble every seven years to hear the law read (31:10–13). Even resident aliens are integrated into the covenant people (cf. 31:12), and all menial laborers are embraced by a traditionally patterned "from . . . to" formula (cf. Josh 9:21, 23, 27).[8]

The assembly is to take on the obligations of Deuteronomy as a "covenant including a curse" (note j). Yahweh makes (literally "cuts"; vv. 11, 13 [ET 12, 14]; cf. 5:2–3) this covenant to "establish" (i.e., "raise up, constitute") Israel as his people (cf. 28:9). Israel, for its part, "enters" this covenant and curse, that is, "passes over into it" (*'ābar*). This verb may reflect a covenant-making ceremony in which one passes between the cut-up pieces of an animal (Gen. 15:17; Jer 34:18–19). The reciprocal responsibilities of the relationship between people and God have been set forth in Deut 26:17–19. Future generations are included in and bound by this agreement, as was sometimes the case with ancient political treaties.[9] In Deuteronomy, of course, this reference to the future is a rhetorical device to include the book's readers.

[15–20 (ET 16–21)] This section traces a temporal sequence from past experience (vv. 15–16 [ET 16–17]) through perilous present (vv. 17–18 [ET 18–19]) to grim future (vv. 19–20 [ET 20–21]). In entering the covenant, Israel also comes under the inescapable curse that upholds obedience (vv. 18–20 [ET 19–21]; cf. the hendiadys of vv. 11, 13 [ET 12, 14]). This curse threatens those who might agree to the covenant with secret reservations, perhaps intending to adhere to a private non-Yahwistic cult or a cult using images, while still participating in the public national religion. The experience of life in Egypt and transit through alien peoples is employed to remind the audience of the horrors of such idolatry.

Moses addresses the generation of those in Moab as well as later readers with the inclusive "we" of shared national history (v. 15 [ET 16]). He depicts the danger of apostasy as an individual or corporate "root," whose oblivious,

---

7. Lohfink, "Bundesschluss," 69.

8. The camp situation (contrast 31:12) fits Israel's circumstances in Moab. A. D. H. Mayes, "Deuteronomy 29, Joshua 9, and the Place of the Gibeonites in Israel," in *Das Deuteronomium*, ed. Lohfink, 321–25, suggests that this text depends on Josh 9 and seeks to reclassify the Gibeonites from slaves into resident aliens incorporated into the cultic community. He points to the comparable role of clothes and shoes and bread and wine in vv. 4–5 and Josh 9.

9. VTE 1, 25, 34, 57 *ANET*, 534, 537–39; Sefire IA, *ANET*, 659.

self-centered inner thoughts are revealed. The comprehensive list of potential wrongdoers expressly includes women, suggesting that they had a reputation for participating in private, nonorthodox worship (cf. 13:7 [ET 6]; 17:2). Language describing one's heart turning away also appears in 30:17. The metaphor of "root" implies an underground and hidden causative factor, perhaps a reemergence of something formerly suppressed (cf. Isa 11:1; 14:29–30). "Poison and wormwood" are figures of bitter experience (Deut 32:32; Ps 69:22 [ET 21]; Jer 9:15). Although v. 18 [ET 19] is obscure (notes q and r), it is clear that this reprobate is laying claim to blessing and security in spite of disobedient conduct and in spite of having heard the curse. In contrast to the outcome of vv. 21–27 [ET 22–28], Yahweh isolates this offender, and the people as a whole remain unscathed. The lawbreaker cannot hide within the larger obedient community. The curses work both impersonally like a hostile creature (v. 19 [ET 20], note t) and as a "script" followed by Yahweh's active fury (v. 20 [ET 21]). Wiping out someone's name is also threatened in 7:24; 9:14; 25:19. Repetition of *kol* ("whole curse," "all the tribes," "all the curses") underscores totality and emphasizes that this script for doom is identical with the book of Deuteronomy.

[21–27 (ET 22–28)] The topic shifts from calamity in the life of an individual offender to the doom of a more distant national future. The transition is abrupt and unexpected, suggesting that vv. 21–27 [ET 22–28] were inserted into the text at a later stage. Verses 17–20 [ET 18–21] take the perspective of Moses and Israel, looking forward from the present in Moab into future possibilities of individual disobedience and doom. Verses 21–27 [ET 22–28] reverse this, describing the perspective of future observers looking back at the collective results of Israel's apostasy in the land. Yet there are still connections between the two sections. The collective service of other gods (v. 25 [ET 26]) is the aggregate of individual choices about worship (v. 17 [ET 18]). The same threats "written in this book," which doom the individual or faction in the short term (vv. 19–20 [ET 20–21]), will also doom the whole nation over the long haul (v. 26 [ET 27]). The resumptive repetition of vv. 19–20 [ET 20–21] by 26 [ET 27] suggests that vv. 21–27 [ET 22–28] were added in the exilic period to update the threats of Deuteronomy in light of defeat and exile. From this "future" perspective, what was only a threatened possibility in chapter 28 has become a reality.

Verses 21–27 [ET 22–28] represent a rhetorical set piece that takes the reader forward into a "future" that is also the exilic reader's present. The vocabulary of Yahweh's wrath makes a concentric pattern: "wrath, hot anger" (vv. 22 and 27 [ET 23, 28]) surround "burning of wrath" (v. 23 [ET 24]) and "wrath burned" (v. 26 [ET 27]).[10] The script of the future is set out, using the verb *āmar*, "say," three times (vv. 21, 23, 24 [ET 22, 24, 25]). First the "next generation" is said to speak (vv. 21–22 [ET 22–23]). What they say, however, is not

10. Braulik, *Deuteronomium II*, 216.

immediately quoted. Rather a description of the terrible sights of the devastated land intervenes, as viewed by both that future generation and visiting foreigners. This interruption of expected sequence rhetorically foregrounds and emphasizes the horrific state of affairs. The "plagues" and "sicknesses" of v. 21 [ET 22] link back to the curses of 28:59, 61. The rhetoric of v. 22 [ET 23] is powerful in its terseness. Perhaps the salt is a human act intended to sterilize or curse (Judg 9:45). More likely, Sodom and Gomorrah are in view, the salt being that of the Dead Sea and the sulfur that described in Gen 19:24. The language of "overthrow" (*hāpak*) is a typical feature of the tradition of Sodom and Gomorrah (Gen 19:21, 25, 29; Isa 13:19; Amos 4:11).

The nations join the next generation in asking why (v. 23 [ET 24]). Then comes the answer (vv. 24–27 [ET 25–28]; note y).[11] Is the reader to think that those who answer still have "this book" (v. 26 [ET 27]) at hand, or does this language collapse the viewpoint of these future speakers with the perspective of the reader? Verse 27 [ET 28] adds exile to the picture of Sodom and Gomorrah. These are still the words of future speakers, but again their perspective merges with that of the exilic reader ("as is the case today"). Israel is "uprooted," metaphorically torn like a plant from the soil (Jer 12:14). The sequence "wrath, hot anger, and great fury" also appears in Jer 21:5; 32:37, further indicating an exilic date for this section.[12]

[28 (ET 29)] Precisely what this poetic parallelism intends to contrast is obscure (note z). Following rabbinic understanding, one could read this as an opposition between concealed and detected human wrongdoing. This would pick up the topic of sin and destruction from vv. 17–27 [ET 18–28]. God punishes secret sins, but humans are responsible for punishing overt ones. Neither sort of sin, however, escapes punishment, so one should obey the law.

A second approach takes this as an opposition between undisclosed realities and divinely revealed truths. If one understands this in terms of the argument presented in chapter 29, the contrast is between a hidden future concealed from humanity and current realities known now. The hidden future remains the realm of God's work in history. But the present is known, and Israel's role in it is to obey the law. In the shadow of a grim potential future, Israel must focus on keeping the law now. One might also take this a step further. Although the

---

11. Both vivid descriptions of curses fulfilled on treaty violators and the question-and-answer format characterize Assyrian political rhetoric. See D. E. Skweres, "Das Motiv der Strafgrunderfragung in biblischen und neuassyrischen Texten," *BZ* 14 (1970): 181–97 (cf. *ANET*, 300). For other parallels, see Weinfeld, *Deuteronomic School*, 100–116. This text is taken up in Jer 22:8–9 and 2 Kgs 9:8–9; see Nelson, *Double Redaction*, 74–75.

12. The language and logic is similar to that of ch. 4. Deuteronomy 4:25–28 and 29:21–27 [ET 22–28] share the topic of the actualization of the curses in history. The speech of the nations is a reversal of their outlook in 4:5–8. The striking notion of gods allotted to nations found in 29:25 [ET 26] also appears in 4:19, and the "wood and stone" of 29:16 [ET 17] in 4:28.

actual course of the future remains hidden, threatening elements of it have been revealed nonetheless. The secret future is in God's hands, but the covenant curses reveal enough about that future to motivate keeping the law.

However, the interpreter might also choose to understand the contrast between "secret" and "revealed" in terms of the proximity of the law and the feasibility of obeying it (cf. 30:11–14). The revealed law of Deuteronomy is readily accessible for Israel to obey. One is simply to keep this law, while setting aside any speculations about secret things that properly concern God alone. Human wisdom has limits that make it impossible for mortals to understand what divine wisdom comprehends (Prov 30:3–4).

I Set Before You Life and Death
30:1–20

If You Return to Yahweh

30:1 When all these things have happened to you, the blessing and the curse that I have set before you, if you take them to heart among all the nations where Yahweh[a] has dispersed you, 2 and return to Yahweh your God and obey him according to all I am commanding you today, both you and your children,[b] with all your heart and with all your being, 3 then Yahweh will restore your fortunes[c] and have compassion on you and gather you again from all the peoples among whom Yahweh has scattered you. 4 Even if your dispersal should be to the ends of the sky, from there Yahweh your God will gather you, and from there he will take you back. 5 Yahweh your God will bring you into the land that your ancestors took over and you will take it over. He will make you more prosperous and numerous than your ancestors.[d]

6 Yahweh will circumcise[e] your heart and the heart of your offspring so you will love Yahweh your God with all your heart and with all your being, so that you may live. 7 Yahweh your God will put these curses[f] on your enemies and on your foes who persecuted you. 8 But you[g] will again obey Yahweh and do his commandments[h] that I am commanding you today. 9 Yahweh will cause you to abound in all your undertakings, in the fruit of your womb, in the fruit of your cattle, and in the fruit of your ground[i] for prosperity. For Yahweh will again take delight[j] in making you prosperous, just as he delighted in your ancestors, 10 if you obey Yahweh your God to keep his commandments and his decrees written[k] in this book of the law, if you turn to Yahweh your God with all your heart and with all your being.[l]

A Matter of Life or Death

11 Indeed, this commandment that I am commanding you today is not too hard for you,[m] nor is it too far away. 12 It is not in heaven that you should say, "Who will go up to heaven for us and get it for us and proclaim it to us that we may do it?" 13 Nor is it beyond the sea that you should say, "Who will cross to the other side of the sea for us and get it for us and proclaim it to us that we may do it?" 14 No, the word is very near to you, in your mouth and in your heart[n] for you to do it.

15 See, I hereby set[o] before you today life and prosperity, and death and calamity. 16 If you obey the commandments of Yahweh your God[p] that I am commanding you today, to love Yahweh your God, to walk in his ways, and to keep his commandments, decrees, and ordinances,[q] then you shall live and multiply, and Yahweh your God will bless you in the land that you are going in to take over. 17 But if your heart turns away and you do not listen, and you let yourself be led astray[r] and bow down to other gods and serve them, 18 I declare to you today that you will surely perish. You will not enjoy long life in the land that you are crossing the Jordan to go in[s] to take over. 19 I call heaven and earth to witness against you today. Life and death, the blessing and the curse, I hereby set before you.[t] Choose life so that you and your offspring may live, 20 by loving Yahweh your God, obeying him, and clinging to him; for that is life for you and length of days for you to live in the land that Yahweh swore to your ancestors, to Abraham, to Isaac, and to Jacob, to give them.

a. Follows OG as the shorter text. OG lacks four of the eight occurrences of *'lhyk*, "your God," found in MT (v. 1, twice in v. 3, v. 6). Tg. Ps.-J. supports OG in v. 1 and in the second instance in v. 3.

b. Follows MT. OG lacks *'th wbnyk*, literally "you and your sons," perhaps omitted by the translator as superfluous.

c. Whether the object noun *šĕbût* comes from *šbh*, "lead away captive," or *šwb*, "return," is disputed, but the meaning of the idiom (determined on literary rather than etymological grounds) is clear: "restore to an earlier state of well-being." See J. M. Bracke, "*Šûb šĕbût:* A Reappraisal," *ZAW* 97 (1985): 233–44.

d. Alternate translation: "make you prosperous and more numerous than."

e. That is, "open your heart up" to remove impediments to obedience. Contrast 10:16, where Israel is commanded to do this. The last words are literally "for the sake of your life"; See Williams, *Hebrew Syntax*, 365.

f. Follows OG. MT expands with *kl*: "*all* these curses."

g. Emphatic "you" in contrast to Yahweh's deeds in vv. 6–7.

h. Follows OG. MT expands with *kl*: "*all* his commandments."

i. Follows MT with the order "womb, cattle, ground," as in 28:11. Sam., OG, 4QDeut[b] (apparently) give these items in the order of 28:4, 18. The absence of *ltwbh*, "for prosperity," in OG is a translation strategy in that this idea is contained in the verb.

j. That is, "be determined to."

k. Follows the grammatically unusual text of MT (supported by Sam.; cf. 29:20 [ET 21]). The feminine singular participle *hktwbh*, "written," refers to two masculine plural nouns, "commandments" and "decrees." Tg., Syr., 4QDeut[b] level this to the expected plural. The participle should be construed as an abstract collective as in 29:20: "the things written" (cf. the quotation formula in Josh 10:13; 2 Sam 1:18).

l. Alternate translations construing the repeated *kî* as temporal or causal rather than conditional: "when you obey . . . when you turn," or "when you obey . . . because you turn," or "because you will obey . . . when you turn."

m. Follows MT and Sam. 4QDeut[b] and OG put *mmk* at the end of the verse: *wl'rhwqh hw' mmk*, "nor is it too far away *from you*."

n. "In your mouth": known by heart through oral learning and reviewing (Josh 1:8). "In your heart": internalized, not merely rote (Jer 31:33).

o. Translating as performative speech. Alternate translation: "I have set."

p. Follows OG: *(w)'šr tšm' 'l mṣwt yhwh 'lhyk*. MT lost this protasis by haplography from '*šr* to '*šr*. For '*šr* as "if" cf. 11:27; 18:22.

q. Follows the MT order of these three items. Sam. and OG give them as "decrees, commandments, ordinances." LXX[B] lost "commandments" through an inner-Greek haplography.

r. Nip'al of *ndh* in a tolerative sense, *IBHS* 23.4f.

s. Follows MT. OG lacks *lb'*, "to go," probably omitted to correspond to 4:26 and other occurrences of this formula (Wevers, *Text History*, p. 90, list 14).

t. A resumptive repetition of v. 15 with the direct object in reverse order.

The introductory verse 28:69 [ET 29:1] at the beginning and the shift to narrative mode in 31:1 at the end mark off chapters 29–30 as a distinct unit of thought. The summary character of 30:15–20 relates appropriately to the summons and address introduced by 29:1 [ET 2]. The sections that make up this division are not well coordinated, however. The transitions between 29:20 and 21 [ET 21 and 22], 29:28 [ET 29] and 30:1, and 30:14 and 15 are exceptionally abrupt. It is generally agreed that the older material consists of 29:1–20 [ET 2–21], 30:11–14, and 15–20, while 29:21–27 (28) [ET 22–28 (29)] and 30:1–10 were added at a later, exilic period. As a whole, chapters 29–30, along with chapter 4, which is associated in topic and language, form a frame around the parenetic and legal core of Deuteronomy.

The final form of chapter 30 is held together by the repetition of "I set before you" (*nātattî lĕpānêkā*; vv. 1, 15, 19), "the blessing and the curse" (vv. 1, 19), and "that I am commanding you today" (vv. 2, 8, 11, 16; cf. 28:1, 13, 14, 15). In this way chapter 30 echoes the language of 11:26–28, so that together these two passages surround the law code as brackets. A sevenfold repetition of "today" (vv. 2, 8, 11, 15, 16, 18, 19) enhances rhetorical intensity. "Love Yahweh your God" appears in vv. 6, 16, and 20.

[1–10] In the context of completed destruction and exile, Israel is challenged to repent and reform. This section takes a step further into the future, beyond the disappointment and failure of 29:21–27 [ET 22–28]. The outlook has shifted from that of chapter 29. Disobedience and its resulting curses are no longer the subjects of warning, but are assumed to have taken place. Verses 1–10 promise a restoration based on repentance and assure prosperity contingent on obedience. These verses are held together by two interlaced concentric structures. The more important of these structures is based on variations of the root *šwb*, the English equivalents for which include "turn," "return," "repent," "do again," and "restore." Both Yahweh and Israel "turn," but Israel makes the first move:

> *Israel* reflects and repents
>   "take [literally *return*] to heart"—v. 1
>   "*return* to Yahweh"—v. 2
> *Yahweh* restores and reverses past action
>   "*restore* your fortunes"—v. 3a
>   "gather you again" (*turn* and gather)—v. 3b
> *Israel* reverses past action
>   "again obey" (*turn* and obey)—v. 8
> *Yahweh* returns to prosper
>   "again take delight" (*turn* to take delight)—v. 9
> *Israel* returns in obedience
>   "*turn* to Yahweh"—v. 10

A second concentric structure plays on "all your heart and being" and surrounds Yahweh's act of circumcision with the conditions and results of obedience:

> "return . . . obey . . . heart and being"—v. 2
> "land . . . make you prosperous (*hêṭibĕkā*). . . your ancestors"—v. 5
> "circumcise . . . heart and being"—v. 6
> "ground . . . make you prosperous (*lĕṭôb*) . . . your ancestors"—v. 9
> "obey . . . turn . . . heart and being"—v. 10[1]

This change in subject involving a subsequent positive future that goes a step beyond the disasters of 29:21–27 [ET 22–28] is unexpected. Now the "book" that was the vehicle of curse in 29:19, 20, 26 [ET 20, 21, 27] becomes the book

---

1. Braulik, *Deuteronomium II*, 219. For other rhetorical structures see T. A. Lenchak, *"Choose Life!": A Rhetorical-Critical Investigation of Deuteronomy 28,69–30,20* (AnBib 129; Rome: Pontifical Biblical Institute Press, 1993), 177–78; G. Vanoni, "Der Geist und der Buchstabe: Überlegungen zum Verhältnis der Testamente und Beobachtungen zu Dtn 30, 1–10," *BN* (1981): 65–98.

that provides an opportunity for new obedience. There is a shift to second-person singular address from the plural of chapter 29. Deuteronomy 30:1–10 closely resembles 4:29–31 in outlook and audience. Both sections speak about the possibilities of a renewed relationship with Yahweh.[2] However, 30:1–10 goes a step further than 4:29–31 to envision a return home from exile. Together, these optimistic passages form an interpretive bracket around the address of Moses.

Because they refer to both "the blessing and the curse," vv. 1–10 attach more directly to chapter 28 than to chapter 29, which incorporates only curses. Accordingly, 30:2, 8, and 10 reply to the similar language of 28:1, 15, 45. Similarly, 30:3 responds to 28:64, 30:5 to 28:62–63, and 30:9 to 28:4, 11, 63. However, chapter 29 intervenes before chapter 30 and thus separates 30:1–10 from chapter 28. This editorial sequence appropriately holds off expressing any consolation until all possible punishments have been articulated.[3]

Verses 1–3 form a long sentence with vv. 1–2 as apodosis and v. 3 as protasis. The path of return is laid out step by step. First (v. 1), Israel will take these blessings and curses to heart in the land of exile. The text refers not just to the curse, but to the whole cycle—first blessing, then curse. Both will occur, and in that order. Second (v. 2), Israel initiates a complete and sincere return to Yahweh through renewed obedience (cf. 4:30). Next (vv. 3–5), Yahweh will gather Israel together and restore it to the land. Those dispersed to earth's farthest margin (cf. 4:32) will return to the land. Since these margins extend to the "ends of the sky," Yahweh's heavenly control extends even to those in far-off exile.[4] The "ancestors" in v. 5 are not the patriarchs, but those who enjoyed the phase of blessing and prosperity in Israel's history.

There is another step (vv. 6, 8). Loving Yahweh and obeying will become second nature, because Yahweh will act to unblock hearts. Circumcising the heart is a metaphor for a radical, interior renewal that makes love and obedience fully possible (cf. Jer 4:4). Circumcision of the heart makes the obedience

---

2. Deuteronomy 4:29–31 represents the same optimistic outlook and theology as 30:1–10 and is probably the work of the same author; see H. W. Wolff, "The Kerygma of the Deuteronomic Historical Work" (trans. F. C. Prussner), in W. Brueggemann and Wolff, *The Vitality of Old Testament Traditions* (2d ed.; Atlanta: John Knox, 1975), 83–100; repr. in *Reconsidering Israel and Judah*, ed. Knoppers and McConville, 62–78. For detailed analysis, see D. Knapp, *Deuteronomium 4*, 137–38, 154–57.

3. Rofé, "Covenant in the Land of Moab," in *Das Deuteronomium*, ed. Lohfink, 311–12.

4. Apparently v. 3 is literarily dependent on Jer 29:13–14a. For associations between vv. 3–4 and Jeremiah, Second Isaiah, and Ezekiel, see N. Mendecki, "Dtn 30:3–4—nachexilisch?" *BZ* 29 (1985): 267–71. Also A. Schenker, "Unwiderrufliche Umkehr und neuer Bund: Vergleich zwischen Dt 4:25–31, 30:1–14; Jer 31:31–34," *FZPhTh* 27 (1980): 93–106.

of 6:5 possible and fulfills the demand made by 10:16. Its positive effects are not just for the short term, but include future generations as well.[5]

In the last step, Yahweh will transfer the curses onto Israel's foes where they "belong" (7:15), but the blessings of prosperity will shower upon Israel (vv. 7, 9).[6] Verse 10 is a summary. All this will occur if Israel obeys and wholeheartedly returns. The essential first step in this movement must be taken by Israel, but only Yahweh's willingness to "have compassion" (v. 3) can lead to restoration and only what Yahweh promises to do in v. 6 can make Israel's love and obedience enduringly possible.

[11–14] Moses abruptly stops portraying the future and returns to the present "Moab moment." He takes up once again the decisive challenge for obedience set forth in 29:1–20 [ET 2–21]. His tone shifts from warning and threatening to persuading and encouraging. The argument is that the law is not beyond human capacity to understand nor is it undisclosed and remote. This is a user-friendly law, easy to grasp and freely available. The essential point is simply to "do it" (the last words of vv. 12, 13, and 14).

"This commandment" is used inclusively for all of Deuteronomy (cf. 5:31–6:2; 11:22; 19:9). It is not "too hard" (literally "wonderful"), connoting something beyond comprehension rather than something too hard to perform. "Wonderful" suggests realities beyond ordinary purview (17:8; Ps 131:1) or human understanding (Ps 139:6; Prov 30:18; Job 42:3). This assertion is at odds with v. 6, which asserts that divine circumcision of the heart is a necessary prerequisite for obedience. "Too wonderful" anticipates the vertical distance to the heavenly realm in v. 12; "too far away" points to the horizontal distance of v. 13. Verses 12 and 13 suggest a sort of heroic and epic quest, rather like that of Gilgamesh. Wisdom literature speaks of the fruitless quest for unreachable wisdom (Job 28:12–28; cf. Ps 139:8–9). The inaccessibility of heaven was a proverbial motif (Prov 30:4). However, the law of Deuteronomy does not involve a remote wisdom (cf. Qoh 7:23) that must be sought out; it is a revealed and known reality. Its proximity correlates with the nearness of Yahweh stressed in Deut 4:7. It is readily available "in the public domain"; no one needs to strive to "proclaim it to us that we may do it" (vv. 12–13). This line of argument may clarify the obscurity of 29:28 [ET 29]; the commandment is not a secret thing, but something accessible, revealed so that

---

5. The theology of v. 6 is similar to that of Jer 31:31–34 and 32:37–41. For an argument that vv. 1–10 represent a post-Deuteronomic theology that sees restoration as a result of Yahweh's actions rather than a process initiated by Israel's repentance, see M. Z. Brettler, "Predestination in Deuteronomy 30:1–10," in *Those Elusive Deuteronomists: The Phenomenon of Pan-Deuteronomism* (ed. L. Schearing and S. McKenzie; JSOTSup 268; Sheffield: Sheffield Academic Press, 1999), 171–88. Brettler argues that the syntax of vv. 1b-2 and 10 is not conditional.

6. Verse 7 may be an addition. It breaks the continuity between vv. 6 and 8 and uses 'ālâ for "curse" (cf. ch. 29) instead of qĕlālâ.

it may be performed. The availability of the law is illustrated by Israel's capacity to memorize and internalize it (v. 14, "in your mouth and in your heart"; note n). The reader is reminded of 6:6–9 and 11:18–19, where verbalized instruction and internal mediation take place in Israel's hearts and mouths.[7]

[15–20] Moses focuses the critical option offered by Deuteronomy into its sharpest form, while amplifying the rhetoric of 11:26–28. Verse 15 sets out the two divergent choices. Verse 16 depicts the future of obedience. Then vv. 17–18 describe the shape of things to come if Israel selects the way of apostasy. Finally, vv. 19–20 admonish the audience to take the only option conceivable: "Choose life!" With this forceful appeal, Moses arrives at the rhetorical goal of 28:69 [ET 29:1]–30:20. A repetition of "today" signifies that now is the moment of decision for both the assembly at Moab and the reader of Deuteronomy: "today I set, today I command, today I declare, today I call to witness" (vv. 15, 16, 18, 19). Moses uses polar opposites to persuade the audience that making the right choice is simplicity itself: life versus death, prosperity (*ṭôb*) opposed to calamity (*rā'*), blessing rather than curse, "length of days" (v. 20) in opposition to "not enjoy long life" (v. 18). The contrast of life and death is a common motivational theme in wisdom literature (Prov 11:19; 14:27; 18:21).

The choice does not involve merely consenting to the covenant, however, but actually obeying it. The option is either "if you obey" (v. 16, literally "listen"; note p) or "if you do not listen" (v. 17). Verse 16 gathers together Deuteronomy's language of obedience (10:12; 11:1, 22) and reward (4:1; 7:13; 8:1). It uses an expansive rhetoric of triplets: three tasks ("love, walk, keep"), three synonyms for law ("commandments, decrees, ordinances"), and three results of obedience ("live, multiply, Yahweh will bless you"). Verse 19 sets this choice into the context of an appeal to heaven and earth as a *merismus* describing the totality of creation (cf. 4:26; 31:28). This appeal to heaven and earth may also allude to their role as witnesses in international treaties. The "love" and "cling" of v. 20 reflects the language of personal affection and loyalty (Gen 34:3; 1 Kgs 11:2; Prov 18:24; cf. Deut 11:22; Josh 22:5).

---

7. For the exilic character of this section and its relationship to Isa 55:10–11, see E. Aurelius, "Heilsgegenwart im Wort: Dtn 30,11–14," in *Liebe und Gebot*, ed. Kratz and Spieckermann, 13–29.

Final Words from Moses and Yahweh 31:1–30

Preparing for the Future

31:1 Moses finished speaking[a] all these words to all Israel. 2 He said to them, "Today I am one hundred twenty years old. I am no longer able to come in and go out.[b] Yahweh has said to me, 'Do not cross this Jordan.' 3 Yahweh your God himself will cross over before you. He will destroy these nations before you, and you will dispossess them. Joshua is the one[c] who will cross over before you, just as Yahweh promised. 4 Yahweh will do to them just as he did to Sihon and Og, the kings of the Amorites, and to their land, when he destroyed them.[d] 5 Yahweh will give them over to you and you shall do to them just as[e] I have commanded you. 6 Be brave and strong! Do not fear or be alarmed about them, because Yahweh your God is the one going with you. He will not abandon you or forsake you."

7 Then Moses summoned Joshua and said to him in the sight of all Israel: "Be brave and strong, for you are the one who will go with[f] this people into the land that Yahweh has sworn to their ancestors to give them; and you will cause them to inherit it. 8 Yahweh is the one who will go before you. He will be with you.[g] He will not abandon you or forsake you. Do not fear or be terrified."

9 Then Moses wrote down this law,[h] and gave it to the priests, the sons of Levi who carry the ark of the covenant of Yahweh, and to the elders[i] of Israel. 10 Moses commanded them saying, "At the end of every seven years, at the time appointed for the year of debt remission, during the Feast of Booths, 11 when all Israel comes to appear[j] before Yahweh your God at the place that he will choose, you shall read this law before all Israel in their hearing. 12 Assemble the people—men, women, and small children, and the alien resident in your towns—so that they may hear and learn to fear[k] Yahweh your God and to be careful to do all the words of this law. 13 Their children also,[l] who do not know it, will hear and learn to fear Yahweh your God, as long as you live[m] in the land that you are crossing the Jordan to take over."

14 Yahweh said to Moses, "Now your time to die has drawn near. Summon Joshua and present yourselves in the tent of meeting, so that I may charge him."[n] So Moses and Joshua went and presented themselves in the tent of meeting. 15 Yahweh appeared[o] in the tent in a pillar of cloud, and the pillar of cloud stood at the entrance of the tent.[p]

Song and Law as Witnesses

16 Yahweh said to Moses, "Soon you are going to lie down with your ancestors. This people will set out to prostitute themselves after the foreign gods in their midst[q] in the land to which they are going. They will forsake me and break my covenant that I have made with them. 17 My wrath will break out against them on that day and I will forsake them and hide my face from them. They will become something to be devoured and many calamities and distresses will happen to them. One will say on that day, "Surely it is because my God[r] is not in my midst that these calamities have happened to me!" 18 I will surely hide my face[s] on that day on account of all the wickedness they have done because they turned to other gods. 19 And now write down this song[t] for yourselves and teach it to the Israelites; put it in their mouths, in order that this song may be a witness for me against the Israelites.[u] 20 When I bring them into the land about which I swore to their ancestors,[v] one flowing with milk and honey, and they have eaten and been satisfied and grown fat, then they will turn to other gods and serve them, and they will despise me and break my covenant. 21 Then when many calamities and distresses happen to them,[w] this song will testify against them as a witness, because it will not be forgotten from the mouth of their offspring. For I know their inclination that they are doing today, even before I have brought them into the land about which I swore."[x] 22 So Moses wrote down this song that very day and taught it to the Israelites.

23 Then Yahweh[y] charged Joshua son of Nun and said, "Be brave and strong, for you will bring the Israelites into the land about which I swore to them. I will be with you."

24 When Moses had finished writing down the words of this law in a book to the very end, 25 Moses commanded the Levites who carry the ark of the covenant of Yahweh, saying, 26 "Take this book of the law and put it beside the ark of the covenant of Yahweh your God and let it be there as a witness against you. 27 For I know your rebellion and your stubbornness. If while I am still alive with you today you are so rebellious toward Yahweh, how much more then after my death! 28 Assemble to me all the elders of your tribes[z] and your officers, that I may speak these words in their hearing and call heaven and earth to witness against them. 29 For I know that after my death you will surely act corruptly and turn aside from the way that I have commanded you. Calamity will happen to you in days to come, because you will do what is evil in Yahweh's opinion, offending him by the work of your hands."

30 Then Moses recited the words of this song to the very end, in the hearing of the whole assembly of Israel.

a. Follows 1QDeut[b] and OG *wykl mšh ldbr* as internally more consistent as a conclusion to what Moses has said so far (cf. 32:45). MT (supported by Sam., Vulg., Syr.) originated as a transposition of *k* and *l*: *wylk mšh wydbr*, "and Moses went and spoke." MT is the easier text because Moses has not actually finished speaking.

b. Alternate, more interpretive translations: "act as a military leader" (Josh 14:11; 1 Kgs 3:7) or "move about freely."

c. Follows Sam. and OG in reading a definite article with the participle to emphasize that Joshua will cross, and not Moses: *wyhwš' hw'h'br*. In v. 3a, however, the preferable text is MT: *yhwh . . . hw' 'br*, without the definite article and the note of contrast: "Yahweh . . . himself will cross" (cf. 7:1; 9:3). These two readings best suit sense and context. There is no syntactical connection between v. 3a and v. 3b, suggesting that these are alternative responses to uneasiness over Moses remaining behind.

d. Alternate translation: "whom he destroyed."

e. Follows the shorter text of OG (supported by Vulg.), *k'šr*, "just as" (cf. 26:14) rather than *kkl-hmṣwt 'šr*, "as the whole commandment that," an MT expansion resembling 26:13.

f. Follows MT *tbw'* (Qal) *'t-h'm*, "you will go with the people." For *bw' 't* as "go with," cf. 19:5. OG supports the Qal verb but reads a different preposition: *lpny h'm*, "in front of the people," perhaps harmonizing with 3:28. Sam., Vulg., Syr. harmonize with v. 23: *tby'* (hip'il) *'t-h'm*, "you will lead the people," a confusion of *y* for *w*. It is possible that MT and OG "corrected" an original hip'il in order to avoid the suggestion that Joshua, and not Yahweh, was Israel's real leader. However, this fails to explain why the hip'il of v. 23 would have remained unrevised. See M. Klein, "Deut 31:7, *tbw'* or *tby'*?" *JBL* 92 (1973): 584–85; L. Laberge, "Le texte de Deutéronome 31 (Dt 31,1–29; 32,44–47)," in *Pentateuchal and Deuteronomistic Studies: Papers Read at the XIIIth IOSOT Congress* (ed. C. Brekelmans and J. Lust; BETL 94; Leuven: Leuven University Press, 1990), 148–49.

g. Follows MT. The shorter OG is the translator's simplification of a redundant text: "Yahweh who will go with you"; see Wevers, *Greek Text*, 494.

h. Follows MT. 4QDeut[h] and OG expand with *'l spr*, "in a book," to harmonize with v. 24. Space considerations show that 4QDeut[h] also agrees with OG in adding *bywm hhw'*, "on that day," after "Moses commanded them" in v. 10 (cf. 27:11).

i. Follows OG. MT supplements with *kl*: "*all* the elders."

j. *BHS* follows a popular conjecture that this verb was originally intended as Qal, "to see the face of Yahweh," rather than nip'al (cf. 16:16 note k). However, the tradition of a passive vocalization is at least as old as Sam. and the LXX translator.

k. Alternate translation: "learn it and so fear."

l. Alternate translation understanding the initial *waw* as emphatic: "especially their children."

m. Follows MT. Sam., OG ,Vulg. witness to an easier text: *hm ḥyym*, "*they* live."

n. Literally "command," either as "commission" or as "instruct."

o. Follows MT. OG reflects elements of Num 12:5. Perhaps this was triggered by a misreading of *wyr'*, "appeared," as *wyrd*, "came down." In place of MT v. 15a, the Greek translator reused the Greek of Num 12:5: "and Yahweh came down in a cloud [Numbers has a 'pillar of cloud'] and stood at the door(s) of the tent of meeting." Then the translator created a repetitious text by continuing with Deut 31:15b (Wevers, *Greek Text*,

498–99). Consequently, the omissions indicated by *BHS* notes 15b and 15c need not be taken seriously. *BHS* note 15d (an expansion picked up from the end of v. 15a) does not represent the true OG (= LXX^B; 848).

p. The verse is not internally consistent. The pillar is "in" the tent, but takes its stand "at the entrance." This may harmonize the JE notion of "at the entrance" (Num 12:5) with the P concept of "in" (Num 1:1). Translators cover this over by rendering v. 15a "at the tent." See A. Rofé, "Textual Criticism in the Light of Historical-Literary Criticism: Deuteronomy 31:14–15," *Eretz Israel* 16 (1982): 173.

q. The position of *bĕqirbô* is ambiguous. An alternate translation connecting the pronomial suffix to "land" (construed as masculine; cf. Gen 13:6): "gods in the midst of the land." Perhaps *bĕqirbô* and *šāmmâ*, "to there," are conflated doublet readings. Here and in the following verses the people are referred to in both singular ("it") and plural ("them"). Smooth English requires a consistently plural translation.

r. Follows MT. 4QDeut^c and OG supplement with the divine name: *yhwh 'lhy*, "Yahweh my God."

s. Follows MT. Sam., OG, Syr., Tg. harmonize with v. 17 by adding *mhm*, "from them."

t. Follows MT. 4QDeut^c and OG expand to match v. 30: *dbry*, "the words of [this song]."

u. The change in MT from plural address ("write for yourselves") to singular ("teach it . . . put it") is logical. Moses and Joshua are to write the song; Moses alone is to teach it. In v. 22 Moses alone writes and teaches, so Syr. levels all of v. 19 into second person singular. Yet in 32:44 both Moses and Joshua recite the song, so 4QDeut^c,OG, Vulg. make all of v. 19 plural.

v. Follows MT. Sam. fills out the expected formula (cf. v. 7): *ltt lhm*, "to give to them." An independent development in the Greek tradition (not OG) led to the same expansion. *BHS* note 20c is an error (Seb for Sam.).

w. Follows MT. OG lost v. 21aα through an inner-Greek haplography from *kai* to *kai*.

x. Secondary expansions softened the abrupt MT: "to its ancestors" (Sam.), "to their ancestors" (OG and Syr.), "to it" (Vulg.).

y. Literally "he." Yahweh is giving orders to Joshua, speaking in the first person (MT and Sam.). This abrupt appearance of Yahweh as grammatical subject shows that v. 23 originally connected directly to vv. 14–15. OG took the subject as Moses (although not explicitly, OG = LXX^B, 963) and so altered the following verbs to "Yahweh swore" and "he will be with you."

z. Follows MT (supported by Sam.) in reading the unique *zqny šbṭykm*, "the elders of your tribes." Some Hebrew MSS read the more common *r'šy*, "heads of" (cf. 1:15; 5:23). 4QDeut^b and OG witness to a text inflated into four groups (cf. 29:9 [ET 10]; Josh 23:2; 24:1): [*r'šy?*] *šbṭykm wzqnykm wšpṭykm wšṭrykm*, "your tribes [or tribal leaders] and your elders and your judges and your officers." This longer text seems to conflate a reversal of the order of "elders" and "tribes" with a misreading of *šbṭykm*, "your tribes," as *špṭykm*, "your judges." The Greek translation of 29:9 [ET 10] (see note g there) probably helped solidify this reading. OG puts *kl*, "all," before "these words," rather than at the beginning of the verse as MT does.

Verse 1 brings to a close the speech of Moses that began in 28:69 [ET 29:1]. The mode of discourse changes in a fundamental way, picking up the flow of narrative from chapters 1–3. The "reported speech" of direct discourse shifts back into "reporting speech" describing action. Speech continues, but now it is embedded within narrative.[1] The horizon of interest changes from lawgiving and covenant making to issues of transition into the future. These topics include the age of Moses and his death, change in leadership, periodic reading of the law, and the need for witnesses to warn against future apostasy. In short, the story of chapters 1–3 begins again in chapter 31 and will culminate in the death of Moses reported in chapter 34. There is a sequence of seven speeches. Moses speaks five times: the three speeches in vv. 2–13 (law, Joshua, law), again in vv. 24–29 (law), and in v. 30 (introduction to the Song of Moses). Yahweh speaks twice, vv. 14–15, 23 (Joshua), and vv. 16–22 (song).

This chapter presents a classic problem in critical analysis. The flow of events is puzzling, and evidence for a complex history of development is extensive.

> Verses 14–15 (Yahweh charges Joshua at the tent) abruptly break into the narrative. At the same time, the connection of vv. 14–15 to v. 23 (where the unexpressed grammatical subject must be Yahweh, not Moses) is interrupted in turn by vv. 16–22 (the song as witness).
> The act of Moses in writing the law (vv. 9–13) is picked up again only in v. 24, after digressions concerning Joshua (vv. 13–14, 23) and the song (vv. 16–22).
> There are doublets: appointing Joshua (vv. 7–8 and 14–15, 23), handing over the law (vv. 9 and 25–26), communication of the song (vv. 22 and 30), and the identity of the future witness (song in v. 19, but law in v. 26).

Four observations are in order. First, the return to the narrative trajectory of chapters 1–3 and interest in Israel's life in the land signals the reappearance of DH as a primary author. Verses 1–13 foreshadow the plot of DH that unfolds in the books of Joshua through Kings. The concerns of DH resurface: transmission of leadership to Joshua (Deut 1:38; 3:21, 28), priests as ark carriers (Josh 3–4, 6), the conquest, and public reading of the law (Josh 8:32–35; 2 Kgs 23:1–2).

Second, because law and song compete for attention as the future witness, one must assume that one interest has been superimposed over the other. The Song of Moses (ch. 32) is a literary piece with its own independent origin that was incorporated into Deuteronomy only after the book had taken its fundamental shape. This suggests that the preamble to the song in vv. 16–22 should be distinguished from vv. 1–13, which reflect the concerns of DH, and from vv. 24–29, where the written law has the same cautionary function as the song Moses is about to recite. That the song had an earlier existence apart from and

---

1. Chapter 27 anticipated this shift to narrative, but chs. 28–30 returned to direct speech.

previous to its present context is demonstrated by the circumstance that the verses that introduce it refer only to its negative content and ignore 32:26–43.

Third, these sections divide into those that use Deuteronomistic language (vv. 2–13, 24–29) and those that do not (vv. 14–15, 23; 16–22). In the latter category, vv. 14–15, 23 reflect the language and interests of JE (pillar, tent of meeting). This suggests that the theophany of vv. 14–15, 23 was added to supplement vv. 7–8 as part of the process that incorporated Deuteronomy into the Pentateuch. Then vv. 16–22 were inserted into vv. 14–15, 23 at an even later stage in order to integrate the Song of Moses into Deuteronomy.

The fourth observation is that vv. 24–29 differ from vv. 9–13 in important ways. Rather than being read publicly to inculcate obedience, the law is archived into storage as a *witness*, giving it the same function the song has in vv. 19, 21. Its guardians are not the "priests, the sons of Levi" (v. 9; cf. 21:5), but the "Levites" (cf. 18:7; 27:14). In vv. 28–29 Moses calls for an assembly of the people for the purpose of reciting "these words," which turn out to be the song. Because assembly to hear the law that Moses has just recited would make no sense, these verses must have the song in view. Moreover, vv. 28–29 have a close counterpart in 32:45–46, which refocus attention from song back to law ("these words," "all the words," "all the words of this law"). One must conclude that vv. 24–29 presuppose the presence of the Song of Moses in the text in the role of witness, and are an even later "corrective" response that seeks to (re)assert the place of the law as a warning for the future alongside the witness of the song. In summary, the present form of chapter 31 is the result of successive acts of supplementation: vv. 1–13 (DH) + vv. 14–15, 23 (JE) + 16–22 (song as witness) + vv. 24–29 (law as witness).[2]

For all its complexity, this chapter does reflect a fairly coherent order imposed on it by the final redactional process. It divides into a positive half (vv. 1–13) and a negative half (vv. 16–30), held together by the theophany of vv. 14–15. There are two transmissions of the law to Levitical personnel, two direct divine speeches (vv. 14 and 23), and two parallel addresses to Joshua (vv. 7–9 and 23–25). In the positive segment (vv. 1–13), the law calls for faithful obedience. In the negative section (vv. 16–30) the law and the song together serve

2. Recent studies include E. Talstra, "Deuteronomy 31: Confusion or Conclusion? The Story of Moses' Threefold Succession," in *Deuteronomy and Deuteronomic Literature*, ed. Vervenne and Lust, 87–110; M. Rose, "Empoigner le Pentateuque par sa fin! L'investiture de Josué et la mort de Moïse," in *Le Pentateuque en question* (ed. A. de Pury; Le Monde de la Bible 19; Geneva: Labor et Fides, 1989), 129–47. J. Levenson, "Who Inserted the Book of the Torah?" *HTR* 68 (1975): 203–33, proposes that the song was incorporated as part of an exilic redactional framework (4:1–40; 29:21–28 [ET 22–29]; 30:1–20; 31:16–22, 24–29) that utilized its vocabulary. A. Rofé, "The Composition of Deuteronomy 31 in Light of a Conjecture about Inversion in the Order of Columns in the Biblical Text," *Shnaton* 3 (1979): 59–76, suggests an accidental transfer of manuscript columns (original order: vv. 14–15, 23–27, 16–22, 28–30).

as witnesses against disobedience. The hinge between these diptych panels is the theophany of vv. 14–15. The theophany stresses the topic of the future, which leads to the shift to a negative outlook. Additionally, the dramatic power of divine manifestation authorizes the unexpected appearance of the Song of Moses as a partner to the Mosaic law.

The seven speeches are each embedded in brief narratives and arranged so that long and short speeches alternate. These speeches begin in a positive mode (vv. 1–6 [long], 7–8 [short], 9–13 [long], 14–15 [short], and then shift to a negative outlook (vv. 16–22 [long], 23 [short], 24–29 [long]). In addition, vv. 9–27 are shaped into a concentric topical pattern with the song in the center:

> law—vv. 9–13
>   Joshua—vv. 14–15
>   Song—vv. 16–22.
>   Joshua—v. 23
> law—vv. 24–27[3]

This redactional arrangement makes law the framework for the appointment of Joshua and associates the song with the law. This arrangement seems to explain why vv. 14–15, 23 were split apart in the redaction process. As a resumptive repetition of v. 9, v. 24 picks up the narrative thread from vv. 9–13 after the theophany and the role of the song in the future has been described. The resumptive frame of 31:30 and 32:44 brackets the song and incorporates it into the narrative.

Even in the complex final form of the text, the reader is able to negotiate a plot featuring frequent shifts of actors and scenes. The emphasis is on successors to Moses that will serve Israel in the future: Joshua, the written law, priests and elders, and the song. The roles of each are articulated and interrelated. Priests and elders are associated with the law (vv. 9, 25) and the elders with the song as well (v. 28). Law and song are associated in their common function as witnesses (v. 26) and by being conveyed by Moses "to the very end" (vv. 24 and 30). Joshua is linked to the song by the plural "write" of v. 19 (and later by 32:44).[4]

---

3. Lohfink, "Bundesschluss in *Studien zum Deuteronomium I*," 48–51.

4. For a reconstruction of the order of events that lies behind the order presented in the text itself, see N. Lohfink, "Zur Fabel in Dtn 31–32," in *Studien zum Deuteronomium IV*, 247–63. He understands the succession of events as vv. 9, 24 (Moses had previously written [pluperfect] the law), vv. 1–8 (the assembly of chs. 29–30), vv. 14–23 (theophany in which Joshua is appointed and the song revealed; v. 22 being proleptic), vv. 9, 24–27 (transfer of law), vv. 28–30 (recitation of the song to the elders), vv. 10–13 (instructions for reading of the law), 32:44 (a second assembly of the people at which Moses and Joshua teach the song), 32:45–47 (last words of Moses). Verses 9–13 and 24–29 would then narrate the same event, reported in two stages. An alternate order of events is suggested by C. J. Labuschagne, "The Setting of the Song of Moses in Deuteronomy," in *Deuteronomy and Deuteronomic Literature*, ed. Vervenne and Lust, 111–29, who proposes that the "torah" in vv. 24–26 actually refers to the song viewed as a "teaching."

[1–8] The text returns the reader from the future vision of chapter 30 to the narrative present on the threshold of conquest. In format, vv. 1–6 are a "war oration," comparable to 1:29–33; 7:17–24; 9:1–6. Verse 1 concludes the address of chapters 29–30 and functions along with 32:45 as an inclusive bracket for chapters 31 and 32.

Moses has reached the age for death (v. 2; Gen 6:3). He cites Yahweh's earlier announcement that he will not cross the Jordan (3:27), but says nothing about the reason given for this in 3:26. The end of his leadership is the result of old age and disability (v. 2a; contrast 34:7), but also a matter of divine veto (v. 2b). Verse 3 describes incursion into the new land with two grammatically unconnected, alternative statements, one about Yahweh and one about Joshua. The statement about Joshua (v. 3b) connects directly to the promise made to him in 3:28. Emphatic grammar (note c) contrasts Joshua's crossing with the fact that Moses will not cross. In v. 3a the emphatic grammar stresses Yahweh's actions ("cross," "destroy") as assurances of divine support. Perhaps v. 3a about Yahweh was added as a corrective supplement to v. 3b.

Verse 5 calls on Israel to perform the acts of destruction commanded in 7:1–5; 12:2–3; 20:16–17. Verse 6 urges courage on the whole nation and reassures them of Yahweh's presence, as a prelude to this same charge and assurance being directed to Joshua in vv. 7–8. "Be brave and strong" (also vv. 7 and 23; 3:28) may derive from the genre of priestly oracle (Pss 27:14; 31:25 [ET 24]). These short, emphatic rallying cries would have been appropriate to crisis situations such as impending battle: "Be brave and strong" (Josh 1:6, 9, 18; 10:25); "do not fear or be alarmed" (Deut 1:29; 7:21; 20:3; Josh 1:9). The assurance that Yahweh will accompany Israel is characteristic of the language of sacral war (cf. Deut 20:4; 23:15 [ET 14]).

Verses 7–8 take up the theme of encouraging Joshua from 3:21–22, 28. Moses obeys Yahweh's command given in 3:28 and communicates publicly to Joshua what he had urged on him (only privately?) in 3:22. Verses 7–8 have same shape as v. 23: a formula of encouragement followed by a description of Joshua's task, which is followed in turn by a formula of support.[5]

[9–13] Moses commands periodic reenactments of the Horeb experience (cf. v. 12 and 4:10: "assemble the people," "hear," "learn/teach," "fear," "words") and imitates the pattern of writing and handing over laws that Yahweh practiced there (5:22; 10:4). The prospect of a future without Moses requires that his multifaceted leadership role be divided among several successors (v. 9). Perhaps

---

5. Lohfink suggests a special formula for appointment to office ("The Deuteronomic Picture of the Transfer of Authority from Moses to Joshua," in *Theology of the Pentateuch*, 234–47). Lohfink also finds his threefold formula in 3:28 and Josh 1:6, 9b, proposing that Joshua's task is divided into two stages: "go over" (conquer) and "cause to inherit" (allot the land). Moses installs Joshua to both tasks in vv. 7–8, but Yahweh installs him only to the first in v. 23 and not to the second until Josh 1:6, 9b. For a rebuttal, see D. J. McCarthy, "An Installation Genre?" *JBL* 90 (1971): 31–41.

the Levitical priests represent the divine side of the covenant relationship (cf. 27:9, 14) and the elders the human side (cf. 5:23; 27:1).[6] Deuteronomy is appropriately entrusted to priests and elders, for they are often responsible for administering its provisions.

Public reading allows the law to continue to be effective for future generations, even though Moses will no longer be present. Writing the law not only makes public reading possible, but also allows the law to be effective in future situations (17:18–20; 28:58, 61; 29:26 [ET 27]; 30:10). Written law can bridge the physical distance between Moab and the new land and the temporal gap between those who first hear it and their descendants. The special capability of written law to transcend time and space also lies behind the inscribed stones of 27:2–4, 8 and the command to write the law on doorposts and display it on hands and foreheads (6:8–9; 11:18, 20).[7] Moses' act of writing helps the reader understand earlier references to a "book of the law" and serves as an etiology for Deuteronomy's existence and a validation of its authority.[8] Because context indicates that the law is already in written form (29:19, 20, 26 [ET 20, 21, 27]; 30:10), one may choose to read Moses' act of writing as a pluperfect: "Moses had already written," (*IBHS* 33.2.3).

This gathering is related to the remission year and inclusive assembly of Booths at the central "place" (vv. 10–11; 15:1–11; 16:13–15). The vocabulary of "appear" seems to derive from 16:16. The list of participants emphasizes totality: "all" appear and "all" are to hear. According to vv. 12–13, there is a "behavioral objective" in this recurring educational experience: "hear" in order to "learn to fear" and "do" (cf. 5:1: "hear . . . learn . . . do"; 17:19: "read . . . learn . . . fear"). The children, as yet less accountable, hear only to "learn to fear" (v. 13), while "to do" is reserved for their elders. The association of written law with children and length of life in the land appears also in 11:18–21 and 17:18–20. There is no hint in the text that any sort of covenant renewal ceremony is envisioned. Because no regularly scheduled gatherings to hear the law are reported elsewhere, this is probably a purely utopian provision.[9]

[14–15] The story line about Moses moves a step forward, from the incapacity

6. N. Lohfink, "Die Ältesten Israels und der Bund: Zum Zusammenhang von Dtn 5,23; 26,17–19; 27,1.9f und 31,9," in *Studien zum Deuteronomium IV*, 265–83.

7. S. Amsler, "Loi orale et loi écrite dans le Deutéronome," in *Das Deuteronomium*, ed. Lohfink, 51–54.

8. For the literary tradition of a dying wise person leaving a written instruction, see S. Weitzman, "Lessons from the Dying: The Role of Deuteronomy 32 in Its Narrative Setting," *HTR* 87 (1994): 377–93.

9. DH delays the dedication of the temple in order to place it into the 448th year after Moses gives this command, a number divisible by seven. Solomon's year 4 was 480 years after the exodus (1 Kgs 6:1) and thus 440 years after Moses spoke Deuteronomy (Deut 1:3). The temple was finished in the eighth month of Solomon's year 11 (1 Kgs 6:38; 447 years), but not dedicated until

of age (v. 2) to the prospect of death. This "death of Moses" plot parallels the patriarchal death scenes in Genesis and leads on to provide an occasion for the Song and the Blessing of Moses (chs. 32 and 33). The theme continues in v. 16 ("lie down with your ancestors"; Gen 47:30), v. 28 (convening for the dying leader's testament; cf. Gen 47:29), and v. 29 (warning about events "in days to come"; Gen 49:1).

Yahweh speaks directly for the first time outside the frame of Moses' words. The appearance of the tent of meeting is totally unexpected—perhaps effecting a surprise appropriate to theophany! The text is related to Exod 33:7–11 (a non-P tradition). This direct theophany removes any doubt over Joshua's authority. Because the tent remains the location of Yahweh's instructions in vv. 16–22 (cf. v. 23), the theophany also endorses the upcoming song as divinely revealed.

[16–22] The future predicted in general terms in 4:25; 8:19; 29:21 [ET 22] is now made specific. The death of Moses will trigger it. These verses view disobedience as something already determined, inevitable. The song is portrayed exclusively in negative terms, reflecting only one aspect of an incorporated independent poem. When Yahweh's face is hidden (v. 18), the song will still be on hand to speak (v. 19). There are verbal connections backward in Deuteronomy and forward to the song itself. Verses 16–17 echo the "alien gods" of 32:12, 16, 22, 23. Verse 17 reflects the payback logic of 32:21, the hidden divine face of 32:20 (along with 31:18), and more generally the calamities of 32:22–25. Verse 20 describes the movement from satiation to apostasy that is typical of Deuteronomy (6:10–13; 8:12–20; 11:14–16), but also present in 32:13–18. The root *nāʾaṣ* ("despise") points to 32:19.

Verse 16 distances Yahweh from Israel with a contemptuous reference to "this people" (cf. 9:13, 27) and condemns them with the language of prostitution (cf. Judg 2:17; 8:27, 33). Time moves quickly forward to the readers' own present; the obedient period under the leadership of Joshua disappears from view. In Deuteronomy the indictment of the people for "breaking" (*prr* hipʿil) the covenant occurs only in vv. 16 and 20. The use of "my God" in the dramatic quotation of the disloyal person is ironic. (Context makes the translation "my gods" improbable.) There is wordplay in v. 18 between "my face" (*pānay*) and "turned" (*pānâ*). "Face" describes Yahweh's attentive presence (32:20). To "turn to" (*pānâ*) is to rely on (Ps 40:5 [ET 4]).

Verse 19 turns attention to the song ("And now"). "In their mouths" (vv. 19, 21) signifies that Israel should be able to recite it from memory. It is to be not merely available, but actually uttered so that it will confront people from their

---

the seventh month of year 12 (8:2, 65; 448 years). The law was actually recited every seven years in the late monarchy according to W. L. Holladay, "A Proposal for Reflections in the Book of Jeremiah of the Seven-Year Recitation of the Law in Deuteronomy (Deut 31,10–13)," in *Das Deuteronomium*, ed. Lohfink, 326–28.

very own mouths. The song will attest to future generations that their sin and the resulting divine judgment had been both foreseen ("I know," v. 21) and foretold ("teach it," v. 19). Joshua joins Moses in writing the song (note u), reminding the reader that the dramatic locale remains the tent of meeting. Verse 21 insinuates that this negative outcome is inevitable, given Israel's existing "inclination" (implicitly toward evil). Because that inclination is already present "today" (v. 21), the song must be written and taught "that very day" (v. 22).

Verse 22 may be taken as proleptic, an assurance that Moses obeyed even though his actual recital is not reported until v. 30. Thus the wording of the song remains hidden from the reader for a while, perhaps as a literary reflection of the private situation of the tent of meeting. Yet the words of Yahweh (vv. 16–21) and of Moses (vv. 28–29) clearly reveal its accusatory character even before Moses recites it.

[23] Verse 23 closes the scene at the tent of meeting; in the final form of the text, this scene incorporates all of vv. 14–23. Only after the all-important song has been introduced (vv. 16–22) does Yahweh finally charge Joshua, something that has been anticipated since v. 14. Recapping the material of vv. 7–8 in the light of newly revealed information about upcoming calamity, Yahweh endorses the commission performed by Moses. The divine oath made to the ancestors (vv. 7, 20) is now understood as having been sworn directly to Israel. Joshua will not just "go with" Israel as in v. 7, but will enable Yahweh's goal of "bringing" them into the land (vv. 20–21).

[24–30] At first, these verses push the song into the background and promote the law instead (vv. 24–26), but finally shift back to introduce a recitation (v. 28) that turns out to be the song (v. 30). Law is associated with the song in being a witness (vv. 19 and 26) and as something communicated "to the very end" (vv. 24 and 30). Verses 24–26 replicate the sequence of vv. 7–9: after a commission given to Joshua, Moses writes the law and entrusts it to Levitical personnel. This reiteration of the action of v. 9 may be taken as a signal that the law must be understood somewhat differently now that Yahweh's theophany has revealed future judgment and the contents of the song. The dreadful future laid bare in the song means that the law must assume the function of being a warning and a witness. The tangible presence of the law book beside the ark will testify that Israel had accepted it and agreed to its terms, yet went on to disobey. For this reason, the law is entrusted here not to priests and elders for public reading, but to Levites for archival storage beside the ark they carry.

In contrast to v. 9, Moses finishes writing the law "in a book to the very end" (v. 24). This suggests that Moses brings to a close a complete and completely transmitted law book that now includes the song, which itself is also completely transmitted (v. 30). Verse 24 is similar to a scribal colophon (cf. Ps 72:20; Jer

51:64; Job 31:40), assuring the reader that the full text of the law has been conveyed in spite of the disconcerting appearance of theophany and song (cf. Deut 5:22). Perhaps because it is to be archived, the law is now explicitly identified as a "book" (contrast vv. 9–13). As an objective witness to expected apostasy, the law book sounds more like a static, iconic document than a living text for ongoing rereading intended to elicit renewed obedience. The notion of Levitical custodianship connects to 10:8 and 17:18 and to the presence of the Decalogue tablets inside the ark (cf. the verbal parallel between v. 26 and 10:2, 5).[10] In association with the portable ark, the law can move forward into Israel's future.

References in v. 27 to "rebellion" (*mrh* hip'il) and "stubbornness" (literally a "stiff neck") are a verbal reminiscence of the golden calf episode (cf., respectively, 9:7, 23, 24 and 9:6, 13). "Act corruptly" (*šḥt* hip'il) and turn aside from the way . . . commanded" and "evil in Yahweh's opinion, offending (*k's* hip'il) him" (v. 29) are cross-references to the same incident (cf. 9:12, 16, 18). This indicates that "the work of your hands" in v. 29 refers to idols (cf. 4:28). Based on the golden calf experience, Moses knows (vv. 27, 29) what Yahweh also knows (v. 21). On the other hand, the language of "act corruptly" and "offend" also appears in the upcoming song (32:5, 16, 21). "These words" (v. 28) turn out to refer to the song and not the law, so that the two entities become associated in the reader's mind. The elders and officers are to hear the song, yet it is also spoken to all (v. 30). Here heaven and earth do not function as witnesses in case of potential disobedience (as in 4:26; 30:19), but witness to the inevitable fact of apostasy instead.

The Song of Moses
32:1–52

Ascribe Greatness to God

32:1 "Listen, O heavens, and I will speak;
  and let the earth hear the words of my mouth.
2 May my teaching drip like rain,
  my speech trickle down like the dew;
  like gentle rain on grass
  and like abundant showers on green plants.
3 For I will proclaim the name of Yahweh.
  Ascribe greatness to our God!

10. C. T. Begg, "The Tables (Deut. x) and the Lawbook (Deut. xxxi)," *VT* 33 (1983): 96–97.

4 The Rock—his work is perfect,
indeed, all his ways are just.
A faithful God and without deceit,
he is righteous and upright.

5 His nonchildren have dealt corruptly with him as their blemish,[a]
a perverse and crooked generation.

6 Is it Yahweh you thus repay,
O foolish and unwise people?
Is not he your father who created you,
he who made you and established you?

Consider the Past: Election, Providence, Apostasy

7 Remember the days of old,
consider the years of each generation.
Ask your father and he will inform you;
your elders, and they will tell you.

8 When the Most High apportioned the nations,
when he divided up humanity,
he fixed[b] the boundaries of peoples
according to the number of the divine beings.[c]

9 Indeed, Yahweh's own portion was his people,
Jacob his surveyed possession.[d]

10 He found him[e] in a desert land,
in a wasteland of howling wilderness.[f]
He shielded him, cared for him,
guarded him as the pupil[g] of his eye.

11 As an eagle protects its nest,
hovers over its young,
he spreads his wings, takes him up,
bears him up on his pinions.

12 Yahweh alone guided him;
and no foreign god was with him.

13 He made him ride over the heights of the land,
and he ate[h] produce of the field.
He suckled him with honey from the crags,
and oil from flinty rock,

14 curds from the herd and milk from the flock,
with fat of lambs and rams,
of Bashan bulls and goats,
along with the choicest wheat;
and grape-blood you drank as foaming wine.

15   Jacob ate and had enough;[i]
        and Jeshurun grew fat and kicked.
        You got fat, you grew thick, you gorged!
    He abandoned God who made him,
        and scorned the Rock of his salvation.

16   They made him jealous with alien things,
        with repugnant things they offended him.

17   They sacrificed to demons, nongods,
        gods they had never known,
    new ones newly arrived,
        whom your[j] ancestors had not dreaded.

18   You were unmindful[k] of the Rock that bore[l] you;
        and you forgot the God who birthed you.

Yahweh Proposes to Destroy Israel

19   Yahweh saw and spurned,[m]
        because of the offensiveness of his sons and daughters.

20   And he said: 'I will hide my face from them,
        I will see what their end will be;
    for they are a perverse[n] generation,
        children with no faithfulness in them.

21   They made me jealous with a nongod,
        offended me with their idols.[o]
    So I will make them jealous with a nonpeople,
        with a foolish nation I will offend them.

22   For a fire is kindled by my anger,
        and burns to the depths of Sheol;
    and it eats up the earth and its produce
        and ignites the foundations of the mountains.

23   I will gather[p] disasters upon them,
        expend my arrows against them:

24   wasting hunger
        and consuming pestilence
        and bitter epidemic
    and the teeth of beasts I will send against them,
        with poison of things that crawl in dust.

25   The sword shall bereave out in the street,
        and terror in the chambers;
    young man and woman alike,
        nursing child with old grayhead.

Yahweh Relents

26   I thought I would strike them down,[q]
       make the memory of them cease from the human race,
27   had I not feared an enemy's offensiveness,
       lest their foes misjudge,
     lest they say, 'Our hand is triumphant
       and it was not Yahweh who did all this.'
28   They are a nation devoid of good counsel,
       and there is no understanding in them.
29   If they were wise, they would understand this;
       they would discern what their end will be.
30   How could one pursue a thousand,
       and two put ten thousand to flight,
     unless their Rock had sold them out,
       and Yahweh had handed them over?
31   Indeed, their rock is not like our Rock,
       as our enemies have assessed.
32   Indeed, their vine comes from the vine stock of Sodom,
       and from the terraces of Gomorrah.
     Their grapes are grapes of poison,
       the clusters are bitter for them.
33   Their wine is the venom of serpents,
       and the cruel poison of asps.
34   Is not this gathered up in store with me,
       sealed in my treasuries?
35   For the day[r] of vindication and recompense,[s]
       for the time when their foot shall slip,
     because the day of their calamity is near,
       and the doom prepared rushes upon them.
36   Indeed, Yahweh will pass favorable judgment on his people,
       and on his servants he will take compassion,
     when he sees that their power is gone,
       and no one left, neither bond nor free.
37   Then he will say: 'Where are their gods,
       the rock where they sought refuge,[t]
38   who ate the fat of their sacrifices,
       drank the wine of their libations?
     Let them rise up and help you;
       let it be your protection!'

Yahweh Vindicates Israel

39   'See now that I, I am the One;
         there is no other god beside me.
      I kill and I make alive;
         I have wounded, but I will heal,
         and no one can deliver from my power.
40   Indeed, I lift up my hand to the sky[u]
         and I say: "As I live forever,
41   when I sharpen my flashing sword
         and my hand holds fast to judgment,
      I will return vindication onto my adversaries
         and will pay back those who hate me.
42   I will make my arrows drunk with blood
         —and my sword shall devour flesh—
      with the blood of slain and captive—
         from the head of the wild-haired enemy."'[v]
43   Raise a shout of joy, O heavens, together with him,
         and bow down to him, all gods!
      For the blood of his children he avenges,
         and returns vindication onto his adversaries;
      and repays those who hate him,
         and makes atonement for the land of his people."[w]

Transition to the Death of Moses

44 Moses came and recited all the words of this song in the hearing of the
people, he and Hoshea son of Nun.[x]

45 When Moses finished speaking these words[y] to all Israel, 46 he said
to them: "Take to heart all the words with which I am admonishing you
today. Command them to your children, so that they may be careful to do
all the words of this law. 47 This is not a trivial matter for you. It is your
very life. By this word you will have long life in the land to which you
are crossing the Jordan to take it over."

48 Yahweh spoke to Moses on that very day, saying,

49 "Go up this mountain of the Abarim, Mount Nebo, which is in the
land of Moab opposite Jericho, and view the land of Canaan, which I am
going to give to the Israelites for a holding. 50 You must die there on the
mountain that you are about to ascend and be gathered to your kinfolk,
just as your brother Aaron died on Mount Hor and was gathered to his
kinfolk, 51 because you committed sacrilege against me among the
Israelites at the waters of Meribath-kadesh in the wilderness of Zin,

because you did not preserve my holiness among the Israelites. 52 Indeed, from a distance you may view the land, but you will not enter it."ᶻ

    a. This translation attempts to render MT, literally "it/he has dealt corruptly with him, his nonchildren, their blemish." (1) Context suggests that *l'* and *bnyw* belong together as a poetic locution: "nonchildren" (cf. v. 17, "nongods"; v. 21, "nonpeople"). Once this expression was no longer understood, transposition of *lw l'* (MT, Sam.) became possible (OG, Syr.). (2) The more difficult singular verb of MT is preferable to the plural read by Sam., OG, Vulg., Syr. (3) MT *bnyw*, "his children," lacks the pronominal suffix in Sam., Syr., and perhaps OG. (4) This translation construes *mwmm*, "their blemish," as modifying the preceding phrase (cf. NRSV, RSV). An alternative would be to take it as the subject of the verb: "their blemish has dealt corruptly" (cf. NJPS, REB). (5) Sam., OG, Syr. read "blemish" without the pronominal suffix, highlighting the possibility of dittography or haplography: *mwm[m]*.

    b. *Yqtl* preterite (cf. vv. 10, 14, etc.), *IBHS* 31.1.1.

    c. Follows 4QDeutʲ, OG (= 848) *bny 'lhym*. For theological reasons this was softened to "angels of God" (LXXᴬᴮ) in the LXX tradition. A similar concern to avoid legitimizing pagan divinities lies behind the MT revision (supported by Sam., Vulg., Syr.) *bny yśr'l*, "sons of Israel," which connects the seventy persons of Deut 10:22 to the traditional number of the nations. Tg. Ps.-J. refers to both seventy angels and seventy sons of Israel. Sirach 17:17 reflects this verse in the context of the nations' divine or angelic rulers.

    d. Follows MT as the shorter text. Sam., OG have "Israel" at the end of the verse: "Yahweh's own portion was his people Jacob, his surveyed possession Israel."

    e. Follows MT, referring to a "finding" election tradition (cf. Hos 9:10; Ezek 16:5–7). Sam., OG have *y'mṣhw*, "he made him strong." This originated as a transposition of letters, but also avoids the suggestion that Yahweh encountered Israel for the first time in the wilderness.

    f. This half line appears in Sam. as *wbthllwt yšmnhw*, "and with praiseworthy deeds he made him fat," a better parallelism to the Sam. reading in v. 10aα.

    g. Literally the "the little man [reflected?] in the eye," the object of one's closest care and attention (Ps 17:8; Prov 7:2).

    h. Follows the abrupt shift of grammatical subject in MT as more difficult. Sam., OG, Syr. have the easier hip'il with object suffix, "he fed him." For MT "he suckled him" (*wnqhw* hip'il) Sam., Syr. have "he sucked it" (*yynqhw* Qal; confusion of *w* and *y*), and OG has *ynqhw*, "they sucked."

    i. Follows Sam., 4QPhyl N, OG in starting the verse with *y'kl y'kb wyśb'*. Although reminiscent of 31:20, this does not have the character of a scribal addition. MT lost this line by haplography caused by the similarity of *wyśb'*, "and had enough," and *wyb't*, "and kicked."

    j. Follows MT. OG, Targ., Vulg. harmonize with the first half of the verse: "their ancestors."

    k. MT treats *tšy* as though the Qal of an unknown verb *šyh*, but it is usually understood as from *nšh/nšyh*, "forget," which makes good parallelism. Sam., 4QPhyl N have *tš'*, the hip'il of *nš'*, "trick, deceive."

l. An alternate translation would be "begot, sired." However, *yld* means "to bear [a child]" more often than "to beget," and this translation fits better with "he suckled him" in v. 13. The parallel verb *ḥwl* pol'el (translated as "birthed") means "experience labor pains."

m. Follows MT *wynṣ* as slightly more difficult. 4QPhyl N has *wyqn*, "was jealous," substituting a verb used three other times in the poem in parallelism with *k's* (vv. 16, 21). OG has two verbs at this point, representing either a double translation of MT (Wevers, *Greek Text*, 520) or a conflation of the two alternate readings *wyqn'* and *wynṣ*. Alternate translations of v. 19: "Yahweh saw and spurned (because of offensiveness) his sons and daughters" or "Yahweh saw (it) and spurned in vexation his sons and daughters."

n. Follows MT *thpkt*. Sam. lacks the initial *t*, reading a different noun from the same root: *hpkwt*, "[generation of] destruction."

o. Follows MT *bhblyhm* literally "their vapors" (cf. 2 Kgs 16:13, 26). By a confusion of gutturals, Sam. has *b'blyhm*, "their mourning rites."

p. The consonantal text is ambiguous. The masoretic vocalization as *sph* hip'il, "I will sweep away/sweep up upon them," represents an odd use of the verb. LXX and Vulg. translate as *'sp* Qal, "I will gather" (cf. Mic 4:6). Another possibility is *ysp* hip'il, "I will multiply."

q. "Strike down" follows an Arabic cognate (*HALOT* 3:907). MT understands *'p'yhm* as a hip'il imperfect of *p'h* ("dash in pieces"?). OG offers a contextual translation, "scatter." Aquila, Syr., Vulg. divide into *'p 'yhm* (or using the consonants of Sam. *'py hm*), "where are they?"

r. Follows Sam., OG (and apparently 4QpaleoDeut[r]), reading *lywm* for better parallelism with "for the time." MT *ly*, "[vengeance is] mine" (cf. Rom 12:19; Heb 10:30), could have originated from the use of *y* as an abbreviation for *ywm* (Tov, *Textual Criticism*, 257). Alternate translation of MT alluding to the "this" of v. 34: "It is to be my vindication."

s. MT understands this as a substantive. OG, Vulg., Syr., Tg. (and Rom 12:19 and Heb 10:30) have "I will repay," either witnessing to a first-person imperfect or construing the consonants of MT as a pi'el infinitive absolute (cf. Sam.).

t. MT is preferable as the shorter text. 4QDeut[q] reads a supplementary *'šr*, "which": *ṣwr 'šr hsyw bw* (supported by OG, Vulg., Syr.). OG omits "rock," which it usually translates as "God," to avoid repetition after "their gods."

u. Follows MT. At this point, OG adds another colon: "and I swore by my right hand" (cf. Isa 62:8), perhaps intended as a clarification of an assumed oath situation.

v. The root *pr'*, "let go, let loose," sometimes refers to "locks of hair" (Num 6:5; Ezek 44:20), suggestive of the unshorn hair of ritually dedicated warriors (Judg 5:2 NRSV). The translation "wild-haired" seeks to capture the verb's connotation of unruliness or disregard, the disheveled hair of reckless combat. Another possibility is "the heads of enemy princes," based on the Greek translation here and Judg 5:2 (*HALOT* 3:970–71). For "the heads of enemy rebels," see J. G. Janzen, "The Root *pr'* in Judges v 2 and Deuteronomy xxxii 42," *VT* 39 (1989): 393–406.

w. See below, Excursus 1: The Text of Deuteronomy 32:43.

x. The redactional strategy of OG was to finish the topic of the Song of Moses completely and only then refer again to the law. Accordingly, it first repeats 31:22 to terminate the song and then translates 32:44, but replaces "song" with "law" so that the lawgiving is concluded as well.

y. Follows Sam., Syr. in omitting the MT harmonizing expansion *kl*, "all." OG lost "all these words" by homoioarchton from *'t kl* to *'l kl*.

z. Follows OG. MT augments with a phrase taken from v. 49: *'l-h'rṣ 'šr-'ny ntn lbny yśr'l*, "to the land that I am going to give to the Israelites." Alternate translation of *min-neged*, "from a distance": "before you" (2 Kgs 2:15).

The Song of Moses (31:30; 32:44) gives theological meaning to Israel's experience of disaster and affirms the potential for restoration. It is a theodicy in the sense that it explains national catastrophe in a way that affirms rather than denies Yahweh as the one and only active and powerful God, who remains both righteous and committed to Israel.[1] As such it seeks to give confidence and build trust in Yahweh. The song aims to move its audience to a praise of Yahweh (v. 3) made possible by accepting its theological case. Recurring themes include the subordination or impotence of other gods (vv. 8, 17, 31, 37–38, 43), Israel's familial relationship to Yahweh (vv. 5, 6, 18, 19, 20, 43), and the image of the Divine Warrior (vv. 22–25, 40–42). The organizing principle is Israel's history with Yahweh: primeval election leading to settlement in the land (vv. 6–14), Israel's apostasy (vv. 15–18), Yahweh's initial plan of destruction (vv. 19–25), and finally Yahweh's change of heart and vengeance on Israel's enemies (vv. 26–43).

The scholarly literature is extensive.[2] Attempts to date the song on the basis of the identity of the enemy or linguistic evidence have been inconclusive. Its archaic or archaizing language is at variance with a postdisaster situation that would appear to be at least exilic.[3] The song's pattern of argument is similar to the genre of prophetic lawsuit.[4] However, a comparison to the book of Psalms suggests that the genre classification of hymn is more appropriate. The song starts with an appeal for attention (cf. Pss 49:2 [ET 1]; 78:1) and begins and

1. J. Luyten, "Primeval and Eschatological Overtones in the Song of Moses (Dt 32,1–43)," in *Das Deuteronomium*, ed. Lohfink, 341–47, considers the song to be a forerunner of apocalyptic literature. On its relationship to changing theological attitudes about the nations, see B. Gosse, "Deutéronome 32,1–43 et les rédactions des livres d'Ezéchiel et d'Isaïe," *ZAW* 107 (1995): 110–17.

2. The most recent monograph is P. Sanders, *The Provenance of Deuteronomy 32* (*OtSt* 37; Leiden: Brill, 1996).

3. S. A. Nigosian, "Linguistic Patterns of Deuteronomy 32," *Bib* 78 (1997): 206–24, suggests between the 10th and 8th centuries. A. Reichert, "The Song of Moses (Dt 32) and the Quest for Early Deuteronomic Psalmody," *Proceedings of the Ninth World Congress of Jewish Studies A* (Jerusalem: World Union of Jewish Studies, 1986), 53–60, proposes the 7th century. S. Hidal, "Some Reflections on Deuteronomy 32," *Annual of the Swedish Theological Institute* 11 (1978): 15–21, opts for the early exile.

4. G. E. Wright, "The Lawsuit of God: A Form-Critical Study of Deuteronomy 32," in *Israel's Prophetic Heritage* (ed. B. W. Anderson et al.; New York: Harper, 1962), 26–67. J. M. Wiebe, "The Form, Setting and Meaning of the Song of Moses," *Studia Biblica et Theologica* 17 (1989): 119–63, dates it to the time of Samuel and connects it to an annual ceremony of covenant renewal. Weitzman, "Lessons from the Dying," indicates that the song is both an accusation and an instructional

ends with a summons to praise (vv. 3, 43). Its historical retrospective is similar to that of Pss 78, 105, 106, 134, 135, although the absence of any reference to the exodus is striking.

[1–6] Verses 1–3 are a prologue or exordium, characterized by a first-person address to a universal audience. Two imperatives ("listen," "ascribe") enclose two first-person declarations ("I will speak," "I will proclaim"), which in turn enclose three wishes in the third person ("hear," "drip," "trickle down").[5] Moses begins with an apostrophe to heaven (cf. Isa 1:2–3; Jer 2:12–13; cf. Mic 6:2). Heaven is also apparently the audience addressed by the summons of v. 3. Heaven and earth are not witnesses here (as in 4:26; 30:19; 31:28), but provide an impartial and objective audience before which the poet sets forth a theological case. They serve as a *merismus* for the whole of creation, a universal forum for an argument from history. "Words of my mouth" characterizes the offering of wisdom (Job 34:2; Ps 49:4 [ET 3]).[6]

Verse 2 anticipates the effectiveness of what is to be spoken (cf. Job 29:22–23; Isa 55:10–11), using life-giving water as a metaphor. There is a link to v. 1 in that this water is first heaven's rain, then earth's dew. The flow is downward, to the earthly plane of the audience and toward the "land" with which the poem concludes (v. 43). "Teaching" (*leqaḥ*) is the communication of the wise sage (Prov 1:5; 4:2; 7:21). "Gentle rain" (*śĕ'îrim*) is sometimes taken to mean "rainstorm" or "welling up of underground water" (*HALOT* 3:1341–42). Verse 3 completes the direct address to the universal audience, revealing that the song will be a doxology, proclaiming the nature and deeds of Yahweh and defending Yahweh's righteousness in the face of catastrophe. The hymnic imperative (cf. Pss 29:1–2; 96:7–8) forms a doxological bracket with the initial imperative of v. 43, which is also addressed to the heavens.

Verse 4 proclaims the theological axiom that governs the poem: "our God" is the "Rock." Rock as a metaphor for refuge and protection occurs seven times (vv. 4, 15, 18, 30, 31 [twice], 37). Being the Rock entails being just (v. 4), the source of salvation (v. 15), the creator of Israel (v. 18), and unlike ineffective pagan gods (vv. 31, 37). The works of the Rock are "perfect" (*tāmîm*, "unimpaired in reliability"; cf. Ps 18:31–32 [ET 30–31]) even in the context of catastrophe (v. 30).

---

testament and draws a parallel with the last words of the legendary sage Ahiqar. A balanced opinion is given by S. A. Nigosian, "The Song of Moses (Dt 32): A Structural Analysis," *ETL* 72 (1996): 5–22: "it appears to be a unique genre: a 'covenant lawsuit' inverted to forge a salvation oracle and the whole presented in the didactic mode" (p. 8). The song thus negotiates the tension between Deuteronomic retribution theology and Israel's election.

5. For an analysis of the prologue, see H. Irsigler, "Das Proömium im Moselied Dtn 32: Struktur, Sprechakte und Redeintentionen von V. 1–3," in *Lingua Restituta Orientalis* (ed. R. Schulz and M. Görg; Ägypten und Altes Testament 20; Wiesbaden: Harrassowitz, 1990), 161–74.

6. For other parallels to wisdom see J. R. Boston, "Wisdom Influence upon the Song of Moses," *JBL* 87 (1968): 198–202.

Verses 5–6 abruptly introduce Israel's apostasy as a negative countertheme to Yahweh's "greatness" (v. 3). Israel behaves as faithless "nonchildren" or "pseudo-children," undermining the parent-child relationship promoted in vv. 6, 10–12, 43. As "perverse and crooked" (cf. Ps 18:27 [ET 26]), they are the opposite of Yahweh, who is "righteous and upright" (v. 4). "Perverse" (*'iqqēš*) literally denotes "twisted," a favorite designation of culpability in the sharply oppositional ethics of wisdom (Prov 10:9; 11:20; 19:1). Verse 6 shifts the address to Israel ("you") and poses a rhetorical question that implies that such ingratitude is unbelievable. As "unwise" (*nābāl*), Israel is foolish and boorish, even villainous (cf. v. 21; the verb from this root appears in v. 15 translated as "scorned"). The literary context ("made," "established"; cf. Ps 119:73) shows that *qānâ* (v. 6) denotes "create" or even "procreate" (cf. Gen 4:1) rather than merely "acquire." "Establish" (*kwn* pol'el) implies "set up to last, fix solidly."

[7–14] The thesis of Yahweh's faithfulness (from v. 4) is developed through a historical review of divine election, providence, and the gift of the land's bounty. "Remember" (v. 7) turns attention to past events, first positive ones (vv. 7–14) and then subsequent negative ones (vv. 15–18). The truth of this story cannot be denied, for it is deeply rooted in the far past. "Of old" (*'ôlām*) describes the oldest history (Amos 9:11; Mic 7:14; 1 Sam 27:8), here reaching back into mythic times (cf. Gen 6:4).[7] Elders would preserve the oldest living tradition (Joel 1:2–3). To "ask" about the past is an effective piece of rhetoric (Deut 4:32; Job 8:8–10).

Verses 8–9 use a mythic setting to emphasize Israel's special affiliation with Yahweh, pushing Israel's election back into primeval times. These verses presuppose the existence of a myth that explained the variety of nationalities (cf. Gen 10; 11:1–9; the Sumerian flood narrative, *ANET*, 43, lines 91–99) and national gods. The divine title "Most High" (*'elyôn*) is appropriate for this foundational act of apportionment.[8] In contrast, "Yahweh" names the one who chooses Israel. Yet both context (including v. 39) and poetic parallelism make clear that these two designations refer to the same God.[9] Thus Israel relates directly to the universal God (who is both "Most High" and Yahweh), while other nations do so only through intermediate divinities to whom they were apportioned. Israel is equivalent to Yahweh's personal real estate, "his allotment surveyed by rope" (*hebel nahălātô*; cf. Ps 105:11).

Verses 10–14 explore the consequences of this special relationship. In v. 10

---

7. The translation "of each generation" takes the *waw* as distributive. See Williams, *Hebrew Syntax*, 101, 442; cf. Ps 90:1.

8. The possible alternate translation, "caused the nations to inherit," does not fit the context of v. 9.

9. For parallel structures between verses, see S. A. Geller, "The Dynamics of Parallel Verse: A Poetic Analysis of Deut 32:6–12," *HTR* 75 (1982): 35–56.

the election tradition of wilderness "finding" (Hos 9:10; Ezek 16:3–6) supplements the election images of fatherlike creation (v. 6) and mythic allotment (vv. 8–9). The chaotic wilderness, howling with wind or the cries of animals and demons, contrasts with the rich land Israel receives in vv. 13–14.

The image of the eagle in v. 11 continues the notion of protection from v. 10b and prefigures Israel's journey in v. 13a. It remains unclear, however, exactly what this eagle is doing with its young. The translation "protects" for *yā'îr* is based on its parallelism with "hover" here (*rḥp* pi'el; cf. Gen 1:2) and its use in Job 8:6 (*HALOT* 2:820). Yahweh's wings offer protection (Ps 91:4). Others translate *yā'îr* as "stirs up," suggesting the image of the eagle shoving baby birds out of the nest for flying lessons and then catching them on its back in v. 11b.[10] It is more likely, however, that v. 11b no longer refers to the eagle but directly to Yahweh as the referent of the image. Yahweh, the winged deity of solar iconography, transports the people with ease and safety (cf. Exod 19:4).

Verse 12 nicely underscores the exclusive nature of the election relationship, while subtly introducing the problem of other gods that will emerge in vv. 15–18. "Foreign god," that is, a god of an alien people, alludes to the "nations" and "divine beings" of vv. 8–9.

Verses 13–14 shift to the topic of the land and its richness. "Make ride over" (or "cause to travel over"; alluded to in Isa 58:14) echoes the image of transport by the winged deity described in v. 11b. An alternate translation would be: "cause to mount upon." A list of the richest food products characteristic of Palestine is introduced by the summary expression "produce of the field." The maternal image of breast-feeding highlights Israel as a receptive and nearly passive object of divine providence. Israel is nurtured even from unpromising places, by bees making honey in crags and olive trees producing oil among rocks.[11]

This rich menu continues in v. 14. The translation follows the line division of the Aleppo Codex (*BHS* breaks the line between "of lambs" and "rams of Bashan") and construes the four animals as a series of nouns in construct with "fat" (cf. the masoretic accentuation). "Choicest wheat" is literally "fat of the kidneys of wheat," that is, the very best portion of the wheat harvest (Isa 34:6; cf. Pss 81:17 [ET 16]; 147:14). In English one would say "the cream of the crop." That "grapeblood" means wine is clear from Gen 49:11. "Foaming" indicates that it is "new wine," still fermenting (*HALOT*

---

10. The question is not whether such an improbable avian procedure actually takes place, but whether ancient people supposed that it did. See H. G. L. Peels, "On the Wings of the Eagle (Dtn 32, 11)—An Old Misunderstanding," *ZAW* 106 (1994): 300–303.

11. "Honey" may denote grape juice or dates thickened into syrup. For similar images of abundance, see Ps 81:17 [ET 16]; Job 29:6.

1:330). The abrupt change to the second person directs the argument at the audience (cf. vv. 15, 18).

[15–18] The poem now turns to the countertheme of faithlessness, which has already been introduced in vv. 5–6. This change is marked by a shift to *waw*-consecutive verbs. Verse 15 describes the startling, negative consequence of the sumptuousness portrayed in vv. 13–14 (cf. 6:11–12; 8:10–14; 11:14–16). In this context, Israel's honorific nickname "Jeshurun" ("the upright"; 33:5, 26; Isa 44:2) is ironic. Fattened up, Jeshurun has a kick like an unruly animal (cf. Hos 4:16). The translation "gorged" derives from an Arabic root; an alternative would be "grew stubborn" as a poetic parallel for "kicked" (*HALOT* 2:502). Traditionally this verb has been derived from *ksh*, "to cover [oneself with fat]."

The alien and repugnant things (gods? practices?) of v. 16 are elucidated by v. 17. Negative rhetoric degrades these false objects of worship: they are third-rate demons,[12] pseudogods, "new-fangled" gods with no record of mighty deeds or reliability. "Dreaded" (root *śʿr*) denotes negative fear, not positive reverence (Jer 2:12; Ezek 27:35; 32:10), perhaps related to "hair-raising" terror or "hairy" goat demons (*HALOT* 3:1344). The accusation of forgetting God is typical of Deuteronomy (6:10–12; 8:11–19).

[19–25] The subject shifts to divine reaction; as a result of what Yahweh "saw," he "spurned" them (cf. Jer 14:21; Lam 2:6). "Offensiveness" (root *kʿs*) refers to intensely negative feelings of provocation and chagrin in an interpersonal relationship, often caused by infidelity. Israel's offensiveness involves other gods and thus provokes Yahweh's jealousy:

> v. 16—"made him jealous . . . they offended him"
> v. 21a—"made me jealous . . . offended me"
> v. 21b—"make them jealous . . . offend them"

Beginning in v. 20, Yahweh describes the nature of this spurning. Yahweh's face is hidden (cf. 31:17–18), either in anger or in revulsion over such behavior. "I will see" suggests a passive waiting for developments (Ps 73:17). "Perverse" means literally "turned upside down," treacherous and false. Israel's *lōʾ-ʾēmun* ("nonfaithfulness") contrasts with Yahweh's nature as *ʾēl ʾĕmûnâ* ("faithful God") in v. 4.

In v. 21 Yahweh shifts from the passive stance of v. 20 to an active reaction fashioned as a fair and balanced payback, as "poetic justice." The same verbs that describe Israel's infidelity ("make jealous," "offend") also portray Yahweh's retaliation. "Nongods" and the folly of insubstantial "vapor idols" (note o) are countered by an invasion by a "nonpeople," a nation of fools. The identity of this group is deliberately obscured, but "non-people" hints at barbarians or raiding

---

12. The Akkadian cognate denotes minor spirits protecting the household.

nomads, while *nābāl*, "foolish," suggests a vicious, "vandal" nation.[13] Yahweh's universal control of nations (v. 8) is turned against Israel. Yet a hint of hope may remain, for the divine plan is to make Israel "jealous."

Yahweh's plan for the destruction of Israel is described using the language of the Divine Warrior. Verse 22 introduces the weapon of fire (Job 31:12; Ps 18:8–9 [ET 7–8]; 50:3; Amos 1:4; 7:4). An alternate translation of "by my anger" would be "from my nostrils." This fire moves downward from its heavenly starting point, down to Sheol and down to earth and its underpinnings. This conflagration extends to the deepest level of the cosmos, even to the world of the dead.

In vv. 23–24 Yahweh's anger turns from its cosmic horizon to focus on Israel itself. The Divine Warrior will use up his quiver of arrows (cf. v. 42; Ezek 5:16; Ps 7:13 [ET 12]; 38:3 [ET 2]; Job 6:4). One thinks immediately of lightning, but the list that follows may enumerate these arrows as an arsenal of weapons. If so, it would be appropriate to translate the verb *šālaḥ*, "send," in v. 24 as "shoot" (Ps 18:15 [ET 14]). The five arrows of the Divine Warrior are:

Wasting hunger. This takes *mĕzê* as a plural construct derived from an unattested root *mzh*, "to suck" (*HALOT* 2:564). The phrase means either "hunger that sucks out" or (as a passive idea) "sucked out by hunger."[14]

Consuming pestilence. The translation of *rešep* as "pestilence" is based on parallelism here and in Hab 3:5. Behind this usage is the figure of the (often sinister) god Resheph, who appears as an attendant of the marching Divine Warrior in Hab 3:5. Perhaps Resheph is portrayed here as a demon in Yahweh's service.[15] On the other hand, one could understand *rešep* as a common noun, "flame," used either metaphorically as "fever, heat," or literally as "bolt of fire" (cf. Ps 76:4 [ET 3]; *HALOT* 3:1297–98). The translation "consuming" takes *lĕḥumê* as a participle with active meaning from *lāḥam*, "to use as food." If the participle is intended as passive, it would denote "consumed by pestilence." Some scholars derive the expression from the homologous root *lḥm*, "to fight," thus "battered by pestilence."[16]

Bitter epidemic. *Qeṭeb*, "epidemic," may also be a demon.[17] A less specific translation would be "destruction."

---

13. J. Marböck, "*nābāl*," *TDOT* 9:157–71.

14. Yahweh's arrows could also be understood as three demonic figures modified by first-person suffixes: "Hunger, my Sucker; Resheph, my Warrior; and the Sting, my Poisonous One." See J. C. de Moor, "O Death, Where Is Thy Sting?" in *Ascribe to the Lord: Biblical and Other Studies in Memory of P. C. Craigie* (ed. L. Eslinger and G. Taylor; JSOTSup 67; Sheffield: JSOT Press, 1988), 99–107.

15. P. Xella, "Resheph," *DDD*, 700–703.

16. J. C. Greenfield, "Smitten by Famine, Battered by Plague (Deuteronomy 32:24)," in *Love and Death in the Ancient Near East* (ed. J. H. Marks; Guilford, Conn.: Four Quarters Press, 1987), 151–52.

17. N. Wyatt, "Qeteb," *DDD*, 673–74; *HALOT* 3:1091–92.

Teeth of beasts. If Resheph and Qeteb are demonic figures, perhaps "beasts" refers to Behemoth, often supposed to be a mythic creature (Job 40:15–24).

Poison of things that crawl in dust. These creeping vermin would be venomous snakes, insects, and scorpions.

The portrayal of brutal slaughter in v. 25 relates to the theme of an invading nation in v. 21 and the "enemy" of v. 27. "Bereave" (*škl* pi'el) denotes "make childless." The text uses language of all-inclusive totality, encompassing the polar opposites of location, sex, and age. This is a paradigm of an invaded city—swords in the streets, fear in the houses. Terror reaches inside to kill where sword cannot reach; "chambers" is a common literary equivalent for a safe haven (1 Kgs 20:30; 22:25; Isa 26:20).

[26–38] With "I thought" (literally "I said" or "I had said"; cf. Exod 13:17; Ezek 20:13) the poet daringly takes the reader into Yahweh's own internal consciousness. Before it is too late, Yahweh reconsiders. Yahweh has second thoughts about the potential consequences to personal reputation and self-interest (vv. 26–27) and takes into account the foolish and vicious character of Israel's foes (vv. 28–33). These agents of Yahweh's anger will themselves face accumulated judgment (vv. 34–35). When Yahweh sees that Israel has reached its low point, Israel's situation changes (vv. 36–38).

The critical turning point of vv. 26–27 has nothing to do with Israel's repentance or reformed behavior. Instead the cause for this reversal is purely theocentric, focusing on what Yahweh cannot tolerate in light of the theological reality expressed in v. 39. Ultimately, Israel's hope depends on Yahweh's intrinsic integrity and concern for personal reputation. However, the pathos of Israel's distressed situation also motivates Yahweh's change of heart (v. 36). In v. 27 the potential "offensiveness" of the enemy counters the offense that Yahweh has experienced from Israel (cf. vv. 16, 19, 21). Israel's foes would "misjudge" (*nkr* pi'el; alternatively, "misrepresent"). Their arrogance (literally "our hand is high"; contrast v. 40) would undermine Yahweh's exclusive claim to be the source of both victory and defeat (v. 39; cf. 8:17 and 9:28).

In light of vv. 31–33, it is more reasonable to understand the dull-witted "nation" of vv. 28–29 as the enemy rather than as Israel, although the latter possibility cannot be excluded. The enemy's misjudgment feared in v. 27 is all the more likely because they lack sense. The *waw* in the second colon of v. 28 may be epexegetical: "in that, that is" (*IBHS* 39.2.4).

The erroneous logic of vv. 27–28 is countered by the correct reasoning of vv. 29–30. Verse 29 introduces the protasis of an unreal condition (*lû*). The enemy (or Israel?) should have perceived "their end" (v. 29). This word (*'aḥărît*) denotes "what happens later" or "the final stage," with either a negative (Ps 73:17–19) or positive (Deut 8:16) implication. This "end" could refer broadly to how things must inevitably turn out for the enemy (or for Israel) or point more immediately to the enemy's military successes or Israel's defeats.

Moreover, the enemy (or Israel) should have recognized the implications of the totality of Israel's defeat (v. 30). The only reasonable explanation for this reversal of the proper pattern of sacral war (contrast Josh 23:10; Judg 7; cf. Isa 30:17) is that Yahweh "their Rock" had "sold them out" (cf. Judg 2:14; 3:8). In the context of Deuteronomy, such panicked retreat on the part of Israel is the result of fulfilled curses (28:7, 25).

Verses 31–33 return to an evaluation of the foe. The defeat of Israel must have been caused by Israel's Rock, for the gods of the enemy could never have won such a victory. Verse 31b is obscure. The noun *pĕlîlîm* seems to mean either "assessors" or "assessments" (*HALOT* 3:932). As "judges" (RSV) of their own situation the enemies have reached an incorrect "assessment" (NJPS). Alternatively, one could translate this word as "fools" on the basis of context and the LXX (NRSV), or even extend the force of the negative of v. 31a to v. 31b: "our enemies are *not* judges." Verse 32 connects the origin of these enemies and their corrupt nature to Sodom and Gomorrah, at the same time hinting that the enemies will share a similar fate. The image of these foes as a bad vine stands in sharp contrast to the customary use of vine and vineyard as images for Israel. *šadĕmōt* "terraces" (*HALOT* 4:1422–23) sounds similar to "Sodom."

Integrated images unite vv. 32–34. Bad vines yield bitter grapes (v. 32), which produce poisonous wine (v. 33). In v. 34 this wine (the referent of *hû'*, "this") is gathered (understanding *kāmus* on the basis of an Akkadian cognate; see *HALOT* 2:481) and sealed up in storage for the foe's eventual doom. This last image suggests either a sealed storeroom or individually sealed wine containers. Sealing connotes identifying and safeguarding with the intent of eventually unsealing (Cant 4:12; cf. Hos 13:12; Job 14:17). Verse 35 proclaims that Yahweh intends to punish nations that have overstepped their bounds as agents of divine wrath (cf. Isa 10:5–19, 24–27; Jer 25:12–14).

Verse 36 returns to the topic of Yahweh's change in plan for Israel (cf. vv. 26–27), emphasizing that they are "his servants" (i.e., those who serve him in worship) and "his people" (cf. vv. 9, 43). The translation "pass favorable judgment" takes the verb *dîn* in its positive sense of "to right a wrong." "Take compassion on" understands *nḥm* hitpaʻel in its positive sense of "relent." Yahweh's mood changes and divine anger moderates (Ps 135:14 duplicates v. 36a). Israel has hit its absolute nadir, but its desperate situation triggers a positive divine response (cf. Judg 10:13–16). The *merismus* "bond or free" clearly means "everyone," but the precise import of this expression remains obscure.[18]

Yahweh may have abandoned the plan of total destruction (vv. 26, 36), but Yahweh's indictment of Israel's apostasy still stands, expressed in accusatory questions (vv. 37–38). In asking "where are their gods . . . who ate" ("who" is a relative, not an interrogative), Yahweh is either speaking sarcastically or, for

18. The expression most likely denotes those under legal or ritual restraint or free from it.

rhetorical purposes, adopting Israel's apostate point of view. Verse 38b returns to the "you" address of vv. 6, 15, 18. The plural "let them rise" applies to the gods of v. 37a, and the singular "let it be" pertains to the "rock" of v. 37b. This shift in number is necessary; the alien gods are numerous (v. 17), but the "rock" metaphor requires the singular (v. 31).

[39–43] The theme of the Divine Warrior reappears at this point, but it now points to Yahweh's saving, positive role. Yahweh turns against those who have harassed and maltreated Israel. "See now" in v. 39 refers to the realities expressed in previous verses. Yahweh is the complete opposite of the absent and impotent gods mocked in vv. 37–38. The repetitive grammar of exclusivity (cf. 2:27; 16:20) proclaims that Yahweh is the sole deity having the powers of the Divine Warrior. "No other god beside me" conveys that Yahweh is not associated with any pantheon, companion god, or consort (cf. v. 12). Israel's downfall does not mean that Yahweh is weak or uncaring. Such a conclusion is disallowed by a restatement of Yahweh's traditional attributes of supreme authority and mercy: "kill and make alive" (1 Sam 2:6–8; Isa 43:10–11, 13), "wound and heal" (Hos 6:1–2). The order of these attributes is not accidental, but reproduces the movement of the poem from catastrophe to restoration. Verse 39 proclaims Yahweh's incomparable activity and power, but not any sort of absolute monotheism.

The Divine Warrior lifts his hand high (v. 40). This act marks a transition, moving from the speech of vv. 37–39 to the warlike action of vv. 41–42. This gesture seems to be an act of oath taking (Gen 14:22; Ezek 36:7), although it could conceivably indicate the martial posture of the Divine Warrior's upraised fighting arm, familiar from ancient Near Eastern iconography (cf. Ps 10:12).[19] Verse 41 gives the content of Yahweh's oath introduced by v. 40b. Yahweh's sword flashes because it is lightning itself (Hab 3:11; cf. Nah 3:3). The nations that Yahweh had utilized to punish Israel are now treated as Yahweh's enemies because of their brutal actions. The sword of v. 25a is turned against them, and the retribution language of v. 35 is picked up once again (the roots *nqm* and *šlm*). "*Return* vindication" (using *šwb* hip'il) is a way of saying that this punishment is warranted, appropriate, and justified. "My hand holds fast to judgment" (or "justice") is a striking phrase, portraying the concept of justice itself being wielded by Yahweh as a metaphorical weapon.[20]

Untangling the poetically intermixed predicates of v. 42 resolves the statement into: "I will make my arrows drunk with blood, with the blood of slain and captive; and my sword shall devour flesh from the head of the wild-haired

---

19. J. Lust, "For I Lift up My Hand to Heaven and Swear: Deut 32:40," in *Studies in Deuteronomy*, ed. García Martínez et al., 155–64; contested by Viberg, *Symbols of Law*, 19–32.

20. NAB emends this to *bā'ašpâ*, "[my] quiver." Alternate translation assuming an ellipsis: "holds it [my sword] fast in judgment."

enemy." The arrows that had been directed against Israel in v. 23 are now turned against the enemy. The powerful images of the ravenous sword (2 Sam 2:26; 11:25; Isa 1:20; 34:5–6; Jer 46:10) and thirsty arrows symbolize bloody, physical violence. The "blood of the captive" may refer to wounded prisoners or captives executed in accordance with the ban of ḥērem.

The poem circles back in v. 43 to the initial apostrophe of vv. 1–3, addressing heaven and heavenly beings and calling on them to praise Yahweh (cf. Job 38:7; Isa 49:13). This conclusion picks up the theme of vindication and payback from v. 41. Significantly, the poem concludes with the words "his people" as the chief focus of Yahweh's concern (cf. vv. 9, 36). The need to "make atonement for the land" may refer to the polluting effects of bloodshed on the land in warfare (cf. Num 35:30–34; 2 Sam 21:1, 14).

[44–47] Verses 44–47 form a bracketing conclusion by reversing the order of "law" and "song" from 31:26, 30 into "song" and "law." Verse 44 by itself also brackets the song by reiterating 31:30. "All the words" echoes "to the end" from 31:30 and stresses that Moses spoke the positive words of the song and not just the negative words that witness against Israel (cf. the parallels to the song in 31:16–21). "Moses came" is puzzling, perhaps conveying "came into the assembly" mentioned in 31:30. The involvement of Hoshea (Joshua) explicitly carries out what is implied by the plural verb of 31:19.

The traditional scene of a leader delivering a final testament (cf. 31:14, 16, 29) reappears in vv. 45–47. "These words" in v. 45 looks back to both song and law (cf. "all the words" in v. 46). Moses has *finished* speaking," moving beyond 31:1 (speaking the law) and 31:24 (writing the law) to achieve a completed declaration of law and song together. Verse 46 alludes to "be careful to do all the words of this law" in 31:12 and the theme of educating children in 31:13 (cf. 4:9; 6:7; 11:19). Verse 47 repeats the language of life "in the land . . . crossing the Jordan . . . to take over" from 31:13. It also looks back to the themes of life and land in the song itself (32:13–14, 39, and 43) and reiterates the challenge of 30:15–20.

[48–52] Deuteronomic language is replaced by expressions characteristic of the Priestly Writing, and attention shifts to the death of Moses.[21] This section corresponds closely to Num 27:12–14 and seems to function as a resumptive repetition of that passage, designed to resume the narrative of the Tetrateuch after the "interruption" of Deuteronomy. It is not surprising that a supplementary explanation for Moses' scandalous death outside the land should appear at

---

21. For parallels to the Priestly Writing, see Tigay, *Deuteronomy*, 518. Mount Hor as the place of Aaron's death corresponds to Num 20:22–28; 33:38, rather than Deut 10:6. The punishment of Moses and Aaron reflects Num 20:12–13, in contrast to Deut 1:37; 9:20; 10:6. From a literary standpoint, of course, the reader could choose to take the assertions of Moses (1:37; 3:26; 4:21) as his own personal perspective and rationale, which is corrected by Yahweh's judgment revealed by the omniscient narrator in 32:51.

this point. Moses' approaching end sets the scene for his final blessing, delivered "before his death" like those of the patriarchs (33:1; cf. Gen 27:10; 50:16). "That very day" (v. 48) equates the day of Moses' proclamation of the law (Deut 1:3) with that of Yahweh's command. The phrase "gathered to your kinfolk" (v. 50) must be taken as a conventional expression that does not speak literally about burial in an ancestral tomb (cf. 31:16).

Excursus: The Text of Deuteronomy 32:43

This verse has generated considerable discussion.[22] The earliest recoverable text consists of six lines, preserved by 4QDeut[q] (cf. NRSV, REB).

1. *hrnynw šmym 'mw*
2. *whšthww lw kl 'lhym*
3. *ky dm bnyw yqwm*
4. *wnqm yšyb lṣryw*
5. *wlmśn 'yw yšlm*
6. *wkpr 'dmtw 'mw*

MT is shorter, having four lines (lines 1, 3, 4, 6; cf. RSV). OG witnesses to a text of eight lines (cf. NJB) because it preserves a second, alternative translation of lines 1–2. The first two lines of OG (designated OG[1–2] below) are a fairly exact rendering of lines 1–2 as given in 4QDeut[q]. The third and fourth lines of OG (designated OG[3–4]) offer a second translation of line 1, although in the form given by MT, followed by an alternative version of line 2 using a different verb.

Line 1. A process of orthodox revision modified MT. The apostrophe to the heavens (4QDeut[q], OG[1–2]) was changed by substituting *gwym*, "peoples," so MT (supported by Sam., Syr., Vulg., OG[3–4]) reads a less offensive "praise, O nations, his people." OG[3–4] has a doublet translation of *'mw* as both "with him" and "his people."

Line 2. The orthodox revision represented by MT eliminated this reference to pagan gods (cf. Ps 97:7). OG[1–2] translates "gods" interpretively as "sons of God," while OG[3–4] renders it as "angels" (cf. Ps 97:7 LXX; Heb 1:6). The verb of OG[3–4], *enischyein* ("confirm, strengthen oneself"), is inexplicable as a translation of 4QDeut[q] *whšthww* and must witness to a different Hebrew text, although what that might have been remains obscure.

22. For example, P. M. Bogaert, "Les trois rédactions conservés et la forme originale de l'envoi du Cantique du Moïse (Dt 32,43)," in *Das Deuteronomium*, ed. Lohfink, 329–40; A. van der Kooij, "The Ending of the Song of Moses: On the Pre-Masoretic Version of Deut. 32:43," in *Studies in Deuteronomy*, ed. García Martínez et al., 93–100; A. Rofé, "The End of the Song of Moses (Deuteronomy 32:43)," in *Liebe und Gebot*, ed. Kratz and Spieckermann, 164–72.

Line 3. MT reads *'bdyw*, "his servants," instead of "his sons" (4QDeut^q, OG). This revision clarified that Israel was to be the beneficiary of God's vindication, not "sons" in the sense of divine beings or some sort of pantheon. "Servants" may have been suggested by v. 36.

Line 4. OG has a doublet translation, employing two verbs for *wnqm*, "and he takes vengeance."

Line 5. The absence of this line in MT is difficult to explain. When paired with line 4, line 5 is very close to v. 41b and has sometimes been taken as an expansion from there (cf. NAB). However, line 5 is needed to complete the parallelism begun by line 4.

Line 6. OG supplements with "Yahweh" as an explicit subject. MT reads *'dmtw 'mw* as a double direct object, "his land, his people." Syr. supports this, although with a dittography of *w* to read "his land *and* his people." 4QDeut^q, Sam., OG, Vulg. read the grammatically simpler *'dmt 'mw*, "the land of his people." MT is adopted here as the more difficult text, but translated as a construct chain (GKC 90o).

The Blessing of Moses
33:1–29

Yahweh Came from Sinai

33:1   This is the blessing that Moses the man of God pronounced on Israel before his death:

2   He said:
      Yahweh came from Sinai,
          and dawned from Seir for them;[a]
      he shone forth from Mount Paran.
      With him were some of the myriads of holy ones;[b]
          on his right side, fire flew out for them.[c]

3   Indeed, O lover of the peoples,[d]
          all his holy ones were in your hand;
      they marched[e] at your feet,
          accepted your sayings.[f]

4   Moses commanded a law to us,
          as an inherited possession for the assembly of Jacob.

5   Then a king arose in Jeshurun,
          when the heads of the people assembled,
          the tribes of Israel together.

The Twelve Tribes

6 May Reuben live, and not die out,
    and yet let his people be few.
7 And this he said of Judah:
O Yahweh, give heed to Judah,
    and bring him to his people.
With his own hands he defends his cause;[g]
    be a help against his adversaries.
8 And of Levi he said:
Give to Levi[h] your Thummim,
    and your Urim to your loyal one,
whom you tested at Massah,
    with whom you contended at the waters of Meribah;
9 who said of his father and mother,
    "I do not regard him."[i]
His kin he disregarded
    and his children[j] he did not acknowledge.
Indeed, they observed your word
    and kept your covenant.
10 They teach your ordinances to Jacob,
    and your law to Israel.
They put the smoke of sacrifice in your nostrils,
    and whole burnt offerings on your altar.
11 Bless, O Yahweh, his wealth,
    and may you favor his endeavors.
Strike the loins of those who rise against him,
    that those who hate him may not rise again.[k]
12 Of Benjamin he said:
The beloved of Yahweh dwells in security
    (who shelters over him all day long),[l]
    and between his shoulders he dwells.
13 And of Joseph he said:
Blessed by Yahweh be his land,
    from the bounty of heaven's dew[m]
    and of the deep that stretches out beneath,
14 with the bounty of the sun's produce
    and the bounty of the months' yield,
15 with the finest[n] of the ancient mountains
    and the bounty of the everlasting hills;
16 with the bounty of the earth and its fullness,
    and the favor of the Dweller[o] in the Bush.

Let it come[p] on the head of Joseph,
  on the crown of the head of the prince among his brothers.

17 The firstborn of his[q] [divine] Bull—majesty is his!
  His horns are the horns of a wild ox;
with them he gores peoples,
  all together[r] the ends of the earth.
These are the ten thousands of Ephraim;
  these are the thousands of Manasseh.

18 And of Zebulun he said:
Rejoice, Zebulun, in your going out;
  and Issachar, in your tents.

19 They call peoples to the mountain;
  there they offer right sacrifices.
Indeed, they suck out the abundance of the seas
  and the hidden treasures of the sand.

20 And of Gad he said:
Blessed be the one who enlarges Gad![s]
  Like a lion he dwells
  and tears at the arm, even at the crown of the head.

21 He chose the best for himself,
  for a portion of a chieftain was there.
The heads of the people assembled;[t]
  he executed the justice of Yahweh
  and his ordinances for Israel.

22 And of Dan he said:
Dan is a lion's cub
  that leaps forth from Bashan.

23 And of Naphtali he said:
O Naphtali, replete with favor
  and full of the blessing of Yahweh,
  take over[u] the west and the south.

24 And of Asher he said:
Most blessed of sons be Asher;
  may he be the favorite of his brothers
  and may he dip his foot in oil.

25 May your gate bolts be iron and bronze,
  your strength as lasting as your days.

Happy Are You, O Israel!

26 There is none like the God of Jeshurun,[v]
  who rides on the skies to your help,

and in his majesty on the clouds.
27 A dwelling place is the ancient God,
and underneath are the eternal arms.ʷ
He drove out the enemy before you
and said, "Destroy!"
28 So Israel lives in safety,
untroubled is the abodeˣ of Jacob,
inʸ a land of grain and wine,
indeed, his skies drop down dew.
29 Happy are you, O Israel! Who is like you,
a people saved by Yahweh?
The shield of your help,
and who isᶻ the sword of your glory!
Your enemies will come fawning to you,
but you will tread on their backs.

a. Follows *lmw* as the more difficult reading, having no formal antecedent. OG, Syr., Tg., Vulg. read *lnw*, "for us" (NRSV), which is less disturbing in light of v. 4. However, the first person plural there refers to giving the law, not to the approach of the Divine Warrior. This variant probably originated as a misreading of *m* as ligature for *nw*. BHS conjectures *l'mw*, "for his people."

b. MT *w'th mrbbt qdš* presents two interlocked problems. (1) Masoretic tradition takes *w'th* as a verb ("and he came"; cf. v. 21). However, other witnesses read a preposition here: OG indicates *'t*, "with (the myriads)"; Sam., Syr., Vulg., Tg. read *w'tw*, "and with him (were the myriads)" (cf. NRSV). (2) MT understands *mrbbt qdš*, as a place name, "from Ribeboth-kadesh." This is sometimes emended to *mmrbt qdš*, "from Meribath-kadesh" (cf. 32:51; BHS). The alternative is to understand this phrase as describing a host of heavenly beings. OG translates as though *'t rbbt qdš*, "with myriads of holy ones," and Syr. *w'tw rbbt qdš*, "and with him (were) myriads of holy ones." Following this line of thinking, Sam. *w'tw mrbbwt qdš* could be taken as "and with him were some of [partitive preposition] the myriads of holy ones." I read with MT, taking *w'th* as an alternate spelling of *w'tw*, "with him" (*h* as a vowel letter for *ô*, GKC 91e; cf. Sam.) and the *m* as partitive.

c. This translation retains MT Qere *mymynw 'š dt lmw* and treats *dāt* as a defective feminine perfect of *d'h*, "fly"; see R. C. Steiner, "*Dāt* and *'ên*: Two Verbs Masquerading as Nouns in Moses' Blessing (Deuteronomy 33:2, 28)," *JBL* 115 (1996): 693–98. The central problem is *'šdt*, which was traditionally resolved into *'š*, "fire," and *dt*, a late Persian loanword for "law" (Vulg., Tg., Aquila, Symmachus). NJPS (cf. RSV, NAB) "lightning flashing" apparently takes *dt* as the survivor of something like *dōleqet* ("burning") or *lappîdōt* ("flames"). OG "angels with him" seems to be a translation based on context, although BHS attempts a retroversion to *'šrw 'lym*, "gods advanced." NRSV draws out of this "a host of his own." If one understands *mymynw* in geographic terms ("from the south of it"), the word *'šd*, "slope," commends itself: "from the south of the slopes to them" or "from south (of it) to them at the slopes."

d. Follows MT. OG suggests 'mw, "his people," consistent with the poem's topic and xenophobic tone (cf. v. 11). Alternate translation: "O favorite among the peoples." Alternate translation of "in your hand": "by your side" (cf. Zech 4:12).

e. Taking MT whm tkw as tkh pu'al (HALOT 4:1730; perhaps "and they crowded together"). OG "they are under you" suggests himtakkû (mkk with an infixed t), "they sink, bow down," although this is probably an instance of translating an unknown word according to context.

f. Follows MT, taking "lift up," nāśā', in the sense of "accept, receive," although the verb could also imply "carry out, execute." Sam. and Vulg. have "they" for "he" and the singular noun "saying" for the plural of MT. OG renders this last word as though mdbryw, "from his words."

g. Understanding rb as the perfect or participle of ryb, "contend" (OG, Vulg., Syr., and the masoretic vocalization). As feminine plural, "hands" is awkward as the subject of rb, which is masculine singular. Consequently, I construe "hands" as an adverbial accusative of manner ("with his hands"; cf. English "handily"). Alternate translation assuming the root rbh ("be many"): "strengthen his hands for him." Another alternate translation applying thyh, "be," to both halves of the line: "Be the hands contending for him and be a help against his adversaries."

h. Follows 4QDeut^h, 4QTest, OG, inserting hbw llwy to achieve better poetic structure. MT lost this through haplography triggered by the preceding wllwy, "and to Levi."

i. Follows MT and Syr. as the more difficult text. 4QDeut^h and OG replace "him" with "you" (singular) as the pronoun appropriate for direct address (cf. Vulg. "you" [plural]). 4QTest supports the "you" suffix, but the reading is made uncertain by erasures and corrections. Sam. l'r'yty lacks the object suffix and highlights the potential for haplography or dittography involving the following w. On the text of vv. 8–21, see J. A. Duncan, "New Readings for the 'Blessing of Moses' from Qumran," JBL 114 (1995): 273–90.

j. That is, "his sons," as in Qere and the ancient versions. Kethib, Sam., 4QDeut^h, 4QTest: "his son."

k. The odd-looking construct "loins of" apparently has an enclitic mêm (IBHS 9.8c). The last word is prefixed with a privative mem having the force "without (the haters of him) rising" (Williams, Hebrew Syntax, 321). Alternate translation dividing the colon into 4 + 2 words: "Strike the loins of . . . and of those who hate him, that they may not rise again."

l. Follows Sam. and Syr. lbth hpp 'lyw kl-hywm, eliminating the first 'lyw of MT. MT 'lyw hpp 'lyw conflates two alternate readings, hpp 'lyw and 'lyw hpp. 4QDeut^h, OG also witness to this conflated text, but instead of the first 'lyw read 'l: "God shelters over him." This hints at an original 'lywn, "Most High" (or the divine name 'ly supposedly present in 1 Sam 2:10). 4QDeut^h follows "God" with mhwpp (Polel participle), suggesting the divine designation 'lm, i.e., 'l plus an enclitic m (Ps 29:1; perhaps 89:7 [ET 6]). The abrupt changes in grammatical subject in this verse are hard to follow. Yahweh is the most natural subject of the middle clause. If Benjamin is the subject of the third clause, this would be an image of divine protection, perhaps a portrayal of sheltering between the shoulders at (or on) Yahweh's back (1 Sam 17:6). If Yahweh is the subject, the image could refer to the location of a sanctuary (Bethel? Jerusalem?) flanked by the slopes (shoulders) of Benjamin's hills. See J. D. Heck, "The Missing Sanctuary of Deut 33:12,"

JBL 103 (1984): 523–29. The verb *ḥpp* could indicate "protect like a canopy" (*ḥuppâ*) or relate to an Arabic verb for "surround" (*HALOT* 1:339).

m. Follows MT, supported by OG (Wevers, *Greek Text*, 547). Vulg., Syr., Tg. conflate *mṭl*, "dew," with an alternate reading *m'l* "from above," a misreading bolstered by Gen 49:25 and a desire to supply a parallel for *tḥt*, "under," in the next line.

n. Follows MT (supported by Sam., OG, Syr., Tg.). 4QDeut[h] leveled to *mmgd* (vv. 14, 16). "Finest of" translates *mērōʾs,* literally "from the head," which could also be translated as "from the tops of."

o. The "*ḥireq* of connection" used in constructs (*IBHS* 8.2e). "Bush," *sěneh*, sounds like "Sinai" and is connected to it by Exod 3. See M. Beek, "Der Dornbusch als Wohnsitz Gottes," *OtSt* 14 (1965): 153–61.

p. Verse 16b equals Gen 49:26b, except for the nonstandard form *tbw'th*, "let it come" (GKC 48d: third-person cohortative). This looks like a blend of *tbw',* "let it come," and either *thy*, "let it be" (as Gen 49:26), or *t'th* ("let it come"). Perhaps the rarer *t'th* was explained with the more common *tbw',* and then the two alternates were conflated. Or it may be that there has been contamination from *tbw't* in v. 14.

q. Follows MT supported by 4QDeut[h] as the more difficult reading. Sam., Syr., Vulg. (and apparently 1QDeut[b]) have *šwr*, "bull," without the puzzling pronominal suffix, applying the image of a bull to Joseph rather than God: "Like a firstborn bull in his majesty."

r. Follows MT. NRSV and REB conjecture a transposition error and read *ydḥh*, "drive." OG and Vulg. interpret by adding "as far as," suggesting an alternate translation: "drives them to the ends of the earth."

s. Or "make space for Gad." Alternate translation pointing as a noun *merḥāb*: "the enlargement of Gad," or transposing the consonants into *mrḥby*: "the broad lands of Gad."

t. Follows OG, which joins *spwn* to the first word of v. 21b: *wyt'spwn*, "when they gathered themselves" (cf. v. 5a). Some scholars eliminate *spwn* ("esteemed" in rabbinic Hebrew) as a gloss on "chieftain." Earlier in this verse, the word translated as "chose" is literally "saw" (*HALOT* 3:1159, §12). "The best" *rēʾšît* could instead signify "[territory of] the firstborn" (i.e., Reuben, Num 32). Another translation possibility for *mḥqq*, "chieftain" (Judg 5:14; *HALOT* 1:347), is "a portion decreed for him" (cf. Isa 10:1).

u. Alternate translation reading *yršh* as a finite verb (OG, Syr., Vulg.): "he takes over." Yām, "west," could also be "sea": "to the sea [i.e., Galilee] and south."

v. Ignoring the masoretic vocalization ("none like God, O Jeshurun") and treating this as a construct expression.

w. The obscurity of this verse has generated many conjectures. Changing *měʿōnâ*, "dwelling," into *mimmaʿal*, "above," produces better parallelism: "Above is the ancient God, and underneath are the eternal arms." Translating "he subdues the ancient gods, shatters the forces of old" (cf. NRSV, REB) treats *m'nh* as a pi'el participle of *'nh*, "humble," transposes the consonants of *wmtḥt* into *wmḥtt,* "who shatters" (pi'el participle of *ḥtt*), and understands "arm" as a metaphor for "powers."

x. This assumes a noun from a presumed root *'wn*, "dwell" (cf. *m'nh* in v. 27), in order to achieve better parallelism. A similar result would be achieved by understanding *'ên* as a perfect stative verb: "Jacob dwells alone." Another translation of this word would be "fountain," possibly a reference to Jacob's well.

y. The preposition *ʾel* may attach to the previous name: "Jacob-el." See D. N. Freedman, "The Original Name of Jacob," *Israel Exploration Journal* 13 (1963): 125–26.

z. Follows the awkward *w'šr* of MT. REB "the Blessed One is your sword" thinks of
the verb *'šr,* "bless." NJB "the sword leads" envisions *'šr,* "march." *W'šr* may have been
absent from the text used by OG and perhaps originated as a vertical dittography of the
first word in the verse.

The Blessing of Moses points forward to the conquest and the land of
promise, promoting the themes of abundance, security, and valor by describing how Israel's life will take shape.[1] Earlier allusions to the tradition of a
dying patriarch passing on his final testament (31:2, 16) have prepared the
reader for this moment. Apart from an explicit reference to Moses (v. 4) and
another possible allusion (v. 21), however, the association of the blessing
with the rest of Deuteronomy is tenuous. It interrupts the connection
between the command to go up to Nebo (32:49–52) and its execution
(34:1–5). These last words of Moses are similar to Jacob's final blessing
(Gen 49) and seem to be part of the redactional process that incorporated
Deuteronomy into the Pentateuch.

Verses 2–5 and 26–29 frame an anthology of tribal blessings.[2] Perhaps these
framing verses were originally an independent hymn into which the blessings
were inserted at the catchphrase "tribes of Israel" (v. 5). Or they may have been
composed to serve as a framework for the blessings in order to help fuse the
references to individual tribes into the unified story of "all Israel."[3] Verse 4 constitutes the fundamental point of connection to Deuteronomy, linking the theophany of the Divine Warrior to Moses, lawgiving, and the gathered nation. In a
similar way, "Sinai" as the mountain of Divine Warrior theophany (v. 2; Judg
5:5; Ps 68:8–9 [ET 7–8]) is associated with the mountain of lawgiving (vv. 3bβ,
4, perhaps 21) and divine self-revelation (v. 16).

1. The most recent major study is S. Beyerle, *Der Mosesegen im Deuteronomium: Eine text-,
kompositions- und formkritische Studie zu Deuteronomium 33* (BZAW 250; Berlin: de Gruyter,
1997). On selected interpretive problems, see B. Margulis, "Gen. xlix 10 / Deut. xxxiii 2–3, " *VT*
19 (1969): 202–10. A. H. J. Gunneweg, "Über den Sitz im Leben der sogenannte Stammessprüche
(Gen 49, Dtn 33, Jdc 5)," *ZAW* 76 (1964): 245–55, postulates a liturgical celebration of theophany
by a tribal assembly. For another approach, see U. Cassuto, "Deuteronomy Chapter xxxiii and the
New Year in Ancient Israel," in *Biblical and Oriental Studies* (trans. I. Abrahams; 2 vols.; Jerusalem: Magnes, 1973–75), 1:47–70.

2. On the framework poem, see D. N. Freedman, "The Poetic Structure of the Framework of
Deuteronomy 33," in *Divine Commitment and Human Obligation, vol. 2: Poetry and Orthography*
(ed. J. Huddlestun; Grand Rapids: Eerdmans, 1997), 85–107; A. S. Van der Woude, "Erwägungen
zum Rahmenpsalm von Deuteronomium 33," in *Studies in Deuteronomy,* 281–88.

3. D. L. Christensen, "Two Stanzas of a Hymn in Deuteronomy 33," *Bib* 65 (1984): 382–89,
concludes that a common meter and a chiastic pattern link vv. 2–5 and 26–29a together as a pre-
existing hymn.

The framework is held together by a concentric structure of proper names: Yahweh in vv. 2 and 29, Jacob in vv. 4 and 28, Jeshurun in vv. 5 and 26. Both introduction and conclusion describe the Divine Warrior approaching to help the people (vv. 2 and 26–27). These framing verses surround the individual tribal sayings with the theme of national unity ("Jeshurun," "Israel together," "people," vv. 5, 26, 28–29) and their particularized blessings with Yahweh's comprehensive blessings of law, kingship, safety, and fertility (vv. 4–5, 28).

The anthology of blessings (vv. 6–25) concentrates on military security or success (vv. 7, 11, 12, 17, 20, 25) and material prosperity (vv. 13–16, 19, 21, 23, 24). There are three basic types. Some blessings are undirected wishes (Reuben, Gad, and vv. 13–16 for Joseph). Others are prayers directed at God (Judah, Levi). The rest are descriptions of tribal lifestyle and situation. In contrast to Gen 49, Yahweh is mentioned directly and there are no indictments of tribal character or behavior. Stylistic irregularities and variation in genre suggest that this catalog represents a compilation of originally independent gnomic or proverbial statements. A tradition of stereotypical aphorisms is evident in Gen 16:12; 27:27–29, 39–40; Judg 5:15b–18. A similar vocabulary of blessing appears in the speech of Balaam (cf. v. 17 with Num 23:22; 24:8; v. 20 with Num 23:24). Except in the case of Levi, the blessings refer to each tribe as an eponymous individual. The northern tribes are congratulated on their prosperity; a future improvement in circumstances is desired for Reuben, Judah, and Gad. Animal images are employed for Joseph, Gad, and Dan. The sequence begins with Reuben, probably as firstborn (and in the context of Deuteronomy the location of Moses' speech). The perspective then moves west of the Jordan to Judah (and Levi), and northward (Benjamin, Joseph, Zebulun and Issachar treated together). The last four tribes (the sons of concubines in Genesis) appear in a counterclockwise, peripheral arc (Gad, Dan, Naphtali, Asher).[4]

The blessings are incorporated into the scene of a final testament by the headings "he said." Reuben lacks such a heading, perhaps because it is the first blessing after the "he said" of v. 2. The perspectives of northern Israel are evident. Joseph and Levi have long and splendid blessings. Judah receives a shorter blessing, one that alludes to its separation from the rest of the "people." Simeon does not appear at all. Reuben still survives, but is threatened with extinction. These circumstances suggest that the collection was assembled between the political breakup of Judah and Israel and the Assyrian conquests of 732 and 722 B.C.E.[5]

---

4. See H.-J. Zobel, *Stammesspruch und Geschichte* (BZAW 95; Berlin: Töpelmann, 1965). This is a collection of bits of ancient folklore according to I. L. Seeligmann, "A Psalm from Pre-Regnal Times," *VT* 14 (1964): 75–92.

5. Dating varies widely. Opinions include D. N. Freedman, "Poetic Structure": 11th century; A. Caquot, "Les bénédictions de Moïse [Deutéronome 33,6–25]," *Sem* 32 (1982): 67–81; 33 (1983): 59–76: no older than the 6th century; Beyerle, *Der Mosesegen*, 279–80: first half of the

[1] This is one of four headings that organize the final form of Deuteronomy (with 1:1; 4:45; 28:69 [ET 29:1]). It incorporates the Blessing of Moses into the plot of his upcoming death and shapes the poem into a patriarchal deathbed testament. Like Jacob, Moses blesses "before his death" (Gen 27:7, 10). As "man of God," Moses is a prophet (Josh 14:6; Ps 90:1 [ET superscription]; cf. Deut 18:15; 34:10). Consequently, his blessing is to be respected as a powerful word that will shape the future.

[2–5] The introductory framework describes the Divine Warrior coming from or via the southern mountains, perhaps Yahweh's ancient pre-Israelite home, to save and deliver (Judg 5:4–5; Hab 3:3–15; Ps 68:8–9, 16–19 [ET 7–8, 15–18]).[6] A mythic pantheon of divine beings is fully subordinated to Yahweh. The kingship of the Divine Warrior is linked to the role of Moses as lawgiver by connecting the Sinai of theophany (v. 2; cf. Ps 68:8–9 [ET 7–8]; Judg 5:5) with the place of lawgiving and national assembly (vv. 3–5).

Verse 2 has not been transmitted correctly and is difficult to translate; the last line (v. 2b) seems to be irretrievably corrupt (note c). The verbs with Yahweh as subject ("came," "dawned," "shone forth") and the repeated preposition "from" emphasize Yahweh's motion away from the southern mountain locale. "Came" indicates the perspective of Israel. The repetition of *lmw*, "for them," stresses that Yahweh's approach is for Israel's sake. "Dawned" and "shone forth" represent Divine Warrior language (Hab 3:3–4; Ps 50:1–2; 80:2–3 [ET 1–2]; 94:1; 104:2–3; Job 37:15; Isa 60:2) and describe Yahweh in terms of a solar deity (cf. 1 Kgs 8:53a LXX; Pss 46:6 [ET 5]; 84:12 [ET 11]; 91:4; 101:8).[7] "Myriads of holy ones" refers to the Divine Warrior's army of minor deities (Num 10:36; 1 Kgs 22:19; Pss 68:18 [ET 17]; 89:8 [ET 7]; Zech 14:5), who appear in art as archers, chariots, and riders on horses.[8]

The translation of v. 3 is also a problem, in part because of a confusion of pronouns. "Your" clearly refers to Yahweh (who is the "lover of peoples" or "favorite among peoples," note d). "His holy ones" alludes to the makeup of Yahweh's army. If these are human troops, "his" could refer to either Yahweh or Israel, but if superhuman powers are meant, "his" must indicate Yahweh. These "holy ones" are in "your" hand (in Yahweh's charge or by Yahweh's side)

11th century. H. Seebass, "Die Stammeliste von Dtn xxxiii," *VT* 27 (1977): 158–69, proposes that Jeshurun stands for Simeon in coalition with non-Israelite tribes and suggests the reign of David and Solomon.

6. L. E. Axelsson, *The Lord Rose Up from Seir: Studies in the History and Traditions of the Negev and Southern Judah* (ConBOT 25; Stockholm: Almqvist & Wiksell, 1987), 48–65.

7. An inscription from Kuntillet 'Ajrud uses this verb: "and when El shines forth, the mountains melt." See G. I. Davies, *Ancient Hebrew Inscripitons* (Cambridge: Cambridge University Press, 1991), 82, no. 8.023.

8. P. D. Miller Jr., "Cosmology and World Order in the Old Testament: The Divine Council as Cosmic-Political Symbol," *Horizons in Biblical Theology* 9, no. 2 (1987): 54–64.

and march (or "fall," note e) at "your" feet, emphasizing the subordinate relationship of these (earthly or heavenly) warriors to Yahweh. Context (v. 19) suggests that "the peoples" denotes the tribes of Israel rather than nations in general (cf. Gen 28:3; 48:4). "Sayings" could refer to orders given to an army or point forward to the law (or instruction) of v. 4.

Israel becomes the speaker in v. 4. The proclamation of law follows immediately upon the arrival of the Divine Warrior, perhaps within the context of a national assembly (v. 5). Verse 4 may be a redactional link, tying the poem to the body of Deuteronomy. However, the parallelism between *tôrâ* and "inherited possession" suggests that *tôrâ* could refer (as "instruction") to the blessings that follow. Last words can be "commanded" (2 Sam 17:23; 2 Kgs 20:1). For *môrāšâ* as "property transferred by inheritance," see *HALOT* 2:561. Traditionally, the Divine Warrior receives kingship after winning victory, so it is more natural to understand "king" in v. 5 in divine rather than human terms (cf. Exod 15:18). However, emerging as king "in Jeshurun" seems like an odd thing to say of universal, divine kingship.[9] "The tribes of Israel together" may have served as a catchphrase that prompted the insertion of the blessings at this point.

[6] The blessing for Reuben has no heading and takes the form of a wish. It reflects Reuben's early decline in population and endangered future (cf. Gen 35:22; 49:3–4).

[7] Judah's blessing is set in the form of a prayer. The heading is different from the others, perhaps stressing Judah's special significance. The reference to Judah's separation reflects a northern Israelite perspective and probably refers to the divided kingdom.

[8–11] The blessing of Levi is fashioned as a prayer. It advocates an explicitly Levitical priesthood, perhaps over against rival priestly claimants. Levi has earned its special role through a former act of fidelity that went so far as to deny family connections (cf. Num 25:1–13; Ezek 44:15; 48:11). Levi's "antifamily" position stands in some tension with the emphasis on "brotherhood" in vv. 16, 24. This perspective on the event at Massah is more similar to that of Ps 81:8 [ET 7] than to that of Deut 6:16. It refers to a tradition having a plot similar to Exod 32:26–29, but not reported in either Exod 17 or Num 20. Wordplay is prominent: you tested at the testing place (Massah) and contended at the site of contention (Meribah).

The shift from the singular language of vv. 8–9a to the plural of vv. 9b–10 suggests a different origin for these respective sections, as does the unexpectedly "secular" direction taken in v. 11. Verse 11 may represent an older materialistic and militaristic blessing, later augmented by vv. 8–9a and then vv.

---

9. According to van der Woude, "Rahmenpsalm," 286–88, the translation "he [Yahweh] *became* king in Jeshurun" (RSV, NJPS) would require the word order *wayĕhî melek bîšurûn*.

9b–10 as priestly oriented supplements. Verses 8–9a authorize the function of priestly divination; vv. 9b-10 add the tasks of instruction and sacrifice.

The alliterated, poetic declaration in v. 9a (*lě'ābîw ûlě'immô lō' rě'îtîw*) sounds like a formal legal proclamation of familial severance. The translation takes *qět̞ôrâ* (v. 10) broadly as smoke from sacrifice (1 Sam 2:15–16; Hos 4:13; 11:2); more narrowly construed it would be incense. The imprecation of v. 11b could be targeted against those who opposed the priestly claims of those with Levitical genealogy. If so, the malediction against their procreative powers ("loins"; 1 Kgs 12:10; Isa 48:1) would be especially apposite. On the other hand, "loins" can also denote "strength" more generally, and Levi's *ḥêl*, "wealth," could mean its military valor. In other words, v. 11 could speak of Levi as a belligerent, secular tribe (cf. Gen 34).

[12] Benjamin's blessing describes its secure situation in its territory. The tribal name occurs only in the heading and not in the blessing itself. Meaning is obscured by textual and grammatical problems (see note l). It seems most natural to take Benjamin as the subject of both occurrences of the verb "dwell" in an *abb 'a'* pattern: "dwells in security . . . between his [Yahweh's] shoulders he dwells."

[13–17] The blessing of Joseph is close to its counterpart in Gen 49:22–26. The topic of fertility in vv. 13–16 coincides with Gen 49:25–26, while that of political status in v. 17 corresponds to Gen 49:22–24. The same images of fertility (vv. 13, 15) and the designation of Joseph as "prince" (v. 16b) appear in Gen 49:25–26.

Verses 13–16 are held together tightly by the repetition of "bounty" (*meged*; for connotations of fecundity, see Cant 4:13, 16; 7:14 [ET 13]). Such "list poetry" is designed to express comprehensiveness. This catalog has a mythic flavor and may engage in a polemic against mythic conceptions of fertility. The bounties of heaven, earth, the "deep" (*těhôm*), the sun, and the moon's monthly cycle are proclaimed to be nothing other than the blessing of Yahweh, the God whom Israel encountered at Sinai (note o). The mythic deep "stretches" or "crouches down" (*rābaṣ*; cf. Gen 49:9, 14) like an animal underneath the world. "Months" or "moons" in v. 14 may refer to different crops ripening in different months or may allude to a putative influence of lunar phases and cycles on plant growth. Alternatively, the reference to sun and moon could signify that crops mature on a regular basis, year by year and month by month. "Mountains" (v. 15) yield wood, stone, and ores, but these are also the primordial mountains where numinous powers dwell (Gen 49:26; Hab 3:6). Verse 16b introduces the topic of political status with "prince of his brothers" (*nāzîr*, one "separated" as highest in status or who wears the *nēzer* or turban of distinction; cf. Gen. 49:26).

If one reads v. 17 without the pronominal suffix (note q), the bull describes Joseph and his aggressive triumphs. If the MT reading "his bull" is accepted, the image could refer to Ephraim as Joseph's favorite son. However, the expression most likely uses "bull" as a divine designation to declare the special status of Joseph as the favorite of his God, Yahweh the divine Bull. Conceiving of a god as a bull is well attested in both the Hebrew Bible and ancient Near Eastern iconographic tradition.[10] As a divine image, the bull conveys strength and assertiveness (rather than fertility). Joseph is subsequently portrayed as a different animal, the wild ox that triumphs over the far-off peoples of "the ends of the earth" (Pss 2:8; 22:28 [ET 27]; Isa 52:10). This same symbolism of goring horns appears in Num 23:22; 24:8. Perhaps Joseph's two horns are Ephraim and Manasseh. Verse 17b subtly alludes to the dominance of Ephraim over Manasseh through a rhetorical "step down" that reverses the usual order of "thousand" and "ten thousand" (contrast 32:30; 1 Sam 18:7; 21:12 [ET 11]; 29:5).

[18–19] The heading refers only to Zebulun, but the blessing involves Issachar as well. These two tribes are commonly paired (Gen 49:13–15; Judg 5:14–15). This blessing apparently portrays the comfortable situation of these tribes before the onset of Assyrian rule. "Going out" and "in your tents" (v. 18) form a *merismus* for a community's whole life, setting off for public activity and staying at home for domestic pursuits. In v. 19 "peoples," most likely members of other Israelite tribes, congregate at the holy mountain of Zebulun and Issachar. This is undoubtedly the important border shrine of Mount Tabor (Josh 19:12, 22; Judg 4:6, 12; Hos 5:1). The sacrifices they offer are "right," either in the sense of being presented in a state of righteousness, offered in rich amounts (Ps 51:21 [ET 19]), or performed in a manner appropriate to the demands of the divine-human relationship (Ps 4:6 [ET 5]).[11] Zebulun and Issachar have easy access along the Jezreel Valley to the riches of the sea and seacoast. They extract ("suck out") assets derived from fishing and trade, perhaps including the famous purple dye produced from shellfish. The translation takes *śĕpûnê* as a by-form of *śpn*, "hide."

[20–21] For a tribe as peripheral as Gad, the length and complexity of this blessing is surprising. It comprises a wish, a comparison to a lion illustrating aggressiveness, a reference to prestigious territory, and a mysterious allusion to tribal governance. The wish (v. 21a) is an indirect blessing on one—perhaps Yahweh—who champions Gad's expansion.[12] Verse 21 is problematic in several ways (note t), and translations vary widely. Perhaps "portion of a chieftain (*mĕḥōqēq*)" signifies land so superb that it would even do for a ruler. However, because *ḥqq* can mean "decree, engrave [laws in stone]," this is sometimes understood as signifying the region of Moses' burial place (in Reuben; Josh

---

10. Keel and Uehlinger, *Gods, Goddesses, and Images of God*, 118–20.

11. W. Zwickel, "Opfer der Gerechtigkeit" (Dtn xxxiii 19; Ps iv 6, li 21)," *VT* 45 (1995): 386–91, interprets as "sacrifices appropriate to a given situation."

12. On successive territorial shifts involving Gad, see C. H. J. de Geus, "Gad," *ABD* 2:864–65.

13:20). If this is indeed a reference to Moses, then perhaps v. 21b alludes to his act of lawgiving and to vv. 4–5. In this case, vv. 4–5 and 21b could function as a refrain or antiphon. This possibility is reinforced by the repetition at both places of "heads of the people" and "gathered together" ('sp hitpa'el, note t).[13]

[22] Dan's blessing is an animal comparison aphorism. His small size (as a "lion's cub") disguises a surprising aggressiveness. The verb zānaq may be a metathesized cognate of Arabic nazaqa, "jump forth" (HALOT 1:276; cf. LXX). Bashan is not a locale of Dan and must be part of the lion metaphor. Perhaps an abundance of cattle led to a corresponding abundance of predators, so that the aggressiveness of lions in Bashan became proverbial. However, the snake comparisons in the parallel text Gen 49:17 suggest that "Bashan" may disguise a cognate to Ugaritic bṭn, "snake" (HALOT 1:165), thus "rushes away from a snake" or "leaps forth [quicker] than a snake."

[23] This is an aphorism about Naphtali's productive land in east Galilee and, perhaps, an encouragement to increase it (note u) to areas "west and south" of Lake Galilee.

[24–25] These verses comprise a wish for prosperity and security.[14] Like Joseph (v. 16b, "prince among his brothers"), Asher's situation is compared with that of other tribes. He is the most blessed of the sons and most popular of the brothers. Perhaps the text conceals an implicit wordplay in that the name Asher is similar to the root 'šr, "call fortunate," and to 'āšur, "footstep." Those words themselves do not actually appear, but the associated concepts of "blessed, favorite" and "foot" are present. The image involving "foot" may simply express general prosperity (Gen 49:11; Job 29:6) or more specifically point to a superabundance of olive trees. The metaphor of bolts in a city gate in v. 25 (min'āl, HALOT 2:602) communicates "secure as though bolted up with bronze and iron." This expression could also allude to Asher's vulnerability to outside attack and its large number of venerable and important cities (Josh 19:25–30). Translating dōbe' as "strength" is a conjecture from context and the ancient versions, with weak backing from Ugaritic (HALOT 1:208).

[26–29] Mention of "Jeshurun" returns attention to the topic of vv. 2–5. The Divine Warrior of vv. 2–3 reappears, riding through the skies like the weather god (Isa 19:1; Pss 18:11 [ET 10]; 68:5, 34 [ET 4, 33]; 104:3). The focus of this concluding framework is security and divine protection. Verses 26 and 29 form a bracket around these final verses with "none like" Yahweh and "who is like" Israel. In other words, the uniqueness of Yahweh (v. 26) entails the uniqueness of elected Israel (v. 29).

13. Z. Weisman, "A Connecting Link in an Old Hymn: Deuteronomy 33:19a, 21b," VT 28 (1978): 365–68, suggests that vv. 5, 19a, and 21b unify the poem as references to a liturgical assembly.

14. J. R. Porter, "The Interpretation of Deuteronomy xxxiii 24–5," VT 44 (1994): 267–70, offers an alternate interpretation that blesses Asher as a matchless warrior rather than as a prosperous tribe.

Verses 26–27 describe Yahweh as Divine Warrior, and vv. 28–29 concern Israel's protection by this Divine Warrior. The poetic parallelism of v. 26 equates "help" for Israel with Yahweh's "majesty" (v. 26b), a theologically powerful offer of comfort. "Underneath" in v. 27 most likely means underneath those whom God supports; the divine arms are Israel's underpinning (cf. Hos 11:3). However, this could also refer to the "primordial arms" of the Divine Warrior's might in battle, perhaps reaching down to strike earthly enemies. Verses 27b–28a describe three connected actions with *waw*-consecutive imperfect verbs: Yahweh "drove out" and "said," and as a result "Israel lives." "Untroubled" (v. 28a) translates *bādād*, "alone," implying either left alone after an enemy has been expelled or unafraid to be alone (cf. Num 23:9). Verse 28b is reminiscent of Isaac's blessing of Jacob in Gen 27:28 (cf. 2 Kgs 18:32; Deut 33:13–16) and connects the triumphs of the Divine Warrior to the rich blessings of the land (for "grain and wine" see Hos 7:14; Ps 4:8 [ET 7]). Verse 29 portrays Israel's especially fortunate state (Pss 33:12; 89:16 [ET 15]; 144:15; 146:5) as a unique people (cf. Deut 4:7) whose distinctiveness consists in being saved by Yahweh. The Divine Warrior embodies a complete armament: the shield of defense and the sword of offense. Perhaps Israel's enemies only pretend submission (thus "feign obedience," *HALOT* 2:469–70), but the emphatic pronoun *wĕ'attâ* ("but you for your part") contrasts Israel's unequivocal supremacy with their ambiguous behavior. Setting one's foot on a defeated enemy's back (*bāmâ*, *HALOT* 1:136, §1a) is a symbol of triumph.[15]

The Death of Moses
34:1–12

34:1 Moses went up from the plains of Moab to Mount Nebo, the top of Pisgah, which is opposite Jericho, and Yahweh showed him the whole land: Gilead as far as Dan, 2 all Naphtali, the land of Ephraim and Manasseh, all the land of Judah as far as the Western Sea, 3 the Negeb, and the Plain—the valley of Jericho, the city of palm trees—as far as Zoar. 4 Yahweh said to him, "This is the land about which I swore to Abraham, to Isaac, and to Jacob, saying, 'To your offspring I will give it.' I have let you see it with your eyes, but you will not cross over to there."

---

15. Joshua 10:24. See O. Keel, *The Symbolism of the Biblical World: Ancient Near Eastern Iconography and the Book of Psalms* (trans. T. J. Hallett; New York: Seabury, 1978), 253–55.

5 Then Moses, the servant of Yahweh, died there[a] in the land of Moab
at the command of Yahweh. 6 He[b] buried him in a valley in the land of
Moab,[c] opposite Beth-peor, but no one knows his place of burial to this
day.

7 Moses was one hundred twenty years old when he died; his eyes
were undimmed and his vital strength had not slipped away.[d] 8 The
Israelites wept for Moses in the plains of Moab thirty days. Then the days
of weeping in mourning for Moses ended. 9 Joshua son of Nun was full
of a spirit of wisdom, because Moses had laid his hands on him, and the
Israelites obeyed him and did just as Yahweh had commanded Moses.

10 Never again[e] has a prophet like Moses arisen in Israel—whom
Yahweh knew[f] face to face[g]—11 with regard to[h] all the signs and wonders
that Yahweh sent him to do in the land of Egypt, against Pharaoh and all
his servants and all his land, 12 and for all his mighty hand and for all the
great deeds of terror that Moses did in the sight of all Israel.

a. Follows MT. OG (= LXX[A]) also reads *šm*, "there." LXX[B] omitted it as an unnecessary word.

b. Follows MT. OG and Tg. Neof. read "*they* buried," interpreting MT as an impersonal expression to avoid the offensive notion of Yahweh burying Moses.

c. Follows MT supported by OG (= LXX[A]). A later Greek textual development
(LXX[B]) lost "in the land of Moab" through a skip caused by the similarity of *en gai*, "in
the valley," and *en gē*, "in the land of."

d. The masoretic pointing takes the verb as *nws*, "flee." Other possibilities are "wrinkled" (i.e., "dried up," from an Arabic root *nss*) or "sicken" (from *nss*, only Isa 10:18).
The subject noun is also problematic: "moistness, vital juices, sap." Most take this as a
reference to life force in general, but sexual potency has also been suggested. Masoretic
tradition points as *lēhōh* with a masculine suffix, but repointing the suffix as feminine
(*lēhāh*) changes the referent to Moses' eye: "and its luster had not gone away." A reference to cheeks or jaw (*lēhî*) is suggested by Vulg. and Syr.: "his cheek had not wrinkled." See J. H. Tigay, "*lō' nās lēhō*, 'He Had Not Become Wrinkled' (Deuteronomy
34:7)," in *Solving Riddles and Untying Knots*, ed. Zerit et al., 345–50.

e. Alternate translation taking the *waw* as contrastive: "*But* never again."

f. Or "single out," literally "know" (cf. Gen 18:19).

g. In the sense of "one on one." Cf. Exod 33:11: "to speak with someone as to a
friend," or Num 12:6–8; Ezek 20:35: "without mediation." The expression in Deut 5:4
is different.

h. Verses 11–12 set forth the reasons that Moses was unequalled, linking back to v.
10a with the preposition *l* (*lāmed* of specification; *IBHS* 11.2.10d).

The death of the incomparable prophet, liberator, and lawgiver concludes
both Deuteronomy and the Pentateuch. However, this ending also marks a transition, a move into the future, into Israel's history that is to be recounted in DH.
As Moses surveys the land on both sides of the Jordan, he also looks forward

to the time when "the whole land" will belong to Israel. Thus this chapter unites the lawgiver of Deuteronomy with the prophetic liberator of oppressed Israel under the perspective of Israel's future life in the land. Chapter 34 is no mere afterthought. The entire theology of Deuteronomy can be comprehended from the perspective of the death of Moses.[1]

The chapter is a fusion of Priestly and Deuteronomistic materials. The future horizon of DH appears clearly in vv. 1b–6 (Jericho, oath to the ancestors). The language and interests of P are visible in vv. 1a, 7–9 (Aaron, "Nebo . . . opposite Jericho," like 32:49; reference to Num 27:15–23). Verses 10–12 are less easy to classify. Using elements of Deuteronomistic language, these verses look back over the entire career of Moses, alluding specifically to the concept of Moses' face-to-face relationship with Yahweh found also in Exod 33:11.

The DH story of the tragic fate of Moses, his viewing the land, and Joshua's succession (1:35–39; 3:23–29; 31:1–8), has been combined with or overlaid by the later Priestly story that consists of Num 20:12–13, 22–29; 27:12–23; and Deut 32:48–52. At points in the Priestly material, there is a tendency to adjust or reframe earlier parts of Deuteronomy. Thus v. 7 corrects 31:2, insisting that Moses was still full of vigor and died only because he had reached humanity's allotted term of years. The happy ending of v. 9 opposes the notion of immediate apostasy implied by 31:16, 29. Such apostasy would not take place for another generation (cf. Josh 24:31, Judg 2:7–10). Verse 10 corrects the impression of Deut 18:15: no prophet totally comparable to Moses ever appeared.[2]

[1–4] Moses' geographical survey expands on the command of 3:27 (DH), but is also consistent with 32:49 (P). His vision is like that of Abraham (Gen 13:14–15), and v. 4 actually quotes Gen 12:7 (cf. Exod 33:1). He looks from right to left, first north, then west, then south. It is not completely evident whether the movement described by "as far as" refers to the sweep of his panorama, as his gaze shifts across the points of the compass, or to "lines of extent" drawn out to points on a mental map. However, the prevalence of similar "lines of extent" in Joshua (1:4; 10:41; 11:17; 12:1–5, etc.) makes the latter option more likely. The first line of extent ("[from] Gilead as far as Dan") designates territories to the north. Supplementary phrases incorporate "all

---

1. D. T. Olson, *Deuteronomy and the Death of Moses* (Overtures to Biblical Theology; Minneapolis: Fortress Press, 1994).

2. For a comprehensive critical analysis, see F. García López, "Deut 34, Dtr History, and the Pentateuch," in *Studies in Deuteronomy*, ed. García Martínez et al., 47–61; T. C. Römer, "Deuteronomium 34 zwischen Pentateuch, Hexateuch und deuteronomistischem Geschichtswerk," *ZABR* 5 (1999): 167–78. R. Lux, "Der Tod des Mose als 'besprochene und erzählte Welte': Literaturwissenschaftliche und theologische Interpretation von Deut 32:48–52 und 34," *ZTK* 84 (1987): 395–425, offers a literary analysis focusing on the verb tenses and discerns a message addressed to exilic fears over dying in the land of exile. P. Stoellger, "Deuteronomium 34 ohne Priesterschrift," *ZAW* 105 (1993): 26–51, analyzes these compositional stages totally within the circle of the Deuteronomistic school.

Naphtali" (i.e., the highlands of Galilee) and then the central highlands. Ephraim and Manasseh are treated as a unit, but listed in order of tribal dominance. The second line of extent includes Judah and runs west out to the Mediterranean. The third line of extent describes the view to the south, starting from the Negeb and the plain of Jericho and running southward to Zoar. Yahweh "showed" Moses all this, giving him phenomenal sharpness of sight, or perhaps prophetic insight into its deeper meaning (cf. Amos 7:1, 4, 7). What can physically be seen from Mount Nebo's location is beside the point. This description is a divinely assisted visualization granted to Moses and a mental map given to the reader.

[5–6] Moses is Yahweh's "servant," perhaps intended in the sense of a royal minister (2 Kgs 22:12). It is unclear whether "at the command of Yahweh" refers to the fact of his death or to its location outside the land. A satisfying ring composition is completed as Moses is buried at the same place where he began speaking (1:5; 3:29). Verse 6 communicates a legendary feature about Moses' burial (*Yahweh* buried him), but then blocks the natural impulse toward a grave cult. Burial by Yahweh not only glorifies Moses, but explains the surprising circumstance that the location of his grave is unknown. Perhaps this also served as polemic against some site once claimed to be the tomb of Moses.

The tradition of the death of Moses and his supernatural burial serves both theological and narratival purposes. Like the death and burial formulas about the minor judges (Judg 10:1–5 and 12:7–15), it helps communicate a continuity of office subsequent to Moses. In the structure of DH, the chain formed by 3:27b–28 to 31:2–3 to Josh 1:2 emphasizes that the removal of Moses from the scene made it possible for Israel to move on under the new leadership of Joshua, so that the next stage of saving history could unfold. For readers of this chapter who have the whole Pentateuch in view, Moses' death and burial clarify that he was not like Abraham, who not only saw the land, but also went through it and was buried in it (Gen 13:14–15, 17; 25:9).[3]

[7–9] Verse 7 breaks the *waw*-consecutive chain of vv. 1–5 with background information about Moses. Heroic legendary motifs about his death correspond to those reported about his birth. Unlike Isaac (Gen 27:1) or Jacob (Gen 48:10), his old age is characterized by freshness and strength. He dies only because he has reached the divinely imposed limit. These legendary motifs continue in vv. 10–12. His relationship to Yahweh was a personal one, and he was a doer of mighty deeds.[4] Of course, from the more practical standpoint of narrative necessity, Moses would also need this good eyesight to view the land!

---

3. For further observations on tradition history, see S. Schwertner, "Erwagungen zu Moses Tod und Grab in Dtn 34, 5.6," *ZAW* 84 (1972): 25–46.

4. G. W. Coats, "Legendary Motifs in the Moses Death Reports," *CBQ* 39 (1977): 34–44; repr. in *Song of Power,* ed. Christensen, 181–91.

The completion of an extralong period of mourning (cf. Num 20:29) brings the narrative about Moses to an end in v. 8, but then v. 9 points forward to another story yet to follow. A grammatical pattern sets up the parallel between Moses (vv. 7–8) and Joshua (v. 9): "Moses son of"[5] is followed by "the Israelites wept," then "Joshua son of" is followed by "the Israelites obeyed." Joshua possesses the royal characteristic of "a spirit of wisdom" in order to govern (Isa 11:1–5; cf. Solomon). This description reflects the investiture described in Num 27:12–23.[6] Yet Joshua's leadership remains derivative in the sense that the people obey what was commanded to Moses.

[10–12] This final tribute to Moses also validates the book of Deuteronomy.[7] "Never again" serves as support for Deuteronomy's unparalleled and permanent authority, perhaps lest 18:15–19 be misunderstood. Prophets like Moses would appear, but none would have his unmediated access to Yahweh's presence ("face"). The repetition of "all" in vv. 11–12 highlights the signs and wonders of Moses as confirming evidence of his prophetic office (in some tension with the outlook of 13:3 [ET 2]). That these deeds were done "in the sight of all Israel" implies that Moses performed them not just to oppose Pharaoh, but so the people would believe him (Exod 4:30–31; 14:31).

---

5. Verse 7 is literally "Moses [was] son of one hundred twenty years."

6. However, Num 27:12–23 describes this as a transferal not of spirit as in Deut 34:9 (cf. Num 27:18), but of authority (Num 27:20). In sacrificial practice, laying *one* hand on a sacrificial animal illustrated ownership and the power of disposal. However, Moses' action of investiture involved both hands (Deut 34:9; Num 27:23).

7. It is similar in purpose to the self-authenticating epilogue of the Code of Hammurabi, *ANET*, 178–80. See J. H. Tigay, "The Significance of the End of Deuteronomy (Deut. 34:10–12)," in *Temples, Texts, and Traditions: A Tribute to Menahem Haran* (ed. M. Fox; Winona Lake, Ind.: Eisenbrauns, 1995), 137–43. Similar self-authenticating statements appear in 4:2; 13:1 [ET 12:32]; 31:24, 30.

INDEX OF ANCIENT SOURCES

INDEX OF MODERN AUTHORS